W9-ADP-898

Georgia Voices

Georgia Voices

Volume One: Fiction

Edited by Hugh Ruppersburg

The University of Georgia Press Athens and London

Designed by Sandra Strother Hudson
Set in Stemple Garamond by Tseng Information Systems, Inc.
Printed and bound by Arcata Graphics/Kingsport
The paper in this book meets the guidelines
for permanence and durability of the Committee on
Production Guidelines for Book Longevity
of the Council on Library Resources.

Printed in the United States of America

96 95 94 93 92 C 5 4 3 2 1
96 95 94 93 92 P 5 4 3 2 1

Library of Congress Cataloging in Publication Data

Georgia voices / edited by Hugh Ruppersburg.
p. cm.
Includes bibliographical references.
Contents: v. 1. Fiction.
ISBN 0-8203-1432-3 (alk. paper). — ISBN 0-8203-1433-1
(pbk.: alk. paper)
1. American literature—Georgia. 2. Georgia—Literary
collections. I. Ruppersburg, Hugh M.
PS558.G4G44 1992
813.008′09758–dc20 91-36688
CIP

British Library Cataloging in Publication Data available

Contents

Part Two
Georgia Writers in the Twentieth Century, 1900–1960

Preface

This book grew from my discovery some years ago that there existed no collection of modern Georgia writers. It grew as well from my conviction that, although collections of writing from the American South often included works by such nationally known Georgians as Sidney Lanier, Carson McCullers, Flannery O'Connor, Alice Walker, and James Dickey, Georgia writing did not end with those few. Other authors deserved attention, people with names like Frances Newman and Byron Herbert Reece and Raymond Andrews, men and women who have produced distinguished and entertaining work that ought to be better appreciated, especially by readers of their own state. A collection of some of the best Georgia writing would bring their work more attention and would attest as well to the rich and diverse literary heritage of the state. Thus this volume of Georgia fiction, and the volumes of nonfiction and poetry that are to follow, came to be.

The writers who appear in this collection either were born in Georgia or spent significant periods of their lives here. Most of them lived out their lives in the state. A few spent considerably less time here. Jean Toomer, the author of *Cane*, spent only three months, but he called that brief stay "the starting point of almost everything of worth that I have done."[1] A widely respected book by one of the earliest African-American novelists, *Cane* is about Georgia and Georgians, so it seemed appropriate to include an excerpt. Conrad Aiken, who left at the age of eleven but returned to live out the winters of his

1. Toomer's letter to the *Liberator* magazine, quoted by Darwin T. Turner, "Introduction" to *Cane* (New York: Liveright, 1975), xvi.

final years in Savannah, hardly wrote about the South at all. (His story "Strange Moonlight" is an exception.) But his prominence as a significant American writer dictates his inclusion. Augusta J. Evans lived only the first five years of her life in the state and spent most of her years in Alabama. Many still think of her as a Georgia writer, and Georgians read her work widely during the second half of the nineteenth century. Thus she has been included as well.

The most important principle governing the selections in this volume was that the selections included should remain entertaining and readable today. I did not look for writers who wrote specifically about Georgia experiences, though most of the pieces here concern the state in some way. I did not want to produce a historical anthology that would feature writers who, though important in their time, are of little interest now. Nor did I want to suggest by the writing this anthology contains that Georgia is a state of cultural homogeneity. Indeed, I hope to have suggested the opposite through the variety of male and female, black and white writers included—writers who reflect the diversity of life in the state.

For the most part this is an anthology of twentieth-century writing. Those nineteenth-century writers included, such as Joel Chandler Harris and Augustus Baldwin Longstreet, appear not only because their work was important and influential but also because it still makes for good reading and because it reflects, often vividly, the early life and history of the state.

An unfortunate but inescapable fact about a collection such as this is that some writers are left out. Often the exclusion is intentional: many nineteenth- and early twentieth-century writers who once were well known have lost their appeal today. Other writers simply did not fit here. The popular nineteenth-century columnist Charles H. Smith, or "Bill Arp," for example, I have reserved for the Georgia nonfiction collection, where he really belongs. Genre fiction—detective writing, science fiction, historical romance, for instance—is not included, though Georgia writers have earned distinction in these areas. I have included many Georgia writers alive and at work today—Mary Hood, Charlie Smith, Alice Walker, and others—but not every living writer could be represented, and a writer's exclusion does not imply a judgment on the quality of his or her work. Future editions of this volume will no doubt reflect changing attitudes toward old and new figures in Georgia fiction.

A number of people played an important part in the preparation of this volume. I thank David Aiken for his help with nineteenth-century Georgia writers, Sheila Bailey for her advice on Margaret Mitchell and *Gone with the Wind*, and Warren Leamon for his suggestions about many aspects of the anthology. Karen Orchard, executive editor of the University of Georgia Press, has been encouraging and supportive from the beginning. Her influence is evident in numerous ways. I am much indebted to Diana Schuh, who labored long and hard to secure publication rights to the contents of the anthology. Coburn Freer and the English department of the University of Georgia provided valuable research time and assistance. Linda Smit searched out hard-to-find items in the library, xeroxed, and proofread. For their help along the way, I am also grateful to Charles East, Darren Felty, Sherrie Ford, Rosemary Franklin, Tony Grooms, James Kilgo, Alice Kinman, Stanley Lindberg, Hubert McAlexander, Rayburn Moore, Jennifer Murphy, David Peterson, and my wife, Patricia, whose opinions, as always, helped shape my own. Most of all I thank my mother, Margaret Caruthers Ruppersburg, who many years ago suggested that I would find great writers in my own backyard, if only I would look. To her, and to the people of this state, this anthology of Georgia fiction is dedicated.

The publication of this volume was supported by
The Friends of the University of Georgia Press

Acknowledgments

The Press and I would like to acknowledge the authors and publishers who gave us permission to include the stories or excerpts from novels that appear in this volume. They are:

"Strange Moonlight" by Conrad Aiken. Copyright 1950 by Conrad Aiken. From *The Collected Short Stories of Conrad Aiken*. Reprinted by permission of Schocken Books, published by Pantheon Books, a division of Random House, Inc.

Excerpt from *Appalachee Red* by Raymond Andrews. Published by Dial Press. Copyright 1978 by Raymond Andrews. Reprinted by permission of the author.

Excerpt from *Swamp Water* by Vereen Bell. Copyright 1940, 1941 by Vereen Bell. Reprinted by permission of Vereen Bell, Jr.

Excerpt from *Cold Sassy Tree* by Olive Ann Burns. Copyright 1984 by Olive Ann Burns. Reprinted by permission of Ticknor & Fields, a Houghton Mifflin Company.

"The Night My Old Man Came Home" and "Wild Flowers" from *Stories of Life: North and South* by Erskine Caldwell. Copyright 1937 and 1938 and renewed 1964 and 1965, respectively, by Erskine Caldwell. Reprinted by permission of McIntosh and Otis, Inc.

Excerpt from *The Prince of Tides* by Pat Conroy. Copyright 1986 by Pat Conroy. Reprinted by permission of Houghton Mifflin Co.

Excerpt from *A Feast of Snakes* by Harry Crews reprinted with permission of Atheneum Publishers, an imprint of the Macmillan Publishing Company. Copyright 1976 by Harry Crews.

Excerpt from *Deliverance* by James Dickey. Copyright 1970 by James Dickey. Reprinted by permission of Houghton Mifflin Co.

"Nobody's Fool," from *And Venus Is Blue* by Mary Hood. Copyright 1986 by Mary Hood. Reprinted by permission of Houghton Mifflin Co.

Excerpt from *The Year the Lights Came On* by Terry Kay. Copyright 1976 by Terry Kay. Reprinted by permission of the author.

Excerpt from *Youngblood* by John O. Killens. Copyright 1954 by John O. Killens. Reprinted by permission of Grace Killens.

"Papaya," from *Unheard Melodies* by Warren Leamon. Copyright 1990 by Warren Leamon. Reprinted by permission of the author.

"The Sojourner," from *The Ballad of the Sad Cafe and Collected Short Stories* by Carson McCullers. Copyright 1936, 1941, 1942, 1950, and 1955 by Carson McCullers. Copyright renewed in 1979 by Floria V. Lasky. Reprinted by permission of Houghton Mifflin Co.

Excerpt from *Lamb in His Bosom* by Caroline Miller. Copyright 1933 by Caroline Miller. Reprinted by permission of the author.

Excerpt from *Gone with the Wind* by Margaret Mitchell. Reprinted by permission of the William Morris Agency, Inc., on behalf of the author. Copyright 1936, 1964 by Margaret Mitchell.

"A Mess of Pardiges" by Marion Montgomery. Copyright 1966 by Marion Montgomery. Reprinted by permission of the author.

Excerpt from *The Hard-Boiled Virgin* by Frances Newman reprinted by permission of Liveright Publishing Corporation. Copyright 1926 by Boni & Liveright, Inc. Copyright 1954 by Louis Rucker.

"The Artificial Nigger," from *A Good Man Is Hard to Find and Other Stories* by Flannery O'Connor. Copyright 1955 by Flannery O'Connor and renewed 1983 by Regina O'Connor. Reprinted by permission of Harcourt Brace Jovanovich, Inc.

Excerpt from *Better a Dinner of Herbs* by Herbert Byron Reece. Copyright 1950 by E. P. Dutton & Co., Inc. Used by permission of the publisher, Dutton, an imprint of New American Library, a division of Penguin Books USA Inc.

"Fubar," from *The Widow's Mite and Other Stories* by Ferrol Sams. Copyright 1987 by Ferrol Sams. Reprinted by permission of the author.

Excerpt from *Shine Hawk* by Charlie Smith. Copyright 1988 by Charlie Smith. Reprinted by permission of the author.

Chapter 29 of *Strange Fruit* by Lillian Smith. Copyright 1944 by Lillian Smith and renewed 1972 by Paula Snelling. Reprinted by permission of Harcourt Brace Jovanovich, Inc.

"Mr. McAllister's Cigarette Holder," from *McAfee County* by Mark Steadman. Copyright 1970, 1971 by Mark Steadman. Reprinted by permission of the author.

"Esther" and "Blood-Burning Moon" are reprinted from *Cane* by Jean Toomer, by permission of Liveright Publishing Corporation. Copyright 1923 by Boni & Liveright. Copyright renewed 1951 by Jean Toomer.

"To Hell with Dying" from *In Love & Trouble: Stories of Black Women* by Alice Walker. Copyright 1967 by Alice Walker. Reprinted by permission of Harcourt Brace Jovanovich, Inc.

"The Starless Air," from *The Warm Country* by Donald Windham. Copyright 1962 by Donald Windham. Reprinted by permission of the author.

"Health Card" by Frank Yerby, from *O. Henry Memorial Award Prize Stories of 1944*, reprinted by permission of the William Morris Agency, Inc., on behalf of the author. Copyright 1944 by Frank Yerby.

Introduction

In its short history Georgia has produced a rich array of writers. Among Southern states, only Mississippi, by virtue of William Faulkner and Eudora Welty, can claim more literary prominence. But with such authors as Conrad Aiken, Flannery O'Connor, Carson McCullers, Alice Walker, and James Dickey (not to mention the ever popular Margaret Mitchell), Georgia holds a second rank of considerable esteem. Georgia writers have written about the same subjects that have interested writers across history and throughout the world: family, war, hardship, ambition, love and death, change, the search for knowledge and meaning. But the state of Georgia has provided its writers with a context of particularity—history and geography, values and codes, social and cultural climates, an environment—that gives their writings an identity based on time and place, a commonly shared heritage and experience that out of all the world's literature and history makes it distinctive and unique.

Writing in Georgia did not develop in isolation from that of the rest of the nation. The same events and forces that influenced the growth of our national literature also influenced the state's literature. The disappearance of the frontier, the expansion of industry, the growth of cities, the trauma of war and depression, the tumultuous changes of the twentieth century—all have shaped Georgia writing. Yet certain factors unique to the state have left their marks. The relatively late founding of the colony of Georgia in 1733 by Sir James Oglethorpe, and the persistence of the frontier well into the nineteenth century, significantly influenced the literature, especially its taste for humor and violence, and its tendency to view rural Georgians as living in isolation, cut off from the flow of events and history in the outer world. The state grew slowly in its early years and even by 1820 showed little promise of achieving the prominence of such older former Southern colonies as Virginia and the Carolinas. In many ways it remained a frontier until just before the Civil War. Atlanta was still a small settlement in 1850. The writings of Georgia humorists William Tappan Thompson and Augustus Baldwin Longstreet bear witness to the reality of the frontier and its proximity to the mainstream of life in the state well into the nineteenth century.

Even for modern writers the frontier remains a vivid memory. We sense its presence in the fiction of Flannery O'Connor, Erskine Caldwell, and Harry Crews. But we discover as well in those writers and many others the strongly rural and agricultural nature of the life that developed in Georgia as the frontier disappeared. The fiction of Caldwell, O'Connor, Crews, Jean Toomer, Caroline Miller, Carson McCullers, Herbert Byron Reece, Alice Walker, Mary Hood, and others is often set in a remote and faceless farm and pine land. James Dickey in *Deliverance* and Charlie Smith in *Shine Hawk* explore in different ways the frontier's place in the modern Southern landscape, though for both the frontier has become as much a domain of the mind as of the wilderness.

The gradual disappearance of the frontier brought slow, sometimes almost imperceptible change to the state. But the Civil War, the central event of the state's history (and the nation's), did quite the opposite. That war's reverberations continue to be felt today, though writers have typically assumed a diverse range of attitudes toward it. Such authors as Augusta J. Evans in the nineteenth century and Margaret Mitchell in the twentieth chronicled its impact and in the process helped to foster a mythic past which even today Georgians and Americans struggle to understand. It is difficult to think of any writer, white or black, who has not in some way been affected by the Civil War's consequences. Yet its reverberations have weakened in the twentieth century, and other events have begun to overshadow it. The growth of such cities as Atlanta, Macon, and Savannah and the increasing importance of industry have been powerfully felt in modern Georgia.

Agriculture remains an important part of the state's economy, but Georgia is no longer a primarily agricultural state. Perhaps no modern phenomenon has brought more sweeping change to the modern South than the civil rights movement, in some sense the dramatic conclusion to events set in motion by the end of the Civil War.

One sign of the change that has transformed the state is the role the city, principally Atlanta, plays in much modern Georgia fiction. This city's importance can be traced back to the idea of the New South popularized by Henry Grady and others in the 1880s. Grady believed that the best prospects for the post–Civil War South lay in commerce, industry, and reconciliation with the North. The New South is a powerful force in Margaret Mitchell's *Gone with the Wind*, especially in the character of Scarlett O'Hara, though Mitchell quite clearly mourns the disappearing traditions and values that the New South is supplanting. For Frances Newman in *The Hard-Boiled Virgin*, Pat Conroy in *The Prince of Tides*, Berry Fleming in *Colonel Effingham's Raid*, and Donald Windham in *The Warm Country*, the city is the primary center of life. Those who live there are, for the most part, as contented as their rural counterparts. They hardly consider themselves refugees or urban prisoners. Yet several Georgia writers have explored the tensions between the southern metropolis and the wilderness and farmlands that lie beyond its borders. A primary theme of James Dickey's *Deliverance* is the disappearing wilderness, receding but nonetheless still there, only a short drive away. Georgia writers do not always agree on the virtues of city and country life. Still, the city figures more prominently in modern Georgia writing than it does in the writing of any other Southern state.

Coupled with the memory of the Civil War, the issue of race has for more than a century gripped the imagination of the state's writers. With the end of the Civil War and the trauma of Reconstruction, the predominantly white Georgia writers in the nineteenth century assumed one of two attitudes toward the freed slaves: they were either a menace to law and order (as Charles H. Smith, or "Bill Arp," argued in his postwar letters), or were dispossessed, comic orphans of the only life-style (slavery) really suited to their natures. Some might feel that Joel Chandler Harris endorses this latter attitude in his story "Free Joe," an attitude typical of much post–Civil War apologist writing in the South. (Although "Free Joe" is about a slave freed before the war, by suggesting that "the problems of one generation are the paradoxes of a succeeding one," Harris makes clear that he is really addressing the problem of freed slaves after the war.) What "Free Joe" concerns is the "Negro question" that so occupied white Southerners in the decades following the war: the question of what to do with the freed slaves, of whether to educate them, of whether they should have been freed to begin with. Describing the misery of a former slave rejected by whites and blacks alike, Harris does not at all imply that the man would have been better off in bondage. Instead, he vividly reveals the cruelties of a system of slavery which makes freedom impossible even for the freed slave: society has no place for him at all. The story genuinely pities Joe's suffering and suggests that he cannot simply be ignored, that a solution to his problem must be found. In this way "Free Joe" and Harris anticipate later treatments of the racial theme by twentieth-century writers.

Modern white Georgia writers often express the racial theme as a struggle for recognition and reconciliation. Black writers typically represent it as a struggle for survival and identity, for establishing cultural roots in a hostile or at least indifferent society. No theme is more often explored by Georgia writers. Only a few simply failed to meet the challenges it posed. Sidney Lanier in his 1867 novel *Tiger-Lilies* portrays blacks simply as comic figures. Margaret Mitchell in *Gone with the Wind* (1936) does no better: for her the great racial tragedy of the Civil War was emancipation and the social upheaval it caused. Other writers treated the issue with attitudes ranging from ambiguity to moral outrage. One of the most dramatic moments in Georgia writing occurs in Flannery O'Connor's "The Artificial Nigger," when an old man from the Georgia mountains and his grandson discover the meaning of racism (of class prejudice in general) in the face of an iron jockey (an "artificial nigger") on the lawn of an affluent Atlanta mansion ("They ain't got enough real ones here," says the old man of the wealthy white owners of the iron figure. "They got to have an artificial one"). In this single discovery O'Connor uncovers the roots of the bias and conflict which have torn humankind since its beginnings. She also parallels the dispossession of Southern blacks to that of the two hill people who feel so lost and out of place in Atlanta. Along with Erskine Caldwell and others, O'Connor recognized that the poor Georgia white was as dispossessed and disadvantaged in most ways as the black.

Black Georgia writers have treated the themes of race and racism in their own ways. A consistent focus in black writing has been the struggle for survival and identity in a predominantly white world. For Raymond Andrews, in his Muskhogean County Trilogy (and for Jean Toomer in *Cane*), survival means defining and preserving a cultural heritage. It means much the same for Alice Walker, who is additionally concerned with the struggle of women for identity and welfare in a world dominated by men. Other Georgia women, such as Augusta J. Evans in *Macaria* and *St. Elmo*, Margaret Mitchell in *Gone with the Wind*, and Frances Newman in *The Hard-Boiled Virgin*, have also explored this theme.

Georgia writers inhabit a particular region with a distinct cultural and historical tradition. The characters, events, and themes they write about are aspects of that tradition. But they are also citizens of the nation and the world. The themes that concern them are not so much Georgia themes as they are American and human themes. The importance of Georgia in the literature of its writers is most often an importance of place, a means of rooting the experience of human life in a specific context of personal and cultural values, of identifying oneself out of all time and place in relation to a region, a nation, and a world.

Part One

Georgia Writers: From the Beginnings to 1900

The proximity of the frontier to early nineteenth century Georgia, and the southeastern United States in general, gave rise to a brand of writing that became the nation's first truly native literature. Sometimes called frontier humor or humor of the old southwest or simply tall-tale humor, old Southern humor is a rowdy, bawdy, vital form of writing that vividly conveys the life of the American frontier. Usually it was written by men who did not consider themselves "literary" authors. They were lawyers or doctors or itinerant salesmen who wrote as a hobby or to pass the time while traveling from one town to another. Not surprisingly, their humor usually takes the form of short sketches and anecdotes. Rarely did they write anything approaching the polish or length of a short story. The typical humorous sketch is more an extended joke, though the very best Southern humor transcends these limitations. The narrator of these sketches is often a relatively educated man who describes the doings of people in small towns and settlements along the frontier. Usually his tone is mildly condescending, as if to make clear that he considers himself above what he is describing. Yet his pleasure in what he describes is often evident. Frequently the tales are clearly *told*—narrated by one person to another. In the Sut Lovingood tales of George Washington Harris, the educated narrator George writes down the stories he hears from his uneducated friend Sut, a prankster of the first magnitude. William Tappan Thompson framed his sketches as letters written to a city newspaper editor by the relatively unsophisticated Major Jones. Georgia humorist Henry Nash Smith ("Bill Arp") also wrote letters as well as newspaper columns (the mid twentieth century Piney Woods Pete was his latter-day successor). The African-American folktales preserved by Joel Chandler Harris in his Uncle Remus stories show how the genre was practiced by black Georgians as well as whites.

The informal, unpolished quality of these tales makes them all the more entertaining. Often at their center is a prankster who enjoys playing nasty tricks—sometimes on pompous and mean-spirited hypocrites and sometimes simply for pleasure. Among the most successful Southern humorists were Alabamian Johnson Jones Hooper and his *Adventures of Simon Suggs*, Tennessean George Washington Harris's *Tales of Sut Lovingood*, and Louisianan Henry Clay Lewis's *Odd Leaves from the Life of a Louisiana Swamp Doctor*. One of the earliest and most popular humorists was Georgian Augustus Baldwin Longstreet, whose 1835 collection of sketches *Georgia Scenes* helped define the southern humor genre (and has remained in print since its publication). Soon after Longstreet came William Tappan Thompson, whose charming Major Jones relates stories about life in rural, backwoods Georgia. Thompson's sketches are unusually gentle for the Southern humor tradition, but they are nonetheless funny. Longstreet's humor is more brutal: in his story "The Fight," the two burliest men in town engage in fierce physical combat. In "The Horse Swap" Longstreet recounts a swindle in which an unsuspecting man is traded a horse with a festering saddle sore (a tale which influenced an episode of William Faulkner's novel *The Hamlet*). In "A Gander-Pulling" he describes a contest near Augusta in which young men ride back and forth past a goose suspended from a tree, competing to be the first to pull off the poor creature's head.

The often grotesque blends of humor and violence in the fiction of many modern Georgia writers is one legacy of the Southern humorists, and of the frontier's persistence in the Southern literary imagination. The influence of frontier humor is apparent throughout American literature. Samuel Clemens was an enthusiastic admirer who practiced his own brand in *Huckleberry Finn*, *Tom Sawyer*, and other fiction. Faulkner, Erskine Caldwell, Eudora Welty, Flannery O'Connor, and Harry Crews were all literary inheritors of the tradition, while Lewis Grizzard, Roy Blount, Ferrol Sams, and the comic strip "Pogo" have practiced it in a more popular vein. To the north, S. J. Perelman, James Thurber, Philip Roth, Joseph Heller, Woody Allen, and many others have carried on their own version of the tradition.

Many readers regarded frontier humor as vulgar, crude, and unsuitable for polite consumption, and they turned to other kinds of writing. One alternative was the popular, sentimental, often romantic fiction of Georgia-Alabama novelist Augusta J. Evans, who wrote in the same tradition as Harriet Beecher Stowe and Fanny Fern. Evans was one of the most popular writers of nineteenth-century America. Her 1866 book *St. Elmo* was a phenomenal success and was read well into this century. The strong heroines at the center of Evans's novels contrast markedly with the female characters in many other American works of the time. They apparently influenced Margaret Mitchell in her portrayal of Scarlett O'Hara, and they show that at least some nineteenth-century Southern women were aware of their inferior social position (although the ultimate goal of Evans's heroines was always a good marriage). Writers such as Evans have received renewed attention recently from readers and critics interested in uncovering authors overlooked because of sexual or racial bias. But Evans was not a great writer. Her fiction is clichéd, flowery, and wooden, her characters flat, her plots melodramatic. (In the first thirty-one pages of *St. Elmo*, the main character, Edna Earle, sees a man killed in a duel, his wife die of paralysis, her grandfather die of old age, and a baby and numerous others killed in a train wreck.) Nonetheless, she offers a revealing view of aspects of nineteenth-century Southern society not always addressed by male authors.

Sidney Lanier's only novel *Tiger-Lilies* (1867) is somewhat more memorable than the novels of Evans; it relates the adventures of a young man in the Civil War and is loosely based on Lanier's own experiences. Strongly influenced by European writers and not yet possessed of the mature vision of his greatest poetry, Lanier still managed to give in his book a vivid sense of the atmosphere in the Civil War South.

Black Georgians played only a minor role in nineteenth-century Georgia writing. There are several slave narratives and some letters, but little else. Late in the century, however, one white writer did work to preserve some of the folk narratives of the African-American slave tradition. Joel Chandler Harris, in the last two decades of the nineteenth century, wrote stories, novels, and sketches considerably more varied than his famous Uncle Remus tales would suggest. The humor of his Uncle Remus tales is clear enough. What is not so clear is that in them Harris sought to document significant aspects of slave folklife and culture. In this sense they are local color stories. Some might argue that they belong to the apologist school of post–Civil War literature which sought to assuage grief over the loss of the war by fabricating a mythical antebellum past. Alice Walker certainly argues this point in her angry essay about Harris, "The Dummy in the Window." But in fact Harris showed at least some awareness of the falsehood of that past. He wrote from a number of perspectives, and his stories about slaves and freed blacks in particular suggest that he recognized their oppression. We encounter that recognition in his story "Free Joe" and its genuine sympathy for a black man as a human being rather than merely as a pathetic symbol of a lost antebellum Eden. For a time Harris's Uncle Remus stories were ignored either as racist appropriations of a tradition belonging to black writers, or as children's writing. In recent years they have been rediscovered and reinterpreted by black and white readers alike. Another late nineteenth century writer who wrote in a similar vein was Will N. Harben, who focused much of his writing on poor Georgia whites, and who dedicated to Harris one of his best-known books, *Northern Georgia Sketches*. Harris and Harben produced some of the best examples of realistic writing in the state at the end of the century.

In comparison with the fiction of the twentieth century, the work that Georgians produced in the nineteenth might seem unimpressive, with a few exceptions. Perhaps Georgians were too busy defending slavery or recovering from the Civil War to commit themselves wholly to the literary arts. Yet in the humor of A. B. Longstreet and William Tappan Thompson, and in the local color realism of Joel Chandler Harris, the state made a significant contribution to regional and national literature.

Augustus Baldwin Longstreet

The Fight

In the younger days of the Republic, there lived in the county of ———, two men, who were admitted on all hands to be the very *best men* in the county—which, in the Georgia vocabulary, means they could flog any other two men in the county. Each, through many a hard fought battle, had acquired the mastery of his own battalion; but they lived on opposite sides of the Court House, and in different battalions; consequently they were but seldom thrown together. When they met, however, they were always very friendly; indeed, at their first interview, they seemed to conceive a wonderful attachment to each other, which rather increased than diminished, as they became better acquainted; so that, but for the circumstance which I am about to mention, the question which had been a thousand times asked "Which is the best man, Billy Stallions, (Stallings,) or Bob Durham?" would probably never have been answered.

Billy ruled the upper battalion, and Bob the lower. The former measured six feet and an inch, in his stockings, and without a single pound of cumbrous flesh about him weighed a hundred and eighty. The latter, was an inch shorter than his rival, and ten pounds lighter; but he was much the most active of the two. In running and jumping, he had but few equals in the county; and in wrestling, not one. In other respects they were nearly equal. Both were admirable specimens of human nature in its finest form. Billy's victories had generally been achieved by the tremendous power of his blows; one of which had often proved decisive of his battles; Bob's, by his adroitness in bringing his adversary to the ground. This advantage he had never failed to gain, at the onset, and when gained, he never failed to improve it to the defeat of his adversary. These points of difference, have involved the reader in a doubt, as to the probable issue of a contest between them. It was not so, however, with the two battalions. Neither had the least difficulty in determining the point by the most natural and irresistible deductions *a priori:* and though, by the same course of reasoning, they arrived at directly opposite conclusions, neither felt its confidence in the least shaken by this circumstance. The upper battalion swore "that Billy only wanted one lick at him to knock his heart, liver and lights out of him; and if he got two at him, he'd knock him into a cocked hat." The lower battalion retorted, "that he wouldn't have time to double his fist, before Bob would put his head where his feet ought to be; and that, by the time he hit the ground, the meat would fly off his face so quick, that people would think it was shook off by the fall." These disputes often led to the *argumentum ad hominem;* but with such equality of success on both sides, as to leave the main question just where they found it. They usually ended, however, in the common way, with a bet; and many a quart of old Jamaica (whiskey had not then supplanted rum) were staked upon the issue. Still, greatly to the annoyance of the curious, Billy and Bob continued to be good friends.

Now there happened to reside in the county, just alluded to, a little fellow, by the name of Ransy Sniffle: a sprout of Richmond, who, in his earlier days, had fed copiously upon red clay and blackberries. This diet had given to Ransy a complexion that a corpse would have disdained to own, and an abdominal rotundity that was quite unprepossessing. Long spells of the fever and ague, too, in Ransy's youth, had conspired with clay and blackberries, to throw him quite out of the order of nature. His shoulders were fleshless and elevated; his head large and flat; his neck slim and translucent; and his arms, hands, fingers and feet, were lengthened out of all proportion to the rest of his frame. His joints were large, and his limbs small; and as for flesh, he could not with propriety be said to have any. Those parts which nature usually supplies with the most of this article—the calves of the legs for example—presented in him the appearance of so many well drawn blisters. His height was just five feet nothing; and his average weight in blackberry season, ninety-five. I have been thus particular in describing him, for the purpose of showing what a great matter a little fire sometimes kindleth. There was nothing on this earth which delighted Ransy so much as a fight. He never seemed fairly alive, except when he was witnessing, fomenting, or talking about a fight. Then, indeed, his deep sunken grey eye, assumed something of a living fire; and his tongue acquired a volubility that bordered upon eloquence. Ransy had been kept for more than a year in the most torturing suspense, as to the comparative manhood of Billy Stallings and Bob Durham. He had resorted to all his usual expedients to bring them in collision, and had entirely failed. He had faithfully reported to Bob all that had been said by the people in the upper battalion "agin him," and "he was sure Billy Stallings started it. He heard Bill say himself to Jim Brown, that he could whip him, *or any other man in his battalion,*" and this he told to Bob—adding, "Dod burn his soul, if he was a little bigger, if he'd let any man *put upon* his battalion in such a way." Bob replied, "If he (Stallings) thought so, he'd better come and try it." This Ransy carried to Billy, and delivered it with a spirit becoming his own dignity, and the character of his battalion, and with a coloring well calculated to give it effect. These, and many other schemes which Ransy laid, for the gratification of his curiosity, entirely failed of their object. Billy and Bob continued friends, and Ransy had begun to lapse into the most tantalizing and hopeless despair, when a circumstance occurred, which led to a settlement of the long disputed question.

It is said that a hundred game cocks will live in perfect harmony together, if you will not put a hen with them: and so it would have been with Billy and Bob, had there been no women in the world. But there were women in the world, and from them, each of our heroes had taken to himself a wife. The good ladies were no strangers to the prowess of their husbands, and strange as it may seem, they presumed a little upon it.

The two battalions had met at the Courthouse, upon a regimental parade. The two champions were there, and their wives had accompanied them. Neither knew the other's lady, nor were the ladies known to each other. The exercises of the day were just over, when Mrs. Stallings and Mrs. Durham stept simultaneously into the store of Zepheniah Atwater, from "down east."

"Have you any Turkey-red?" said Mrs. S.

"Have you any curtain calico?" said Mrs. D. at the same moment.

"Yes, ladies," said Mr. Atwood, "I have both."

"Then help me first," said Mrs. D., "for I'm in a hurry."

"I'm in as great a hurry as she is," said Mrs. S., "and I'll thank you to help me first."

"And pray, who are you, madam!" continued the other.

"Your betters, madam," was the reply.

At this moment Billy Stallings stept in. "Come," said he, "Nancy, let's be going; it's getting late."

"I'd o' been gone half an hour ago," she replied, "if it hadn't been for that impudent huzzy."

"Who do you call an impudent huzzy? you nasty, good-for-nothing, snaggle-toothed gaub of fat, you," returned Mrs. D.

"Look here woman," said Billy, "have you got a husband here? If you have, I'll *lick* him till he learns to teach you better manners, you *sassy* heifer you." At this moment something was seen to rush out of the store, as if ten thousand hornets were stinging it; crying "Take care—let me go—don't hold me—where's Bob Durham?" It was Ransy Sniffle, who had been listening in breathless delight, to all that had passed.

"Yonder's Bob, setting on the Courthouse steps," cried one. "What's the matter?"

"Don't talk to me!" said Ransy. "Bob Durham, you'd better go long yonder, and take care of your wife. They're playing h——l with her there, in Zeph. Atwater's store. Dod deternally durn my soul, if any man was to talk to my wife as Bill Stallions is talking to yours, if I didn't drive blue blazes through him in less than no time."

Bob sprang to the store in a minute, followed by a hundred friends; for the bully of a county never wants friends.

"Bill Stallions," said Bob, as he entered, "what have you been saying to my wife?"

"Is that your wife?" inquired Billy, obviously much surprised, and a little disconcerted.

"Yes, she is, and no man shall abuse her, I don't care who he is."

"Well," rejoined Billy, "it an't worth while to go over it—I've said enough for a fight: and if you'll step out, we'll settle it!"

"Billy," said Bob, "are you for a fair fight?"

"I am," said Billy. "I've heard much of your manhood, and I believe I'm a better man than you are. If you will go into a ring with me, we can soon settle the dispute."

"Choose your friends," said Bob; "make your ring, and I'll be in it with mine, as soon as you will."

They both stept out, and began to strip very deliberately; each battalion gathering round its champion—except Ransy, who kept himself busy, in a most honest endeavor to hear and see all that transpired in both groups, at the same time. He ran from one to the other, in quick succession—peeped here, and listened there—talked to this one—then to that one—and then to himself—squatted under one's legs, and another's arms; and in the short interval between stripping and stepping into the ring, managed to get himself trod on by half of both battalions. But Ransy was not the only one interested upon this occasion:—the most intense interest prevailed every where. Many were the conjectures, doubts, oaths and imprecations uttered, while the parties were preparing for the combat. All the knowing ones were consulted as to the issue; and they all agreed to a man, in one of two opinions: either that Bob would flog Billy, or Billy would flog Bob. We must be permitted, however, to dwell for a moment upon the opinion of 'Squire Thomas Loggins; a man, who it was said, had never failed to predict the issue of a fight, in all his life. Indeed, so unerring had he always proved, in this regard, that it would have been counted the most obstinate infidelity, to doubt for a moment, after he had delivered himself. 'Squire Loggins was a man who said but little; but that little was always delivered with the most imposing solemnity of look and cadence. He always wore the aspect of profound thought, and you could not look at him without coming to the conclusion, that he was elaborating truth from its most intricate combinations.

"Uncle Tommy," said Sam Reynolds, "you can tell us all about it, if you will—how will the fight go?"

The question immediately drew an anxious group around the 'Squire. He raised his teeth slowly from the head of his walking cane, on which they had been resting—pressed his lips closely and thoughtfully together—threw down his eye brows—dropped his chin—raised his eyes to an angle of twenty three degrees—paused about half a minute, and replied: "Sammy, watch Robert Durham close in the beginning of the fight—take care of William Stallions in the middle of it—and see who has the wind at the end." As he uttered the last member of the sentence, he looked slyly at Bob's friends, and winked very significantly; whereupon they rushed, with one accord, to tell Bob what Uncle Tommy had said. As they retired, the 'Squire turned to Billy's friends, and said, with a smile: "Them boys think I mean that Bob will whip."

Here the other party kindled into joy, and hastened to inform Billy how Bob's friends had deceived themselves as to Uncle Tommy's opinion. In the meantime, the principals and seconds, were busily employed in preparing themselves for the combat. The plan of attack and defence, the manner of improving the various turns of the conflict, "the best mode of saving wind," &c. &c. were all discussed and settled. At length, Billy announced himself ready, and his crowd were seen moving to the centre of the Court House Square; he and his five seconds in the rear. At the same time, Bob's party moved to the same point, and in the same order. The ring was now formed, and for a moment the silence of death reigned through both battalions. It was soon interrupted, however, by the cry of "clear the way!" from Billy's seconds; when the ring opened in the centre of the upper battalion (for the order of march had arranged the centre of the two battalions on opposite sides of the circle) and Billy stept into the ring from the east, followed by his friends. He was stript to the trowsers, and exhibited an arm, breast and shoulders, of the most tremendous portent. His step was firm, daring and martial; and as he bore his fine form a little

in advance of his friends, an involuntary burst of triumph broke from his side of the ring; and at the same moment, an uncontrollable thrill of awe, ran along the whole curve of the lower battalion.

"Look at him!" was heard from his friends—"just look at him."

"Ben, how much you ask to stand before that man two seconds?"

"Pshaw, don't talk about it! Just thinkin' about it's broke three o' my ribs a'ready!"

"What's Bob Durham going to do, when Billy lets that arm loose upon him?"

"God bless your soul, he'll think thunder and lightning a mint julip to it."

"Oh, look here men, go take Bill Stallions out o' that ring, and bring in Phil Johnson's stud horse, so that Durham may have some chance! I don't want to see the man killed right away."

These and many other like expressions, interspersed thickly with oaths of the most modern coinage, were coming from all points of the upper battalion, while Bob was adjusting the girth of his pantaloons, which walking had discovered, not to be exactly right. It was just fixed to his mind, his foes becoming a little noisy, and his friends a little uneasy at his delay, when Billy called out, with a smile of some meaning, "Where's the bully of the lower battalion? I'm getting tired of waiting."

"Here he is," said Bob, lighting, as it seemed from the clouds in the ring, for he had actually bounded clear of the head of Ransy Sniffle, into the circle. His descent was quite as imposing as Billy's entry, and excited the same feelings, but in opposite bosoms.

Voices of exultation now rose on his side.

"Where did he come from?"

"Why," said one of the seconds (all having just entered), "we were girting him up, about a hundred yards out yonder, when he heard Billy ask for the bully; and he fetched a leap over the Courthouse, and went out of sight; but I told them to come on, they'd find him here."

Here the lower battalion burst into a peal of laughter, mingled with a look of admiration, which seemed to denote their entire belief of what they had heard.

"Boys, widen the ring, so as to give him room to jump."

"Oh, my little flying wild cat, hold him if you can! and when you get him fast, hold lightning next."

"Ned what you think he's made of?"

"Steel-springs and chicken-hawk, God bless you!"

"Gentlemen," said one of Bob's seconds, "I understand it is to be a fair fight; catch as catch can, rough and tumble:—no man touch 'till one or the other hollos."

"That's the rule," was the reply from the other side.

"Are you ready?"

"We are ready."

"Then blaze away my game cocks."

At the word, Bob dashed at his antagonist at full speed; and Bill squared himself to receive him with one of his most fatal blows. Making his calculation from Bob's velocity, of the time when he would come within striking distance, he let drive with tremendous force. But Bob's onset was obviously planned to avoid this blow; for contrary to all expectations, he stopt short just out of arms reach; and before Billy could recover his balance—Bob had him "all under-hold." The next second, sure enough, "found Billy's head where his feet ought to be." How it was done, no one could tell; but as if by supernatural power, both Billy's feet were thrown full half his own height in the air, and he came down with a force that seemed to shake the earth. As he struck the ground, commingled shouts, screams and yells burst from the lower battalion, loud enough to be heard for miles. "Hurra my little hornet!"—"Save him!"—"Feed him!—Give him the Durham physic till his stomach turns!" Billy was no sooner down than Bob was on him, and lending him awful blows about the face and breast. Billy made two efforts to rise by main strength, but failed. "Lord bless you man, don't try to get up!—*Lay* still and take it!—you *bleege* to have it."

Billy now turned his face suddenly to the ground, and rose upon his hands and knees. Bob jerked up both his hands and threw him on his face. He again recovered his late position, of which Bob endeavored to deprive him as before; but missing one arm, he failed, and Billy rose. But he had scarcely resumed his feet before they flew up as before, and he came again to the ground. "No fight gentlemen!" cried Bob's friends, "the man can't stand up!—Bouncing feet are bad things to fight in." His fall, however, was this time comparatively light; for having thrown his right arm round Bob's neck, he carried his head down with him. This grasp, which was obstinately maintained, prevented Bob from getting on him, and they lay head to head, seeming, for a time, to do nothing. Presently they rose, as if by mutual consent; and as they rose, a shout broke from both battalions. "Oh, my lark!" cried the east, "has he foxed you? Do you begin to feel him! He's only beginning to fight—He ain't got warm yet."

"Look yonder!" cried the west—"didn't I tell you so! He hit the ground so hard, it jarred his nose off. Now ain't he a pretty man as he stands! He shall have my sister Sall just for his pretty looks. I want to get in the breed of them sort o' men, to drive ugly out of my kin folks."

I looked and saw that Bob had entirely lost his left ear, and a large piece from his left cheek. His right eye was a little discolored, and the blood flowed profusely from his wounds.

Bill presented a hideous spectacle. About a third of his nose, at the lower extremity, was bit off, and his face so swelled and bruised, that it was difficult to discover in it any thing of the human visage—much more the fine features which he carried into the ring.

They were up only long enough for me to make the foregoing discoveries, when down they went again, precisely as before. They no sooner touched the ground than Bill relinquished his hold upon Bob's neck. In this, he seemed to all, to have forfeited the only advantage which put him upon an equality with his adversary. But the movement was soon explained. Bill wanted this arm for other purposes than defence; and he had made arrangements whereby he knew that he could make it answer these purposes; for when they rose again, he had the middle finger of Bob's left hand in his mouth. He was now secure from Bob's annoying trips; and he began to lend his adversary most tremendous blows, every one of which was hailed by a shout from his friends. "Bullets!—*Hoss* kicking!—Thunder!"—"That'll do for the face—now feel his short ribs, Billy!"

I now considered the contest settled. I deemed it impossible for any human being to withstand for five seconds, the loss of blood which issued from Bob's ear, cheek, nose and finger, accompanied with such blows as he was receiving. Still he maintained the conflict, and gave blow for blow with considerable effect. But the blows of each became slower and weaker, after the first three or four; and it became obvious, that Bill wanted the room, which Bob's finger occupied, for breathing. He would therefore, probably, in a short time, have let it go, had not Bob anticipated his politeness, by jerking away his hand, and making him a present of the finger. He now seized Bill again, and brought him to his knees—but he recovered. He again brought him to his knees; and he again recovered. A third effort, however, brought him down, and Bob on top of him. These efforts seemed to exhaust the little remaining strength of both; and they lay, Bill undermost, and Bob across his breast, motionless, and panting for breath. After a short pause, Bob gathered his hand full of dirt and sand, and was in the act of grinding it in his adversary's eyes, when Bill cried "Enough!"—Language cannot describe the scene which followed—the shouts, oaths, frantic jestures, taunts, replies and little fights; and therefore I shall not attempt it. The champions were borne off by their seconds, and washed: when many a bleeding wound, and ugly bruise, was discovered on each, which no eye had seen before.

Many had gathered round Bob, and were in various ways congratulating and applauding him, when a voice from the centre of the circle cried out: "Boys, hush and listen to me!" It proceeded from 'Squire Loggins, who had made his way to Bob's side, and had gathered his face up into one of its most flattering and intelligible expressions. All were obedient to the 'Squire's command. "Gentlemen," continued he, with a most knowing smile, "is—Sammy—Reynold—in—this—company—of—gentlemen." "Yes," said Sam, "here I am." "Sammy," said the 'Squire, winking to the company, and drawing the head of his cane to his mouth with an arch smile, as he closed, "I—wish—you—to tell—cousin—Bobby—and—these—gentlemen here present—what—your—uncle—Tommy—said—before—the—fight—began." "Oh! get away, Uncle Tom," says Sam, smiling, (the 'Squire winked,) "you don't know nothing about *fighting*." (The 'Squire winked again.) "All you know about it, is how it'll begin; how it'll go on; how it'll end; that's all. Cousin Bob, when you going to fight again, just go to the old man, and let him tell you all about it. If he can't, don't ask nobody else nothing about it, I tell you." The 'Squire's foresight was complimented in many ways by the by-standers; and he retired, advising "the boys to be at peace, as fighting was a bad business."

Durham and Stallings kept their beds for several weeks, and did not meet again for two months. When they met, Billy stepped up to Bob and offered his hand, saying: "Bobby you've *licked* me a fair fight; but you wouldn't have done it, if I hadn't been in the wrong. I oughtn't to have treated your wife as I did; and I felt so through the whole fight; and it sort o' cowed me."

"Well Billy," said Bob, "let's be friends. Once in the fight, when you had my finger in your mouth, and was pealing me in the face and breast, I was going to hollo; but I thought of Betsy, and knew the house would be too hot for me, if I got whipt, when fighting for her, after always whipping when I fought for myself."

"Now, that's what I always love to see," said a by-stander: "It's true, I brought about the fight; but I wouldn't have done it, if it hadn't o' been on account of *Miss* (Mrs.) Durham. But dod eternally durn my soul, if I ever could stand by and see any woman put upon—much less *Miss* Durham. If Bobby hadn't been there, I'd o' took it up myself, be durned if I wouldn't, even if I'd o' got whipt for it—But we're all friends now." The reader need hardly be told, this was Ransy Sniffle.

Thanks to the Christian religion, to schools, colleges, and benevolent associations, such scenes of barbarism and cruelty, as that which I have been just describing, are now of rare occurrence: though they may still be occasionally met with in some of the new counties. Wherever they prevail, they are a disgrace to that community. The peace officers who countenance them, deserve a place in the Penitentiary.

William Tappan Thompson

From *Major Jones' Courtship*

Major Jones Pops the Question

Pineville, December 27th, 1842

To Mr. Thompson:—*Dear Sir*—Crismus is over, and the thing's ded. You know I told you in my last letter I was gwine to bring Miss Mary up to the chalk a Crismus. Well, I done it, slick as a whistle, though it come mighty nigh bein a serious undertakin. But I'll tell you all about the whole circumstance.

The fact is, I's made my mind up more'n twenty times to jest go and come rite out with the whole bisness, but whenever I got whar she was, and whenever she looked at me with her witchin eyes, and kind o' blushed at me, I always felt sort o' skeered and fainty, and all what I made up to tell her was forgot, so I couldn't think of it to save me. But you's a married man, Mr. Thompson, so I couldn't tell you nothin bout poppin the question, as they call it. Its a mighty grate favor to ax of a rite pretty gall, and to people as aint used to it, it goes monstrous hard, don't it? They say widders don't mind it no more'n nothin. But I'm making a transgression as the preacher ses.

Crismus eve I put on my new suit and shaved my face as slick as a smoothin iron and went over to old Miss Stallionses. As soon as I went into the parler whar they was all setin round the fire, Miss Carline and Miss Kesiah both laughed rite out—

"There, there," ses they, "I told you so, I knew it would be Joseph."

"What's I done, Miss Carline," ses I.

"You come under little sister's chicken bone, and I do blieve she knew you was comin when she put it over the dore."

"No I didn't—I didn't no such thing, now," ses Miss Mary, and her face blushed red all over.

"Oh, you needn't deny it," ses Miss Kesiah, "you 'long to Joseph now, jest as sure as ther's any charm in chicken bones."

I knowd that was a first rate chance to say something, but the dear little creater looked so sorry and kep blushin so, I couldn't say nothin zactly to the pint, so I tuck a chair and reached up and tuck down the bone and put it in my pocket.

"What are you gwine to do with that old bone now, Majer?" ses Miss Mary.

"I'm gwine to keep it as long as I live," ses I, "as a Crismus present from the handsomest gall in Georgia."

When I sed that, she blushed worse and worse.

"Aint you shamed, Majer?" ses she.

"Now you ought to give *her* a Crismus gift, Joseph, to keep all *her* life," ses Miss Carline.

"Ah," ses old Miss Stallions, "when I was a gall we used to hang up our stockins—"

"Why, mother!" ses all of 'em, "to say stockins rite afore—"

Then I felt a little streaked too, cause they was all blushin as hard as they could.

"Highty-tity!" ses the old lady—"what finement. I'd like to know what harm ther is in stockins. People now-a-days is gittin so mealy-mouthed they can't call nothin by its name, and I don't see as they's any better than the old time people was. When I was a gall like you, child, I use to hang up my stockins and git 'em full of presents."

The gals kep laughin.

"Never mind," ses Miss Mary, "Majer's got to give me a Crismus gift—won't you Majer?"

"Oh, yes," ses I, "you know I promised you one."

"But I didn't mean *that,*" ses she.

"I've got one for you, what I want you to keep all your life, but it would take a two bushel bag to hold it," ses I.

"Oh, that's the kind," ses she.

"But will you keep it as long as you live?" ses I.

"Certainly I will, Majer."

"Monstrous finement now-a-days—old people don't know nothin bout perliteness," said old Miss Stallions, jest gwine to sleep.

"Now you hear that, Miss Carline," ses I. "She ses she'll keep it all her life."

"Yes, I will," ses Miss Mary—"but what is it?"

"Never mind," ses I, "you hang up a bag big enuff to hold it and you'll find out what it is, when you see it in the mornin."

Miss Carline winked at Miss Kesiah, and then whispered to her—then they both laughed and looked at me as mischievous as they could. They spected somethin.

"You'll be sure to give it to me now, if I hang up a bag," ses Miss Mary.

"And promise to keep it," ses I.

"Well, I will, cause I know you wouldn't give me nothin that wasn't worth keepin."

They all agreed they would hang up a bag for me to put Miss Mary's Crismas present in, on the back porch, and bout nine o'clock I told 'em good evenin and went home.

I sot up till mid-night, and when they was all gone to bed I went softly into the back gate, and went up to the porch and thar, shore enuff, was a grate big meal bag hangin to the jice. It was monstrous unhandy to git into it, but I was tarmined not to back out. So I sot some chairs on top of a bench and got hold of the rope and let myself down into the bag; but jest as I was gittin in, the bag swung agin the chairs, and down they went with a terrible racket. But no body didn't wake up but old Miss Stallionses grate big cur dog, and here he cum rippin and tarin through the yard like rath, and round and round he went trying to find what was the matter. I sot down in the bag and didn't breathe louder nor a kitten, for fear he'd find me out, and after a while he quit barkin. The wind begun to blow bominable cold, and the old bag kep turnin round and swinging so it made me sea-sick as the mischief. I was afraid to move for fear the rope would brake and let me fall, and thar I sot with my teeth ratlin like I had a ager. It seemed like it would never come daylight, and I do blieve if I didn't love Miss Mary so powerful I would froze to deth; for my hart was the only spot that felt warm, and it didn't beat more'n two licks a minit, only when I thought how she would be sprised in the mornin, and then it went in a canter. Bimeby the cussed old dog come up on the porch and begun to smell bout the bag, and then he barked like he thought he'd treed something. "Bow! wow! wow!" ses he.—Then he'd smell agin, and try to git up to the bag. "Git out!" ses I, very low, for fear they would hear me. "Bow! wow! wow!" ses he. "Be gone! you bominable fool," ses I, and I felt all over in spots, for I spected every minit he'd nip me, and what made it worse, I didn't know whar bouts he'd take hold. "Bow! wow! wow!"—Then I tried coaxin—"come here, good feller," ses I, and whistled a little to him, but it wan't no use. Thar he stood and kep up his eternal whinin and barkin, all night. I couldn't tell when daylight was breakin, only by the chickens crowin, and I was monstrous glad to hear 'em, for if I'd had to stay thar one hour more, I don't blieve I'd ever got out o' that bag alive.

Old Miss Stallions come out fust, and as soon as she saw the bag, ses she,

"What upon yeath has Joseph put in that bag for Mary? I'll lay its a yearlin or some live animal, or Bruin wouldn't bark at it so."

She went in to call the galls, and I sot thar, shiverin all over so I couldn't hardly speak if I tried to—but I didn't say nothin. Bimeby they all come runnin out.

"My lord, what is it?" ses Miss Mary.

"Oh, it's alive!" ses Miss Kesiah, "I seed it move."

"Call Cato, and make him cut the rope," ses Miss Carline, "and less see what it is. Come here Cato and git this bag down."

"Don't hurt it for the world," ses Miss Mary.

Cato untied the rope that was round the jice, and let the bag down easy on the floor, and I tumbled out all covered with corn meal, from hed to foot.

"Goodness gracious!" ses Miss Mary, "if it aint the Majer himself!"

"Yes," ses I, "and you know you promised to keep my Crismas present as long as you lived."

The galls laughed themselves almost to deth and went to brushin off the meal as fast as they could, sayin they was gwine to hang that bag up every Crismas till they got husbands too. Miss Mary—bless her bright eyes—she blushed as butiful as a morninglory, and sed she'd stick to her word. She was rite out o' bed, and her hair wasn't comed, and her dress wasn't fixt at all, but the way she looked pretty was rale distractin. I do blieve if I was froze stif, one look at her charmin face, as she stood lookin down to the floor with her rogish eyes, and her bright curls fallin all over her snowy neck, would fotch'd me too. I tell you what, it was worth hangin' in a meal bag from one Crismas to another to feel as happy as I have ever since.

I went home after we had the laugh out, and set by the fire till I got thawed. In the forenoon all the Stallionses come over to our house and we had one of the gratest Crismus Dinners that ever was seed in Georgia, and I don't blieve a happier company ever sot down to the same table. Old Miss Stallions and mother settled the match, and talked over everything that ever happened in ther families, and laughed at me and Mary, and cried bout ther ded husbands, cause they wasn't alive to see ther children married.

Its all settled now, cept we haint sot the weddin day. I'd like to have it all over at once, but young galls always like to be engaged awhile, you know, so I spose I must wait a month or so. Mary (she ses I mustn't call her Miss Mary now) has been a good deal of trouble and botheration to me, but if you could see her, you wouldn't think I ought to grudge a little sufferin to git sich a sweet little wife.

You must come to the weddin if you possibly kin. I'll let you know when. No more from

Your frend til deth,

JOS. JONES

N.B. I've ben thinkin bout your proposal for me to edit that little paper what you want to start. I should like to blige you if it won't be no more trouble than you say, but Mary ses she thinks I better not, cause editers dont never make nothin, and are always poor as Jobe's turky. I would like the bisness mighty well, if it would pay, but if I do go into it I wont have a single scriber what dont pay rite up when he takes the paper. When my weddin's over, I'll have considerable time to rite, and if I was certain that a rite spunky little paper, full of fun and good pieces, could git scribers enuf at sich a low price, to pay for the cost and trouble, I'd go into it like a two-year-old in a cane break.

I like to forgot to tell you bout cousin Pete. He got snapt on egnog when he heard of my gagement, and he's ben as meller as hosapple ever sense.

The Major Avenged

Pineville, February 2nd, 1843

To Mr. Thompson—*Dear Sir*—Ever sense I writ my last letter to you, things is gone on jest as strate as a shingle, and the only thing what troubles me is, I'm fraid it's all too good to last. It's always ben the way with me ever sense I can remember, whenever I'm the happyest sum cussed thing seems to turn up jest to upset all my calculations, and now, though the day is sot for the weddin, and the Stallionses is gittin every thing reddy as fast as they can, I wouldn't be sprised much if some bominable thing was to happen, some yeathquake or something, jest to bust it all up agin, though I should hate it monstrous.

Old Miss Stallions red that piece in the Miscellany bout the mistake in parson Miller's figers, and I do blieve she's as glad bout it as if she was shore she would live a whole thousand years more herself. She ses she hain't got no objection to the weddin now, for me and Mary'll have plenty of time to make a fortin for our children and rais 'em up as they ought to be. She ses she always wondered how Mr. Miller could cifer the thing out so strait, to the very day, without a single mistake, but now he's made sich a terrible blunder of a whole thousand years, she ses she knows he aint no smarter nor other people, if he was raised at the north.

It's really surprisin how mazin poplar it does make a body to be engaged to be married to a butiful young lady. Sense the thing's leaked out, every body's my tickeler frend, and I can't meet nobody wherever I go, but what wants to gratilate me on my good fortin, cept cousin Pete and two or three other fellers, who look sort o' like they wanted to laugh and couldn't. Almost every night Mary and me is invited to a party. Tother night we went to one to old Squire Rogerses, whar I got my dander up a little the worst I've had it for some time. I don't blieve you have ever hearn of jest sich a fool trick as they played on me. Ther was a good many thar, and as the Squire don't 'low dancin, they all played games and tricks, and sich foolishness to pass away the time, which to my notion's a bominable site worse than dancin.

Cousin Pete was thar splurgin bout in his biggest, and with his dandy cut trowsers and big whiskers, and tried to take the shine off everybody else, jest as he always does. Well, bimeby he ses,

"Spose we play brother Bob—let's play brother Bob."

"Yes, lets play that," ses all of 'em, "won't you be brother Bob, Majer?"

"Who's brother Bob?" ses I, for I didn't know nothing bout it, and that's the way I cum to be so bominably tuck in.

"I tell you," ses he, "you and some body else must set down in the chairs and be blindfolded, and the rest must all walk round and round you, and keep tappin you on the head with sumthing til you gess who bob'd you."

"But how bob me?" ses I.

"Why," ses he, "when any one taps you, you must say, brother, I'm bob'd! and then they'll ax, who bob'd you? and if you gess the rite one, then they must take your place and be bob'd til they gess who bob'd 'em. If you'll be blindfolded I will," ses he, "jest for fun."

"Well," ses I, "anything for fun," and cousin Pete sot out two chairs into the middle of the room, and we sot down, and they tied a handkercher round my eyes tite as the mischief, so I couldn't see to gess no more'n if I had no eyes at all.

I hadn't sot no time fore cawhalux! some one tuck me rite side o' the hed with a dratted big book. The fire flew out o' my eyes in big live coals and I like to keeled over out of the chair. I felt my blood risin like a mill-tail but they all laughed mightily at the fun, and after a while ses I, "brother I'm bob'd." "Who bob'd you?" ses they. I guessed the biggest-fisted feller in the room, but it wasn't him. The next minit spang went the book agin cousin Pete's head. "Whew!" ses he, "brother I'm bob'd." "Who bob'd you?" ses they. But cousin Pete didn't gess rite nother, and the fust thing I knowed, whang they tuck me agin. I was dredful anxious to gess rite, but it was no use, I missed it every time, and so did cousin Pete, and the harder they hit the harder they laughed. One time they hit me a great deal softlier than the rest. "Brother, I'm bob'd!" ses I. "Who bob'd you?" ses they. "Miss Mary Stallions," ses I. "No I never," ses she, and they all roared out worse than ever.

I begin to git monstrous tired of sich fun, which seemed so much like the frogs in the spellin book—for it was fun to them but it was deth to me—and I don't know what I would done if Mary hadn't come up and ontied the hankercher.

"Lets play something else," ses she, and her face was as red as fire, and she looked sort o' mad out of her eyes.

I seed ther was something wrong in a minit.

Well, they all went on playin "pawns" and " 'pon honor," and "Here we go round the gooseberry bush," and "Oh sister Feby, how merry we be," and sich nonsense til they played all they knowed, and while they was playin Mary told me all how cousin Pete bob'd me himself.

It was the most oudacious take in I ever hearn of. Do you think the cus didn't set rite down beside me and never blindfolded himself at all, and hit me every lick himself, now and then hittin his knee with the book, to make me blieve he was bob'd too! My hed was a singin with the licks when she told me how he done me, and I do blieve if it hadn't ben for her I'd gin cousin Pete sich a lickin rite thar in that room as he never had afore in his born days. Blazes! but I was mad at fust. But Mary begged me not to raise no fus bout it, now it was all over, and she would fix him for his smartness. I hadn't no sort of a ide how she was gwine to do it, but I knowd she was enuff for cousin Pete any time, so I jest let her go ahed. Well, she tuck the bominable fool off to one side and whispered to him like she was gwine to let him into the secret. She told him bout a new play what she learned down to Macon when she was at the college, called "Interduction to the King and Queen," what she sed was a grate deal funnyer than "Brother Bob," and swaded him to help to git 'em all to play.

After she and him made it all up, cousin Pete put out three chairs close together in a roe for a throne, and Mary she put a sheet over 'em to make 'em look a little grand. Bill Byers was to be King and Mary was to be Queen.

"Now you must all come in tother room," ses cousin Pete, "only them what belongs to the court, and then you must come in and be interduced, one at a time."

"I aint gwine," ses Tom Stallions, "for ther's some trick in it."

"No ther aint," ses cousin Pete, "I'll give you my word ther aint no trick, only a little fun."

"Well," ses I, "I's had fun enough for one nite."

Mary looked at me and kind o' winked, and ses she "you're one of the court you know, Majer, but jest go out till the court is sumonsed before the throne."

Well we all went out, and bimeby Bill Biers called out the names of all the lords and ladys what belonged to the court, and we all went in and tuck chairs on both sides of the throne.

Cousin Pete was to be the first one interduced, and Samuwell Rogers was to be the feller what interduced the company. Well bimeby the dore opened and in come cousin Pete, bowin and scrapin, and twistin and rigglein and putin on more ares nor a French dancin master—he beat Crotchett all to smash. The King sot on one side of the throne and the Queen on tother, leavin room in the middle for some one else. Sam was so full of laugh at cousin Pete's anticks that he couldn't hardly speak.

"Doctor Peter Jones," ses he, "I interduce you to ther Majestys the King and Queen."

Cousin Pete scraped about a while and then drapt on one knee, rite afore 'em.

"Rise gallant knight," ses Bill Byers, "rise, we dub you knight of the royal bath."

Cousin Pete got up and bowed and scraped a few more times, and went to set down between 'em, but they ris up jest as he went to set down, and the fust thing he knowd, kerslosh he went, rite into a big tub full of cold water, with nothing but his hed and heels stickin out.

He tried to kiss Mary as he was takin his seat, and if you could jest seed him as he went into that tub with his arms reached out to her, and his mouth sot for a kiss, I do blieve you'd laughed more'n you ever did afore in your life. The fellers was all so spicious that some trick was gwine to be played, that they left the dore open and when the thing tuck place they all run in shoutin and laughin like they would bust ther sides.

Pete got out as quick as he could, and I never seed a feller so wilted down in all my life. He got as mad as a hornet, and sed it was a d——d mean trick to sarve enny body so, specially in cold wether. And he went rite off home by himself to dry.

Mary made the niggers take out the middle chair and put the tub of water thar when we was all in tother room. Pete didn't spicion the trick was gwine to turn out that way—he thought the queen was gwine to sentence every feller what didn't kiss her as he sot down, to do something that would make fun for the rest, and he was jest gwine to open the game. I felt perfectly satisfied after that, and I don't think cousin Pete will be quite so fond of funny tricks the next time.

But I like to forget to tell you, my weddin is to take place—pervidin ther aint no more yeath quakes nor unaccountabel things to prevent—on the 22 of this month, which you know is a famous day what ought to be celebrated by every genewine patriot in the world. I shall look for you to come, and I hope you will be sure to be thar, for I know you wouldn't grudge the ride jest to see Miss Mary Jones what is to be. We's gwine to have a considerable getherin, jest to please the old folks, and old Miss Stallions ses she's gwine to give us a real Georgia weddin of the old time fashion. No more from

Your frend til deth,

JOS. JONES

P.S.—I went over tother nite to see 'em all, and they was as bisy as bees in a tar barrel sowin and makin up finery. Mary was sowin something mighty fine and white with ruffles and jigamarees all round it. "What kind of a thing is that?" ses I. The gals looked at one another and laughed like they would die, and my poor little Mary (bless her soul) kep getherin it up in a heap and blushin dredful.—"Tell him, sis," ses Miss Carline, but Mary looked rite down and didn't say nothin. "I'll tell him," ses Miss Kesiah—"It's a—" "No you shant now—stop, stop," ses Mary, and she put her pretty little hand rite on Miss Kesiah's mouth, and looked like she'd cry for a little. I felt so sorry for her, I told 'em I didn't want to know, and they put the things away, and bimeby I went home, but I kep thinkin all the way what upon yeath it could be. I spose I'll find out some day.

Cousin Pete Goes Courting

Pineville, December 29th, 1843

To Mr. Thompson:—*Dear Sir*—Well, Crismus and New Years is gone, and a heap of fun has gone with 'em. Down here in Pineville we had real times, you may be sure. Every body tuck Crismus, specially the niggers, and sich other carryins on—sich dancin and singin, and shootin poppers and skyrackets—you never did see. But the best joke was the way cousin Pete got tuck in 'bout gettin in sister Keziah's Crismus bag. Pete had a kind of sneakin notion of her for some time, but the dratted fool don't know no more about courtin nor a hown pup does bout 'stronomy. He was over to our hous Crismus eve, gwine on with his nonsense, and botherin sister Kiz til she got rite tired of him—tellin her how he wanted to git marryed so bad he didn't know what would come of him, and how he wished somebody would hang up a bag for him, like Mary did for me.

"Oh, yes," ses she, "you want to fool somebody now, don't you—but you'r mighty mistaken."

"No, Miss Keziah," ses he, "if I ain't in good yearnest, I never was in my life."

"But, now, Doctor, would you give yourself away to any young lady for a Crismus gift like brother Joseph did?"

"That I would," ses he, "and glad of the chance."

"Ah," ses she, "I'm fraid you want to play some trick—you young doctors is so monstrous hard to please." And then she looked round at me and kind o' winked her pretty black eyes and smiled.

Pete looked in the glass, and sort o' slicked down his whiskers, and then ses he, "All the galls ses that; but the fact is, Miss Keziah, we's sceptible to female charms jest like common men, I can asshore you. And the fact is, I'm termined to marry the first gal that will have me for a Crismus present."

"Now, you all hear that," ses Keziah.

"Yes," we all said.

"Now mind," ses she to cousin Pete, "you ain't foolin."

I never seed Pete look so quare—he looked sort o' skeered and sort o' pleased, and he trembled all over and his voice was so husky he couldn't hardly speak.

"No, I is down right yearnest—you see if I aint."

"Well," ses she, "we'll see."

Pete seemed monstrous fidgety, and bimeby he 'lowed it was time to go, and after bidin us all good night, ses he, "Now remember, Miss Keziah," and away he went with a hart as light as a handfull of chicken feathers.

He hadn't been gone more'n no time afore Sister Keziah, bust rite out a laughin.

"Now," ses she, "if I don't fix Dr. Pomposity good, then I aint Keziah Stallions, that's all. He's always been cavortin about and makin so much of himself, as who but he! and now I'll take him down a peg."

"Why, aint you gwine to hang up no bag?" ses sister Carline.

"That I aint," ses she.

"Oh, now, sis, that's too bad to disappint him so."

"But the doctor shant be disappinted, for I'll make aunt Prissy hang up one for him to take an airin in till murnin if he's a mind to, and then we'll see if he'll be as good as his word."

And shore enuff, she called aunt Prissy and made her go up in the loft and empty the feather-bag, and fix a rope in it, and go and hang it on the porch for cousin Pete. Then she told Priss all how she must do in the mornin, and we all went to bed.

I couldn't sleep for thinkin what a bominable fool they was gwine to make out of poor Pete. Mary sed it was a great shame to serve anybody so, but she didn't blieve Keziah would quit being wild and mischievous.

It wasn't no great time fore I heard the gate squeak, and the next minit there was a monstrous racket among the dogs, and I know'd Pete was come. I could here the gals titterin and laughin in ther room, and the next thing bang went something agin the fence, and then one of the dogs set up a ki-ey! like something had hurt him, and all was still for a few minits. Then I heard Pete steppin about very cautious on the porch, and movin the table and chairs, and then the jice shuck with his weight, as he drapped into the bag. All was still agin for a little while, cept the galls snickerin in ther room, and then I heard Pete sneeze, and the dogs barked, and I thought the galls would laugh so loud he'd hear 'em, but he kep a sneezin in spite of all he could do.

"Now," ses Mary, "aint that too bad, to fool anybody that way—jest think how you would feel in that old bag what's been full of stinkin old chicken feathers for so long."

"That's a fact," ses I, but I couldn't help laughin all the time.

Pete cleared his throte a time or two, and every now and then he fetched a kind of a smothered up sneeze, and then the dogs would bark. You better keep your mouth shut, old feller, thinks I, if you don't want to git your windpipe lined with chicken feathers. Every now and then the jice would shake as Pete kep turnin and twistin round, tryin to git fixed comfortable, but I knew ther was no comfort in that bag, even if it had no fethers in it; and then when I thought what a terrible disappintment was waitin for him in the mornin, I couldn't help pityin him from the bottom of my hart.

It was a long time before we could go to sleep, but I drapt off after a while, and didn't wake til mornin. I was mighty anxious to see how the thing was gwine to turn out, and got reddy long before aunt Prissy come to see what was in her bag—the galls was up by daylight too, to see the fun. Nobody went out till all the niggers from the kitchen had got round the bag.

"Whoop-e-e-e!" ses little nigger Ned, "Mammy! see what's dat hangin on de porch."

"Kih!" ses old ant Hetty, "dat mus be ole Santa-claus heself, fell in dar when he was putting lasses candy for Pris, and can't git out."

Pete never said nothin, waitin for the galls to come.

"Oh! Miss Calline and Miss Keziah, come see what I got in my bag," ses Pris. "I spec its something what uncle Friday fotch from Gusta; he sed he was gwine to give me a Crismus."

By this time the galls was on the porch, and the niggers unswung the bag, and out tumbled Pete, all kivered with feathers from head to foot, so you couldn't see his eyes, mouth, whiskers, nor nothin else.

"Whew!" ses he, as soon as he got his hed out, and the fethers flew all over the floor, which skeered the little niggers so they split to the kitchen squallin like the very old devil was after 'em.

"God Lord, massa Pete!" ses ant Prissy, "dat you in my bag? I thought 'em was something good."

"Your bag!" ses Pete, "drat your infernal picter, who told you to hang up a bag, for white folks to go and git into? Never mind, Miss Keziah, I was only in fun, anyway," ses he, while they was all laughin fit to die, and he was trying to brush off the feathers. "Never mind, I was only jokin with you, but I had a better opinion of you than to think you would serve a body so, and ding my feathers if I aint glad I've found you out. Never mind, Miss," ses he, and he gin her a look like he could bit her hed off, and then he blowed his nose a time or two and put out.

"But aint you gwine to be as good as your word, doctor?" ses she.

"You jest go to grass," ses he; and that's the last we've seed of cousin Pete sense Crismus morning.

Mary gave the galls a rite good settin down for servin him so. But for my part I think it aint no great matter, for he is such a bominable fool, that a few pretty hard lessons won't do him no harm.

I sed ther wasn't nothin new down here—well ther haint been much—but ther was one of the curiousest live things here tother day from Augusta that ever was seen in these parts. It was sort o' tween a dandy and a gote, but on a slight examination it would have passed very well for a old monkey with its tail cut off or tucked up under its cote. The most distinguished feature about it was a little impertinent lookin gote-knot that stuck rite strate out from its chin, jest like them little gotes what they have in the mountains with tails drawed up so tight that ther hind feet don't hardly touch the ground. It had a cap on its head and a outlandish lookin bag cote. It went round town without anybody with it, and I never was so glad Mary was to home at the plantation. At first my pinter dog tried his best to set it, but soon as it turned round so he could see its face he just snuffed a little and drapped his tail and walked off. The fact was, he couldn't make out what sort of a varmint it was. Bimeby it spoke to somebody, and then Spike know'd it was some kind of a human, but he kep his eye on him all the time. I never did 'blieve in Metemsichosisism as they call it, before lately, but now I can't help but 'blieve ther's something in it. Whether people really do turn into animals or not after they're dead, I won't pretend to say; but one thing I'm certain of, and that is, that some people git to be monstrous nigh monkeys and gotes before they do die. All that little feller what was down here tother day wanted to make a complete billy gote out of him, was to have his cote-tail cut to a pint and turned up behind. If they can help it, I don't see what our young dandies make sich gotes of themselves for. If it's to be conspicuous, they don't gain nothing by it—for people is sure to ask questions about 'em, and then ther're sure to find out, that they aint much—generally some nincomnoddle, that's sprung from nothing and don't know how to live in decent people's circumstances. No more from

Your friend, til deth

JOS. JONES

P.S. Mary's in rite good spirits, considerin. I expect to rite you a letter one of these days, old feller, that'll make your hair stand on eend with joy and gratification. But as the old sayin is, we mustn't count our chickens fore they're hatcht.

Sidney Lanier

From *Tiger-Lilies*

Book II

CHAPTER I

Thou shalt not kill.
Love your enemies.
Father, forgive them: they know not what they do.
Christ

The early spring of 1861 brought to bloom, besides innumerable violets and jessamines, a strange, enormous, and terrible flower.

This was the blood-red flower of war, which grows amid thunders; a flower whose freshening dews are blood and hot tears, whose shadow chills a land, whose odors strangle a people, whose giant petals droop downward, and whose roots are in hell.

It is a species of the great genus sin-flower, which is so conspicuous in the flora of all ages and all countries, and whose multifarious leafage and fruitage so far overgrow a land that the violet, or love-genus, has often small chance to show its quiet blue.

The cultivation of this plant is an expensive business, and it is a wonder, from this fact alone, that there should be so many fanciers of it. A most profuse and perpetual manuring with human bones is absolutely necessary to keep it alive, and it is well to have these powdered, which can be easily done by hoofs of cavalry-horses and artillery-wheels, not to speak of the usual method of mashing with cannon-balls. It will not grow, either, except in some wet place near a stream of human blood; and you must be active in collecting your widows' tears and orphans' tears and mothers' tears to freshen the petals with in the mornings.

It requires assiduous working; and your labor-hire will be a large item in the expense, not to speak of the amount disbursed in preserving the human bones alive until such time as they may be needed, for, I forgot to mention, they must be fresh, and young, and newly-killed.

It is, however, a hardy plant, and may be grown in any climate, from snowy Moscow to hot India.

It blooms usually in the spring, continuing to flower all summer until the winter rains set in: yet in some instances it has been known to remain in full bloom during a whole inclement winter, as was shown in a fine specimen which I saw the other day, grown in North America by two wealthy landed proprietors, who combined all their resources of money, of blood, of bones, of tears, of sulphur and what not, to make this the grandest specimen of modern horticulture, and whose success was evidenced by the pertinacious blossoms which the plant sent forth even amid the hostile rigors of snow and ice and furious storms. It is supposed by some that seed of this American specimen (now dead) yet remain in the land; but as for this author (who, with many friends, suffered from the unhealthy odors of the plant), he could find it in his heart to wish fervently that these seed, if there be verily any, might perish in the germ, utterly out of sight and life and memory and out of the remote hope of resurrection, forever and ever, no matter in whose granary they are cherished!

But, to return.

It is a spreading plant, like the banyan, and continues to insert new branch-roots into the ground, so as sometimes to overspread a whole continent. Its black-shadowed jungles afford fine cover for such wild beasts as frauds and corruptions and thefts to make their lair in; from which, often, these issue with ravening teeth and prey upon the very folk that have planted and tended and raised their flowery homes!

Now, from time to time, there have appeared certain individuals (wishing, it may be, to disseminate and make profit upon other descriptions of plants) who have protested against the use of this war-flower.

Its users, many of whom are surely excellent men, contend that they grow it to protect themselves from oppressive hailstorms, which destroy their houses and crops.

But some say the plant itself is worse than any hailstorm; that its shades are damp and its odors unhealthy, and that it spreads so rapidly as to kill out and uproot all corn and wheat and cotton crops. Which the plant-users admit; but rejoin that it is cowardly to allow hailstorms to fall with impunity, and that manhood demands a struggle against them of some sort.

But the others reply, fortitude is more manly than bravery, for noble and long endurance wins the shining love of God; whereas brilliant bravery is momentary, is easy to the enthusiastic, and only dazzles the admiration of the weak-eyed since it is as often shown on one side as the other.

But then, lastly, the good war-flower cultivators say, our preachers recommend the use of this plant, and help us mightily to raise it in resistance to the hailstorms.

And reply, lastly, the interested other-flower men, that the preachers should preach Christ; that Christ was worse hailed upon than anybody, before or since; that he always refused to protect himself, though fully able to do it, by any war-banyan; and that he did, upon all occasions, not only discourage the resort to this measure, but did inveigh against it more earnestly than any thing else, as the highest and heaviest crime against Love—the Father of Adam, Christ, and all of us.

Friends and horticulturists, cry these men, stickling for the last word, if war was ever right, then Christ was always wrong; and war-flowers and the vine of Christ grow different ways, insomuch that no man may grow with both!

CHAPTER II

King Henry.—How now, good Blunt? Thy looks are full of speed.
Blunt.—So hath the business that I come to speak of.
Lord Mortimer of Scotland hath sent word
That Douglas and the English rebels met,
The eleventh of this month, at Shrewsbury:
A mighty and a fearful head they are,
If promises be kept on every hand,
As ever offered foul play in a state.

King Henry IV

But these sentiments, even if anybody could have been found patient enough to listen to them, would have been called sentimentalities, or worse, in the spring of 1861, by the inhabitants of any of those States lying between Maryland and Mexico. An afflatus of war was breathed upon us. Like a great wind, it drew on and blew upon men, women, and children. Its sound mingled with the solemnity of the church-organs and arose with the earnest words of preachers praying for guidance in the matter. It sighed in the half-breathed words of sweethearts conditioning impatient lovers with war-services. It thundered splendidly in the impassioned appeals of orators to the people. It whistled through the streets, it stole in to the firesides, it clinked glasses in bar-rooms, it lifted the gray hairs of our wise men in conventions, it thrilled through the lectures in college halls, it rustled the thumbed book-leaves of the school-rooms.

This wind blew upon all the vanes of all the churches of the country, and turned them one way—toward war. It blew, and shook out, as if by magic, a flag whose device was unknown to soldier or sailor before, but whose every flap and flutter made the blood bound in our veins.

Who could have resisted the fair anticipations which the new war-idea brought? It arrayed the sanctity of a righteous cause in the brilliant trappings of military display; pleasing, so, the devout and the flippant which in various proportions are mixed elements in all men. It challenged the patriotism of the sober citizen, while it inflamed the dream of the statesman, ambitious for his country or for himself. It offered test to all allegiances and loyalties; of church, of state; of private loves, of public devotion; of personal consanguinity; of social ties. To obscurity it held out eminence; to poverty, wealth; to greed, a gorged maw; to speculation, legalized gambling; to patriotism, a country; to statesmanship, a government; to virtue, purity; and to love, what all love most desires—a field wherein to assert itself by action.

The author devoutly wishes that some one else had said what is here to be spoken—and said it better. That is: if there was guilt in any, there was guilt in nigh all of us, between Maryland and Mexico; that Mr. Davis, if he be termed the ringleader of the rebellion, was so not by virtue of any instigating act of his, but purely by the unanimous will and appointment of the Southern people; and that the hearts of the Southern people bleed to see how their own act has resulted in the chaining of Mr. Davis, who was as innocent as they, and in the pardon of those who were as guilty as he!

All of us, if any of us, either for pardon or for punishment: this is fair, and we are willing.

But the author has nought to do with politics; and he turns with a pleasure which he hopes is shared by the Twenty-four-thousand-nine-hundred-and-ninety-nine, to pursue the adventures of Paul Rübetsahl and company.

CHAPTER VI

Russet yeas and honest kersey noes.
Love's Labor's Lost

Cain Smallin was the most indefatigable of scouts. He was always moving; the whole country side knew him. His good-natured face and communicative habits procured for him a cordial welcome at every house in that quiet country, where as yet only the distant roar of the war had been heard, where all was still and sunny and lonesome, where the household-talk was that of old men and women, of girls and children, whose sons and brothers were all away in the midst of that dimly-heard roaring. In this serene land a soldier's face that had been in front of cannon and bullets was a thing to be looked at twice, and a soldier's talk was the rare treasure of a fireside. The gunboats in the river, upon which these neighbors looked whenever they walked the river bank, had ceased to be objects of alarm, or even of curiosity. They lay there quietly and lazily, day after day, making no hostile sign; and had lain so since Norfolk fell. And as for the evening-gun at Fortress Monroe—that had boomed every sunset for many a year before the war.

On his way to the Point which terminates between Burwell's Bay and Smithfield Creek, and which afforded store of succulent grass and clover for the horses, Cain Smallin passed the house of a neighbor who had particularly distinguished himself in kindness to our little party of scouts. The old gentleman was seated in the open doorway, in midst of a pile of newspapers.

"Good mornin'! Mr. Smallin. Could n't stand it any longer, you see, so I sent Dick away up to Ivor yesterday to try and get some papers. Here's another stinger in the "Examiner." Sit down here; I want you to read it."

"Thank'ee, sir, don't care if I do rest a leetle; tollubble warm walkin' this mornin'," replied the mountaineer, and fell to reading—a slow operation for him whose eye was far more accustomed to sighting a rifle than deciphering letters.

"Massy me!" said he, after some silence, "our men's desertin' mighty fast, up yan, f'om the army. Here's nigh to a whole column full of 'Thirty Dollars Rewards' for each deserter. Let's see if I know any of 'em."

Cain's lip moved busily, in what might well have been called a spell of silence. Suddenly he dropped the paper and looked piteously upward.

"May be I spelt it wrong, le'm me look again," muttered he, and snatched the paper up to gaze again upon that dreadful Thirty Dollar column.

It was there.

"Thirty-Dollars Reward.

"Deserted from the ——— Regiment, ——— Volunteers, Gorm Smallin, who enlisted," &c., &c.

Cain Smallin dropped his newspaper and strode hastily out of the door, unheeding the surprise of his host.

He walked rapidly, and aimlessly. The cruel torture would not permit him to rest; his grief drove him about; it lashed him with sharp thongs. Across fields and marshes, through creeks and woods, with bent head, with hands idly hanging, with unsteady step, he circled. A tear emerged from his eye. It stopped in a furrow, and glistened. Occasionally he muttered to himself,—

"We was poor. We aint never had much to live on but our name, which it was good as gold. An' now it aint no better'n rusty copper; hit'll be green an' pisenous. An' who's done it? Gorm Smallin! Nobody but Gorm Smallin! My own brother, Gorm Smallin! Gorm,—Gorm." He repeated this name a hundred times, as if his mind wandered and he wished to fix it.

The hours passed on and still the mountaineer walked. His simple mountain-life had known few griefs. This was worse than any sorrow. It was disgrace. He knew no sophistries to retire into, in the ostrich-fashion wherewith men avoid dishonor. He had lost all. Not only he, but all whom he loved, would suffer.

"What will the Sterlin's say? Old John Sterlin'; him that stuck by us when corn was so scurce in the Cove? an' Philip! him that I've hunted with an' fished with an' camped with, by ourselves, in yan mountains? And Miss Felix! Miss Felix!"

The man dwelt on this name. His mind became a blank, except two luminous spots which were rather feelings than thoughts. These were, a sensation of disgrace and a sensation of loveliness: the one embodied in the name Gorm, the other in the name Felix. He recoiled from one; he felt as if religion demanded that he should also recoil from the other. He suffered more than if he had committed the crime himself. For he was innocence, and that is highly tender and sensitive, being unseared.

At length the gathering twilight attracted his attention. He looked around, to discover his locality. Leaping a fence he found himself in the main road, and a short walk brought him to a low house that stood in a field on the right. He opened the gate, and knocked at the door. "Here's whar he said he'd stay," he muttered. Gorm himself came to the door.

"Put on your hat, Gorm!"

The stern tone of his voice excited his brother's surprise.

"What fur, Cain?"

"I want you to walk with me, a little piece. Hurry!"

Gorm took down his hat and came out.

"Whar to, brother Cain?"

"Follow me," replied Cain, with a motion of displeasure at the wheedling tone of his brother.

Leaving the road, he struck into a path leading to the Point from which he had wandered. As he walked his pace increased, until it required the most strenuous exertions on the part of his companion to keep up with his long and rapid strides.

"Whar the devil air you gwine to, Cain? Don't walk so fast, anyhow; I'm a'most out o' breath a'ready!"

The mountaineer made no reply, but slackened his pace. He only muttered to himself: "Hits eight mile across; ye'll need your strength to git thar, may be."

The path wound now amongst gloomy pines, for some distance, until suddenly they emerged upon the open beach. They were upon the extreme end of the lonely Point. The night was dark; but the sand-beach glimmered ghastly white through the darkness. Save the mournful hooting of an owl from his obscure cell in the woods, the place was silent. Hundreds of huge tree-stumps, with their roots upturned in the air, lay in all fantastic positions upon the white sand, as the tide had deposited them. These straggling clumps had been polished white by salt air and waves. They seemed like an agitated convention of skeletons, discussing the propriety of flesh. A small boat rested on the beach, with one end secured by a "painter" to a stake driven in the sand.

"Little did I think, when I found it in the marsh this mornin' an' brought it thar, thinkin' to git it round to camp to-night, what use I was gwine to put it to," said Cain Smallin to himself.

As he led the way to the boat, suddenly he stopped and turned face to face with his recreant brother. His eyes glared into Gorm's. His right hand was raised, and a pistol-barrel protruded from the long fingers.

"Gorm Smallin," he said, with grating voice, "have ye ever know'd me to say I'd do anything an' then not to do it?"

"I—I—no, I have n't, Cain," stuttered the deserter, cowering with terror and surprise.

"Remember them words. Now answer my questions, and don't say nothin' outside o' them. Gorm Smallin, whar was you born?"

"What makes you ax me sich foolish questions, Cain? I was born in Tennessy, an' you know it!"

"Answer my questions, Gorm Smallin! Who raised you, f'om a little un?"

"Mother an' father, o' course."

"Who's your mother and father? what's ther name?"

"Cain, air you crazy? ther name's Smallin."

"Gorm Smallin, did you ever know any o' the Smallins to cheat a man in a trade?"

"No, Cain; we've always been honest."

"Did ye ever know a Smallin to swar to a lie afore the Jestis?"

"No."

"Did ye ever know one to steal another man's horse, or his rifle, or anything?"

"No."

"Did ye ever know one to sneak out f'om a rightful fight?"

"No."

"Did ye ever know one to"—the words came like lightning with a zigzag jerk—"to desert f'om his rigiment?"

The flash struck Gorm Smallin. He visibly sank into himself like a jointed cane. He trembled, and gazed apprehensively at the pistol in his brother's right hand which still towered threateningly aloft. He made no reply.

"Ye don't like to say yes this time!" continued Cain. "Gorm Smallin, altho' I say it which I'm your brother,—ye lied every time ye said no, afore. *You* has cheated in a dirty trade; *you* has swore to a lie afore God that's better than the Jestis; *you* has stole what's better 'n any rifle or horse; *you* has sneaked out f'om the rightfullest fight ye ever was in; *you* has deserted f'om your rigiment, an' that when yer own brother an' every friend ye had in the world was fightin' along with ye.

"Gorm Smallin, you has cheated me, an' ole father an' mother an' all, out of our name which it was all we had; you has swore to a lie, for you swore to me 'at the colonel sent you down here to go a-scoutin' amongst the Yankees; you has stole our honest name, which it is more than ye can ever make to give to your wife's baby; you has sneaked out f'om a fight that we was fightin' to keep what was our'n an' to pertect them that has been kind to us an' them that raised us; you has deserted f'om your rigiment which it has fought now gwine on four year an' fought manful, too, an' never run a inch.

"Gorm Smallin, you has got your name in the paper 'ith thirty dollars reward over it, in big letters; big letters, so 'at father's ole eyes can read it 'ithout callin' sister Ginny to make it out for him. Thar it is, for every man, woman, *and* child in the whole Confederacy to read it, an' by this time they *has* read it, may be, an' every man in the rigiment has cussed you for a sneak an' a scoundrel, an' wonderin' whether Cain Smallin will do like his brother!

"Gorm Smallin, you has brung me to that, that I haint no sperrit to fight hearty an' cheerful. Ef ye had been killed in a fa'r battle, I mought ha' been able to fight hard enough for both of us, for every time I cried a-thinkin' of you, I 'd ha' been twice as strong an' twice as clear-sighted as I was buffore. But—sich things as these"—the mountaineer wiped off a tear with his coat-sleeve—"burns me an' weakens me an' hurts my eyes that bad that I kin scarcely look a man straight forrard in the face. Hit don't make much diff'ence to me now, whether we whips the Yanks or they whips us. What good 'll it do ef we conquer 'em? Everybody 'll be a-shoutin' an' a-hurrahin' an' they 'll leave *us* out o' the frolic, for we is kin to a deserter! An' the women 'll be a-smilin' on them that has lived to git home, one minute, an' the next they 'll be a-weepin' for them that's left dead in Virginy an' Pennsylvany an' Tennessy,—but *you* won't git home, an' *you* won't be left dead nowher; they cain't neither smile at you nor cry for you; what 'll they do ef anybody speaks yer name? Gorm Smallin, they 'll lift their heads high an' we 'll hang our'n low. They 'll scorn ye an' we 'll blush for ye.

"Had n't ye better be dead? Had n't I better kill ye right here an' bury ye whar ye cain't do no more harm to the fambly name?

"But I cain't shoot ye, hardly. The same uns raised us an' fed us. I cain't do it; an' I'm sorry I cain't!

"You air 'most on yer knees, anyhow; git down on 'em all the way. Listen to me. God A'mighty's a-lookin' at you out o' the stars yan, an' he's a listenin' at you out o' the sand here, an' he won't git tired by mornin' but he 'll keep a-listenin' an' a-lookin' at ye to-morrow all day. Now mind ye. I'm gwine to put ye in this boat here, an' you can paddle across to yan side the river, easy. Ef ye 'll keep yer eye on yan bright star that's jest a-risin' over Bullitt Pint, ye 'll strike t'other shore about the right place. Ef ye paddle out o' the way, the guard on yan gunboat 'll be apt to fire into ye; keep yer eye on the star. Ye 'll git to the beach on t' other side, an' lay down under a tree an' sleep till mornin'—ef ye *can* sleep. In the mornin' ye 'll walk down the road, an' the Yankee pickets 'll see yer gray coat an' take ye to Head-quarters. The officer at Head-quarters 'll examine ye, an' when you tell him you air a deserter he 'll make ye take the oath, an' ef he know'd how many oaths ye've already broke I think he would'n' take the trouble! Howsumdever, I'm gwine to do the same foolishness, for it's all I kin do. Now when ye take the oath the officer 'll likely make ye sign yer name to it, or write yer name somewhar. Gorm Smallin, when ye write that name ye *shall* not write your own name; ye must write some other name. Swar to it, now, while ye air kneelin' buffore God A'mighty! Raise up yer hands, both of 'em; swar to it, that ye 'll write some other name in the Yankee deserter-book, or I 'll shoot ye, thar, right down!"

Cain had placed the muzzle of his pistol against his brother's forehead.

The oath was taken.

"Don't git up yet; kneel thar. Hit would'n' be right to put any other man's name in the deserter-book in place o' yourn, for ye mought be robbin' some other decent fambly of ther good name. Le'ss see. We must git some name that nobody ever was named afore. Take a stick thar an' write it in the sand, so you won't forgit it. The fust name don't make no diff'ence. Write Sam'l."

It was written in great scrawling letters.

"Now write J, an' call out as you write, so you won't forgit it. For I'm gwine to captur' that deserter-book on' see ef your name's in it. Write J, an' call out."

"J."

"O."

"O."

"X."

"X."

"O."

"O."

"B."

"B."

"B, agin."

"B, agin."

"le, -bul!"

"le, -bul!"

"Sam'l Joxo—Joxy—I cain't call it, but you can write it—hit'll do. Git it by heart."

Cain paused a moment.

"Now git up. Git in the boat. Gorm Smallin, don't never come back home, don't never come whar I may be! I cain't shake hands with ye; but I'll shove ye off."

Cain loosened the head of the boat from the sand, turned her round, and gave a mighty push, running with her till he was waist deep in the water. He came out dripping, folded his arms, and stood still, watching the dusky form in the receding boat.

Gorm Smallin was a half-mile from shore. Suddenly he heard his brother's voice, across the water.

"Gorm!"

"Hello!"

"Joxo—Joxobabbul!" cried Cain Smallin at the top of his voice, bending down to read the inscription on the sand.

Augusta J. Evans

From *St. Elmo*

CHAPTER I

"He stood and measured the earth: and the everlasting mountains were scattered, the perpetual hills did bow."

These words of the prophet upon Shigionoth were sung by a sweet, happy, childish voice, and to a strange, wild, anomalous tune—solemn as the Hebrew chant of Deborah, and fully as triumphant.

A slender girl of twelve years' growth steadied a pail of water on her head, with both dimpled arms thrown up, in ancient classic Caryatides attitude; and, pausing a moment beside the spring, stood fronting the great golden dawn—watching for the first level ray of the coming sun, and chanting the prayer of Habakkuk. Behind her in silent grandeur towered the huge outline of Lookout Mountain, shrouded at summit in gray mist, while centre and base showed dense masses of foliage, dim and purplish in the distance—a stern cowled monk of the Cumberland brotherhood. Low hills clustered on either side, but immediately in front stretched a wooded plain, and across this the child looked at the flushed sky, rapidly brightening into fiery and blinding radiance. Until her wild song waked echoes among the far-off rocks, the holy hush of early morning had rested like a benediction upon the scene, as though nature laid her broad finger over her great lips, and waited in reverent silence the advent of the sun. Morning among the mountains possessed witchery and glories which filled the heart of the girl with adoration, and called from her lips rude but exultant anthems of praise. The young face, lifted toward the cloudless east, might have served as a model for a pictured Syriac priestess—one of Baalbec's vestals, ministering in the olden time in that wondrous and grand temple at Heliopolis.

The large black eyes held a singular fascination in their mild, sparkling depths, now full of tender, loving light and childish gladness; and the flexible red lips curled in lines of orthodox Greek perfection, showing remarkable versatility of expression; while the broad, full, polished forehead with its prominent, swelling brows, could not fail to recall, to even casual observers, the calm, powerful face of Lorenzo de' Medicis, which, if once looked on, fastens itself upon heart and brain, to be forgotten no more. Her hair, black, straight, waveless as an Indian's, hung around her shoulders, and glistened as the water from the dripping bucket trickled through the wreath of purple morning-glories and scarlet cypress, which she had twined about her head, ere lifting the cedar pail to its resting-place. She wore a short-sleeved dress of yellow striped homespun, which fell nearly to her ankles, and her little bare feet gleamed pearly white on the green grass and rank dewy creepers that clustered along the margin of the bubbling spring. Her complexion was unusually transparent, and early exercise and mountain air had rouged her cheeks till they matched the brilliant hue of her scarlet crown. A few steps in advance of her stood a large, fierce yellow dog, with black, scowling face, and ears cut close to his head; a savage, repulsive creature, who looked as if he rejoiced in an opportunity of making good his name "Grip." In the solemn beauty of that summer morning the girl seemed to have forgotten the mission upon which she came; but as she loitered, the sun flashed up, kindling diamond fringes on every dew-beaded chestnut leaf and oak-bough, and silvering the misty mantle which enveloped Lookout. A moment longer that pure-hearted Tennessee child stood watching the gorgeous spectacle, drinking draughts of joy, which mingled no drop of sin or selfishness in its crystal waves; for she had grown up alone with nature—utterly ignorant of the roar and strife, the burning hate and cunning intrigue of the great world of men and women, where, "like an Egyptian pitcher of tamed vipers, each struggles to get its head above the other." To her, earth seemed very lovely; life stretched before her like the sun's path in that clear sky, and, as free from care or forebodings as the fair June day, she walked on, preceded by her dog—and the chant burst once more from her lips:

"He stood and measured the earth: and the everlasting mountains were scattered, the perpetual hills—"

The sudden, almost simultaneous report of two pistol-shots rang out sharply on the cool, calm air, and startled the child so violently that she sprang forward and dropped the bucket. The sound of voices reached her from the thick wood bordering the path, and, without reflection, she followed the dog, who bounded off toward the point where it issued. Upon the verge of the forest she paused, and, looking down a dewy green glade where the rising sun darted the earliest arrowy rays, beheld a spectacle which burned itself indelibly upon her memory. A group of five gentlemen stood beneath the dripping chestnut and sweet-gum arches; one leaned against the trunk of a tree, two were conversing eagerly in undertones, and two faced each other fifteen paces apart, with pistols in their hands. Ere she could comprehend the scene, the brief conference ended, the seconds resumed their places to witness another fire, and like the peal of a trumpet echoed the words:

"Fire! One!—two!—three!"

The flash and ringing report mingled with the command and one of the principals threw up his arms and fell. When with horror in her wide-strained eyes and pallor on her lips, the child staggered to the spot, and looked on the prostrate form, he was dead. The hazel eyes stared blankly at the sky, and the hue of life and exuberant health still glowed on the full cheek; but the ball had entered the heart, and the warm blood, bubbling from his breast, dripped on the glistening grass. The surgeon who knelt beside him took the pistol from his clenched fingers, and gently pressed the lids over his glazing eyes. Not a word was uttered, but while the seconds sadly regarded the stiffening form, the surviving principal coolly drew out a cigar, lighted and placed it between his lips. The child's eyes had wandered to the latter from the pool of blood, and now in a shuddering cry she broke the silence:

"Murderer!"

The party looked around instantly, and for the first time perceived her standing there in their midst, with loathing and horror in the gaze she fixed on the perpetrator of the awful deed. In great surprise he drew back a step or two, and asked gruffly:

"Who are you? What business have you here?"

"Oh! how dared you murder him? Do you think God will forgive you on the gallows?"

He was a man probably twenty-seven years of age—singularly fair, handsome, and hardened in iniquity, but he cowered before the blanched and accusing face of the appalled child; and ere a reply could be framed, his friend came close to him.

"Clinton, you had better be off; you have barely time to catch the Knoxville train, which leaves Chattanooga in half an hour. I would advise you to make a long stay in New York, for there will be trouble when Dent's brother hears of this morning's work."

"Aye! Take my word for that, and put the Atlantic between you and Dick Dent," added the surgeon, smiling grimly, as if the anticipation of retributive justice afforded him pleasure.

"I will simply put this between us," replied the homicide, fitting his pistol to the palm of his hand; and as he did so, a heavy antique diamond ring flashed on his little finger.

"Come, Clinton, delay may cause you more trouble than we bargained for," urged his second.

Without even glancing toward the body of his antagonist, Clinton scowled at the child, and, turning away, was soon out of sight.

"Oh, sir! will you let him get away? will you let him go unpunished?"

"He cannot be punished," answered the surgeon, looking at her with mingled curiosity and admiration.

"I thought men were hung for murder."

"Yes—but this is not murder."

"Not murder? He shot him dead! What is it?"

"He killed him in a duel, which is considered quite right and altogether proper."

"A duel?"

She had never heard the word before, and pondered an instant.

"To take a man's life is murder. Is there no law to punish 'a duel'?"

"None strong enough to prohibit the practice. It is regarded as the only method of honorable satisfaction open to gentlemen."

"Honorable satisfaction?" she repeated—weighing the new phraseology as cautiously and fearfully as she would have handled the bloody garments of the victim.

"What is your name?" asked the surgeon.

"Edna Earl."

"Do you live near this place?"

"Yes, sir, very near."

"Is your father at home?"

"I have no father, but grandpa has not gone to the shop yet."

"Will you show me the way to the house?"

"Do you wish to carry him there?" she asked, glancing at the corpse, and shuddering violently.

"Yes, I want some assistance from your grandfather."

"I will show you the way, sir."

The surgeon spoke hurriedly to the two remaining gentlemen, and followed his guide. Slowly she retraced her steps, refilled her bucket at the spring, and walked on before the stranger. But the glory of the morning had passed away; a bloody mantle hung between the splendor of summer sunshine and the chilled heart of the awe-struck girl. The forehead of the radiant, holy June day had been suddenly red-branded like Cain, to be henceforth an occasion of hideous reminiscences; and with a blanched face and trembling limbs the child followed a narrow, beaten path, which soon terminated at the gate of a rude, unwhitewashed paling. A low, comfortless looking three-roomed house stood within, and on the steps sat an elderly man, smoking a pipe, and busily engaged in mending a bridle. The creaking of the gate attracted his attention, and he looked up wonderingly at the advancing stranger.

"Oh, grandpa! there is a murdered man lying in the grass, under the chestnut trees, down by the spring."

"Why! how do you know he was murdered?"

"Good morning, sir. Your granddaughter happened to witness a very unfortunate and distressing affair. A duel was fought at sunrise, in the edge of the woods yonder, and the challenged party, Mr. Dent, of Georgia, was killed. I came to ask permission to bring the body here, until arrangements can be made for its interment; and also to beg your assistance in obtaining a coffin."

Edna passed on to the kitchen, and as she deposited the bucket on the table, a tall, muscular, red-haired woman, who was stooping over the fire, raised her flushed face, and exclaimed angrily:

"What upon earth have you been doing? I have been half-way to the spring to call you, and hadn't a drop of water in the kitchen to make coffee! A pretty time of day Aaron Hunt will get his breakfast! What do you mean by such idleness?"

She advanced with threatening mien and gesture, but stopped suddenly.

"Edna, what ails you? Have you got an ague? You are as white as that pan of flour. Are you scared or sick?"

"There was a man killed this morning, and the body will be brought here directly. If you want to hear about it, you had better go out on the porch. One of the gentlemen is talking to grandpa."

Stunned by what she had seen, and indisposed to narrate the horrid details, the girl went to her own room, and seated herself in the window, tried to collect her thoughts. She was tempted to believe the whole affair a hideous dream, which would pass away with vigorous rubbing of her eyes; but the crushed purple and scarlet flowers she took from her forehead, her dripping hair and damp feet assured her of the vivid reality of the vision. Every fibre of her frame had received a terrible shock, and when noisy, bustling Mrs. Hunt ran from room to room, ejaculating in astonishment, and calling on the child to assist in putting the house in order, the latter obeyed silently, mechanically, as if in a state of somnambulism.

Mr. Dent's body was brought up on a rude litter of boards, and temporarily placed on Edna's bed, and toward evening when a coffin arrived from Chattanooga, the remains were removed, and the coffin rested on two chairs in the middle of the same room. The surgeon insisted upon an immediate interment near the scene of combat;

but the gentleman who had officiated as second for the deceased expressed his determination to carry the unfortunate man's body back to his home and family, and the earliest train on the following day was appointed as the time for their departure. Late in the afternoon Edna cautiously opened the door of the room which she had hitherto avoided, and with her apron full of lilies, white poppies and sprigs of rosemary, approached the coffin, and looked at the rigid sleeper. Judging from his appearance, not more than thirty years had gone over his handsome head; his placid features were unusually regular, and a soft, silky brown beard fell upon his pulseless breast. Fearful lest she should touch the icy form, the girl timidly strewed her flowers in the coffin, and tears gathered and dropped with the blossoms, as she noticed a plain gold ring on the little finger, and wondered if he were married—if his death would leave wailing orphans in his home, and a broken-hearted widow at the desolate hearthstone. Absorbed in her melancholy task, she heard neither the sound of strange voices in the passage, nor the faint creak of the door as it swung back on its rusty hinges; but a shrill scream, a wild, despairing shriek, terrified her, and her heart seemed to stand still as she bounded away from the side of the coffin. The light of the setting sun streamed through the window, and over the white, convulsed face of a feeble but beautiful woman, who was supported on the threshold by a venerable, gray-haired man, down whose furrowed cheeks tears coursed rapidly. Struggling to free herself from his restraining grasp, the stranger tottered into the middle of the room.

"O Harry! My husband! my husband!" She threw up her wasted arms, and fell forward senseless on the corpse.

They bore her into the adjoining apartment, where the surgeon administered the usual restoratives, and though finally the pulse stirred and throbbed feebly, no symptom of returning consciousness greeted the anxious friends who bent over her. Hour after hour passed, during which she lay as motionless as her husband's body, and at length the physician sighed, and pressing his fingers to his eyes, said sorrowfully to the grief-stricken old man beside her: "It is paralysis, Mr. Dent, and there is no hope. She may linger twelve or twenty-four hours, but her sorrows are ended; she and Harry will soon be reunited. Knowing her constitution, I feared as much. You should not have suffered her to come; you might have known that the shock would kill her. For this reason I wished his body buried here."

"I could not restrain her. Some meddling gossip told her that my poor boy had gone to fight a duel, and she rose from her bed and started to the railroad depot. I pleaded, I reasoned with her that she could not bear the journey, but I might as well have talked to the winds. I never knew her obstinate before, but she seemed to have a presentiment of the truth. God pity her two sweet babes!"

The old man bowed his head upon her pillow, and sobbed aloud.

Throughout the night Edna crouched beside the bed, watching the wan but lovely face of the young widow, and tenderly chafing the numb, fair hands which lay so motionless on the coverlet. Children are always sanguine, because of their ignorance of the stern, inexorable realities of the untried future, and Edna could not believe that death would snatch from the world one so beautiful and so necessary to her prattling, fatherless infants. But morning showed no encouraging symptoms, the stupor was unbroken, and at noon the wife's spirit passed gently to the everlasting reunion.

Before sunrise on the ensuing day, a sad group clustered once more under the dripping chestnuts, and where a pool of blood had dyed the sod, a wide grave yawned. The coffins were lowered, the bodies of Henry and Helen Dent rested side by side, and, as the mound rose slowly above them, the solemn silence was broken by the faltering voice of the surgeon, who read the burial service.

"Man, that is born of a woman, hath but a short time to live, and is full of misery. He cometh up, and is cut down, like a flower; he fleeth as it were a shadow, and never continueth in one stay. Yet, O Lord God most holy, O Lord most mighty, O holy and most merciful Savior, deliver us not into the pains of eternal death!"

The melancholy rite ended, the party dispersed, the strangers took their departure for their distant homes, and quiet reigned once more in the small, dark cottage. But days and weeks brought to Edna no oblivion of the tragic events which constituted the first great epoch of her monotonous life. A nervous restlessness took possession of her, she refused to occupy her old room, and insisted upon sleeping on a pallet at the foot of her grandfather's bed. She forsook her whilom haunts about the spring and forest, and started up in terror at every sudden sound; while from each opening between the chestnut trees the hazel eyes of the dead man, and the wan, thin face of the golden-haired wife, looked out beseechingly at her. Frequently, in the warm light of day, ere shadows stalked to and fro in the thick woods, she would steal, with an apronful of wild flowers, to the solitary grave, scatter her treasures in the rank grass that waved above it, and hurry away with hushed breath and quivering limbs. Summer waned, autumn passed, and winter came, but the girl recovered in no degree from the shock which had cut short her chant of praise on that bloody June day. In her morning visit to the spring, she had stumbled upon a monster which custom had adopted and petted—which the passions and sinfulness of men had adroitly draped and fondled, and called Honorable Satisfaction; but her pure, unperverted, Ithuriel nature pierced the conventional mask, recognized the loathsome lineaments of crime, and recoiled in horror and amazement, wondering at the wickedness of her race and the forbearance of outraged Jehovah. Innocent childhood had for the first time stood face to face with Sin and Death, and could not forget the vision.

Edna Earl had lost both her parents before she was old enough to remember either. Her mother was the only daughter of Aaron Hunt, the village blacksmith, and her father, who was an intelligent, promising young carpenter, accidentally fell from the roof of the house which he was shingling, and died from the injuries sustained. Thus Mr. Hunt, who had been a widower for nearly ten years, found himself burdened with the care of an infant only six months old. His daughter had never left him, and after her death the loneliness of the house oppressed him painfully, and for the sake of his grandchild he resolved to marry again. The middle-aged widow whom he selected was a kind-hearted and generous woman, but indolent, ignorant, and exceedingly high-tempered; and while she really loved the little orphan committed to her care, she contrived to alienate her affection, and to tighten the bonds of union between her husband and the child. Possessing a remarkably amiable and equable disposition, Edna rarely vexed Mrs. Hunt, who gradually left her more and more to the indulgence of her own views and caprices, and contented herself with exacting a certain amount of daily work, after the accomplishment of which she allowed her to amuse herself as childish whims dictated. There chanced to be no children of her own age in the neighborhood, consequently she grew up without companionship, save that furnished by her grandfather, who was dotingly fond of her, and would have utterly spoiled her, had not her temperament fortunately been one not easily injured by unrestrained liberty of action. Before she was able to walk, he would take her to the forge, and keep her for hours on a sheep-skin in one corner, whence she watched, with infantile delight, the blast of the furnace, and the shower of sparks that fell from the anvil, and where she often slept, lulled by the monotonous chorus of trip and sledge. As she grew older, the mystery of bellows and slack-tub engaged her attention, and at one end of the shop on a pile of shavings, she collected a mass of curiously shaped bits of iron and steel, and blocks of wood, from which a miniature shop threatened to rise in rivalry; and finally, when strong enough to grasp the handles of the bellows, her greatest pleasure consisted in rendering the feeble assistance which her grandfather was always so proud to accept at her hands. Although ignorant and uncultivated, Mr. Hunt was a man of warm, tender feelings, and rare nobility of soul. He regretted the absence of early advantages which poverty had denied him; and in teaching Edna to read and to write, and to cipher, he never failed to impress upon her the vast superiority which a thorough education confers. Whether his exhortations first kindled her ambition, or whether her aspiration for knowledge was spontaneous and irresistible, he knew not; but she manifested very early a fondness for study and thirst for learning which he gratified to the fullest extent of his limited ability. The blacksmith's library consisted of the family Bible, Pilgrim's Progress, a copy of Irving's Sermons on Parables, Guy Mannering, a few tracts, and two books which had belonged to an itinerant minister who preached occasionally in the neighborhood, and who, having died rather suddenly at

Mr. Hunt's house, left the volumes in his saddle-bags, which were never claimed by his family, residing in a distant State. Those books were Plutarch's Lives and a worn school copy of Anthon's Classical Dictionary; and to Edna they proved a literary Ophir of inestimable value and exhaustless interest. Plutarch especially was a Pisgah of letters, whence the vast domain of learning, the Canaan of human wisdom, stretched alluringly before her; and as often as she climbed this height, and viewed the wondrous scene beyond, it seemed, indeed,

> *. . . an arch where through*
> *Gleams that untraveled world, whose margin fades*
> *Forever and forever when we move.*

In after years she sometimes questioned if this mount of observation was also that of temptation, to which ambition had led her spirit, and there bargained for and bought her future. Love of nature, love of books, an earnest piety and deep religious enthusiasm were the characteristics of a noble young soul, left to stray through the devious, checkered paths of life without other guidance than that which she received from communion with Greek sages and Hebrew prophets. An utter stranger to fashionable conventionality and latitudinarian ethics, it was no marvel that the child stared and shivered when she saw the laws of God vetoed, and was blandly introduced to murder as Honorable Satisfaction.

Joel Chandler Harris

The Wonderful Tar-Baby Story

"Didn't the fox *never* catch the rabbit, Uncle Remus?" asked the little boy the next evening.

"He come mighty nigh it, honey, sho's you born—Brer Fox did. One day atter Brer Rabbit fool 'im wid dat calamus root, Brer Fox went ter wuk en got 'im some tar, en mix it wid some turkentime, en fix up a contrapshun wat he call a Tar-Baby, en he tuck dish yer Tar-Baby en he sot 'er in de big road, en den he lay off in de bushes fer to see what de news wuz gwineter be. En he didn't hatter wait long, nudder, kaze bimeby here comes Brer Rabbit pacin' down de road—lippity-clippity, clippity-lippity—dez ez sassy ez a jay-bird. Brer Fox, he lay low. Brer Rabbit come prancin' 'long twel he spy de Tar-Baby, en den he fotch up on his behime legs like he wuz 'stonished. De Tar-Baby, she sot dar, she did, en Brer Fox, he lay low.

" 'Mawnin'!' sez Brer Rabbit, sezee—'nice wedder dis mawnin',' sezee.

"Tar-Baby ain't sayin' nothin', en Brer Fox, he lay low.

" 'How duz yo' sym'tums seem ter segashuate?' sez Brer Rabbit, sezee.

"Brer Fox, he wink his eye slow, en lay low, en de Tar-Baby, she ain't sayin' nothin'.

" 'How you come on, den? Is you deaf?' sez Brer Rabbit, sezee. 'Kaze if you is, I kin holler louder,' sezee.

"Tar-Baby stay still, en Brer Fox, he lay low.

" 'Youer stuck up, dat's w'at you is,' says Brer Rabbit, sezee, 'en I'm gwineter kyore you, dat's w'at I'm a gwinter do,' sezee.

"Brer Fox, he sorter chuckle in his stummuck, he did, but Tar-Baby ain't sayin' nothin'.

" 'I'm gwineter larn you howter talk ter 'specttubble fokes ef hit's de las' ack,' sez Brer Rabbit, sezee. 'Ef you don't take off dat hat en tell me howdy, I'm gwineter bus' you wide open,' sezee.

"Tar-Baby stay still, en Brer Fox, he lay low.

"Brer Rabbit keep on axin' 'im, en de Tar-Baby, she keep on sayin' nothin', twel present'y Brer Rabbit draw back wid his fis', he did, en blip he tuck 'er side er de head. Right dar's whar he broke his merlasses jug. His fis' stuck, en he can't pull loose. De tar hilt 'im. But Tar-Baby, she stay still, en Brer Fox, he lay low.

" 'Ef you don't lemme loose, I'll knock you agin,' sez Brer Rabbit, sezee, en wid dat he fotch 'er a wipe wid de udder han', en dat stuck. Tar-Baby, she ain't sayin' nothin', en Brer Fox, he lay low.

" 'Tu'n me loose, fo' I kick de natal stuffin' outen you,' sez Brer Rabbit, sezee, but de Tar-Baby, she ain't sayin' nothin'. She des hilt on, en den Brer Rabbit lose de use er his feet in de same way. Brer Fox, he lay low. Den Brer Rabbit squall out dat ef de Tar-Baby don't tu'n 'im loose he butt 'er cranksided. En den he butted, en his head got stuck. Den Brer Fox, he sa'ntered fort', lookin' des ez innercent ez one er yo' mammy's mockin'-birds.

" 'Howdy, Brer Rabbit,' sez Brer Fox, sezee. 'You look sorter stuck up dis mawnin',' sezee, en den he rolled on de groun', en laughed en laughed twel he couldn't laugh no mo'. 'I speck you'll take dinner wid me dis time, Brer Rabbit. I done laid in some calamus root, en I ain't gwineter take no skuse,' sez Brer Fox, sezee."

Here Uncle Remus paused, and drew a two-pound yam out of the ashes.

"Did the fox eat the rabbit?" asked the little boy to whom the story had been told.

"Dat's all de fur de tale goes," replied the old man. "He mout, en den agin he moutent. Some say Jedge B'ar come 'long en loosed 'im—some say he didn't. I hear Miss Sally callin'. You better run 'long."

Free Joe and the Rest of the World

The name of Free Joe strikes humorously upon the ear of memory. It is impossible to say why, for he was the humblest, the simplest, and the most serious of all God's living creatures, sadly lacking in all those elements that suggest the humorous. It is certain, moreover, that in 1850 the sober-minded citizens of the little Georgian village of Hillsborough were not inclined to take a humorous view of Free Joe, and neither his name nor his presence provoked a smile. He was a black atom, drifting hither and thither without an owner, blown about by all the winds of circumstances and given over to shiftlessness.

The problems of one generation are the paradoxes of a succeeding one, particularly if war, or some such incident, intervenes to clarify the atmosphere and strengthen the understanding. Thus, in 1850, Free Joe represented not only a problem of large concern, but, in the watchful eyes of Hillsborough, he was the embodiment of that vague and mysterious danger that seemed to be forever lurking on the outskirts of slavery, ready to sound a shrill and ghostly signal in the impenetrable swamps, and steal forth under the midnight stars to murder, rapine, and pillage,—a danger always threatening, and yet never assuming shape; intangible, and yet real; impossible, and yet not improbable. Across the serene and smiling front of safety, the pale outlines of the awful shadow of insurrection sometimes fell. With this invisible panorama as background, it was natural that the figure of Free Joe, simple and humble as it was, should assume undue proportions. Go where he would, do what he might, he could not escape the finger of observation and the kindling eye of suspicion. His lightest words were noted, his slightest actions marked.

Under all the circumstances it was natural that his peculiar condition should reflect itself in his habits and manners. The slaves laughed loudly day by day, but Free Joe rarely laughed. The slaves sang at their work and danced at their frolics, but no one ever heard Free Joe sing or saw him dance. There was something painfully plaintive and appealing in his attitude, something touching in his anxiety to please.

He was of the friendliest nature, and seemed to be delighted when he could amuse the little children who had made a play-ground of the public square. At times he would please them by making his little dog Dan perform all sorts of curious tricks, or he would tell them quaint stories of the beasts of the field and birds of the air; and frequently he was coaxed into relating the story of his own freedom. The story was brief, but tragical.

In the year of our Lord 1840, when a negro-speculator of a sportive turn of mind reached the little village of Hillsborough on his way to the Mississippi region, with a caravan of likely negroes of both sexes, he found much to interest him. In that day and at that time there were a number of young men in the village who had not bound themselves over to repentance for the various misdeeds of the flesh. To these young men the negro-speculator (Major Frampton was his name) proceeded to address himself. He was a Virginian, he declared; and, to prove the statement, he referred all the festively inclined young men of Hillsborough to a barrel of peach-brandy in one of his covered wagons. In the minds of these young men there was less doubt in regard to the age and quality of the brandy than there was in regard to the negro-trader's birthplace. Major Frampton might or might not have been born in the Old Dominion—that was a matter for consideration and inquiry—but there could be no question as to the mellow pungency of the peach-brandy.

In his own estimation, Major Frampton was one of the most accomplished of men. He had summered at the Virginia Springs; he had been to Philadelphia, to Washington, to Richmond, to Lynchburg, and to Charleston, and had accumulated a great deal of experience which he found useful. Hillsborough was hid in the woods of middle Georgia, and its general aspect of innocence impressed him. He looked on the young men who had shown their readiness to test his peach-brandy, as overgrown country boys who needed to be introduced to some of the arts and sciences he had at his command. Thereupon the Major pitched his tents, figuratively speaking, and became, for the time being, a part and parcel of the innocence that characterized Hillsborough. A wiser man would doubtless have made the same mistake.

The little village possessed advantages and seemed to be providentially arranged to fit the various enterprises that Major Frampton had in view. There was the auction-block in front of the stuccoed court-house, if he desired to dispose of a few of his negroes; there was a quarter-track, laid out to his hand and in excellent order, if he chose to enjoy the pleasures of horse-racing; there were secluded pine thickets within easy reach, if he desired to indulge in the exciting pastime of cock-fighting; and various lonely and unoccupied rooms in the second story of the tavern, if he cared to challenge the chances of dice or cards.

Major Frampton tried them all with varying luck, until he began his famous game of poker with Judge Alfred Wellington, a stately gentleman with a flowing white beard and mild blue eyes that gave him the appearance of a benevolent patriarch. The history of the game in which Major Frampton and Judge Alfred Wellington took part is something more than a tradition in Hillsborough, for there are still living three or four who sat around the table and watched its progress. It is said that at various stages of the game Major Frampton would destroy the cards with which they were playing, and send for a new pack, but the result was always the same. The mild blue eyes of Judge Wellington, with few exceptions, continued to overlook "hands" that were invincible—a habit they had acquired during a long and arduous course of training from Saratoga to New Orleans. Major Frampton lost his money, his horses, his wagons, and all his negroes but one, his body-servant. When his misfortune had reached this limit, the major adjourned the game. The sun was shining brightly, and all nature was cheerful. It is said that the major also seemed to be cheerful. However this may be, he visited the court-house and executed the papers that gave his body-servant his freedom. This being done, Major Frampton sauntered into a convenient pine thicket, and blew out his brains.

The negro thus freed came to be known as Free Joe. Compelled, under the law, to choose a guardian, he chose Judge Wellington, chiefly because his wife Lucinda was among the negroes won from Major Frampton. For several years Free Joe had what may be called a jovial time. His wife Lucinda was well provided for, and he found it a comparatively easy matter to provide for himself; so that, taking all the circumstances into consideration, it is not matter for astonishment that he became somewhat shiftless.

When Judge Wellington died, Free Joe's troubles began. The judge's negroes, including Lucinda, went to his half-brother, a man named Calderwood, who was a hard master and a rough customer generally—a man of many eccentricities of mind and character. His neighbors had a habit of alluding to him as "Old Spite"; and the name seemed to fit him so completely that he was known far and near as "Spite" Calderwood. He probably enjoyed the distinction the name gave him, at any rate he never resented it, and it was not often that he missed an opportunity to show that he deserved it. Calderwood's place was two or three miles from the village of Hillsborough, and Free Joe visited his wife twice a week, Wednesday and Saturday nights.

One Sunday morning he was sitting in front of Lucinda's cabin, when Calderwood happened to pass that way.

"Howdy, marster?" said Free Joe, taking off his hat.

"Who are you?" exclaimed Calderwood abruptly, halting and staring at the negro.

"I'm name' Joe, marster, I'm Lucindy's ole man."

"Who do you belong to?"

"Marse John Evans is my gyardeen, marster."

"Big name—gyardeen. Show your pass."

Free Joe produced the document, and Calderwood read it aloud slowly, as if he found it difficult to get at the meaning:

"*To whom it may concern: This is to certify that the boy Joe Frampton has my permission to visit his wife Lucinda.*"

This was dated at Hillsborough, and signed "*John W. Evans.*"

Calderwood read it twice, and then looked at Free Joe, elevating his eyebrows, and showing his discolored teeth.

"Some mighty big words in that there. Evans owns this place, I reckon. When's he comin' down to take hold?"

Free Joe fumbled with his hat. He was badly frightened.

"Lucindy say she speck you wouldn't min' my comin', long ez I behave, marster."

Calderwood tore the pass in pieces and flung it away.

"Don't want no free niggers 'round here," he exclaimed. "There's the big road. It'll carry you to town. Don't let me catch you here no more. Now, mind what I tell you."

Free Joe presented a shabby spectacle as he moved off with his little dog Dan slinking at his heels. It should be said in behalf of Dan, however, that his bristles were up, and that he looked back and growled. It may be that the dog had the advantage of insignificance, but it is difficult to conceive how a dog bold enough to raise his bristles under Calderwood's very eyes could be as insignificant as Free Joe. But both the negro and his little dog seemed to give a new and more dismal aspect to forlornness as they turned into the road and went towards Hillsborough.

After this incident Free Joe seemed to have clear ideas concerning his peculiar condition. He realized the fact that though he was free he was more helpless than any slave. Having no owner, every man was his master. He knew that he was the object of suspicion, and therefore all his slender resources (ah! how pitifully slender they were!) were devoted to winning, not kindness and appreciation, but toleration; all his efforts were in the direction of mitigating the circumstances that tended to make his condition so much worse than that of the negroes around him—negroes who had friends because they had masters.

So far as his own race was concerned, Free Joe was an exile. If the slaves secretly envied him his freedom (which is to be doubted, considering his miserable condition), they openly despised him, and lost no opportunity to treat him with contumely. Perhaps this was in some measure the result of the attitude which Free Joe chose to maintain toward them. No doubt his instinct taught him that to hold himself aloof from the slaves would be to invite from the whites the toleration which he coveted, and without which even his miserable condition would be rendered more miserable still.

His greatest trouble was the fact that he was not allowed to visit his wife; but he soon found a way out of this difficulty. After he had been ordered away from the Calderwood place, he was in the habit of wandering as far in that direction as prudence would permit. Near the Calderwood place, but not on Calderwood's land, lived an old man named Micajah Staley and his sister Becky Staley. These people were old and very poor. Old Micajah had a palsied arm and hand; but, in spite of this, he managed to earn a precarious living with his turning-lathe.

When he was a slave Free Joe would have scorned these representatives of a class known as poor white trash, but now he found them sympathetic and helpful in various ways. From the back door of the cabin he could hear the Calderwood negroes singing at night, and he fancied he could distinguish Lucinda's shrill treble rising above the other voices. A large poplar grew in the woods some distance from the Staley cabin, and at the foot of this tree Free Joe would sit for hours with his face turned toward Calderwood's. His little dog Dan would curl up in the leaves near by, and the two seemed to be as comfortable as possible.

One Saturday afternoon Free Joe, sitting at the foot of this friendly poplar, fell asleep. How long he slept he could not tell; but when he awoke little Dan was licking his face, the moon was shining brightly, and Lucinda his wife stood before him laughing. The dog, seeing that Free Joe was asleep, had grown somewhat impatient, and he concluded to make an excursion to the Calderwood place on his own account. Lucinda was inclined to give the incident a twist in the direction of superstition.

"I'z settin' down front er de fireplace," she said, "cookin' me some meat, w'en all of a sudden I year sumpin at de do'—scratch, scratch. I tuck'n tu'n de meat over, en make out I aint year it. Bimeby it come dar 'gin—scratch, scratch. I up en open de do', I did, en, bless de Lord! dar wuz little Dan, en it look like ter me dat his ribs done grow tergeer. I gin 'im some bread, en den, w'en he start out, I tuck'n foller 'im, kaze I say ter myse'f, maybe my nigger man mought be some'rs 'roun'. Dat ar little dog got sense, mon."

Free Joe laughed and dropped his hand lightly on Dan's head. For a long time after that, he had no difficulty in seeing his wife. He had only to sit by the poplar tree until little Dan could run and fetch her.

But after a while the other negroes discovered that Lucinda was meeting Free Joe in the woods, and information of the fact soon reached Calderwood's ears. He said nothing; but one day he put Lucinda in his buggy, and carried her to Macon, sixty miles away. He carried her to Macon, and came back without her; and nobody in or around Hillsborough, or in that section, ever saw her again.

For many a night after that Free Joe sat in the woods and waited. Little Dan would run merrily off and be gone a long time, but he always came back without Lucinda. This happened over and over again. The "willis-whistlers" would call and call, like phantom huntsmen wandering on a far-off shore; the screech-owl would shake and shiver in the depths of the woods; the night-hawks, sweeping by on noiseless wings, would snap their beaks as though they enjoyed the huge joke of which Free Joe and little Dan were the victims; and the whip-poor-wills would cry to each other through the gloom. Each night seemed to be lonelier than the preceding, but Free Joe's patience was proof against loneliness. There came a time, however, when little Dan refused to go after Lucinda. When Free Joe motioned him in the direction of the Calderwood place, he would simply move about uneasily and whine; then he would curl up in the leaves and make himself comfortable.

One night, instead of going to the poplar-tree to wait for Lucinda, Free Joe went to the Staley cabin, and, in order to make his welcome good, as he expressed it, he carried with him an armful of fat-pine splinters. Miss Becky Staley had a great reputation in those parts as a fortune-teller, and the school-girls, as well as older people, often tested her powers in that direction, some in jest and some in earnest. Free Joe placed his humble offering of light-wood in the chimney-corner, and then seated himself on the steps, dropping his hat on the ground outside.

"Miss Becky," he said presently, "whar in de name er gracious you reckon Lucindy is?"

"Well, the Lord he'p the nigger!" exclaimed Miss Becky, in a tone that seemed to reproduce, by some curious agreement of sight with sound, her general aspect of peakedness. "Well, the Lord he'p the nigger! haint you been a-seein' her all this blessed time? She's over at old Spite Calderwood's, if she's anywhere, I reckon."

"No'm, dat I aint, Miss Becky. I aint seen Lucindy in now gwine on mighty nigh a mont'."

"Well, it haint a-gwine to hurt you," said Miss Becky, somewhat sharply. "In my day an' time it wuz allers took to be a bad sign when niggers got to honeyin' 'roun' an' gwine on."

"Yessum," said Free Joe, cheerfully assenting to the proposition—"yessum, dat's so, but me an' my ole 'oman, we 'uz raise tergeer, en dey aint bin many days w'en we 'uz 'way fum one 'n'er like we is now."

"Maybe she's up an' took up wi' some un else," said Micajah Staley from the corner. "You know what the sayin' is, 'New master, new nigger.' "

"Dat's so, dat's de sayin', but taint wid my ole 'oman like 'tis wid yuther niggers. Me en her wuz des natally raise up tergeer. Dey's lots likelier niggers dan w'at I is," said Free Joe, viewing his shabbiness with a critical eye, "but I know Lucindy mos' good ez I does little Dan dar—dat I does."

There was no reply to this, and Free Joe continued—

"Miss Becky, I wish you please, ma'am, take en run yo' kyards en see sump'n in'er 'bout Lucindy; kaze ef she sick, I'm gwine dar. Dey ken take en take me up en gimme a stroppin', but I'm gwine dar."

Miss Becky got her cards, but first she picked up a cup, in the bottom of which were some coffee grounds. These she whirled slowly round and round, ending finally by turning the cup upside down on the hearth and allowing it to remain in that position.

"I'll turn the cup first," said Miss Becky, "and then I'll run the cards and see what they say."

As she shuffled the cards the fire on the hearth burned slow, and in its fitful light the gray-haired, thin-featured woman seemed to deserve the weird reputation which rumor and gossip had given her. She shuffled the cards for some moments, gazing intently in the dying fire; then, throwing a piece of pine on the coals, she made three divisions of the pack, disposing them about in her lap. Then she took the first pile, ran the cards slowly through her fingers, and studied them carefully. To the first she added the second pile. The study of these was evidently not satisfactory. She said nothing, but frowned heavily; and the frown deepened as she added the rest of the cards until the entire fifty-two had passed in review before her. Though she frowned, she seemed to be deeply interested.

Without changing the relative position of the cards, she ran them over again. Then she threw a larger piece of pine on the fire, shuffled the cards afresh, divided them into three piles, and subjected them to the same careful and critical examination.

"I can't tell the day when I've seed the cards run this a-way," she said after a while. "What is an' what aint, I'll never tell you; but I know what the cards sez."

"W'at does dey say, Miss Becky?" the negro inquired, in a tone the solemnity of which was heightened by its eagerness.

"They er runnin' quare. These here that I'm a lookin' at," said Miss Becky, "they stan' for the past. Them there, they er the present; and the t'others, they er the future. Here's a bundle"—tapping the ace of clubs with her thumb—"an' here's a journey as plain as the nose on a man's face. Here's Lucinda"—

"Whar she, Miss Becky?"

"Here she is—the queen of spades."

Free Joe grinned. The idea seemed to please him immensely.

"Well, well, well!" he exclaimed. "Ef dat don't beat my time! De queen er spades! W'en Lucindy year dat hit'll tickle 'er, sho'!"

Miss Becky continued to run the cards back and forth through her fingers.

"Here's a bundle an' a journey, and here's Lucinda. An' here's ole Spite Calderwood."

She held the cards toward the negro and touched the king of clubs.

"De Lord he'p my soul!" exclaimed Free Joe with a chuckle. "De faver's dar. Yesser, dat's him! W'at de matter 'long wid all un um, Miss Becky?"

The old woman added the second pile of cards to the first, and then the third, still running them through her fingers slowly and critically.

By this time the piece of pine in the fireplace had wrapped itself in a mantle of flame, illuminating the cabin and throwing into strange relief the figure of Miss Becky as she sat studying the cards. She frowned ominously at the cards and mumbled a few words to herself. Then she dropped her hands in her lap and gazed once more into the fire. Her shadow danced and capered on the wall and floor behind her, as if, looking over her shoulder into the future, it could behold a rare spectacle. After a while she picked up the cup that had been turned on the hearth. The coffee grounds, shaken around, presented what seemed to be a most intricate map.

"Here's the journey," said Miss Becky, presently; "here's the big road, here's rivers to cross, here's the bundle to tote." She paused and sighed. "They haint no names writ here, an' what it all means I'll never tell you. Cajy, I wish you'd be so good as to han' me my pipe."

"I haint no hand wi' the kyards," said Cajy, and he handed the pipe, "but I reckon I can patch out your misinformation, Becky, bekaze the other day, whiles I was a-fishin' up Mizzer Perdue's rolling-pin, I hearn a rattlin' in the road. I looked out, an' Spite Calderwood was a-drivin' by in his buggy, an' thar sot Lucinda by him. It'd in-about drapt out er my min'."

Free Joe sat on the door-sill and fumbled at his hat, flinging it from one hand to the other.

"You haint see um gwine back, is you, Marse Cajy?" he asked after a while.

"Ef they went back by this road," said Mr. Staley, with the air of one who is accustomed to weigh well his words, "it must 'a' bin endurin' of the time whiles I was asleep, bekaze I haint bin no furder from my shop than to yon bed."

"Well, sir!" exclaimed Free Joe in an awed tone, which Mr. Staley seemed to regard as a tribute to his extraordinary power of statement.

"Ef it's my beliefs you want," continued the old man, "I'll pitch 'em at you fair and free. My beliefs is that Spite Calderwood is gone an' took Lucindy outen the county. Bless your heart and soul! when Spite Calderwood meets the Old Boy in the road they'll be a turrible scuffle. You mark what I tell you."

Free Joe, still fumbling with his hat, rose and leaned against the door-facing. He seemed to be embarrassed. Presently he said:

"I speck I better be gittin' 'long. Nex' time I see Lucindy, I'm gwine tell 'er w'at Miss Becky say 'bout de queen er spades—dat I is. If dat don't tickle 'er, dey aint no nigger 'oman never bin tickle'."

He paused a moment, as though waiting for some remark or comment, some confirmation of misfortune, or, at the very least, some endorsement of his suggestion that Lucinda would be greatly pleased to know that she had figured as the queen of spades; but neither Miss Becky nor her brother said anything.

"One minnit ridin' in de buggy, 'longside er Mars Spite, en de nex' high-falutin' 'roun' playin' de queen er spades. Mon, deze yer nigger gals gittin' up in de pictur's; dey sholy is."

With a brief "Good-night, Miss Becky, Mars Cajy," Free Joe went out into the darkness, followed by little Dan. He made his way to the poplar, where Lucinda had been in the habit of meeting him, and sat down. He sat there a long time; he sat there until little Dan, growing restless, trotted off in the direction of the Calderwood place. Dozing against the poplar in the gray dawn of the morning, Free Joe heard Spite Calderwood's fox-hounds in full cry a mile away.

"Shoo!" he exclaimed, scratching his head, and laughing to himself, "dem ar dogs is des a-warmin' dat old fox up."

But it was Dan the hounds were after, and the little dog came back no more. Free Joe waited and waited, until he grew tired of waiting. He went back the next night and waited, and for many nights thereafter. His waiting was in vain, and yet he never regarded it as in vain. Careless and shabby as he was, Free Joe was thoughtful enough to have his theory. He was convinced that little Dan had found Lucinda, and that some night when the moon was shining brightly through the trees, the dog would rouse him from his dreams as he sat sleeping at the foot of the poplar-tree, and he would open his eyes and behold Lucinda standing over him, laughing merrily as of old; and then he thought what fun they would have about the queen of spades.

How many long nights Free Joe waited at the foot of the poplar-tree for Lucinda and little Dan no one can ever know. He kept no account of them and they were not recorded by Micajah Staley or by Miss Becky. The season ran into summer and then into fall. One night he went to the Staley cabin, cut the two old people an armful of wood, and seated himself on the door-steps, where he rested. He was always thankful—and proud, as it seemed—when Miss Becky gave him a cup of coffee, which she was sometimes thoughtful enough to do. He was especially thankful on this particular night.

"You er still layin' off for to strike up wi' Lucindy out thar in the woods, I reckon," said Micajah Staley, smiling grimly. The situation was not without its humorous aspects.

"Oh, dy er comin', Mars Cajy, dey er comin', sho," Free Joe replied, "I boun' you dey'll come; en w'en dey does come, I'll des take en fetch um yer, whar you kin see um wid you own eyes, you en Miss Becky."

"No," said Mr. Staley, with a quick and emphatic gesture of disapproval. "Don't! don't fetch 'em anywheres. Stay right wi' 'em as long as may be."

Free Joe chuckled, and slipped away into the night, while the two old people sat gazing in the fire. Finally Micajah spoke:

"Look at that nigger; look at 'im. He's pine-blank as happy now as a kildee by a mill-race. You can't 'feze 'em. I'd in-about give up my t'other hand ef I could stan' flat-footed, an' grin at trouble like that there nigger."

"Niggers is niggers," said Miss Becky, smiling grimly, "an' you can't rub it out; yet I lay I've seed a heap of white people lots meaner'n Free Joe. He grins,—an' that's nigger,—but I've ketched his under jaw a-trimblin' when Lucindy's name uz brung up. An' I tell you," she went on bridling up a little, and speaking with almost fierce emphasis, "the Old Boy's done sharpened his claws for Spite Calderwood. You'll see it."

"Me, Rebecca?" said Mr. Staley, hugging his palsied arm; "me? I hope not."

"Well, you'll know it then," said Miss Becky, laughing heartily at her brother's look of alarm.

The next morning Micajah Staley had occasion to go into the woods after a piece of timber. He saw Free Joe sitting at the foot of the poplar, and the sight vexed him somewhat.

"Git up from there," he cried, "an 'go an' arn your livin'. A mighty purty pass it's come to, when great big buck niggers can lie a-snorin' in the woods all day, when t'other folks is got to be up an' a-gwine. Git up from there!"

Receiving no response, Mr. Staley went to Free Joe, and shook him by the shoulder; but the negro made no response. He was dead. His hat was off, his head was bent, and a smile was on his face. It was as if he had bowed and smiled when death stood before him, humble to the last. His clothes were ragged; his hands were rough and callous; his shoes were literally tied together with strings; he was shabby in the extreme. A passer-by, glancing at him, could have no idea that such a humble creature had been summoned as a witness before the Lord God of Hosts.

Will N. Harben

The Heresy of Abner Calihan

Neil Filmore's store was at the crossing of the Big Cabin and Rock Valley roads. Before the advent of Sherman into the South it had been a grist-mill, to which the hardy mountaineers had regularly brought their grain to be ground, in wagons, on horseback, or on their shoulders, according to their conditions. But the Northern soldiers had appropriated the miller's little stock of toll, had torn down the long wooden sluice which had conveyed the water from the race to the mill, had burnt the great wheel and crude wooden machinery, and rolled the massive grinding-stones into the deepest part of the creek.

After the war nobody saw any need for a mill at that point, and Neil Filmore had bought the property from its impoverished owner and turned the building into a store. It proved to be a fair location, for there was considerable travel along the two main roads, and as Filmore was postmaster his store became the general meeting-point for everybody living within ten miles of the spot. He kept for sale, as he expressed it, "a little of everything, from shoe-eyes to a sack of guano." Indeed, a sight of his rough shelves and unplaned counters, filled with cakes of tallow, beeswax and butter, bolts of calico, sheeting and ginghams, and the floor and porch heaped with piles of skins, cases of eggs, coops of chickens, and cans of lard, was enough to make an orderly housewife shudder with horror.

But Mrs. Filmore had grown accustomed to this state of affairs in the front part of the house, for she confined her domestic business, and whatever neatness and order were possible, to the room in the rear, where, as she often phrased it, she did the "eatin' an' cookin', an' never interfeer with pap's part except to lend 'im my cheers when thar is more'n common waitin' fer the mail-carrier."

And her chairs were often in demand, for Filmore was a deacon in Big Cabin Church, which stood at the foot of the green-clad mountain a mile down the road, and it was at the store that his brother deacons frequently met to transact church business.

One summer afternoon they held an important meeting. Abner Calihan, a member of the church and a good, industrious citizen, was to be tried for heresy.

"It has worried me more'n anything that has happened sence them two Dutchmen over at Cove Spring swapped wives an' couldn't be convinced of the'r error," said long, lean Bill Odell, after he had come in and borrowed a candle-box to feed his mule in, and had given the animal eight ears of corn from the pockets of his long-tailed coat, and left the mule haltered at a hitching-post in front of the store.

"Ur sence the widder Dill swore she was gwine to sue Hank Dobb's wife fer witchcraft," replied Filmore, in a hospitable tone. "Take a cheer; it must be as hot as a bake-oven out thar in the sun."

Bill Odell took off his coat and folded it carefully and laid it across the beam of the scales, and unbuttoned his vest and sat down, and proceeded to mop his perspiring face with a red bandanna. Toot Bailey came in next, a quiet little man of about fifty, with a dark face, straggling gray hair, and small, penetrating eyes. His blue jean trousers were carelessly stuck into the tops of his clay-stained boots, and he wore a sack-coat, a "hickory" shirt, and a leather belt. Mrs. Filmore put her red head and broad, freckled face out of the door of her apartment to see who had arrived, and the next moment came out dusting a "split-bottomed" chair with her apron.

"How are ye, Toot?" was her greeting as she placed the chair for him between a jar of fresh honey and a barrel of sorghum molasses. "How is the sore eyes over yore way?"

"Toler'ble," he answered, as he leaned back against the counter and fanned himself with his slouch hat. "Mine is about through it, but the Tye childern is a sight. Pizen-oak hain't a circumstance."

"What did ye use?"

"Copperas an' sweet milk. It is the best thing I've struck. I don't want any o' that peppery eye-wash 'bout my place. It'd take the hide off'n a mule's hind leg."

"Now yore a-talkin'," and Bill Odell went to the water-bucket on the end of the counter. He threw his tobacco-quid away, noisily washed out his mouth, and took a long drink from the gourd dipper. Then Bart Callaway and Amos Sanders, who had arrived half an hour before and had walked down to take a look at Filmore's fish-pond, came in together. Both were whittling sticks and looking cool and comfortable.

"We are all heer," said Odell, and he added his hat to his coat and the pile of weights on the scale-beam, and put his right foot on the rung of his chair. "I reckon we mought as well proceed." At these words the men who had arrived last carefully stowed their hats away under their chairs and leaned forward expectantly. Mrs. Filmore glided noiselessly to a corner behind the counter, and with folded arms stood ready to hear all that was to be said.

"Did anybody inform Ab of the object of this meeting?" asked Odell.

They all looked at Filmore, and he transferred their glances to his wife. She flushed under their scrutiny and awkwardly twisted her fat arms together.

"Sister Calihan wuz in here this mornin'," she deposed in an uneven tone. "I 'lowed somebody amongst 'em ort to know what you-uns wuz up to, so I up an' told 'er."

"What did she have to say?" asked Odell, bending over the scales to spit at a crack in the floor, but not removing his eyes from the witness.

"Law, I hardly know what she didn't say! I never seed a woman take on so. Ef the last bit o' kin she had on earth wuz suddenly wiped from the face o' creation, she couldn't 'a' tuk it more to heart. Sally wuz with 'er, an' went on wuss 'an her mammy."

"What ailed Sally?"

Mrs. Filmore smiled irrepressibly. "I reckon you ort to know, Brother Odell," she said, under the hand she had raised to hide her smile. "Do you reckon she hain't heerd o' yore declaration that Eph cayn't marry in no heretic family while yo're above ground? It wuz goin' the round at singin'-school two weeks ago, and thar hain't been a thing talked sence."

"I hain't got a ioty to retract," replied Odell, looking down into the upturned faces for approval. "I'd as soon see a son o' mine in his box. Misfortune an' plague is boun' to foller them that winks at infidelity in any disguise ur gyarb."

"Oh, shucks! don't fetch the young folks into it, Brother Odell," gently protested Bart Callaway. "Them two has been a-settin' up to each other ever sence they wuz knee-high to a duck. They hain't responsible fer the doin's o' the old folks."

"I hain't got nothin' to take back, an' Eph knows it," thundered the tall deacon, and his face flushed angrily. "Ef the membership sees fit to excommunicate Ab Calihan, none o' his stock 'll ever come into my family. But this is dilly-dallyin' over nothin'. You fellers 'll set thar cocked up, an' chaw an' spit, an' look knowin', an' let the day pass 'thout doin' a single thing. Ab Calihan is either fitten or unfitten, one ur t'other. Brother Filmore, you've seed 'im the most, now what's he let fall that's undoctrinal?"

Filmore got up and laid his clay pipe on the counter and kicked back his chair with his foot.

"The fust indications I noticed," he began, in a raised voice, as if he were speaking to some one outside, "wuz the day Liz Wambush died. Bud Thorn come in while I wuz weighing up a side o' bacon fur Ab, an' 'lowed that Liz couldn't live through the night. I axed 'im ef she had made her peace, and he 'lowed she had, entirely, that she wuz jest a-lyin' thar shoutin' Glory ever' breath she drawed, an' that they all wuz glad to see her reconciled, fer you know she wuz a hard case speritually. Well, it wuz right back thar at the fireplace while Ab wuz warmin' hisse'f to start home that he 'lowed that he hadn't a word to say agin Liz's marvelous faith, nur her sudden speritual spurt, but that in his opinion the doctrine o' salvation through faith without actual deeds of the flesh to give it backbone wuz all shucks, an' a dangerous doctrine to teach to a risin' gineration. Them wuz his words as well as I can remember, an' he cited a good many cases to demonstrate that the members o' Big Cabin wuzn't any more ready to help a needy neighbor than a equal number outside the church. He wuz mad kase last summer when his wheat wuz spilin' everybody that come to he'p wuz uv some other denomination, an' the whole lot o' Big Cabin folks made some excuse ur other. He 'lowed that you—"

Filmore hesitated, and the tall man opposite him changed countenance.

"Neil, hain't you got a bit o' sense?" put in Mrs. Filmore, sharply.

"What did he say ag'in' me—the scamp?" asked Odell, firing up.

Filmore turned his back to his scowling wife, and took an egg from a basket on the counter and looked at it closely, as he rolled it over and over in his fingers.

"Lots that he ortn't to, I reckon," he said, evasively.

"Well, what wuz *some* of it? I hain't a-keerin' what he says about me."

"He 'lowed, fer one thing, that yore strict adheerance to doctrine had hardened you some, wharas religious conviction, ef thar wuz any divine intention in it, ort, in reason, to have a contrary effect. He 'lowed you wuz money-lovin' an' uncharitable an' unfergivin' an', a heap o' times, un-Christian in yore persecution o' the weak an' helpless—them that has no food an' raiment—when yore crib an' smokehouse is always full. Ab is a powerful talker, an'—"

"It's the devil in 'im a-talkin'," interrupted Odell, angrily, "an' it's plain enough that he ort to be churched. Brother Sanders, you intimated that you'd have a word to say; let us have it."

Sanders, a heavy-set man, bald-headed and red-bearded, rose. He took a prodigious quid of tobacco from his mouth and dropped it on the floor at the side of his chair. His remarks were crisp and to the point.

"My opinion is that Ab Calihan hain't a bit more right in our church than Bob Inglesel. He's got plumb crooked."

"What have you heerd 'im say? That's what we want to git at," said Odell, his leathery face brightening.

"More'n I keered to listen at. He has been readin' stuff he ortn't to. He give up takin' the *Advocate*, an' wouldn't go in Mary Bank's club when they've been takin' it in his family fer the last five year, an' has been subscribin' fer the *True Light* sence Christmas. The last time I met 'im at Big Cabin, I think it wuz the second Sunday, he couldn't talk o' nothin' else but what this great man an' t'other had writ somewhar up in Yankeedom, an' that ef we all keep along in our little rut we'll soon be the laughin'-stock of all the rest of the enlightened world. Ab is a slippery sort of a feller, an' it's mighty hard to ketch 'im, but I nailed 'im on one vital p'int."

Sanders paused for a moment, stroked his beard, and then continued: "He got excited sorter, an' 'lowed that he had come to the conclusion that hell warn't no literal, burnin' one nohow, that he had too high a regyard fer the Almighty to believe that He would amuse Hisse'f roastin' an' feedin' melted lead to His creatures jest to see 'em squirm."

"He disputes the Bible, then," said Odell, conclusively, looking first into one face and then another. "He sets his puny self up ag'in' the Almighty. The Book that has softened the pillers o' thousands; the Word that has been the consolation o' millions an' quintillions o' mortals of sense an' judgment in all ages an' countries is a pack o' lies from kiver to kiver. I don't see a bit o' use goin' furder with this investigation."

Just then Mrs. Filmore stepped out from her corner.

"I hain't been axed to put in," she said, warmly; "but ef I wuz youuns I'd go slow with Abner Calihan. He's nobody's fool. He's too good a citizen to be hauled an' drug about like a dog with a rope round his neck. He fit on the right side in the war, an' to my certain knowledge has done more to'ds keepin' peace an' harmony in this community than any other three men in it. He has set up with the sick an' toted medicine to 'em, an' fed the pore an' housed the homeless. Here only last week he got hisse'f stung all over the face an' neck helpin' that lazy Joe Sebastian hive his bees, an' Joe an' his triflin' gang didn't git a scratch. You may see the day you'll regret it ef you run dry shod over that man."

"We simply intend to do our duty, Sister Filmore," said Odell, slightly taken aback; "but you kin see that church rules must be obeyed. I move we go up thar in a body an' lay the case squar before 'im. Ef he is willin' to take back his wild assertions an' go 'long quietly without tryin' to play smash with the religious order of the whole community, he may stay in on probation. What do you-uns say?"

"It's all we kin do now," said Sanders; and they all rose and reached for their hats.

"You'd better stay an' look atter the store," Filmore called back to his wife from the outside; "somebody mought happen along." With a reluctant nod of her head she acquiesced, and came out on the little porch and looked after them as they trudged along the hot road toward Abner Calihan's farm. When they were out of sight she turned back into the store. "Well," she muttered, "Abner Calihan *may* put up with that triflin' layout a-interfeerin' with 'im when he is busy a-savin' his hay, but ef he don't set his dogs on 'em he is a better Christian 'an I think he is' an' he's a good un. They are a purty-lookin' set to be a-dictatin' to a man like him."

A little wagon-way, which was not used enough to kill the stubbly grass that grew on it, ran from the main road out to Calihan's house. The woods through which the little road had been cut were so thick and the foliage so dense that the overlapping branches often hid the sky.

Calihan's house was a four-roomed log building which had been weather-boarded on the outside with upright unpainted planks. On the right side of the house was an orchard, and beneath some apple-trees near the door stood an old-fashioned cider-press, a pile of acid-stained rocks which had been used as weights in the press, and numerous tubs, barrels, jugs, and jars, and piles of sour-smelling refuse, over which buzzed a dense swarm of honey-bees, wasps, and yellow-jackets. On the other side of the house, in a chip-strewn yard, stood cords upon cords of wood, and several piles of rich pine-knots and charred pine-logs, which the industrious farmer had on rainy days hauled down from the mountains for kindling-wood. Behind the house was a great log barn and a stable-yard, and beyond them lay the cornfields and the lush green meadow, where a sinuous line of willows and slender cane-brakes marked the course of a little creek.

The approach of the five visitors was announced to Mrs. Calihan and her daughter by a yelping rush toward the gate of half a dozen dogs which had been napping and snapping at flies on the porch. Mrs. Calihan ran out into the yard and vociferously called the dogs off, and with awed hospitality invited the men into the little sitting-room.

Those of them who cared to inspect their surroundings saw a rag carpet, walls of bare, hewn logs, the cracks of which had been filled with yellow mud, a little table in the center of the room, and a cottage organ against the wall near the small window. On the mantel stood a new clock and a glass lamp, the globe of which held a piece of red flannel and some oil. The flannel was to give the lamp color. Indeed, lamps with flannel in them were very much in vogue in that part of the country.

"Me an' Sally wuz sorter expectin' ye," said Mrs. Calihan, as she gave them seats and went around and took their hats from their knees and laid them on a bed in the next room. "I don't know what to make of Mr. Calihan," she continued, plaintively. "He never wuz this away before. When we wuz married he could offer up the best prayer of any young man in the settlement. The Mount Zion meetin'-house couldn't hold protracted meetin' without 'im. He fed more preachers an' the'r hosses than anybody else, an' some 'lowed that he wuz jest too natcherly good to pass away like common folks, an' that when his time come he'd jest disappear body an' all." She was now wiping her eyes on her apron, and her voice had the suggestion of withheld emotions. "I never calculated on him bringin' sech disgrace as this on his family."

"Whar is he now?" asked Odell, preliminarily.

"Down thar stackin' hay. Sally begun on 'im ag'in at dinner about yore orders to Eph, an' he went away 'thout finishin' his dinner. She's been a-cryin' an' a-poutin' an' takin' on fer a week, an' won't tech a bite to eat. I never seed a gal so bound up in anybody as she is in Eph. It has mighty nigh driv her pa distracted, kase he likes Eph, an' Sally's his pet." Mrs. Calihan turned her head toward the adjoining room: "Sally, oh, Sally! are ye listenin'? Come heer a minute!"

There was silence for a moment, then a sound of heavy shoes on the floor of the next room, and a tall rather good-looking girl entered.

Her eyes and cheeks were red, and she hung her head awkwardly, and did not look at any one but her mother.

"Did you call me, ma?"

"Yes, honey; run an' tell yore pa they are all heer,—the last one of 'em, an' fer him to hurry right on to the house an' not keep 'em a-waitin'."

"Yes-sum!" And without any covering for her head the visitors saw her dart across the back yard toward the meadow.

With his pitchfork on his shoulder, a few minutes later Abner Calihan came up to the back door of his house. He wore no coat, and but one frayed suspender supported his patched and baggy trousers. His broad, hairy breast showed through the opening in his shirt. His tanned cheeks and neck were corrugated, his hair and beard long and reddish brown. His brow was high and broad, and a pair of blue eyes shone serenely beneath his shaggy brows.

"Good evenin'," he said, leaning his pitch-fork against the door-jamb outside and entering. Without removing his hat he went around and gave a damp hand to each visitor. "It is hard work savin' hay sech weather as this."

No one replied to this remark, though they all nodded and looked as if they wanted to give utterance to something struggling within them. Calihan swung a chair over near the door, and sat down and leaned back against the wall, and looked out at the chickens in the yard and the gorgeous peacock strutting about in the sun. No one seemed quite ready to speak, so, to cover his embarrassment, he looked farther over in the yard to his potato-bank and pig-pens, and then up into the clear sky for indications of rain.

"I reckon you know our business, Brother Calihan," began Odell, in a voice that broke the silence harshly.

"I reckon I could make a purty good guess," and Calihan spit over his left shoulder into the yard. "I hain't heerd nothin' else fer a week. From all the talk, a body'd 'low I'd stole somebody's hawgs."

"We jest *had* to take action," affirmed the self-constituted speaker for the others. "The opinions you have expressed," and Odell at once began to warm up to his task, "are so undoctrinal an' so p'int blank ag'in' the articles of faith that, believin' as you seem to believe, you are plumb out o' j'int with Big Cabin Church, an' a resky man in any God-feerin' community. God Almighty"—and those who saw Odell's twitching upper lip and indignantly flashing eye knew that the noted "exhorter" was about to become mercilessly personal and vindictive—"God Almighty is the present ruler of the universe, but sence you have set up to run ag'in' Him it looks like you'd need a wider scope of territory to transact business in than jest heer in this settlement."

The blood had left Calihan's face. His eyes swept from one stern, unrelenting countenance to another till they rested on his wife and daughter, who sat side by side, their faces in their aprons, their shoulders quivering with soundless sobs. They had forsaken him. He was an alien in his own house, a criminal convicted beneath his own roof. His rugged breast rose and fell tumultuously as he strove to command his voice.

"I hain't meant no harm—not a speck," he faltered, as he wiped the perspiration from his quivering chin. "I hain't no hand to stir up strife in a community. I've tried to be law-abidin' an' honest, but it don't seem like a man kin he'p thinkin'. He—"

"But he kin keep his thinkin' to hisse'f," interrupted Odell, sharply; and a pause came after his words.

In a jerky fashion Calihan spit over his shoulder again. He looked at his wife and daughter for an instant, and nodded several times as if acknowledging the force of Odell's words. Bart Callaway took out his tobacco-quid and nervously shuffled it about in his palm as if he had half made up his mind that Odell ought not to do all the talking, but he remained mute, for Mrs. Calihan had suddenly looked up.

"That's what I told him," she whimpered, bestowing a tearful glance on her husband. "He mought 'a' kep' his idees to hisse'f ef he had to have 'em, and not 'a' fetched calumny an' disgrace down on me an' Sally. When he used to set thar atter supper an' pore over the *True Light* when ever'body else wuz in bed, I knowed it'd bring trouble, kase some o' the doctrine wuz scand'lous. The next thing I knowed he had lost intrust in prayer-meetin', an' 'lowed that Brother Washburn's sermons wuz the same thing over an' over, an' that they mighty nigh put him to sleep. An' then he give up axin' the blessin' at the table—somethin' that has been done in my fam'ly as fur back as the oldest one kin remember. An' he talked his views, too, fer it got out, an' me nur Sally narry one never cheeped it, fer we wuz ashamed. An' then ever' respectable woman in Big Cabin meetin'-house begun to sluff away from us as ef they wuz afeerd o' takin' some dreadful disease. It wuz hard enough on Sally at the start, but when Eph up an' tol' her that you had give him a good tongue-lashin', an' had refused to deed him the land you promised him ef he went any further with her, it mighty nigh prostrated her. She hain't done one thing lately but look out at the road an' pine an' worry. The blame is all on her father. My folks has all been good church members as fur back as kin be traced, an' narry one wuz ever turned out."

Mrs. Calihan broke down and wept. Calihan was deeply touched; he could not bear to see a woman cry. He cleared his throat and tried to look unconcerned.

"What step do you-uns feel called on to take next to—to what you are a-doin' of now?" he stammered.

"We 'lowed," replied Odell, "ef we couldn't come to some sort o' understandin' with you now, we'd fetch up the case before preachin' to-morrow an' let the membership vote on it. The verdict would go ag'in' you, Ab, fer thar hain't a soul in sympathy with you."

The sobbing of the two women broke out in renewed volume at the mention of this dreadful ultimatum, which, despite their familiarity with the rigor of Big Cabin Church discipline, they had up to this moment regarded as a vague contingent rather than a tangible certainty.

Calihan's face grew paler. Whatever struggle might have been going on in his mind was over. He was conquered.

"I am ag'in' bringin' reproach on my wife an' child," he conceded, a lump in his throat and a tear in his eye. "You all know best. I reckon I have been too forward an' too eager to heer myself talk." He got up and looked out toward the towering cliffy mountains and into the blue indefiniteness above them, and without looking at the others he finished awkwardly: "Ef it's jest the same to you-uns you may let the charge drap, an'—an' in future I'll give no cause fer complaint."

"That's the talk" said Odell, warmly, and he got up and gave his hand to Calihan. The others followed his example.

"I'll make a little speech before preachin' in the mornin'," confided Odell to Calihan after congratulations were over. "You needn't be thar unless you want to. I'll fix you up all right."

Calihan smiled faintly and looked shame-facedly toward the meadow, and reached outside and took hold of the handle of his pitchfork.

"I want to try to git through that haystack 'fore dark," he said, awkwardly. "Ef you-uns will be so kind as to excuse me now I'll run down and finish up. I'd sorter set myself a task to do, an' I don't like to fall short o' my mark."

Down in the meadow Calihan worked like a tireless machine, not pausing for a moment to rest his tense muscles. He was trying to make up for the time he had lost with his guests. Higher and smaller grew the great haystack as it slowly tapered toward its apex. The red sun sank behind the mountain and began to draw in its long streamers of light. The gray of dusk, as if fleeing from its darker self, the monster night, crept up from the east, and with a thousand arms extended moved on after the receding light.

Calihan worked on till the crickets began to shrill and the frogs in the marshes to croak, and the hay beneath his feet felt damp with dew. The stack was finished. He leaned on his fork and inspected his work mechanically. It was a perfect cone. Every outside straw and blade of grass lay smoothly downward, like the hair on a well-groomed horse. Then with his fork on his shoulder he trudged slowly up the narrow field-road toward the house. He was vaguely grateful for the darkness; a strange, new, childish embarrassment was on him. For the first time in life he was averse to meeting his wife and child.

"I've been spanked an' told to behave ur it 'ud go wuss with me," he muttered. "I never wuz talked to that away before by nobody, but I jest had to take it. Sally an' her mother never would 'a' heerd the last of it ef I had let out jest once. No man, I reckon, has a moral right to act so as to make his family miserable. I crawfished, I know, an' on short notice; but law me! I wouldn't have Bill Odell's heart in me fer ever' acre o' bottom-lan' in this valley. I wouldn't 'a' talked to a houn' dog as he did to me right before Sally an' her mother."

He was very weary when he leaned his fork against the house and turned to wash his face and hands in the tin basin on the bench at the side of the steps. Mrs. Calihan came to the door, her face beaming.

"I wuz afeerd you never would come," she said, in a sweet, winning tone. "I got yore beans warmed over an' some o' yore brag yam taters cooked. Come on in 'fore the coffee an' biscuits git cold."

"I'll be thar in a minute," he said; and he rolled up his sleeves and plunged his hot hands and face into the cold spring-water.

"Here's a clean towel, pa; somebody has broke the roller." It was Sally. She had put on her best white muslin gown and braided her rich, heavy hair into two long plaits which hung down her back. There was no trace of the former redness about her eyes, and her face was bright and full of happiness. He wiped his hands and face on the towel she held, and took a piece of a comb from his vest pocket and hurriedly raked his coarse hair backward. He looked at her tenderly and smiled in an abashed sort of way.

"Anybody comin' to-night?"

"Yes, sir."

"Eph Odell, I'll bet my hat!"

The girl nodded, and blushed and hung her head.

"How do you know?"

"Mr. Odell 'lowed I mought look fer him."

Abner Calihan laughed slowly and put his arm around his daughter, and together they went toward the steps of the kitchen door.

"You seed yore old daddy whipped clean out to-day," he said, tentatively. "I reckon yo're ashamed to see him sech a coward an' have him sneak away like a dog with his tail tucked 'tween his legs. Bill Odell is a power in this community."

She laughed with him, but she did not understand his banter, and preceded him into the kitchen. It was lighted by a large tallow-dip in the center of the table. There was much on the white cloth to tempt a hungry laborer's appetite—a great dish of greasy string-beans, with pieces of bacon, a plate of smoking biscuits, and a platter of fried ham in brown gravy. But he was not hungry. Slowly and clumsily he drew up his chair and sat down opposite his wife and daughter. He slid a quivering thumb under the edge of his inverted plate and turned it half over, but noticing that they had their hands in their laps and had reverently bowed their heads, he cautiously replaced it. In a flash he comprehended what was expected of him. The color surged into his homely face. He played with his knife for a moment, and then stared at them stubbornly, almost defiantly. They did not look up, but remained motionless and patiently expectant. The dread of the protracted silence, for which he was becoming more and more responsible, conquered him. He lowered his head and spoke in a low, halting tone:

"Good Lord, Father of us all, have mercy on our sins, and make us thankful fer these, Thy many blessings. Amen."

Part Two

Georgia Writers in the Twentieth Century, 1900–1960

Modern Georgia writers have been citizens of both a particular region and of the world at large. The regional aspects of their writing distinguish it from the writing of other parts of the nation and give it a particular character. Henry Grady's "New South" address in 1886 marked at least the symbolic beginning of the modern age for Georgia. Defeat in the Civil War and a bitter decade of Reconstruction left many Georgians disaffected. Others were more practical, more able and willing to adjust to the times and get on with their lives, to seize the opportunities that industry and business from the North brought their way. This did not mean they began discarding their past. Far from it. Georgia writing is the history of a continuous struggle with the past, of how to relate it to the present and carry it forward into the future. This struggle continues today.

Most modern Georgia writers have been hard realists in style and attitude. The modern era and all its problems left little room for romanticism or nostalgia. The central and most traumatic issue of the century was that of race. Encouraged by their race's slow but undeniable economic and cultural progress in Atlanta and other large cities of the state, and by the Harlem Renaissance to the north, black Georgians began to write in every genre. Georgia Douglas Johnson received national attention for her poetry. Walter White published two successful novels, *Fire in the Flint* (1924) and *Flight* (1926), before turning his energies to a long career in the NAACP. The famous writer and philosopher W. E. B. Du Bois, on the faculty of Atlanta University from 1897 to 1910, was only one of a number of individuals who encouraged the development of a cultural and political identity for blacks in Atlanta and the rest of the state early in the century.

Black writers had to contend with an array of complicated issues. Foremost among them was the question of identity. What stance should they take toward a society largely oppressive to them? Separatism, assimilation, or some position in between? What attitude should they take toward the past and slavery? What should be the relationship of black culture to white culture? Quite apart from the perhaps metaphysical issues of identity was the more practical issue of survival. Such writers as Jean Toomer, Frank Yerby, and John Oliver Killens addressed these issues directly and indirectly. Toomer's novel *Cane* is a powerful celebration of the black folk culture of rural Georgia, a culture he valued for its own independent vitality from the white. Killens is directly concerned with the forces that a young black man confronts in a white racist society, and Yerby in his early stories is similarly concerned.

Race was an issue for white writers too, though they often approached it in different ways. The white writer who, for her time, gave the most controversial treatment to the issue was Lillian Smith, whose 1944 novel *Strange Fruit* explored the subject of interracial love, and whose nonfiction work *Killers of the Dream* (1949) addressed with fierce indignation the racism of the pre–civil rights South. Smith was an exception to the white rule, for the most part. While a few writers ignored the issue entirely, most were still exploring and attempting to understand the relationship of whites and blacks in a society predicated on racial separateness. Flannery O'Connor's "The Artificial Nigger," despite its title, which she wisely retained though John Crowe Ransom urged her to change it to something less offensive, is a powerful study from a white perspective of racial isolation in the state before 1960. Racial ambivalence often led white writers to the creation of deeply moving fiction. Byron Herbert Reece's second novel *The Hawk and the Sun* and Carson McCullers's *A Member of the Wedding* owe their power at least in part to this ambivalence.

Change has been a major theme throughout the history of literature. Each generation mourns the one that has just passed, and confronts the fear of its own mortality. But the American Civil War made change a particularly poignant issue for writers in the South. Defeat radically altered Southern society. The gradual shrinking of the rural agricultural South as the new urban South began to replace it was one modern consequence. The importance of this theme was expressed in 1930 in a book called *I'll Take My Stand*, a collection of essays by twelve Southerners who had gathered together in Nashville, Tennessee, and called themselves "agrarians." The agrarians regarded traditional Southern culture as threatened by the encroachment of Northern industry and values, and argued that the South should act to preserve its culture, even at the cost of isolation from the rest of the world. Although there was no Georgian among these twelve agrarians, many Georgians sympathized with them. Even those who did not still worried over the challenges the modern world posed.

Agrarianism is almost everywhere evident among modern Southern writers, even among black writers, who stood the most to gain from the arrival of change in the South. With its emphasis on regional culture, agrarianism encouraged writers to document the details and textures of Southern life. This interest seems to have been important to such writers as Jean Toomer, Erskine Caldwell, Vereen Bell, and Byron Herbert Reece, for example. Toomer's recognition that Georgia black folk culture would soon irretrievably change helped motivate the writing of his novel *Cane*. In an autobiography he explained, "The folk-spirit was walking in to die on the modern desert. That spirit was so beautiful. Its death was so tragic. Just this seemed to sum life for me. And this was the feeling which I put into 'Cane.' 'Cane' was a swan-song.' "[1] The desire to preserve those aspects of Southern life and character that may soon pass away has, if anything, grown among Georgia writers of the last thirty years.

The writers of *I'll Take My Stand* provided such a compelling metaphor for the dilemmas of the modern South that agrarianism for a time seemed to blot out other perspectives. It argued for a unified, coherent Southern culture which responded to the threats of the modern world with a single, unflinching voice. Many Southern teachers and

1. Quoted in Darwin T. Turner, "Introduction" to *Cane* (New York: Liveright, 1975), xxii.

critics of literature were strongly swayed by it, and they frequently favored those Southern writers whose agrarian sentiments supported the notion of a unified Southern culture. But the often dissenting voices of such writers as Frances Newman, Margaret Mitchell, and Lillian Smith undercut the myth of cultural coherence and expressed other, quite different viewpoints. At first these writers were either ignored or dismissed. In recent years, as new attitudes toward literature and Southern culture developed, such writers as Mitchell and Newman have received reevaluation. Black writers have also received increasing attention. The resulting discord, with many Southern voices speaking in contrast and disagreement, gives a far more real and authentic sense of Georgia life.

Margaret Mitchell did and did not fit the agrarian mold. On the one hand, her desire to preserve the memory of the pre–Civil War South motivated her writing of *Gone with the Wind*. On the other, she was much interested in the place of women in a male-dominated society. Feminist concerns were not part of the agrarian agenda. Scarlett O'Hara may fit in some ways the stereotype of the Southern belle, but she is also a willful and conniving woman who understands the practicalities of life in the vanquished South well enough to do what is necessary to protect her family and her land. With the exception of Rhett Butler, the men in the novel are weak and unable to adjust to change and defeat. Most of the women, including Melanie Wilkes, are also too weak to adjust, a rigidity that Mitchell seems to identify as characteristic of the Old South in general. Only Scarlett, with her fierce devotion to her homeland and her instinctive understanding of the forces that threaten her way of life, is able to endure, though at a great cost which the novel makes clear.

Gone with the Wind from this viewpoint is a feminist study of the forces that govern relations between the sexes and that bind a society together. But it is not great literature, and its political, historical, and racial perceptions are not profound. Despite several brilliant and descriptive episodes, it is marred by stereotyped characters, imperceptive portrayals of blacks, and a flawed vision of the South and the Civil War. Nonetheless, its portrayal of the fiercely independent Scarlett is undeniably compelling. Many may question its literary merit, but its popularity among millions of readers testifies to the power of its story.

Like Mitchell, Frances Newman was also concerned with the role of women in a male-dominated society, especially in her novel *The Hard-Boiled Virgin*, whose protagonist is a modern counterpart to Scarlett O'Hara. Newman's protagonist, Katharine Faraday, is a young woman growing up in upper-class Atlanta society. Her family and her social class hold clear expectations concerning the role she is to play. If she defies those expectations, she risks expulsion from society, disgrace—risks she is ultimately willing to run. Newman's novel is a subtle analysis of relations between the sexes in the urban South. Even more, it is a study of a young woman's difficult struggle to become a fully independent individual. In pursuit of that end, Katharine must sever all links to those conventions that give traditional womanhood meaning: family, high society, education, marriage, even love. Only when she is finally unencumbered by illusion can she begin to define herself, a definition that the determined but shallow Scarlett never achieves. (Newman, who worked for years as a librarian at Georgia Tech, is probably the most distinctive prose stylist of all the state's writers. Her difficult, precise, heavily subordinated prose is best described by comparison to the stream of consciousness writing of James Joyce and Virginia Woolf, whose work she apparently knew well.)

The importance of place and the effects of change always seem to have a role in Georgia fiction. In many ways the story in this anthology that most eloquently expresses these themes is Carson McCullers's "The Sojourner." Not set in the South or in Georgia, it is nonetheless intensely Southern. It concerns a Southern-born man who lives in Europe but returns to Georgia to attend his father's funeral and then visits his former wife and her new family in New York City. Although he prides himself on his cosmopolitan life, his travels, and his success in business, he leaves America deeply shaken at the end of his visit. He returns to Paris and seeks out the child of the woman he thinks he might marry, the son who he thinks might become his own: "Again, the terror, the acknowledgment of wasted years and death. Valentin, responsive and confident, still nestled in his arms. His cheek touched the soft cheek and felt the brush of the delicate eyelashes. With inner desperation he pressed the child close—as though an emotion as protean as his love could dominate the pulse of time." His father's death and his encounter with his former wife remind him of the place and the family he has lost, of his own mortality, and his transient existence in the modern world. These are central impulses in modern Georgia writing, and in Southern and American writing as well.

Jean Toomer

From *Cane*

Esther

I

Nine

Esther's hair falls in soft curls about her high-cheek-boned chalk-white face. Esther's hair would be beautiful if there were more gloss to it. And if her face were not prematurely serious, one would call it pretty. Her cheeks are too flat and dead for a girl of nine. Esther looks like a little white child, starched, frilled, as she walks slowly from her home towards her father's grocery store. She is about to turn in Broad from Maple Street. White and black men loafing on the corner hold no interest for her. Then a strange thing happens. A clean-muscled, magnificent, black-skinned Negro, whom she had heard her father mention as King Barlo, suddenly drops to his knees on a spot called the Spittoon. White men, unaware of him, continue squirting tobacco juice in his direction. The saffron fluid splashes on his face. His smooth black face begins to glisten and to shine. Soon, people notice him, and gather round. His eyes are rapturous upon the heavens. Lips and nostrils quiver. Barlo is in a religious trance. Town folks know it. They are not startled. They are not afraid. They gather round. Some beg boxes from the grocery stores. From old McGregor's notion shop. A coffin-case is pressed into use. Folks line the curb-stones. Business men close shop. And Banker Warply parks his car close by. Silently, all await the prophet's voice. The sheriff, a great florid fellow whose leggings never meet around his bulging calves, swears in three deputies. "Wall, y cant never tell what a nigger like King Barlo might be up t." Soda bottles, five fingers full of shine, are passed to those who want them. A couple of stray dogs start a fight. Old Goodlow's cow comes flopping up the street. Barlo, still as an Indian fakir, has not moved. The town bell strikes six. The sun slips in behind a heavy mass of horizon cloud. The crowd is hushed and expectant. Barlo's under jaw relaxes, and his lips begin to move.

"Jesus has been awhisperin strange words deep down, O way down deep, deep in my ears."

Hums of awe and of excitement.

"He called me to His side an said, 'Git down on your knees beside me, son, Ise gwine t whisper in your ears.'"

An old sister cries, "Ah, Lord."

"'Ise agwine t whisper in your ears,' he said, an I replied, 'Thy will be done on earth as it is in heaven.'"

"Ah, Lord. Amen. Amen."

"An Lord Jesus whispered strange good words deep down, O way down deep, deep in my ears. An He said, 'Tell em till you feel your throat on fire.' I saw a vision. I saw a man arise, an he was big an black an powerful—"

Some one yells, "Preach it, preacher, preach it!"

"—but his head was caught up in th clouds. An while he was agazin at th heavens, heart filled up with th Lord, some little white-ant biddies came an tied his feet to chains. They led him t th coast, they led him t th sea, they led him across th ocean an they didnt set him free. The old coast didnt miss him, an th new coast wasnt free, he left the old-coast brothers, t give birth t you an me. O Lord, great God Almighty, t give birth t you an me."

Barlo pauses. Old gray mothers are in tears. Fragments of melodies are being hummed. White folks are touched and curiously awed. Off to themselves, white and black preachers confer as to how best to rid themselves of the vagrant, usurping fellow. Barlo looks as though he is struggling to continue. People are hushed. One can hear weevils work. Dusk is falling rapidly, and the customary store lights fail to throw their feeble glow across the gray dust and flagging of the Georgia town. Barlo rises to his full height. He is immense. To the people he assumes the outlines of his visioned African. In a mighty voice he bellows:

"Brothers an sisters, turn your faces t th sweet face of the Lord, an fill your hearts with glory. Open your eyes an see th dawnin of th mornin light. Open your ears—"

Years afterwards Esther was told that at that very moment a great, heavy, rumbling voice actually was heard. That hosts of angels and of demons paraded up and down the streets all night. That King Barlo rode out of town astride a pitch-black bull that had a glowing gold ring in its nose. And that old Limp Underwood, who hated niggers, woke up next morning to find that he held a black man in his arms. This much is certain: an inspired Negress, of wide reputation for being sanctified, drew a portrait of a black madonna on the courthouse wall. And King Barlo left town. He left his image indelibly upon the mind of Esther. He became the starting point of the only living patterns that her mind was to know.

2

Sixteen

Esther begins to dream. The low evening sun sets the windows of McGregor's notion shop aflame. Esther makes believe that they really are aflame. The town fire department rushes madly down the road. It ruthlessly shoves black and white idlers to one side. It whoops. It clangs. It rescues from the second-story window a dimpled infant which she claims for her own. How had she come by it? She thinks of it immaculately. It is a sin to think of it immaculately. She must dream no more. She must repent her sin. Another dream comes. There is no fire department. There are no heroic men. The fire starts. The loafers on the corner form a circle, chew their tobacco faster, and squirt juice just as fast as they can chew. Gallons on top of gallons they squirt upon the flames. The air reeks with the stench of scorched tobacco juice. Women, fat chunky Negro women, lean scrawny white women, pull their skirts up above their heads and display the most ludicrous underclothes. The women scoot in all directions from the danger zone. She alone is left to take the baby in her arms. But what a baby! Black, singed, woolly, tobacco-juice baby—ugly as sin. Once held to her breast, miraculous thing: its breath is sweet and its lips can nibble. She loves it frantically. Her joy in it changes the town folks' jeers to harmless jealousy, and she is left alone.

Twenty-two

Esther's schooling is over. She works behind the counter of her father's grocery store. "To keep the money in the family," so he said. She is learning to make distinctions between the business and the social worlds. "Good business comes from remembering that the white folks dont divide the niggers, Esther. Be just as black as any man who has a silver dollar." Esther listlessly forgets that she is near white, and that her father is the richest colored man in town. Black folk who drift in to buy lard and snuff and flour of her, call her a sweet-natured, accommodating girl. She learns their names. She forgets them. She thinks about men. "I dont appeal to them. I wonder why." She recalls an affair she had with a little fair boy while still in school. It had ended in her shame when he as much as told her that for sweetness he preferred a lollipop. She remembers the salesman from the North who wanted to take her to the movies that first night he was in town. She refused, of course. And he never came back, having found out who she was. She thinks of Barlo. Barlo's image gives her a slightly stale thrill. She spices it by telling herself his glories. Black. Magnetically so. Best cotton picker in the county, in the state, in the whole world for that matter. Best man with his fists, best man with dice, with a razor. Promoter of church benefits. Of colored fairs. Vagrant preacher. Lover of all the women for miles and miles around. Esther decides that she loves him. And with a vague sense of life slipping by, she resolves that she will tell him so, whatever people say, the next time he comes to town.

After the making of this resolution which becomes a sort of wedding cake for her to tuck beneath her pillow and go to sleep upon, she sees nothing of Barlo for five years. Her hair thins. It looks like the dull silk on puny corn ears. Her face pales until it is the color of the gray dust that dances with dead cotton leaves.

3

Esther is twenty-seven

Esther sells lard and snuff and flour to vague black faces that drift in her store to ask for them. Her eyes hardly see the people to whom she gives change. Her body is lean and beaten. She rests listlessly against the counter, too weary to sit down. From the street some one shouts, "King Barlo has come back to town." He passes her window, driving a large new car. Cut-out open. He veers to the curb, and steps out. Barlo has made money on cotton during the war. He is as rich as anyone. Esther suddenly is animate. She goes to her door. She sees him at a distance, the center of a group of credulous men. She hears the deep-bass rumble of his talk. The sun swings low. McGregor's windows are aflame again. Pale flame. A sharply dressed white girl passes by. For a moment Esther wishes that she might be like her. Not white; she has no need for being that. But sharp, sporty, with get-up about her. Barlo is connected with that wish. She mustnt wish. Wishes only make you restless. Emptiness is a thing that grows by being moved. "I'll not think. Not wish. Just set my mind against it." Then the thought comes to her that those purposeless, easy-going men will possess him, if she doesnt. Purpose is not dead in her, now that she comes to think of it. That loose women will have their arms around him at Nat Bowle's place to-night. As if her veins are full of fired sun-bleached southern shanties, a swift heat sweeps them. Dead dreams, and a forgotten resolution are carried upward by the flames. Pale flames. "They shant have him. Oh, they shall not. Not if it kills me they shant have him." Jerky, aflutter, she closes the store and starts home. Folks lazing on store windowsills wonder what on earth can be the matter with Jim

Crane's gal, as she passes them. "Come to remember, she always was a little off, a little crazy, I reckon." Esther seeks her own room, and locks the door. Her mind is a pink meshbag filled with baby toes.

Using the noise of the town clock striking twelve to cover the creaks of her departure, Esther slips into the quiet road. The town, her parents, most everyone is sound asleep. This fact is a stable thing that comforts her. After sundown a chill wind came up from the west. It is still blowing, but to her it is a steady, settled thing like the cold. She wants her mind to be like that. Solid, contained, and blank as a sheet of darkened ice. She will not permit herself to notice the peculiar phosphorescent glitter of the sweet-gum leaves. Their movement would excite her. Exciting too, the recession of the dull familiar homes she knows so well. She doesnt know them at all. She closes her eyes, and holds them tightly. Wont do. Her being aware that they are closed recalls her purpose. She does not want to think of it. She opens them. She turns now into the deserted business street. The corrugated iron canopies and mule- and horse-gnawed hitching posts bring her a strange composure. Ghosts of the commonplaces of her daily life take stride with her and become her companions. And the echoes of her heels upon the flagging are rhythmically monotonous and soothing. Crossing the street at the corner of McGregor's notion shop, she thinks that the windows are a dull flame. Only a fancy. She walks faster. Then runs. A turn into a side street brings her abruptly to Nat Bowle's place. The house is squat and dark. It is always dark. Barlo is within. Quietly she opens the outside door and steps in. She passes through a small room. Pauses before a flight of stairs down which people's voices, muffled, come. The air is heavy with fresh tobacco smoke. It makes her sick. She wants to turn back. She goes up the steps. As if she were mounting to some great height, her head spins. She is violently dizzy. Blackness rushes to her eyes. And then she finds that she is in a large room. Barlo is before her.

"Well, I'm sholy damned—skuse me, but what, what brought you here, lil milk-white gal?"

"You." Her voice sounds like a frightened child's that calls homeward from some point miles away.

"Me?"

"Yes, you Barlo."

"This aint th place fer y. This aint th place fer y."

"I know. I know. But I've come for you."

"For me for what?"

She manages to look deep and straight into his eyes. He is slow at understanding. Guffaws and giggles break out from all around the room. A coarse woman's voice remarks, "So thats how th dictie niggers does it." Laughs. "Mus give em credit fo their gall."

Esther doesnt hear. Barlo does. His faculties are jogged. She sees a smile, ugly and repulsive to her, working upward through thick licker fumes. Barlo seems hideous. The thought comes suddenly, that conception with a drunken man must be a mighty sin. She draws away, frozen. Like a somnambulist she wheels around and walks stiffly to the stairs. Down them. Jeers and hoots pelter bluntly upon her back. She steps out. There is no air, no street, and the town has completely disappeared.

Blood-Burning Moon

I

Up from the skeleton stone walls, up from the rotting floor boards and the solid hand-hewn beams of oak of the pre-war cotton factory, dusk came. Up from the dusk the full moon came. Glowing like a fired pine-knot, it illumined the great door and soft showered the Negro shanties aligned along the single street of factory town. The full moon in the great door was an omen. Negro women improvised songs against its spell.

Louisa sang as she came over the crest of the hill from the white folks' kitchen. Her skin was the color of oak leaves on young trees in fall. Her breasts, firm and up-pointed like ripe acorns. And her singing had the low murmur of winds in fig trees. Bob Stone, younger son of the people she worked for, loved her. By the way the world reckons things, he had won her. By measure of that warm glow which came into her mind at thought of him, he had won her. Tom Burwell, whom the whole town called Big Boy, also loved her. But working in the fields all day, and far away from her, gave him no chance to show it. Though often enough of evenings he had tried to. Somehow, he never got along. Strong as he was with hands upon the ax or plow, he found it difficult to hold her. Or so he thought. But the fact was that he held her to factory town more firmly than he thought for. His black balanced, and pulled against, the white of Stone, when she thought of them. And her mind was vaguely upon them as she came over the crest of the hill, coming from the white folks' kitchen. As she sang softly at the evil face of the full moon.

A strange stir was in her. Indolently, she tried to fix upon Bob or Tom as the cause of it. To meet Bob in the canebrake, as she was going to do an hour or so later, was nothing new. And Tom's proposal which she felt on its way to her could be indefinitely put off. Separately, there was no unusual significance to either one. But for some reason, they jumbled when her eyes gazed vacantly at the rising moon. And from the jumble came the stir that was strangely within her. Her lips trembled. The slow rhythm of her song grew agitant and restless. Rusty black and tan spotted hounds, lying in the dark corners of porches or prowling around back yards, put their noses in the air and caught its tremor. They began plaintively to yelp and howl. Chickens woke up and cackled. Intermittently, all over the countryside dogs barked and roosters crowed as if heralding a weird dawn or some ungodly awakening. The women sang lustily. Their songs were cotton-wads to stop their ears. Louisa came down into factory town and sank wearily upon the step before her home. The moon was rising towards a thick cloud-bank which soon would hide it.

Red nigger moon. Sinner!
Blood-burning moon. Sinner!
Come out that fact'ry door.

2

Up from the deep dusk of a cleared spot on the edge of the forest a mellow glow arose and spread fan-wise into the low-hanging heavens. And all around the air was heavy with the scent of boiling cane. A large pile of cane-stalks lay like ribboned shadows upon the ground. A mule, harnessed to a pole, trudged lazily round and round the pivot of the grinder. Beneath a swaying oil lamp, a Negro alternately whipped out at the mule, and fed cane-stalks to the grinder. A fat boy waddled pails of fresh ground juice between the grinder and the boiling stove. Steam came from the copper boiling pan. The scent of cane came from the copper pan and drenched the forest and the hill that sloped to factory town, beneath its fragrance. It drenched the men in circle seated around the stove. Some of them chewed at the white pulp of stalks, but there was no need for them to, if all they wanted was to taste the cane. One tasted it in factory town. And from factory town one could see the soft haze thrown by the glowing stove upon the low-hanging heavens.

Old David Georgia stirred the thickening syrup with a long ladle, and ever so often drew it off. Old David Georgia tended his stove and told tales about the white folks, about moonshining and cotton picking, and about sweet nigger gals, to the men who sat there about his stove to listen to him. Tom Burwell chewed cane-stalk and laughed with the others till some one mentioned Louisa. Till some one said something about Louisa and Bob Stone, about the silk stockings she must have gotten from him. Blood ran up Tom's neck hotter than the glow that flooded from the stove. He sprang up. Glared at the men and said, "She's my gal." Will Manning laughed. Tom strode over to him. Yanked him up and knocked him to the ground. Several of Manning's friends got up to fight for him. Tom whipped out a long knife and would have cut them to shreds if they hadnt ducked into the woods. Tom had had enough. He nodded to Old David Georgia and swung down the path to factory town. Just then, the dogs started barking and the roosters began to crow. Tom felt funny. Away from the fight, away from the stove, chill got to him. He shivered. He shuddered when he saw the full moon rising towards the cloud-bank. He who didnt give a godam for the fears of old women. He forced his mind to fasten on Louisa. Bob Stone. Better not be. He turned into the street and saw Louisa sitting before her home. He went towards her, ambling, touched the brim of a marvelously shaped, spotted, felt hat, said he wanted to say something to her, and then found that he didnt know what he had to say, or if he did, that he couldnt say it. He shoved his big fists in his overalls, grinned, and started to move off.

"Youall want me, Tom?"

"Thats what us wants, sho, Louisa."

"Well, here I am—

"An here I is, but that aint ahelpin none, all th same."

"You wanted to say something? . ."

"I did that, sho. But words is like th spots on dice: no matter how y fumbles em, there's times when they jes wont come. I dunno why. Seems like th love I feels fo yo done stole m tongue. I got it now. Whee! Louisa, honey, I oughtnt tell y, I feel I oughtnt cause yo is young an goes t church an I has had other gals, but Louisa I sho do love y. Lil gal, Ise watched y from them first days when youall sat right here befo yo door befo th well an sang sometimes in a way that like t broke m heart. Ise carried y with me into th fields, day after day, an after that, an I sho can plow when yo is there, an I can pick cotton. Yassur! Come near beatin Barlo yesterday. I sho did. Yassur! An next year if ole Stone'll trust me, I'll have a farm. My own. My bales will buy yo what y gets from white folks now. Silk stockings an purple dresses—course I dont believe what some folks been whisperin as t how y gets them things now. White folks always did do for niggers what they likes. An they jes cant help alikin yo, Louisa. Bob Stone likes y. Course he does. But not th way folks is awhisperin. Does he, hon?"

"I dont know what you mean, Tom."

"Course y dont. Ise already cut two niggers. Had t hon, t tell em so. Niggers always tryin t make somethin out a nothin. An then besides, white folks aint up t them tricks so much nowadays. Godam better not be. Leastawise not with yo. Cause I wouldnt stand f it. Nassur."

"What would you do, Tom?"

"Cut him jes like I cut a nigger."

"No, Tom—"

"I said I would an there aint no mo to it. But that aint th talk f now. Sing, honey Louisa, an while I'm listenin t y I'll be makin love."

Tom took her hand in his. Against the tough thickness of his own, hers felt soft and small. His huge body slipped down to the step beside her. The full moon sank upward into the deep purple of the cloud-bank. An old woman brought a lighted lamp and hung it on the common well whose bulky shadow squatted in the middle of the road, opposite Tom and Louisa. The old woman lifted the well-lid, took hold the chain, and began drawing up the heavy bucket. As she did so, she sang. Figures shifted, restlesslike, between lamp and window in the front rooms of the shanties. Shadows of the figures fought each other on the gray dust of the road. Figures raised the windows and joined the old woman in song. Louisa and Tom, the whole street, singing:

Red nigger moon. Sinner!
Blood-burning moon. Sinner!
Come out that fact'ry door.

3

Bob Stone sauntered from his veranda out into the gloom of fir trees and magnolias. The clear white of his skin paled, and the flush of his cheeks turned purple. As if to balance this outer change, his mind became consciously a white man's. He passed the house with its huge open hearth which, in the days of slavery, was the plantation cookery. He saw Louisa bent over that hearth. He went in as a master should and took her. Direct, honest, bold. None of this sneaking that he had to go through now. The contrast was repulsive to him. His family had lost ground. Hell no, his family still owned the niggers, practically. Damned if they did, or he wouldnt have to duck around so. What would they think if they knew? His mother? His sister? He shouldnt mention them, shouldnt think of them in this connection. There in the dusk he blushed at doing so. Fellows about town were all right, but how about his friends up North? He could see them incredible, repulsed. They didnt know. The thought first made him laugh. Then, with their eyes still upon him, he began to feel embarrassed. He felt the need of explaining things to them. Explain hell. They wouldnt understand, and moreover, who ever heard of a Southerner getting on his knees to any Yankee, or anyone. No sir. He was going to see Louisa to-night, and love her. She was lovely—in her way. Nigger way. What way was that? Damned if he knew. Must know. He'd known her long enough to know. Was there something about niggers that you couldnt know? Listening to them at church didnt tell you anything. Looking at them didnt tell you anything. Talking to them didnt tell you anything—unless it was gossip, unless they wanted to talk. Of course, about farming, and licker, and craps—but those werent nigger. Nigger was something more. How much more? Something to be afraid of, more? Hell no. Who ever heard of being afraid of a nigger? Tom Burwell. Cartwell had told him that Tom went with Louisa after she reached home. No sir. No nigger had ever been with his girl. He'd like to see one try. Some position for him to be in. Him, Bob Stone, of the old Stone family, in a scrap with a nigger over a nigger girl. In the good old days . . . Ha! Those were the days. His family had lost ground. Not so much, though. Enough for him to have to cut through old Lemon's canefield by way of the woods, that he might meet her. She was worth it. Beautiful nigger gal. Why nigger? Why not, just gal? No, it was because she was nigger that he went to her. Sweet . . . The scent of boiling cane came to him. Then he saw the rich glow of the stove. He heard the voices of the men circled around it. He was about to skirt the clearing when he heard his own name mentioned. He stopped. Quivering. Leaning against a tree, he listened.

"Bad nigger. Yassur, he sho is one bad nigger when he gets started."

"Tom Burwell's been on th gang three times fo cuttin men."

"What y think he's agwine t do t Bob Stone?"

"Dunno yet. He aint found out. When he does—Baby!"

"Aint no tellin."

"Young Stone aint no quitter an I ken tell y that. Blood of th old uns in his veins."

"Thats right. He'll scrap, sho."

"Be gettin too hot f niggers round this away."

"Shut up, nigger. Y dont know what y talkin bout."

Bob Stone's ears burned as though he had been holding them over the stove. Sizzling heat welled up within him. His feet felt as if they rested on red-hot coals. They stung him to quick movement. He circled the fringe of the glowing. Not a twig cracked beneath his feet. He reached the path that led to factory town. Plunged furiously down it. Halfway along, a blindness within him veered him aside. He crashed into the bordering canebrake. Cane leaves cut his face and lips. He tasted blood. He threw himself down and dug his fingers in the ground. The earth was cool. Cane-roots took the fever from his hands. After a long while, or so it seemed to him, the thought came to him that it must be time to see Louisa. He got to his feet and walked calmly to their meeting place. No Louisa. Tom Burwell had her. Veins in his forehead bulged and distended. Saliva moistened the dried blood on his lips. He bit down on his lips. He tasted blood. Not his own blood; Tom Burwell's blood. Bob drove through the cane and out again upon the road. A hound swung down the path before him towards factory town. Bob couldnt see it. The dog loped aside to let him pass. Bob's blind rushing made him stumble over it. He fell with a thud that dazed him. The hound yelped. Answering yelps came from all over the countryside. Chickens cackled. Roosters crowed, heralding the bloodshot eyes of southern awakening. Singers in the town were silenced. They shut their windows down. Palpitant between the rooster crows, a chill hush settled upon the huddled forms of Tom and Louisa. A figure rushed from the shadow and stood before them. Tom popped to his feet.

"Whats y want?"

"I'm Bob Stone."

"Yassur—an I'm Tom Burwell. Whats y want?"

Bob lunged at him. Tom side-stepped, caught him by the shoulder, and flung him to the ground. Straddled him.

"Let me up."

"Yassur—but watch yo doins, Bob Stone."

A few dark figures, drawn by the sound of scuffle, stood about them. Bob sprang to his feet.

"Fight like a man, Tom Burwell, an I'll lick y."

Again he lunged. Tom side-stepped and flung him to the ground. Straddled him.

"Get off me, you godam nigger you."

"Yo sho has started somethin now. Get up."

Tom yanked him up and began hammering at him. Each blow sounded as if it smashed into a precious, irreplaceable soft something. Beneath them, Bob staggered back. He reached in his pocket and whipped out a knife.

"Thats my game, sho."

Blue flash, a steel blade slashed across Bob Stone's throat. He had a sweetish sick feeling. Blood began to flow. Then he felt a sharp twitch of pain. He let his knife drop. He slapped one hand against his neck. He pressed the other on top of his head as if to hold it down. He groaned. He turned, and staggered towards the crest of the hill in the direction of white town. Negroes who had seen the fight slunk into their homes and blew the lamps out. Louisa, dazed, hysterical, refused to go indoors. She slipped, crumbled, her body loosely propped against the woodwork of the well. Tom Burwell leaned against it. He seemed rooted there.

Bob reached Broad Street. White men rushed up to him. He collapsed in their arms.

"Tom Burwell. . . ."

White men like ants upon a forage rushed about. Except for the taut hum of their moving, all was silent. Shotguns, revolvers, rope, kerosene, torches. Two high-powered cars with glaring search-lights. They came together. The taut hum rose to a low roar. Then nothing could be heard but the flop of their feet in the thick dust of the road. The moving body of their silence preceded them over the crest of the hill into factory town. It flattened the Negroes beneath it. It rolled to the wall of the factory, where it stopped. Tom knew that they were coming. He couldnt move. And then he saw the search-lights of the two cars glaring down on him. A quick shock went through him. He stiffened. He started to run. A yell went up from the mob. Tom wheeled about and faced them. They poured down on him. They swarmed. A large man with dead-white face and flabby cheeks came to him and almost jabbed a gun-barrel through his guts.

"Hands behind y, nigger."

Tom's wrists were bound. The big man shoved him to the well. Burn him over it, and when the woodwork caved in, his body would drop to the bottom. Two deaths for a godam nigger. Louisa was driven back. The mob pushed in. Its pressure, its momentum was too great. Drag him to the factory. Wood and stakes already there. Tom moved in the direction indicated. But they had to drag him. They reached the great door. Too many to get in there. The mob divided and flowed around the walls to either side. The big man shoved him through the door. The mob pressed in from the sides. Taut humming. No words. A stake was sunk into the ground. Rotting floor boards piled around it. Kerosene poured on the rotting floor boards. Tom bound to the stake. His breast was bare. Nails' scratches let little lines of blood trickle down and mat into the hair. His face, his eyes were set and stony. Except for irregular breathing, one would have thought him already dead. Torches were flung onto the pile. A great flare muffled in black smoke shot upward. The mob yelled. The mob was silent. Now Tom could be seen within the flames. Only his head, erect, lean, like a blackened stone. Stench of burning flesh soaked the air. Tom's eyes popped. His head settled downward. The mob yelled. Its yell echoed against the skeleton stone walls and sounded like a hundred yells. Like a hundred mobs yelling. Its yell thudded against the thick front wall and fell back. Ghost of a yell slipped through the flames and out the great door of the factory. It fluttered like a dying thing down the single street of factory town. Louisa, upon the step before her home, did not hear it, but her eyes opened slowly. They saw the full moon glowing in the great door. The full moon, an evil thing, an omen, soft showering the homes of folks she knew. Where were they, these people? She'd sing, and perhaps they'd come out and join her. Perhaps Tom Burwell would come. At any rate, the full moon in the great door was an omen which she must sing to:

Red nigger moon. Sinner!
Blood-burning moon. Sinner!
Come out that fact'ry door.

Frances Newman

From *The Hard-Boiled Virgin*

Although Katharine Faraday had never been thought decorative enough to become even a flower-girl before, she managed to follow six white uniformed groomsmen and six white-frocked and crimson-hatted bridesmaids up the aisle of Saint Michael's Church without once looking towards the box-pews she was passing, and nevertheless to arrive at the altar with the first version of the phrases in which she would tell Captain Edward Cabot just the point in the rehearsal when she had decided that no blood is blue enough to take the place of elementary education, and just the point in her progress up the aisle when she had decided that no blood is blue enough to take the place of cold cream, or even of curling irons. When she turned to face the white satin in which Sarah Rutledge was approaching Second Lieutenant Henry Simpson, and which Katharine Faraday did not think was worthy of being folded in blue tissue paper and preserved for Sarah Rutledge's ascension from Magnolia Cemetery on the day of judgment, she was wondering if Captain Cabot was too remotely descended from the Cabots of Massachusetts to enjoy having her tell him that after three days of inspection Charleston did not seem an uncommonly patriotic or an uncommonly martial town, but that apparently its customs allowed a commission in the United States Army to take the place of a whole family tree, and that apparently the most highly placed Charlestonian girl could marry an army officer without even one grandfather who had signed his name to the Declaration of Independence—if only the officer had been born outside the boundaries of South Carolina. When she slipped her own bouquet of well-wired crimson roses into the crook of her left arm and took the bouquet of well-wired white roses which she supposed Sarah Rutledge would hardly have chosen except as public proof that ten years of residence in Atlanta had not given her a taste for flowers so hysterical as orchids or so High Church as lilies, she was wondering if Sarah Rutledge could be thinking of anything except the dreadful sounds which had come through the opening and closing door of Mrs. Pinckney Rutledge's room on the night before Harriet Rutledge was born. When she turned back the veil which had sheltered all those ladies of the Rutledge family who had achieved weddings, and which had successfully drooped its leaves and roses between Sarah Rutledge's lack of timidity and the interest natural in a congregation of her relations, she was rewarded by a remarkably mature example of the gracious condescension a wedded wife smiles at a spinster. She realised then that she had suffered a defeat more damaging than the defeat she suffered on the day Sarah Rutledge became a woman, and that no matter how many babies and no matter how many other calamities she might fear her union with Henry Simpson would bring her, Sarah Rutledge was triumphant in the realization that she was married. Katharine Faraday had not forgotten the afternoons and the nights when she had planned the yellow chiffon frocks and the yellow-plumed hats behind which she would walk down the aisle of the First Presbyterian Church beside the yellow stripes of the United States cavalry, but she did not regret the August night when she decided that she could never again endure the suspense of waiting for the miracle of a letter from James Fuller, and that she could not endure the possibility of his suspecting her of wanting to marry him if he did not want to marry her, and that she could never answer the letter which had escaped a thousand miles of dangers and which was pressed against the spot that was no longer tender and that was rose and yellow instead of blue. But when she laid her left hand against Captain Cabot's white sleeve—just as much more lightly than propriety demanded as Eleanor Faraday's experienced instruction specified—and told him she was sure he must have noticed how perfectly Sarah Rutledge's smile echoed Mendelssohn's triumphant nuptial waterfall, she regretted that neither propriety nor loyalty, nor Eleanor Faraday's instruction about hiding her more elaborate mental processes, allowed her to tell him she was sure he could not have guided so many bridegrooms to altars without wondering how Mendelssohn's chords managed to dash down half an organ, and nevertheless to shout out a pride of achievement exactly as triumphant as the pride a hen manages to convey in an ascending stutter. When she was arranging Sarah Rutledge's two yards of shining satin in a curve she had admired in a large flat magazine called The Spur, she was too much annoyed by Caroline Rutledge's interest in Captain Cabot's sword to find any conversational inspiration in the celebrated white marble mantel which Sarah Rutledge's maternal grandmother considered a fitting background for brides and for coffins. And when she sat down beside Captain Cabot on the lowest step of the piazza which looked down on the garden and on the little orange-tree which provided Sarah Rutledge's grandmother with one of the smaller reasons for a complacence that was noticeable even in Charleston, Katharine Faraday did not remember that she owed a satisfactory back-drop to a gentleman who was confidently awaiting a glorious resurrection on the left side of Saint Michael's churchyard. Neither did she realize that this James Monroe back-drop was set for the third act of the play which had begun beside the tall rubber-tree in the drawing room of the West Point Hotel, or that Edward Cabot was playing the part of the martial hero whose more youthful scenes had been played by James Fuller. But when Edward Cabot told her stories of the days when he was a yearling corporal and stories of the days when he had left West Point too late for the Spanish but in plenty of time for the Filipinos, she listened with an attention as visible as if she were not engaged in laying the memory of Sarah Rutledge's triumphant smile beside the memory that Henry Simpson was a second lieutenant and that Edward Cabot was captain of his battery. When the sunlight left the orange-tree which was not identified by oranges or by orange-blossoms, but which was a nicely symbolical proscenium arch, she enjoyed feeling cool enough to be wrapped in the martial cape which Edward Cabot proved his experience by turning on its crimson side. And she enjoyed the public isolation of a darkness she did not think about as a screen for the possible touch of Edward Cabot's experienced hand. When the attentions a maid of honour must show her bride obliged her to walk up the celebrated stairway which was another of the smaller reasons for the complacence of Sarah Rutledge's grandmother, Katharine Faraday was entirely occupied in wondering if Edward Cabot would really come over to Atlanta and dance with her in her white débutante's frock. But when she ran down the celebrated stairway with her red rosebud of rice, she had not forgotten the little grey box Sarah Rutledge had laid in her bag beside her bridal nightgown and her bridal negligé, and she had not forgotten Sarah Rutledge's assurance that it would delay the advent of Rutledge Simpson until he could be born in the quarters of a first lieutenant.

On the third Wednesday afternoon in November, Katharine Faraday dressed herself in a white crêpe de chine frock which had been made in Atlanta, and in which she was officially introduced to all those ladies whom she already knew and who could reasonably be expected to ask the right kind of young men to sit beside her at dinner or to sit behind her in theatre and opera boxes during the uncomfortable years when she would be professionally engaged in looking about for a husband, and in which she was also introduced to those ladies who could only be expected to ask her to lunch and to play bridge with girls who might ask her to dinner. On the third Wednesday evening in November, her mother and her mammy and her two sisters helped her into a white chiffon frock which had been made in Baltimore, and in which she was introduced to all those members of the Piedmont Driving Club whom she already knew and whose fathers had not worn policemen's uniforms or presided over their own green-groceries or lived over their own lime-kilns within the tenacious memory of Katharine Faraday's mother, and whose uncles had always been saved from the consequences of their misappropriations by the influence of their families. She was also introduced to an aging, wasting and presumably virgin spinster, whose gift for rolling saplings so loudly that she seemed to be rolling logs would probably have made her a cardinal if she had not suffered the misfortune of being born a woman, and whose descriptions of dinners and dances and weddings filled such elaborately bound scrap-books that she had attained every social honour except marriage. But since Katharine Faraday knew that journalists who described dances were not yet allowed the pleasure of choosing any of their adjectives on the impolite side of the pages which journalists who described plays seemed to memorize in the newer editions of Roget's thesaurus, she knew that Edward Cabot would be provided with a satisfactory description of her white chiffon frock and her crimson roses and her brunette beauty, and she allowed her failure to ask for breakfast on the morning of the third Thursday in November to suggest that she was still asleep. She lay in the bird's-eye maple bed in the pink room to which she always retired before the arrival of a visitor, and she thought about Edward Cabot's beautifully brushed yellow hair and his attentive blue eyes, and about the hours when she had sat beside him on the terrace instead of using the strategic advantage of her own début dance against a young lawyer who was called Neal Lumpkin as evidence that he was sure to get on in the world, and against a young man who was called Grant Jordan as evidence that his father had made too many paper bags for him to have any occasion to get on in the world. She thought about Edward Cabot's remarkable resemblance to the golden-haired tenor who was so tall and so fair that he was not likely to sing in the Metropolitan Opera House, but whom she had first seen in the white uniform of Lieutenant Pinkerton, and she wondered if the resemblance and the white uniform could possibly mean that she was ever likely to spend such a night of suspense as the night Madame Butterfly had very naturally failed to survive when such depressing music and the observation of a contralto were added to her natural anxiety. But when she found herself unable to stop wondering if Edward Cabot's legs could be like the legs her father still revealed by continuing to follow the strange custom which stopped nocturnal masculine costumes at the knee, and if he could be modelled precisely like George Faraday and the clear illustrations in Gray's Anatomy, she decided that the laws of hospitality would not allow her to put off knocking on the door of the blue room in which Isabel Ambler was presumably having her coffee. Katharine Faraday thought that a taste for coffee was evidence of an upbringing unbecoming an Ambler, and although she had never questioned the beauty of the nineteenth-century bed on which Isabel Ambler was lying between two of Mrs. Alexander Faraday's four linen sheets, she had never slept soundly on it since the day when she had learned that it was the birthplace of her mother and of her mother's six brothers and three sisters. But she sat down on it and leaned against one of the rosewood posts which might have been intended to support the ceiling instead of the blue satin tester that had once been the gown in which Marian Faraday first led a cotillion. And then she politely set about her belated duty of congratulating Isabel Ambler on her public conquest of a thin young man who was called Grantland Lamar as evidence that his grandfathers had both shed blood of the best quality on the red clay of half the counties to which their grandfathers had given their names, but that one of his great-grandfathers had known better than to buy any of the bonds printed by the Confederate States of America. She knew that Isabel Ambler would enjoy her congratulations, but that she would feel obliged to answer them by talking about the sufferings she had endured on Sunday morning when she had not been able to start for Saint Paul's Church at ten o'clock and stop to lay eighteen pink carnations on her lost Harrison's perfectly kept grave in Hollywood Cemetery. She also knew that the customs of Richmond do not require politeness of a girl whose great-grandmother had proved herself its ideal of southern womanhood by combining a degree of beauty which charmed George Washington with a degree of intelligence which refused the hand of George Washington. And since she did not know herself that she was entirely faithful to the martial hero of Katharine Faraday's second romantic tragedy and that Edward Cabot was only playing the rôle of the hero in the third act of the drama whose first two acts had been played by James Fuller, she was not surprised when Isabel Ambler's ideas of politeness did not require her to congratulate Katharine Faraday on an admirer who had remembered to bring his crimson-lined cape all the way from Fort Moultrie, and who had remembered to turn it on its crimson side when he wrapped it around her white chiffon frock before he sat down beside her in a white vest of which even George Faraday had not been able to disapprove. And since Edward Cabot was thirty-three years old, he had not made the mistake of mentioning Isabel Ambler's red hair or her white neck, and Katharine Faraday was not wishing for revenge when she began to admire the rose-coloured velvet in which she thought that Isabel Ambler looked like a young mother who was doing her duty by her children. But on the evening of the third Thursday in November, Katharine Faraday did not think of her own white lace between Isabel Ambler's rose-coloured velvet and Nellie Clark's apple-green satin, and she did not think about the play, which was called King Lear, or about its celebrated interpreter, who was called Robert Mantell, and she was not distressed because the audience was not made up of people who would realize that Katharine Faraday was sitting in the third box on the right side of the Grand Opera House. She was not thinking of anything except that she would not see Edward Cabot again until she went down to Sullivan's Island in January and stayed with Sarah Rutledge for the first Saint Cecilia Ball, and that she must look at his beautifully brushed hair and his blue eyes as often as she could before the terrible minute she would have to live through when a door closed behind him, and which she knew would be so coldly different from the minute before when he was still in the same room with her.

If journalistic custom had allowed chroniclers of dances to print the verdict of the experienced jury whom Mrs. Alexander Faraday had invited to inspect her youngest daughter on the third Wednesday in November, Atlanta would probably have read in the public prints of the third Thursday in November that Katharine Faraday's beauty would not be the occasion of increased civic pride which Eleanor Faraday's golden beauty had been for ten years, and that her dancing would never inspire orchestra leaders as Marian Faraday's dancing was still inspiring them after three years of unsatisfactory marriage.

If journalistic custom had allowed the experienced spinster to print a reasoned review of Katharine Faraday instead of a polite description of Katharine Faraday's début dance, the conclusion of the sagacity which had won every social honour except marriage would almost certainly have been that Katharine Faraday's conversation was not interesting to her and that it was not likely to be interesting to the members of the Piedmont Driving Club, or even to the decreasingly important members of the Capital City Club, and that it was therefore not interesting. If Katharine Faraday had been privileged to hear the verdict which was spoken so often that it did not need to be printed except for her own enlightenment, she would not have been able to console herself with the realisation that interest is a completely transitive verb. But during her first official week of dinners and dances and theatres and Sunday afternoon callers, she discovered that she was less interesting to the members of the Piedmont Driving Club than she had been to the young men who came to Mrs. Randolph's dances and the young men who came to Mrs. Rutherford Cobb's dinners and the young men who came to West Point Hops. She gave herself up for lost on the evening when she realized that she could usually keep herself from talking to them about the things in which her mother said they could not possibly be interested, but that she could not give up thinking about Edward Cabot long enough to think up amusing remarks about the things they might be interested in. Whenever she opened an envelope which had already shot its blazing disappointment through her eyes down her whole body as she saw that it was not addressed by Edward Cabot or even postmarked in Fort Moultrie, and when she read a card which invited her to another dance, she felt a terror of anticipation she would not have felt if her dentist had set his awful chair in the midst of Peachtree Street and invited her world to stop and see how Katharine Faraday supported his borings. And when she was provided with the member of the Piedmont Driving Club without whom she could not walk into a ballroom as respectably as she could have walked in without two stockings, she knew her world must realize that she would not go to dances unless she wanted to be danced with, but she knew she could not walk away as she had walked away from the line of children in the Calhoun Street School's yard before they could discover that she might not have received the tap on the head which would have made her eligible to play Prisoner's Base. When she lay down on the nineteenth-century bed for the hour's sleep her mother considered the best beautifier for a ball-room, she always felt that she could not leave even that bed's depressing shelter for a room she knew would seem very cold. But the prospect of an awakening which might follow a victorious evening always made her slip into the white chiffon frock around which Edward Cabot had wrapped his cape, or into the crimson crêpe de chine shirred with gold threads or into the yellow crêpe satin he had never seen, and then go out and try to talk to men who did not seem to know that she had been tingling with radiance half an hour before, but whom she must please if she hoped to check off safely partnered dances as convicts may check off days without lashes. She had never suspected that men choose their partners for anything except pretty faces and pretty frocks and obedient dancing and the right conversation and the right quantity and volume of laughter, and when she smiled up at a young man with a smile which only meant that she wanted him to dance with her again, the answering pressure of his left arm was the first confirmation of her suspicion that membership in the Piedmont Driving Club was not a complete social reference, and to a new fear that she would always appeal to the wrong kind of man. But when a newspaper left all its other pages blank by failing to mention the town of Charleston or the artillery of the United States, she still saw announcements that the Atlanta Theatre or the Grand Opera House would shortly present a celebrated actor in an unsuccessful play or a successful play without any celebrated actor. She still remembered that her world would be waiting to see whether she walked into the play's first performance with one of the Piedmont Driving Club's younger members, and she began to listen for a ringing telephone as soon as she had stopped listening for the postman who would leave her whole body burning from the blazing fall of her disappointment, or who would leave it an alabaster lamp for the rising and falling glow of its electric spray.

Erskine Caldwell

The Night My Old Man Came Home

The dogs barked at a little before midnight, and Ma got up to look out the window. It was a snowy night about two weeks before Christmas. The wind had died down a little since supper, but not enough to keep it from whistling around the eaves every once in a while. It was just the kind of white winter night when it felt good to be in bed with plenty of covers to keep warm.

The light was burning in the hall, because we always kept one light on all night. Ma did not turn on the light in the room right away. She could see better what was going on outside when the room was dark.

She did not say a word for quite a while. The dogs growled some, and then started in barking again. They were kept chained at the side of the house all night; if they had been allowed to run loose, they would have chewed up a lot of people who came out that way after dark. It was a good thing for my old man, too; they would have chewed him up as quick as they would have somebody they had never smelt before. My old man was away from home so much he was just like a stranger, anyway. The last time he was there was in the summer, and he only stayed about five minutes then. He came back for a pair of pants he had left hanging on a nail in the woodshed the winter before.

"That's him, all right," Ma said, tapping the window-sill with the door key. She was no more mad than usual, but that was enough. When she tapped the woodwork with things like the door key, it was the only sign anybody needed to know how she was feeling.

Presently there was a rumble that sounded like a two-horse wagon crossing a plank bridge. Then a jar shook the house like somebody had taken a sledge hammer and knocked most of the foundation from under it.

That was my old man trying out the front steps and porch in the dark to see if they would hold his weight. He was always afraid somebody was going to set a trap for him when he came home, something like loosening the boards on the porch in such a way that he would fall through and have to lie there until Ma could reach him with the broom or something.

"He's going to come home like this just once too many some of these times," Ma said. "I'm getting sick and tired of it."

"I want to get up and see him," I said. "Please, Ma, let me."

"You stay right where you are, William, and pull those covers up over your head," Ma said, tapping some more on the sill with the door key. "When he gets in here, he's not going to be any fit sight for you to look at."

I got up on my knees and elbows and pulled the covers over my head. When I thought Ma had stopped looking that way, I pulled the covers back just enough so I could see out.

The front door banged open, almost breaking the glass in the top part. My old man never did act like he cared anything about the glass in the door, or about the furniture, or about anything else in the house. He came home once and picked Ma's sewing machine to pieces, and Ma had a dickens of a time saving up enough to get it fixed.

I never knew my old man could make so much racket. It sounded like he was out in the hall jumping up and down to see if he could stomp the floor clear through the ground. All the pictures on the wall shook, and some of them turned cockeyed. Even the big one of Grandpa turned sidewise.

Ma turned the light on and went to the fireplace to kindle the fire. There were lots of embers in the ashes that glowed red when she fanned them with a newspaper and laid some kindling over them. As soon as the kindling began to blaze, she put on two or three chunks of wood and sat down on the hearth with her back to the fire to wait for my old man to come into the room.

He was banging around out in the hall all that time, sounding like he was trying to kick all the chairs down to the far end next to the kitchen. In the middle of it he stopped and said something to somebody he had with him.

Ma got up in a hurry and put her bathrobe on. She looked in the mirror a time or two and straightened her hair. It was a big surprise for him to bring somebody home with him like that.

"You cover up your head and go to sleep like I told you, William," Ma said.

"I want to see him," I begged her.

"Don't argue with me, William," she said, patting her bare foot on the floor. "Go and do like I told you once already."

I pulled the covers up, but slipped them back enough to see out.

The door to the hall opened a couple of inches. I got up on my knees and elbows again so I could see better. Just then my old man kicked the door open with his foot. It flew back against the wall, knocking loose dust that nobody knew was there before.

"What do you want, Morris Stroup?" Ma said, folding her arms and glaring at him. "What do you want this time?"

"Come on in and make yourself comfortably at home," my old man said, turning around and jerking somebody into the room by the arm. "Don't be backward in my own house."

He pulled a girl about half the size of Ma into the room and pushed her around until they were over against Ma's sewing machine. Ma turned on her feet, watching them just like she had been a weathervane following the wind.

It was pretty serious to watch my old man drunk and reeling, and to see Ma so mad she could not get a word out of her mouth.

"Say 'Howdy,' " he told the girl.

She never said a thing.

My old man put his arm around her neck and bent her over. He kept it up, making her bow like that at Ma, and then he got to doing it too, and pretty soon they were keeping time bowing. They did it so much that Ma's head started bobbing up and down, just like she could not help herself.

I guess I must have snickered out loud, because Ma looked kind of silly for a minute, and then she went and sat down by the fire.

"Who's she?" Ma asked, acting like she was pretty anxious to find out. She even stopped looking cross for a little while. "Who is she, Morris?"

My old man sat down heavy enough to break the bottom out of the chair.

"She?" he said. "She's Lucy. She's my helper nowadays."

He turned around in the chair and looked over at me on my knees and elbows under the cover.

"Howdy, son," he said. "How've you been?"

"Pretty well," I said, squeezing down on my knees and trying to think of something to say so I could show him how glad I was to see him.

"Still growing, ain't you, son?" he said.

"A little, I reckon," I told him.

"That's right. That's the thing to do. Just keep it up, son. Some day you'll be a man before you know it."

"Pa, I—"

Ma picked up a piece of kindling and slung it at him. It missed him and hit the wall behind him. My old man jumped up on his feet and danced around like it had hit him instead of the wall. He reeled around like that until he lost his footing, and then he slid down the wall and sat on the floor.

He reached over and got his hands on a straight-back chair. He looked it over carefully, and then he started pulling the rungs out. Every time he got one loose, he pitched it into the fireplace.

When all the rungs and legs were out, he started picking the slats out of the back and throwing them into the fire. Ma never said a word. She just sat and looked at him all the time.

"Let's go, Morris," the girl Lucy said. It was the first thing she had said since she got there. Both Ma and me looked at her sort of surprised, and my old man cut his eyes around too, like he had forgotten she was there. "Morris, let's go," she said.

Lucy looked all but scared to death, it was easy to see. Everybody had stared at her so much, and Ma was acting so mad, that it was no wonder.

"Sit down and make yourself comfortable," my old man told her. "Just sit, Lucy."

She reached for one of the chairs and sat down just like he told her to.

The way she was sitting there, and Ma's mad streak on, and my old man picking the chair to pieces was a funny sight to see. I guess I must have snickered again out loud, because Ma turned around at me and shook her finger and motioned for me to pull the covers up over my head, and to go to sleep too, I guess. But I could never go to sleep while all that was going on, when I had not seen my old man for so long a time, and Ma must have known it. I just squeezed down on my elbows and knees as much as I could, and kept on looking.

"When you get that chair picked to pieces, Morris Stroup, you can just hand me over seven dollars to pay for a new one," Ma said, rocking back and forth.

"Shucks, Martha," my old man said. "Shucks, I don't believe there's a chair in the whole world that I'd give more than a dollar, maybe two, for."

Ma jerked out of her spell like a snapped finger. She jumped up and grabbed the broom from the side of the mantelpiece and started for him. She beat him over the head with it until she saw how much damage she was doing to the broomstraw, and then she stopped. She had beat out so much straw that it was scattered all over the floor. After that she turned the broom around and began poking him with the handle.

My old man got up in a hurry and staggered across the room to the closet, throwing what was left of the chair into the fire as he passed it. He opened the closet door and went inside. He did something to the lock, because no matter how hard Ma tried, she could not make the door open after he had closed it.

By that time Ma was so mad she did not know what she was doing. She sat down on the edge of the bed and pinned her hair up a little.

"This is nice goings-on at this time of night, Morris Stroup!" she yelled at him through the door. "What kind of a child can I raise with things like this going on in the house?"

She did not even wait for my old man to answer her. She just spun around toward Lucy, the girl my old man had brought along with him.

"You can have him," Ma said, "but you've got to keep him away from here."

"He told me he wasn't married," Lucy told Ma. "He said he was a single man all the time."

"Single man!" Ma yelled.

She got red in the face again and ran to the fireplace for the poker. Our poker was about three feet long and made of thick iron. She jabbed it into the crack of the closet and pried with it.

My old man began to yell and kick in the closet. I never heard such a racket as when the dogs started their barking again. People who heard them must have thought robbers were murdering all of us that night.

About then Lucy jumped up, crying.

"Stop that!" she yelled at Ma. "You're hurting him in that closet!"

Ma just turned around, swinging her elbow as she went.

"You leave me be!" Ma told her. "I'll attend to what I'm doing, sister!"

I had to squirm all around to the other side of the bed to keep up with what they were doing at the closet door. I never saw two people carry on so funny before. Both of them were mad, and scared to do much about it. They acted like two young roosters that wanted to fight but did not know how to go about it. They were just flapping around, trying to scare each other.

But Ma was as strong as the next one for her size. All she had to do when she made up her mind was drop the poker, grab Lucy, and give her a shove. Lucy sailed across the room and landed up against the sewing machine. She looked scared out of her wits when she found herself there so quick.

Ma picked up the poker again and she pried with all her might and, *bang!* the door sprang open. There was my old man backed up against the closet wall all tangled up in Ma's clothes, and he looked like he had been taken by surprise and caught red-handed with his fist in the grocer's cash drawer. I never saw my old man look so sheepish before in all my life.

As soon as Ma got him out of the closet and into the room, she went for Lucy.

"I'm going to put you out of my house," Ma told her, "and put a stop to this running around with my husband. That's one thing I won't stand for!"

She grabbed at Lucy, but Lucy ducked out of reach. Then they came back at each other just exactly like two young roosters that had finally got up enough nerve to start pecking. They jumped around on the floor with their arms flapping like wings and Ma's bathrobe and Lucy's skirt flying around like loose feathers. They hopped around in a circle for so long that it looked like they were riding on a merry-go-round. About that time they got their hands in each other's hair and started pulling. I never heard so much screaming before. My old man's eyes had just about got used to the light again, and he could see them, too, every once in a while. His head kept going around and around, and he missed a lot of it.

Ma and Lucy worked across the room and out the door into the hall. Out there they scuffled some more. While it was going on, my old man stumbled across the room, feeling for another chair. He picked up the first one he could put his hands on. It was Ma's high-back rocker, the one she sat in all the time when she was sewing and just resting.

By that time Ma and Lucy were scuffling out on the front porch. My old man shut the door to the hall and locked it. That door was a thick, heavy one with a spring thumb lock as well as a keyhole lock.

"No use talking, son," he said, sitting down on the bed and pulling off his shoes, "there's nothing else in the world like a couple of females at odds. Sometimes—"

He slung his shoes under the bed and turned out the light. He felt his way around the bed, dragging Ma's high-back rocker with him. I could hear the wood creak in the chair when he strained on the rungs. He pulled the covers up, then began picking the chair to pieces and throwing them toward the fire. Once in a while one of the pieces hit the mantelpiece; as often as not one of them struck the wall.

By then Ma and Lucy had got the dogs started again. They must have been out in the front yard scuffling by that time, because I could not hear them on the porch.

"Sometimes, son," my old man said, "sometimes it appears to me like the good Lord ought never put more than one woman in the world at a time."

I snuggled down under the covers, hugging my knees as tight as I could, and hoping he would stay at home all the time, instead of going off again.

My old man broke the back off the rocker and slung it in the dark toward the fireplace. It hit the ceiling first, and then the mantelpiece. He began picking the seat to pieces next.

It sure felt good being there in the dark with him.

Wild Flowers

The mockingbird that had perched on the roof top all night, filling the clear cool air with its music, had flown away when the sun rose. There was silence as deep and mysterious as the flat sandy country that extended mile after mile in every direction. Yesterday's shadows on the white sand began to reassemble under the trees and around the fence posts, spreading on the ground the lacy foliage of the branches and the fuzzy slabs of the wooden fence.

The sun rose in leaps and bounds, jerking itself upward as though it were in a great hurry to rise above the tops of the pines so it could shine down upon the flat country from there to the Gulf.

Inside the house the bedroom was light and warm. Nellie had been awake ever since the mockingbird had left. She lay on her side with one arm under her head. Her other arm was around the head beside her on the pillow. Her eyelids fluttered. Then for a minute at a time they did not move at all. After that they fluttered again, seven or eight or nine times in quick succession. She waited as patiently as she could for Vern to wake up.

When Vern came home sometime late in the night, he did not wake her. She had stayed awake waiting for him as long as she could, but she had become so sleepy her eyes would not stay open until he came.

The dark head on the pillow beside hers looked tired and worn. Vern's forehead, even in sleep, was wrinkled a little over his nose. Around the corners of his eyes the skin was darker than it was anywhere else on his face. She reached over as carefully as possible and kissed the cheek closest to her. She wanted to put both arms around his head and draw him to her, and to kiss him time after time and hold his dark head tight against her face.

Again her eyelids fluttered uncontrollably.

"Vern," she whispered softly. "Vern."

Slowly his eyes opened, then quickly closed again.

"Vern, sweet," she murmured, her heart beating faster and faster.

Vern turned his face toward her, snuggling his head between her arm and breast, and moving until she could feel his breath on her neck.

"Oh, Vern," she said in a whisper.

He could feel her kisses on his eyes and cheek and forehead and mouth. He was comfortably awake by then. He found her with his hands and they drew themselves tightly together.

"What did he say, Vern?" she asked at last, unable to wait any longer. "What, Vern?"

He opened his eyes and looked at her, fully awake at last.

She could read what he had to say on his face.

"When, Vern?" she said.

"Today," he said, closing his eyes and snuggling his head into her warmth once more.

Her lips trembled a little when he said it. She could not help herself.

"Where are we going to move to, Vern?" she asked like a little girl, looking closely to his lips for his answer.

He shook his head, pushing it tightly against her breasts and closing his eyes against her body.

They both lay still for a long time. The sun had warmed the room until it was almost like summer again, instead of early fall. Little waves of heat were beginning to rise from the weatherworn windowsill. There would be a little more of summer before winter came.

"Did you tell him—?" Nellie said. She stopped and looked down at Vern's face. "Did you tell him about me, Vern?"

"Yes."

"What did he say?"

Vern did not answer her. He pushed his head against her breast and held her tighter, as though he were struggling for food that would make his body strong when he got up and stood alone in the bare room.

"Didn't he say anything, Vern?"

"He just said he couldn't help it, or something like that. I don't remember what he said, but I know what he meant."

"Doesn't he care, Vern?"

"I guess he doesn't, Nellie."

Nellie stiffened. She trembled for a moment, but her body stiffened as though she had no control over it.

"But you care what happens to me, don't you, Vern?"

"Oh, God, yes!" he said. "That's all I do care about now. If anything happens—"

For a long time they lay in each other's arms, their minds stirring them wider and wider awake.

Nellie got up first. She was dressed and out of the room before Vern knew how quickly time had passed. He leaped out of bed, dressed, and hurried to the kitchen to make the fire in the cookstove. Nellie was already peeling the potatoes when he got it going.

They did not say much while they ate breakfast. They had to move, and move that day. There was nothing else they could do. The furniture did not belong to them, and they had so few clothes it would not be troublesome to carry them.

Nellie washed the dishes while Vern was getting their things ready. There was nothing to do after that except to tie up his overalls and shirts in a bundle, and Nellie's clothes in another, and to start out.

When they were ready to leave, Nellie stopped at the gate and looked back at the house. She did not mind leaving the place, even though it had been the only home she and Vern had ever had together. The house was so dilapidated that probably it would fall down in a few years more. The roof leaked, one side of the house had slipped off the foundation posts, and the porch sagged all the way to the ground in front.

Vern waited until she was ready to leave. When she turned away from the house, there were tears in her eyes, but she never looked back at it again. After they had gone a mile, they had turned a bend in the road, and the pines hid the place from sight.

"Where are we going, Vern?" she said, looking at him through the tears.

"We'll just have to keep on until we find a place," he said. He knew that she knew as well as he did that in that country of pines and sand the farms and houses were sometimes ten or fifteen miles apart. "I don't know how far that will be."

While she trudged along the sandy road, she could smell the fragrance of the last summer flowers all around her. The weeds and scrub hid most of them from sight, but every chance she got she stopped a moment and looked along the side of the ditches for blossoms. Vern did not stop, and she always ran to catch up with him before she could find any.

In the middle of the afternoon they came to a creek where it was cool and shady. Vern found her a place to lie down and, before taking off her shoes to rest her feet, scraped a pile of dry pine needles for her to lie on and pulled an armful of moss from the trees to put under her head. The water he brought her tasted of the leaves and grasses in the creek, and it was cool and clear. She fell asleep as soon as she had drunk some.

It was late afternoon when Vern woke her up.

"You've been asleep two or three hours, Nellie," he said. "Do you think you could walk a little more before night?"

She sat up and put on her shoes and followed him to the road. She felt a dizziness as soon as she was on her feet. She did not want to say anything to Vern about it, because she did not want him to worry. Every step she took pained her then. It was almost unbearable at times, and she bit her lips and crushed her fingers in her fists, but she walked along behind him, keeping out of his sight so he would not know about it.

At sundown she stopped and sat down by the side of the road. She felt as though she would never be able to take another step again. The pains in her body had drawn the color from her face, and her limbs felt as though they were being pulled from her body. Before she knew it, she had fainted.

When she opened her eyes, Vern was kneeling beside her, fanning her with his hat. She looked up into his face and tried to smile.

"Why didn't you tell me, Nellie?" he said. "I didn't know you were so tired."

"I don't want to be tired," she said. "I just couldn't help it, I guess."

He looked at her for a while, fanning her all the time.

"Do you think it might happen before we get some place?" he asked anxiously. "What do you think, Nellie?"

Nellie closed her eyes and tried not to think. They had not passed a house or farm since they had left that morning. She did not know how much farther it was to a town, and she was afraid to think how far it might be even to the next house. It made her afraid to think about it.

"I thought you said it would be another two weeks . . . ?" Vern said. "Didn't you, Nellie?"

"I thought so," she said. "But it's going to be different now, walking like this all day."

His hat fell from his hand, and he looked all around in confusion. He did not know what to do, but he knew he had to do something for Nellie right away.

"I can't stand this," he said. "I've got to do something."

He picked her up and carried her across the road. He found a place for her to lie under a pine tree, and he put her down there. Then he untied their bundles and put some of their clothes under her head and some over her feet and legs.

The sun had set, and it was becoming dark. Vern did not know what to do next. He was afraid to leave her there all alone in the woods, but he knew he had to get help for her.

"Vern," she said, holding out her hand to touch him.

He grasped it in his, squeezing and stroking her fingers and wrist.

"What is it, Nellie?"

"I'm afraid it is going to happen . . . happen . . . happen right away," she said weakly, closing her eyes before she could finish.

He bent down and saw that her lips were bloodless and that her face was whiter than he had ever seen anyone's face. While he watched her, her body became tense and she bit her mouth to keep from screaming with pain.

Vern jumped up and ran to the road, looking up it and down it. The night had come down so quickly that he could not tell whether there were any fields or cleared ground there as an indication of somebody's living near. There were no signs of a house or people anywhere.

He ran back to Nellie.

"Are you all right?" he asked her.

"If I could go to sleep," she said, "I think I would be all right for a while."

He got down beside her and put his arms around her.

"If I thought you wouldn't be afraid, I'd go up the road until I found a house and get a car or something to carry you. I can't let you stay here all night on the ground."

"You might not get back—in time!" she cried frantically.

"I'd hurry as fast as I could," he said. "I'll run until I find somebody."

"If you'll come back in two or three hours," she said, "I'd be able to stand it, I think. I couldn't stand it any longer than that alone, though."

He got up.

"I'm going," he said.

He ran up the road as fast as he could, remembering how he had pleaded to be allowed to stay in the house a little longer so Nellie would not have to go like that. The only answer he had got, even after he had explained about Nellie, was a shake of the head. There was no use in begging after that. He was being put out, and he could not do anything about it. He was certain there should have been some money due him for his crop that fall, even a few dollars, but he knew there was no use in trying to argue about that, either. He had gone home the night before, knowing they would have to leave. He stumbled, falling heavily, headlong, on the road.

When he picked himself up, he saw a light ahead. It was only a pale ray from a board window that had been closed tightly. But it was a house, and somebody lived in it. He ran toward it as fast as he could.

When he got to the place, a dog under the house barked, but he paid no attention to it. He ran up to the door and pounded on it with both fists.

"Let me in!" he yelled. "Open the door!"

Somebody inside shouted, and several chairs were knocked over. The dog ran out from under the house and began snapping at Vern's legs. He tried to kick the dog away, but the dog was just as determined as he was, and came back at him more savagely than before. Finally he pushed the door open, breaking a button lock.

Several Negroes were hiding in the room. He could see heads and feet under the bed and behind a trunk and under a table.

"Don't be scared of me," he said as calmly as he could. "I came for help. My wife's down the road, sick. I've got to get her into a house somewhere. She's lying on the ground."

The oldest man in the room, a gray-haired Negro who looked about fifty, crawled from under the bed.

"I'll help you, boss," he said. "I didn't know what you wanted when you came shouting and yelling like that. That's why I didn't open the door and let you in."

"Have you got a cart, or something like that?" Vern asked.

"I've got a one-horse cart," the man said. "George, you and Pete go hitch up the mule to the cart. Hurry and do it."

Two Negro boys came from their hiding places and ran out the back door.

"We'll need a mattress, or something like that to put her on," Vern said.

The Negro woman began stripping the covers from the bed, and Vern picked up the mattress and carried it out the front door to the road. While he waited for the boys to drive the cart out, he walked up and down, trying to assure himself that Nellie would be all right.

When the cart was ready, they all got in and drove down the road as fast as the mule could go. It took less than half an hour for them to reach the grove where he had left Nellie, and by then he realized he had been gone three hours or longer.

Vern jumped to the ground, calling her. She did not answer. He ran up the bank and fell on his knees beside her on the ground.

"Nellie!" he said, shaking her. "Wake up, Nellie! This is Vern, Nellie!"

He could not make her answer. Putting his face down against hers, he felt her cold cheek. He put his hands on her forehead, and that was cold, too. Then he found her wrists and held them in his fingers while he pressed his ear tightly against her breast.

The Negro man finally succeeded in pulling him backward. For a while he did not know where he was or what had happened. It seemed as if his mind had gone completely blank.

The Negro was trying to talk to him, but Vern could not hear a word he was saying. He did know that something had happened, and that Nellie's face and hands were cold, and that he could not feel her heart beat. He knew, but he could not make himself believe that it was really true.

He fell down on the ground, his face pressed against the pine needles, while his fingers dug into the soft damp earth. He could hear voices above him, and he could hear the words the voices said, but nothing had any meaning. Sometime—a long time away—he would ask about their baby—about Nellie's—about their baby. He knew it would be a long time before he could ask anything like that, though. It would be a long time before words would have any meaning in them again.

Caroline Miller

From *Lamb in His Bosom*

CHAPTER I

Cean turned and lifted her hand briefly in farewell as she rode away beside Lonzo in the ox-cart. Her mother and father and Jasper and Lias stood in front of the house, watching her go. The old elder who had married Cean to Lonzo was in the house somewhere, leaving the members of the family to themselves in their leave-taking of Cean. But the youngest of the family, Jake, was not there; he had fled away, his thin face hard with grief. He had laid his deepest curse on Lonzo Smith's head. Now he lay on his face under a budding willow on a sandbank of the river that ran two miles from his father's place. He hoped, with a fiendish hope that was a curse, that hairy, red worms would find out the holes in Lonzo Smith's ears, that they would crawl in and grow horny heads and furry tails, and eat out Lonzo's in'ards. But Cean would hate that; she would brew all kinds of yerb teas for him to drink. There wasn't anything to do. Cean had gone and done it; she had made her bed; now let her lie in it. She wouldn't ever know he cared, neither. She wasn't his sister any more; she was all Lonzo's. Now she would sleep in Lonzo's bed instead of Jake's. At this thought, misery almost suffocated the child; he found it hard to draw his breath out of his lungs. For he could shut his eyes and feel her body warming his body under the covers. She had a way of rounding his head into her shoulder, of catching his legs up against her with her strong, lean hand, and they would sleep so, their bodies fitted one to the other. In the night they might turn, and then his thin body would fit in a protecting curve along her back.

He opened his eyes, and there was the white sand against his face, magnified into little hills and valleys before his eyes. There were the budding willow branches above him, rising and falling in lifts of wind that ran down the river. He blew on a hill of sand close beside his mouth, and it fluttered down. He'd go on back and bring up the calves. They'd think that's where he was.

Cean's and Lonzo's bodies jounced gently in the slow motion of the wooden-wheeled cart. The way to their new home lay across the woods, close around the edge of the great swamp of cypress, through a little creek, and across a rise where there were huckleberries and rattlesnakes in hot weather. Farther on there were tall timbers and fine grazing; and there, six miles to the west of her mother's home, Lonzo had set up Cean's house with its broad clay-stuck chimney. There was a spring at the side under a smother of elder bushes and sweet bays; a new-set fig bush and Seven Sisters rose cuttings and a bed of pinks were beginning to take root by Cean's back door where her mother had set them. Lonzo had cut down every tree for the house, and Cean's brothers had helped him to notch them and lock them into the sturdy walls, and to line the walls with heavy planks riven from heart-pine. They had split the rails for the cow-pen, and Betsey was there now with her little pied-ed calf close against her. Lonzo would set up a springhouse for Cean, for the milk and butter, when he had his seed in the ground; and in the late summer, Cean's brothers would help him with the crib for the corn that he would raise in the new ground, corn for meal and grits, corn for feed for the ox. Pumpkins, peas, potatoes, melons—they would raise fields full of them; they would fare fine. Cean would water and tend such things. Her mother had told her that a woman must see to things like that—fruit, a garden-patch, milk and butter and the children; men must raise and butcher the meat and make and gather in the crops.

Cean's new bonnet was hot about her neck. She slipped it back off her head, tied the strings together under her chin, and let it swing free down her back. Her face was brown and full and bright; her mouth was wide and closed firmly over her teeth. Her hair blowsed over her temples from where it was parted in the middle. Her bright brown eyes went shyly about, seeking gentle satisfaction in the soft air, the sunshine, the thick plodding of the hooves of the ox on the slick brown pine-needles and soft sand. Her happy glance slipped shyly to Lonzo's bearded face. His neck, browned by sunlight, was moist in fine beads of sweat. Her glance moved upward to his coarse black hair that came down from under the fine hat he had bargained for last fall on the Coast. She saw the set of his large head, the set of his strong shoulders, then her eyes hurried away, a little frightened by that nearness, by the coarse black hair, the strong male shoulders, the sturdy silence of the man beside her who was her husband.

Now she was married. The elder that came through twice a year had said the marriage words over them: "Do you take this woman, Tillitha Cean Carver . . . ? . . ." After that, she belonged to him, to cook his victuals and to wash his clothes. After that, she belonged to herself, too. Now she was a woman and would churn her own butter, scald her own milk-crocks and set them in the sun to make them smell sweet and clean; now she would own and tend her little patch of herbs and melons, drop corn behind her own man, and watch it grow, and hoe the grass out from around the sharp, clean blades cutting through the earth. She would have her own corn, her own man, her own way of living from now on, but her eyes hurried away from his strong, sinewy neck going down into his shirt, his strong, sinewy body wet with fine-beaded new sweat.

The trail hugged the edge of the swamp, and the undergrowth pressed in close about them. It was cool and sweet here. The air was wet from the swamp water and the black, spongy bogs. Yellow jessamine sprawled high on the trees and swarms of its sweet-smelling bright blooms burst out through the green. The cypresses were new-feathered on their pale high trunks. All the swamp seemed stirred into sweet unease. In the summer it lay sluggish and fevered in muck; alligators drowsed in the mud and moccasins slipped through the water. In winter the swamp was dismal and forbidding, with the beasts screaming in the cold, and the water black and still. But now, on Cean's marriage day, yellow jessamine smothered the tops of the pine trees, maples burned aloft in the cool gloom, and all the little saplings and all the giant pines lifted the candles of their wax-colored leaf-buds, white candles on the tip of every tree, on the end of every limb, burning with slow fire into new growth. Orioles chittered carelessly. A cardinal stitched a bar of song over and over, reiterating spring. Close about them Cean heard the stealthy, hurrying feet of little creatures escaping from their path; bushes rustled in brief panic, then stilled. Coveys of partridges whirred away in sudden, frantic haste; Lonzo would trap them when the crops were laid by. And there were turkeys in the swamp and squirrels and fish—all manner of meat. Oh, they would fare fine!

Cean drew her legs closer to herself so that her skirt might escape the bamboo's little thorns that came over the cart's side to pluck at her. Her leg under heavy skirts pressed close against Lonzo's right leg along the seat beside her. The road to the creek bore sharply to the left, and she pressed hard on Lonzo, leaning against her will. Fear moved through her as she felt herself so close upon him. She tried to move back from him, but could not, for the incline was more than a little steep. Her breathing came and went close against his shoulder. The ox halted and lowered his head in the little stream to drink. Bright-brown water flowed beneath them; bay leaves shone green above them. A creeper of bamboo swam on the current. Here the afternoon light was stifled to clear, pale green. Cean saw the sandy bottom of the stream worn into little ruffles by the water's slow flowing. A little way down the branch, she heard squirrels bark and swing through the tree-tops. For the first time since they had started their journey Lonzo turned his black eyes on her. He said:

"Gettin' tired?"

She flushed and looked far down the little stream.

"No, I ain't a-tired."

There was silence as his eyes went after hers down the stream. She had a feeling that his thoughts were close on the trail of her thoughts. She was too shy now to move farther from him. She said:

"This is a first-rate place fer yore hogs to waller in when hit's hot."

His voice was proud:

"Our hogs, ye'd better say."

Cean's eyes clouded over with shyness. She was miserable under the glance of his eyes and the tone of his voice. He said:

"The hogs'll help keep out snakes fer ye . . . if ye're scared of 'em."

"I ain't a-scared. . . ."

His black eyes shone.

"Ye ain't a-scared of nothin', air ye?"

She shook her head and dropped her eyes miserably. He watched her for a moment and spoke heavily and sweetly:

"Little un!"

He turned his head quickly and chucked to the ox; the three of them moved up to the bank where the sand was washed white, and on up the rise where the palmettos whispered in clumps, where new leaves of the scrub oaks were pale yellow and green, where pines soughed aloft on their great rough trunks and grass was springing, heavy and green in the open spaces, where Cean's cow would graze.

Smoke from Lonzo's slow-burning stumps in the new ground drifted far across the swamp. Cean saw it—a thin fog in the lowlands. And off there she saw her house, bright-yellow as the sun, new in the sun, the logs fresh from the bark, the chimney fresh from the clay in Lonzo's hands. At the back the bright new fence rails held in her cow and calf. Far and wide about the house, holes where the stumps had been were smoking in the still air. The undergrowth had been grubbed out, the labor leaving Lonzo's hands horny and hard, and his heavy shoulders a little stooped. The ground was broken into dark clods, ready for the seeds, yellow, black, white, to burst into bright green down the furrows. Cean could think of the house as almost hidden from sight by rows and rows of rough, rustling corn. There would be cotton at the back, and a patch of tobacco for Lonzo to dry and twist for his own taste. She would root a grape vine to spread across her back yard on posts, and tomorrow she would drop the little handful of sunflower seeds to grow for the hens and rooster her mother had given her.

The ox plodded on across the rising ground and struck into the new ground. The cart jolted them roughly as it went over the uneven plowed ground, making the first road to the door of their house. The house came nearer to Cean, the logs of it golden in the afternoon sunlight, the roof of it sloping sharply down to thwart the soaking rains, the doors and shutters tightly chinked to shut out the sharpest wind of winter.

Finally, there was the yard, cleared but with the soil unturned by the plow. And there was the clean, new block that led from the ground into the house. The chickens scurried past the door, feeling strange away from the great flock that was Cean's mother's. The cow lowed lonesomely down in the pen. Lonzo lifted one of his long legs over the side of the cart and jumped to the ground. He turned back to Cean, and his lips spread a little, almost disclosing his teeth in his soft, thick beard. A little shyly he held out his arms to Cean, saying:

"Come, little un!" And she gave her weight to his arms and slipped through them to the ground.

She went into the house where the floor of split logs had never been scrubbed and yet was clean, where Lonzo had set the bedplace in the corner with its depth of dry cornshucks soaked and softened in water, and dried again in recent suns. Over these shucks, that would rustle softly with the turn of their bodies, was spread the thick mattress of soft new cotton, caught between its homespun ticking with strong thread in the hands of Cean's mother. Atop the cotton mattress lay Cean's feather bed, the feathers saved from every goose for years gone. Atop this were homespun sheets and Cean's quilts, one of them the bright and dark scraps of the Widow's Trouble pattern, sewn by Cean's fingers through her girlhood. She had two other quilts—Star of the East, and Maiden's Tear—that she had pieced herself. That would be more than enough cover for these bright, cool nights, and before winter came again she would make other quilts. Lonzo's mother had promised wool for two comforts when the sheep should be sheared in April.

Before the deep fireplace were set the well-built chairs that Lonzo had made, the wood bright and new, the cow-hide bottoms only lately stretched and cured. There was a low, wide chest along the wall, for quilts or any such thing. Across the hearth were set the iron pots and the big hoecake spider. From the rafters hung the sides of meat their parents had given them, and there was a keg of shelled corn in the corner; and a grist-mill was to be found in the yard to grind their corn, if Cean would but swing the rock around. From the Smiths or the Carvers, Lonzo could have as many more cartloads of corn as they should need until the crops were made and gathered in. Cean could go to her mother's any day for greens, and her own patch would soon be sown, and green in a month.

The house was ready for living. Cean's mother had made the bed and set out the pots on the fireplace. Betsey would give no milk tonight, because the calf had not been parted off, but after today Cean would be milking.

Cean unrolled the bundle of clothing she had brought with her, and placed it in the chest. She hung her bonnet on a wooden peg by the head of the bed alongside Lonzo's new hat and old coonskin cap. She took off her fine new shoes, brushed the thin dust from them, and set them in the chest. The floor was cool to her feet as she walked about.

It was near dark. Lonzo brought firewood and set fire for cooking. Then he went out again to the cow-pen. Her mother had sent along plenty of cold food for supper, but Cean would cook on her own fireplace this first night in her new home. She sliced meat, and mixed meal and water and salt for cornbread. A song pushed up in her throat as she worked, but she held still because she was afraid Lonzo might notice. When the meal was spread on the eating-table, she called him briefly:

"Supper's done."

He came, and they ate, their glances dropping away, each from the other's, to their victuals, their hands clumsy at breaking the bread and sopping the meat grease.

As night fell the fire on the fireplace was built up and filled the room with soft, pulsing light. Cean cleared the table and brought water to wash her feet.

Lonzo went to the bed and, stooping, brought out a roll of goods.

He brought them to Cean's chair by the fire, and spread them on the floor for her to see:

"I thought ye mought like somethin' sorter fer ye-self."

There was a clean-washed rug of sheepskin. There was a little chest of cherrywood not a foot high, with carved knobs and rings across the lid, and a little catch with a piece of wood no bigger than your little finger to slip in and hold it shut. There was a pearly trinket carved from a cow's horn. There were six hairpins of cedar wood. And there were two knitting-needles of cedar, polished and shining.

Cean handled the things, each to itself. She could not decide which pleased her most. Lonzo had a turn with his hand. He could make most anything.

She moved the slender needles of cedar in the motions of knitting. The wood slipped, cool and quick, through her fingers. She spoke shyly:

"I'll be knittin' ye stockin's 'fore cold weather."

He watched her hands in stubborn embarrassment:

"Better knit ye some, ye own self. . . ."

She said:

"I wasn't askin' fer no pretty things such as these, Lonzo."

He explained, simply:

"I jes' give 'em to ye, to be a-givin', little un."

She laid the pretty things in the chest, and spread the rug beside the bed. She washed her feet before the fire; going to the shadows by the bed, she dropped her dress about her feet and slipped a shift that her mother's hands had woven over her head and down her body. She slid beneath the cover while the soft shucks whispered huskily, and turned her face to the wall until Lonzo should come.

When Cean moved from the fire into the shadows by the bed, Lonzo left the house and walked through the dark to the cow-pen. The night was a thin and gauzy blackness, not dark and heavy as are moonless nights. There was not much of a moon, though, only a little one, cool and high, that foretold rain in the open, downward swing of its curved blade. Before it was full, that moon would empty itself of rain, soaking the new ground. Lonzo must put in his seed. He must spread a shelter for Betsey and her calf in the near side of the cow-pen. The cow was used to rain, doubtless, but the little pied-ed feller might not like it, and a lean-to would keep rain off of Cean at milking-time.

Lonzo walked to the rough rails of the cow-pen, and leaned upon them. Betsey, hearing his footsteps, came to the fence and answered his low-spoken "Coa" with a plaintive moo. He fingered her ear, roughing the short, coarse hair with his fingernail. He moved his hand down across the bony sockets of her eyes. Always the feel of a cow's forehead reminded him of the sightless stare of bleached skulls that he sometimes saw far from any clearing, where critters had wandered off to die. Dumb things don't like to die with others looking on. They'll drag off by a branch somewhere, and lie down, and nobody will ever know until you see the buzzards circling lower and lower above some thin cypress, or sitting in solemn black rows along dead limbs, glossing their greasy-black feathers, one by one. There beneath, if you have a mind to, you can find a hide ripped open, and lank bones picked clean.

Lonzo could hear the little calf nuzzling his mother's bag. He wasn't hungry; but he'd better suck while he could. Tomorrow he'd be shut up while his mother went to crop grass on the slope toward the swamp.

Lonzo turned and faced his fields, leaning his weight upon his elbows on the fence. His eyes went through the thin darkness and saw his land ready for planting—through the thin dark, and saw the crops leaning heavy above the soil. The corn would go in there, and the cotton across yonder, and a pea-patch close beyond the cow-pen. Peas would bring partridges in the fall. He'd have to fix a garden-patch for Cean's seeds and a washing-shed by the spring. He'd have to clear out some of the brush; a moccasin will slip up on you if you give him a chance. He must fix Cean a cypress wash-block like his mother's, and a dug-out wash trough with a soap-rack. He had the tree picked out; all there was to do was to strip it and dig it out and set it up on four legs. He had enough to do to keep him busy till frost, what with Cean's little jobs. And there was the land to fence, once and for all, with no tellin' how many rails to be split.

The little moon hung lonesome in the early night, unwearied in fulling and shrinking over woods and waters. Lonzo found it over his left shoulder through space clear of tree or cloud; it meant good luck—rain and good luck. He walked back to the house with slow eagerness. He would put the old brood sow's pen on the other side of the spring; she'd rake straw in another month. He walked heavily across the back yard, and pushed in the back door with unwanted roughness. He'd get a hound-puppy or two to chase rabbits and to keep the house from seeming so still.

Cean heard his coming, and her lashes quivered on her cheeks. Hidden under the thin white coverlids with their soft fringe of lashes, her eyes were warm and bright.

Margaret Mitchell

From *Gone with the Wind*

CHAPTER XXIV

The bright glare of morning sunlight streaming through the trees overhead awakened Scarlett. For a moment, stiffened by the cramped position in which she had slept, she could not remember where she was. The sun blinded her, the hard boards of the wagon under her were harsh against her body, and a heavy weight lay across her legs. She tried to sit up and discovered that the weight was Wade who lay sleeping with his head pillowed on her knees. Melanie's bare feet were almost in her face and, under the wagon seat, Prissy was curled up like a black cat with the small baby wedged in between her and Wade.

Then she remembered everything. She popped up to a sitting position and looked hastily all around. Thank God, no Yankees in sight! Their hiding place had not been discovered in the night. It all came back to her now, the nightmare journey after Rhett's footsteps died away, the endless night, the black road full of ruts and boulders along which they jolted, the deep gullies on either side into which the wagon slipped, the fear-crazed strength with which she and Prissy had pushed the wheels out of the gullies. She recalled with a shudder how often she had driven the unwilling horse into fields and woods when she heard soldiers approaching, not knowing if they were friends or foes—recalled, too, her anguish lest a cough, a sneeze or Wade's hiccoughing might betray them to the marching men.

Oh, that dark road where men went by like ghosts, voices stilled, only the muffled tramping of feet on soft dirt, the faint clicking of bridles and the straining creak of leather! And, oh, that dreadful moment when the sick horse balked and cavalry and light cannon rumbled past in the darkness, past where they sat breathless, so close she could almost reach out and touch them, so close she could smell the stale sweat on the soldiers' bodies!

When, at last, they had neared Rough and Ready, a few camp fires were gleaming where the last of Steve Lee's rear guard was awaiting orders to fall back. She had circled through a plowed field for a mile until the light of the fires died out behind her. And then she had lost her way in the darkness and sobbed when she could not find the little wagon path she knew so well. Then finally having found it, the horse sank in the traces and refused to move, refused to rise even when she and Prissy tugged at the bridle.

So she had unharnessed him and crawled, sodden with fatigue, into the back of the wagon and stretched her aching legs. She had a faint memory of Melanie's voice before sleep clamped down her eyelids, a weak voice that apologized even as it begged: "Scarlett, can I have some water, please?"

She had said: "There isn't any," and gone to sleep before the words were out of her mouth.

Now it was morning and the world was still and serene and green and gold with dappled sunshine. And no soldiers in sight anywhere. She was hungry and dry with thirst, aching and cramped and filled with wonder that she, Scarlett O'Hara, who could never rest well except between linen sheets and on the softest of feather beds, had slept like a field hand on hard planks.

Blinking in the sunlight, her eyes fell on Melanie and she gasped, horrified. Melanie lay so still and white Scarlett thought she must be dead. She looked dead. She looked like a dead, old woman with her ravaged face and her dark hair snarled and tangled across it. Then Scarlett saw with relief the faint rise and fall of her shallow breathing and knew that Melanie had survived the night.

Scarlett shaded her eyes with her hand and looked about her. They had evidently spent the night under the trees in someone's front yard, for a sand and gravel driveway stretched out before her, winding away under an avenue of cedars.

"Why, it's the Mallory place!" she thought, her heart leaping with gladness at the thought of friends and help.

But a stillness as of death hung over the plantation. The shrubs and grass of the lawn were cut to pieces where hooves and wheels and feet had torn frantically back and forth until the soil was churned up. She looked toward the house and instead of the old white clapboard place she knew so well, she saw there only a long rectangle of blackened granite foundation stones and two tall chimneys rearing smoke-stained bricks into the charred leaves of still trees.

She drew a deep shuddering breath. Would she find Tara like this, level with the ground, silent as the dead?

"I mustn't think about that now," she told herself hurriedly. "I mustn't let myself think about it. I'll get scared again if I think about it." But, in spite of herself, her heart quickened and each beat seemed to thunder: "Home! Hurry! Home! Hurry!"

They must be starting on toward home again. But first they must find some food and water, especially water. She prodded Prissy awake. Prissy rolled her eyes as she looked about her.

"Fo' Gawd, Miss Scarlett, Ah din' spec ter wake up agin 'cept in de Promise Lan'."

"You're a long way from there," said Scarlett, trying to smooth back her untidy hair. Her face was damp and her body was already wet with sweat. She felt dirty and messy and sticky, almost as if she smelled bad. Her clothes were crushed and wrinkled from sleeping in them and she had never felt more acutely tired and sore in all her life. Muscles she did not know she possessed ached from her unaccustomed exertions of the night before and every movement brought sharp pain.

She looked down at Melanie and saw that her dark eyes were opened. They were sick eyes, fever bright, and dark baggy circles were beneath them. She opened cracking lips and whispered appealingly: "Water."

"Get up, Prissy," ordered Scarlett. "We'll go to the well and get some water."

"But, Miss Scarlett! Dey mout be hants up dar. Sposin' somebody daid up dar?"

"I'll make a hant out of you if you don't get out of this wagon," said Scarlett, who was in no mood for argument, as she climbed lamely down to the ground.

And then she thought of the horse. Name of God! Suppose the horse had died in the night! He had seemed ready to die when she unharnessed him. She ran around the wagon and saw him lying on his side. If he were dead, she would curse God and die too. Somebody in the Bible had done just that thing. Cursed God and died. She knew just how that person felt. But the horse was alive—breathing heavily, sick eyes half closed, but alive. Well, some water would help him too.

Prissy climbed reluctantly from the wagon with many groans and timorously followed Scarlett up the avenue. Behind the ruins the row of whitewashed slave quarters stood silent and deserted under the overhanging trees. Between the quarters and the smoked stone foundations, they found the well, and the roof of it still stood with the bucket far down the well. Between them, they wound up the rope, and when the bucket of cool sparkling water appeared out of the dark depths, Scarlett tilted it to her lips and drank with loud sucking noises, spilling the water all over herself.

She drank until Prissy's petulant: "Well, Ah's thusty, too, Miss Scarlett," made her recall the needs of the others.

"Untie the knot and take the bucket to the wagon and give them some. And give the rest to the horse. Don't you think Miss Melanie ought to nurse the baby? He'll starve."

"Law, Miss Scarlett, Miss Melly ain' got no milk—ain' gwine have none."

"How do you know?"

"Ah's seed too many lak her."

"Don't go putting on any airs with me. A precious little you knew about babies yesterday. Hurry now. I'm going to try to find something to eat."

Scarlett's search was futile until in the orchard she found a few apples. Soldiers had been there before her and there was none on the trees. Those she found on the ground were mostly rotten. She filled her skirt with the best of them and came back across the soft earth, collecting small pebbles in her slippers. Why hadn't she thought of putting on stouter shoes last night? Why hadn't she brought her sun hat? Why hadn't she brought something to eat? She'd acted like a fool. But, of course, she'd thought Rhett would take care of them.

Rhett! She spat on the ground, for the very name tasted bad. How she hated him! How contemptible he had been! And she had stood there in the road and let him kiss her—and almost liked it. She had been crazy last night. How despicable he was!

When she came back, she divided up the apples and threw the rest into the back of the wagon. The horse was on his feet now but the water did not seem to have refreshed him much. He looked far worse in the daylight than he had the night before. His hip bones stood out like an old cow's, his ribs showed like a washboard and his back was a mass of sores. She shrank from touching him as she harnessed him. When she slipped the bit into his mouth, she saw that he was practically toothless. As old as the hills! While Rhett was stealing a horse, why couldn't he have stolen a good one?

She mounted the seat and brought down the hickory limb on his back. He wheezed and started, but he walked so slowly as she turned him into the road she knew she could walk faster herself with no effort whatever. Oh, if only she didn't have Melanie and Wade and the baby and Prissy to bother with! How swiftly she could walk home! Why, she would run home, run every step of the way that would bring her closer to Tara and to Mother.

They couldn't be more than fifteen miles from home, but at the rate this old nag traveled it would take all day, for she would have to stop frequently to rest him. All day! She looked down the glaring red road, cut in deep ruts where cannon wheels and ambulances had gone over it. It would be hours before she knew if Tara still stood and if Ellen were there. It would be hours before she finished her journey under the broiling September sun.

She looked back at Melanie who lay with sick eyes closed against the sun and jerked loose the strings of her bonnet and tossed it to Prissy.

"Put that over her face. It'll keep the sun out of her eyes." Then as the heat beat down upon her unprotected head, she thought: "I'll be as freckled as a guinea egg before this day is over."

She had never in her life been out in the sunshine without a hat or veils, never handled reins without gloves to protect the white skin of her dimpled hands. Yet here she was exposed to the sun in a broken-down wagon with a broken-down horse, dirty, sweaty, hungry, helpless to do anything but plod along at a snail's pace through a deserted land. What a few short weeks it had been since she was safe and secure! What a little while since she and everyone else had thought that Atlanta could never fall, that Georgia could never be invaded. But the small cloud which appeared in the northwest four months ago had blown up into a mighty storm and then into a screaming tornado, sweeping away her world, whirling her out of her sheltered life, and dropping her down in the midst of this still, haunted desolation.

Was Tara still standing? Or was Tara also gone with the wind which had swept through Georgia?

She laid the whip on the tired horse's back and tried to urge him on while the waggling wheels rocked them drunkenly from side to side.

CHAPTER XXV

The next morning Scarlett's body was so stiff and sore from the long miles of walking and jolting in the wagon that every movement was agony. Her face was crimson with sunburn and her blistered palms raw. Her tongue was furred and her throat parched as if flames had scorched it and no amount of water could assuage her thirst. Her head felt swollen and she winced even when she turned her eyes. A queasiness of the stomach reminiscent of the early days of her pregnancy made the smoking yams on the breakfast table unendurable, even to the smell. Gerald could have told her she was suffering the normal aftermath of her first experience with hard drinking but Gerald noticed nothing. He sat at the head of the table, a gray old man with absent, faded eyes fastened on the door and head cocked slightly to hear the rustle of Ellen's petticoats, to smell the lemon verbena sachet.

As Scarlett sat down, he mumbled: "We will wait for Mrs. O'Hara. She is late." She raised an aching head, looked at him with startled incredulity and met the pleading eyes of Mammy, who stood behind Gerald's chair. She rose unsteadily, her hand at her throat and looked down at her father in the morning sunlight. He peered up at her vaguely and she saw that his hands were shaking, that his head trembled a little.

Until this moment she had not realized how much she had counted on Gerald to take command, to tell her what she must do, and now— Why, last night he had seemed almost himself. There had been none of his usual bluster and vitality, but at least he had told a connected story and now—now, he did not even remember Ellen was dead. The combined shock of the coming of the Yankees and her death had stunned him. She started to speak, but Mammy shook her head vehemently and raising her apron dabbed at her red eyes.

"Oh, can Pa have lost his mind?" thought Scarlett and her throbbing head felt as if it would crack with this added strain. "No, no. He's just dazed by it all. It's like he was sick. He'll get over it. He must get over it. What will I do if he doesn't?—I won't think about it now. I won't think of him or Mother or any of these awful things now. No, not till I can stand it. There are too many other things to think about—things that can be helped without my thinking of those I can't help."

She left the dining room without eating, and went out onto the back porch where she found Pork, barefooted and in the ragged remains of his best livery, sitting on the steps cracking peanuts. Her head was hammering and throbbing and the bright sunlight stabbed into her eyes. Merely holding herself erect required an effort of will power and she talked as briefly as possible, dispensing with the usual forms of courtesy her mother had always taught her to use with negroes.

She began asking questions so brusquely and giving orders so decisively Pork's eyebrows went up in mystification. Miss Ellen didn't never talk so short to nobody, not even when she caught them stealing pullets and watermelons. She asked again about the fields, the gardens, the stock, and her green eyes had a hard bright glaze which Pork had never seen in them before.

"Yas'm, dat hawse daid, lyin' dar whar Ah tie him wid his nose in de water bucket he tuhned over. No'm, de cow ain' daid. Din' you know? She done have a calf las' night. Dat why she beller so."

"A fine midwife your Prissy will make," Scarlett remarked caustically. "She said she was bellowing because she needed milking."

"Well'm, Prissy ain' fixin' ter be no cow midwife, Miss Scarlett," Pork said tactfully. "An' ain' no use quarrelin' wid blessin's, 'cause dat calf gwine ter mean a full cow an' plen'y buttermilk fer de young Misses, lak dat Yankee doctah say dey' need."

"All right, go on. Any stock left?"

"No'm. Nuthin' 'cept one ole sow an' her litter. Ah driv dem inter de swamp de day de Yankees come, but de Lawd knows how we gwine git dem. She mean, dat sow."

"We'll get them all right. You and Prissy can start right now hunting for her."

Pork was amazed and indignant.

"Miss Scarlett, dat a fe'el han's bizness. Ah's allus been a house nigger."

A small fiend with a pair of hot tweezers plucked behind Scarlett's eyeballs.

"You two will catch the sow—or get out of here, like the field hands did."

Tears trembled in Pork's hurt eyes. Oh, if only Miss Ellen was here! She understood such niceties and realized the wide gap between the duties of a field hand and those of a house nigger.

"Git out, Miss Scarlett? Whar'd Ah git out to, Miss Scarlett?"

"I don't know and I don't care. But anyone at Tara who won't work can go hunt up the Yankees. You can tell the others that too."

"Yas'm."

"Now, what about the corn and the cotton, Pork?"

"De cawn? Lawd, Miss Scarlett, dey pasture dey hawses in de cawn an' cah'ied off whut de hawses din' eat or spile. An' dey driv dey cannons an' waggins 'cross de cotton till it plum ruint, 'cept a few acres over on de creek bottom dat dey din' notice. But dat cotton ain' wuth foolin' wid, 'cause ain' but 'bout three bales over dar."

Three bales. Scarlett thought of the scores of bales Tara usually yielded and her head hurt worse. Three bales. That was little more than the shiftless Slatterys raised. To make matters worse, there was the question of taxes. The Confederate government took cotton for taxes in lieu of money, but three bales wouldn't even cover the taxes. Little did it matter though, to her or the Confederacy, now that all the field hands had run away and there was no one to pick the cotton.

"Well, I won't think of that either," she told herself. "Taxes aren't a woman's job anyway. Pa ought to look after such things, but Pa— I won't think of Pa now. The Confederacy can whistle for its taxes. What we need now is something to eat."

"Pork, have any of you been to Twelve Oaks or the MacIntosh place to see if there's anything left in the gardens there?"

"No, Ma'm! Us ain' lef' Tara. De Yankees mout git us."

"I'll send Dilcey over to MacIntosh. Perhaps she'll find something there. And I'll go to Twelve Oaks."

"Who wid, chile?"

"By myself. Mammy must stay with the girls and Mr. Gerald can't—"

Pork set up an outcry which she found infuriating. "There might be Yankees or mean niggers at Twelve Oaks. She mustn't go alone."

"That will be enough, Pork. Tell Dilcey to start immediately. And you and Prissy go bring in the sow and her litter," she said briefly, turning on her heel.

Mammy's old sunbonnet, faded but clean, hung on its peg on the back porch and Scarlett put it on her head, remembering, as from another world, the bonnet with the curling green plume which Rhett had brought her from Paris. She picked up a large split-oak basket and started down the back stairs, each step jouncing her head until her spine seemed to be trying to crash through the top of her skull.

The road down to the river lay red and scorching between the ruined cotton fields. There were no trees to cast a shade and the sun beat down through Mammy's sunbonnet as if it were made of tarlatan instead of heavy quilted calico, while the dust floating upward sifted into her nose and throat until she felt the membranes would crack dryly if she spoke. Deep ruts and furrows were cut into the road where horses had dragged heavy guns along it and the red gullies on either side were deeply gashed by the wheels. The cotton was mangled and trampled where cavalry and infantry, forced off the narrow road by the artillery, had marched through the green bushes, grinding them into the earth. Here and there in the road and fields lay buckles and bits of harness leather, canteens flattened by hooves and caisson wheels, buttons, blue caps, worn socks, bits of bloody rags, all the litter left by the marching army.

She passed the clump of cedars and the low brick wall which marked the family burying ground, trying not to think of the new grave lying by the three short mounds of her little brothers. Oh, Ellen—She trudged on down the dusty hill, passing the heap of ashes and the stumpy chimney where the Slattery house had stood, and she wished savagely that the whole tribe of them had been part of the ashes. If it hadn't been for the Slatterys—if it hadn't been for that nasty Emmie who'd had a bastard brat by their overseer—Ellen wouldn't have died.

She moaned as a sharp pebble cut into her blistered foot. What was she doing here? Why was Scarlett O'Hara, the belle of the County, the sheltered pride of Tara, tramping down this rough road almost barefoot? Her little feet were made to dance, not to limp, her tiny slippers to peep daringly from under bright silks, not to collect sharp pebbles and dust. She was born to be pampered and waited upon, and here she was, sick and ragged, driven by hunger to hunt for food in the gardens of her neighbors.

At the bottom of the long hill was the river and how cool and still were the tangled trees overhanging the water! She sank down on the low bank, and stripping off the remnants of her slippers and stockings, dabbled her burning feet in the cool water. It would be so good to sit here all day, away from the helpless eyes of Tara, here where only the rustle of leaves and the gurgle of slow water broke the stillness. But reluctantly she replaced her shoes and stockings and trudged down the bank, spongy with moss, under the shady trees. The Yankees had burned the bridge but she knew of a footlog bridge across a narrow point of the stream a hundred yards below. She crossed it cautiously and trudged uphill the hot half-mile to Twelve Oaks.

There towered the twelve oaks, as they had stood since Indian days, but with their leaves brown from fire and the branches burned and scorched. Within their circle lay the ruins of John Wilkes' house, the charred remains of that once stately home which had crowned the hill in white-columned dignity. The deep pit which had been the cellar, the blackened field-stone foundations and two mighty chimneys marked the site. One long column, half-burned, had fallen across the lawn, crushing the cape jessamine bushes.

Scarlett sat down on the column, too sick at the sight to go on. This desolation went to her heart as nothing she had ever experienced. Here was the Wilkes pride in the dust at her feet. Here was the end of the kindly, courteous house which had always welcomed her, the house where in futile dreams she had aspired to be mistress. Here she had danced and dined and flirted and here she had watched with a jealous, hurting heart how Melanie smiled up at Ashley. Here, too, in the cool shadows of the trees, Charles Hamilton had rapturously pressed her hand when she said she would marry him.

"Oh, Ashley," she thought, "I hope you are dead! I could never bear for you to see this."

Ashley had married his bride here but his son and his son's son would never bring brides to this house. There would be no more matings and births beneath this roof which she had so loved and longed to rule. The house was dead and to Scarlett, it was as if all the Wilkeses, too, were dead in its ashes.

"I won't think of it now. I can't stand it now. I'll think of it later," she said aloud, turning her eyes away.

Seeking the garden, she limped around the ruins, by the trampled rose beds the Wilkes girls had tended so zealously, across the back yard and through the ashes to the smokehouse, barns and chicken houses. The split-rail fence around the kitchen garden had been demolished and the once orderly rows of green plants had suffered the same treatment as those at Tara. The soft earth was scarred with hoof prints and heavy wheels and the vegetables were mashed into the soil. There was nothing for her here.

She walked back across the yard and took the path down toward the silent row of whitewashed cabins in the quarters, calling "Hello!"

as she went. But no voice answered her. Not even a dog barked. Evidently the Wilkes negroes had taken flight or followed the Yankees. She knew every slave had his own garden patch and as she reached the quarters, she hoped these little patches had been spared.

Her search was rewarded but she was too tired even to feel pleasure at the sight of turnips and cabbages, wilted for want of water but still standing, and straggling butter beans and snap beans, yellow but edible. She sat down in the furrows and dug into the earth with hands that shook, filling her basket slowly. There would be a good meal at Tara tonight, in spite of the lack of side meat to boil with the vegetables. Perhaps some of the bacon grease Dilcey was using for illumination could be used for seasoning. She must remember to tell Dilcey to use pine knots and save the grease for cooking.

Close to the back step of one cabin, she found a short row of radishes and hunger assaulted her suddenly. A spicy, sharp-tasting radish was exactly what her stomach craved. Hardly waiting to rub the dirt off on her skirt, she bit off half and swallowed it hastily. It was old and coarse and so peppery that tears started in her eyes. No sooner had the lump gone down than her empty outraged stomach revolted and she lay in the soft dirt and vomited tiredly.

The faint niggery smell which crept from the cabin increased her nausea and, without strength to combat it, she kept on retching miserably while the cabins and trees revolved swiftly around her.

After a long time, she lay weakly on her face, the earth as soft and comfortable as a feather pillow, and her mind wandered feebly here and there. She, Scarlett O'Hara, was lying behind a negro cabin, in the midst of ruins, too sick and too weak to move, and no one in the world knew or cared. No one would care if they did know, for everyone had too many troubles of his own to worry about her. And all this was happening to her, Scarlett O'Hara, who had never raised her hand even to pick up her discarded stockings from the floor or to tie the laces of her slippers—Scarlett, whose little headaches and tempers had been coddled and catered to all her life.

As she lay prostrate, too weak to fight off memories and worries, they rushed at her like buzzards waiting for death. No longer had she the strength to say: "I'll think of Mother and Pa and Ashley and all this ruin later—Yes, later when I can stand it." She could not stand it now, but she was thinking of them whether she willed it or not. The thoughts circled and swooped above her, dived down and drove tearing claws and sharp beaks into her mind. For a timeless time, she lay still, her face in the dirt, the sun beating hotly upon her, remembering things and people who were dead, remembering a way of living that was gone forever—and looking upon the harsh vista of the dark future.

When she arose at last and saw again the black ruins of Twelve Oaks, her head was raised high and something that was youth and beauty and potential tenderness had gone out of her face forever. What was past was past. Those who were dead were dead. The lazy luxury of the old days was gone, never to return. And, as Scarlett settled the heavy basket across her arm, she had settled her own mind and her own life.

There was no going back and she was going forward.

Throughout the South for fifty years there would be bitter-eyed women who looked backward, to dead times, to dead men, evoking memories that hurt and were futile, bearing poverty with bitter pride because they had those memories. But Scarlett was never to look back.

She gazed at the blackened stones and, for the last time, she saw Twelve Oaks rise before her eyes as it had once stood, rich and proud, symbol of a race and a way of living. Then she started down the road toward Tara, the heavy basket cutting into her flesh.

Hunger gnawed at her empty stomach again and she said aloud: "As God is my witness, as God is my witness, the Yankees aren't going to lick me. I'm going to live through this, and when it's over, I'm never going to be hungry again. No, nor any of my folks. If I have to steal or kill—as God is my witness, I'm never going to be hungry again."

In the days that followed, Tara might have been Crusoe's desert island, so still it was, so isolated from the rest of the world. The world lay only a few miles away, but a thousand miles of tumbling waves might have stretched between Tara and Jonesboro and Fayetteville and Lovejoy, even between Tara and the neighbors' plantations. With the old horse dead, their one mode of conveyance was gone, and there was neither time nor strength for walking the weary red miles.

Sometimes, in the days of backbreaking work, in the desperate struggle for food and the never-ceasing care of the three sick girls, Scarlett found herself straining her ears for familiar sounds—the shrill laughter of the pickaninnies in the quarters, the creaking of wagons home from the fields, the thunder of Gerald's stallion tearing across the pasture, the crunching of carriage wheels on the drive and the gay voices of neighbors dropping in for an afternoon of gossip. But she listened in vain. The road lay still and deserted and never a cloud of red dust proclaimed the approach of visitors. Tara was an island in a sea of rolling green hills and red fields.

Somewhere was the world and families who ate and slept safely under their own roofs. Somewhere girls in thrice-turned dresses were flirting gaily and singing "When This Cruel War Is Over," as she had done only a few weeks before. Somewhere there was a war and cannon booming and burning towns and men who rotted in hospitals amid sickening-sweet stinks. Somewhere a barefoot army in dirty homespun was marching, fighting, sleeping, hungry and weary with the weariness that comes when hope is gone. And somewhere the hills of Georgia were blue with Yankees, well-fed Yankees on sleek cornstuffed horses.

Beyond Tara was the war and the world. But on the plantation the war and the world did not exist except as memories which must be fought back when they rushed to mind in moments of exhaustion. The world outside receded before the demands of empty and half-empty stomachs and life resolved itself into two related thoughts, food and how to get it.

Food! Food! Why did the stomach have a longer memory than the mind? Scarlett could banish heartbreak but not hunger and each morning as she lay half asleep, before memory brought back to her mind war and hunger, she curled drowsily expecting the sweet smells of bacon frying and rolls baking. And each morning she sniffed so hard to really smell the food she woke herself up.

There were apples, yams, peanuts and milk on the table at Tara but never enough of even this primitive fare. At the sight of them, three times a day, her memory would rush back to the old days, the meals of the old days, the candle-lit table and the food perfuming the air.

How careless they had been of food then, what prodigal waste! Rolls, corn muffins, biscuits and waffles, dripping butter, all at one meal. Ham at one end of the table and fried chicken at the other, collards swimming richly in pot liquor iridescent with grease, snap beans in mountains on brightly flowered porcelain, fried squash, stewed okra, carrots in cream sauce thick enough to cut. And three desserts, so everyone might have his choice, chocolate layer cake, vanilla blanc mange and pound cake topped with sweet whipped cream. The memory of those savory meals had the power to bring tears to her eyes as death and war had failed to do, and the power to turn her ever-gnawing stomach from rumbling emptiness to nausea. For the appetite Mammy had always deplored, the healthy appetite of a nineteen-year-old girl, now was increased fourfold by the hard and unremitting labor she had never known before.

Hers was not the only troublesome appetite at Tara, for wherever she turned hungry faces, black and white, met her eyes. Soon Carreen and Suellen would have the insatiable hunger of typhoid convalescents. Already little Wade whined monotonously: "Wade doan like yams. Wade hungwy."

The others grumbled, too:

"Miss Scarlett, 'ness I gits mo' to eat, I kain nuss neither of these chillun."

"Miss Scarlett, ef Ah doan have mo' in mah stummick, Ah kain split no wood."

"Lamb, Ah's perishin' fer real vittles."

"Daughter, must we always have yams?"

Only Melanie did not complain, Melanie whose face grew thinner and whiter and twitched with pain even in her sleep.

"I'm not hungry, Scarlett. Give my share of the milk to Dilcey. She needs it to nurse the babies. Sick people are never hungry."

It was her gentle hardihood which irritated Scarlett more than the nagging whining voices of the others. She could—and did—shout them down with bitter sarcasm but before Melanie's unselfishness she was helpless, helpless and resentful. Gerald, the negroes and Wade clung to Melanie now, because even in her weakness she was kind and sympathetic, and these days Scarlett was neither.

Wade especially haunted Melanie's room. There was something wrong with Wade, but just what it was Scarlett had no time to discover. She took Mammy's word that the little boy had worms and dosed him with the mixture of dried herbs and bark which Ellen always used to worm the pickaninnies. But the vermifuge only made the child look paler. These days Scarlett hardly thought of Wade as a person. He was only another worry, another mouth to feed. Some day when the present emergency was over, she would play with him, tell him stories and teach him his A B C's but now she did not have the time or the soul or the inclination. And, because he always seemed underfoot when she was most weary and worried, she often spoke sharply to him.

It annoyed her that her quick reprimands brought such acute fright to his round eyes, for he looked so simple minded when he was frightened. She did not realize that the little boy lived shoulder to shoulder with terror too great for an adult to comprehend. Fear lived with Wade, fear that shook his soul and made him wake screaming in the night. Any unexpected noise or sharp word set him to trembling, for in his mind noises and harsh words were inextricably mixed with Yankees and he was more afraid of Yankees than of Prissy's hants.

Until the thunders of the siege began, he had never known anything but a happy, placid, quiet life. Even though his mother paid him little attention, he had known nothing but petting and kind words until the night when he was jerked from slumber to find the sky aflame and the air deafening with explosions. In that night and the day which followed, he had been slapped by his mother for the first time and had heard her voice raised at him in harsh words. Life in the pleasant brick house on Peachtree Street, the only life he knew, had vanished that night and he would never recover from its loss. In the flight from Atlanta, he had understood nothing except that the Yankees were after him and now he still lived in fear that the Yankees would catch him and cut him to pieces. Whenever Scarlett raised her voice in reproof, he went weak with fright as his vague childish memory brought up the horrors of the first time she had ever done it. Now, Yankees and a cross voice were linked forever in his mind and he was afraid of his mother.

Scarlett could not help noticing that the child was beginning to avoid her and, in the rare moments when her unending duties gave her time to think about it, it bothered her a great deal. It was even worse than having him at her skirts all the time and she was offended that his refuge was Melanie's bed where he played quietly at games Melanie suggested or listened to stories she told. Wade adored "Auntee" who had a gentle voice, who always smiled and who never said: "Hush, Wade! You give me a headache" or "Stop fidgeting, Wade, for Heaven's sake!"

Scarlett had neither the time nor the impulse to pet him but it made her jealous to see Melanie do it. When she found him one day standing on his head in Melanie's bed and saw him collapse on her, she slapped him.

"Don't you know better than to jiggle Auntee like that when she's sick? Now, trot right out in the yard and play, and don't come in here again."

But Melanie reached out a weak arm and drew the wailing child to her.

"There, there, Wade. You didn't mean to jiggle me, did you? He doesn't bother me, Scarlett. Do let him stay with me. Let me take care of him. It's the only thing I can do till I get well, and you've got your hands full enough without having to watch him."

"Don't be a goose, Melly," said Scarlett shortly. "You aren't getting well like you should and having Wade fall on your stomach won't help you. Now, Wade, if I ever catch you on Auntee's bed again, I'll wear you out. And stop sniffling. You are always sniffling. Try to be a little man."

Wade flew sobbing to hide himself under the house. Melanie bit her lip and tears came to her eyes, and Mammy standing in the hall, a witness to the scene, scowled and breathed hard. But no one talked back to Scarlett these days. They were all afraid of her sharp tongue, all afraid of the new person who walked in her body.

Scarlett reigned supreme at Tara now and, like others suddenly elevated to authority, all the bullying instincts in her nature rose to the surface. It was not that she was basically unkind. It was because she was so frightened and unsure of herself she was harsh lest others learn her inadequacies and refuse her authority. Besides, there was some pleasure in shouting at people and knowing they were afraid. Scarlett found that it relieved her overwrought nerves. She was not blind to the fact that her personality was changing. Sometimes when her curt orders made Pork stick out his under lip and Mammy mutter: "Some folks rides mighty high dese days," she wondered where her good manners had gone. All the courtesy, all the gentleness Ellen had striven to instill in her had fallen away from her as quickly as leaves fall from trees in the first chill wind of autumn.

Time and again, Ellen had said: "Be firm but be gentle with inferiors, especially darkies." But if she was gentle the darkies would sit in the kitchen all day, talking endlessly about the good old days when a house nigger wasn't supposed to do a field hand's work.

"Love and cherish your sisters. Be kind to the afflicted," said Ellen. "Show tenderness to those in sorrow and in trouble."

She couldn't love her sisters now. They were simply a dead weight on her shoulders. And as for cherishing them, wasn't she bathing them, combing their hair and feeding them, even at the expense of walking miles every day to find vegetables? Wasn't she learning to milk the cow, even though her heart was always in her throat when that fearsome animal shook its horns at her? And as for being kind, that was a waste of time. If she was overly kind to them, they'd probably prolong their stay in bed, and she wanted them on their feet again as soon as possible, so there would be four more hands to help her.

They were convalescing slowly and lay scrawny and weak in their bed. While they had been unconscious, the world had changed. The Yankees had come, the darkies had gone and Mother had died. Here were three unbelievable happenings and their minds could not take them in. Sometimes they believed they must still be delirious and these things had not happened at all. Certainly Scarlett was so changed she couldn't be real. When she hung over the foot of their bed and outlined the work she expected them to do when they recovered, they looked at her as if she were a hobgoblin. It was beyond their comprehension that they no longer had a hundred slaves to do the work. It was beyond their comprehension that an O'Hara lady should do manual labor.

"But, Sister," said Carreen, her sweet childish face blank with consternation. "I couldn't split kindling! It would ruin my hands!"

"Look at mine," answered Scarlett with a frightening smile as she pushed blistered and calloused palms toward her.

"I think you are hateful to talk to Baby and me like this!" cried Suellen. "I think you are lying and trying to frighten us. If Mother were only here, she wouldn't let you talk to us like this! Split kindling, indeed!"

Suellen looked with weak loathing at her older sister, feeling sure Scarlett said these things just to be mean. Suellen had nearly died and she had lost her mother and she was lonely and scared and she wanted to be petted and made much of. Instead, Scarlett looked over the foot of the bed each day, appraising their improvement with a hateful new gleam in her slanting green eyes and talked about making beds, preparing food, carrying water buckets and splitting kindling. And she looked as if she took a pleasure in saying such awful things.

Scarlett did take pleasure in it. She bullied the negroes and harrowed the feelings of her sisters not only because she was too worried and strained and tired to do otherwise but because it helped her to forget her own bitterness that everything her mother had told her about life was wrong.

Nothing her mother had taught her was of any value whatsoever now and Scarlett's heart was sore and puzzled. It did not occur to her that Ellen could not have foreseen the collapse of the civilization in which she raised her daughters, could not have anticipated the disappearings of the places in society for which she trained them so well. It did not occur to her that Ellen had looked down a vista of placid future years, all like the uneventful years of her own life, when she had taught her to be gentle and gracious, honorable and kind, modest and truthful. Life treated women well when they had learned those lessons, said Ellen.

Scarlett thought in despair: "Nothing, no, nothing, she taught me is of any help to me! What good will kindness do me now? What value is gentleness? Better that I'd learned to plow or chop cotton like a darky. Oh, Mother, you were wrong!"

She did not stop to think that Ellen's ordered world was gone and a brutal world had taken its place, a world wherein every standard, every value had changed. She only saw, or thought she saw, that her mother had been wrong, and she changed swiftly to meet this new world for which she was not prepared.

Only her feeling for Tara had not changed. She never came wearily home across the fields and saw the sprawling white house that her heart did not swell with love and the joy of homecoming. She never looked out of her window at green pastures and red fields and tall tangled swamp forest that a sense of beauty did not fill her. Her love for this land with its softly rolling hills of bright-red soil, this beautiful red earth that was blood colored, garnet, brick dust, vermilion, which so miraculously grew green bushes starred with white puffs, was one part of Scarlett which did not change when all else was changing. Nowhere else in the world was there land like this.

When she looked at Tara she could understand, in part, why wars were fought. Rhett was wrong when he said men fought wars for money. No, they fought for swelling acres, softly furrowed by the plow, for pastures green with stubby cropped grass, for lazy yellow rivers and white houses that were cool amid magnolias. These were the only things worth fighting for, the red earth which was theirs and would be their sons', the red earth which would bear cotton for their sons and their sons' sons.

The trampled acres of Tara were all that was left to her, now that Mother and Ashley were gone, now that Gerald was senile from shock, and money and darkies and security and position had vanished overnight. As from another world she remembered a conversation with her father about the land and wondered how she could have been so young, so ignorant, as not to understand what he meant when he said that the land was the one thing in the world worth fighting for.

"For 'tis the only thing in the world that lasts . . . and to anyone with a drop of Irish blood in them the land they live on is like their mother. . . .'Tis the only thing worth working for, fighting for, dying for."

Yes, Tara was worth fighting for, and she accepted simply and without question the fight. No one was going to get Tara away from her. No one was going to set her and her people adrift on the charity of relatives. She would hold Tara, if she had to break the back of every person on it.

Conrad Aiken

Strange Moonlight

It had been a tremendous week—colossal. Its reverberations around him hardly yet slept—his slightest motion or thought made a vast symphony of them, like a breeze in a forest of bells. In the first place, he had filched a volume of Poe's tales from his mother's bookcase, and had had in consequence a delirious night in inferno. Down, down he had gone with heavy clangs about him, coiling spouts of fire licking dryly at an iron sky, and a strange companion, of protean shape and size, walking and talking beside him. For the most part, this companion seemed to be nothing but a voice and a wing—an enormous jagged black wing, soft and drooping like a bat's; he had noticed veins in it. As for the voice, it had been singularly gentle. If it was mysterious, that was no doubt because he himself was stupid. Certainly it had sounded placid and reasonable, exactly, in fact, like his father's explaining a problem in mathematics; but, though he had noticed the orderly and logical structure, and felt the inevitable approach toward a vast and beautiful or terrible conclusion, the nature and meaning of the conclusion itself always escaped him. It was as if, always, he had come just too late. When, for example, he had come at last to the black wall that inclosed the infernal city, and seen the arched gate, the voice had certainly said that if he hurried he would see, through the arch, a far, low landscape of extraordinary wonder. He had hurried, but it had been in vain. He had reached the gate, and for the tiniest fraction of an instant he had even glimpsed the wide green of fields and trees, a winding blue ribbon of water, and a gleam of intense light touching to brilliance some far object. But then, before he had time to notice more than that every detail in this fairy landscape seemed to lead toward a single shining solution, a dazzling significance, suddenly the infernal rain, streaked fire and rolling smoke, had swept it away. Then the voice had seemed to become ironic. He had failed, and he felt like crying.

He had still, the next morning, felt that he might, if the opportunity offered, see that vision. It was always just round the corner, just at the head of the stairs, just over the next page. But other adventures had intervened. Prize-day, at school, had come upon him as suddenly as a thunderstorm—the ominous hushed gathering of the entire school into one large room, the tense air of expectancy, the solemn speeches, all had reduced him to a state of acute terror. There was something unintelligible and sinister about it. He had, from first to last, a peculiar physical sensation that something threatened him, and here and there, in the interminable vague speeches, a word seemed to have eyes and to stare at him. His prescience had been correct—abruptly his name had been called, he had walked unsteadily amid applause to the teacher's desk, had received a small black pasteboard box; and then had cowered in his chair again, with the blood in his temples beating like gongs. When it was over, he had literally run away—he didn't stop till he reached the park. There, among the tombstones (the park had once been a graveyard) and trumpet-vines, he sat on the grass and opened the box. He was dazzled. The medal was of gold, and rested on a tiny blue satin cushion. His name was engraved on it—yes, actually cut into the gold; he felt the incisions with his fingernail. It was an experience not wholly to be comprehended. He put the box down in the grass and detached himself from it, lay full length, resting his chin on his wrist, and stared first at a tombstone and then at the small gold object, as if to discover the relation between them. Humming-birds, tombstones, trumpet-vines, and a gold medal. Amazing. He unpinned the medal from its cushion, put the box in his pocket, and walked slowly homeward, carrying the small, live, gleaming thing between fingers and thumb as if it were a bee. This was an experience to be carefully concealed from mother and father. Possibly he would tell Mary and John. . . . Unfortunately, he met his father as he was going in the door, and was thereafter drowned, for a day, in a glory without significance. He felt ashamed, and put the medal away in a drawer, sternly forbidding Mary and John to look at it. Even so, he was horribly conscious of it—its presence there burned him unceasingly. Nothing afforded escape from it, not even sitting under the peach tree and whittling a boat.

II.

The oddest thing was the way these and other adventures of the week all seemed to unite, as if they were merely aspects of the same thing. Everywhere lurked that extraordinary hint of the enigma and its shining solution. On Tuesday morning, when it was pouring with rain, and he and Mary and John were conducting gigantic military operations in the back hall, with hundreds of paper soldiers, tents, cannon, battleships, and forts, suddenly through the tall open window, a goldfinch flew in from the rain, beat wildly against a pane of glass, darted several times to and fro above their heads, and finally, finding the open window, flashed out. It flew to the peach tree, rested there for a moment, and then over the outhouse and away. He saw it rising and falling in the rain. This was beautiful—it was like the vision in the infernal city, like the medal in the grass. He found it impossible to go on with the Battle of Gettysburg and abandoned it to Mary and John, who instantly started to quarrel. Escape was necessary, and he went into his own room, shut the door, lay on his bed, and began thinking about Caroline Lee.

John Lee had taken him there to see his new air-gun and a bag of BB shot. The strange house was dim and exciting. A long winding dark staircase went up from near the front door, a clock was striking in a far room, a small beautiful statue of a lady, slightly pinkish, and looking as if it had been dug out of the earth, stood on a table. The wallpaper beside the staircase was rough and hairy. Upstairs, in the playroom, they found Caroline, sitting on the floor with a picture book. She was learning to read, pointing at the words with her finger. He was struck by the fact that, although she was extraordinarily strange and beautiful, John Lee did not seem to be aware of it and treated her as if she were quite an ordinary sort of person. This gave him courage, and after the air-gun had been examined, and the bag of BB shot emptied of its gleaming heavy contents and then luxuriously refilled, he told her some of the words she couldn't make out. "And what's this?" she had said—he could still hear her say it, quite clearly. She was thin, smaller than himself, with dark hair and large pale eyes, and her forehead and hands looked curiously transparent. He particularly noticed her hands when she brought her five-dollar goldpiece to show him, opening a little jewel box which had in it also a necklace of yellow beads from Egypt and a pink shell from Tybee Beach. She gave him the goldpiece to look at, and while he was looking at it put the beads round her neck. "Now, I'm an Egyptian!" she said, and laughed shyly, running her fingers to and fro over the smooth beads. A fearful temptation came upon him. He coveted the goldpiece, and thought that it would be easy to steal it. He shut his hand over it and it was gone. If it had been John's, he might have done so, but, as it was, he opened his hand again and put the goldpiece back in the box. Afterwards, he stayed for a long while, talking with John and Caroline. The house was mysterious and rich, and he hadn't at all wanted to go out of it, or back to his own humdrum existence. Besides, he liked to hear Caroline talking.

But although he had afterwards for many days wanted to go back to that house, to explore further its dim rich mysteriousness, and had thought about it a great deal, John hadn't again suggested a visit, and he himself had felt a curious reluctance about raising the subject. It had been, apparently, a vision that was not to be repeated, an incursion into a world that was so beautiful and strange that one was permitted of it only the briefest of glimpses. He had, almost, to reassure himself that the house was really there, and for that reason he made rather a point of walking home from school with John Lee. Yes, the house was there—he saw John climb the stone steps and open the huge green door. There was never a sign of Caroline, however, nor any mention of her; until one day he heard from another boy that she was ill with scarlet fever, and observed that John had stayed away from school. The news didn't startle or frighten him. On the contrary, it seemed just the sort of romantic privilege in which such fortunate people would indulge. He felt a certain delicacy about approaching the house, however, to see if the red quarantine sign had been affixed by the door, and carefully avoided Gordon Square on his way home from school. Should he write her a letter or send her a present of marbles? For neither action did there seem to be sufficient warrant. But he found it impossible to do nothing, and later in the afternoon, by a very circuitous route which took him past the county jail—where he was thrilled by actually seeing a prisoner looking out between the gray iron bars—he slowly made his way to Gordon Square and from a safe distance, more or less hiding himself behind a palmetto tree, looked for a long while at the wonderful house, and saw, sure enough, the red sign.

Three days later he heard that Caroline Lee was dead. The news stunned him. Surely it could not be possible? He felt stifled, frightened, and incredulous. In a way, it was just what one would expect of Caroline, but none the less he felt outraged. How was it possible for anyone, whom one actually knew, to *die*? Particularly anyone so vividly and beautifully remembered! The indignity, the horror, of death obsessed him. *Had* she actually died? He went again to Gordon Square, not knowing precisely what it was that he expected to find, and saw something white hanging by the green door. But if, as it appeared, it was true that Caroline Lee, somewhere inside the house, lay dead, lay motionless, how did it happen that he, who was so profoundly concerned, had not at all been consulted, had not been invited to come and talk with her, and now found himself so utterly and hopelessly and forever excluded—from the house, as from her? This was a thing which he could not understand. As he walked home, pondering it, he thought of the five-dollar goldpiece. What would become of it? Probably John would get it, and, if so, he would steal it from him. . . . All the same, he was glad he hadn't taken it.

To this reflection he came back many times, as now once more with the Battle of Gettysburg raging in the next room. If he had actually taken it, what a horror it would have been! As it was, the fact that he had resisted the temptation, restored the goldpiece to the box, seemed to have been a tribute to Caroline's beauty and strangeness. Yes, for nobody else would he have made the refusal—nobody on earth. But, for her, it had been quite simple, a momentary pang quickly lost in the pleasure of hearing her voice, watching her pale hands twisting the yellow beads, and helping her with her reading. "And what's this?" she had said, and "Now I'm an Egyptian!" . . . What was death that could put an end to a clear voice saying such things? . . . Mystery was once more about him, the same mystery that had shone in the vision of the infernal city. There was something beautiful which he could not understand. He had felt it while he was lying in the grass among the tombstones, looking at the medal; he had felt it when the goldfinch darted in from the rain and then out again. All these things seemed in some curious way to fit together.

III.

The same night, after he had gone to bed, this feeling of enormous and complicated mystery came upon him again with oppressive weight. He lay still, looking from his pillow through the tall window at the moonlight on the white outhouse wall, and again it seemed to him that the explanation for everything was extraordinarily near at hand if he could only find it. The mystery was like the finest of films, like the moonlight on the white wall. Surely, beneath it, there was something solid and simple. He heard someone walk across the yard, with steps that seemed astoundingly far apart and slow. The steps ceased, a door creaked. Then there was a cough. It was old Selena, the Negro cook, going out for wood. He heard the sticks being piled up, then the creak of the door again, and again the slow steps on the hard baked ground of the yard, æons apart. How did the peach tree look in the moonlight? Would its leaves be dark, or shiny? And the chinaberry tree? He thought of the two trees standing there motionless in the moonlight, and at last felt that he must get out of bed and look at them. But when he had reached the hall, he heard his mother's voice from downstairs, and he went and lay on the old sofa in the hall, listening. Could he have heard aright? His mother had just called his father "Boy!" Amazing!

"It's two parties *every* week, and sometimes three or four, that's excessive. You know it is."

"Darling, I *must* have *some* recreation!"

His father laughed in a peculiar angry way that he had never heard before—as strange, indeed, as his mother's tone had been.

"Recreation's all right," he said, "but you're neglecting your family. If it goes on, I'll have another child—that's all."

He got off the sofa and went softly down the stairs to the turn of the railing. He peered over the banisters with infinite caution, and what he saw filled him with horror. His mother was sitting on his father's knee, with her arms about his neck. She was kissing him. How awful! . . . He couldn't look at it. What on earth, he wondered as he climbed back into bed, was it all about? There was something curious in the way they were talking, something not at all like fathers and mothers, but more like children, though he couldn't in the least understand it. At the same time, it was offensive.

He began to make up a conversation with Caroline Lee. She was sitting under the peach tree with him, reading her book. What beautiful hands she had! They were transparent, somehow, like her forehead, and her dark hair and large pale eyes delighted him. Perhaps she *was* an Egyptian!

"It must be nice to live in your house," he said.

"Yes, it's very nice. And you haven't seen half of it, either."

"No, I haven't. I'd like to see it all. I liked the hairy wallpaper and the pink statue of the lady on the table. Are there any others like it?"

"Oh, yes, lots and lots! In the secret room downstairs, where you heard the silver clock striking, there are fifty other statues, all more beautiful than that one, and a collection of clocks of every kind."

"Is your father very rich?"

"Yes, he's richer than anybody. He has a special carved ivory box to keep his collars in."

"What does it feel like to die—were you sorry?"

"Very sorry! But it's really quite easy—you just hold your breath and shut your eyes."

"Oh!"

"And when you're lying there, after you've died, you're really just pretending. You keep very still, and you have your eyes *almost* shut, but really you know everything! You watch the people and listen to them."

"But don't you want to talk to them, or get out of bed, or out of your coffin?"

"Well, yes, at first you do—but it's nicer than being alive."

"Why?"

"Oh, I don't know! You understand everything so easily!"

"How nice that must be!"

"It is."

"But after they've shut you up in a coffin and sung songs over you and carried you to Bonaventure and buried you in the ground, and you're down there in the dark with all that earth above you—isn't that horrible?"

"Oh, no! . . . As soon as nobody is looking, when they've all gone home to tea, you just get up and walk away. You climb out of the earth just as easily as you'd climb out of bed."

"That's how you're here now, I suppose."

"Of course!"

"Well, it's very nice."

"It's lovely. . . . Don't I look just as well as ever?"

"Yes, you do."

There was a pause, and then Caroline said:

"I know you wanted to steal my goldpiece—I was awfully glad when you put it back. If you had asked me for it, I'd have given it to you."

"I like you very much, Caroline. Can I come to Bonaventure and play with you?"

"I'm afraid not. You'd have to come in the dark."

"But I could bring a lantern."

"Yes, you could do that."

. . . It seemed to him that they were no longer sitting under the peach tree, but walking along the white shell-road to Bonaventure. He held the lantern up beside a chinquapin tree, and Caroline reached up with her pale, small hands and picked two chinquapins. Then they crossed the little bridge, walking carefully between the rails on the sleepers. Mossy trees were all about them; the moss, in long festoons, hung lower and lower, and thicker and thicker, and the wind made a soft, seething sound as it sought a way through the gray ancient forest.

IV.

It had been his intention to explore, the next morning, the vault under the mulberry tree in the park—his friend Harry had mentioned that it was open, and that one could go down very dusty steps and see, on the dark floor, a few rotted boards and a bone or two. At breakfast he enlisted Mary and John for the expedition; but then there were unexpected developments. His father and mother had abruptly decided that the whole family would spend the day at Tybee Beach. This was festive and magnificent beyond belief. The kitchen became a turmoil. Selena ran to and fro with sugar sandwiches, pots of deviled ham, cookies, hard-boiled eggs, and a hundred other things; piles of beautiful sandwiches were exquisitely folded up in shining, clean napkins, and the wicker basket was elaborately packed. John and Mary decided to take their pails with them, and stamped up and downstairs, banging the pails with the shovels. He himself was a little uncertain what to take. He stood by his desk wondering. He would like to take Poe's tales, but that was out of the question, for he wasn't supposed to have the book at all. Marbles, also, were dismissed as unsuitable. He finally took his gold medal out of its drawer and put it in his pocket. He would keep it a secret, of course.

All the way to the station he was conscious of the medal burning in his pocket. He closed his fingers over it, and again felt it to be a live thing, as if it were buzzing, beating invisible wings. Would his fingers have a waxy smell, as they did after they'd been holding a June bug, or tying a thread to one of its legs? . . . Father carried the basket, Mary and John clanked their pails, everybody was talking and laughing. They climbed into the funny, undignified little train, which almost immediately was lurching over the wide, green marshes, rattling over red-iron bridges enormously complicated with girders and trusses. Great excitement when they passed the gray stone fort, Fort Pulaski. They'd seen it once from the river, when they were on the steamer going to the cotton islands. His father leaned down beside Mary to tell her about Fort Pulaski, just as a cloud shadow, crossing it, made it somber. How nice his father's smile was! He had never noticed it before. It made him feel warm and shy. He looked out at the interminable green marshes, the flying clouds of rice-birds, the channels of red water lined with red mud, and listened intently to the strange complex rhythm of the wheels on the rails and the prolonged melancholy wail of the whistle. How curious it all was! His mother was sitting opposite him, very quiet, her gray eyes turned absently toward the window. She wasn't looking at things—she was thinking. If she had been looking at things, her eyes would have moved to and fro, as Mary's were doing.

"Mother," he said, "did you bring our bathing suits?"

"Yes, dear."

The train was rounding a curve and slowing down. They had suddenly left the marshes and were among low sand dunes covered with tall grass. He saw a man, very red-faced, just staggering over the top of one of the dunes and waving a stick. . . . It was hot. They filed slowly off the train and one by one jumped down into the burning sand. How strange it was to walk in! They laughed and shrieked, feeling themselves helpless, ran and jumped, straddled up the steep root-laced sides of dunes and slid down again in slow, warm avalanches of lazy sand. Mother and father, picking their way between the dunes, walked slowly ahead, carrying the basket between them—his father pointed at something. The sunlight came down heavily like sheets of solid brass and they could feel the heat of the sand on their cheeks. Then at last they came out on the enormous white dazzling beach with its millions of shells, its black-and-white-striped lighthouse, and the long, long sea, indolently blue, spreading out slow, soft lines of foam, and making an interminable rushing murmur like trees in a wind.

He felt instantly a desire, in all this space and light, to run for miles and miles. His mother and father sat under a striped parasol. Mary and

John, now barefooted, had begun laborious and intense operations in the sand at the water's edge, making occasional sallies into the sliding water. He began walking away along the beach close to the waves, keeping his eye out for any particularly beautiful shell, and taking great care not to step on jellyfish. Suppose a school of flying fish, such as he had seen from the ship, should swim in close to the beach and then, by mistake, fly straight up onto the sand? How delightful that would be! It would be almost as exciting as finding buried treasure, a rotten chest full of goldpieces and seaweed and sand. He had often dreamt of thrusting his hand into such a sea-chest and feeling the small, hard, beautiful coins mixed with sand and weed. Some people said that Captain Kidd had buried treasure on Tybee Beach. Perhaps he'd better walk a little closer to the dunes, where it was certainly more likely that treasure would have been hidden. . . . He climbed a hot dune, taking hold of the feathery grass, scraping his bare legs on the coarse leaves, and filling his shoes with warm sand. The dune was scooped at the top like a volcano, the hollow all ringed with tall, whistling grass, a natural hiding place, snug and secret. He lay down, made excessively smooth a hand's breadth of sand, then took the medal out of his pocket and placed it there. It blazed beautifully. Was it as nice as the five-dollar goldpiece would have been? He liked especially the tiny links of the little gold chains by which the shield hung from the pin-bar. If only Caroline could see it! Perhaps if he stayed here, hidden from the family, and waited till they had gone back home, Caroline would somehow know where he was and come to him as soon as it was dark. He wasn't quite sure what would be the shortest way from Bonaventure, but Caroline would know—certainly. Then they would spend the night here, talking. He would exchange his medal for the five-dollar goldpiece, and perhaps she would bring, folded in a square of silk, the little pink statue. . . . Thus equipped, their house would be perfect. . . . He would tell her about the goldfinch interrupting the Battle of Gettysburg.

V.

The chief event of the afternoon was the burial of his father, who had on his bathing suit. He and Mary and John all excitedly labored at this. When they had got one leg covered, the other would suddenly burst hairily out, or an arm would shatter its mold, and his father would laugh uproariously. Finally they had him wholly buried, all except his head, in a beautiful smooth mound. On top of this they put the two pails, a lot of pink shells in a row, like the buttons of a coat, and a collection of seaweeds. Mother, lying under her parasol, laughed lazily, deliciously. For the first time during the day she seemed to be really happy. She began pelting small shells at father, laughing in an odd, delightful, teasing way, as if she was a girl, and father pretended to be furious. How exactly like a new grave he looked! It was singularly as Caroline had described it, for there he was all alive in it, and talking, and able to get up whenever he liked. Mary and John, seeing mother throw shells, and hearing her teasing laughter, and father's comic rage, became suddenly excited. They began throwing things wildly—shells, handfuls of seaweed, and at last sand. At this, father suddenly leapt out of his tomb, terrifying them, scattered his grave clothes in every direction, and galloped gloriously down the beach into the sea. The upturned brown soles of his feet followed him casually into a long, curling green wave, and then his head came up shaking like a dog's and blowing water, and his strong white arms flashed slowly over and over in the sunlight as he swam far out. How magnificent! . . . He would like to be able to do that, to swim out and out and out, with a sea-gull flying close beside him, talking.

Later, when they had changed into their clothes again in the salty-smelling wooden bathhouse, they had supper on the veranda of the huge hotel. A band played, the colored waiters bowed and grinned. The sky turned pink, and began to dim; the sea darkened, making a far sorrowful sound; and twilight deepened slowly, slowly into night. The moon, which had looked like a white thin shell in the afternoon, turned now to the brightest silver, and he thought, as they walked silently toward the train, of which they could see the long row of yellow windows, that the beach and dunes looked more beautiful by moonlight than by sunlight. . . . How mysterious the flooded marshes looked, too, with the cold moon above them! They reminded him of something, he couldn't remember what. . . . Mary and John fell asleep in the train; his father and mother were silent. Someone in the car ahead was playing a concertina, and the plaintive sound mingled curiously with the clacking of the rails, the rattle of bridges, the long, lugubrious cry of the whistle. Hoo-o! Hoo-o! Where was it they were going—was it to anything so simple as home, the familiar house, the two familiar trees, or were they, rather, speeding like a fiery comet toward the world's edge, to plunge out into the unknown and fall down and down forever?

No, certainly it was not to the familiar. . . . Everything was changed and ghostly. The long street, in the moonlight, was like a deep river, at the bottom of which they walked, making scattered, thin sounds on the stones, and listening intently to the whisperings of elms and palmettos. And their house, when at last they stopped before it, how strange it was! The moonlight, falling through the two tall swaying oaks, cast a moving pattern of shadow and light all over its face. Slow swirls and spirals of black and silver, dizzy gallops, quiet pools of light abruptly shattered, all silently followed the swishing of leaves against the moon. It was like a vine of moonlight, which suddenly grew all over the house, smothering everything with its multitudinous swift leaves and tendrils of pale silver, and then as suddenly faded out. He stared up at this while his father fitted the key into the lock, feeling the ghostly vine grow strangely over his face and hands. Was it in this, at last, that he would find the explanation of all that bewildered him? Caroline, no doubt, would understand it; she was a sort of moonlight herself. He went slowly up the stairs. But as he took the medal and a small pink shell out of his pocket, and put them on his desk, he realized at last that Caroline was dead.

Vereen Bell

From *Swamp Water*

The swamp, with its morasses, and jungle growths so thick they said you had to back up to bat your eyes, wasn't easily invaded. But the swamp was full of water, slow-flowing water; and this had to come out somewhere. So Ben paddled steadily up the black little Suwannee River.

Every hour or so he stopped to blow the cow horn that was slung with a piece of rawhide around his neck, then to listen for the far-off answering bay of a lost hound dog. The sound startled the cat squirrels that frolicked in the tupelo trees, and once brought to the surface a big alligator turtle with its corrugated shell and malignant stare. A joree ran along the leaf-littered sandbank, chirping with absent-minded friendliness and twisting his black-hooded head.

The sun rode high. Ben went ashore and unwrapped his ham-and-biscuit lunch, and ate, squatting by the water's edge and watching the redbellies that rose with popping mouths to take his crumbs. When he had finished, he blew the horn some more, and listened, stock-still, but no sound came back except the scream of a fish eagle.

Again he paddled, now beginning to feel doubtful about the wisdom of following the river. After a while, though, the firm sandbanks sank and became low muck, bordered with lush green maiden cane. Instead of tupelo bushes there were runty bays, and titi bushes, and paintroot. Ahead rose tall trees—the tallest he had ever seen. The boat was entering a long, narrow lake, and he knew he was in the swamp. The wild majesty of it caught at his throat.

On the left side of the lake were the cypresses, taller than highland pines, savagely graceful from their wet swollen boles to their slim tops with distant greener-than-grass foliage and graybeard moss, gently waving. There was row after row of them, as far as the eye could see, each of them kingly, casting their green shadows into the still, bonnet-covered water. Hundreds of wood ducks flew about in them, squealing, lighting on the slender branches, their thin cries echoing throughout the vast green cathedral. A poor-joe bird rose in agitation, squawling indignantly back at the boatman.

On the right side of the lake was a jungle wall of many colors, of bright bay and amber berries and yellow jessamine and scarlet ivy trumpets and pink hurrah blossoms. The white of the Cherokee roses was spattered everywhere. He paddled on, uneasily. The gators in the lake watched him curiously. They sank before his boat, and presently came up behind it, hissing. Once he brought up a two-foot gator on his paddle blade.

Three half-grown bears in a bee tree stopped their busy work to regard the visitor, raising their noses high to catch scent of him. A huge cottonmouth, big around as a man's neck, lay near the boat, rocking gently in the undulating water, and watching Ben with a stare of cold hate. Its tongue licked in and out like live rubber. Ben swung the paddle against the flat, evil head. "Git!" he said, and the snake fled in zigzag alarm into the dense water grass.

The wood ducks were quiet now, and a weird hush fell over the swamp. The silence grew, like a dumb monster watching solemnly from the cypresses. Ben shivered. He struck the side of the boat with the paddle, just to hear a noise, but even that sound seemed smothered.

This'd be a ideal time to give a good hard blow on the horn, while everything's so unnatural quiet. He raised the cool horn to his mouth, then hesitated, his animal instincts warning him not to make his presence conspicuous. But how would he find Trouble if he didn't blow the horn?

Finally, he blew. The sound was incredibly loud, echoing and re-echoing, until the sky was full of startled birds, ducks and limpkins and bitterns and ibises. They disappeared, and again the silence came, broken only by something like the faint far-off honking of a wild goose.

Ben jumped. The wild-goose sound was a distant dog's baying. Excitedly he blew the horn again, and presently the answer came again, floating thinly to him, then suddenly breaking off. He blew the horn repeatedly, and got no further answer. But now he had the direction. He started paddling.

The lake narrowed, became shallow. Ben changed from paddle to pole, and sent the boat through the black water, rustling against the lily pads. On one side of the narrow run the thicket persisted. On the other now the cypresses were gone, and instead there was a vast bogland of half-petrified logs and charred stumps and stagnant water. Ben figured that Trouble had been obliged to go through the thicket at one time or another. Perhaps, by going on all fours, he himself could get through.

He shoved the boat under the bushes to the bank, and stepped out onto the semisolid earth. At the weight of his step, bushes thirty feet away trembled. On his knees, he saw a small opening, a tunnel through the low bushes of the thicket. He squeezed into it, and wriggled his way along for several feet. The thorns fought at him, and the muscular vines seemed deliberately to entwine his hands and feet.

Abruptly he heard a noise, and at the same time he noticed that the ground beneath him was wavering, like a gentle ocean swell. Coming toward him in the tunnel was a big gator, running with his flat head parallel to the ground, his great jaw agape so that Ben could see the yellow stoblike teeth and beefy tongue. Before Ben could think at all, the monster was at him, and Ben instinctively rolled sidewise, pressing his body hard into the matted vines and thorns. The claws of the gator's hurrying back foot raked against his thigh, ripping the denim trousers. Then there was a splash outside somewhere, and silence.

Trembling, Ben turned around and headed out. *Might meet another old son of a gun that don't want to be cut off from the water.*

Two hundred yards farther on, he found an opening in the thicket, and through it he could see high land—palmetto clumps and a pine forest. He looked at the sun—halfway down. He shoved his boat up on the bank and got out.

Gun under his arm, he stepped through the opening in the thicket. There was a quick movement somewhere near him. Ben whirled, and met a brilliant, abrupt shattering of consciousness.

It was almost dusk when Ben opened his eyes. His hands were tied behind him tightly; his back was against an oak sapling. A fire flickered around a blackened pot. Beyond stood a rough palmetto-roof shelter; to one of its cabbage-palm supports was tied the hound, Trouble, who lay quietly panting, watching Ben. A big buck deer hung between two live oaks, its skin in places loose and wrinkled, as if it had been rolled back to expose the saddle meat.

The man stood down near the water's edge, a tall alert figure in a rough-cut buckskin shirt and short buckskin trousers that were hardly trousers at all; barefooted. He was so dark Ben at first thought he was an Indian. His beard was thin, and in tufts, a spot of it on each jaw, another on his chin. The man came back to the fire, walking absolutely without sound, almost as if he were not actually touching the earth; but his steps were springy, exuberant. His legs were very long and hard and knotty; his knees bulged, like two apples in a pair of stockings. There was no one else; it was a one-man camp.

Ben's head throbbed; his eyeballs moved in little puddles of pain, and he seemed to hear his eyelids open and close, as if they were paper. A thick matting of dried blood and hair covered the aching back of his head.

Ben watched the man stirring the pot, almost too sick to be interested. He wouldn't have believed any living thing could have got as close to him, without his knowing it, as the man must have been.

"If you've done hurt that dog," Ben said, "you damn shore better be careful how you untie me from here!"

The man came to him. "Thought once I might've knocked your brains clean out, the way you done," he said. "That dog's all right, less'n a full belly is bad for him."

Ben flexed his wrists. "How come you give me that lick on the head?"

The man went back to the fire, inspecting the big pot, and then the smaller earthen one in the embers. He took an absorbed interest in the cooking. He would squat there motionlessly, like some sort of bony, graceful animal, then in that springy step move around to the other side, and squat again, watching.

"Hit's a long time since I tasted coffee. My God, hit smells good. When I found it in your boat, I et a handful of grounds."

Ben said, slowly, "We was wondering, the other night, what ever went with you."

The man looked down his shoulder at him, sharply. "Did you come at me?"

"I come at my dog, that's all."

Tom Keefer squatted in silence, staring thoughtfully into the fire, his mind no longer on the coffee. Finally he ate, and fed Trouble. Then he began sharpening his hunting knife, slowly and carefully.

"Bud, I'm mighty sorry you turnt out to know me," Keefer said.

Ben watched the knife. The blade shone, the thin red light from the fire dancing along the edge like blood.

"If you was to let me take my dog and go, I'd promise not to tell it on you about hiding in Okefenokee," Ben suggested.

"I don't expect I could do that," Keefer told him. He wiped the knife clean, and looked at Ben appraisingly, as at a hog about to be butchered.

Chill sweat stood on Ben's upper lip. *Father, let him do it with a quick lick.*

An hour passed.

Still Tom Keefer delayed, cutting little pieces of bark off to test the knife edge. He went down to the water's edge and drank, his long, angular frame flat on the black wet muck. When he came back, he again sharpened the knife, with painful deliberation.

Tom Keefer muttered, "I can still see that other fellow flopping around and thumping on the floor boards, see him like it was last night, and he God shore needed killing. What you reckon I'll have on my mind from now on, when the owls is chuckling and gators is noisy and I cain't git to sleep?" Finally he shoved his knife into its wild-hog-hide sheath purposefully. "Well, hit won't be no boy with a cut throat on my mind."

"You ain't goan do it?"

"No, I ain't."

Ben was too sick to feel relief.

After a while, Keefer said, "But you're in Okefenokee for good, Bud. If I let you go back, you'll tell it on me, first thing."

"Not if I said I wouldn't."

"I wouldn't trust nobody. Your word don't mean nothing to me, not when my living er hanging's independent on it."

"I ain't goan stay. I'll git away sometime, if I have to bust you on the head when you ain't looking."

"Bud, when we git where we're going, they ain't but one way to find your way outn this swamp—and that's with me showing you. Maybe you don't know, but Okefenokee's a mighty big wet place. They's seven hundred square miles of it, and not no signposts ner nobody to tell you. I don't believe the man is alive that can catch me when I ain't looking, but if you was to, you'd parish to death trying to git out by yourself. I ain't just running off at the mouth; you'll see."

Ben did see. That night they moved camp. In Keefer's boat for two hours they delved deeper into the mysterious swamp, while the night was alive and ominous around them. Ben tried to keep his sense of direction, but finally he gave up; the swamp all looked alike. Keefer had not been lying. Only by purest luck would a man live to find his way out. But, Ben thought, that didn't matter. If he got a chance, he meant to try it.

In the days that followed, he learned that Keefer was more swamp animal than man. Without his ever seeming to be particularly alert, even when they were out visiting Keefer's quail and turkey traps, there was never a moment when Ben felt that he had an opportunity to attack. Keefer had of course taken the gun, and kept the ax and any other possible weapons out of Ben's reach.

If it hadn't been that he was a prisoner, the life wouldn't have been so bad. The forays for food with Trouble and Keefer occupied some of the time.

"I give out of gunpowder months ago," Keefer said. "Learned to do plumb without it. We'll save yourn till we need it to keep from gitting panther-et er something."

They were searching for a bee tree near a pond. A swamp bear appeared on the opposite side, to hunt the soft bank for turtle eggs, but he caught scent of them, and disappeared with a great crackling of brush. After a while, a small drove of wood ducks came into the pond, whimpering, and lit. The drakes moved about busily, their bright feathers and head tufts catching the morning sun.

Presently there was another movement of wings, and a large bird dropped into the water a few feet from the brush-covered shore, straightening pink feathers. For a moment then it waited motionlessly, and finally thrust its spoon-shaped bill down into the water.

"We goan have curlew for dinner," Keefer whispered. Screened by bay bushes, he crept around the edge of the pond on his belly, moving when the curlew had its head down feeding, lying immobile when its head was up. After what seemed to Ben an interminable time, Keefer was within five yards of the bird, shielded by the low brush. In his hand he held a three-foot piece of lightwood, and now, quickly, he rose and threw. The missile struck the surprised bird's head. Beating its pink wings upon the water, the curlew flopped out toward the center of the pond and then died with a feeble trembling.

Keefer shrugged out of his meager buckskin shirt and trousers, and slid into the water like an otter, and swam toward the curlew. When he came back, Ben was waiting with the sheath knife Keefer had left with his clothes. When Keefer reached the shallower water and stood up Ben jabbed the knife point hard against a long scar on the naked brown belly, and drops of blood mingled with the dripping water.

"Now's a good time to make up your mind where you want to take me out of here peaceable," Ben said, "er have me bury this blade in your guts a little bit at the time until you decide to."

Keefer dropped the curlew. "I thought about that knife in my clothes right after I got in the water," he said.

Later, when Ben was thinking back, he figured just about what must have happened. Keefer's iron hand, all of a sudden, was clamped around Ben's wrist. At the same time, Keefer sucked his belly in, away from the knife, and before Ben could shove the blade forward against the steely grip, Keefer had slipped sideways. Keefer's hard elbow struck Ben's jaw with jolting force. As Ben fell back, Keefer snapped the arm that held the knife around behind Ben's back, and shoved upward with such savage force that Ben's fingers sprang open in sudden, agonized pain, and the knife leaped into the bay bush.

"You see there?" Keefer said, breathing easily.

"Not quite yet!" Ben said, turning quickly, dragging his arm out of Keefer's grasp, feeling the burning pain that raced through strained ligaments.

For several minutes, then, they fought. Quick as a timber rattler, Keefer was almost impossible to hit; and, being wet and naked, hard to hold. Furthermore, those long, ropy muscles held power and what seemed to be absolute tirelessness. Just when Ben thought he was getting slightly the upper hand, he found himself on his back in the silty water, with Keefer's hard hands around his throat, and he knew he either had to quit or be immediately drowned.

Standing over him, Keefer said, "You're a good man, Bud, but you got to give it up now." He released his hold, pulled Ben upright, and stepped on the bank. "Come on."

That afternoon, Ben lay in the shade of the live oak, half sick, his strength gone like blood from his veins. Keefer pulled a fat tick from Trouble's neck, and said:

"Don't know as I ever seen a better hound dog than thisn. How come I happen to have him, I seen him and that buck deer coming acrost Billy's Lake, him onto the buck's ear, and the buck trying to hook him off. When they got to the bank, wasn't neither one of 'em could hardly move, and they just laid there, plumb give out. I killed the deer with a light'rd knot. Plenty hounds'll run a deer for you, but thisn's the first I seen that'd purely catch one and hold 'im fer you," he mused in profound admiration. He rose and stretched.

Presently he said, "Guess I'll go git a drink of swamp water."

Ben dozed.

When he woke, Keefer was bent over the pot, slowly and deliberately stirring a tea of hais-law. Keefer's left cheek was puffed and bloody, and his eyes held a curious dullness. He drank the tea and painfully arose, and stupidly, like a man with no brain, walked to his pine-straw bed and lay down.

"What's got into you?" Ben asked.

Keefer's eyes opened, but there was no light in them. He didn't answer. Finally Ben thought to follow the path to the water's edge. Half mashed into the soft muck of the bank was a dead cottonmouth moccasin, his head beaten to shapelessness. Already the blowflies were busy about it, and Ben knew that he must have been asleep for an hour or so. The prints of Keefer's big hands were in the muck, filled with water, where he had knelt to drink when the snake struck his cheek. The sheath knife lay where it had dropped after Keefer cut his cheek to bleed the wound.

Ben went back to camp and after a while he located his gun. Then he began the search for Keefer's boat, carrying Trouble with him on a leash of rawhide.

He found the boat shoved deep into a brush-covered inlet. Three soft-shelled turtles slid off it into the water. The boat was a shallow cypress dugout; you could still see spots of blackened wood where the log had been burned and then dressed out. The stob pole floated beside the boat.

They got into the boat and started poling, heading toward the long lake that would lead them out of the swamp. *Reckon my girl's wondering what come of me.* It was the first time he had thought of Mabel McKenzie in days.

Far overhead, two buzzards wheeled slowly, almost motionless against the white clouds. Ben stood still a moment, letting the pole trail in the dying wake of the boat. He looked at the buzzards again.

"I don't expect I ought to just go right off and leave him there. Somebody ought to kind of bury him. From his looks he'll be dead by morning," he thought, uneasily.

Resolutely, he turned the boat back toward camp. Keefer lay in exactly the same position. His breathing was hardly audible. It occurred to Ben that he was dying mighty easy for a man that had been cottonmouth-bit.

Before dawn, Ben rose and looked at Keefer again. He didn't touch him, but no breathing was audible. Ben began working on a makeshift grave. Daylight had come when he finished it, and he decided he better say some sort of funeral speech.

I'm going to git him, now, Lord, and put him down in it. A dead soul's a-coming, and hit ain't nobody but Tom Keefer but he died without no hollering ner cutting the fool, just like a natural man. He killed a fellow in his day, and stole many a pig, Lord. I wouldn't tell it on him, but you know it good as I do. I ain't going to hold nothing against him, not even him trying to steal old Trouble. So if you want to go sort of light on him, too, hit'll be all right with me. Amen.

Ben hesitated, then went to the camp. Tom Keefer was half sitting up, resting on his elbow, his eyes dazed.

"Never thought to see you around here no more," Keefer said slowly.

"I sort of stayed to bury you," Ben muttered. "Looks like I went to the trouble for nothing."

Keefer sat up, painfully. "If I let them things kill me, I'd a been dead a long time ago. I bet I been cottonmouth-bit a dozen times," he said. "Ain't no doctors out here. I just make up my mind to git well, and think hard on it, and maybe pray some. I'll be up from here afore night."

Ben stared at him, not sure whether to be glad or sorry that Keefer was alive.

While he built the fire, Keefer watched him. "Ben," he said weakly, "you had a chancet to leave me, and you never took it. I ain't going to keep you here. When I git a little better I'll show you the way out. I know you ain't going to tell them about me, if you say you ain't."

"I ain't going to tell."

"Maybe sometime another you'll come back, and we'll have us some hunts, me and you and Trouble."

"I been thinking. They's one gracious heap of coon and otter in this here place. I could bring us some traps in here, and my God at the hides we could catch! I'd take them out to sell, and we'd split the money. Don't know what you'd want with money out here, though, come to think of it."

"I got a good use for it, if I ever git a-holt of any," Keefer said, slowly.

Carson McCullers

The Sojourner

The twilight border between sleep and waking was a Roman one this morning: splashing fountains and arched, narrow streets, the golden lavish city of blossoms and age-soft stone. Sometimes in this semi-consciousness he sojourned again in Paris, or war German rubble, or Swiss skiing and a snow hotel. Sometimes, also, in a fallow Georgia field at hunting dawn. Rome it was this morning in the yearless region of dreams.

John Ferris awoke in a room in a New York hotel. He had the feeling that something unpleasant was awaiting him—what it was, he did not know. The feeling, submerged by matinal necessities, lingered even after he had dressed and gone downstairs. It was a cloudless autumn day and the pale sunlight sliced between the pastel skyscrapers. Ferris went into the next-door drugstore and sat at the end booth next to the window glass that overlooked the sidewalk. He ordered an American breakfast with scrambled eggs and sausage.

Ferris had come from Paris to his father's funeral which had taken place the week before in his home town in Georgia. The shock of death had made him aware of youth already passed. His hair was receding and the veins in his now naked temples were pulsing and prominent and his body was spare except for an incipient belly bulge. Ferris had loved his father and the bond between them had once been extraordinarily close—but the years had somehow unraveled this filial devotion; the death, expected for a long time, had left him with an unforeseen dismay. He had stayed as long as possible to be near his mother and brothers at home. His plane for Paris was to leave the next morning.

Ferris pulled out his address book to verify a number. He turned the pages with growing attentiveness. Names and addresses from New York, the capitals of Europe, a few faint ones from his home state in the South. Faded, printed names, sprawled drunken ones. Betty Wills: a random love, married now. Charlie Williams: wounded in the Hürtgen Forest, unheard of since. Grand old Williams—did he live or die? Don Walker: a B.T.O. in television, getting rich. Henry Green: hit the skids after the war, in a sanitarium now, they say. Cozie Hall: he had heard that she was dead. Heedless, laughing Cozie—it was strange to think that she too, silly girl, could die. As Ferris closed the address book, he suffered a sense of hazard, transience, almost of fear.

It was then that his body jerked suddenly. He was staring out of the window when there, on the sidewalk, passing by, was his ex-wife. Elizabeth passed quite close to him, walking slowly. He could not understand the wild quiver of his heart, nor the following sense of recklessness and grace that lingered after she was gone.

Quickly Ferris paid his check and rushed out to the sidewalk. Elizabeth stood on the corner waiting to cross Fifth Avenue. He hurried toward her meaning to speak, but the lights changed and she crossed the street before he reached her. Ferris followed. On the other side he could easily have overtaken her, but he found himself lagging unaccountably. Her fair brown hair was plainly rolled, and as he watched her Ferris recalled that once his father had remarked that Elizabeth had a "beautiful carriage." She turned at the next corner and Ferris followed, although by now his intention to overtake her had disappeared. Ferris questioned the bodily disturbance that the sight of Elizabeth aroused in him, the dampness of his hands, the hard heartstrokes.

It was eight years since Ferris had last seen his ex-wife. He knew that long ago she had married again. And there were children. During recent years he had seldom thought of her. But at first, after the divorce, the loss had almost destroyed him. Then after the anodyne of time, he had loved again, and then again. Jeannine, she was now. Certainly his love for his ex-wife was long since past. So why the unhinged body, the shaken mind? He knew only that his clouded heart was oddly dissonant with the sunny, candid autumn day. Ferris wheeled suddenly and, walking with long strides, almost running, hurried back to the hotel.

Ferris poured himself a drink, although it was not yet eleven o'clock. He sprawled out in an armchair like a man exhausted, nursing his glass of bourbon and water. He had a full day ahead of him as he was leaving by plane the next morning for Paris. He checked over his obligations: take luggage to Air France, lunch with his boss, buy shoes and an overcoat. And something—wasn't there something else? Ferris finished his drink and opened the telephone directory.

His decision to call his ex-wife was impulsive. The number was under Bailey, the husband's name, and he called before he had much time for self-debate. He and Elizabeth had exchanged cards at Christmastime, and Ferris had sent a carving set when he received the announcement of her wedding. There was no reason *not* to call. But as he waited, listening to the ring at the other end, misgiving fretted him.

Elizabeth answered; her familiar voice was a fresh shock to him. Twice he had to repeat his name, but when he was identified, she sounded glad. He explained he was only in town for that day. They had a theater engagement, she said—but she wondered if he would come by for an early dinner. Ferris said he would be delighted.

As he went from one engagement to another, he was still bothered at odd moments by the feeling that something necessary was forgotten. Ferris bathed and changed in the late afternoon, often thinking about Jeannine: he would be with her the following night. "Jeannine," he would say, "I happened to run into my ex-wife when I was in New York. Had dinner with her. And her husband, of course. It was strange seeing her after all these years."

Elizabeth lived in the East Fifties, and as Ferris taxied uptown he glimpsed at intersections the lingering sunset, but by the time he reached his destination it was already autumn dark. The place was a building with a marquee and a doorman, and the apartment was on the seventh floor.

"Come in, Mr. Ferris."

Braced for Elizabeth or even the unimagined husband, Ferris was astonished by the freckled red-haired child; he had known of the children, but his mind had failed somehow to acknowledge them. Surprise made him step back awkwardly.

"This is our apartment," the child said politely. "Aren't you Mr. Ferris? I'm Billy. Come in."

In the living room beyond the hall, the husband provided another surprise; he too had not been acknowledged emotionally. Bailey was a lumbering red-haired man with a deliberate manner. He rose and extended a welcoming hand.

"I'm Bill Bailey. Glad to see you. Elizabeth will be in, in a minute. She's finishing dressing."

The last words struck a gliding series of vibrations, memories of the other years. Fair Elizabeth, rosy and naked before her bath. Half-dressed before the mirror of her dressing table, brushing her fine, chestnut hair. Sweet, casual intimacy, the soft-fleshed loveliness indisputably possessed. Ferris shrank from the unbidden memories and compelled himself to meet Bill Bailey's gaze.

"Billy, will you please bring that tray of drinks from the kitchen table?"

The child obeyed promptly, and when he was gone Ferris remarked conversationally, "Fine boy you have there."

"We think so."

Flat silence until the child returned with a tray of glasses and a cocktail shaker of Martinis. With the priming drinks they pumped up conversation: Russia, they spoke of, and the New York rainmaking, and the apartment situation in Manhattan and Paris.

"Mr. Ferris is flying all the way across the ocean tomorrow," Bailey said to the little boy who was perched on the arm of his chair, quiet and well behaved. "I bet you would like to be a stowaway in his suitcase."

Billy pushed back his limp bangs. "I want to fly in an airplane and be a newspaperman like Mr. Ferris." He added with sudden assurance, "That's what I would like to do when I am big."

Bailey said, "I thought you wanted to be a doctor."

"I do!" said Billy. "I would like to be both. I want to be a atom-bomb scientist too."

Elizabeth came in carrying in her arms a baby girl.

"Oh, John!" she said. She settled the baby in the father's lap. "It's grand to see you. I'm awfully glad you could come."

The little girl sat demurely on Bailey's knees. She wore a pale pink crêpe de Chine frock, smocked around the yoke with rose, and a matching silk hair ribbon tying back her pale soft curls. Her skin was summer tanned and her brown eyes flecked with gold and laughing. When she reached up and fingered her father's horn-rimmed glasses, he took them off and let her look through them a moment. "How's my old Candy?"

Elizabeth was very beautiful, more beautiful perhaps than he had ever realized. Her straight clean hair was shining. Her face was softer, glowing and serene. It was a madonna loveliness, dependent on the family ambiance.

"You've hardly changed at all," Elizabeth said, "but it has been a long time."

"Eight years." His hand touched his thinning hair self-consciously while further amenities were exchanged.

Ferris felt himself suddenly a spectator—an interloper among these Baileys. Why had he come? He suffered. His own life seemed so solitary, a fragile column supporting nothing amidst the wreckage of the years. He felt he could not bear much longer to stay in the family room.

He glanced at his watch. "You're going to the theater?"

"It's a shame," Elizabeth said, "but we've had this engagement for more than a month. But surely, John, you'll be staying home one of these days before long. You're not going to be an expatriate, are you?"

"Expatriate," Ferris repeated. "I don't much like the word."

"What's a better word?" she asked.

He thought for a moment. "Sojourner might do."

Ferris glanced again at his watch, and again Elizabeth apologized. "If only we had known ahead of time—"

"I just had this day in town. I came home unexpectedly. You see, Papa died last week."

"Papa Ferris is dead?"

"Yes, at Johns Hopkins. He had been sick there nearly a year. The funeral was down home in Georgia."

"Oh, I'm so sorry, John. Papa Ferris was always one of my favorite people."

The little boy moved from behind the chair so that he could look into his mother's face. He asked, "Who is dead?"

Ferris was oblivious to apprehension; he was thinking of his father's death. He saw again the outstretched body on the quilted silk within the coffin. The corpse flesh was bizarrely rouged and the familiar hands lay massive and joined above a spread of funeral roses. The memory closed and Ferris awakened to Elizabeth's calm voice.

"Mr. Ferris' father, Billy. A really grand person. Somebody you didn't know."

"But why did you call him *Papa* Ferris?"

Bailey and Elizabeth exchanged a trapped look. It was Bailey who answered the questioning child. "A long time ago," he said, "your mother and Mr. Ferris were once married. Before you were born—a long time ago."

"Mr. Ferris?"

The little boy stared at Ferris, amazed and unbelieving. And Ferris' eyes, as he returned the gaze, were somehow unbelieving too. Was it indeed true that at one time he had called this stranger, Elizabeth, Little Butterduck during nights of love, that they had lived together, shared perhaps a thousand days and nights and—finally—endured in the misery of sudden solitude the fiber by fiber (jealousy, alcohol and money quarrels) destruction of the fabric of married love?

Bailey said to the children, "It's somebody's suppertime. Come on now."

"But Daddy! Mama and Mr. Ferris—I—"

Billy's everlasting eyes—perplexed and with a glimmer of hostility—reminded Ferris of the gaze of another child. It was the young son of Jeannine—a boy of seven with a shadowed little face and nobby knees whom Ferris avoided and usually forgot.

"Quick march!" Bailey gently turned Billy toward the door. "Say good night now, son."

"Good night, Mr. Ferris." He added resentfully, "I thought I was staying up for the cake."

"You can come in afterward for the cake," Elizabeth said. "Run along now with Daddy for your supper."

Ferris and Elizabeth were alone. The weight of the situation descended on those first moments of silence. Ferris asked permission to pour himself another drink and Elizabeth set the cocktail shaker on the table at his side. He looked at the grand piano and noticed the music on the rack.

"Do you still play as beautifully as you used to?"

"I still enjoy it."

"Please play, Elizabeth."

Elizabeth arose immediately. Her readiness to perform when asked had always been one of her amiabilities; she never hung back, apologized. Now as she approached the piano there was the added readiness of relief.

She began with a Bach prelude and fugue. The prelude was as gaily iridescent as a prism in a morning room. The first voice of the fugue, an announcement pure and solitary, was repeated intermingling with a second voice, and again repeated within an elaborated frame, the multiple music, horizontal and serene, flowed with unhurried majesty. The principal melody was woven with two other voices, embellished with countless ingenuities—now dominant, again submerged, it had the sublimity of a single thing that does not fear surrender to the whole. Toward the end, the density of the material gathered for the last enriched insistence on the dominant first motif and with a chorded final statement the fugue ended. Ferris rested his head on the chair back and closed his eyes. In the following silence a clear, high voice came from the room down the hall.

"Daddy, how *could* Mama and Mr. Ferris—" A door was closed.

The piano began again—what was this music? Unplaced, familiar, the limpid melody had lain a long while dormant in his heart. Now it spoke to him of another time, another place—it was the music Elizabeth used to play. The delicate air summoned a wilderness of memory. Ferris was lost in the riot of past longings, conflicts, ambivalent desires. Strange that the music, catalyst for this tumultuous anarchy, was so serene and clear. The singing melody was broken off by the appearance of the maid.

"Miz Bailey, dinner is out on the table now."

Even after Ferris was seated at the table between his host and hostess, the unfinished music still overcast his mood. He was a little drunk.

"*L'improvisation de la vie humaine*," he said. "There's nothing that makes you so aware of the improvisation of human existence as a song unfinished. Or an old address book."

"Address book?" repeated Bailey. Then he stopped, noncommital and polite.

"You're still the same old boy, Johnny," Elizabeth said with a trace of the old tenderness.

It was a Southern dinner that evening, and the dishes were his old favorites. They had fried chicken and corn pudding and rich, glazed candied sweet potatoes. During the meal Elizabeth kept alive a conversation when the silences were overlong. And it came about that Ferris was led to speak of Jeannine.

"I first knew Jeannine last autumn—about this time of the year—in Italy. She's a singer and she had an engagement in Rome. I expect we will be married soon."

The words seemed so true, inevitable, that Ferris did not at first acknowledge to himself the lie. He and Jeannine had never in that year spoken of marriage. And indeed, she was still married—to a White Russian money-changer in Paris from whom she had been separated for five years. But it was too late to correct the lie. Already Elizabeth was saying: "This really makes me glad to know. Congratulations, Johnny."

He tried to make amends with truth. "The Roman autumn is so beautiful. Balmy and blossoming." He added, "Jeannine has a little boy of seven. A curious trilingual little fellow. We go to the Tuileries sometimes."

A lie again. He had taken the boy once to the gardens. The sallow foreign child in shorts that bared his spindly legs had sailed his boat in the concrete pond and ridden the pony. The child had wanted to go in to the puppet show. But there was not time, for Ferris had an engagement at the Scribe Hotel. He had promised they would go to the guignol another afternoon. Only once had he taken Valentin to the Tuileries.

There was a stir. The maid brought in a white-frosted cake with pink candles. The children entered in their night clothes. Ferris still did not understand.

"Happy birthday, John," Elizabeth said. "Blow out the candles."

Ferris recognized his birthday date. The candles blew out lingeringly and there was the smell of burning wax. Ferris was thirty-eight years old. The veins in his temples darkened and pulsed visibly.

"It's time you started for the theater."

Ferris thanked Elizabeth for the birthday dinner and said the appropriate good-byes. The whole family saw him to the door.

A high, thin moon shone above the jagged, dark skyscrapers. The streets were windy, cold. Ferris hurried to Third Avenue and hailed a cab. He gazed at the nocturnal city with the deliberate attentiveness of departure and perhaps farewell. He was alone. He longed for flighttime and the coming journey.

The next day he looked down on the city from the air, burnished in sunlight, toylike, precise. Then America was left behind and there was only the Atlantic and the distant European shore. The ocean was milky pale and placid beneath the clouds. Ferris dozed most of the day. Toward dark he was thinking of Elizabeth and the visit of the previous evening. He thought of Elizabeth among her family with longing, gentle envy and inexplicable regret. He sought the melody, the unfinished air, that had so moved him. The cadence, some unrelated tones, were all that remained; the melody itself evaded him. He had found instead the first voice of the fugue that Elizabeth had played—it came to him, inverted mockingly and in a minor key. Suspended above the ocean the anxieties of transience and solitude no longer troubled him and he thought of his father's death with equanimity. During the dinner hour the plane reached the shore of France.

At midnight Ferris was in a taxi crossing Paris. It was a clouded night and mist wreathed the lights of the Place de la Concorde. The midnight bistros gleamed on the wet pavements. As always after a transocean flight the change of continents was too sudden. New York at morning, this midnight Paris. Ferris glimpsed the disorder of his life: the succession of cities, of transitory loves; and time, the sinister glissando of the years, time always.

"*Vite! Vite!*" he called in terror. "*Dépêchez-vous.*"

Valentin opened the door to him. The little boy wore pajamas and an outgrown red robe. His gray eyes were shadowed and, as Ferris passed into the flat, they flickered momentarily.

"*J'attends Maman.*"

Jeannine was singing in a night club. She would not be home before another hour. Valentin returned to a drawing, squatting with his crayons over the paper on the floor. Ferris looked down at the drawing—it was a banjo player with notes and wavy lines inside a comic-strip balloon.

"We will go again to the Tuileries."

The child looked up and Ferris drew him closer to his knees. The melody, the unfinished music that Elizabeth had played, came to him suddenly. Unsought, the load of memory jettisoned—this time bringing only recognition and sudden joy.

"Monsieur Jean," the child said, "did you see him?"

Confused, Ferris thought only of another child—the freckled, family-loved boy. "See who, Valentin?"

"Your dead papa in Georgia." The child added, "Was he okay?"

Ferris spoke with rapid urgency: "We will go often to the Tuileries. Ride the pony and we will go into the guignol. We will see the puppet show and never be in a hurry any more."

"Monsieur Jean," Valentin said. "The guignol is now closed."

Again, the terror, the acknowledgment of wasted years and death. Valentin, responsive and confident, still nestled in his arms. His cheek touched the soft cheek and felt the brush of the delicate eyelashes. With inner desperation he pressed the child close—as though an emotion as protean as his love could dominate the pulse of time.

Lillian Smith

From *Strange Fruit*

TWENTY-NINE

As night fell, Bill Talley and Dee and the others went to their homes back in the county or to the sawmill and Ellatown. Bill and Dee driving home in the buggy out to Shaky Pond. Wheels grinding through sand, grinding through shadows and lights along road and swamp. Bill and Dee not talking, only hoofs and creak of wheels breaking the silence as the buggy moved under moss hanging low from great oaks, past ponds, past black clumps of palmetto . . . cotton fields . . . to the old house.

Lias met them at the lane to take the horses.

"Well, Lias," Bill said, "I hear they burned a nigger over to town today," voice mighty casual. Bill lifted his great weight out of the buggy.

Lias's hand fumbled for the bridle.

"Made a big fire, they say."

Lias had the bridle now.

"Watcha say, Lias?"

"Nothin, Mr. Bill. Yassuh—yassuh, Mr. Bill, sho must've."

Dee laughed, pulled his long thin legs from behind the buckboard, eased to the ground.

"Well," said Bill, "reckon we better get to pickin, a Monday."

"Yassuh, Boss."

"Reckon you can round up plenty hands, don't you? Won't be no trouble about gittin plenty?"

"Nossuh, Boss. Kin git all we kin use, yassuh."

Dee laughed, walked away.

Bill said, "Better put the horses up. They're wore out."

"Yassuh, Mr. Bill."

"And rub em down. They're tired. Don't like to see my horses git so tired. Damned hot weather!"

"Yassuh, Mr. Bill; thankee, Boss."

Miss Sadie went to bed early. She would like to go to sleep if she could, for there'd been little sleep for her the night before at the switchboard. And maybe sleep would help her forget what she had seen from her office window. She shouldn't have watched, but she had watched; and now her eyes were full of a black body swinging from the old cypress . . . full of the swinging and full of flames; of man's cruelty and anger. Maybe a little sleep would help her get it out of her mind, and her eyes. She turned over and pulled the sheet straight and as she did, someone knocked on her door.

It was Belle. Belle in her nightgown with a pink summer coat over her.

"You'll just have to let me sleep with you, Sadie, for I can't stay another minute in that house by myself, I'm so nervous I'm ajumping all over and I got to thinking now we're likely to have a raping tonight after this, with the niggers all aroused, you know, it's really not right, Sadie, for a woman to stay alone and you need somebody with you too so I—"

"You're welcome to stay, Belle. Just crawl in and turn off the light."

Belle crawled in and turned off the light.

Sadie edged over to her side of the bed. Maybe in a moment now she'd get to sleep and—

"Wasn't it just awful!" Belle crawled closer to Sadie. "I stood there on my piazza and watched and I was so close, Sadie, that I could hear that nigger's scream, and it made my blood—"

"Let's try to go to sleep, Belle, we're both worn out." Sadie edged over nearer the rim of the bed.

"Yes, we do need sleep all right, after all we've been through," Belle agreed.

Belle pulled down her nightgown and turned her pillow over. "My, it was terrible—terrible—you know, Sadie, I'll never forget this in all my life, it's one of those things you carry with you to your gr—"

"Yes, I know. But let's try to sleep now if we can."

Belle turned over.

Sadie smoothed the sheet once more. Maybe in a minute, now, she'd go to sleep. It's hard to believe the men you've seen downtown every day—so pleasant and agreeable to you, always doing something kind for you—could do a thing like this. What was it in folks that made them cruel? What did it satisfy in them? Must be something in a person that needed to hate—to make him want to hurt somebody weaker than himself—

"And, Sadie, the flames got so high I thought for the life of me they'd touch the sky, I did, and Sadie, you know—I smelled it, yes I did—terrible—it was just awful—just like barbecue—just exactly—made me think of all the times I'd eaten—it turned my stomach inside out and—"

Miss Sadie sat straight up and faced her guest. "Hush your mouth, Belle Strickland! You hear! If you make one more sound tonight—if you—I'll—I'll—I'll do something bad to you—I'll—" Shocked at herself, Miss Sadie suddenly lay down.

Miss Belle did not move. Nor did she speak another word.

The swing on the Pusey's dark porch whined on relentlessly.

"It's the Lord's will," Mrs. Pusey said in her patient, skimmed-milk voice; "he wasn't a good boy, Dottie, and would have caused you a life of trouble . . . They found his body out to Colored Town. You know what that means."

Creak, creak—back and forth in the darkness.

"Many a woman would thank God for being spared—what you've

been spared. Look at Mrs. Sug Rushton . . . Some men, Dottie, can't keep away from nigger women—can't keep away—"

Creak—creak creak—

"It's the Lord's will, Dottie. A day will come when you'll see what you've been saved from. When you're older and know what I know about men . . . you'll be thankful that God spared you from the kind of life some women have to bear. Men are hard to live with, all of them, but some men are worse than others and those that run after . . ."

But Dottie's low sobs went on, a little endless stream of sorrow threading its way between the creaks of the porch swing and Mrs. Pusey's plaintive words.

Preacher Livingston and Roseanna sat on their shed in the dark. Roseanna had sent the twins to bed early, and now she had opened the shutters and let in some air, for though she could hear the girls talking softly in their bed, they had undressed in the dark as she bade them do.

"Ned," she said, "I want to get the twins up to Atlanta, soon as we can."

"A month fo school! They can't go now, Rosie."

"I won't have them stay another minute in this place! I can't stand the worry."

Preacher Livingston turned to his wife. "There ain no runnin away from white folks, Rosie, you oughter know that well as me. There's ways to git along wid white folks if you hunts round for um. I've spent my whole life ahuntin . . . and I've found some—glad to say—I've found a few."

"I know you have," Roseanna said, and hesitated. "But they're ways we don want our chudren atakin . . . do we, Ned?" Roseanna was talking very simply now and without her airs. "We want something better for the twins than we had, don we? Sometimes I feel—" she hesitated again, "sometimes I most feel I'd rather kill them with my own hands than have them—go through," her voice sank very low, "what I've—been through . . . and other colored women like me."

Preacher Livingston moved uneasily in his chair.

"There's ways to git along, I'm tellin you! Colored folks don have to git in trouble wid white folks. Hit's their own fault when they does. There's ways. There's always been ways . . ."

From where Willie Echols and his wife Mollie sat—and their friends—under the chinaberry tree, you could see the glare of the dry-kiln, plain.

"Tom Harris musta turned out a million feet of lumber right there this summer," Lewis said, and wheeled his go-cart around to see the glow better.

"Yeah. But to hear him talk . . . when Saddy night comes, there ain't a dollar."

"Rich folks always talks hard times. You git used to it." Lewis laughed good-naturedly.

"I never have and don aim to git used to it. I aims to git a few of them dollars one of these days. What we need is to organize for a living wage. If we was to—"

Mollie laughed a deep fat laugh. "Willie's all time talkin bout organizin. I tell him he's wastin his breath. All Tom Harris ud do would be to turn him off and hire a nigger in his place."

"Oughter run the last one out the county," old Mrs. Lewis said firmly.

"Ma, you gittin kinder hard on—"

"Reckon we got one less anyway!"

"God yes! Warn't it a sight!"

"I never seen it," Mollie said. "Musta been terrible! Never could bear to wring a chicken's neck, and I knowed it ud be moren I could stand."

"I went," gray-haired Mrs. Lewis said, and her lips grew grim. "It was a turrible sight, but you coulda stood it."

Lewis laughed, and lifted a stump of a leg over the side of the go-cart where it could get the air. "I never went. Never did like to mix up in a thing like that. But Ma always said atter she seed me come outa that belt with both legs tore off she could look at anything."

Ma looked at Lewis now. "Well, you warn't no purty play-thing, I tell ye that."

"It coulda been worse," Lewis said. "It shore coulda been worse. And I'm about afeared of them wild talkers as anything. Now you take Tom Harris. He done purty good by me. Give me a hundard dollars and paid my doctor bill. And I reckon he'll be givin me a job as night watchman purty soon."

"A hundard dollar won't buy you no new legs," his wife retorted.

Lewis did not answer at once, and when he spoke, he spoke softly. "Well, Ma, mebbe hit don do no good to talk of it."

They were quiet for a time, just sitting there resting and watching the glow from the kiln.

Echols laughed. "It was a sight, that nigger! Swingin there. Got what he deserved. What every one of em deserve. But Mollie woulda fainted dead away when he begun to smell."

"Lawd, don't talk about it!" Mollie said, and made a face. With a plump hand she eased up one of her breasts a little where it was chafed.

"Mommy, mommy, mommy, mommy," screamed a child inside the house.

"I declare! J. L.'s havin a nightmare agin! That boy bolts his rations so fas he—"

"Mommy, mommy," sobbed the little fellow as he came running out of the house and down the steps, "they'll git me . . . they'll git me . . . I seed em . . ."

"Nobody aimin to git ye! Hit's niggers they burn—they ain't agoin to burn you. Get on back with ye to bed, boy." Echols laughed, gave the boy a playful push.

Nobody had ever seen Willie in better spirits, and everybody joined in the laughter as Mollie turned the little fellow around and sent him back.

"Well," said Mrs. Lewis, "we better be agittin home and to bed ourselves. It's atter nine o'clock."

Mollie and Willie sat on for a time under the chinaberry tree, until the Nine O'clock passed.

"Late tonight," Mollie said.

"Late half the time." Willie stood up. "Never was a train to run on time. How about bed, old woman?"

"Well, I don't care if I do." Mollie pulled her two hundred pounds out of the low cane-bottom chair and followed Will into the house.

It did not take them long to get to bed. Nor long for Willie to pull Mollie's big soft body to him.

"My!" Mollie sighed after a time, "my . . . you ain't been like this in a year!"

"Ain't felt like this in a year," Willie laughed and reached for her again.

Tom Harris sat on the south porch of the Harris home while his wife watered her pot plants. Although it was dark and long after supper, Anne was carefully watering each fern, begonia, geranium, night-blooming cereus. Slowly and carefully. And Tom knew that she was deeply troubled.

He sat in his big porch rocker as she moved from shadowy pot to pot, herself a deeper shadow.

She emptied the watering-pot on the asparagus fern, sat down near him, rocked slowly back and forth in the darkness. Tom waited, knowing Anne was trying to say something; after a time she would find slow words.

Beyond them, on College Street, a car stopped. A voice called, "Harriet!" Waited. Moved on.

"I don't want the girls to go out tonight," he said.

"They're both here. I've told them."

"Tom," Anne said, "I worry about Charlie. If one of my boys turned out—I wish you'd speak to him."

"What do you want me to speak about, Anne?"

"I don't know . . . he never goes to church—doesn't take interest in the things we've taught our children to believe in."

"Charlie's all right, Anne."

"How do you know? Sometimes I wonder if we ever know our children . . ."

"All we can do, Anne, is the best we can and trust God to do the rest. Charlie's all right. Fine boy."

"I'm a little tired," Anne was standing now, "I think I'll go to bed. Papa," she was at the door, "try to talk to Charlie."

Tom sat on the porch after Anne had gone, looking into a darkness that was too black for his eyes to see through.

Charlie came out of the house, sat down. "Hello, Dad."

"Howdy, Son."

You could hear the singing over at the tent. From the sound of it, not many people were at the meeting.

"Dad, you were right—reckless, this afternoon."

"Well . . . I don't know."

"I don't think many men would have done what you did."

"It didn't do any good."

"They might have killed you. Pretty ugly crowd."

"It didn't do any good."

"Maybe it did more than you know. Maybe some of those watching felt . . . as I did."

"I don't know, Charlie. I'm too old to know—anything."

"You're younger than any child you've got—and a better man."

"Too old to figure out things like this."

Praise God from whom all blessings flow,

Praise Him, all creatures here below . . .

"Some of the boys doing that burning, Son, were our men from the mill. Hard-working. Good to their families. Two of them stewards in Sarah Chapel."

Praise Him above, ye heavenly . . .

"I can't understand why they'd want to do it." Tom sighed.

Praise Father, Son and . . .

"So many leaving the county, it's got folks nervous—" He stopped.

"Sometimes, Dad, when I think of the South all I can see is a white man kneeling on a nigger's stomach. Every time he raises his arms in prayer he presses a little deeper in the black man's belly."

"Hate to hear you say a thing like that, Charlie. There're things hard to understand about the South . . . I know. But without God, it'd be worse. Lot worse."

"Trouble is, you can't be a Christian in the South. You can't be one even if you want to, in the setup we've got down here! Everybody gouging his living out of somebody beneath him—singing hymns as he gouges—"

"It's your saying things like that, Son, that worries your mother. Know you don't mean it way it sounds. Know you mean something else. I've lived a long time, Charlie, I can't live without God. Can't live without Him," Tom's voice was a whisper. After a moment he went on, "A lynching's a terrible thing. I know it's wrong to kill a man, no matter what his color. I know you got to be fair to him. But you can't make a Negro your social equal!"

"Why?"

"You know you can't do it! Turn em loose down here and before you know it, you'd have—" Tom stopped.

"What you reckon would happen, Dad? What you reckon?"

Tom didn't answer.

The two men sat looking out into the darkness.

Harriet came from the living room where she had been reading, and slipped into a chair. "I've always wondered how a lyncher feels," she said. "Now I know."

The two men did not answer.

"Every Southerner knows, of course. We lynch the Negro's soul every day of our lives."

The men did not answer.

"In all this town no one had the courage to try to stop it."

Charlie said quickly, "Except your own Dad—"

"Son, I'd rather you didn't discuss such things with your sister."

"Oh, Dad, don't be silly! What did he do, Charlie?"

Charlie hesitated, glanced at his father, told her briefly.

Harriet sat without speaking; then quietly went over to her father and kissed his bald head.

"I was too late," Tom said softly.

No one spoke again. After a while, Tom stood. "I hope some day you young folks will find the answer. Hope some day you'll find how come it all started and what can be done about it. Well . . . think I'll turn in. Kinda tired out. Good night, Sister."

"Good night, darling."

"Night, Son."

"Night, Dad."

Brother and sister sat on in a long silence.

"Too late," Harriet whispered. "What's the answer, Charlie?"

"I don't know one. Only thing I can see for anybody with sense to do is to get out!"

"Run away . . . Nice and easy. Smart people run away. Or maybe it isn't so smart. You can't run away from a thing like this. It'll follow you all over the world."

"Right now, I have some ideas," Charles said slowly. "If I stay here twenty years, I won't have them. Now I see things without color getting in the way—I won't be able to, then. It'll get me. It gets us all. Like quicksand. The more you struggle, the deeper you sink in it—I'm damned scared to stay—" He laughed.

"Everybody's scared," Harriet went on softly. "White man's blown himself up to such a size, now his own shadow scares him. Scared to do the decent thing for fear it will only do—harm. When every day by not doing—"

The only sound on the porch was the crunch of their rockers.

"Did you see it, Charlie?"

"From the edge."

"Who did it?"

"Mill folks—farm folks—Bill Talley and his crowd got it going."

"Was it—pretty bad?"

"Thing that got me the most," Charlie said slowly, "was the hate on folks' faces. Even on the women's. It wasn't Henry they were hating—or any Negro. It was—I don't know. Being poor couldn't do it—"

"It might help."

He went on after a little. "Yeah, but it couldn't do it. Not that kind of hate. Some of those men were at that revival last night at the altar . . . praying to be saved. This afternoon they burned a man to ash."

"You remember—" Harriet was feeling her way now, "the time we went with Gus to Milledgeville to see his mother? We saw a man there in the asylum who said he was God—you remember? He was out in the ward—they let him go loose—putting everybody 'in their place' . . . Telling everybody where they could sit and stand and how to speak to him. They said he picked up a chair one day and almost killed a woman because she wouldn't stay where he had put her . . . The doctors called it paranoia. It doesn't seem to me white folks are very different—from him."

"All of us nuts, huh?" Charlie laughed.

"I don't think there's much difference," Harriet said. "How about giving your sister a cigarette?"

"I'm willing—but you know how Mother feels . . ."

"O.K. Pass it up." She laughed, sighed. "What would happen, Charlie," she said after a little, "if for one day here in Maxwell you and I would do the human thing? Just act human and sane and decent—for one day. Would you have the courage?"

Charles laughed. "Let's go in. You ask too many questions."

Brother Saunders quick-stepped until his left foot synchronized with the evangelist's.

"Of course," he said, "this trouble is bound to hurt the revival, though the crowds will pick up better than that handful tonight."

The two men walked on in silence across the business blocks and down College Street.

"I doubt though," Brother Saunders said, "that we'll get back the enthusiasm we had."

Brother Dunwoodie pulled a strand of moss from above his head, dropped bits of it on the sidewalk as they went down College Street.

Suddenly he spoke. "I don't condone a thing like this afternoon. I feel nothing but condemnation for such blood-thirstiness."

"Nor I," Brother Saunders replied. "But it doesn't do any good to criticize people—not at a time like this. Only stirs up more bad feeling between the races. It don't do to *talk* about these things. Makes them worse! Now it's always been my policy to keep out of controversies and politics. A servant of God has no business mixing in such matters. Our job is the winning of souls to Christ."

Brother Dunwoodie sighed, "And sometimes it seems to me the devil can beat us all out of sight! Well," he raised his voice to a more cheerful level, "here's my corner. Good night."

"Good night," Brother Saunders said.

It was not far from the Harrises' side gate to the porch but far enough for Brother Dunwoodie to hear his steps echo in hollow mockery the minister's words—and his own.

"Yes," he sighed, "everywhere you turn, the devil's setting a trap for you."

Sam Perry sat before his desk. He had been there all evening. And though Aunt Easter now and then came to the door she did not go in, for there was a look on Sam's face which made Easter walk softly and stay on her side of the house. Once he said, "Go to bed, Auntie, I don't want supper." And Mrs. Perry had not urged him to eat.

Someone knocked on the door, and Sam put his hand to his gun. It was only Dan, who smiled at the gesture, came in.

"I was afraid you was asleep, Sam, but I had to come. Tempy's been so nervy all night I can't do nothin with her. She screamin and takin on like she done time she went dumb, and I feared she might be going off again into one of her spells. Maybe if you'd give her some of those powders, Sam, to make her drop off to sleep—"

Sam said yes, she probably needed to sleep, and turned to prepare something for her.

Dan sat there quietly, his dark brown face sagged with fatigue, hands resting on his knees.

"Dessie's not come home," he said evenly, "but I reckon she to the Harrises'." He rubbed his hand slowly over the bald part of his head. "If she ain't, I reckon there's nothin I kin do about it."

Sam measured the powder and rolled it in little papers.

"I reckon in a time like this, better tend my own business and leave other folks' alone."

"That's right, Dan. You're dead right," Sam said. "Tend your own business and to hell with everybody else's."

"Well, I don know," Dan half smiled, "but I sorter figure long as it's hot and folks needs plenty ice and I kin go round and ring a bell and sell um ten to fifty pounds and save a little money and keep my mouf shut and tend to Tempy I'll likely stay out of trouble and git along. Least I figure it that way."

"Yes, Dan, you'll always get along, I believe." Sam suddenly smiled. "I believe you always will."

The air was still. Down by the branch it would be cooler, but here at the office the day's dust still lay in the air.

In one of the cabins somebody lit a lantern. One of the sick ones worse maybe, or dying. Sam Perry mighty near right. Two more had died and five more sick. Well, they'd all been stuck with that needle now, so maybe it wouldn't get worse. But what a carryin on! Thought they'd sure have to hog-tie one wench and—

Even when you try to help the darkies, they buck it. Like the privies. Never would use them. Lot rather squat behind a palmetto. A lot rather! More like children than grown people. Maybe more like animals than either. But likeable. Yeah . . .

Cap'n Rushton chuckled. Couldn't help but like the crazy fools. Reckon that's why he stayed out at the still so much. Rather be around them than most folks in Maxwell.

He laid down his pipe. Better get to bed for the little rest that was left him. He went to the edge of the shed. Everything quiet. Shacks stretched a row of shadows down each side of the road, hardly bigger than shadows made by palmetto or sleeping cows. Well, glad it was over now. Saw when he went to town yesterday that Bill was out to git a nigger. You could see it in Bill's eye. You'd seen it before. Bill had a habit of killing one off now and then. Used to say there was too dadburn many of em. String one up now and then or drop him in the pond to the gators—made the others flourish like pruning a tree. Bill took things pretty far. Did as a boy. Kill a dog easy as that if he happened to step on the dog's tail—turn on him as if the dog had done something to *him*! Remembered seeing that once. But a lynching now and then did seem to settle things . . . Bad as it was, and it was bad, it did settle things. And things needed settling. Ever since the war the niggers had been restless. He'd been dead-set against sending them to France with the A.E.F., said then, they'd get ideas the South would pay high for. God knows, plenty things crawling in their heads without mixing em with the French variety! Well, the Yankees who run things in Washington didn't believe it or didn't care. God-durn fools promised the nigger the vote if he'd go. And now the cussed idiot expected it. Restless . . . swarming North like flies to a dirty pot. Thinking because they'd strutted around in khaki and ogled French women they could eat dinner with a white man. Like as not. Yeah. Thought they had a right now to look at white girls . . . Saw one of them a Saturday on the street staring straight at a bunch of girls in a car down at the drugstore. Bound to be trouble. Just a wonder it hadn't come before. Hands short for the pickin—short at the still—short everywheres. Some of the towns had stopped letting them buy railroad tickets to the North—turning them back.

Well, he'd kept out of it himself, for a lynching wasn't to his liking. One of those things that seem necessary now and then, but you let the other fellow do it. Like sticking a pig—much as you liked your cracklin' bread, you couldn't stand a hog-killing. Just hoped they got the right nigger. Maybe they did. Maybe they didn't. More likely Tracy Deen had come to his death in another way—from things being whispered round town today. Folks were talking a little about one of the Anderson niggers. Not saying much for the sake of the Deens, but a little something. Get a woman mad enough, she'd do you in, in a minute. Now that's a boy who'd never had a chance—with a mother like Alma Deen always trying to make him fit some fool picture she had in her mind . . . And Tut too easy on Alma! Ought to take a woman like Alma and—

He eased off his shoes. Might as well let women be.

Sometimes he wondered, maybe, if he ought to tell Della what Tut had said. Trouble is—if he told her he had less than a year to live—she'd take on like he was a prize package! Make him drink that durned mess Tut had fixed up; be fixing up messes of her own prescription for him—and fret and worry until it'd be like sitting up with your own corpse every day! As it was, Della made out well enough by herself in town. If he stayed away all the time, she'd never miss him—with her club and her missionary society and her garden, and the cook's worrisome ways and Della's old uncle, so childish he couldn't even feed himself without spilling it down his clothes. Altogether, they kept

Della pretty happy. But if she thought he wasn't going to live long, she'd make him stay in town, and he couldn't abide the place! Be nursing him and fixing doo-daddles—and first thing you know they'd both be at each other's throat, or wanting to be . . .

Glad he was back here where it was quiet. He'd kept as far from the ball ground today as he could, but folks told him about it. Told him about Tom Harris rushing in there, trying to stop it. Some folks are satisfied with the world as it is; some have to work themselves to death afixin it over. And Tom has always been one of the fixers. Trying to make things over. Reform. Didn't seem able to see that it's all of a piece. You take the strain off here—you put an extra strain there. Like prohibition. Tom worked himself half to death for local option, and then for prohibition—and got it. But what did he get! What you going to give a man when you take his drink from him! Take his whisky away . . . you ain't changed him a bit. He'll just have to hunt something else . . .

Cap'n Rushton fixed the mosquito net tight around his bed and lay down. As for lynching . . . There'll be lynchings long as white folks and black folks scrouge each other—everybody scrambling for the same penny.

He stretched out and groaned. Felt good to get a bed under you. Yeah. Felt good. He turned on his side to ease the hurting. Turned back. Sighed. Sometimes he wondered what it was folks mourned over when a man died. Hard to believe it was the corpse.

They sat on the screen porch, the three of them, saying nothing. Only their rockers crunched now and then against the floor.

Tut looked at Alma, so quiet, so composed. He'd like to go to her and put his hand on her shoulder. Like to kiss her and remind her that he was still here—to give her what comfort he could. Been a long time since he'd kissed Alma like that. A long time. He'd like to be close to her now, to share this grief with her. He knew it was harder for a woman to lose her son than for a man—and that was hard enough . . .

The air was sweet with damp honeysuckle from the near-by trellis, but Tut smelled only the heavy fragrance of wreaths and sprays. Their boy. Made of her and him, grown to a man, unknown, tumultuous, weak maybe. Yet loving and sweet. Both children seemed mighty loving and sweet, to Tut. Things they said when they were little . . . the manly things young Tracy used to do . . . way he'd trudge after you when you went hunting, keep right up to you, never complain . . . way he'd take up for his mother if he thought you were against her—and him no more than two years old . . . way he'd give his playthings to Henry . . .

Tears were rolling down Tut's face, but he didn't know it, as he lived over his life with his boy . . . seeing the good things . . . the lovable things. He was gently replacing Tracy in Alma's womb, re-creating him, making him the boy he might have been. He was seeing him in all the beauty of man's tenderest dream. Tut would never see his son in any other way.

The telephone rang. Someone needed Dr. Deen.

Laura said, "Want me to go with you, Daddy?"

"Better stay with your mother, Sister." Tut picked up his bag.

They heard the car door slam, the buzz of the starter, the rattle of wheels sliding on gravel; watched the taillight turn the corner.

Prentiss Reid picked up his pencil. Began to draw a man on a sheet of paper.

And after a time Maxwell Georgia slept. As still as only the weary can be, it lay—splotched dark against flat stretches of cotton; tied to them by roads which wound their white threads through cottonfields, past black pinelands, around ponds, under great oaks, on, on, on, in the night.

Covered by darkness, Maxwell slept . . . in tired peace. The night freight chuffed up Sandy Hill, clanked its short-lived signal of commerce, passed on to the North. The moon came up above the line of pinelands in the east, slowly moved across the town, making luminous and beautiful the thin white steeples of Baptist and Methodist churches, throwing wayward bright shafts of light on roofs, glinting the railroad track, whitening the big revival tent, washing away all trace of the day and its black sin.

Frank Yerby

Health Card

Johnny stood under one of the street lights on the corner and tried to read the letter. The street lights down in the Bottom were so dim that he couldn't make out half the words, but he didn't need to: he knew them all by heart anyway.

"Sugar," he read, "it took a long time but I done it. I got the money to come to see you. I waited and waited for them to give you a furlough, but it look like they don't mean to. Sugar, I can't wait no longer. I got to see you. I got to. Find a nice place for me to stay—where we can be happy together. You know what I mean. With all my love, Lily."

Johnny folded the letter up and put it back in his pocket. Then he walked swiftly down the street past all the juke joints with the music blaring out and the G.I. brogans pounding. He turned down a side street, scuffing up a cloud of dust as he did so. None of the streets down in Black Bottom was paved, and there were four inches of fine white powder over everything. When it rained the mud would come up over the tops of his army shoes, but it hadn't rained in nearly three months. There were no juke joints on this street, and the Negro shanties were neatly whitewashed. Johnny kept on walking until he came to the end of the street. On the corner stood the little white-washed Baptist Church, and next to it was the neat, well-kept home of the pastor.

Johnny went up on the porch and hesitated. He thrust his hand in his pocket and the paper crinkled. He took his hand out and knocked on the door.

"Who's that?" a voice called.

"It's me," Johnny answered; "it's a sodjer."

The door opened a crack, and the woman peered out. She was middle-aged and fat. Looking down, Johnny could see that her feet were bare.

"Whatcha want, sodjer?"

Johnny took off his cap.

"Please, ma'am, lemme come in. I kin explain it t'yuh better settin' down."

She studied his face for a minute in the darkness.

"Aw right," she said; "you kin come in, son."

Johnny entered the room stiffly and sat down on a corn-shuck-bottomed chair.

"It's this way, ma'am," he said. "I got a wife up Nawth. I been tryin' an' tryin' t' git a furlough so I could go t' see huh. But they always put me off. So now she done worked an' saved enuff money t' come an' see me. I wants t' ax you t' rent me a room, ma'am. I doan' know nowheres t' ax."

"This ain't no hotel, son."

"I know it ain't. I cain't take Lily t' no hotel, not lak hotels in this heah town."

"Lily yo wife?"

"Yes'm. She my sho' nuff, honest t' Gawd wife. Married in th' Baptist Church in Deetroit."

The fat woman sat back, and her thick lips widened into a smile.

"She a good girl, ain't she? An' you doan' wanta take her t' one o' these heah ho'houses they calls hotels."

"That's it, ma'am."

"Sho' you kin bring huh heah, son. Be glad t' have huh. Reveren' be glad t' have huh too. What yo' name, son?"

"Johnny. Johnny Green. Ma'am—"

"Yas, son?"

"You understands that I wants t' come heah too?"

The fat woman rocked back in her chair and gurgled with laughter. "Bless yo' heart, chile, I ain't always been a ole woman! And I ain't always been th' preacher's wife neither!"

"Thank you, ma'am. I gotta go now. Time fur me t' be gittin' back t' camp."

"When you bring Lily?"

"Be Monday night, ma'am. Pays you now if you wants it."

"Monday be aw right. Talk it over wit th' Reveren', so he make it light fur yuh. Know sodjer boys ain't got much money."

"No ma'am, sho' Lawd ain't. G' night, ma'am."

When he turned back into the main street of the Negro section the doors of the joints were all open and the soldiers were coming out. The girls were clinging onto their arms all the way to the bus stop. Johnny looked at the dresses that stopped halfway between the pelvis and the knee and hugged the backside so that every muscle showed when they walked. He saw the purple lipstick smeared across the wide full lips, and the short hair stiffened with smelly grease so that it covered their heads like a black lacquered cap. They went on down to the bus stop arm in arm, their knotty bare calves bunching with each step as they walked. Johnny thought about Lily. He walked past them very fast without turning his head.

But just as he reached the bus stop he heard the whistles. When he turned around he saw the four M.P.s and the civilian policemen stopping the crowd. He turned around again and walked back until he was standing just behind the white men.

"Aw right," the M.P.s were saying, "you gals git your health cards out."

Some of the girls started digging in their handbags. Johnny could see them dragging out small yellow cardboard squares. But the others just stood there with blank expressions on their faces. The soldiers started muttering, a dark, deep-throated sound. The M.P.s started pushing their way through the crowd, looking at each girl's card as they passed. When they came to a girl who didn't have a card they called out to the civilian policemen:

"Aw right, mister, take A'nt Jemima for a little ride."

Then the city policemen would lead the girl away and put her in the Black Maria.

They kept this up until they had examined every girl except one. She hung back beside her soldier, and the first time the M.P.s didn't see her. When they came back through one of them caught her by the arm.

"Lemme see your card, Mandy," he said.

The girl looked at him, her little eyes narrowing into slits in her black face.

"Tek yo' han' offen me, white man," she said.

The M.P.'s face crimsoned, so that Johnny could see it, even in the darkness.

"Listen, black gal," he said, "I told you to lemme see your card."

"An' I tole you t' tek yo' han' offen me, white man!"

"Gawddammit, you little black bitch, you better do like I tell you!"

Johnny didn't see very clearly what happened after that. There was a sudden explosion of motion, and then the M.P. was trying to jerk his hand back, but he couldn't, for the little old black girl had it between her teeth and was biting it to the bone. He drew his other hand back and slapped her across the face so hard that it sounded like a pistol shot. She went over backwards and her tight skirt split, so that when she got up Johnny could see that she didn't have anything on under it. She came forward like a cat, her nails bared, straight for the M.P.'s eyes. He slapped her down again, but the soldiers surged forward all at once. The M.P.s fell back and drew their guns and one of them blew a whistle.

Johnny, who was behind them, decided it was time for him to get out of there and he did; but not before he saw the squads of white M.P.s hurling around the corner and going to work on the Negroes with their clubs. He reached the bus stop and swung on board. The minute after he had pushed his way to the back behind all the white soldiers he heard the shots. The bus driver put the bus in gear and they roared off toward the camp.

It was after one o'clock when all the soldiers straggled in. Those of them who could still walk. Eight of them came in on the meat wagon, three with gunshot wounds. The colonel declared the town out of bounds for all Negro soldiers for a month.

"Dammit," Johnny said, "I gotta go meet Lily, I gotta. I cain't stay heah. I cain't!"

"Whatcha gonna do," Little Willie asked, "go A.W.O.L.?"

Johnny looked at him, his brow furrowed into a frown.

"Naw," he said, "I'm gonna go see th' colonel!"

"Whut! Man, you crazy! Colonel kick yo' black ass out fo' you gits yo' mouf open."

"I take a chanct on that."

He walked over to the little half mirror on the wall of the barracks. Carefully he readjusted his cap. He pulled his tie out of his shirt front and drew the knot tighter around his throat. Then he tucked the ends back in at just the right fraction of an inch between the correct pair of buttons. He bent down and dusted his shoes again, although they were already spotless.

"Man," Little Willie said, "you sho' is a fool!"

"Reckon I am," Johnny said; then he went out of the door and down the short wooden steps.

When he got to the road that divided the colored and white sections of the camp his steps faltered. He stood still a minute, drew in a deep breath, and marched very stiffly and erect across the road. The white soldiers gazed at him curiously, but none of them said anything. If a black soldier came over into their section it was because somebody sent him, so they let him alone.

In front of the colonel's headquarters he stopped. He knew what he had to say, but his breath was very short in his throat and he was going to have a hard time saying it.

"Whatcha want, soldier?" the sentry demanded.

"I wants t' see th' colonel."

"Who sent you?"

Johnny drew his breath in sharply.

"I ain't at liberty t' say," he declared, his breath coming out very fast behind the words.

"You ain't at liberty t' say," the sentry mimicked. "Well I'll be damned! If you ain't at liberty t' say, then I ain't at liberty t' let you see th' colonel! Git tha hell outa here, nigger, before I pump some lead in you!"

Johnny didn't move.

The sentry started toward him, lifting his rifle butt, but another soldier, a sergeant, came around the corner of the building.

"Hold on there," he called. "What tha hell is th' trouble here?"

"This here nigger says he wants t' see tha colonel an' when I ast him who sent him he says he ain't at liberty t' say!"

The sergeant turned to Johnny.

Johnny came to attention and saluted him. You aren't supposed to salute N.C.O.s, but sometimes it helps.

"What you got t' say fur yourself, boy?" the sergeant said, not unkindly. Johnny's breath evened.

"I got uh message fur th' colonel, suh," he said; "I ain't s'posed t' give it t' nobody else but him. I ain't even s'posed t' tell who sont it, suh."

The sergeant peered at him sharply.

"You tellin' tha truth, boy?"

"Yassuh!"

"Aw right. Wait here a minute."

He went into H.Q. After a couple of minutes he came back out.

"Aw right, soldier, you kin go on in."

Johnny mounted the steps and went into the colonel's office. The colonel was a lean, white-haired soldier with a face tanned to the color of saddle leather. He was reading a letter through a pair of horn-rimmed glasses which had only one earhook left, so that he had to hold them up to his eyes with his hand. He put them down and looked up. Johnny saw that his eyes were pale blue, so pale that he felt like he was looking into the eyes of an eagle or some other fierce bird of prey.

"Well?" he said, and Johnny stiffened into a salute. The colonel half smiled.

"At ease, soldier," he said. Then: "The sergeant tells me that you have a very important message for me."

Johnny gulped in the air.

"Beggin th' sergeant's pardon, suh," he said, "but that ain't so."

"What!"

"Yassuh," Johnny rushed on, "nobody sent me. I come on m' own hook. I had t' talk t' yuh, Colonel, suh! You kin sen' me t' th' guardhouse afterwards, but please, suh, lissen t' me fur jes' a minute!"

The colonel relaxed slowly. Something very like a smile was playing around the corners of his mouth. He looked at his watch.

"All right, soldier," he said, "you've got five minutes."

"Thank yuh, thank yuh, suh!"

"Speak your piece, soldier; you're wasting time!"

"It's about Lily, suh. She my wife. She done worked an' slaved fur nigh onto six months t' git the money t' come an' see me. An now you give th' order that none o' th' cullud boys kin go t' town. Beggin' yo' pahdon, suh, I wasn't in none o' that trouble. I ain't never been in no trouble. You kin ax my cap'n, if you wants to. All I wants is permission to go into town fur one week, an' I'll stay outa town fur two months if yuh wants me to."

The colonel picked up the phone.

"Ring Captain Walters for me," he said. Then: "What's your name, soldier?"

"It's Green, suh. Private Johnny Green."

"Captain Walters? This is Colonel Milton. Do you have anything in your files concerning Private Johnny Green? Oh yes, go ahead. Take all the time you need."

The colonel lit a long black cigar. Johnny waited. The clock on the wall spun its electric arms.

"What's that? Yes. Yes, yes, I see. Thank you, Captain."

He put down the phone and picked up a fountain pen. He wrote swiftly. Finally he straightened up and gave Johnny the slip of paper.

Johnny read it. It said: "Private Johnny Green is given express permission to go into town every evening of the week beginning August seventh and ending August fourteenth. He is further permitted to remain in town overnight every night during said week, so long as he returns to camp for reveille the following morning. By order of the commanding officer, Colonel H. H. Milton."

There was a hard knot at the base of Johnny's throat. He couldn't breathe. But he snapped to attention and saluted smartly.

"Thank you, suh," he said at last. Then: "Gawd bless you, suh!"

"Forget it, soldier. I was a young married man once myself. My compliments to Captain Walters."

Johnny saluted again and about-faced, then he marched out of the office and down the stairs. On the way back he saluted everybody—privates, N.C.O.s, and civilian visitors, his white teeth gleaming in a huge smile.

"That's sure one happy darky," one of the white soldiers said.

Johnny stood in the station and watched the train running in. The yellow lights from the windows flickered on and off across his face as the alternating squares of light and darkness flashed past. Then it was slowing and Johnny was running beside it, trying to keep abreast of the Jim Crow coach. He could see her standing up, holding her bags. She came down the steps the first one and they stood there holding each other, Johnny's arms crushing all the breath out of her, holding her so hard against him that his brass buttons hurt through her thin dress. She opened her mouth to speak but he kissed her, bending her head backward on her neck until her little hat fell off. It lay there on the ground, unnoticed.

"Sugah," she said, "sugah. It was awful."

"I know," he said, "I know."

Then he took her bags and they started walking out of the station toward the Negro section of town.

"I missed yuh so much," Johnny said, "I thought I lose m' mind."

"Me too," she said. Then: "I brought th' marriage license with me like yuh tole me. I doan' want th' preacher's wife t' think we bad."

"Enybody kin look at yuh an' see yuh uh angel!"

They went very quietly through all the dark streets and the white soldiers turned to look at Johnny and his girl.

Lak a queen, Johnny thought, lak a queen. He looked at the girl beside him, seeing the velvety nightshade skin, the glossy black lacquered curls, the sweet, wide hips and the long, clean legs, striding beside him in the darkness. I am black, but comely, O ye daughters of Jerusalem!

They turned into the Bottom where the street lights were dim blobs on the pine poles and the dust rose up in little swirls around their feet. Johnny had his head half turned so that he didn't see the two M.P.s until he had almost bumped into them. He dropped one bag and caught Lily by the arm. Then he drew her aside quickly and the two men went by them without speaking.

They kept on walking, but every two steps Johnny would jerk his head around and look nervously back over his shoulder. The last time he looked the two M.P.s had stopped and were looking back at them. Johnny turned out the elbow of the arm next to Lily so that it hooked into hers a little and began to walk faster, pushing her along with him.

"Wha's yo' hurry, sugah?" she said. "I be heah a whole week!"

But Johnny was looking over his shoulder at the two M.P.s. They were coming toward them now, walking with long, slow strides, their reddish-white faces set. Johnny started to push Lily along faster, but she shook off his arm and stopped still.

"I do declare, Johnny Green! You th' beatiness man! Whut you walk me so fas' fur?"

Johnny opened his mouth to answer her, but the military police were just behind them now, and the sergeant reached out and laid his hand on her arm.

"C'mon, gal," he said, "lemme see it."

"Let you see whut? Whut he mean, Johnny?"

"Your card," the sergeant growled, "lemme see your card."

"My card?" Lily said blankly. "Whut kinda card, mister?"

Johnny put the bags down. He was fighting for breath.

"Look heah, Sarge," he said; "this girl my wife!"

"Oh yeah? I said lemme see your card, sister!"

"I ain't got no card, mister. I dunno whut you talkin' 'bout."

"Look, Sarge," the other M.P. said, "th' soldier's got bags. Maybe she's just come t' town."

"These your bags, gal?"

"Yessir."

"Aw right. You got twenty-four hours to git yourself a health card. If you don't have it by then we hafta run you in. Git goin' now."

"Listen," Johnny shouted; "this girl my wife! She ain't no ho'! I tell you she ain't—"

"What you say, nigger—" the M.P. sergeant growled. "Whatcha say?" He started toward Johnny.

Lily swung on Johnny's arm.

"C'mon, Johnny," she said; "they got guns. C'mon, Johnny, please! Please, Johnny!"

Slowly she drew him away.

"Aw, leave 'em be, Sarge," the M.P. corporal said; "maybe she *is* his wife."

The sergeant spat. The brown tobacco juice splashed in the dirt not an inch from Lily's foot. Then the two of them turned and started away.

Johnny stopped.

"Lemme go, Lily," he said, "lemme go!" He tore her arm loose from his and started back up the street. Lily leaped, her two arms fastening themselves around his neck. He fought silently but she clung to him, doubling her knees so that all her weight was hanging from his neck.

"No, Johnny! Oh, Jesus no! You be kilt! Oh, Johnny, listen t' me, sugah! You's all I got!"

He put both hands up to break her grip but she swung her weight sidewise and the two of them went down in the dirt. The M.P.s turned the corner out of sight.

Johnny sat there in the dust staring at her. The dirt had ruined her dress. He sat there a long time looking at her until the hot tears rose up back of his eyelids faster than he could blink them away, so he put his face down in her lap and cried.

"I ain't no man!" he said. "I ain't no man!"

"Hush, sugah," she said. "You's a man aw right. You's my man!"

Gently she drew him to his feet. He picked up the bags and the two of them went down the dark street toward the preacher's house.

Berry Fleming

Strike Up a Stirring Music

All down the lines of the parked automobiles the civilians had run up their windows against Georgia's February wind; one or two that she could see had left a crack open at the top from which an almost imperceptible blue cigarette smoke oozed and then was whisked away. Some of them probably had their heaters running. Even the general looked cold when she stole a glance at him, though his dignity prevented his swinging his arms about as some of the younger officers did, standing there casually beside the armored car with his gloved hands clasped in front of him, enduring the wind, his head slightly depressed with the weight of the helmet. She could almost have touched him, touched him and whispered, "My husband is Second Lieutenant Marsh. I hope you are going to take good care of him——"

"All right, gentlemen, please," somebody said with a lifted finger, and the colonels and majors and captains moved round in front of the reviewing stand, and the driver of the armored car started his motor. She looked at the wrist watch he had given her on their second anniversary; it was three minutes to ten. They did things on time—which must have pleased Lieutenant Marsh. A year ago when he came home that evening from the advertising office on Forty-third Street and handed her the plain white stampless envelope addressed to "2nd Lt. John B. Marsh, FA-Reserves," handed it to her and hammered hard at a cigarette while she read the contents with parted lips, a year ago she would have thought the only military characteristic he had was a rather annoying respect for promptness.

She could hardly believe the words she saw. John in uniform! It was almost funny. He wasn't the soldier type. There was nothing cold about him, nothing rigid or precise. He walked along with great strides that she couldn't keep up with, a hand often in his pocket, his coat collar often turned up in a hangover of a casual undergraduate fashion. He was just a college boy who had taken "military science" as a snap course toward a degree, who had accepted his reserve commission with something of a smile, accepted it and put it away with his degree and forgotten both. He hadn't even thought of mentioning it to her until they had been married a year, and she happened to see one of those envelopes in a wastebasket she was emptying. "What's this?" she asked him when he came home. "Have I married a soldier?"

"That's a wild oat from my college days."

"But what do they want?"

"They want to know if I'd like to spend two weeks at camp this summer as a guest of the U.S.A."

"You aren't going to do it."

"Of course not."

She had hardly ever thought about it again, though the question came up once more the next spring; he wondered if he ought to go and get his promotion. He was getting on to the age limit for second lieutenant.

"But you don't believe in war."

"There's not going to be any war." Hitler hadn't anything to fight with; Germany was broke. And even if there should be a war in Europe . . .

Four beautiful notes, wistfully on the wind, from a bugler far out in the middle of the parade ground, standing there under his globular helmet like a little round-topped peg, like one of the markers on her father's cribbage board, back, back on winter evenings in Ohio when she was doing fractions on a five-cent pad in the dining room—fifteen thousand olive-colored cribbage pegs, but not shiny like olives, glossless, dusty-looking. You could hardly see them; you looked out with your eye prepared to see an empty field, because there was not a sound from over there, not a movement, not even, from that side, a stir in the wind of the few red leaves still clinging to the Georgia blackjacks. Then all of a sudden your eye, as if it were only getting used to the light, perceived, with almost the shock of a flash of fire, that there in front of you, as far away again as the bugler, stretching in a low colorless rim interminably to the left, and to the right over the shallow rise—the division, Lieutenant Marsh's division. It looked larger than at Benning, but that was just because the shallow rise kept you from seeing the end of the front.

The general lifted and lowered a quiet hand in answer to the energetic salute of a little peg a stone's throw in front of the stand that looked forlorn and utterly lonely in the tramped expanse of brown grass and the wind, like a bird alone in the sky, like the first gull coming out of the mist below Land's End when she knew the voyage was over and this junior from Princeton named Marsh was going on to Havre and she and her mother were landing at Plymouth—a little shy, avoiding her all the way across until the last day, then taking those long strides about the deck that she couldn't keep step with.

And she was going to lose him again soon, and in the same way: she was getting off, he was going on—as she had lost him now, melted into the dark rim running along the field. She knew approximately where he was standing because she could count down by the three clusters of points that sparkled in the fitful sun and that in a few minutes now would strike up a stirring music. *Ricominciate il suono!* It wouldn't be the "suono" that Mozart was thinking of, but it would be a stirring music, too, in its way. Counting to the right from the third regimental band, you came to the first artillery battalion, then the second battalion; he was standing in front of the third battery, not even distinguishable now as a figure, melting into the rest like a blade of wheat in a field, like somebody walking off into the dark of the first break of day. . . .

Clinging to him for a minute in the weakening light of the naked bulbs over the breakfast table, while the window grew pearl with the dawn, clinging to the chilly smoothness of his field jacket: "You'll be back tonight."

"Sure, oh sure."

She smiled at asking and at his reply; they both knew he could never be certain whether he would be back or not. All she knew was that one day he wouldn't.

"When the time comes we shan't get home, you know," he warned her once, months ago at another camp.

"You mean one day you'll just go out that door in the morning and ——"

"We couldn't have everybody calling all over town; even if the telephone system would stand it, it's not to get out when we are moving."

One night when she asked him about it again he said, "We aren't going yet. We're just up to war strength."

"But war strength——" She could hardly say it without her throat contracting.

He smiled at her, hammering hard at a cigarette as he had done that other time. "Twenty per cent over, for foreign service."

As long as she lived she would never forget that phrase. She had never heard anything like it for condensing the hurt of war into a few innocent words; that twenty percent was to be the torn dead, the swathed passengers of the hospital trains. . . .

The general crawled into the front of the armored car, pulled himself up through a sort of ring, and getting his feet, not as spryly as Lieutenant Marsh would have done but still getting them, answered the salute of a sergeant on the ground who had banged the steel door, and was driven off over the gray field, the long pole of the radio antenna whipping with the roll of the ground. She turned and mounted the two or three steps into the stand; she could take her choice of seats: there were hardly a dozen people there, most of them women, "army wives" with an especially small nod for the wife of a second lieutenant, a few civilians with their coat collars turned up, having trouble with their cigarettes in the wind.

The general would come back; he would come home someday. A lieutenant's chances were—well, they weren't quite so good—with the music blowing away on the wind and washing back now and then in a faint rhythmic boom of the drum, and the heavy car driving down the line toward the rise and, after a while, over it in a brief silhouette.

This was the last stop all right. This was as far as she went. Moving about from one Southern town to another, nobody seemed to know why, or to ask. One parade ground, then another; one flimsy little Southern house, then another, rented from amateur landlords who had plastered on a thin coat of paint and doubled the rent, or who threw up a pasteboard partition and created an "apartment"—John tiptoeing down the hall in the daybreak, letting himself through the front door like a fugitive, not to wake up the civilian population. Not to wake up Mr. Rogers, who would begin to stir at about the time John was marching in from the first drill period and be served a hot breakfast and drive into town and a warm office about nine-thirty, nine-thirty or a quarter to ten, a few minutes one way or the other didn't matter—to the civilian population. Not to wake up Mrs. Rogers, who would be finishing her breakfast coffee at about the time the "young lieutenant's wife" got back from the "tea store."

"You're up mighty early," was the cheery greeting at first. Sometimes she was handed a camellia if she happened to be a little later than usual and found Mrs. Rogers with her scissors and basket and gloves among her flowers. Then, when they got it through their heads that the young lieutenant began his day's work before the cook was awake—"Is everything all right? You must let me know if you need anything," as if she and John were down South on some personal holiday, on a hunting trip, up betimes to get into the rice fields by sunrise. . . . Oh, maybe she was too hard on them; they were nice about asking you to "supper" and all that. But . . .

"We'll win all right," said Mr. Rogers reassuringly, lighting a cigar. "Just give us a little time, and we'll wipe 'em off the map."

But John was taking his yellow-fever shots, and "map" was not a piece of slick paper to run your finger over; "map" was sand and heat and thirst and John in mortal danger—and she somewhere or other, married and not married. . . .

This was as far as she went. "From here on the division is on its own." He smiled when she told him that, picking her up against the stiff leather of his belts and straps, there in the indifferent town, going its way while the division went theirs, talking about the war as if it were a baseball game.

"Just give us a little time, and we'll wipe 'em off the map!" Tune in tomorrow, same time, same station, this crisis of the age brought to them by the courtesy of the First National Bank.

Who's "we," Mr. Rogers? She could hardly keep from saying it. . . .

The car pulled up under its gleaming whip, the general folded himself out of it, straightened his helmet, returned to the stand. The bugler floated his golden notes across the field. The first band moved into position. Then the top of the dark rim lifted almost imperceptibly, like the hair bristling between the shoulders of a hunting dog her father had had when the cat came near, lifted and grayed, and she knew the division had shouldered its bayonets. She heard the solid boom of car doors closing now; the civilians began to emerge.

She watched, fascinated, though she had seen the parade many times—watched the band begin to play, almost in make-believe, for they stepped off with all the motions of a stirring music, yet there was no sound, watched the light glint on the porcupine quills of the leading mass as the square changed direction with a curious combination of the cumbersome and the supple, heard the music more clearly then, from far away like the band at the fair when they were late on account of her mother and the hair ribbon pulling her hair with a Sunday prudery, circus bands, college bands, a faraway band one spring at the races, holiday bands—all but this one; this one, when it came abreast, would have saddle-colored holsters at its hip swinging with a heavy grace to the bright music.

The women in the stand rose to their feet, rose in pairs, each pair homogeneous in a battling, fleeting way, like the warmth of a day in spring and a day in autumn—more pairs than had been in the stand last time. The mothers were coming down now, the "army wives'" mothers, coming down very casually, just for a little visit. It was almost something to smile about, how the mothers were beginning to gather; when the mothers gathered the transports gathered too.

But they were a little premature this time; only two nights before, knitting a pair of socks in front of the hideous coal stove the landlord had graciously consented to install in front of the blocked-up fireplace, she had asked him as she did occasionally, "Are you twenty per cent over yet?" And he had teased her with "That's information of value and comfort to the enemy," but he had laughed and she knew he was telling her they were not—they weren't quite ready for the mothers and the ships yet.

She didn't know why she wanted to prolong this walking-along-the-edge existence, this imperceptible drawing nearer—while the little town grew fat to bursting and new houses sprang up over land where the pine stumps were still bleeding, all the town cheery in a Christmas mood, publishing in the papers every payday the amount of the divisional pay roll, the fat-throated politicians with the sinister eyes counting the "take" from the dens and the tourist cabins and the trailer parks—while the young men drilled and dug in and fired and lay in the rain and marched through the night and wandered about the town looking forlornly at the houses and the gardens with the late camellias. But no; let even all that go on forever. . . .

And here they came now, as if they would come on forever, like a wide ribbon of some silver-topped grain swaying slightly in the wind, stirring with the stirring music. Down the field in a steady measured flow, past the civilians looking on, past the general lifting and lowering his hand benevolently, the bright-tipped quills of their bayonets shining, the whole mass of them holding, beneath the music, an implacable, rock-ribbed, somehow amazing silence. They trudged by; in time to the music, but not with a light step. "The sand is soft," he said; you had to push against it to keep from losing distance—and now there was a haze of dust rising about the knees and waists of the men in the rear ranks of the squares, dust rising and blowing away. One of the squares, as it thrust by, lost some of its shape as the far side lagged, and a civilian voice behind her muttered at them, "Watch that line!"—as if they were cadets at a military school, instead of an army that nine months before had been riding the subways and plowing the fields, an army that now, however its line might lag, had sweated through a summer in the Alabama lowlands, camped among the snakes and the tarantulas and the scorpions, maneuvered through many a night and gone into action without breakfast, the warm rain collecting in drops on their beards. "One night," he told her with a laugh, "we killed eleven rattlers in one battery area."

She wanted to turn and look at this man over her shoulder, just look at him. But she didn't; another thought drove him out of her mind, a half-formed thought that occurred to her in the midst of the stirring music, in the midst of watching their lines, a little wavy, watching the short sway of the spades and hatchets at their belts: they seemed to be passing more slowly than usual.

Which was impossible. The bands played to a certain cadence, and the division would march past in almost the same length of time to a second. She had better quit imagining things and look sharp or she would miss him; sometimes she did.

But this time she saw him, on the far side of the second artillery square beyond the third man with the guidon—saw him trudging by to that curious throb of the mass that was not so much the pulse of the music as the very pulse of the division, saw him for a moment just before he was hidden by the nearer officers, marching by now still with a trace of that civilian stride by which she had recognized him among the Fifth Avenue crowds on many a summer evening, waiting in front of the library—saw him now and felt her throat catch as she made out the little surreptitious waving of three fingers of the hand saluting the general, saw him and lost him again as the front of the square moved on.

Then with her throat still tight she saw something else, and she laid her hand on the cold rim of the chair back before her. She had never counted the ranks of his battalion, but she had a feeling about the size of it; she knew well the way it looked from the stand, the space it occupied in your vision. . . . His battalion was longer than last time.

And it was as if somebody had expressed in words something she had been unconsciously thinking for a long time. Now she understood. The whole division was "twenty per cent over"; that was why it had stretched so far over the shallow rise, that was why it seemed to move past so slowly, why the last rank of his battalion was only now crossing her sight—bent backward at the far end, a steam of dust rising about their knees.

And she could feel a sickening tumble of something inside her, and her eyes seemed to flood with nothing at all, and she laid both hands on the rim of the chair back.

She sat down and waited for a minute, the stirring music pounding in her ears. After a while she stood up again and watched the gray quills moving over the rise against the gray sky, moving with a pulsing motion, the banners streaming on the wind.

Byron Herbert Reece

From *Better a Dinner of Herbs*

Uncle Enid

From time to time as he drove Uncle Enid rested his forearm against the money belt he had made from a sugar sack and strings and tied about his middle before setting out. The belt contained all the money he had got for the farm and the animals and the house plunder. It was a sizable sum, containing, besides, all he had saved through years of frugal living. The weight of the money pulled against his flesh and he could see in his mind the nest of greenbacks and the cluster of silver pieces in the bag. The money represented his freedom from the small and great tyrannies of life on the farm and the fine bulk of it resting in safety against his body set up a pleasurable feeling that tingled in his nerve ends.

Yet a gold piece that had been his particular treasure was missing from the hoard. He remembered clearly his sharp sense of loss when he first discovered it was gone from among the pieces of money. When he thought of the gold piece there was an emptiness in him like that of hunger. He went back in his mind now to the day, shortly after he had sold the farm to Tully, when he went to the crock that served him as a bank to reassure himself of his great fortune:

The money was all there except the gold piece. Its glow was absent from the flash of the silver and the dull-green shining of the bills. He was stunned. He let the silver pour through his fingers again but the gold piece did not reappear among the silver coins, as he knew it would not though he could not accept the fact that it was missing from the nest of coins. He crushed the bills in his hands, thinking if the gold piece was invisible among their folds he would feel its golden bulk resisting the pressure of his fingers. He did feel the curving edge of a coin as his fingers tightened on the bills and he was dizzy with relief, but when he had straightened the bills out one by one to come on the coin he found it to be yet another coin of silver. For a moment he hated the silver coin because it was not the gold piece.

"It's gone," he said to himself. He stood looking at the pile of money that bulked on the cupboard shelf, opening and closing his fingers as he regarded it. He seemed to be waiting for the silver coins and the green bills to say where the gold piece had gone from among them. He looked at them a long time. Then he put the money in the crock again and stuffed the old gingham rag in the top and replaced it on the cupboard shelf.

"Gone," he said to himself, turning from the crock and the cupboard toward the door through which a shaft of winter sunlight as gold as the lost coin was pouring. He made as if to go out the door, then turned back to the cupboard and removed the crock and searched carefully the shelf on which the crock rested. The coin was not there.

"Somebody stole it," he said. He pulled the gingham rag from the crock and shook it carefully, but nothing fell from its folds. Only a little dust went up, golden in color, dullish golden.

Then he began to count the money feverishly. He made the silver pieces clink against each other in a fury of clinking. He had only been admiring the money when he discovered the gold piece missing. For moments after the discovery he had hoped that it was only misplaced, had fallen on the shelf or by some chance got entangled in the old rag that served both to stop the top of the crock and disguise its contents. But someone must have taken the gold piece, and if so, how much more besides? The coins rattled against each other in his haste of counting. The bills slap-slap-slapped against each other as he ran up their total in his mind.

Nothing was missing but the gold piece.

It was damned queer.

He selected a dollar at random from the silver and stood throwing it into the air and catching it as it came down. He took particular pains to make it reverse itself in the air with each throw, yet his mind was not on the silver dollar. His mind had gone in search of the gold piece.

There had been but the one gold piece in all the money.

It had shone like the moon when the air is smoky at its rising.

He began to follow it from the beginning in his mind in hopes of tracing it down, even to the place where it must now be, eluding him.

He was crouching on the ground, on his heels, with his neighbor Tully facing him. They had concluded the interminable palaver that is the ritual of the country tradesman and agreed upon terms for the transference of the farm from his possession to Tully's.

"Three hundred in greenbacks," Tully said, counting it out on his knee in fives, tens, and ones.

"Twenty-five in silver," Tully had the silver in a little bag tied with a drawstring. He poured the contents of the bag on the ground and stacked it in piles, each coin after its kind, dime upon dime, quarter upon quarter, half dollar upon half dollar and silver dollars after their kind. Their bright milled edges glittered in the sun.

There was a pause, and Uncle Enid looked at Tully expectantly while he rested on his heels, his hands hanging slack between his open knees, not yet rising to go exploring his pocket for the remaining money. After a moment Tully raised his hand to the pocket on the bib of his overalls and reached into it with stubby forefinger and slowly brought forth the gold piece from the pocket's depth. It emerged from between the denim-blue lips of the pocket like the sun emerging from between two thunderheads.

That was the first he had seen of the gold piece.

Tully held the coin in the palm of his cupped hand and his eyes dwelt on it fondly. He, too, looked at the coin, admiring its clean stamp and the fine shine of its alloy. He suddenly wanted the coin very much. In all his life he had never possessed a gold piece.

"I meant to keep the gold piece," Tully said. "If I could have raised the money without throwing in the gold piece . . ." he held it still in his hand, turning it from side to side. "Got it a long time ago in a trade with Old Harkins. Dead now. You remember Old Harkins?"

He remembered and nodded. His own palm tingled with desire to feel the weight of the gold piece.

"Kept it for a good-luck piece," Tully went on. "Never spent it, hard up a lot of times but never did spend the gold piece."

Uncle Enid nodded again, keeping his eyes on the gold piece. He might hang it from his watch chain.

"No sense being foolish about a piece of money, though," Tully said. He stretched out his hand, slowly, reluctantly, and transferred the gold piece from his own palm to Uncle Enid's. "Did mean to keep it," he said, "but it spends as good as greenback."

"Twenty in gold."

And so the deal by which Tully came into possession of his farm was completed.

"Well," he had said, "you've got yourself a fine farm. With the land you've bought added to what you had already nobody in the county's got a better."

Tully, pleased, nodded his head three times and the thought of the land he now owned returned a greater shining to his eyes than the surrender of the gold piece had taken away.

He left Tully then, and on the way to the farm that had been his own his heart sank to think that the ancestral acres that had underwritten the security of his forefathers for generations were no longer his. But the weight of the silver and the bulk of the greenbacks reassured him; and nestled in his watch pocket was the twenty-dollar gold piece. Finally it came in his mind to represent the freedom he had bought with the sale of the farm. A man has a right to a while of freedom before he dies, he thought. As long as a man is young and able security can dwell in his muscles as well as in property. Inside himself he felt the strength of his body, firm and supple as a hickory sapling, and his fear disappeared. He carried his freedom, minted in a mint, printed on a press, along the country road and when he reached the house where he was born he stored it in the old crock he had used to bank his extra change. He placed the coins and the bills in the crock and stuffed an old gingham rag into its throat and placed the crock where it had always rested on the top shelf of the kitchen cupboard.

All except the gold piece.

He kept the gold piece in his watch pocket. He had not yet decided what to do with it. Besides, he wanted it on his person so he could hold it in his hand from time to time.

That was how he had come into possession of the gold piece, and now it was gone.

He stood, still with the silver dollar in his hand, and went back in his mind to take up the history of the gold piece.

It was too much money to hang on a watch chain. If it had been a two-dollar-and-a-half piece or even a five-dollar one it would have made a fine charm to hang at the chain's end. But not a twenty-dollar piece. It would be putting on airs. Yet he held the coin to the end of the chain to try out how it would look, and all his dark ancestors came from the cells of his body and the fields of his flesh and looked at him and said, "Ha!" He was almost as outraged as they by the look of a twenty-dollar gold piece at his chain's end, and he put the coin in his pocket again and the scorn left the faces of his dark ancestors and they faded away.

Instead of a charm for his watch chain he would keep it as a shield against the worm of want, should the strength that dwelt in his body fail for a time. And it was big enough to hide Danny, to enfold him for a long time against hunger, and it had the power to hire his healing if he should become ill. He had a momentary vision of Danny in that golden robe, his fine face shining with a goldish cast through the gold of the coin encompassing him.

So he gave up the idea of hanging the coin from his watch chain, but he carried it in his watch pocket as he went about his work, the tasks life on the farm demanded doing in the old age of the year. He gathered corn and stored roughage in the cavernous barn loft with a peculiar zest, thinking: The last time, the last time. On leaving the farm he meant to work at a sawmill or go to the smelters at the copper works not far away and work there.

He often took the coin from his pocket when Danny was not with him to see the action and looked at it and admired it. He took the coin as gold and round as the day and held it in his hand and let the two medallions, the day and the coin, flash fire from each other. It became dearer each day and finally it came to represent all the money, itself, the silver and the greenbacks safe in the glazed crock.

After he had carried the coin for a month he lost it.

A certain night he took his watch from his pocket to wind it. As he was winding the watch he noticed there were fine scratches on the watch crystal. The coin, he concluded, was scratching the face of the watch. He must think of a way to keep them separated in his pocket. Wrap the coin in a piece of cloth perhaps. He probed into the pocket with his forefinger, reaching for the coin.

It was not there.

He sat down, filled with dismay.

The gold piece would be difficult to find. He had had it at noon that day. At noon he had taken it from his pocket and rested himself by looking at it. When he looked at the coin the tiredness flowed out of his muscles like the water from a pool when its dam is broken. That day he had finished hauling the corn from the south bottom. He could have lost it in the field. He could have lost it in the wagon bed, stooping over it to throw the corn from the bed into the crib. It could have lodged in the husk of an ear of corn and traveled with it into the crib. If so he would never find it.

His dismay deepened. He rose as if to go in search of the coin. The night was too dark. There was no use going in search of the bright coin in that unbroken darkness. Even so gold a coin could not penetrate the night and announce itself by dazzles of golden light. He must wait for day.

He was up before the sun and said he must go out and Danny stood watching him intently as he went from the house, searching the ground in the frosty light of early morning for the coin. He retraced the wagon tracks along the road to the south bottom, walking slowly, examining the tracks with undivided attention. Once he looked ahead and saw a shining in the right wagon track a few yards ahead. It sent shafts of light from the sun into the absorbing air. His heart lifted and he hurried toward the object.

It was a piece of mica set in a pebble of sandstone that glittered in the sun.

He did not find it in the field, nor in the wagon bed, nor about the crib.

"Tully begrudged me the gold piece," he said at the end of the first day of the Days of the Lost Gold Piece. In the days that followed he went about his work as usual but his eyes were always searching for the missing coin; even where he had not been on the day of loss he sought it.

One night he took the crock from the shelf and looked into it. "If I had put the gold piece with the other money," he said, and replaced the crock.

Then on a morning he took his pail and went to the feed room of the barn for morning feed for the cow. The room was littered with straws and slivers of shucks, and when he moved a golden dust rose up from his feet into the block of sunlight that prisoned in the door. As he stooped to put the meal in the feed pail he saw the coin.

It was lying in the straw litter.

It had fallen from his pocket earlier as he bent above the feed pail. He scooped it up with a short cry of joy. The hand that retrieved the gold piece trembled, and the trembling increased the glittering of the gold piece as it rested in his hand in the glow of the morning sun.

That was the first time he had lost it but not the last by two.

He had returned the gold piece to his pocket wrapped in a fold of his linen handkerchief. He returned it with a sense of thankfulness and because its bulk was increased by the wrapping he had only to put his hand against the pocket to know it was there, safe in his bosom like the salvation of the Lord prisoned in the bosom of saints.

The days wheeled one after the other like great golden coins in the weeks following, the Days of the Found Gold Piece. The days were like his coin except their reverse sides showed obsidian, like the stone of the arrows left in his fields by the Indians, themselves shot by the bowstring of time beyond the land of their nativity. He was busy with gathering the harvest into the barn, to the last ear of corn, to the last golden pumpkin, to the last bronze bundle of fodder. His kitchen walls were strung with dried beans and slender scarlet peppers that hung like beads about the slender necks of nails driven into the wall to hold them. He paused at times to wonder who would reap the benefits of his careful husbandry of the autumn harvest, since he could not carry in his faring a tithe of all he had gathered.

When he saw Tully infrequently he observed about him the airs of an owner of extensive property. He did not resent these airs, though in the days before he had sold him the farm Tully and he met as equals, their relationship long established on the basis of ownership of equal possessions. These airs that Tully now gave himself were the reward of long skimping in order to save enough money to buy Uncle Enid's property.

"If I could take possession right away," Tully would say, "I could get some plowing done before spring. It's going to push me to get all the land in, now there are so many acres to plow."

"Most any time now," he would say, keeping in mind the terms of their agreement whereby he could not be evicted before the New Year, but seeming to wish to oblige Tully. "Got to have a sale and be rid of the corn and plunder."

"I need to extend the ditch in the south bottom," Tully would say. "Ground's a little sobby beyond the head of the ditch. If I could take over right away. . . ."

"Right at once now," he would answer.

So he was busy as the days of late autumn wheeled into winter. He thought of the gold piece less often, and in the press of several busy days not at all.

He was catching water from the trough when his eyes fell upon something at the edge of the pond. It was vaguely familiar, it moved something in his mind but he stood preoccupied with the song of the water from the trough against the sides of the bucket, a tune running from treble to bass as the level of the water rose. As he took the bucket from the trough his eyes brushed the scrap at the pond's edge and something electric swept through him. He set the bucket down, spilling the water, and took up the linen scrap from the pond. He unfolded the cloth to the gold piece within, and the film of wetness added to the sheen of its luster.

He did not know when he had lost it, but he went to the crock and placed the gold piece in the nest of greenbacks with the silver pieces. Its golden shine warred with the flashing of the silver coins.

Thereafter he went without fear of the coin slipping from his pocket.

So he followed the gold piece in his mind to the time when it was deposited in the crock. He yearned to see beyond the crock then to the coin itself, wherever it was. But he had followed it in vain in his mind. He found no clue that would be helpful in locating the gold piece. His vision of it, lying lost and golden in a cleft of darkness, faded to nothing.

It could not have been lost from the crock.

Someone had taken it.

He skirted the possible thief in his mind. He felt suddenly tired as he stood looking into the crock. As he made a motion toward the crock a cloud came over the sun.

The gold was even gone out of the day.

He made to lift the crock and replace it in its usual position on the top cupboard shelf. Then for the first time he was aware of the silver dollar in his hand. He removed the gingham rag and flung the coin angrily into the crock. It rang against the glazed sides of the crock and came to rest with a final dull clank among the other coins. He took the crock into his hands then, but instead of placing it on the cupboard shelf he turned abruptly to his own room. There he placed the crock on a shelf of the clothes press and pulled his shirts over it. They hid the crock in a random fold of their disarray.

"I coveted it too much. The Lord wouldn't let me keep it," he said, taking leave of the gold piece. He turned then and went through the door looking for Danny. He had it in his mind to leave the farm as soon as possible.

When the time of their going forth arrived, as the first preparation for the journey he took the money less the gold piece and placed it in the bag he had made for it, and tied it about his middle. Now he rode in the wagon through the falling snow and the loss of the gold piece was in his mind, and he could think of nothing to do with the loss except endure it to dullness and at length to dust.

Danny

To remember, Danny thought.

He had been preoccupied with the promise in the sky when Uncle Enid came that day from visiting the crock and passed like a wraith through the field of his vision. Clouds fluffy and soft as sheep's wool scudded before the wind from the sky's northwest corner. A tentative snowdrop fell now and then from the racing clouds. These represented partial payment of a note the sky had signed on a blustery day early in October, when a few flakes, the first of the year, fell to disappear as soon as fallen.

It was his hope that now the sky meant to pay the note in full, and yet the hope ran counter to his weather wisdom. The clouds were rough and jumbled like a field of boulders, and he had come to expect a respectable snow only from a sky cloud as smooth as glass, gray and unmoving. The turbulence of the air was a factor against the fulfillment of his hope also, for snow wants stillness to fall through. Should his hope prevail over the natural obstacles to its fulfillment he was prepared to pay the sky a full measure of delight.

Later through his speculation the voice of Uncle Enid came up from the barn, calling his name. He stood at the woodpile under the larger of two golden maples that stood at the flank of the house like guards posted to hold it from surprise attack from the elements, hearing the voice that came to him soft and rounded by its passage through the space from the barn to the house. He did not respond to the call. I am here already, he thought, and he filed the call away in the part of his brain reserved for unfinished matters and carried an armful of wood from the woodpile to the back porch. Ordinarily the business of getting wood for the night was a dull chore but the promise of snow made it exciting, lifted it into the realm of important matters, as if he laid in food against a siege.

His uncle's voice came to him again, rounded and modulated by its thrust through the space from his uncle to himself, and he listened carefully, but this time his uncle was not calling his name. He was calling the hogs in the lot for their afternoon feed. Having gone to the barn on other matters and not being able to fulfill them his uncle nevertheless refused to waste the energy that had carried him there, and so he was feeding the hogs and no doubt would feed the other animals their evening feed before returning to the house in the quest of himself, Danny.

This switch of attention on his uncle's part freed him for moments from the constraint of his authority. But the purity of his release from his uncle was colored with speculation concerning his want with him at all.

For punishment?

For reward?

Through the exercise of these two powers his uncle validated their relationship as father and son, though they were not father and son, but the fact that both seemed to him now beyond the periphery of likelihood left him to fruitless speculation that itched like a rash in his mind. He made a small mountain of wood rise on the back porch, then in the silence that came up from the barn like a tide in the wake of his uncle's voice he went into the kitchen by way of the hall that ran from the back to the front porch, dividing the short end of the L-shaped structure from the long end that served as the living quarters of the house. On his way through the hall he passed the door of his own room and had a momentary vision of himself lying in his bed asleep. He looked at the mirror features of his face a moment before the vision was lost in a switch of interest. He passed Uncle Enid's room on the other side of the hall exactly opposite his own, and the two Nobody's Rooms lying on either side of the hall, dark foreboding domains of mystery.

When he entered the kitchen he looked first at the cupboard, and it assumed its familiar image in his mind, yet it was not exactly the same. He stood regarding the cupboard while the hunger that had brought him to the kitchen subsided and was forgotten in the effort to determine what made the cupboard strange in its familiarity. Suddenly his mind restored the object missing from the image of the cupboard.

The crock that flowered with an old gingham rag was gone.

When he discovered this a tendril of an emotion he did not understand began to grow in his mind. He turned his head from where he stood and looked through the door, and because his uncle was not on the path a feeling of relief swept through him like a gust of wind. He took a piece of sweetbread from the second shelf of the cupboard and went through the hall nibbling at it.

Something of stealth came over him then; there was a dread of his uncle on his spirit. In a pause he made to listen he heard that silence still flowed from the barn. Then he heard his uncle wading in the silence and, urged away from him, he stepped from the porch on the side of the house opposite the path side. He went toward the barn as his uncle came from there. They moved in opposite directions, the house between them.

And Danny was first aware then that between them was the lost and the taken, the gold piece.

On the path to the barn he heard his uncle call him again, his voice rising loud and urgent from the doorway of the house. He tried to ignore the call altogether but it remained, a cord binding their two entities that were otherwise planetary in their separate orbits of action.

With the cord of his uncle's voice binding them he went to the barn.

Besides his Uncle Enid, who was at its center, his world was populated by these others: Bessie the cow, the bull who was known as Blackie, the mare, without name since she was not a primary character, and Five-Pigs the sow and her current offspring. With the exception of the latter these lived in the nether regions of the barn, in the stables that were dark and stuffy under the huge loft that smelled of fodder and hay.

He paused at the hog lot where Five-Pigs was eating the corn his uncle had fed her. She placed a large divided foot on the ears and bit the grains from the cobs. As he leaned over the fence the sow grunted in recognition, and he climbed the fence and stood among the pigs that were too young to eat the corn. They tugged at their mother's side, and he pulled them away and offered them the remainder of his sweetbread. They smelled of it and made tentative efforts to take it into their mouths, then returned to the wrinkled dugs of their mother.

He stooped and tickled a pig on its pink belly and it leaned against his hand, leaning harder and harder until he removed his hand and the pig lay for a moment on its side on the ground.

"Old Five-Pigs," he said to the sow. There was logic in the name because for some reason she always gave birth to five pigs. She was large and shaggy, a sandstone color; her ears hung before her face hiding her little eyes that looked out small and mean from between straggly eyebrows. The expression of her eyes belied her nature for she was friendly and gentle and bore with his pranking with as much grace as an old woman shows to the idle and foolish pranking of the young.

"Old Five-Pigs," he said again and laid his hand on her leathery back, folding his fingers into her rough hair. The sow replied with a grunt and a flipping of her crusty tail.

At that moment his uncle called him yet again and his voice had grown sharp. He made the gesture of Not Coming which consisted of an impatient screwing up of his face and entered the barn. The hallway was littered with straw and fodder shatters and numberless worn plows and broken pieces of iron saved for emergencies of mending that never occurred stuck from cracks in the wall. He went through the tunnel of hallway, looking first toward the house. His uncle was nowhere in sight and he climbed then into the loft and threw down three bronze bundles of fodder.

These he gave to the forage-eating animals that lived in the barn. One to Bessie, so named because his uncle had bought her from a woman of the neighborhood named Bessie Teague. Bessie was a claybank with a dull-white star in her forehead. She did not converse with him in her language, as the sow did, but she had eloquent eyes. As he threw the bundle of fodder into her stall she looked at him with a clear grateful stare. He closed the door upon her and as he did so it occurred to him suddenly that her udder was like a pot in which his uncle did their washings by the brook's side.

The second bundle of fodder he gave to the bull. He had discovered Blackie two years before by an elder clump in the pasture where he had been birthed by Bessie. He was totally black except for a smudge of white that stained the purity of his color near his right flank.

Blackie was playful like himself and though he had been warned that the bull might hurt him he disregarded the warning. When the bull was turned to pasture they would play together, feinting toward each other, butting their heads together lightly in a pantomime of fight.

He fed the third bundle of fodder to the mare, not lingering at the door of her stall because of all the animals she was most a stranger. Not that there was any evil in her, she was almost as placid as the cow, yet because she contained great potentials of strength and speed he was afraid of her.

After the mare there was nothing more to feed, and he went from the hallway into the light of the enormous round day. The barnyard fowls converged around him as he came from the barn but he paid no attention to them. He had never been able to establish any sort of contact with the fowls, as he had with the other inhabitants of the farmstead. Because of this lack of understanding between them he even disliked the fowls, especially the speckled guineas that scattered to the woods when disturbed and cried pot-rack-pot-rack-pot-rack for hours with ear-shattering shrillness.

He was already on his way to the house when his uncle called him again, shouting, the irritation that was beginning to grow in him riding the waves of his voice. He had entirely lost the trace of the strange emotion that stirred him as he beheld the absence of the crock. His spirit was warmed and lifted through contact with the animals. The image of the coin guilt had minted in his mind had melted and run down into the slag of his subconscious.

"Danny!" his uncle shouted from the kitchen door. He smiled faintly and then put on the empty face with which he confronted his uncle when in doubt of his reception. It began to snow again in great erratic drops and he removed the nothing from his face and let delight shine there for a moment. The snow touched him with a chaste cool touch and as he ran along the path he clapped his hands together and sang out, "The Old Woman in the sky is picking her geese!"

Now in the wagon the gold piece was between them again. It rested now in the purse his uncle had given to encourage him in thrift. It rested there with the three pennies that had comprised his whole fortune before he had taken the gold piece. He did not know the value of the gold piece. He had taken it because it was beautiful.

He wished the gold piece back in the crock and its taking washed from his mind and removed from between him and his uncle, who drove the mare through the falling snow withdrawn and partially lost to him by the act that defiled and punished him, and was all the more regrettable because it was as irrevocable as the hour in which he stole.

The gold piece had not been between them as they sat at the long kitchen table, on the eve of the promising sky, eating by lamplight. They sat at the table in the house that did not know the touch of women eating from an excessively clean table covered with green oilcloth. The small brass lamp rested in the center of the table, in an island of darkness that was the shadow of its base. Uncle Enid sat on the side next the stove in order to be handy to it and Danny faced him from the opposite side of the table. They never ate side by side for if they had they would have been unable to see each other without a craning and bending of necks and part of the communication between them would have been lost.

He says things without speaking, Danny thought. I finger about in my plate and his face darkens because I am supposed to use my fork and not my fingers. He doesn't say anything but I look at his darkened face and it makes me uncomfortable. I pick up my fork and use it to corner the fat back in the peas on my plate and his face lightens and we are together again. His own face darkened and lightened like fields when clouds are many but broken and sweep intermittently between the earth and sun.

They talked little in words at meals for there was nothing much to talk about and through the years that they had lived together they had come to understand each other's gestures and facial expressions and words were unnecessary between them.

Yet Danny had stumbled on a new discovery in the act of listening to his uncle call him from the barn earlier in the afternoon. He had been aware for some time of the possibility of the thing he had discovered, but it burst upon him suddenly like all discoveries do and it excited him greatly.

"I know what color talking is," he said as he helped himself to a plate of black-eyed peas.

"What color, then?" Uncle Enid said. It was a trait of his that he never showed surprise. If someone had announced, as to the fowls in the fairy story, that the sky was falling he would have turned without haste to look and see for himself.

"It's black," Danny said. "When you say, bring a bucket of water, the words sound black."

Uncle Enid smiled and looked at him with amusement growing in his eyes.

"When you yell," Danny said, "it sounds red."

"It does, does it?" Uncle Enid said.

"Except not exactly," Danny said. "It sounds like red and yellow mixed."

"What color does a baby cry?" Uncle Enid said.

"Why, it cries about the same color of a rock," Danny said. He was afraid that his uncle was beginning to make fun of him. The light of amusement grew in his eyes. It danced there like a swarm of midges early in the morning.

"Rocks are all colors," Uncle Enid said.

"It cries the color of a flint rock," Danny said.

"Gray or white or yellow?" Uncle Enid said.

"Gray," Danny said, taking his choice of the colors of flint. He was not anxious to continue the description of the colors of sound. He wanted more time to listen and determine the colors the sounding world made.

They sat in silence for a long while after they had finished eating. Danny began to droop with sleepiness. He made rings in the leavings in his plate with a slender forefinger and the figures he made ran together and then separated, closed and exploded as his consciousness wavered in the nelson bend of sleep.

After a while Uncle Enid lifted him and warmed him before the fire as he would an inanimate bundle. Then he carried him through the hall to his room and turned back the covers.

"I don't want to go to bed," Danny said on his way through the dark hall.

"Time," Uncle Enid said.

"It's too cold," Danny said.

"It's not much cold," Uncle Enid said, but he could tell from the way the wind struck the corner of the house that it had veered from southwest to north. It whistled in a lamenting cold voice about the eaves.

"Will it snow?" Danny said.

"Not while the wind's from the north," Uncle Enid said.

"I want it to snow," Danny said.

"All boys want it to snow," Uncle Enid said.

He lifted Danny and held him under the arms while he unbuttoned his overalls and let them slip from his body to the floor. "I've got to quit this foolishness of putting you to bed," he said.

"I can get in bed," Danny said. But he stood on the sheepskin before his bed and made no move to crawl between the covers.

Uncle Enid lifted him and placed him in bed, then he tucked the covers around him to keep out the cold. He stood with the brass lamp in his hand and looked at Danny in silence. Danny regarded him in turn with a light quizzical stare.

"You forgot something," Uncle Enid said.

Danny closed his eyes and said swiftly in a subdued voice:

"Now I lay me down to sleep
I pray the Lord the watch to keep.
If I should die before I wake
I pray the Lord my soul to take.
God bless Uncle Enid and God bless me."

Uncle Enid sighed. He meant to tell Danny that tomorrow he would go and arrange the sale and when they were rid of the goods they would go and try their luck in the wide world. Instead he turned to leave the room.

"Night," he said.

"Night," Danny said, and one listening could not have told whether they were commenting on the time of day or taking leave of each other for the solitary journey across the continent of sleep.

When Uncle Enid left him in the darkness Bessie and the sow and the pigs and Blackie and the mare passed like specters through his mind and he asked that they be blessed along with Uncle Enid and himself. Then from a sense of justice he summoned the fowls also. From this spectral procession a guinea took disturbed flight but its progress dissolved into nothingness and a wail of the north wind was sliced clean from its source by sleep which is a knife and nothing.

Uncle Enid

Nor was the gold piece between them the following morning when the day of their faring was closer by one. Uncle Enid rose in the half-light of dawn, shivering in the cold air, the flesh of his legs pimpling where they were bare below his shirt. He stood on the outer rims of his feet, his insteps drawn away from the icy floor, hesitating to draw on his overalls. They were slick with cold as if with filth. The cold flowing about him urged him at last and he put first one leg through a hollow of cloth and then the other. He felt as if he were encased in ice. He stood trembling, trying to contract his flesh to bring it away from contact with the cold cloth. When the warmth of his flesh had communicated itself to the cloth he bent to ease his feet into his shoes, iron from the cold. When he made the first steps in them they would not bend.

When he stepped onto the porch for wood to build a fire the wind caught him, a wind so cold it felt wet to the skin. He hastened a back-stick from the pile and overlaid the andirons with small sticks and lit the fire with rich pine knots he had gathered from fallen trees on the mountains. While he was outside getting wood for the fire he saw that a powder of snow lay on the low matted grass of the fields. There was snow as light as frost on the woodpile under the maples and the straw pile by the barn smoked in the chilly fire of snow.

When the fire roared at last, he sat with his hands folded over the end of the fire shovel, resting his head on his hands. He spread his legs wide to the heat, and as the warmth began to collect in his clothing he suddenly brought his knees together to shut it out. He was troubled and a little outraged at the suggestiveness the warm cloth imparted to his body where it bound against his crotch.

He rose and turned to build a fire in the stove.

He made biscuits and put them in a pan and took sausage from a mason jar where they were buried in a fog of grease and put them in another, setting the pan toward the back of the stove where the heat was less. When he was finished with his morning chores the food would be cooked. Though he was not now pressed for time he persisted in following the patterns of his habits. In the times of great activity on the farm his method of cooking gained him precious minutes in the fields.

In all his years he had never cooked a meal without feeling slightly outraged at performing what he considered a woman's task. It was his only ability developed to a high state of perfection of which he was not proud. He did not boast of his ability to cook among men as he did his ability to cradle wheat. His proficiency at cooking displeased him, as if it impugned his masculinity.

Thinking then of his desire to surrender his distaff duties brought inexplicably the sensation he had experienced before the fire.

While the food cooked on the stove he went to the barn and fed the animals. He stood at the opened doors of the stalls, observing with wonder the great gouts of breath the animals sent vivid into the cold morning air. In the vapor of their breathing that dissolved, not from edge to center but all at once, he saw suddenly a metaphor for the dispersal of life into the wide air of death.

On his way through the house again he called Danny and told him it was time to rise. He stood before his door, listening. There was no sound of activity within, and he went into the kitchen and set the table and placed the food upon it. Then he entered Danny's room and turned the covers from him. As the air struck his body Danny turned immediately from the pose of sleep and rose and clung to him for warmth until he held him away at arm's length and slapped him smartly on the buttocks and helped him into his overalls.

Going to the kitchen Danny saw that the niggard sky had failed to fulfill its promise.

"I wanted it to snow," he said.

"It didn't oblige you," Uncle Enid said in a bantering tone but his nephew looked at him with an affronted stare and he knew that he was very disappointed. Then he remembered with a dim sense of hurt because it came no more the sense of joy with which he had awakened to a morning of snow in the days of his boyhood.

"I guess snow's a boy's weather, all right," he said. Then he continued, "There isn't any snow but it's a special day still."

"What kind of a special day?" Danny said.

"I'll go and arrange a sale and when we are rid of the house plunder we will go away. We will go where there are things to do and people to see every day." He spoke in the spell of his own dreaming. It was later that he remembered the look his nephew flashed him, and so he was never able to determine whether it spoke of anxiety or disbelief.

Uncle Enid

Neither could he say when he had come to accept the fact that Danny had taken the gold piece. Now with the house behind them and becoming already the property of memory he thought of the gold piece again and he was certain that Danny had taken it. I could say to him let me have the gold piece, he thought, and he would give it to me. But what would I say then? Then I would have proof that he had taken it and I would have to punish him yet not much for if I hurt him I hurt myself

If I never mention it

If I never
He will not say here it is and shrink from me and hurt me
Because he is hurt.

Yet in stealing the coin Danny had also stolen of his love for him. The sum of the money was less and his love was less, even by the smallest degree, and the restoring of the first would not restore the second. Nothing would restore it.

Nothing will restore the taken away, he thought. And he thought of all he had ever lost, the little and the much, and though for some he had been recompensed the lost had never been returned.

Behold what has gone through a door.

Behold what has slipped from the hand.

He turned his mind then from loss and the gold piece and began to think about the days that led to their departure.

John Oliver Killens

From *Youngblood*

CHAPTER ONE

Laurie Lee Barksdale began this life along with the brand new century. About one minute after twelve, a black cold night, in Tipkin, Georgia, January the first, nineteen hundred and zero-zero. As the church bells rang and the pistols fired and the whistles blew all over town, the new baby cried. But she didn't cry much. The mother smiled at the father as he walked in nervously from the back porch. The old midwife said, "She sure is a pretty youngun." And the mother's mother wiped her brow and said, "Umph—Aah Lord——" And the mother lay in the bed and smiled. The father's name was Dale. He kissed his wife on her forehead, went to the chest and got his gun, went out on the back porch and shot into the night, till his fingers got tired and his strong hand trembled. Load and reload. He had expected a boy, but it didn't matter much. She sure was a funny looking baby. Just as red as a beet. Didn't favor a thing.

Got to work twice as hard now, Dale Barksdale. Got to give her all the chances you didn't have in spite of these crackers. His face filled up and his throat and his shoulders. He felt weak, helpless, and scared, he felt strong and mighty. As the whistles still blew and the church bells rang and the guns fired out, he raised his gun and BANG BANG BANG. And—a Great God Almighty, what you gonna name this pretty little child?

The years jumped by, and the girl grew pretty and strong and healthy, and Dale and Martha were as proud as punch. Everywhere they went people said—That child sure got a pretty head on her shoulders, and mother-wit too. They would look at Dale and say—Whachoo swelling up so about? She don't look like you. She Martha up and down. Well, Dale would tell them, that's all right about that.

When she was four years old she said a long recitation by heart in church at an Easter exercise, and she didn't seem nervous. Right then and there folks said she was going to be a school teacher.

When she was eight years old, she was pretty as a peach and round and plump, except for her slender hands, her long tapering fingers. Folks told Dale and Martha that God had given their little girl a gift and she was born to play pretty music, be a great musician. And Dale believed it. On her ninth birthday he brought home a second or third or fourth-hand piano and got Professor Larkins to give her music lessons. And how she loved to tickle those keys. So it was church recitals and playing for the B.Y.P.U. and this and that and everything else. When her nimble fingers ran up and down those keys, she made you laugh and sing, she made you cry and shout, she filled your eyes with shamefaced tears.

Dale was good to his children, Laurie and Tim, worked hard like a dog. Folks would say to him—Dale Barksdale, you sure ain't got no sense at all, working so hard. Ain't got the sense you were born with. You ought to sit down and rest a little while. Children these days ain't worth all them sacrifices, I do declare. Grow up to be something, turn they back on you sure as you born to die.

That's all right about that, Dale would tell them. I ain't looking for no rewards. Just want them to do better than I did. Git an education. Be something else 'sides a workhorse for white folks. Thatta be good enough reward for me. And he meant that thing.

Laurie Lee Barksdale: eleven years old now, and her old mischievous grandmother told her that very morning at the breakfast table. "Gal, you jes beginning to smell your pee, you old pretty thing you!" Later that morning she was coming from town. There wasn't a prettier girl her age in all Johnson County no matter the color. Feeling good and walking with bouncing steps through Woodley's Lane, with the sun reaching down into the alley and resting on her face and her neck and her shoulders. Thinking about next Sunday's recital, mixed up with thoughts about the pretty-faced boy in the ninth grade always smiling at her. She was about halfway through the alley. She saw a tall lanky white man walking towards her, but she didn't think about it, till he walked right up to her, and he grabbed hold of her before she knew it in broad open daylight—Lord Lord Lord!

"Turn me loose, man! Turn me loose!" Struggling with an anger and fright and strength hitherto unknown to her. She looked desperately around her—not a soul in sight, but two great big old alley cats on top of a garbage can.

Nicely dressed, middle-aged white man with brown squinting eyes, mixed with whiskey-red. He mumbled to himself as he grabbed her plump buttocks. And he wouldn't let her go. Scared crazy with her heart in her mouth and blood flowing in the well of her stomach. Greatgodalmighty! She kicked him on his shins, she kneed him in his groin, but he wouldn't turn her loose.

"Turn me loose!"

His hand found her young breasts, a recently developed wonder to her. He squeezed them till they hurt. "Come on, yaller bitch, you got something good and I know it. Ain't no needer keeping it to yourself." Grabbing at her skirt and fumbling at his fly.

She could hear other voices now. "Damn I reckin—Thassa fiery little nigger heffer."

"She sure is pretty."

"Leave her lone, Mr. Hill, you old no-good hound."

Breathing and snorting in her face and on her neck and her ears. His breath smelled like whiskey puke. *Upped her skirt and peed on her thighs*!

She raked her fingernails down his long scrawny face, drawing his blood, and she sunk her teeth deep into his arm, and she got away from him. Jesus Have Mercy, she got away!

"Goddamn no-good nigger bitch! Come back here. Doncha run from me." She heard crackers laughing till she turned the corner.

Running and crying most of the way home—Through the heart of

Crackertown, across the railroad track and through Tucker's Field, she reached Colored town. She stopped running and crying, and she leaned against an evergreen tree, and she looked at the shanties scattered over the valley, but her eyes saw nothing.

"What's the matter, Laurie Lee?"

"Nothing, Miss Susie. I'm all right, I thank you."

Somehow she straightened up just before she reached the house, because she didn't want the folks to know; wanted nobody in the whole wide world to hear about it. Sneaked around the side of the house and into the woodshed. She looked hard at the axe. She should chop off her legs. Whack them off clean up to her belly. A sharp chill ran across her shoulders and down her back. She stripped off her clothes, and she got into a washtub full of water, and she scrubbed the skin off her young brown body with washing powder and lye soap. Her legs and her thighs were on fire. Standing in the tub now, naked and trembling. One thing sure, she wouldn't tell the folks.

Later that evening after the chickens got quiet and a little old unexpected breeze got busy and stirring, she sat on the back porch listening to her Mama and her Big Mama talk. Looking straight into Big Mama's mouth like she usually did. Big Mama doing most of the talking. "You listen to these-shere rich white folks, honey, talking about slavery was a good thing—talking about good-hearted marsters. Won' no sicha thing. I done told you that a million times. If a marster was good, he wouldna had no slaves—he'da sot em all free. Crackers always talking about the slaves cried when Marster Lincoln sot us free. We cried all right, honey. Aah Lord—we cried. Won' a Negro's eyes dry that time. We cried for joy and shouted hallelujah." She glanced down at Laurie Lee and she rocked back and forth, singing to herself:

Free at last. . . .
Free at last. . . .
Thank Godamighty
I'm free at last. . . .

Listening to Big Mama, Laurie Lee felt like she was being lifted upon a great silvery cloud, going higher and higher, sailing around and around and higher and higher towards a bright purple moon—

Big Mama stopped singing and she laughed that short dry laugh of hers and she looked down at Laurie. "Aah Lord, doll baby, all this time and we ain't free yet." Suddenly, all that had happened to Laurie Lee in the alley that day came back to her, the evil old white man and everything else. Her bosom became heavy and her face filled up and she turned her head—didn't want to let on.

"What's the matter, doll baby?" Big Mama asked her.

She started to say, nothing Big Mama, but her voice choked off and her eyes filled up and she couldn't hold it back. Steamed up and boiling right over. Telling it now, bit by bit, then fast and fiercely, pouring it angrily out of her system.

There was a pitiful scared look in her mother's eyes, anxious and terrifying, as she begged and pleaded with the girl—"Don't say nothing to your Papa about it, please, sugar pie. Do, he'll go outer here and get himself kilt, sure as gun's iron!"

Laurie Lee looked up at her slavery-time grandmother, as she sat in her rocker, with her wrinkled-up face drawn tight towards the going-down sun, with those deep-dark, at-the-present-time, completely black eyes. Talking between puffs on her corn cob pipe. Speaking with a calmness, nurtured painfully in hatred and meanness and born-in-slavery militance. "Donchoo cry, honey," she said, as she rubbed Laurie Lee's shoulders with her rough bony hands. "Git mad, yes Godamighty, but donchoo waste a single tear. Crying all the time don't do a damn bitter good."

She puffed twice on her pipe, watched the gray smoke, her eyes almost closing. "Hit's always been thataway, doll baby. Aah Lord, honey, goddammit—Crackers make way with the black women folks, and black man bet not even now say a mumbling word!"

Laurie Lee looked sideways up into Mama's eyes, desperate, wide and pitiful. Mama—Mama—Mama! She looked up at Big Mama, felt the strength from the old woman flow into her young body. She got up and walked through the kitchen into the big room, and she cried no more.

NINETEEN TWELVE WAS A YEAR AND A HALF—A COW AND A CALF. It was the year that white men came to the house and took her piano away, while Big Mama cussed. And it didn't matter that Mama went around all day long shaking her head in a helpless fashion, or that Big Mama kept telling Laurie Lee, Donchoo cry honey, or that Papa was mean and cross with everybody for over a week, the piano was gone and it stayed gone. Laurie Lee felt like dying, but she felt like living, and she kept on living, 'cause it was better than dying.

Laurie Lee got a job that summer working for old Lady Tucker over in Radcliffe Heights. Taking care of her little old eight year old girl. It was a real hot summer, burning up, and old Lady Tucker was fat in the stomach, just as big as a house.

"Laurie Lee—ee—"

Laurie was in the great big beautiful kitchen feeding the white child and also getting something to eat for herself. What did that contrary old white woman want this time? Laurie Lee this and Laurie Lee that—

"You Laurie Lee—ee—ee—"

She could hear Mrs. Tucker coming down the stairs and shuffling through the hall. Well let her come. Laurie Lee wasn't going to be running up and down those stairs every time Mrs. Tucker had an urge to call her. Bring me this and take care of that—

"Laurie Lee, didn't you hear me calling you?"

Laurie looked up from the plate, stared the white woman straight in the face, then looked brazenly and contemptuously at her big fat belly. Mrs. Tucker changed colors from white to red. She used to be slender and pretty, but lately her stomach hung down and poked out terribly, and her eyes carried great big double rings around them.

"No mam, Miss Sarah, I didn't hear nothing."

"You must be deaf. Need to wash out your ears."

"Yes, mam."

The white woman's eyes roved around the big kitchen, rested on the little white girl, then roved some more, and back to Laurie Lee. "Laurie Lee, you know Becky, I mean Rebecca, she *is* getting to be a mighty big girl." She paused, catching her breath, waiting for Laurie to express agreement, but the girl said nothing, just kept on looking straight at Mrs. Tucker.

"What I mean is, Laurie Lee, it doesn't look right for you to be calling her Becky and she getting to be a young Miss already." White woman cleared her throat.

Laurie Lee cut her eyes over at the little gray-eyed girl, who kept on eating. "She ain't that big, Miss Sarah."

"What I mean is, don't you think you ought to be calling her Miss Rebecca, instead of keep on calling her Becky like you do?"

"No, mam, I don't see it thataway at all."

White woman sighed heavily and breathed deeply, her fat stomach going in and out like an old dog sleeping. She wished the girl would cooperate. It was so darn hot. "How come, Laurie Lee?"

"She isn't nearbout big as I am. Don't see how come I got to be *Missing* her."

"But—but—but you work for her."

"She don't pay me no wages."

Sarah Tucker wiped the sweat from her brow. "Well, Mr. Tucker and I discussed it last night, and we decided that you start calling our big beautiful girl *Miss* Rebecca. That's all there is to it."

Laurie Lee's nose popped out with sweat, as she looked at the sloppy white woman and away again. "I hate that about you," she muttered to the woman.

"What did I hear you say?" The woman shuffled towards her.

"I said I hate that about you. That's what I said. Thinking I'm going to be calling a little pee-behind white gal *Miss,* you got another thought coming." She stood wide-legged and defiant. Scared, mean and desperate.

Miss Sarah grabbed her by the shoulders. "You *going* to call her Miss Rebecca," she screamed, "you sassy little nigger!" Shaking Laurie Lee by the shoulders now.

Laurie Lee pulled away from the white woman, but the woman stood between her and the door. Laurie's voice trembled. "Don't you shake me," she said. "My Mama don't do that to me."

Miss Sarah picked up the broom leaning against the wall. "Teach you a lesson." She struck Laurie Lee on the side of the head. "You *going* to call her Miss Rebecca. I'm going to tell Mr. Tucker. . . ."

The girl backed up. Red hot all over and covered with sweat. Head going around like a flying jenny. "I hate that hole in your dirty old drawers. Tell Mr. Tucker—You—you better tell Mr. Tucker stop trying to pat me on my behind. I—I'm too big for that . . ." She was ready for anything. The big wide beautiful kitchen was little and stuffy now, and Laurie wanted room and breathing space. The sharp sweaty odor of the white woman surrounded her. Let me out! Let me out!

Miss Sarah let out a gasp and crowded in on Laurie Lee. "Don't you say that about Mr. Tucker! Don't you dare!" Swinging the broom wildly, she hemmed Laurie Lee up in a corner. "Sassy little nigger!" *Swish—Swish* on the head—on the legs—on the shoulders—"Sassy little nigger!"

"Sassy little nig—" Laurie ducked under the broom and closed her eyes and rammed her fist deep into Miss Sarah's stomach. The white woman yelled and fell out on the floor, and the gray-eyed girl opened her pretty mouth and screamed. Laurie ran out of the kitchen through the hall and down the front steps and all the way home.

Mama gave her a good whipping, because she shouldn't have struck the white woman like that in the stomach, knowing she was big and going to have a baby. Took Laurie out in the woodshed to keep Big Mama from interfering. Big Mama broke the door down. Wrestling with Mama all over the woodshed.

"Don' whup that child! Stop whupping that child! Ain' done nuthing wrong. She jes shoulda kilt that evil old bitch!"

That night Big Mama got Laurie Lee off to herself in the kitchen, with the rest of the folks out on the front porch, and she told Laurie Lee—"Honey, don' choo never let em walk over you—don' choo do it—Fight em, honey—Fight em every inch of the way, especially the big rich ones—like—like them Tuckers. They the one took over where ol' marster left off. They lynch us, they starve us and they work us to death, and it ain-na gonna change till you young Negroes gits together and beat some sense in they heads. So fight em, sugar pie. Aah Lordy, honey."

Laurie looked past the kerosene lamp across the table where Big Mama sat. Her eyelashes blinked as a chill went across her round girlish shoulders. An old candle-fly went around and around the lamp chimney, flapping his dusty wings.

"That's right, honey. Don' choo pay your Mama no never mind. And another thing, baby doll, all this crying and praying and shouting and who-shot-John—Ain' none of it gon change these white folks' heart—they don't believe in it nohow."

NINETEEN TWELVE WAS SOMETHING ELSE AGAIN—Mama died towards the end of the year and Big Mama passed four months following. Big Mama Big Mama Big Mama! The sweet hated smell of death in Laurie's nostrils. Standing in that lonely death-kissed room, smelling those flowers that Big Mama couldn't smell. Big Mama's eyes, those dark-black eyes, staring at her through death-sealed lids, lying there in that dark-gray casket, Laurie saw her part her colorless swollen lips and heard her speak in that strong young-folks voice of hers—"Doncha cry, honey. Don' choo waste a single tear!" And she tried not to cry, awfully hard, but she just couldn't help it. Feeling Miss Susie's arm around her shoulders. "Don' cry no more, pretty thing. She ain' dead. She jes gone away on a little short journey. Gone to that land where she never grow old."

Year after next Laurie Lee's brother, Tim, went to the reformatory for rockbattling white boys and breaking old man McWhorter's window. They kept him there for two whole years, and when he came out he was as mean as a bull dog. Tim Barksdale had been the nicest sweetest boy in the world before that reformatory got hold of him. Friendly and shamefaced and so tenderhearted, he couldn't even wring off the neck of a frying-sized chicken. The only boy in Tipkin that wouldn't tie a string to an old ugly juney bug and listen to him zoon. Laurie Lee never would forget the time one summer when she and her baby sister, Bertie, and Tim had spent a couple of weeks down in the country with Uncle Leo and Aunt Jenny Mae—

One July Saturday morning, Uncle Leo had gotten up early and said—"What we gon have for breakfast this morning?—Let's have one them nice frying chickens"—He started to sing some funny words to an old church tune: "There's not a friend like a frying-size chicken——

GLORY TO HIS NAME——GLORY TO HIS NAME——PRECIOUS NAME——"

Tim laughed at Uncle Leo and said, "That's just what the doctor ordered." He had grown into a nice looking boy, long and slim, and all the girls liked him.

Uncle Leo said, "All right, boy, let's me and you take care of breakfast for a change. You kill the chicken and I'll fry that scound. Show these womenfolks how to cook. They think they so tight when it come to the kitchen. Just go out in the chicken yard and pick out any one of them fryers you want—git the prettiest in the bunch and wring that scound's neck clean off."

Tim said, "All right Uncle Leo." And Bertie and Laurie Lee heard him and they giggled to themselves because they knew Tim had never killed a chicken in all his life. Tim went out into the chicken yard. Aunt Jenny and Uncle Leo had all kinds of chicken.

Five minutes passed and Uncle Leo called out—"Got him ready, boy?"

Tim called back, "Not yet, Uncle Leo." A tremble in his voice.

"All right, boy," Uncle Leo said, "Christmas is coming."

About five more minutes. "Got him ready, son?"

"Just a few more minutes, Uncle."

"What's the matter, boy—you got to hatch that chicken?" Uncle Leo came out on the back porch. The girls had been watching Tim from the window. They came out on the porch.

A nice-sized fryer popped out of Tim's frightened grasp and Tim chased him desperately, but unconvincingly, across the yard, sweat pouring from all over his body.

"What's the matter, Tim? Hem that fat rascal up and wring his neck off."

"Yessir." Tim followed the chicken and hemmed him up between a corner of the yard and a big fig tree. Chicken mess was all over the yard and Tim was trying to keep from stepping in it. He was the most nice-nasty boy in the whole wide world. He made a half-hearted lunge for the chicken and the young chicken jumped straight up in the air and yelled out loud, striking Tim in his breast, and poor Tim jumped back, giving the chicken just enough room to get by him and the chase was on all over again. Bertie and Laurie Lee were rolling all over the back porch laughing to beat the band.

Uncle Leo walked down the back steps. "What's the matter, boy—you scared of that chicken?"

"No——Sir——he——he——he just slipped by me that time." Tim caught up with the chicken again and this time he grabbed the chicken and held on desperately, both of their hearts beating a hundred miles an hour, his and the chicken's.

Laurie Lee had stopped laughing now, sympathizing with Tim.

"That's right, boy," Uncle Leo shouted, "now wring his neck off——ain't nothing to it——ought to have you down here during hog killing time——Greatgodamighty—"

Tim's face was blank, he looked like he would rather have been anywhere else in the world excepting that chicken yard. He held the poor chicken out at arm's length and his arm went around and around and around. "That's right, boy. That's what I'm talking about——you done killed him now——let him fall to the ground. I knew you could do it."

Tim let the chicken go and the chicken dropped to the ground and kicked around like a chicken with his neck wrung off and then he lay right still. Tim looked around, scared to death, and stooped to pick him up, and the chicken let out a cry and jumped and ran away and it was Tim and the chicken all over that yard. Tim never did kill that chicken or any other chicken. But the one thing Tim wasn't ever chicken-hearted about was white folks. Just as soon fight a white boy as to look at one. And that was what got him into all that trouble. Papa encouraged him in his meanness towards white folks, but Big Mama was the main one. She always told him: "Don't take no stuff offa 'em, Timmie. Not a damn drap." Everybody said that's what led him to the reformatory. And what happened to him in the reformatory? Greatgodalmighty they made that nice boy ugly and mean and heartless and don't-care, and when he got out he wouldn't listen to anybody.

When he came home he started running around with fast no-good women almost twice his own age, and when Papa got after him, he would cuss under his breath at Papa and tell him to mind his own damn business, and he would stay out all night long and some time come home two days later, and he and Papa would argue and shout at each other for hours at a time. But the one thing that stayed with Laurie Lee more than anything else was the time a big field rat jumped out of the wood box in the kitchen behind the stove and started brazenly across the kitchen floor, and Tim, who used to be so squeamish and nice-nasty, met the big rat in the middle of the floor and brought his foot down and stomped that rat, and stood there crushing him till the blood gushed out and his entrails oozed out over the floor. And Laurie ran out of the kitchen into the next room and passed out cold. When she came to herself, Tim laughed at her. "Since when did you get so chicken-hearted and high-toned? In the institution that was our favorite sport—rat squashing. Don't be for that we'da had to sleep with them bastards. I 'member one time a big old rat ran up a boy's pants leg named Yaller Joe. Old Yaller Joe caught that skeester just before he struck gold—way up his britches legs. He grabbed that rat away up on his thigh and he mashed that rat up against his thigh and he didn't turn him loose till he mashed him flat and the stuff ran down his legs into his shoes." Laurie lay on the bed holding her stomach, her head going around and around. "Get out of here Tim—Go away! Go away! Get out of my sight." But Tim just stood there laughing and jeering at her.

A few days later he ran away from home. Just up and left without saying a word. And nobody ever heard from him. With Mama and Big Mama gone on to Glory, there was nobody left at home but Papa and Bertie, Laurie's younger sister.

Laurie Lee graduated from high school in the tenth grade at the head of her class, and she made a big speech at the exercises. She surely had grown into a pretty young woman. She missed Mama and Big Mama more than ever at graduation time. Papa swore he was going to send her right on to college, and if he didn't there wasn't a cow in Texas, but he couldn't quite make it the very first year. He would send her the next year just as sure as you were born. She got a job teaching school right there in Johnson County. She was a darn good teacher, everybody said so, and the school children liked her.

On Sunday evenings the big boys hung around the house like flies around sugar. Some after Bertie, but most of them after the pretty little school teacher. Ray Morrison was the most persistent. He wouldn't be discouraged——didn't care what. He got further than the others, but he didn't get far. Then one day Ray upped and went off to war, and folks said Laurie had chased him away. She laughed at them and said, "Never mind." But she worried about it.

Joseph (No Middle Name) Youngblood was born in Glenville, Georgia, ninety miles from Tipkin on the Central Line, not even a whistle stop, on April Fools Day, and it rained all day long that day, but he never was anybody's fool. Never had any formal education to speak of, he graduated from the School of Hard Knocks. His Papa died when he was six years old, and his Mama passed when he was nine. His only relative, Uncle Rob, who really was his second cousin, told him when he was eleven years old, seated at the breakfast table on a bright September morning, the early-morning sun casting slicey shadows through the shingled roof—"Son, I hate to say it, Lord knows I do, but things is tough and money is sca'ce and times is tight and the old man ain't so sporty no more."

The soft-eyed black boy looked up in the old man's face, stared across the table through a transparent ladder of dusty rays of sunshine reaching from the roof to the table, and he didn't say anything.

Uncle Rob looked at the boy, and his old wrinkled eyes filled up, and the hairy, shapeless bush over his old mouth quivered. "What I mean is, boy, I want you to go fiward and git ahead, but——but——you know what I mean—"

The boy said, "Yessir." It was early in the morning, but hot already, a day no different from any other day.

The man blew his nose two or three times, because nothing was in it. Tried to look tough and stern with his eyes and his jaws. "Doggonnit, boy, you eat like a man . . . Eat us outa house and home . . . I'm telling you, son, just can't afford it . . . I'm right poorly 'long in now . . .'bout to give up the ghost . . . School be opening fore long——What I mean you won't be going, cause you gotta go to work."

"Thatta be all right, Uncle Rob. I go to work. Get me a job most any old place."

Uncle Rob sucked his teeth and shook his head. "Old man Rickerson just saying yestiddy——Sure could use that boy in the field powerfully much. Need every hand wrestle with that cotton. Time he broke in good. What's the useter waiting? Like I always said——"

Joe Youngblood's face flushed hot and tight, almost giving him away, but it didn't, because his eyes remained quiet like they always did. He'd sooner die than work in old Man Rickerson's cotton field again. One white man whose guts he hated. His mind was traveling a mile a minute, but he didn't say a thing. Late that night long after the town had tucked in and gone completely to sleep, he tiptoed down the front steps, his heart in his mouth, and walked down that long dark lonesome road and the only light he had was the lightning bugs, and he never took a single look back at the one room, fresh-air shack he had shared with Uncle Rob. He hated to put Uncle Rob down, but he just couldn't help it.

He didn't forget Uncle Rob. He wrote to him three weeks later from Waycross, Georgia, sent a little money in the letter, but the letter came back unopened, because Uncle Rob had passed on. Joe sat down and wondered. There was no one left, not a chicken nor a child.

He lived in Waycross, Georgia, working sun-up to sundown, from one job to the next, even did a little sharecropping a few miles out of Waycross, but he hated that kind of work most of all. Grew strong and big and tall by the day. The collard greens and the black-eyed peas and the fat back seemed to stick to his ribs and spread into his shoulders and his arms and his chest, filling them out and the rest of his body. Went to church on Sunday, sang bass in the glee club, played baseball on Saturday afternoons, smiled at the girls and the girls smiled back, thinking he was older than he actually was.

When he was sixteen years old he met a man from Detroit, Michigan. A colored man who drove for a drummer. Met him one night in Hoot's Pool Room. Told Joe in a friendly kind of a way, thought he was talking to a full grown man—"Man, you ain't nothing but a sucker, and I don't mean maybe." Told him about the glories of the Promised Land, Up the Country, where freedom was natural fact, and a man was a man. Colored man get a job 'most any old place—any kind of a job.

And Joe just looked at the man quiet-like and said, "Is it sure 'nough?" A million thoughts running around in his head. Was there really such a place where a colored man could get any kind of a job? Could he ever go to that place?—Good Lord, would he ever?

The man looked at him unbelievingly and said in a kind of sing-song—"Well I done tole you all about it, and it's right there for you, and if you don't get it, it ain't no fault of mine."

And all Joe said was—"Is it, sure 'nough?" His mind was working a mile a minute but his face didn't show it. Plans jumping around in his head already. . . .

Joe dreamed about it and saved and scratched every penny without telling a living soul, because God wasn't exactly living. It was a Saturday afternoon around the last of September when a war was in the world, a great big war, and it was all Germany's fault, and President Wilson promised to keep us out of it, but Germany just wouldn't let us stay out, because she wanted us in, and it looked like we just had to make the world safe for democracy, and everywhere people felt patriotic and they sang that song—*Well I wish I was in Dixie—Look Away—Look Away*——Joe Youngblood walked up to the depot, strapping six feet–two inches, eighteen years old black man, with his clothes tied up in an old beat-up suitcase, his face and his body scrubbed till it hurt, money in his pocket for a ticket to Chicago and a little bit extra to tide him over.

Station Master looked friendly-like at Joe's serious face, smiled and said, "Whew—eee! Boy, you going so far you gon fall off the side of the world."

But Joe didn't crack a single smile.

The station master chuckled, "Boy, where you steal so much money from?"

But Joe didn't smile.

Looking out of the train window now at the fields of cotton and the fields of corn, leaving it behind—Greatgodalmighty! The tall pine trees and the shingled shacks, and the little out-houses with the burlap doors—leaving all that behind a mile a minute. The red clay hills and the country roads, winding and weaving, and the country towns and the big pretty houses and the little ugly houses and the red-faced crackers at the country stations, leaving all that behind, going north every minute, and a lump in his throat and a chill in his shoulders and a knot in his stomach. Feeling good-good-good. Leaning back in his seat in a jim crow coach, but not thinking hard about it being jim crow, because it was taking him up the country. Rocking and reeling and puffing and snorting and clackety clack. Good old, powerful old going-north train.

The fat man seated next to Joe wiped his face with a big red-and-blue handkerchief, looked out of the window and said to Joe—"In Tennessee now—Just crossed the line."

It seemed to Joe he could feel the difference, out of Georgia already. Proved he was going north. He felt excited like a young kid—Is it really you, Joe Youngblood? You old up-the-country fool. You really going up north? But all he said to the fat man beside him was—"Is we sure 'nough?"

The soot from the engine close by got all over him, in his face and his eyes, on his neck and his hands, blackened his clothes, but he really didn't mind. Joe was hot and sweat poured out of his head and all over his body. He felt dirty and sooty, but that was all right. A barefoot black woman stood in front of a one room shack with her baby in her arms. Both of them waved at the jim crow coach and Joe waved back, his eyes filling up watery-like, and he had never seen the woman before, and never would again, but somehow in the pit of his stomach and all through his shoulders she felt to him like a mother or an aunt or a long lost sister. He took a deep breath and closed his eyes in excited weariness, then peace and contentment, like going home at last and the next thing he knew the train was stopping and the porter was yelling Wayman, Tennessee. He thought he was dreaming as he looked out of the window and saw a bunch of white men coming toward the train with shotguns and rifles. He looked at the fat man next to him, whose eyes were wide and nervous now. Everybody else had worried looks on their faces and he knew he wasn't dreaming. The train slowed down to a nervous stop, started up again, jerked a few feet forward and stopped again, puffing and blowing. And the men kept coming towards the jim crow coach.

They boarded the coach from both ends, rifles and shotguns leveled, as Joe and his kind of people waited. A short, square-shouldered, heavy-set man with a handle-bar mustache was the leader of the bunch. He said, "All right all you niggers, git your stuff and git off. We got jobs for every one of you." Like he was saying to them have a drink of nice cold lemonade.

One Negro said, "But I ain't looking for no job, I'm visiting my folks."

"You wuz visiting your folks, but, boy, you ain't visiting your folks no more, lessen they live on Mr. Buck's plantation."

A couple of white men laughed. The rest were grim. Not a Negro had moved. "All right," said the peck with the red mustache, friendly like. "Ain't no hard feelings lessen you boys want to make it like that."

A young Negro with glasses on, looked like a doctor, got up and walked over to the cracker. "Look," he said, "you got the wrong man. I'm not a southerner." Talked proper and straight, looked the cracker in the eye. "I'm on my way home to Chicago. I go to college." Didn't even say please sir.

Cracker looked at him like he had seen a ghost. Cracker batted his eyes, looked away for a moment. "That's what's the trouble, too many niggers going north already. Well, a little stop-over on Mr. Buck's plantation ain't gonna hurt none. Don't need no education nohow."

Joe sat still, face unmoved, everything tumbling down around him. Two whole years of corn bread and syrup, of hoping and conscious scheming, and dreaming and planning and stinching and going without—More than two years——Maybe a lifetime. He had had his doubts all along, but once he got on the train, he had thought that all he had to do was sit back and just ride his way to the Promised Land, never mind what he'd find when he got there. He was more angry than afraid, and wanted to take a stand alongside this nicely dressed Negro, say something, but he didn't know what to say; do something, but he didn't know what to do.

He felt good and strong, though frightened for the young Negro, who turned to the rest of the people in the coach and said—"Are you going to let them get away with this? After all we're American citi—"

The rifle went off. The explosion temporarily deafened Joe. The young Negro slumped down in the aisle, his right arm a shattered, bloody mass at the elbow. Joe jumped from his seat. The cracker with the mustache looked up at him. "See what I mean," he said to Joe, motioning with his rifle towards the young Negro. "Had to shoot one of the youngest and strongest bucks in the group. Won' no needer that neither." He turned to a couple of his men. "Git him offa here fore he bleed up the train. Won't no call for that at all, and Mr. Buck ain't gon like it. See how bad education is for niggers?"

Joe stood there in a silent, helpless, maddening rage, hating the other Negroes for not doing something and hating himself twice as much and double times again. Smothered with hate for this cracker till he could hardly breathe. The jaw muscles of his strong face flexing under the tautness of his black skin. His eyes still quiet except for little, angry crinkles in the corners. Sweat, sweat, sweat——everywhere sweat. Cracker looked at Joe. Joe looked at cracker. First time Joe ever looked at a cracker so straight in the eye. Cracker's eyes shifted.

He licked his mustache and prodded Joe with his rifle. "All right, Goddammit, all you niggers, let's git going."

Joe smiled as he always had a way of doing when he was really good and mad, and he laughed—"*Hingh*"—almost like a dry cough, and he swung his mighty fist, and the man went one way and his rifle the other. But even as the cracker fell he shouted, "Don't shoot that nigger. Mr. Buck won't like it. Just mess him up good fashion."

Fear had gone by now and Joe didn't give a good goddamn, and he swung his fist in every direction, but they cut him down like a strong, sturdy oak. They beat on his shoulders with their guns and rifles, on his head and about his body, till he didn't feel anything, and his knees buckled and they chopped him down, as the sunlight spilled in through the windows along with the smoke and the cinders, and some poor colored fool yelled police.

The lights came on slowly, but everywhere was dark. He opened his eyes. It was night and he wondered where he was—I up north already? Couldn't be on no train . . . Couldn't be up north, because the north is different, and there is something familiar about the way the floor creaks when I move my aching body, the way the moon peeps in through the shingled roof and the smattering of stars. Am I back with Uncle Rob? But Uncle Rob been dead a long time ago. Maybe I'm dead too . . . His body felt like it had been trampled on from head to foot, his shoulders pained like an aching tooth. Dead man couldn't feel. His face was numb. He tried to move his arm, but a pain knifed him so hard he groaned unconsciously. Where the hell was he? It even hurt him to think, but he couldn't help from thinking. Where the hell was he? He heard breathing over here and snoring over there, and the smell of too many people sleeping close together entered his nostrils. *Goddammit, where the hell am I?* Now the moonlight helped him, slivering through the roof and identifying a black face on this side of the shack and a brown face on the other and a body in the corner. Suddenly he was vaguely concerned about a young Negro who was going up north to college, and it all came back to him. The train, the crackers with their guns, the young Negro on his way to college, the explosion, the shattered, bloody arm. And after that what happened? What happened?

He lay there thinking, hurting all over. Goddammit, if nothing had happened he would have been long gone by now. He would have been in Chicago already. He felt God or fate or whatever it was, with its long, claw-like fingers, tightening around his throat, cutting off his breath, like it had always done, choking off his life, his hope, his spirit, and he swore under his breath it wouldn't be like that. If only he had caught the train before that particular one, or the one right after. How come them peckerwoods had to pick on that particular train just because he happened to be on it? Wonder what happened to that Negro on his way to college—Sure talked up to them peckerwoods—From way off he heard the long drawn-out crow of a rooster and another one answer from close by. Another one, then another and another, separate and all together. Must be getting on towards morning. Got to think with a clear head, cause one thing sure, I ain't staying on no Mr. Buck's plantation—Onh-onh—I ain't coming. Got to keep a clear head——Got to——Got to——keep a clear head——hurt—hurt—hurt——pain all over——clear——head—

Noise outside interrupted his thoughts. A flashlight dipped into the shack from one sleeping face to the other. Joe closed his eyes before it got to him. He heard a loud-mouthed cracker say—"Here's that *baaad* nigger. We git through with him his pee gon be like water. We sure got what it takes for a bad ass nigger." He was talking very loud, as if he knew everybody was playing possum. He was all dressed up like a cowboy picture with a black and white holster and gleaming gun.

"All right, all you niggers," he sang out, nudging Joe in the side with his big heavy boot. "All you monkeys—Git up and piss on the rock—it ain' quite day——But it's four o'clock—" Cracker laughed to himself. "Damn sure is one ugly bunch of monkeys, I swan. Smell like billy goats." And the peckerwood laughed again.

"Come on in here, Jim," the cracker called out, "and give these monkeys somethinteat. Goddamn they ugly."

A short, stocky Negro with a narrow mouse-like face came in the shack with a kerosene lantern. He went out and came back in again with a pot of hominy grits and a pan of corn bread. Then he brought in tin plates and dropped them on the floor. Meanwhile the cracker stood playing with his flashlight, blinking it off and on, throwing its glare from face to face while the angry men grumbled underneath their breaths. Joe's body was so full of pain he could hardly move. He managed to get his right hand up to his face, felt the caked-up blood on the side of his head. He wasn't gonna stay in this goddamn place—guarantee anybody.

"All right, you nigger, quit assing around and git that slop down your craw. You ain't in Atlanta at the Biltmore, goddammit, we got work to do."

Every day except Sunday they went out into the cotton fields, while the rooster still crowed and the old dogs howled and before the day broke, with a stomach full of corn bread and hominy grits and worked and sweated till the sun went down and the chickens had gone to bed. On the ninth day during lunch, Joe sat his pan down and started walking, saying nothing to anybody. He walked about a mile past fields of cotton and fields of corn, row upon row of them, wave after wave, acre after acre, everywhere he looked. Where the hell did old man Buck's plantation end? He walked on further till he saw a big iron gate and he started out of it.

"Hey, you, old nigger, where you think you going?" It was the medium sized man with the handle-bar mustache. Where did these crackers get so many guns? Thought the goddamn war was in Europe.

"Just looking around."

"What you looking for?"

"Nothing particular."

"Git your black ass back to work."

Joe muttered to himself, "You got everything right now, Mr. Charlie. Got the world in a jug, got the stopper in your hand. But my day's coming."

That evening when they knocked off work, they took him and they beat him in front of the other Negroes. Cut his back up like raw hamburger, chopped him down to the ground with a long buggy whip, and he didn't say a mumbling word. They dragged him to the shack, blood pouring from his back, and they dumped him in. Late that night about one o'clock, when everybody was asleep, he dragged himself out of the shack, straightened his battered body up, and he walked till daybreak, thinking while he walked . . . looking back at his own life which had not been anybody's bed of roses.

A hard life—hard work—Everything hard——hard. Thinking as the sun rose higher and he left the dusty highway and took to the woods, that he would volunteer for the army, if they were taking colored men. What the hell—he didn't have nothing to hold him back, not a chicken nor a child—Damn good idea——Make the world safe for democracy——Wonder how you went about it? He walked past cotton fields and corn fields and tobacco, rolling far and wide, as if the entire world were made of cotton and corn and tobacco, a beautiful world to look at. Walked till he was weak from hunger and his legs gave out, his shirt all sweaty and sticking to the blood caked up on his back. Shoulda brought some of them other Negroes with me from old man Buck's plantation. Should have talked it over with them, but what the hell would I'da said. He dropped right where he was—Shoulda brought some of them with me . . . Shoulda talked them into it . . . Gotta learn how to talk to people . . . Went right down to his knees and stretched his great body out on the grass and slept till morning and the sun shone on him.

He sat up and blinked his eyes and rubbed them with his knuckles, becoming awake gradually, hurting so bad he could hardly move. He looked all around him at the trees and the fields, and the dew-kissed grass gleaming in the sunshine, his face and arms wet from the dew. How about going into the *man's* army? Make the world safe for democracy, make the whole wide world safe for democracy—that's all that old cracker he used to work for in Waycross talked about. He could see him now, with his toothless grin and his evil blue eyes. Bald headed old bastard. Make the world safe for democracy—Well to hell with that bullshit. I ain't coming—unh—unh. I ain't got no democracy to make the world safe for, no-damn-how. He got to his feet, walked to the next town, caught a freight back to Georgia and settled in Crossroads.

It was 1918 when Laurie Lee Barksdale met Joe Youngblood, the first Saturday in May at a big church picnic. Big-city man from Crossroads, Georgia. Big powerful black handsome man with soft quiet eyes. It was as hot as any day in the middle of August. A few snowy clouds drifting in a big blue sky, sun shining everywhere. Clean and clear and Sundayish looking.

First time she noticed him was at the baseball game. When he came to bat, he stood there at the plate as cool as a cucumber, wide-stanced and pigeon-toed, and he hit that ball a country mile, way up into the big blue sky and far and wide and away over yonder. When he wasn't at bat or playing in the field, he would stand off and seem to be thinking to himself, but every now and then she would catch him looking at her, halfway smiling to himself, and she would feel funny and steal glances at him when he wasn't looking. The other men on his team would come over to him and say something to him or ask him something, and he would say something but he wouldn't say much. He was a part of the team but he seemed stand-offish. He was the biggest in the bunch, and somehow she sensed his tremendous power.

The people yelled themselves hoarse when he came to bat, and they clapped their hands and waved their arms.

And groups of people from Crossroads, Georgia, shouted at him—"Come on, Joe Youngblood! You got the business!"

And—"Crossroads can' lose—For the stuff we use!" And—"Tipkin can' win—For the shape they in!"

Some of them got together and sang at the top of their voices:

Joe Youngblood gon shine tonight . . .
Joe Youngblood gon shine . . .
Joe Youngblood gon shine tonight . . .
Out on the line. . . .
When the moon comes up . . .
And the sun goes down . . .
Joe Youngblood gon shine. . . .

Everybody talking about Joe Youngblood.

Laurie just couldn't keep her eyes off Joe. He was a big strong sturdy oak tree way up above the rest of the forest. As she watched this man, this stranger to her, her heartbeat quickened, her face grew warm, her mouth tasted different. He stirred her soul. Hundreds of men, women and children laughing and talking and playing all around her. . . .

Later in the afternoon they had glee club singing. The boys from Crossroads won the glee club contest. Joe sang bass. Great big thundering powerful bass. All the while stealing glances at Laurie, upsetting her poise.

Laurie had not intended to go to the dance that night, but she reckoned she might as well go along with Bertie. No need of acting stuck-up like she thought she was better than anybody else. Everybody was there, including Joe Youngblood. It was hot and close and nobody felt like dancing, but everybody danced except Joe Youngblood. He just stood around looking important, like he was sweet on himself, as Laurie imagined he was. Watching the man play the piano and stealing glances at Laurie, keeping time with the music with his great big feet, and talking and laughing with people when they came up to him.

About middle ways the dance he got up his courage, walked over to where she was standing and held out his hand, didn't open his mouth. She looked up into his soft dark eyes and away again.

"Sorry," she said. "I'm saving this dance for somebody else. He just went to get me some lemonade."

Joe mumbled something and turned away.

Her narrow eyes flickered. Her nose perspired. She grabbed his arm. "All right," she said, "he can wait till we finish. Lemonade won't spoil."

Joe was a smooth dancer, but he was so darn quiet. There was a soft sweet smell of corn likker on his breath, but she didn't mind a bit, although she knew she should have. He danced the next round with her and the next round and the next, till they both got hot and burning up and their legs got tired, but they kept on dancing. She never did go back for her lemonade. A scandalous shame.

Poorly-lit hall, feet scraping over splintery floor, old piano going bomalama bomalama, couple of hundred people dancing and sweating. Eyebrows raising—Look at Laurie Lee—Look at Miss Laurie—unh—unh—Who woulda thunk it?—Well I do declare—Every now and then she would glance up into his calm quiet face, painfully conscious of herself in his arms and their bodies close together from head to feet and the size of this man in contrast to her own little five-feet three. Swaying together this way and that. Stupid—silly—ridiculous—Making a fool out of herself in front of everybody—What did she know about this man? That he was a good baseball player, that he was a smooth dancer, that she felt excitingly comfortable in his arms, that he gave her a sense of tremendous power, stirring her depths, exciting her bosom. The nearness of his body—the nearness of his body—the rhythm of the dance—What did she know about this great big powerful calm-looking black man? Hardly his name. . . .

They walked together to her house that night up the long dusty road with trees and fields on both sides of them and crickets jabbering and an old locust moaning and lightning bugs blinking, saying very little to each other, but thinking so hard you could almost hear them. They stood on her front porch, the black night all around them. It had cooled off a little, and the old dog was stirring around in the backyard. A brand new quarter moon shone silvery and lonesome-like through a big fig tree.

She didn't want to say goodnight. "I had a good time, Joe. A very lovely time."

"Me too, Miss Laurie." Big, soft, beautiful eyes looking every whichaway. Big, strong, powerful, baby-faced-looking man. He was the quietest young man she had ever met.

"Don't call me *Miss* Laurie."

"Yes, mam." Fumbling with his cap in his hand like one of the big boys in her school. Tissue paper inside of his brand new cap sounded like somebody eating salted soda crackers. His feet toed inward and pawing the porch. . . .

She laughed at him lightly, didn't feel like laughing. "When you coming back to visit our little old town?" Saying the words flippantly, making a joke about it.

Joe looked at her and away again. Greatgodamighty, they had danced and danced and danced, and he could have danced all night long with her. She was just a little biddy armful to Joe Youngblood—a pretty little armful—with beautiful narrow slanting eyes that seemed to know everything, and they looked straight through him when he wasn't looking, and black heavy hair beginning high on her forehead, and the prettiest curviest mouth he had ever laid eyes on. She wasn't bigger than a minute but she was stacked up solid and well put together.

He turned his cap around and around. "Next year I reckin—when the picnic is."

"You going to wait so long?" Never felt this way about a man before—the taste in her mouth, the fullness, the warmth like never before. But she knew it didn't mean anything, because he wasn't her type.

His feet toed in worse than ever. "Ain't got nobody to come to see in Tipkin."

"Oh," she said, "so the town too little for you and the folks too country."

"No'm. No, mam, you know it ain't that."

"You can come and visit us then." Ashamed of her own self for being so forward.

"Can I sure 'nough? I mean I sure be glad to." And she knew that he meant it.

"Goodnight, Joe. Look to see you soon." She held out her hand and took his limp one, and she squeezed it hard and he squeezed hers harder.

He cleared his throat. "How about next Saturday night?" An anxious note in his deep rumbling voice, making a great big lie out of the calm in his eyes.

She said, "That would be just fine."

He came to see her every Saturday and sometimes on Sunday. He had to quit the baseball team because it only played on Saturday afternoons. She didn't want to take him seriously at first. He wasn't educated, didn't have any polish. Just a hard-working man. She had no idea he would be so persistent. She didn't know Joe Youngblood. Sometimes they would be sitting around talking, and she would catch herself correcting his English, trying to polish him up, and he would draw himself inward and stop talking to her. She came to appreciate his unaffected dignity, fierce and proud. And after she got to know him better, she learned of the things that happened to him in his young life, jam-crammed-full. She became familiar with his solid power, his stubborn ways. He reminded her of Big Mama. He wasn't talkative like Big Mama—but there was something about him. Something big and fierce like a keg of dynamite inside of him, and his mother-wit that no amount of education could take the place of. She was in deep deep water before she knew it. Subtle, powerful, unsuspected, he slipped up on her.

Sometimes he would take her by surprise and break out in a rash of conversation, and she couldn't stop him even if she wanted to and the stories he would tell her about himself made her blood run cold. But these times were few and far between. Her old man liked Joe from the very start. But that didn't mean he was ready to hand his favorite child over to Joe or to anybody else. No-sir-ree-bob. He liked Joe as a man, crazy about him, but not as a son-in-law, past, present or future. Dale Barksdale didn't think there was a man living on God's green earth good enough for his Laurie Lee. But that didn't stop Joe Youngblood a single minute.

Because Joe was as stubborn as a Georgia mule and he never was as slow, or even as quiet as he seemed to be. He was like greased lightning. Once he got started, Laurie didn't have a chance. He took Dale's daughter, the pride of Tipkin, clean away from him and made him like it. They got married in October, and he took her to live in Crossroads, Georgia. People in Tipkin just shook their heads.

Flannery O'Connor

The Artificial Nigger

Mr. Head awakened to discover that the room was full of moonlight. He sat up and stared at the floor boards—the color of silver—and then at the ticking on his pillow, which might have been brocade, and after a second, he saw half of the moon five feet away in his shaving mirror, paused as if it were waiting for his permission to enter. It rolled forward and cast a dignifying light on everything. The straight chair against the wall looked stiff and attentive as if it were awaiting an order and Mr. Head's trousers, hanging to the back of it, had an almost noble air, like the garment some great man had just flung to his servant; but the face on the moon was a grave one. It gazed across the room and out the window where it floated over the horse stall and appeared to contemplate itself with the look of a young man who sees his old age before him.

Mr. Head could have said to it that age was a choice blessing and that only with years does a man enter into that calm understanding of life that makes him a suitable guide for the young. This, at least, had been his own experience.

He sat up and grasped the iron posts at the foot of his bed and raised himself until he could see the face on the alarm clock which sat on an overturned bucket beside the chair. The hour was two in the morning. The alarm on the clock did not work but he was not dependent on any mechanical means to awaken him. Sixty years had not dulled his responses; his physical reactions, like his moral ones, were guided by his will and strong character, and these could be seen plainly in his features. He had a long tube-like face with a long rounded open jaw and a long depressed nose. His eyes were alert but quiet, and in the miraculous moonlight they had a look of composure and of ancient wisdom as if they belonged to one of the great guides of men. He might have been Vergil summoned in the middle of the night to go to Dante, or better, Raphael, awakened by a blast of God's light to fly to the side of Tobias. The only dark spot in the room was Nelson's pallet, underneath the shadow of the window.

Nelson was hunched over on his side, his knees under his chin and his heels under his bottom. His new suit and hat were in the boxes that they had been sent in and these were on the floor at the foot of the pallet where he could get his hands on them as soon as he woke up. The slop jar, out of the shadow and made snow-white in the moonlight, appeared to stand guard over him like a small personal angel. Mr. Head lay back down, feeling entirely confident that he could carry out the moral mission of the coming day. He meant to be up before Nelson and to have the breakfast cooking by the time he awakened. The boy was always irked when Mr. Head was the first up. They would have to leave the house at four to get to the railroad junction by five-thirty. The train was to stop for them at five forty-five and they had to be there on time for this train was stopping merely to accommodate them.

This would be the boy's first trip to the city though he claimed it would be his second because he had been born there. Mr. Head had tried to point out to him that when he was born he didn't have the intelligence to determine his whereabouts but this had made no impression on the child at all and he continued to insist that this was to be his second trip. It would be Mr. Head's third trip. Nelson had said, "I will've already been there twict and I ain't but ten."

Mr. Head had contradicted him.

"If you ain't been there in fifteen years, how you know you'll be able to find your way about?" Nelson had asked. "How you know it hasn't changed some?"

"Have you ever," Mr. Head had asked, "seen me lost?"

Nelson certainly had not but he was a child who was never satisfied until he had given an impudent answer and he replied, "It's nowhere around here to get lost at."

"The day is going to come," Mr. Head prophesied, "when you'll find you ain't as smart as you think you are." He had been thinking about this trip for several months but it was for the most part in moral terms that he conceived it. It was to be a lesson that the boy would never forget. He was to find out from it that he had no cause for pride merely because he had been born in a city. He was to find out that the city is not a great place. Mr. Head meant him to see everything there is to see in a city so that he would be content to stay at home for the rest of his life. He fell asleep thinking how the boy would at last find out that he was not as smart as he thought he was.

He was awakened at three-thirty by the smell of fatback frying and he leaped off his cot. The pallet was empty and the clothes boxes had been thrown open. He put on his trousers and ran into the other room. The boy had a corn pone on cooking and had fried the meat. He was sitting in the half-dark at the table, drinking cold coffee out of a can. He had on his new suit and his new gray hat pulled low over his eyes. It was too big for him but they had ordered it a size large because they expected his head to grow. He didn't say anything but his entire figure suggested satisfaction at having arisen before Mr. Head.

Mr. Head went to the stove and brought the meat to the table in the skillet. "It's no hurry," he said. "You'll get there soon enough and it's no guarantee you'll like it when you do neither," and he sat down across from the boy whose hat teetered back slowly to reveal a fiercely expressionless face, very much the same shape as the old man's. They were grandfather and grandson but they looked enough alike to be brothers and brothers not too far apart in age, for Mr. Head had a youthful expression by daylight, while the boy's look was ancient, as if he knew everything already and would be pleased to forget it.

Mr. Head had once had a wife and daughter and when the wife died, the daughter ran away and returned after an interval with Nelson. Then one morning, without getting out of bed, she died and left Mr. Head with sole care of the year-old child. He had made the mistake of telling Nelson that he had been born in Atlanta. If he hadn't told him that, Nelson couldn't have insisted that this was going to be his second trip.

"You may not like it a bit," Mr. Head continued. "It'll be full of niggers."

The boy made a face as if he could handle a nigger.

"All right," Mr. Head said. "You ain't ever seen a nigger."

"You wasn't up very early," Nelson said.

"You ain't ever seen a nigger," Mr. Head repeated. "There hasn't been a nigger in this county since we run that one out twelve years ago and that was before you were born." He looked at the boy as if he were daring him to say he had ever seen a Negro.

"How you know I never saw a nigger when I lived there before?" Nelson asked. "I probably saw a lot of niggers."

"If you seen one you didn't know what he was," Mr. Head said, completely exasperated. "A six-month-old child don't know a nigger from anybody else."

"I reckon I'll know a nigger if I see one," the boy said and got up and straightened his slick sharply creased gray hat and went outside to the privy.

They reached the junction some time before the train was due to arrive and stood about two feet from the first set of tracks. Mr. Head carried a paper sack with some biscuits and a can of sardines in it for their lunch. A coarse-looking orange-colored sun coming up behind the east range of mountains was making the sky a dull red behind them, but in front of them it was still gray and they faced a gray transparent moon, hardly stronger than a thumbprint and completely without light. A small tin switch box and a black fuel tank were all there was to mark the place as a junction; the tracks were double and did not converge again until they were hidden behind the bends at either end of the clearing. Trains passing appeared to emerge from a tunnel of trees and, hit for a second by the cold sky, vanish terrified into the woods again. Mr. Head had had to make special arrangements with the ticket agent to have this train stop and he was secretly afraid it would not, in which case, he knew Nelson would say, "I never thought no train was going to stop for you." Under the useless morning moon the tracks looked white and fragile. Both the old man and the child stared ahead as if they were awaiting an apparition.

Then suddenly, before Mr. Head could make up his mind to turn back, there was a deep warning bleat and the train appeared, gliding very slowly, almost silently around the bend of trees about two hundred yards down the track, with one yellow front light shining. Mr. Head was still not certain it would stop and he felt it would make an even bigger idiot of him if it went by slowly. Both he and Nelson, however, were prepared to ignore the train if it passed them.

The engine charged by, filling their noses with the smell of hot metal and then the second coach came to a stop exactly where they were standing. A conductor with the face of an ancient bloated bulldog was on the step as if he expected them, though he did not look as if it mattered one way or the other to him if they got on or not. "To the right," he said.

Their entry took only a fraction of a second and the train was already speeding on as they entered the quiet car. Most of the travelers were still sleeping, some with their heads hanging off the chair arms, some stretched across two seats, and some sprawled out with their feet in the aisle. Mr. Head saw two unoccupied seats and pushed Nelson toward them. "Get in there by the winder," he said in his normal voice which was very loud at this hour of the morning. "Nobody cares if you sit there because it's nobody in it. Sit right there."

"I heard you," the boy muttered. "It's no use in you yelling," and he sat down and turned his head to the glass. There he saw a pale ghost-like face scowling at him beneath the brim of a pale ghost-like hat. His grandfather, looking quickly too, saw a different ghost, pale but grinning, under a black hat.

Mr. Head sat down and settled himself and took out his ticket and started reading aloud everything that was printed on it. People began to stir. Several woke up and stared at him. "Take off your hat," he said to Nelson and took off his own and put it on his knee. He had a small amount of white hair that had turned tobacco-colored over the years and this lay flat across the back of his head. The front of his head was bald and creased. Nelson took off his hat and put it on his knee and they waited for the conductor to come ask for their tickets.

The man across the aisle from them was spread out over two seats, his feet propped on the window and his head jutting into the aisle. He had on a light blue suit and a yellow shirt unbuttoned at the neck. His eyes had just opened and Mr. Head was ready to introduce himself when the conductor came up from behind and growled, "Tickets."

When the conductor had gone, Mr. Head gave Nelson the return half of his ticket and said, "Now put that in your pocket and don't lose it or you'll have to stay in the city."

"Maybe I will," Nelson said as if this were a reasonable suggestion.

Mr. Head ignored him. "First time this boy has ever been on a train," he explained to the man across the aisle, who was sitting up now on the edge of his seat with both feet on the floor.

Nelson jerked his hat on again and turned angrily to the window.

"He's never seen anything before," Mr. Head continued. "Ignorant as the day he was born, but I mean for him to get his fill once and for all."

The boy leaned forward, across his grandfather and toward the stranger. "I was born in the city," he said. "I was born there. This is my second trip." He said it in a high positive voice but the man across the aisle didn't look as if he understood. There were heavy purple circles under his eyes.

Mr. Head reached across the aisle and tapped him on the arm. "The thing to do with a boy," he said sagely, "is to show him all it is to show. Don't hold nothing back."

"Yeah," the man said. He gazed down at his swollen feet and lifted the left one about ten inches from the floor. After a minute he put it down and lifted the other. All through the car people began to get up and move about and yawn and stretch. Separate voices could be heard here and there and then a general hum. Suddenly Mr. Head's serene expression changed. His mouth almost closed and a light, fierce and cautious both, came into his eyes. He was looking down the length of the car. Without turning, he caught Nelson by the arm and pulled him forward. "Look," he said.

A huge coffee-colored man was coming slowly forward. He had on a light suit and a yellow satin tie with a ruby pin in it. One of his hands rested on his stomach which rode majestically under his buttoned coat, and in the other he held the head of a black walking stick that he picked up and set down with a deliberate outward motion each time he took a step. He was proceeding very slowly, his large brown eyes gazing over the heads of the passengers. He had a small white mustache and white crinkly hair. Behind him there were two young women, both coffee-colored, one in a yellow dress and one in a green. Their progress was kept at the rate of his and they chatted in low throaty voices as they followed him.

Mr. Head's grip was tightening insistently on Nelson's arm. As the procession passed them, the light from a sapphire ring on the brown hand that picked up the cane reflected in Mr. Head's eye, but he did not look up nor did the tremendous man look at him. The group proceeded up the rest of the aisle and out of the car. Mr. Head's grip on Nelson's arm loosened. "What was that?" he asked.

"A man," the boy said and gave him an indignant look as if he were tired of having his intelligence insulted.

"What kind of a man?" Mr. Head persisted, his voice expressionless.

"A fat man," Nelson said. He was beginning to feel that he had better be cautious.

"You don't know what kind?" Mr. Head said in a final tone.

"An old man," the boy said and had a sudden foreboding that he was not going to enjoy the day.

"That was a nigger," Mr. Head said and sat back.

Nelson jumped up on the seat and stood looking backward to the end of the car but the Negro had gone.

"I'd of thought you'd know a nigger since you seen so many when you was in the city on your first visit," Mr. Head continued. "That's his first nigger," he said to the man across the aisle.

The boy slid down into the seat. "You said they were black," he said in an angry voice. "You never said they were tan. How do you expect me to know anything when you don't tell me right?"

"You're just ignorant is all," Mr. Head said and he got up and moved over in the vacant seat by the man across the aisle.

Nelson turned backward again and looked where the Negro had

disappeared. He felt that the Negro had deliberately walked down the aisle in order to make a fool of him and he hated him with a fierce raw fresh hate; and also, he understood now why his grandfather disliked them. He looked toward the window and the face there seemed to suggest that he might be inadequate to the day's exactions. He wondered if he would even recognize the city when they came to it.

After he had told several stories, Mr. Head realized that the man he was talking to was asleep and he got up and suggested to Nelson that they walk over the train and see the parts of it. He particularly wanted the boy to see the toilet so they went first to the men's room and examined the plumbing. Mr. Head demonstrated the ice-water cooler as if he had invented it and showed Nelson the bowl with the single spigot where the travelers brushed their teeth. They went through several cars and came to the diner.

This was the most elegant car in the train. It was painted a rich egg-yellow and had a wine-colored carpet on the floor. There were wide windows over the tables and great spaces of the rolling view were caught in miniature in the sides of the coffee pots and in the glasses. Three very black Negroes in white suits and aprons were running up and down the aisle, swinging trays and bowing and bending over the travelers eating breakfast. One of them rushed up to Mr. Head and Nelson and said, holding up two fingers, "Space for two!" but Mr. Head replied in a loud voice, "We eaten before we left!"

The waiter wore large brown spectacles that increased the size of his eye whites. "Stan' aside then please," he said with an airy wave of the arm as if he were brushing aside flies.

Neither Nelson nor Mr. Head moved a fraction of an inch. "Look," Mr. Head said.

The near corner of the diner, containing two tables, was set off from the rest by a saffron-colored curtain. One table was set but empty but at the other, facing them, his back to the drape, sat the tremendous Negro. He was speaking in a soft voice to the two women while he buttered a muffin. He had a heavy sad face and his neck bulged over his white collar on either side. "They rope them off," Mr. Head explained. Then he said, "Let's go see the kitchen," and they walked the length of the diner but the black waiter was coming fast behind them.

"Passengers are not allowed in the kitchen!" he said in a haughty voice. "Passengers are NOT allowed in the kitchen!"

Mr. Head stopped where he was and turned. "And there's good reason for that," he shouted into the Negro's chest, "because the cockroaches would run the passengers out!"

All the travelers laughed and Mr. Head and Nelson walked out, grinning. Mr. Head was known at home for his quick wit and Nelson felt a sudden keen pride in him. He realized the old man would be his only support in the strange place they were approaching. He would be entirely alone in the world if he were ever lost from his grandfather. A terrible excitement shook him and he wanted to take hold of Mr. Head's coat and hold on like a child.

As they went back to their seats they could see through the passing windows that the countryside was becoming speckled with small houses and shacks and that a highway ran alongside the train. Cars sped by on it, very small and fast. Nelson felt that there was less breath in the air than there had been thirty minutes ago. The man across the aisle had left and there was no one near for Mr. Head to hold a conversation with so he looked out the window, through his own reflection, and read aloud the names of the buildings they were passing. "The Dixie Chemical Corp!" he announced. "Southern Maid Flour! Dixie Doors! Southern Belle Cotton Products! Patty's Peanut Butter! Southern Mammy Cane Syrup!"

"Hush up!" Nelson hissed.

All over the car people were beginning to get up and take their luggage off the overhead racks. Women were putting on their coats and hats. The conductor stuck his head in the car and snarled, "Firstopppppmry," and Nelson lunged out of his sitting position, trembling. Mr. Head pushed him down by the shoulder.

"Keep your seat," he said in dignified tones. "The first stop is on the edge of town. The second stop is at the main railroad station." He had come by this knowledge on his first trip when he had got off at the first stop and had had to pay a man fifteen cents to take him into the heart of town. Nelson sat back down, very pale. For the first time in his life, he understood that his grandfather was indispensable to him.

The train stopped and let off a few passengers and glided on as if it had never ceased moving. Outside, behind rows of brown rickety houses, a line of blue buildings stood up, and beyond them a pale rose-gray sky faded away to nothing. The train moved into the railroad yard. Looking down, Nelson saw lines and lines of silver tracks multiplying and criss-crossing. Then before he could start counting them, the face in the window started out at him, gray but distinct, and he looked the other way. The train was in the station. Both he and Mr. Head jumped up and ran to the door. Neither noticed that they had left the paper sack with the lunch in it on the seat.

They walked stiffly through the small station and came out of a heavy door into the squall of traffic. Crowds were hurrying to work. Nelson didn't know where to look. Mr. Head leaned against the side of the building and glared in front of him.

Finally Nelson said, "Well, how do you see what all it is to see?"

Mr. Head didn't answer. Then as if the sight of people passing had given him the clue, he said, "You walk," and started off down the street. Nelson followed, steadying his hat. So many sights and sounds were flooding in on him that for the first block he hardly knew what he was seeing. At the second corner, Mr. Head turned and looked behind him at the station they had left, a putty-colored terminal with a concrete dome on top. He thought that if he could keep the dome always in sight, he would be able to get back in the afternoon to catch the train again.

As they walked along, Nelson began to distinguish details and take note of the store windows, jammed with every kind of equipment—hardware, drygoods, chicken feed, liquor. They passed one that Mr. Head called his particular attention to where you walked in and sat on a chair with your feet upon two rests and let a Negro polish your shoes. They walked slowly and stopped and stood at the entrances so he could see what went on in each place but they did not go into any of them. Mr. Head was determined not to go into any city store because on his first trip here, he had got lost in a large one and had found his way out only after many people had insulted him.

They came in the middle of the next block to a store that had a weighing machine in front of it and they both in turn stepped up on it and put in a penny and received a ticket. Mr. Head's ticket said, "You weigh 120 pounds. You are upright and brave and all your friends admire you." He put the ticket in his pocket, surprised that the machine should have got his character correct but his weight wrong, for he had weighed on a grain scale not long before and knew he weighed 110. Nelson's ticket said, "You weigh 98 pounds. You have a great destiny ahead of you but beware of dark women." Nelson did not know any women and he weighed only 68 pounds but Mr. Head pointed out that the machine had probably printed the number upsidedown, meaning the 9 for a 6.

They walked on and at the end of five blocks the dome of the terminal sank out of sight and Mr. Head turned to the left. Nelson could have stood in front of every store window for an hour if there had not been another more interesting one next to it. Suddenly he said, "I was born here!" Mr. Head turned and looked at him with horror. There was a sweaty brightness about his face. "This is where I come from!" he said.

Mr. Head was appalled. He saw the moment had come for drastic action. "Lemme show you one thing you ain't seen yet," he said and took him to the corner where there was a sewer entrance. "Squat down," he said, "and stick your head in there," and he held the back of the boy's coat while he got down and put his head in the sewer. He drew it back quickly, hearing a gurgling in the depths under the sidewalk. Then Mr. Head explained the sewer system, how the entire city was underlined with it, how it contained all the drainage and was full of rats and how a man could slide into it and be sucked along down endless pitchblack tunnels. At any minute any man in the city might be sucked into the sewer and never heard from again. He described it so well that Nelson was for some seconds shaken. He connected the sewer passages with the entrance to hell and understood for the first time how the world was put together in its lower parts. He drew away from the curb.

Then he said, "Yes, but you can stay away from the holes," and his face took on that stubborn look that was so exasperating to his grandfather. "This is where I come from!" he said.

Mr. Head was dismayed but he only muttered, "You'll get your fill," and they walked on. At the end of two more blocks he turned to the left, feeling that he was circling the dome: and he was correct for in a half-hour they passed in front of the railroad station again. At first Nelson did not notice that he was seeing the same stores twice but when they passed the one where you put your feet on the rests while the Negro polished your shoes, he perceived that they were walking in a circle.

"We done been here!" he shouted. "I don't believe you know where you're at!"

"The direction just slipped my mind for a minute," Mr. Head said and they turned down a different street. He still did not intend to let the dome get too far away and after two blocks in their new direction, he turned to the left. This street contained two- and three-story wooden dwellings. Anyone passing on the sidewalk could see into the rooms and Mr. Head, glancing through one window, saw a woman lying on an iron bed, looking out, with a sheet pulled over her. Her knowing expression shook him. A fierce-looking boy on a bicycle came driving down out of nowhere and he had to jump to the side to keep from being hit. "It's nothing to them if they knock you down," he said. "You better keep closer to me."

They walked on for some time on streets like this before he remembered to turn again. The houses they were passing now were all unpainted and the wood in them looked rotten; the street between was narrower. Nelson saw a colored man. Then another. Then another. "Niggers live in these houses," he observed.

"Well come on and we'll go somewheres else," Mr. Head said. "We didn't come to look at niggers," and they turned down another street but they continued to see Negroes everywhere. Nelson's skin began to prickle and they stepped along at a faster pace in order to leave the neighborhood as soon as possible. There were colored men in their undershirts standing in the doors and colored women rocking on the sagging porches. Colored children played in the gutters and stopped what they were doing to look at them. Before long they began to pass rows of stores with colored customers in them but they didn't pause at the entrances of these. Black eyes in black faces were watching them from every direction. "Yes," Mr. Head said, "this is where you were born—right here with all these niggers."

Nelson scowled. "I think you done got us lost," he said.

Mr. Head swung around sharply and looked for the dome. It was nowhere in sight. "I ain't got us lost either," he said. "You're just tired of walking."

"I ain't tired, I'm hungry," Nelson said. "Give me a biscuit."

They discovered then that they had lost the lunch.

"You were the one holding the sack," Nelson said. "I would have kepaholt of it."

"If you want to direct this trip, I'll go on by myself and leave you right here," Mr. Head said and was pleased to see the boy turn white. However, he realized they were lost and drifting farther every minute from the station. He was hungry himself and beginning to be thirsty and since they had been in the colored neighborhood, they had both begun to sweat. Nelson had on his shoes and he was unaccustomed to them. The concrete sidewalks were very hard. They both wanted to find a place to sit down but this was impossible and they kept on walking, the boy muttering under his breath, "First you lost the sack and then you lost the way," and Mr. Head growling from time to time, "Anybody wants to be from this nigger heaven can be from it!"

By now the sun was well forward in the sky. The odor of dinners cooking drifted out to them. The Negroes were all at their doors to see them pass. "Whyn't you ast one of these niggers the way?" Nelson said. "You got us lost."

"This is where you were born," Mr. Head said. "You can ast one yourself if you want to."

Nelson was afraid of the colored men and he didn't want to be laughed at by the colored children. Up ahead he saw a large colored woman leaning in a doorway that opened onto the sidewalk. Her hair stood straight out from her head for about four inches all around and she was resting on bare brown feet that turned pink at the sides. She had on a pink dress that showed her exact shape. As they came abreast of her, she lazily lifted one hand to her head and her fingers disappeared into her hair.

Nelson stopped. He felt his breath drawn up by the woman's dark eyes. "How do you get back to town?" he said in a voice that did not sound like his own.

After a minute she said, "You in town now," in a rich low tone that made Nelson feel as if a cool spray had been turned on him.

"How do you get back to the train?" he said in the same reed-like voice.

"You can catch you a car," she said.

He understood she was making fun of him but he was too paralyzed even to scowl. He stood drinking in every detail of her. His eyes traveled up from her great knees to her forehead and then made a triangular path from the glistening sweat on her neck down and across her tremendous bosom and over her bare arm back to where her fingers lay hidden in her hair. He suddenly wanted her to reach down and pick him up and draw him against her and then he wanted to feel her breath on his face. He wanted to look down and down into her eyes while she held him tighter and tighter. He had never had such a feeling before. He felt as if he were reeling down through a pitchblack tunnel.

"You can go a block down yonder and catch you a car take you to the railroad station, Sugarpie," she said.

Nelson would have collapsed at her feet if Mr. Head had not pulled him roughly away. "You act like you don't have any sense!" the old man growled.

They hurried down the street and Nelson did not look back at the woman. He pushed his hat sharply forward over his face which was already burning with shame. The sneering ghost he had seen in the train window and all the foreboding feelings he had on the way returned to him and he remembered that his ticket from the scale had said to beware of dark women and that his grandfather's had said he was upright and brave. He took hold of the old man's hand, a sign of dependence that he seldom showed.

They headed down the street toward the car tracks where a long yellow rattling trolley was coming. Mr. Head had never boarded a streetcar and he let that one pass. Nelson was silent. From time to time his mouth trembled slightly but his grandfather, occupied with his own problems, paid him no attention. They stood on the corner and neither looked at the Negroes who were passing, going about their business just as if they had been white, except that most of them stopped and eyed Mr. Head and Nelson. It occurred to Mr. Head that since the streetcar ran on tracks, they could simply follow the tracks. He gave Nelson a slight push and explained that they would follow the tracks on into the railroad station, walking, and they set off.

Presently to their great relief they began to see white people again and Nelson sat down on the sidewalk against the wall of a building. "I got to rest myself some," he said. "You lost the sack and the direction. You can just wait on me to rest myself."

"There's the tracks in front of us," Mr. Head said. "All we got to do is keep them in sight and you could have remembered the sack as good as me. This is where you were born. This is your old home town. This is your second trip. You ought to know how to do," and he squatted down and continued in this vein but the boy, easing his burning feet out of his shoes, did not answer.

"And standing there grinning like a chim-pan-zee while a nigger woman gives you directions. Great Gawd!" Mr. Head said.

"I never said I was nothing but born here," the boy said in a shaky voice. "I never said I would or wouldn't like it. I never said I wanted to come. I only said I was born here and I never had nothing to do with that. I want to go home. I never wanted to come in the first place. It was all your big idea. How you know you ain't following the tracks in the wrong direction?"

This last had occurred to Mr. Head too. "All these people are white," he said.

"We ain't passed here before," Nelson said. This was a neighborhood of brick buildings that might have been lived in or might not. A few empty automobiles were parked along the curb and there was an occasional passerby. The heat of the pavement came up through Nelson's thin suit. His eyelids began to droop, and after a few minutes his head tilted forward. His shoulders twitched once or twice and then he fell over on his side and lay sprawled in an exhausted fit of sleep.

Mr. Head watched him silently. He was very tired himself but they could not both sleep at the same time and he could not have slept anyway because he did not know where he was. In a few minutes Nelson would wake up, refreshed by his sleep and very cocky, and would begin complaining that he had lost the sack and the way. You'd have a mighty sorry time if I wasn't here, Mr. Head thought; and then another idea occurred to him. He looked at the sprawled figure for several minutes; presently he stood up. He justified what he was going to do on the grounds that it is sometimes necessary to teach a child a lesson he won't forget, particularly when the child is always reasserting his position with some new impudence. He walked without a sound to the corner about twenty feet away and sat down on a covered garbage can in the alley where he could look out and watch Nelson wake up alone.

The boy was dozing fitfully, half conscious of vague noises and black forms moving up from some dark part of him into the light. His face worked in his sleep and he had pulled his knees up under his chin. The sun shed a dull dry light on the narrow street; everything looked like exactly what it was. After a while Mr. Head, hunched like an old monkey on the garbage can lid, decided that if Nelson didn't wake up soon, he would make a loud noise by bamming his foot against the can. He looked at his watch and discovered that it was two o'clock. Their train left at six and the possibility of missing it was too awful for him to think of. He kicked his foot backwards on the can and a hollow boom reverberated in the alley.

Nelson shot up onto his feet with a shout. He looked where his grandfather should have been and stared. He seemed to whirl several times and then, picking up his feet and throwing his head back, he dashed down the street like a wild maddened pony. Mr. Head jumped off the can and galloped after but the child was almost out of sight. He saw a streak of gray disappearing diagonally a block ahead. He ran as fast as he could, looking both ways down every intersection, but without sight of him again. Then as he passed the third intersection, completely winded, he saw about half a block down the street a scene that stopped him altogether. He crouched behind a trash box to watch and get his bearings.

Nelson was sitting with both legs spread out and by his side lay an elderly woman, screaming. Groceries were scattered about the sidewalk. A crowd of women had already gathered to see justice done and Mr. Head distinctly heard the old woman on the pavement shout, "You've broken my ankle and your daddy'll pay for it! Every nickel! Police! Police!" Several of the women were plucking at Nelson's shoulder but the boy seemed too dazed to get up.

Something forced Mr. Head from behind the trash box and forward, but only at a creeping pace. He had never in his life been accosted by a policeman. The women were milling around Nelson as if they might suddenly all dive on him at once and tear him to pieces, and the old woman continued to scream that her ankle was broken and to call for an officer. Mr. Head came on so slowly that he could have been taking a backward step after each forward one, but when he was about ten feet away, Nelson saw him and sprang. The child caught him around the hips and clung panting against him.

The women all turned on Mr. Head. The injured one sat up and shouted, "You sir! You'll pay every penny of my doctor's bill that your boy has caused. He's a juve-nile delinquent! Where is an officer? Somebody take this man's name and address!"

Mr. Head was trying to detach Nelson's fingers from the flesh in the back of his legs. The old man's head had lowered itself into his collar like a turtle's; his eyes were glazed with fear and caution.

"Your boy has broken my ankle!" the old woman shouted. "Police!"

Mr. Head sensed the approach of the policeman from behind. He stared straight ahead at the women who were massed in their fury like a solid wall to block his escape. "This is not my boy," he said. "I never seen him before."

He felt Nelson's fingers fall out of his flesh.

The women dropped back, staring at him with horror, as if they were so repulsed by a man who would deny his own image and likeness that they could not bear to lay hands on him. Mr. Head walked on, through a space they silently cleared, and left Nelson behind. Ahead of him he saw nothing but a hollow tunnel that had once been the street.

The boy remained standing where he was, his neck craned forward and his hands hanging by his sides. His hat was jammed on his head so that there were no longer any creases in it. The injured woman got up and shook her fist at him and the others gave him pitying looks, but he didn't notice any of them. There was no policeman in sight.

In a minute he began to move mechanically, making no effort to catch up with his grandfather but merely following at about twenty paces. They walked on for five blocks in this way. Mr. Head's shoulders were sagging and his neck hung forward at such an angle that it was not visible from behind. He was afraid to turn his head. Finally he cut a short hopeful glance over his shoulder. Twenty feet behind him, he saw two small eyes piercing into his back like pitchfork prongs.

The boy was not of a forgiving nature but this was the first time he had ever had anything to forgive. Mr. Head had never disgraced himself before. After two more blocks, he turned and called over his shoulder in a high desperately gay voice, "Let's us go get us a Co' Cola somewheres!"

Nelson, with a dignity he had never shown before, turned and stood with his back to his grandfather.

Mr. Head began to feel the depth of his denial. His face as they walked on became all hollows and bare ridges. He saw nothing they were passing but he perceived that they had lost the car tracks. There was no dome to be seen anywhere and the afternoon was advancing. He knew that if dark overtook them in the city, they would be beaten and robbed. The speed of God's justice was only what he expected for himself, but he could not stand to think that his sins would be visited upon Nelson and that even now, he was leading the boy to his doom.

They continued to walk on block after block through an endless section of small brick houses until Mr. Head almost fell over a water spigot sticking up about six inches off the edge of a grass plot. He had not had a drink of water since early morning but he felt he did not deserve it now. Then he thought that Nelson would be thirsty and they would both drink and be brought together. He squatted down and put his mouth to the nozzle and turned a cold stream of water into his throat. Then he called out in the high desperate voice, "Come on and getcher some water!"

This time the child stared through him for nearly sixty seconds. Mr. Head got up and walked on as if he had drunk poison. Nelson, though he had not had water since some he had drunk out of a paper cup on the train, passed by the spigot, disdaining to drink where his grandfather had. When Mr. Head realized this, he lost all hope. His face in the waning afternoon light looked ravaged and abandoned. He could feel the boy's steady hate, traveling at an even pace behind him and he knew that (if by some miracle they escaped being murdered in the city) it would continue just that way for the rest of his life. He knew that now he was wandering into a black strange place where nothing was like it had ever been before, a long old age without respect and an end that would be welcome because it would be the end.

As for Nelson, his mind had frozen around his grandfather's treachery as if he were trying to preserve it intact to present at the final judgment. He walked without looking to one side or the other, but every now and then his mouth would twitch and this was when he felt, from some remote place inside himself, a black mysterious form reach up as if it would melt his frozen vision in one hot grasp.

The sun dropped down behind a row of houses and hardly noticing, they passed into an elegant suburban section where mansions were set back from the road by lawns with birdbaths on them. Here everything was entirely deserted. For blocks they didn't pass even a dog. The big white houses were like partially submerged icebergs in the distance. There were no sidewalks, only drives, and these wound around and around in endless ridiculous circles. Nelson made no move to come nearer to Mr. Head. The old man felt that if he saw a sewer entrance he would drop down into it and let himself be carried away; and he could imagine the boy standing by, watching with only a slight interest, while he disappeared.

A loud bark jarred him to attention and he looked up to see a fat man approaching with two bulldogs. He waved both arms like someone shipwrecked on a desert island. "I'm lost!" he called. "I'm lost and can't find my way and me and this boy have got to catch this train and I can't find the station. Oh Gawd I'm lost! Oh hep me Gawd I'm lost!"

The man, who was bald-headed and had on golf knickers, asked him what train he was trying to catch and Mr. Head began to get out his tickets, trembling so violently he could hardly hold them. Nelson had come up to within fifteen feet and stood watching.

"Well," the fat man said, giving him back the tickets, "you won't have time to get back to town to make this but you can catch it at the suburb stop. That's three blocks from here," and he began explaining how to get there.

Mr. Head stared as if he were slowly returning from the dead and when the man had finished and gone off with the dogs jumping at his heels, he turned to Nelson and said breathlessly, "We're going to get home!"

The child was standing about ten feet away, his face bloodless under the gray hat. His eyes were triumphantly cold. There was no light in them, no feeling, no interest. He was merely there, a small figure, waiting. Home was nothing to him.

Mr. Head turned slowly. He felt he knew now what time would be like without seasons and what heat would be like without light and what man would be like without salvation. He didn't care if he never made the train and if it had not been for what suddenly caught his attention, like a cry out of the gathering dusk, he might have forgotten there was a station to go to.

He had not walked five hundred yards down the road when he saw, within reach of him, the plaster figure of a Negro sitting bent over on a low yellow brick fence that curved around a wide lawn. The Negro was about Nelson's size and he was pitched forward at an unsteady angle because the putty that held him to the wall had cracked. One of his eyes was entirely white and he held a piece of brown watermelon.

Mr. Head stood looking at him silently until Nelson stopped at a little distance. Then as the two of them stood there, Mr. Head breathed, "An artificial nigger!"

It was not possible to tell if the artificial Negro were meant to be young or old; he looked too miserable to be either. He was meant to look happy because his mouth was stretched up at the corners but the chipped eye and the angle he was cocked at gave him a wild look of misery instead.

"An artificial nigger!" Nelson repeated in Mr. Head's exact tone.

The two of them stood there with their necks forward at almost the same angle and their shoulders curved in almost exactly the same way and their hands trembling identically in their pockets. Mr. Head looked like an ancient child and Nelson like a miniature old man. They stood gazing at the artificial Negro as if they were faced with some great mystery, some monument to another's victory that brought them together in their common defeat. They could both feel it dissolving their differences like an action of mercy. Mr. Head had never known before what mercy felt like because he had been too good to deserve any, but he felt he knew now. He looked at Nelson and understood that he must say something to the child to show that he was still wise and in the look the boy returned he saw a hungry need for that assurance. Nelson's eyes seemed to implore him to explain once and for all the mystery of existence.

Mr. Head opened his lips to make a lofty statement and heard himself say, "They ain't got enough real ones here. They got to have an artificial one."

After a second, the boy nodded with a strange shivering about his mouth, and said, "Let's go home before we get ourselves lost again."

Their train glided into the suburb stop just as they reached the station and they boarded it together, and ten minutes before it was due to arrive at the junction, they went to the door and stood ready to jump off if it did not stop; but it did, just as the moon, restored to its full splendor, sprang from a cloud and flooded the clearing with light. As they stepped off, the sage grass was shivering gently in shades of silver and the clinkers under their feet glittered with a fresh black light. The treetops, fencing the junction like the protecting walls of a garden, were darker than the sky which was hung with gigantic white clouds illuminated like lanterns.

Mr. Head stood very still and felt the action of mercy touch him again but this time he knew that there were no words in the world that could name it. He understood that it grew out of agony, which is not denied to any man and which is given in strange ways to children. He understood it was all a man could carry into death to give his Maker and he suddenly burned with shame that he had so little of it to take with him. He stood appalled, judging himself with the thoroughness of God, while the action of mercy covered his pride like a flame and consumed it. He had never thought himself a great sinner before but he saw now that his true depravity had been hidden from him lest it cause him despair. He realized that he was forgiven for sins from the beginning of time, when he had conceived in his own heart the sin of Adam, until the present, when he had denied poor Nelson. He saw that no sin was too monstrous for him to claim as his own, and since God loved in proportion as He forgave, he felt ready at that instant to enter Paradise.

Nelson, composing his expression under the shadow of his hat brim, watched him with a mixture of fatigue and suspicion, but as the train glided past them and disappeared like a frightened serpent into the woods, even his face lightened and he muttered, "I'm glad I've went once, but I'll never go back again!"

Part Three

Contemporary Georgia Writers, 1960–1989

With the civil rights movement, the growth of Atlanta into a national and world city, the crisis in farming, the arrival of the so-called information age in which no home is isolated from the flux of world events and culture, and the threat of nuclear war, Georgia plunged headlong into modernity. No longer could anyone regard it as a provincial enclave, separate and apart from the world. Increasingly it faced the prospect of losing the culture and history that made it distinctive. Mountain forests were clear-cut in the north. Swamps and marshes were drained to irrigate farm lands in the south. Rivers were dammed for recreation and energy, polluted by industry, drained by cities in need of water. The summer air over Atlanta took on an enduring tone of brown. Throughout the state, citizens concerned with preserving the architecture and land of their heritage contended with developers and other commercial interests who wanted to build malls, subdivisions, office parks. Suburban Atlanta threatened to become indistinguishable from suburban Los Angeles, Dallas, and Long Island. People talked of "two Georgias," one in the prosperous metropolitan areas, the other in the economically depressed rural hinterlands which remained much as they had been for a hundred years. Some Georgians, aware of how much a part of the world they had become, felt more disaffected than ever.

Georgia fiction of the last three decades does not overtly reflect the tumult the state has experienced. Only a few writers, such as James Dickey and Pat Conroy, address openly the challenges of the modern world, but most Georgia authors, in one way or another, write about them. They turn increasingly to the past as a way of discovering their identities, or they examine the difficulties of survival in a rapidly changing society, or they chronicle regional scenes and characters that the modern world threatens to push out of the way. No longer does the state's regional character seem such a mark of separateness. Now it becomes a source of identity, of place, a way of discovering one's home address in a larger national phone book. Such writers as Raymond Andrews, Ferrol Sams, Olive Ann Burns, and Alice Walker turn to the past in various ways to recover and define their origins, to place themselves more securely in the modern landscape. Alice Walker's *The Color Purple* engages in such a process. So does her story "Everyday Use," not included here because it has been so frequently anthologized elsewhere. "Everyday Use" contrasts two attitudes toward the past, both embodied in a family quilt. The educated, cosmopolitan daughter Dee (who has renamed herself Wangero Leewanika Kemanjo to escape the name she says the white man has given her) returns to her mother's dilapidated shack in search of artifacts to take back to her city friends as quaint proof of her lowly origins, and as folk art to decorate her apartment. The mother and her plain, slow daughter Maggie value the quilt as an heirloom made from pieces of clothing their ancestors once wore ("scraps of dresses Grandma Dee had worn fifty and more years ago. Bits and pieces of Granpa Jarrell's Paisley shirts. And one teeny faded blue piece . . . from Great Granpa Ezra's uniform that he wore in the Civil War"). The quilt links them to the past. It is a source of meaning in a world to which they otherwise do not belong. The educated daughter's desire to use the quilt as decoration, her rejection of her grandmother's name, is evidence of her own loss of heritage and identity. In a different way, to the narrator in "To Hell with Dying," the death of an old man to whom she was close in her childhood signifies a similar loss of meaning.

Other writers have turned to documenting the folkways of rural Georgia life. In a highly poetic style, this is what we find in the two novels of the north Georgia mountain poet Byron Herbert Reece: *Better a Dinner of Herbs* (1950) and *The Hawk and the Sun* (1955). These are intensely introspective studies of the inner lives of people in the hills and small towns of North Georgia. They are difficult to describe: they echo Faulkner, Thornton Wilder, Edgar Lee Masters, Carl Sandburg, and the King James Old Testament. But they are also distinctly original and beautifully written. An example is this short passage from *Better a Dinner of Herbs*, about the coming of spring to the North Georgia hills:

> A phrase came in [the boy's] mind when he first noted the change in the deadness of the winter landscape. "When Spring begins to stain." That was all the phrase. It came to no period of completed thought, was never finished, yet it had meaning. When spring begins to stain, he thought, and as if called forth by his thinking spring came like a seep, a stain of color upon the winter world. Looking out on the hills one day he saw them with their mantle of infant green about them, yet when he looked another day he could not be sure. It was as if there had been a greenish smoke that clung to the trees like one of August's least efficient fogs and the winds of March had blown it clear.

Like his poetry, Reece's novels deserve to be better known. Other, more recent, writers have also written about rural Georgia, though in distinctly different ways. In Harry Crews's novel *A Feast of Snakes* a rattlesnake roundup in a remote Georgia town becomes a symbol of modern estrangement and dislocation. Crews's characters exist in a piney woods void, indifferent to tradition, beset with despair and hopelessness, living only for the next day. They are the citizens of an economically, culturally, and spiritually depressed South, similar to those Georgians Flannery O'Connor wrote about in such stories as "Revelation," "Parker's Back," and "Good Country People." In many ways both O'Connor and Crews are pessimists. O'Connor may see the hope of spiritual redemption for her characters, no matter how miserable or benighted their lives. Crews finds only despair for most of the people he writes about. Mary Hood, in the stories of her books *How Far She Went* and *Venus Is Blue*, writes with a similar but muted pessimism, though from a more humane perspective, and on occasion she admits the possibility of earthly happiness.

But an equal number of writers have turned to the urban dimension of Georgia life. For Pat Conroy, in part of *The Prince of Tides*, and Donald Windham, in many of the stories of *The Warm Country*, this dimension is centered in the city of Atlanta. Windham effectively uses Atlanta as a setting, subtly evoking its character without especially dwelling on it. In his fine story "The Starless Air," modeled loosely on James Joyce's "The Dead," Windham interweaves a description of a family Christmas dinner with the death, alcoholism, and financial jealousy that threaten to tear the family apart. In Conroy's *The Prince of Tides*, the murderous violence of city life—in the form of a maniacal rapist—menaces a family. Conroy's tale is terrifying, and all too indicative of how many have come to view the dangers of modern city life. Except for details of setting, the story could have occurred in any large American city. The same is true of Windham's fiction. This is another reflection of the change that has swept the state. Both writers associate the instability of modern Southern life with the decay of the family and the fear that time may wipe away every detail that once made life secure and assuring.

Three writers have dominated the literary landscape of contemporary Georgia. Flannery O'Connor, of course, was a major force not only in modern Southern fiction but in American writing in general. Her characters, her use of the grotesque, her fusion of comedy and tragedy, her dark gothic visions of a fallen modern world, and the moral structure of her stories made her one of the century's finest writers of short fiction. Alice Walker, Harry Crews, and Marion Montgomery are only three of a number of Georgians who stand in her debt. O'Connor took the change occurring in Georgia and the South as one of her major subjects, though for her change was a metaphor through which she pursued her greater concern with the general human condition. For O'Connor, the South and the rest of the modern world had become a place of abandoned faith and lost souls, with no hope of earthly redemption.

James Dickey regards redemption in the modern world as possible only through physical action and experience that enable one to regain a long lost primal vitality and knowledge. This is a central theme of much of his poetry ("Springer Mountain," for example) and of his

1970 novel *Deliverance*. In that book four businessmen from a large Southern city go to the woods for a weekend of canoeing and companionship. They want to "get back to nature," to be challenged. Yet they get more than they expected when they encounter hostile residents of the hill country near the river. Their ordeal gives at least one of them a deepened insight into the ambiguities of modern life. The backdrop of the action is the Appalachian Mountains and a wild river soon to be submerged by a hydroelectric reservoir. Obliteration is a threat throughout the book: obliteration if the men cannot defeat the river and those who seek to kill them, obliteration when the rising waters of the hydroelectric impoundment cover forever the forests and the small towns and the ways of life associated with them. Dickey's point seems ambiguous: the men from the city have lost some primeval essence by their separation from nature, from their past, yet that primal essence also threatens them with death. Dickey has explored similar themes throughout his poetry, and he remains today one of the major Southern and American poets of the modern century.

The third dominant figure in Georgia writing has been Alice Walker. She has written novels, short fiction, poetry, criticism, and personal essays. She and Toni Morrison are among the first major black women writers to emerge on the American scene. Her style is varied, ranging from a traditional realism to experimental stream-of-consciousness and postmodernist techniques. Her novel *The Color Purple*, for instance, is told through a series of letters. Walker writes from a number of perspectives. As a person of African heritage, she has explored the nature of life for the black American in the modern world. As a feminist, she has examined the plight of women—especially racially and economically oppressed women—in a male-dominated society. Her treatment of women has been so sympathetic, and her treatment of men sometimes so severe, that she has occasionally been criticized as a man-hater. Walker also writes from a Southern perspective. She values tradition, kinship, and place. In *The Color Purple* her characters find satisfaction not through flight to the city and rejection of their rural heritage but through coming to terms—terms distinctly their own—with the land of their births, even with those men who have oppressed them. In this context, Walker's essay "The Black Writer and the Southern Experience" is especially significant. She observes, "No one could wish for a more advantageous heritage than that bequeathed to the black writer in the South: a compassion for the earth, a trust in humanity beyond our knowledge of evil, and an abiding love of justice. We inherit a great responsibility as well, for we must give voice to centuries not only of silent bitterness and hate but also of neighborly kindness and sustaining love."

Like Walker, many black writers have sought to reaffirm and rediscover their origins by returning imaginatively in their writings to the past. Raymond Andrews in particular sought to preserve a folk and cultural tradition in his Muskhogean County trilogy, a humorous sweeping chronicle of black life in a small rural county of the state. But white writers have done much the same thing. Olive Ann Burns was clearly concerned with recovering the details of life long past in her novel *Cold Sassy Tree*. For most Georgians the days she describes are simply beyond recall—those days before automobiles and expressways and electricity. So different are they that at times they seem, as she describes them, remote and almost absurd. Yet they were real, as her novel reminds us, part of a heritage in need of preserving. Terry Kay in *The Year the Lights Came On*, Warren Leamon in *Unheard Melodies*, and Ferrol Sams in *Run with the Horsemen* and *Whisper of the River* engage in a similar process of preservation.

Without the radical change that has swept the state, the past would not seem remote. Nor would it stand in need of recovery. The writers of the last few decades in Georgia have seemed more aware than any of their predecessors that the state's distinctive character might fade. They have written with increasing vigor about that character, as if to record it is to ensure its survival. Yet they have in no way been backward-looking. Life in their state has moved them. They have addressed problems common to the nation and world at large, and they have done so in a way that repeatedly confirms the distinctiveness as well as the universality of life in Georgia.

Marion Montgomery

A Mess of Pardiges

"Well, pull on up here where you can get warm," Billy McKay said while Rhoda finished getting supper on the table. "It's going to be another cold winter."

"You say that every year," Elic McKay said, inching the other rocking chair a little closer to the fire.

The old man sat very straight, frowning at his son. "You noticed the corn shucks this year? Thick as mud. How many times have I missed it?"

"I wish you could predict elections," his son said. "This one is going to be a hard one."

"This will be my ninety-third winter," the old man said, "and if I have missed calling a bad one in the past seventy years, I don't know it."

"The thermometer on the back porch says it is still seventy degrees and the sun has been down over an hour," Elic said.

"That's on the back porch," the old man said. "Throw another piece of wood on the fire."

His son obediently got a quarter of a pine log from the woodbox and laid it in the fireplace, loosening his collar as he sat down.

"Howcome you're getting so sloppy," his father said. "It's about got so I can't tell you from Jefferson. Rolling up your sleeves. Wearing your collar open that way. You're going to catch pneumonia and die before he does."

On Sunday mornings when Elic or Jefferson drove him and Rhoda to church, he wore a shoestring tie. He still had it on. Any other time, he wore his collar buttoned and his sleeves.

"Jefferson never has amounted to much," the old man kept on, "and one of the reasons is that he is so sloppy. If it wasn't that you're county road commissioner, where would he be? Second deputy sheriff is not much to brag about."

"Well, he's not going to be that for long if he votes the way he is telling everybody he's going to."

"His man going to win?" the old man asked.

"That's one thing corn shucks just will not tell you. I wish to God they would." They both sat staring into the fire, Elic about to move his chair back a little when the old man caught him at it. "Well, he ain't going to win in this county, no matter what," Elic said.

"I been listening to my radio," Billy said. "They have just plain got a lot on your man."

"When you do as much for this state as my man has," Elic said, "there's just naturally going to be some things that don't go right."

The old man rocked quietly, his hands folded across his stomach, waiting for Elic to ask him.

"You know," Elic finally said, inching his rocker closer to the old man's, "you know, I have heard it that Jefferson is giving it out that you are going to vote for his man."

"Is that so," Billy said, looking around in surprise. He relaxed and began rocking again.

"Now, that sort of thing can get folks uneasy," Elic said. "All that talk about clearing out the highway department and what it is going to do to a county like this one if his man goes in and the county has voted on the losing side. There are at least a half dozen men in this county that work for the state, and where is that going to leave me year after next if . . ."

"You know that old patch of vetch down the road there on the other side of the barn?" the old man said.

Elic sighed and sat back.

"Listen," the old man said, leaning forward. He looked toward the kitchen to make sure Rhoda was still back there. "There must be twenty of them in one covey."

"I've told you before, Papa. You know Rhoda would have a fit. I'm just not going to be the one that takes you down there."

"Last summer I heard them every evening," the old man said. "One time the bob white got up on the fence post just beyond the apple tree and set there calling for an hour. They nested right there and the young ones are just coveying up and beginning to get to ranging."

"It is September and the season won't start for six weeks," Elic said.

"Never mind that," Billy said. "You know my birthday is next week, don't you? Well, you know exactly what I want for a birthday present? A mess of pardiges."

"I will get you a mess," Elic said.

"No. I want to get it myself. I have killed me a mess of pardiges for my birthday ever since I can remember and . . ."

"Yes, and you remember what Rhoda said last year. That damned ten gauge nearly ruined your shoulder. She'll leave, and then where will you be?"

"Oh, she won't leave," the old man said. "Where would she go? All you have got to do is drive me down there and let me stand by the fence and you jump them."

"How do you know they're there now?"

"Rhoda went up there yesterday to see about some apples and she jumped them. Little old plump birds that have never been shot into. I can get three on the rise. I know it."

"I am just not willing to take the responsibility, Papa," Elic said. "Rhoda is right. You get down in the bed, and it'll be up to her to take care of you."

"I never thought I'd see the day my youngest son would turn against his father," Billy McKay said shortly. "We'll see what Jefferson will say."

"You mean to tell me that you would vote for that . . . for Jefferson's man if he takes you out there to get double pneumonia and a broken shoulder?" Elic demanded.

"Never mind," the old man said. "Poke up the fire."

"It is as hot as hell in here now," Elic said.

"You poke up that fire," Billy said.

Elic took the poker and prized the logs around so that a new shower of sparks and yellow flames shot up the chimney. Then he caught his chair and was about to move it back when he saw the car lights in the front yard. Instead of moving the chair, he sat down wearily and waited for Jefferson to come in.

Jefferson McKay came in with his sleeves buttoned tightly around his wrists and a tie on. He was sixty-seven years old, two years older than his brother Elic and four years older than their sister Rhoda.

"Evening, Papa," he said. "Elic," he added, nodding to his brother. He held out his hands to the flame and rubbed them together briskly. "A little chilly tonight," he said.

"Why don't you just set down," Elic said.

Jefferson pulled another chair up toward the hearth.

"I'm sorry to say it, Elic," he said when he was settled, "but it looks like my man is going to win in a walk."

"Howcome he's running so scared, then?" Elic said.

"He's got so much corruption on your man he has got to talk fast to get it all said before the election," Jefferson said.

"A pack of lies," Elic said. "And let me tell you another thing, don't you be surprised in the least when you find out where this leaves you next Wednesday morning when the votes are all counted."

"It just may be I'll have a job with the highway department, and if I do, you can begin to figure where *that* is going to leave you next election."

"You boys ought not to quarrel like this before supper," Billy said. "The least you could do is get along with each other when you come out here to have supper with me and Rhoda. Grown brothers fussing and fighting like that."

"Well, who started it," Rhoda said. She was standing in the door. "Who is it that has been playing brother against brother for two weeks, trying to get one or the other to take you out yonder where you can kill your fool self with that shotgun?"

"Don't talk like that to me, daughter," Billy said, his voice rising with authority.

"If I didn't you'd be down in yonder in the bed right now with your head on a pillow and me feeding you like a baby, or maybe dead. You forget what it done to you last year, but I don't. I'm telling you every one right now that I'll not stay in this house and be a slave to a bed patient. I have been pretty much a slave for the past thirty years as it is. But I refuse . . ."

"A wise virgin would have had her lamp full and waiting a long time ago," Elic said.

"You stop that," Rhoda said. "I can tell you it ain't the least bit funny."

"It gets funnier every year," Elic said.

"Now every one of you just shut up," Billy said. "You hear me? Stop it right now. I have lived ninety-three years. And for what? To hear my own children bickering and arguing every time they get together. It is enough to make your poor mother turn over in her grave."

"I'm sorry, Papa," Jefferson said.

"Ha," Elic said.

"You big politicians come on in here and eat," Rhoda said, "so I can clean up the kitchen. But you can just leave your politics in here by the fire."

"We'll talk what we damn well please at the supper table," Billy McKay said, getting up from his rocking chair. Elic took one arm and Jefferson the other, but he shook them both off. "And if you haven't got me a cup of hot coffee," he said to Rhoda's back, "instead of that baby drink you keep trying to feed me, I won't touch a morsel."

"Now Papa," Jefferson said.

"Why don't you just shut up," Elic said.

They went in the dining room and Billy sat down at the head, with a son on each side of him. Rhoda sat at the end where her mother used to sit. Billy said a blessing and reached for the meat platter.

"Just howcome you're so sure your man is going to win, Jefferson?" he said.

"Well, Jefferson thinks the city vote is going to do it," Elic said, "but there is about as much chance of him winning as of women voting."

"Women do vote everywhere I hear about but in this county," Rhoda said.

"Women ought to stay out of politics," Billy said.

"My man," Jefferson said, "has got the goods on the incumbent. Your governor is a crook, and the evidence is thick enough to curdle vinegar."

"He's depending on the women to elect him," Elic said.

"Is that howcome your man has got that woman in the race—to split the vote?" Jefferson demanded.

"My man wouldn't do a foolish thing like that. There won't be enough women voting in this state to stir a washpot. At least my man is smart," Elic said.

"Both of them put together are not as smart as that woman," Rhoda said. "Talk about prosperity and raising salaries and paving roads out one side of their mouth and reducing taxes out the other. At least she makes some sense."

"Women ought to stay out of politics," Billy said.

"Talking about legalizing horse racing," Elic said. "Next thing there'll be slot machines and prostitutes in every hotel in the state the way there are in Atlanta."

"Don't you talk that way at my table," Rhoda said.

"I don't approve," Jefferson said, "but I'd rather it would be open that way than underhanded the way that state parks graft was. Talk about gambling! I'd rather run this state on gambling money than be responsible for the mess that has been uncovered."

"Next thing I'll hear is that you have switched over to run that woman's campaign in the county," Elic said.

"There's nobody in this county fool enough to vote for a woman," Billy said. "Now where's my coffee?"

Rhoda pushed back her chair and went to the kitchen to bring the coffee pot.

"I don't know, Papa," Elic said. "There is at least one fool in every county." He was looking across at Jefferson when he said it.

"Papa is right," Jefferson said. "There never has been but one or two women that voted in this county, and I never met a woman yet that I thought would vote for another woman. If that woman gets a single vote here I'll . . . why, I'll take Papa bird hunting."

"Now that is about as safe a offer as I have heard all day," Elic said.

"If she gets a vote in this county, I'll take him tiger hunting."

"Women have got no right mixing in politics," Billy said. He cut off a piece of meat and began chewing it, waiting for his coffee. Rhoda came back and poured his cup up to the brim and filled the other men's cups. She sat down and began eating again.

"Children," Billy McKay said, setting his cup down. "Not to change the subject, but I have been thinking about something all day. It has been preying on my mind. Next Tuesday is going to be my ninety-third birthday, and I don't . . ."

"And you don't think you'll be around for your ninety-fourth," Rhoda said.

Billy glared at her.

"Well, I have heard it for two weeks, let alone every birthday since I can remember," Rhoda said.

"I'm sorry if I have disappointed you," Billy said. "But this time it just happens that it is true. It stands to reason that a man's chances get pretty slim, and with a cold winter coming on."

"You ought not to talk like that, Papa," Jefferson said. "You're going to be around a long time yet."

"No," Billy said, "No. It's no use denying that what must be must be. But somehow it just seems to me that I would rest easier if I could go hunting just one more time. You know how I have loved it."

"I have had my say," Rhoda said. "Pass me the biscuits."

"So," Billy continued, ignoring her, "I am making this offer to you. I will vote for whichever one of you will take me down yonder beyond the barn so I can have just one more shot at that young covey of pardiges."

"But, Papa," Jefferson said.

"Just one shot is all I'm asking. Rhoda went down there to get some apples yesterday, and they jumped up right under that tree. I watched from that window in the kitchen back there. Must have been twenty of them. Then I heard the old bird calling them back up before Rhoda got back to the house. They roost right there by the fence in that vetch."

"I never hoped to live to see the day that my own father would do a thing like this," Rhoda said.

"Why don't you quit bullying him?" Elic said to her.

"Because I know the consequences," Rhoda said. "He'd be dead in a week, and you know it. If he got out there on his feet, a team of mules couldn't stop him. He'd be climbing that fence before the feathers settled."

"I could get right in the front seat of the truck," Billy said. "And you could walk them up, and I will bet you a pretty I could get three of them on the rise. Easy as dropping a bean in a bucket."

"Somebody has already give it out in the county that you are supporting the incumbent," Jefferson said, frowning across the table at Elic. "What's going to come of all that?"

"I heard it the other way around," Elic said.

"He'd vote for both of them and not bat an eye if he could get somebody to take him out yonder where he could kill himself for doing it," Rhoda said. "Why he'd even vote for that woman if . . ."

"Now, Rhoda, you are going too far," Jefferson said.

"He would," she insisted, raising her voice. She began raking scraps into a bowl.

"I'm waiting," Billy said, "to hear which one of you is interested in getting my vote and influence."

The two men looked at their sister.

"Never mind her," Billy said. "She's not going to leave. I have got sick and tired of her telling me when I can do something and when I can't. Which one of you is going to take me?"

"I would like to, Papa," Elic said finally. "But she's right. Think about her. Here she'd be with an invalid to . . ."

"Listen," Billy said. "She says invalid, but the day has never come when I couldn't shoot that gun. We could pick a sunny morning right after breakfast, and . . ."

"Well, say something, Jefferson," Elic demanded.

"Papa," Jefferson said, looking sheepishly toward Rhoda, "You know there is nothing else in the world I'd rather do than take you bird hunting."

"Except get your man elected," Elic said.

"But Baby Sister is right," Jefferson went on.

"What they mean," Rhoda said, "is that if I leave they'll end up having to take care of you, and they have got too much to do to be burdened down with an old . . ."

"Well, why don't you just leave, Baby Sister," Billy said. "Go on. I'd as soon take care of myself as be . . ."

"Now you just settle down, Papa," Rhoda said. "You know you're not going to sleep a wink all night already, drinking two cups of black coffee that way. You get to hollering like that and you may end up with a heart attack."

"I'd . . . I'd vote for that woman, damned if I wouldn't," he added, glaring at Rhoda, who sat glaring back fiercely from the other end of the table.

"Women have got no place in politics," Elic said. "What would folks say, Papa?"

"They'd say that a little common sense had got squeezed in somehow," Rhoda said.

"You keep out of this," Jefferson said.

"I would," Billy said, settling down to finish the last dark drop of his coffee. He was watching Rhoda. "I'd even vote for that woman."

Monday morning after the polls were open, Elic paid a man out in the county to kill some birds for his daddy. The man brought them in a brown paper sack. Right after noon he drove out with them so Rhoda could have them to cook for the next evening. She was dressing five quail on the back porch when he got there.

"Papa's resting," she said. "You better not go in."

"Where'd you get these?" Elic asked.

"None of your business," Rhoda said. She wouldn't look at him but kept her eyes on the bird she was singeing over a piece of burning newspaper.

"Well, here are six more to go with them," Elic said.

"You just take them right on back to town," Rhoda said. "Give them to some of the politicians that are hanging around the ballot box. By morning they are going to need them."

He took the birds home and put them in the refrigerator and called Jefferson to see if he knew where Rhoda had got the quail. He finally got up with him at the drugstore next door to where they were counting the ballots.

"You better come on down here," Jefferson told him. "Things don't look so good."

"I figured that would be your tune about now," Elic said.

"Oh, your man is carrying the county all right," Jefferson said. "I never said he wouldn't. What I'm talking about is that somebody voted for that woman. So far one vote for her out of a hundred and sixty-three. They're giving it out that Papa voted for her."

"That's a damn lie," Elic said. "I knew I should have let you get the birds."

"I drove him in myself right after twelve o'clock," Jefferson said, "like we agreed. And they had counted all the ballots up to then and when they started counting again, this vote was right in the bottom, folded the way old man Wilson said he saw Papa fold it."

"I won't believe he could do a thing like that to us till he tells me to my face," Elic said and hung up the phone before Jefferson could answer.

The next evening Billy sat at the head of the table. "On the rise," he said. "*Blam!* Two of 'em just as they crossed, and then *blam!* Another one. They flew right down along the road and settled by the fence—two did. Rhoda got her apples gathered for this pie and got them three birds and I got in the truck and she drove on down to about where they went down and I leaned up against the fender and she walked along just the other side of the fence." He winced slightly as he lifted the coffee cup.

"I hear by the radio," Rhoda said, "that your man got beat pretty bad, Elic."

"Not in this county he didn't," Elic said. He had been gloomy all evening. "I don't see how you could have done it, Rhoda. After all you have been saying. If he has got a busted shoulder, which is what it looks like to me . . ."

"It was his idea, and he was going to walk if I didn't take him."

"Well, you didn't have to meddle," Jefferson said. "Talk is already all over town."

"First a single got up," Billy said, "and *wham*. Down he went."

"At least he didn't carry this county," Elic said. "Your man didn't get enough votes to amount to a hill of beans."

"He will know that I campaigned for him, though," Jefferson said.

"Well, from what I have been hearing over the radio for a month and from what your man said this morning when they had him on, you might as well not ask him for a thing. He's out to get these little county politicians, and I doubt he'll be impressed by the twelve votes he got from you," Rhoda said.

"It will be a long time before we live this down—what they're saying about Papa in town," Elic said.

"You all cut out that racket about the election. It is over with and done except for another bird hunt and maybe a tiger hunt," Billy said. "Now listen here. After Rhoda got that first single picked up, she wanted to quit. 'No sir ree,' I said. 'Not when there are two more birds right along here by the road that are not smart enough to run off in the field and squat.' So she took about five more steps, saying all right, if I was going to climb the ditch that way she would. Another one got up, and I got it. Never missed a shot."

"I still don't see how you could do a thing like that, Rhoda, his own flesh and blood," Elic said.

"If nobody is going to eat it," Billy said, "pass me that other pardige. And go heat up the coffee, Rhoda."

Donald Windham

The Starless Air

Quivi sospiri, pianti, e alti guai
risonavan per l'aer senza stelle.

The house was painted dark green, but, like the dark green leaves of the sterile magnolia tree in the front yard, it was almost black with the soot of the city. Dark with cynicism and impunity it stood, the only private residence remaining in a block of boarding houses and stores guarded at each corner by a filling station. The ornate and superior structure of the building had always dominated the neighbourhood of comfortable homes which grew up and declined about it, and now it added the obscure distinction of being obsolete. A deep veranda ran the length of the front and half way back on either side. Over the front door the original street number, 910, appeared in a semi-circle of coloured glass. Peachtree Street had been renumbered years ago and the new address was nailed in metal numerals on one of the square columns which, with their connecting balustrades, enclosed the porch; but the family still referred to the homeplace by its original number. Above and beyond the slate roof of the porch, half a dozen second storey windows, each surmounted by a semi-circle of coloured glass, flanked a small upstairs veranda obscured by a wooden spiderweb of knobbed spindles. The third storey was used only as an attic, but it also opened onto two balconies: one was bannistered on three sides by diamond shaped openings, the other forced upward through a series of oval frameworks into a small turret which reached above the top branches of surrounding oaktrees.

The hall was cold. The house had been built for utility and comfort; it had served as the centre of life for a large family where meals were eaten and comfortable evenings spent, but it had no furnace. No furnace had been needed in the days when fires were built in all the rooms and their heat warmed the corridors. But now that only a few rooms were used, the hall was icy.

A woman whose face was puckered but relaxed with a baffled resignation came out of the living-room and closed the door. She hurried to the back end of the cold hall and passed, again closing the door behind her, into a one storey wing which ran behind the main square of the house alongside of a grassless stretch of ground where Papa's hunting dogs had been kept. The fence was gone from around the dog yard and only one tarpaper-roofed dog house was visible in the grey morning twilight which greeted her through the dining-room window as she entered. The fire burned brightly in the room, however, and she knew that her sister was downstairs. She pushed through the first swinging door into the pantry and through the second into the kitchen.

"Merry Christmas, Hannah," she cried. "I didn't know you were down already."

"Merry Christmas, Lois," Hannah answered, turning from the fire which she was lighting in the wood stove. "I thought we'd get an early start this morning, but there's no sign of that Mamie."

Hannah was tall and thin with a thornlike face and figure and a sharp voice. She was the oldest of four sisters and contrasted to Lois who was the youngest and whose plump, fruitlike figure was not yet accustomed to the weight it was adding. With two children each, they lived alone in the large house. They ate together and shared the dining-room and kitchen; otherwise, they lived as separately as possible. Lois *had* the downstairs bedrooms and living-room. Hannah *had* the parlour and library and two bedrooms upstairs. The rest of the house was empty.

"I don't think I'll light the gas oven till we start cooking," Hannah said. "It's warm enough this morning. Mamie doesn't even have the excuse of bad weather."

"No, we needn't have wrapped the pipes in crocus sacking if the weather keeps up like this," Lois agreed.

"Well, it doesn't hurt to be on the safe side," the older sister said.

"No," the younger replied. "And it'll be nice to be able to have the children play outside."

Hannah, who had gone to the sink to wash her hands, frowned.

"Mine are still asleep."

"Well, they've outgrown Santa Claus," Lois said. Then, suddenly remembering their brother, she asked: "What about Bobby?"

Hannah clicked her tongue against the roof of her mouth.

"He's still asleep. I looked in and covered him up. He'd kicked all the covers off onto the floor."

"I declare, it's a wonder they don't catch pneumonia when they're like that," Lois lamented. "I'm glad Mama didn't live to see him do it."

"Well, if Mama were still alive," Hannah said, going to the little pantry and coming back with her arms full of meat, "you can be sure that he wouldn't dare turn up here that way. Christmas hasn't been the same since Mama died."

"No," Lois agreed. "There's less spirit. It seems like there's less of everything but people, and every year there's more of them. How many are coming today?"

"I haven't stopped to count," Hannah said as she poked a fat turkey with her bony finger.

"Let's see," Lois suggested and held up her hands to count on. "There's nine of us brothers and sisters, two aunts and Cousin Ella, my two children, your two, Bobby's five, Ivy's husband and two children, Audrey's husband and Fred junior, Henry's wife and child and Stuart's wife and child. Why, that's thirty in all."

"You've forgotten Cy's wife," Hannah said.

"Yes, Cy's wife. Thirty-one. You know, I don't believe there were ever more than two dozen when Mama was alive. But you know she'd be happy to know we've all stayed together."

"Do you know where the onion board is?" Hannah interrupted.

She could not start the turkey dressing without the onion board and they were still looking for it when the doorbell rang.

"There's the doorbell," Hannah said. "Can you go? It might be Audrey, though I don't know how she ever got away from that Fred Bronson this early."

It was Audrey. Lois let her in, and both of them had to make two trips to the car to carry in all the cakes which she had brought. Her husband, who had driven her over, would not get out of the car.

"Who's staying with Fred junior?" Lois asked.

"That Eustasia," Audrey answered, pronouncing the name as though it were a foreign word. "I don't understand her or any of Fred's sisters. She's just as sweet as sugar, now, though."

"Isn't that the way," Lois said.

She set the huge fourteen-pound fruitcake down on the table beneath the full-length life-sized portrait of Papa so she could close the front door. When she entered the kitchen with the cake Hannah, who had found the onion board where it usually stayed, pointed at the roasting pan in which the cake was cooked and announced that that was what she wanted.

"Now I can finish this dressing and get the turkey in the oven."

"Oh, I meant to tell you," said Lois, "the all-blue lights look real nice on your tree."

"I think they're nice," Hannah agreed. "That's the way the Stantons do their tree now."

"Oh, is that so?"

The Stantons were the family of Hannah's husband from whom she took all her uppity ways, and Lois did not see why Hannah spent so much time with them when her husband had been dead ten years.

Hannah was mixing the sharp oyster dressing for the turkey, Audrey was soaking sweet wine in the fruitcake and loosening it to turn out of the pan, Lois was cutting up fragrant pineapple, oranges and dates for the ambrosia, when Mamie arrived. The negro stood in the open doorway letting the fresh air blow into the kitchen and stir the rich odours.

"Christmas gift, Miss Hannah! Christmas gift, Miss Lois! Christmas gift, Miss Audrey!"

Audrey shivered and cried:

"I'll Christmas gift you, Mamie, if you don't come in here and shut that door. I'm freezing already."

Hannah and Lois exchanged a look over their sister's head. Audrey's steamheated house was so hot that they almost suffocated each time they went to see her.

"It'll be warm as toast in here in a little," Lois said. "Shut the door, Mamie, and come on in. There's plenty for you to do. The children haven't had their breakfast yet."

Mamie went into the servant's room back of the kitchen to change her clothes. After the gust of fresh air, the kitchen was more redolent of food than before. Lois put the ambrosia in the icebox in the little pantry and came back into the kitchen for the bowl in which to mix the dough for the rolls. By habit and without looking, she reached her hand to the shelf by the red flaking wall and found it. There was enough cooking on a routine day to keep the sisters in the kitchen all the time they were not at housekeeping, cleaning rooms, making beds, sorting dirty clothes in the large wicker basket for the washwoman. The familiar dun-coloured plaster of the kitchen walls showed through where the paint had cracked and peeled away and it seemed to be imbued with moisture like the steps at the end of the porch where the children had tried to start a fire one day by holding lit matches to the wood, which had been so wet and earthlike it had only smoked. Within them, the routine of eating kept the air forever dark and whirling, like a whirlpool filled with dust, and no violence which happened outside the house could prevent the sisters from concentrating blindly on their own existence.

"Just let me show you something," Lois said, standing in the middle of the room.

In one hand she held the bowl. With the other she lifted her skirt to reveal a purple and green bruise on the white fat-scarred flesh of her thigh. Audrey, whose body, widowed in a different way, was also beginning to expand in a vegetable growth without resemblance to the human skeleton, gasped in commiseration.

"Why, Lois, however in the world?"

"Bobby."

"Was he . . . ?"

She formed the last word with her lips but did not speak it.

"Yes."

"Did he pinch you?"

"No," Lois said, dropping her dress. "He came in last night and left a box in the dark hallway and I fell over it. I was so mad at him I could have killed him."

"He might have broken her leg," Hannah added from the stove.

"Isn't it the truth," Audrey agreed.

"But I had to forgive him when I saw what it was. A box of toys for his children. When I saw that even in that condition he had remembered them, I had to forgive him."

"Bobby's not bad," Audrey said. "He never acted like that when Margaret was alive."

"Well, what do you reckon makes him do it now?" Lois asked, shaking her head. "Those poor children."

She had gone into the big pantry from which she called back these last words. The big pantry, lined with shelves on which utensils and staple foods were stored, smelled like a musty gourd; and somewhere on one of the top shelves was stored the gourd dipper which had been used at the well when they were children. She pushed the biscuit board from the top of the flour barrel and reached down to fill the sifter with flour.

"Let me tell you something I promised not to tell," Audrey said, standing halfway between Hannah at the stove and Lois in the pantry. She put her hand on the back of a chair with a hairy cowhide seat and waited until her sisters stopped to listen.

Lois knew that Audrey had always had a temper and she heard the familiar tone of anger in Audrey's voice. She remembered the night when Audrey had run away in a fit of temper and married because

Mama had scolded her at a party. They said that her husband's bad blood had been responsible for her invalid child. Lois forgave Audrey her temper whenever she remembered that Audrey was trapped in life with that Fred Bronson and had to spend all of her days tied to him.

"I went down to Bobby's house last week to try and get him straightened out," Audrey said dramatically. "And the house—the house was such a mess that I don't see how those children live in it."

"It shouldn't be," Lois objected. "They've got Edith there all the time with nothing to do but take care of them."

"She's just a good for nothing *nigger*," Hannah whispered, looking toward the back room.

"Anyway," Audrey went on, "ever since Margaret died I've said that what Bobby needs is a job to keep him occupied and I decided to do something about it. I went down there and sent him over to see Cy."

At the name of their oldest brother the other two sisters both tried to speak at once.

"A fine older brother *he* is," Hannah cried, drowning out Lois. "He hasn't been to see us for months. And when I called to see if he was coming to Christmas dinner and to ask him to bring the kick for the eggnog, he said that he would but that he'd have to leave early because he is going to have a drink with the mayor. The *mayor,* mind you."

"Wait till you hear the rest of this," Audrey said. "After all, Bobby is Cy's brother, his own flesh and blood. He ought to help him even if nobody else will. And he's in charge of the hiring for all the construction work the city does."

"It's a shame none of the boys but Cy finished college," Lois sighed.

"Well, that wouldn't have helped much in this case. Do you know what your brother Cy had the nerve to tell Bobby?"

Audrey paused and her sisters looked at her gravely.

"He said that there is a city ordinance which forbids anyone hiring any of his own relatives."

"It's a city ordinance I never heard of," Lois admitted.

"It's a city ordinance *no* one ever heard of," Audrey hissed.

"I'll bet he's got plenty of *her* relatives on the pay-roll," Hannah whispered and leaned her head forward. "I'll bet there's no law against *that*."

"Well, we'll just have to call Cy aside while he's here today and tell him that he has to do something about Bobby," Lois said. "If he can't give him a job let him advance him enough money from the body of the estate to set him up in some kind of business. A filling station, or something."

"But do you think he'll do it?"

"If we tell him to do it, he'll have to," Audrey stated. "You speak to him. I'm not speaking to him, but you speak to him and I'll stand behind you."

The sisters agreed on this, and Lois went into the back room to see what in the world was keeping Mamie. Mamie's mother had lived in the back room; but, for some reason the sisters could not understand, Mamie preferred to live in a shack in Niggertown; and the room was now used for storage. Its odour of old newspapers stacked on trunks and broken leather and horsehair couches was pierced by the sharp scent seeping from an earthenware jar of home brew in the corner. Sitting on a bottomless chair across which a stack of newspapers were folded, Mamie was looking through her pocketbook. Lois stared at her and demanded:

"Mamie, what are you doing? Come on in here and cook the children's breakfast before you freeze and they starve."

She returned to the pantry and hurriedly made the rolls which would have to set and rise. In the kitchen she heard Audrey ask Mamie what she thought of a man who would not give his own brother a job, and heard Mamie laugh and answer:

"Yessam."

When the children had eaten, Lois and Mamie cleared the dining-room table to put in the extra leaves. With them, the round table extended into an oval which filled the room from fireplace to sideboard and from door to windows. Before they finished, the doorbell rang and Bobby's children arrived. Lois let them in. Neat and uncomfortable with respect for 910, they stood in the front hall and assured her that they had eaten breakfast, so Lois told them that their father was still asleep and led them into the living-room to get their presents. She was glad that their presents were waiting for them under her tree rather than under Hannah's. Hannah had the fine rooms and received the grownups, she told herself, but it was Aunt Lois that the children liked and to her side of the house that they came.

The living-room was warm with the odour of pinetree. She had lit the fire and watched her children, in their bathrobes and bedroom slippers, open their presents before she had gone back to the kitchen to help Hannah. They were dressed now. Her oldest boy was standing by the tree before one of the six windows which looked out onto the front porch; but the youngest was lying on the floor by the fireplace arranging coloured marbles along the pattern of the hot rug. She sat down and asked him to come and sit in her lap for a minute. As he climbed up she felt his forehead and thought that he had a fever. A terrible fear of death and the outside world swept over her. Growing up in the comfortable life of the homeplace had not bred in her the faculty of resisting. She accepted the inevitable. Together with her brothers and sisters, she felt no capacity or desire to extend the limitations of her existence; she desired only to keep what she already had. She would rather cut off her right arm, she often said, than have to choose between her two boys or have anything happen to either of them. But as she sat by the glowing fire stroking her son's forehead she realized that he was merely hot from the fire and if he was pale it was probably that his stomach was upset from overeating. Her fears subsided, but she promised herself that she would look at him again in a little while and if he was still pale she would put him to bed.

When she reached the dining-room Mamie had set the table with the everyday silver.

"Mamie! what do you think I made you polish the good silver for yesterday?"

She sent Mamie back to the kitchen to wash the cake stands and she set the table herself. She was thinking about Bobby's children as she turned from the table to go to the kitchen and she was startled to see

Bobby leaning in the hall doorway watching her.

"For goodness sake, Bobby," she gasped, "you startled me."

Her brother leaned in the doorway without replying and smiled at her. His large-pored red face was bloated beneath his stubble of brown silver beard, his small blue eyes were bloodshot, and even at this distance she could see that his smile was intoxicated. Slowly, he heaved his weight away from the doorframe and entered the room like a falling object. He came to rest against the sideboard and Mama's cutglass cups rang perilously against the side of Mama's cutglass punchbowl. His smile widened with defiance and he launched himself off again from the sideboard toward Lois. She could have dodged, but she knew that if she did he would land on the table and break Lord knows what, so she stood still and let him land with his arms about her waist. The reek of sweat and whisky breath engulfed her.

"Bobby, wherever did you get a drink in this house at this hour of the morning?" she asked in despair.

For answer he pinched her thigh.

"Bobby! Your children are here. You don't want them to see you like this. Come on back upstairs with me. Audrey's in the kitchen. You don't want her to see you like this."

"Where's Audrey?" he shouted and let go of Lois. "She loves her brother."

For a second he stood on his own. Then his equilibrium collapsed and he careened through the swinging door into the little pantry. He bumped into the right side of the first doorframe and into the left side of the second. There the door swung open and he stood facing two frozen gazes of admonition. He replied with a half completed gesture, aware of the impossibility of his situation but unable to escape it. His face puckered between crying, shouting, and remaining silent; then he produced a bottle of whisky out of his trousers pocket and whispered:

"Once a year, remember? Have a friendly little drink with your brother Bobby."

With an insufficient disguise of dryness, Audrey said:

"All right, Bobby, give me the bottle and I'll pour us a drink."

The other sisters caught on. Hannah stood firm while Audrey advanced and Lois furnished a rear guard. Their brother stumbled forward in momentary excitement and laughter and flung his arms in a bear hug about Audrey's head as he bit her neck. She screamed and struggled to escape. Undeceived, he held her fast and with his hands free behind her turned up the bottle to his mouth.

"Ha, ha, ha," he laughed as the whisky gurgled and overflowed his mouth, ran through the beard along his chin, and dribbled onto his sister's back.

He twisted and turned, but the sisters had him surrounded and as he turned from Hannah he faced Lois who wrenched the bottle from his grasp. He reached after her, but Audrey was still in his arms and hindered his pursuit. Lois disappeared through the dining-room into the hall. She was almost to the front when she remembered that the children were there. She turned and retraced her steps to the back where she entered the bedroom.

The shade was down and the room dark. Faint glows illuminated the pinpricks in the green cloth through which the sun shot in shafts on bright days. Panting and listening to her heart beat, she leaned against the heavy carved foot of the bed; but her breath would not come slowly nor her heart cease pounding. She reached out one hand and raised the shade. The day was so dark that no more light entered and she lowered the shade again. The reek of man—whisky, smoke, and sweat—had brought back all the melodrama of marriage in the barren landscape of Florida. Her nostrils cringed, and looking down she saw the open bottle clutched in her hand. She crossed to her wardrobe trunk which stood open with its back sides against the wall. Its drawers and closet, covered in a pattern of bluebirds flitting in the branches of trees, faced out into the room; and out of sight, down behind the shoe rack on the closet side, she set the bottle. Mama had given her the trunk as a wedding present. That had been in a different world, peopled with different people. In it had been only pleasure; from it had been banned all which demanded decisions. She remembered sitting on the front porch with Cousin Ella the first time she saw her husband. It was summer. She did not remember the month, but he was dressed all in white and in his hand he carried a small black case like a portable typewriter. (A

Vanaphone—they ceased to exist long ago.) He came smiling up the walk toward her, as handsome as could be, and he asked her mother if he could call on her the next day. Till late that night she read *Elsie Dinsmore*, the only book she loved. She remembered leaving through the white picket fence and down the tree-lined dirt street on her honeymoon. Melodrama and guilt faded with the Florida sky. Reality and innocence returned with her return to the homeplace. Here were no interminable oceans, no brick walls, only the lightning vine spreading across the vacant lot which had been the pasture. The picket fence was gone, the street paved. An electric trolley roared past beneath the overarching trees. She borrowed money from Mama and paid the bad debts her husband had left in all the towns through which they had passed in five years. Mama said that she need not ever leave the homeplace again. But the homeplace was a different world. Papa died and Mama died. At each funeral she sent the children down to the back end of the vacant lot where the cherry trees had bloomed when she was a girl. She did not want them to feel sorrow. The people she had known moved from the neighbourhood. Autumn after autumn, her brothers married and moved from the house, leaving their rooms empty. Spring after spring, they returned, alone, in the middle of the night, drunk, seeking the immunity they had once known, falling asleep across her bed and vomiting in her shoes.

She turned away from the dark cloth of bluebirds and stood up. Before she left the room she opened the small top drawer of the trunk where she kept her scarfs and summer handkerchiefs. In a little lidded compartment at the end, among her rings, earrings, pearshaped rhinestone buttons and glass beads, she found a small black bank book and looked in it. For many months of all the years since she had returned home, the figures on the pages, varying in the first numeral, repeated insistently the three noughts. This reassured her, and she went to the living-room to see how her son was.

The other children were in the front yard playing; she could see them through the windows; but he still lay before the fire. Frightened by what she had felt before, she made him lie down on the couch and tucked a blanket about him. He faced toward the fire and could not see the Christmas tree behind him, so she hung the two stockings bulging with apples, oranges, toy automobiles and hard candies, back over the mantel, one anchored beneath each front leg of the big clock.

"Who is that?" he asked, pointing to an oval gold-framed photograph above him, half way up the wall toward the high ceiling.

"That's Uncle Todd," she told him as she had many times before.

"He was a twin, wasn't he?"

"Yes. His brother's name was Dunk and they had only one picture taken because they looked so much alike."

"Dunk and Todd are funny names."

"I guess so, Sugar," she said and kissed him.

She was nearly to the dining-room when she heard his voice calling: "Moooother!"

She hurried back up the hall wondering what could be wrong. She stood in the open door asking him while he looked at her without answering. Finally he said:

"I love you."

The meal was progressing and the air was turgid with the aroma of cooking turkey and ham. Mamie was washing vegetables at the sink and Hannah was cutting up potatoes on a marble slab.

"Did you get Bobby back to bed?" Lois asked.

"Audrey's upstairs with him now."

"I don't know what makes him do it. And I think Sonny's sick."

Hannah clicked her tongue on the roof of her mouth in sympathy, and suspiciously watched Lois who had opened the oven door and was basting the ham. Just then the doorbell rang and the sisters sent Mamie to answer it.

"It's Miss Ivy," she said on her return.

The sisters hurried up the hall. The front door stood open, letting in the cold air, and at the steps Ivy was being helped up by her daughter.

"Merry Christmas," she shouted in a voice weak with laughter.

"All right, Mama, you've got to step up just a little," her daughter said with amusement. "I'm helping, but you've got to step up just a little."

"Tony," Hannah called to Ivy's husband who was parking the car in the driveway. "Drive on to the backyard so the others can get in."

Tony was Ivy's second husband. They disagreed on everything. When they reached the parlour Ivy sat on the loveseat and he retired to the corner and did not speak except to answer questions. Ivy took charge of the conversation and in a nasal voice repeated what the doctors had told her about her fallen colon. She illustrated with imaginary diagrams on her black and white print dress. When she finished, Audrey came in and she had to repeat it all. Together, the four sisters resembled each other very closely. Their figures varied from Hannah's tall and thin to Ivy's short and fat; but their faces were alike and they all wore their hair the same, in lifeless regular waves with a few carefully disordered curls just behind their ears.

"Does it hurt?" Lois asked.

"Pshaw, no, except I feel so faintified," Ivy laughed. "I don't get to eat hardly a thing."

"Isn't that a shame."

Lois and Audrey took the coats to Lois's bedroom and threw them across the bed.

"Did you get Bobby back upstairs?" Lois asked.

"Yes, but he's not asleep. The Lord only knows when he'll come barging down again."

"I declare. Whatever in the world do you reckon makes him do it?"

When they returned to the parlour, Hannah was telling about Bobby and they joined her in explaining their plan to Ivy. Ivy did not like being told about the plan after it was formulated and her voice was petulant.

"I guess you're right," she said, "but Bobby ought to be ashamed of himself. He doesn't have a worse time than the rest of us. I've been sick for weeks and I'm going to have all these doctor bills."

"But, Ivy, we have to do something about Bobby."

"I admit that," Ivy admitted. "But the way I feel is that the Lord helps those who help themselves."

She struggled delicately to lift her short legs from the floor and sat with them stuck defiantly along the loveseat. Suddenly she turned to her husband with a little shriek.

"Where's Cousin Ella?"

"I left her in the kitchen," he replied.

"Well, for Heaven's sake keep her away from me," she told her sisters. "She's nearly driven me out of my mind."

"Oh, Mama, you shouldn't let her bother you," her daughter said.

"You wouldn't say that if you were helpless in bed and couldn't get away from her," Ivy cried. "I know now why she comes and helps when there's anyone sick or dead. It's not because anyone wants her but because the people she's staying with at the time make sure she goes. Do you know what she was doing this morning? Christmas morning? When the children got up early she was already out, had fixed herself a pot of coffee and drank it, and was sweeping the front yard. And she wouldn't come in, either. I called to her that there was no need for her to do that, but she just went right ahead and finished. And *then* she went around the house and swept the backyard. I get so nervous that I know she's keeping me from getting well, and I don't know what the neighbours think."

"I hope she doesn't find out that Sonny's sick," Lois said. "He's scared of her. Once when she was here I heard her telling him that the reason she never got married was that the only thing she loves is coffee."

"Shush," Hannah shushed them. "I think I hear her coming."

Cousin Ella was thin and wild and wore a long dress made out of a stiff material no longer seen anywhere else except in an occasional square of a crazy quilt. She kissed the sisters and started chattering; but as soon as Hannah said that she had to go back to the kitchen to remind Mamie to put the boiling bacon in the vegetables, as she always forgot, Cousin Ella said that she would help and followed her out.

"Well, thank goodness," Ivy sighed. "But I doubt if we'll ever get any dinner now."

Everyone laughed.

Aunt Lil and Sally arrived next. Lois let them in and led them to the parlour. Everyone shouted at once in greeting, but all voices were lost beneath Aunt Sally's insistent announcement that she had never seen a Christmas day with such weather and that the air outside was a regular brown fog. She moved forward as unobstructably as an elemental force till she reached the comfortable chair near the fire and made Ivy's daughter move so she could sit there.

"So this is Ivy's girl," she said patting her arm. "Honey, you've grown so since last time I saw you I wouldn't have known you. Now run back to the kitchen and do Aunt Sally a favour. Just tell them that you want a coffee can for her and Aunt Lil. They'll know what you mean."

Henry and his wife arrived, then Stuart and his wife. The children stayed in the yard. Lois and Hannah were very polite to the wives for they did not like them. They came from other towns and were not their kind. But, as Hannah said, if their brothers were going to act the way they acted, you couldn't expect any other kind of women to marry them. Jefferson had a very nice bride, but then Jefferson was a very nice boy.

There was a great deal of loud talk in the parlour and Lois told Aunt Sally that Sonny was sick at his stomach. The old woman did not wait for her to finish speaking but shouted with the unquestionable authority of a woman who had outlived a husband, two children and three grandchildren:

"Give him calomel! Tomorrow morning give him a good dose of salts. That's what I always gave my Carl and there wasn't a stronger boy in these parts."

"But calomel makes him nauseated, Aunt Sal . . ."

"Give him calomel, and a piece of Juicyfruit gum after it and he'll like it. I raised eight younguns and never found a one that didn't like it. Here, let me fix it and give it to him for you."

She placed a hand on each arm of her chair and pushed her body up, grunting loudly. When she was standing she followed the grunts with a long, low whistle.

"It's becoming a powerful effort for me to get around," she complained.

Aunt Lil, who was thin, had sat across the fire in a straight chair.

"The trouble with you, Sally, is you're getting fat," she cried in a dry voice.

She sat very straight and leaned forward from the hips as she shifted the snuff to the other side of her mouth and spat toward the coffee can on the hearth. Two drops of the brown liquid splattered on the ash dusted hearth like raindrops on dusty earth.

"That's the funny thing," she continued. "I can't understand it. Sally and I both had all our teeth out, and ever since she's been getting fatter and I've been getting thinner. Had just the opposite effects on us, and done to us both just what we didn't need."

"Aunt Lil," Henry said, "what you need is a bottle of Hannah's good home brew."

A few minutes later, Lois and Sally returned to find everyone with a bottle of home brew in his hand. Sally wanted one too.

"Don't give Sally one," Lil screamed. "She'll break that chair when she sits down if she gets any fatter."

"I don't care," Sally replied. "I want one, and I don't care."

"Sally, Sally," Lil cried, standing up, turning round and laughing. "Look how fat it's making me already."

"Remember the last time Anna came to see us," Audrey said through tears of mirth. "Uncle Tom drove her in from the country one Sunday to have dinner with us, and when they got here she couldn't get out of the car. She got stuck in the door and couldn't move in or out. . . ."

Her voice trailed off in helpless laughter. Everyone joined her: the men in mild deep voices, the women cackling high and shrill.

"Mercy me. How'd she ever get in in the first place?" Lil asked.

"I don't know," Audrey sobbed.

"What's more interesting," Henry said low beneath the women's laughter, "is how she got out."

It was a minute before Audrey could answer.

"We had to send one of the children, around through the other door . . . to push her. . . ."

"When is the last time anybody's been out to see Uncle Tom?" Sally asked woefully.

Audrey sobered.

"Aunt Sally, I don't reckon I've seen him since Anna's funeral."

"We haven't either," Lil said. "We ought to get together some Sunday and drive out to see him."

"We ought to," Lois agreed. "He'd like that."

Lois kissed Jefferson and his bride when they arrived and took them straight to her bedroom to leave their coats. Jefferson was nearest to her age and her favourite. She did not hold it against him, as some of the others did, because Mama had promised him a thousand dollars for his twenty-first birthday and he had gotten it from the estate after she died. While he was still a boy he had come to Florida and spent the summer with her the year her second child was born. It had been the best time of her married life. They went fishing up the St. John River and her husband had been just as nice as he could be. She could talk to Jefferson; she was explaining to him about Bobby when Audrey came in to get her hat and coat.

"Audrey, where are you going?" Lois asked.

Outside an automobile horn sounded impatiently.

"That's Fred."

"Well, but what are you putting on your hat and coat for? Jefferson'll go out and help him bring in Fred junior."

"He's not coming in," Audrey said briskly. "We're going to his sister's house for dinner."

"Audrey Bronson!" Lois exclaimed. "Do you mean to tell me that after having brought all those cakes and having spent the whole morning here cooking . . . ?"

"I've spent half the day with my family, and I'll be fair and spend half the day with his."

Her voice was short. She hurried into the hall. Lois and Jefferson followed.

"Audrey . . ."

The doorbell rang as Audrey opened the door and walked past her husband on the porch.

"Didn't you hear me honking?" he asked.

"I was getting my hat and coat."

She continued across the porch and down the walk toward the car. Fred remained at the door, speaking to Lois. She could barely face him she was so angry, but she was not going to give him the satisfaction of knowing it.

"Lois, I want to ask you something."

His voice was serious.

"What is it, Fred?"

She did not intend to let him ruffle her.

"I wonder if you can tell me why the Indian on the buffalo nickel has such a sneer on his face?"

He had taken out a nickel and held it in his hand. She looked from it to the sneer on his face but could think of no answer. He flipped the nickel over and his sneer broke into a snicker.

"Because his nose is so near to the buffalo's ass."

"Fred Bronson!"

Touching her fingertips to the bannisters, Lois led Jefferson up the long staircase. At the head of the stairs they could see into the room which had been his until he married. It was bare; he had taken the furniture. The floor ran from the doorsill to the hearth in orderly emptiness. At the room where Bobby was in bed they looked in and found him asleep, so they walked quietly along the hall to the stairs. Hannah and her daughter clattered upward toward them with Cousin Ella following.

"You shouldn't talk that way to your mother, Honey," Cousin Ella called.

"Lady Jane! Listen to me."

Lady Jane stopped at the head of the stairs and stared at her mother.

"When your friends come I want you to bring them in and introduce them to me. Do you hear?"

"Yes," Lady Jane answered in anguish.

She ran down the upper hall to her room and slammed the door. Lois feared that Bobby would wake.

"Do what your mother tells you," Cousin Ella called after her.

"What's wrong?" Lois asked.

"She doesn't want to bring her friends in and introduce them to me before she goes out this afternoon," Hannah said. "But I'm not having her go out with any little buttermilks before I'm introduced to them."

She turned and started down the stairs. The others followed.

"She doesn't want them to see Lil and Sally using snuff," Cousin Ella whispered loudly to Lois.

Hannah stopped and turned. They stood strewn out along the stairs.

"Please, Cousin Ella, don't let Aunt Lil or Sally know anything about this."

"Oh, I wouldn't for the world," Cousin Ella protested. "I wouldn't say a word to anyone."

They clattered on down the stairs from vacancy to plentitude.

The sliding doors between the parlour and library were pushed open and the fire lit in the library. Besides more of the inlaid chairs and sofas of the other room, the library contained a large glass-doored bookcase flat against the wall, in which were kept a set of the Book of Knowledge and a set of law books as well as a typewritten bound history of the family of Hannah's husband. Both rooms were crowded now. The air curled with smoke and vibrated with voices loud and faint. The announcement of Audrey's departure broke in a wave of indignant sound which continued to agitate the merriment until Cy arrived. Hannah went out to his car with him to get the whisky for the eggnog and when she returned she whispered to Lois that she had told Cy they wanted to speak to him and he had agreed. It seemed that he wanted to speak to them, too. Lois did not quite hear what Hannah whispered, for names were bouncing from wall to wall of the room, rising higher and higher, but she gathered Hannah's meaning from her expression of knowing surprise.

When the sisters announced that dinner was ready, the entire assembly trouped back to the dining-room carrying the air of consanguinity with them. The circle closed about the table. All the grownups except Hannah and Lois ate at first serving; they waited on table. At first there was one empty chair, for Cousin Ella wanted to help them; but at their insistence she finally sat down, asserting that it was only to keep the others company as she was not the least hungry. She did accept a cup of coffee beside her empty plate. Everyone except Hannah, who had learned from her husband to prefer it afterwards, drank coffee with the meal. And everyone continued to talk as the food was passed, so that only occasionally was a whole sentence by one person audible. Cousin Ella consented to take a little of the dark turkey and a buttered roll, just to keep up her constitution. Ivy's negro and Mamie stayed in the kitchen and dished up the food while the sisters passed the roast and ham, the green vegetables and potatoes, the yams with marshmallow topping, then more turkey and dressing, the rolls, the condiments and jellies. They circled the table, complacently stupified by the richness of the food before they had eaten any. Their movements and voices became infantile. Commanding and begging, they drawled back into the secure past as they sighed and lamented at the smallness of the portions taken. Cousin Ella refused more turkey but took a little dressing. When Henry's wife suggested that someone should be sent to wake Bobby, as it was a shame for anyone to miss such a feast, the sisters exchanged glances, for they did not want someone like her to know; but they felt no apprehension. Perhaps Ivy had talked. They smiled benignly and suggested that he might not feel like eating. Henry's wife said that she guessed maybe he didn't, and laughed raucously. The sisters dreamily moved on, serving in opposite directions. Cousin Ella took a little ham to go with her second cup of coffee. The meal became the happiest they remembered since Mama's death. Someone said that it was going to snow, and they all looked out the window past the empty dog yard which was perilously near to being overrun by the lightning vine. It was certainly dark, but the sisters did not think that it would snow. When they cleared the table Cousin Ella helped them, tossing into her mouth continual bits of bread and meat against the insatiable hunger which she feared might someday be unstaved. Hannah served the ambrosia. Lois put out the mince-meat pie, the chocolate cake, devil's food cake, coconut cake and walnut cake, the fruits and nuts. Aunt Sally declared that she must have gained ten pounds, and popped a glazed cherry into her mouth.

Rapidly, intent on dessert, at the second table the children ate. When they had finished, Hannah and Lois cleared the dining-room table and set the negroes to washing dishes. Every surface in the kitchen was stacked with dirty plates and silver, and the sisters began to put the ingredients for eggnog, the platters, bowls and wire whisks, out on the table in the dining-room. The late afternoon was falling and they turned on the chandelier. Cy and his wife appeared in the doorway to say that Audrey had returned and that they would have to leave soon.

The talk about Bobby no longer seemed as urgent to the sisters.

"We've got all the things out to make eggnog now," Hannah said.

"We can talk while you're making it."

"If you like," Hannah agreed.

Cy's wife stayed with Hannah and Lois while they waited for Cy to return with the family. As the wife of the only successful one of the brothers, she talked to Hannah and Lois as though she thought she was as superior to them as they felt they were to her, and the conversation was punctuated by a great deal of polite laughter. Cy's wife said that she envied them the wonderful eggnog they made and Hannah replied that in that case she could watch and see how they made it. The click of fork and whirl of eggbeater filled a short silence. Then Cy's wife said that she had never seen so large a sugar can. Lois laughed. It was small to them. When she had first married it had seemed so silly to go the grocery store and come home with a little brown bag of sugar or a few slices of bacon wrapped in paper. Everything had been bought in barrels when they were girls: barrels of sugar, barrels of flour, barrels of meal, barrels of apples, everything—and whole sides of bacon.

Cy's wife waited until the whole family was in the dining-room, just as though she were one of them, then left with an air of already knowing what was to be said. Hannah and Lois pursed their lips at each other but could not say anything with everyone there. Cy sat at the head of the table again. Hannah's fork continued to click and Lois's eggbeater to whine.

Cy began by saying that he did not know what they wanted to talk to him about, but that as he had to leave soon he would make his own say brief.

"We can make our say brief, too," Hannah said.

Her wrist did not stop beating. Henry said:

"I didn't know we had anything to say. I thought Cy just wanted to talk to us."

Cy glanced toward Hannah. Without looking up from her work, she said:

"We sisters agreed to speak to Cy about Bobby."

"Something has to be done about him," Lois backed her up; "and if no one person is willing to help him the estate will have to."

"Help him how?" Henry asked.

"By advancing him enough money to start a filling station, or something."

"It looks like you just have to stay drunk to get what you want in this family."

"Henry, how can you say that?" Lois objected, not allowing herself to think that he had tried it enough to know.

"Think of Bobby's children," Hannah added and put down her fork.

Henry looked around at his brothers for support, but they did not like discussions. They preferred to take what was given them and to ask no questions. Then, if things went wrong, they could complain freely.

Triumphantly, Hannah dumped the yellow mixture into the cutglass punchbowl.

"Well, I see what Henry means," Ivy whined. "Bobby's not the only one. I've been sick for weeks and I've got all these doctor bills to pay."

"Well, you're not the only one, either," Hannah said, stirring in the whisky. "All of us have our troubles."

"I didn't say I was the only one," Ivy corrected her. "I said that Bobby wasn't."

"Let's not digress," Lois said. "Let's talk about Bobby like we agreed."

Ivy, huddled malignantly in her chair, twisted her head to face Lois.

"Oh, you and Hannah can afford not to *digress*. You live here in the homeplace and it doesn't cost you a cent. That makes a lot of difference, don't you forget that."

Lois had never thought Ivy would turn on her like that. She replied with tears in her voice:

"Well, I certainly never thought you resented us living here. All the rest of you can live here. The only reason you don't is that you've got better places. And if we move out you'll only have to pay a caretaker."

"No one wants you to move out," Ivy said. "I'm just stating facts."

Jefferson reminded them that they were to talk about Bobby. Lois would not have been surprised then if someone had made a remark about favourites, but no one did. Hannah folded the egg whites into the bowl. Cy stood up. Left with nothing to do, Lois held out the nutmeg which Hannah did not yet need.

"Well, I'm here to tell you that there's less money, not more," Cy said, "so if whatever you want to do for Bobby takes money, you'd better forget it."

Audrey had sat in her seat with her lips pressed defiantly together, but now she parted them.

"Why?" she snapped. "Is it your money? I'd like to know why."

Ivy moaned to indicate that the whole discussion was too much for an invalid. But Cy was angry.

"Any time anyone wants to take charge of the estate I'll be glad to put the whole damned mess into his hands," he said.

"Mess? How did it get into a mess?" Audrey asked quickly.

"I worry about the estate all year around. Then, once a year, you all get excited about money, money, money, and start complaining. Well, you can take charge of it. All of it."

Lois tried to deny that she had ever complained, but Audrey was leaning across the table shaking her finger at Cy.

"You needn't be so high and mighty just because you have a lot coming in and the rest of us only have it going out," she cried. "Just let me remind you that if it hadn't been for your brothers and sisters working for you up to midnight on the very eve of election you wouldn't have that job of yours. And maybe if everything was above board and honest you wouldn't still have it anyway. It's mighty funny to me that before the next election you made your opponent that you'd said all those awful things about into your assistant and the position was changed to a permanent one. Everybody doesn't have such good *luck*."

"Audrey!" Lois exclaimed. "That's your own brother you're talking to. Leave politics to politicians."

Cy grew red in the face and slammed his fist to the table.

"If you're suggesting that I've done anything illegal with Mama's estate I can show you papers for every transaction I've made. And I can give you an account of my own time and money spent."

"Cy," Hannah pleaded, "Audrey didn't mean what she said."

"Yes, I did," Audrey cried. "I'd like to see his accounts. If we all need money, I'd like to know why we can't all have it. It's Mama's money, not Cy's. It's ours."

"Mama would turn over in her grave if she heard us talking like this to each other," Lois said.

"Sit down and let Cy talk," Stuart said to Audrey.

"Let him talk," Audrey said. "Let him talk. I'm ready to listen."

Cy stood for a long time, silent, staring at Audrey who had no intention of being outstared. At last he looked around the circle at the table and spoke shortly.

"What I was going to say before Audrey's outburst was that Mama's securities have dropped in value. Lawyer Smith made some bad investments. You have either to take lower incomes or to sell a piece of property. All the property that's left just eats up money in taxes, anyway."

"What about our income from the Grand Hotel? What about that?" Audrey demanded. "We still own half of that, don't we?"

"That place isn't worth anything except as land, and you can't sell unless Lawyer Smith agrees to sell his half."

"I don't know anything about business," Audrey said, "but it's mighty funny to me that there isn't any income from a hotel that's doing business all the time."

"You don't know anything about what kind of place that hotel is! It's not even on the street. You have to go down an alley to reach it."

"Let's hear what Cy has to say," Hannah told Audrey.

There was another silence.

"Let Audrey say. It's not up to me."

In the cutglass bowl, the eggnog, unstirred, separated, yellow to the bottom cream to the top.

At last Cy repeated that Mama's securities had dropped in value until there was no income beyond that which was necessary to pay the yearly taxes on her property. If the brothers and sisters were to continue receiving money, property would have to be sold. The best piece to begin with would be the vacant lot over on Georgia Avenue. It was not worth much, but it never would be worth much; and it would bring in enough to pay this year's taxes and give each of them a small sum. But not a sum large enough to set anyone up in business. If they wanted to do that there was only one piece of property valuable enough. The homeplace.

"I don't believe a word you're saying," Audrey said. "You just say that because you know none of us want to sell the homeplace."

"Then I won't say any more."

Cy went out through the door to the hall and closed it softly behind him. Lois caught up with him on the front porch just as he was leaving the house. Outside in the world, she saw his wife already waiting for him in their car. Cy did not stop when she called his name. She ran down the steps and along the herringbone brick walk which divided the yard and placed her hand on his arm. He stopped and turned to face her but he did not say anything.

"Cy, you're not going to sell the homeplace, are you?"

"I think it would be a very foolish thing to do until the right time," he replied.

For a while everyone was separated, like children after a quarrel. Standing in the bay of windows beside her Christmas tree, Lois looked out at the unpierced night sky. Snow had begun to fall. Slowly, the ornaments of the boarding house across the street were outlined in white and the house itself disappeared against the black sky. And suddenly she was crying without thinking why, crying as though the cause of her grief lay in the cold window glass and bare yard, the water faucet wrapped in crocus sacking, and the buildings disappearing in the snow. Toward the snow of falling cornices and fading spindles she felt the fear which she had felt toward strange places and people not her kind. In the white disappearing of gables and mansards, the walls of the homeplace dissolved and left her bare to the world. All the things which she loved had come from that world: her children; her diamond rings and pearshaped buttons; the ornaments on the tree at her side, saved year after year since the first Christmas of her marriage. But she had thought that she would never leave the homeplace again, that she and her children would stay here always with the many people death had undone in the house, and she did not understand what had happened.

The room was dark except for the fire and the ornamental lights. She turned toward the door to switch on the chandelier. As she passed the tree her arm brushed against a metal bird with spring legs and a spun glass tail, and as she crossed the room the bird wobbled up and down, this way and that.

"Mother?"

She stopped beside the couch and kissed her son's forehead.

"Yes, darling."

"Where are you going?"

"Nowhere, darling. Mother's going to stay right here with you."

"What's the matter?"

"Nothing, darling. Mother just wants you to get well. Hush now and go back to sleep."

From the silence of the house, Hannah's footsteps echoed. The door opened and a din of voices, exclamations, cries of disbelief and laughter came in a tumult of sound across the hall.

"Wasn't that scene a shame!" Hannah said, striking her hands together. "Audrey can't learn to hold her temper. But she's forgotten it already. She's in there talking and laughing with Aunt Lil and Sally as though nothing has happened."

Her face bereft of expression, Lois looked up at her sister.

"Hannah, what are we going to do if Cy sells the homeplace?"

"There's no chance of his doing that anytime soon," Hannah said.

"But, Hannah, what are we going to do?"

"Well," Hannah said, "I'm going back now and dish up the eggnog. As soon as you think I've had time to cut the fruitcake, tell them all to come on back."

James Dickey

From *Deliverance*

With my cheek on one shoulder, I lay there on my side in the crevice, facing out, not thinking about anything, solid on one side with stone and open to the darkness on the other, as though I were in a sideways grave. The glass of the bow was cold in my hands, cold and familiar. The curves were beautiful to the touch, a smooth chill flowing, and beside the curves the arrow lay—or stood—rigidly, the feathers bristling when I moved a little, and the points pricking at me. But it was good pain; it was reality, and deep in the situation. I simply lay in nature, my pants' legs warm and sopping with my juices, not cold, not warm, but in a kind of hovering. Think, I said, think. But I could not. I won't think yet; I don't have to for a while. I closed my eyes and spoke some words, and they seemed to make sense, but were out of place. I believe I was saying something about some bank advertising Thad and I were not in agreement on, but it might not have been that at all; there is no way to tell.

The first words I really remember were said very clearly. What a view. *What* a view. But I had my eyes closed. The river was running in my mind, and I raised my lids and saw exactly what had been the image of my thought. For a second I did not know what I was seeing and what I was imagining; there was such an utter sameness that it didn't matter; both were the river. It spread there eternally, the moon so huge on it that it hurt the eyes, and the mind, too, flinched like an eye. What? I said. Where? There was nowhere but here. Who, though? Unknown. Where can I start?

You can start with the bow, and work slowly into the situation, working back and working up. I held the bow as tightly as I could, coming by degrees into the realization that I was going to have to risk it again, before much longer. But not now. Let the river run.

And let the moonlight come down for a little while. I had the bow and I had one good arrow and another one I might risk on a short shot. The thought struck me with my full adrenaline supply, all hitting the veins at once. Angelic. Angelic. Is that what it means? It very likely does. And I have a lot of nylon rope, and a long knife that was held at my throat and stuck by a murderer in the tree beside my head. It is not in the tree now; it is at my side. It is not much duller for having been in the river, and if I wanted to shave hair with it, I could. Does it still hurt, where that woods rat, that unbelievable redneck shaved across me with it? I felt my chest, and it hurt. Good. Good. Am I ready? No. No. Not yet, Gentry. It doesn't have to be yet. But soon.

It was easy to say I don't understand, and I did say it. But that was not really relevant. It just came down to where I was, and what I was doing there. I was not much worried. I was about 150 feet over the river, as nearly as I could tell, and I believed that if I could get that far I could get the rest of the way, even though the cliff was steeper here than it was lower down. Let me look, now. That is all there is to do, right at this moment. That is all there is to do, and that is all that needs to be done.

What a view, I said again. The river was blank and mindless with beauty. It was the most glorious thing I have ever seen. But it was not seeing, really. For once it was not just seeing. It was beholding. I *beheld* the river in its icy pit of brightness, in its far-below sound and indifference, in its large coil and tiny points and flashes of the moon, in its long sinuous form, in its uncomprehending consequence. What was there?

Only that terrific brightness. Only a couple of rocks as big as islands, around one of which a thread of scarlet seemed to go, as though outlining a face, a kind of god, a layout for an ad, a sketch, an element of design. It was a thread like the color of sun-images underneath the eyelids. The rock quivered like a coal, because I wanted it to quiver, held in its pulsing border, and what it was pulsing with was me. It might have looked something like my face, in one of those photographs lit up from underneath. My face: why not? I can have it as I wish: a kind of three-quarter face view, set in the middle of the moon-pit, that might have looked a little posed or phony, but was yet different from what any mirror could show. I thought I saw the jaw set, breathing with the river and the stone, but it might also have been a smile of some kind. I closed my eyes and opened them again, and the thread around the rock was gone, but it had been there. I felt better; I felt wonderful, and fear was at the center of the feeling: fear and anticipation—there was no telling where it would end.

I turned back. I turned back to the wall and the cliff, and into my situation, trying to imagine how high the cliff had seemed to be the last time I had seen it by daylight, and trying to estimate where I was on it. I thought I surely must be three quarters of the way up. I believed I could stand upright in the crevice, and this would give me three or four more feet.

Why not? Was there a bulge above me? If I could get on top of that, who knows what might not be possible? I let my hand go up, and it felt the top of the crevice. What are you sending me? I said. It feels good. It feels like something I might be able to work up on top of, if I went to the left, and took one moment of pure death. There is going to be that moment, but that is not bad. I have had so many in the past few hours: so many decisions, so many fingers groping over this insignificant, unwatched cliff, so many muscles straining against the stone.

Where was Drew? He used to say, in the only interesting idea I had ever heard him deal with, that the best guitar players were blind men: men like Reverend Gary Davis and Doc Watson and Brownie McGhee, who had developed the sense of touch beyond what a man with eyes could do. I have got something like that, I said. I have done what I have done, I have got up here mostly by the sense of touch, and in the dark.

Are they below? Is Lewis still twisting into the sand? Is Bobby sitting on the rock beside him trying to think what to do? Is his head in his hands? Or has his jaw set, believing that we can all get out, even now?

Who knows that? But we have laid a plan, and that is all we have been able to do. If that doesn't work, we will probably all be killed, or if I can get back down the cliff when nothing happens, we will all just go a few miles downriver in the canoe, take a few days in the city to recover, report Drew as drowned and get back into the long, declining routine of our lives. But we were cast in roles, and first we must do something about them.

I was a killer. There were deaths involved: one certain murder and probably another. I had the cold glass of the bow in my hand, and I was lying belly-up in a crevice in a cliff above a river, and it could be that everything was with me.

I could get there, in my mind. The whole thing focused, like an old movie that just barely held its own on the screen. The top of the gorge was wild and overgrown and lumpy, and I remembered it also thickly wooded. I wanted to give myself something definite to do when I got to the top, and lying there, I tried to fix on what would be the best thing and the first thing to do when I got there.

I had to admit it: I thought that there was really no danger involved, at least from anything human. I didn't actually believe that the man who had shot Drew would stay around all night for another shot at us, or that he would come back in the early light, either. But then I remembered what I had told Bobby, and I was troubled again. *If it were me* was the main thing I thought. I went over everything in my mind, and as far as I could tell, I was right. There was a lot more reason for him to kill the rest of us than there was for him to let us go. We were all acting it out.

I turned. Well, I said to the black stone at my face, when I get to the top the first thing I'll do will be not to think of Martha and Dean again, until I see them. And then I'll go down to the first stretch of calm water and take a look around before it gets light. When I finish that, I'll make a circle inland, very quiet, and look for him like I'm some kind of an animal. What kind? It doesn't matter, as long as I'm quiet and deadly. I could be a snake. Maybe I can kill him in his sleep. That would be the easiest thing to do, but could I do it? How? With the bow? Or would I put the hardware store knife through him? Could I do it? Or would I like to do it? I asked this.

But the circling—what about that? If I got too far from the river, and the sound of the river, I would almost surely lose myself. And then what? A circle? *What* circle? What principle guides you, when you try to make a circle—a *circle*—in the woods? I didn't have it. Suppose I got inland from the river far enough to lose track of myself? Had I shot the whole thing, right there?

But I could see myself killing, because I had no real notion I would have to. If he was close to the cliff edge, as he would at some place and time have to be, the high-rising sound of water would help me get close enough to him for a killing shot. I wanted to kill him exactly as Lewis had killed the other man: I wanted him to suspect nothing at all until the sudden terrible pain in his chest that showed an arrow through him from behind, come from anywhere.

Oh what a circle, I thought. All in the woods, with the leaves waiting, the wind waiting, for me to draw it. That is leaving too much to chance. It won't work, I knew as I considered it. It will never work.

What then, art director? Graphics consultant? What is the layout? It is this: to shoot him from behind, somewhere on the top of the gorge. He almost certainly would get himself into the prone position in order to shoot down onto the river. There are these various kinds of concentration. While he was deep in his kind, I would try to get within twenty or thirty feet of him and put my one good arrow through his lower rib cage—for what would save the shot would be exactness—and then fall back and run for it into the woods, and sit down and wait until he had time enough to die.

That was as far ahead as I could think. In a way, it seemed already settled. It was settled as things in daydreams always are, but it could be settled only because the reality was remote. It was the same state of mind I had had when I had hunted the deer in the fog. These were worthy motions I was going through, but only motions, and it was shocking to remind myself that if I came on him with the rifle I would have to carry them through or he would kill me.

I slid farther into the crack to draw from the stone a last encouragement, but I was already tired of being there. It would be best to stand up and get on with it.

I got on one knee and went cautiously outward, rising slowly with both hands palm-up on the underside of the fissure top. I was up, slanting backward, and I felt along and around the bulge over my head. To the right there was nothing I could do, but I was glad to be back. To the left the crevice went on beyond where I could reach, and the only thing to do was to edge along it, sidestepping inch by inch until only my toes, very tired again, were in the crack. But I was able to straighten from my back-leaning position to an upright one—really upright—and then to lean surprisingly forward at the waist, as I edged to the left. This was unexpected and exhilarating. The stone came back at me strong. I got on the rock with my knees instead of my toes and fingertips, and had a new body position. With it, I wormed. I went to the left and then to the right, and the river-pit blazed. It was slow going, for the handholds were not good, and the broadheads gored me under the arms a good deal, but there was a trembling and near-perfect balance between gravity—or my version of it—and the slant of the stone: I was at the place where staying on the wall and falling canceled each other out in my body, yet were slightly in favor of my staying where I was, and edging up. Time after time I lay there sweating, having no handhold or foothold, the rubber of my toes bending back against the soft rock, my hands open. Then I would begin to try to inch upward again, moving with the most intimate motions of my body, motions I had never dared use with Martha, or with any other human woman. Fear and a kind of enormous moon-blazing sexuality lifted me, millimeter by millimeter. And yet I held madly to the human. I looked for a slice of gold like the model's in the river: some kind of freckle, something lovable, in the huge serpent-shape of light.

Above me the darks changed, and in one of them was a star. On both sides of that small light the rocks went on up, black and solid as ever, but their power was broken. The high, deadly part of the cliff I was on bent and rocked steadily over toward life, and toward the hole with the star in it, where, as I went, more stars were added until a constellation like a crown began to form. I was now able to travel on knees—my knees after all—the bow scraping the ground beside me.

I was crying. What reason? There was not any, for I was really not ashamed or terrified; I was just there. But I lay down against the cliff to get my eyesight cleared. I turned and propped on my elbow like a tourist, and looked at it again. Lord, Lord. The river hazed and danced into the sparkle of my eyelashes, the more wonderful for being unbearable. This was something; it was something.

But eventually you have to turn back to your knees, and on cliffs they carry you better than any other part of the body, on cliffs of a certain slant; I got on my knees.

It was painful, but I was going. I was crawling, but it was no longer necessary to make love to the cliff, to fuck it for an extra inch or two in the moonlight, for I had some space between me and it. If I was discreet, I could offer it a kick or two, even, and get away with it.

My feet slanted painfully in one direction or another. Guided by what kind of guesswork I could not say, I kept scrambling and stumbling upward like a creature born on the cliff and coming home. Often a hand or foot would slide and then catch on something I knew, without knowing, would be there, and I would go on up. There was nothing it could do against me, in the end; there was nothing it could do that I could not match, and, in the twinkling of some kind of eye-beat. I was going.

By some such way as this, I got into a little canyon. Yes, and I stood up. I could not see much, but it *felt* like the little draw where I had hunted the deer in the fog. The bottom underfoot—under *foot*—was full of loose rocks and boulders, but I was walking it. At each shoulder, the walls were wanting to come down, but they did not. Instead, they started to fill with bushes and small, ghostly, dense trees. These were solid, and I came up to them, little by little. Then their limbs were above me. I was out.

I picked up the bow, out of the crook of my arm. Everything was with me; the knife at my side said what it was. And there was rope, for nothing, or for something. And I looked out, on the mindlessness and the beauty.

Upriver, I could see only the ragged, blinding V of the rapids that had thrown us, and there was nothing to look at there, except only the continual, almost-silent pouring of the water, through and through. I faced around and for what I judged an equal amount of time looked into the woods. I went back into the pines growing on solid ground, leaned my forehead on a tree and then put my forearm between the tree and it.

Where? I went back to look down on the river. Trees, fewer and fewer, were growing to the edge of the cliff. The moon shone down through their needles on the Cahulawassee. I thought for the first time seriously of the coming destruction on the river, of the water rising to the place I was standing now, lifting out of its natural bed up over the stones that had given us such a hard time in the white water, and slowly also up the cliff, the water patiently and inevitably searching out every handhold I had had, then coming to rest where I was standing in the moonlight. I sat on a cold rock at the edge, looking down. I believed, in the great light, that if I fell I could instinctively reach to the cliff and catch on to something that would hold: that, among all the places in the world that could kill me, there was one that could not.

I came back by degrees to the purpose.

First, I assumed that the man who had shot Drew knew that he had shot him. That was a beginning. I also assumed that he knew we hadn't all been killed in the rapids. What then? He might be waiting above the calm where Bobby and Lewis were—where I was, more or less—planning to draw down on them when they started out. If that were the case he would kill them both, though if Bobby gauged the change in the light well enough and set out when there was enough visibility to use the canoe but not enough to shoot by, they might have a chance to get past him, through the next stretch of rapids—the ones now a little downstream from me—and on down. Our whole hope rested on our being able to second-guess the man, and, now that I was on top of the gorge, it seemed to me that we had guessed right, or as right as it was possible for us to do. If Bobby moved out in the very early half-light, the chances of making a good shot down onto the water would be greatly reduced, and big gaps in the upper part of the wall, small deep ravines such as the one I had come up, would keep him from getting downstream at anything like the speed the canoe could make. I counted on his knowing this, and on the idea that he would try to solve the problem by setting up his shots downstream at calm water, where the target would be moving at a more constant speed and not leaping and bobbing. Below me, except for one rush of whiteness cramped between two big hedges of stone, the rapids seemed comparatively gentle, in places—so far as I could tell—scarcely more than a heavy-twilled rippling. But even this would be disconcerting for a marksman because of the bobbing it would cause. If I were going to kill somebody from this distance and this angle I would want to draw a long bead. Under those conditions, and if he was a good shot, there was no reason he couldn't get Bobby and Lewis both, and within a few seconds of each other, if he took his time and dropped the first one cleanly. That would take calm water, as slow as possible, and it would have to be downstream, out of sight around the next turn.

That's it then, I thought. I had to ambush him in some way, if possible from behind, and this depended on my being able to locate the place he would pick to shoot from, and on luck. And I would have to get him as he was steadying down to fire, which cut the margin of safety for Bobby and Lewis very thin.

I had thought so long and hard about him that to this day I still believe I felt, in the moonlight, our minds fuse. It was not that I felt myself turning evil, but that an enormous physical indifference, as vast as the whole abyss of light at my feet, came to me: an indifference not only to the other man's body scrambling and kicking on the ground with an arrow through it, but also to mine. If Lewis had not shot his companion, he and I would have made a kind of love, painful and terrifying to me, in some dreadful way pleasurable to him, but we would have been together in the flesh, there on the floor of the woods, and it was strange to think of it. Who was he? An escaped convict? Just a dirt farmer out hunting? A bootlegger?

Since I needed to be in a place where I could see the river, and as much of it as possible, in order to know whether or not the canoe was in sight of the man, I wanted to get as high as possible, and out of sight, and that meant a rock with an overlook, or a tree. I remembered that when the bow-hunting of deer from tree stands first hit our state, a lot of hunters who had never been near an animal in the woods bagged deer the first time they tried it. Deer are supposed to have no natural enemies in trees, and so seldom look up. This was not much to go on, but there were plenty of trees growing near the edge of the cliff. First, though, I would have to get down the river and find the right spot.

I began to make my way over the boulders at the edge, paralleling the rapids, which went on and on as far as I could see. Most of the time it was not as hard going as I would have thought. The rocks were very big ones, and I stepped and jumped from one dark mass to another with a sureness of foot that astonished me, for there seemed nothing at all to be afraid of. The only thing that bothered me now and then was the harshness of my breath, in which there was still the sound of panic, and this appeared to have nothing to do with the actions of my body. It took me a good while—at least an hour, maybe two—to get down past the rapids. When the moon smoothed out below me, and the rising sound fell back, I had the river where I wanted it. What now?

The top was mostly boulders, and there were a lot of them I could have hidden behind, but I would have had almost no visibility. I decided to go downstream a little farther just to get a look at what was there, and then to come back to about where I was now standing.

This time the traveling was much rougher; there were some very bad places: big hacked-feeling boulders with fallen trees wedged between them, and at one spot there was a kind of natural wall, high like a stone barricade, that I didn't think I'd be able to get over. Both going downriver and coming back I had to feel my way inland twenty or thirty yards to find a way to get over it. There were saplings growing near it on both sides, though, and with the help of these—which gave me something to hold on to as my feet were climbing the rock—I got on top of it and slid down the other side. All the time I was traveling I was looking at the river, and unless the man lay on top of the stone wall—where visibility was not good, the river showing only as a faint movement like the leaves of a tree seen through another tree—he would have to get somewhere on the edge itself to have a wide enough view of the stream to sight and lead accurately. Of the part of the calm water I had been back and forth over, there was only one place that looked right for this. It was surrounded on the upstream side by jumbled rocks, but was easier to get to from inland, as far as I could tell. There was a pale sandy platform at the very edge that looked down on the river through a thicket of grass about a yard high. As far as I was concerned, this was it. We were still far enough from houses and highways not to be heard, but I was fairly sure that we were not awfully far, even so, and the closer we were the less likely he would be to take a chance. If he doesn't come here, I thought, but picks another calm place downstream, Bobby and Lewis have had it.

Yes, I thought with a cowardly but good feeling, *they've* had it. After all, I would have done all I could, and as a last resort could work my way out of the woods, following the river down to the first highway bridge. I was not particularly afraid of the man's hunting me down after killing the others—though I was afraid to some extent, imagining suddenly his moving along my uncertain tracks in the windless underbrush and dark foliage—for he wouldn't know where I was. Though he most likely recalled that there'd been four people in the canoes, one of us could easily have been drowned in the rapids; after all, the three of us nearly *had* drowned there. My life was safer than anyone's unless the toothless man and I came on each other by chance.

Or unless I took a shot at him and missed. That chilled me; I felt my tongue thicken at the possibility. I thought about starting the trek out of the woods now, but the back of my mind told me that I had not gone through enough of the right motions yet; if Bobby and Lewis died, I wanted to be able to say to myself that I had done more than just climb up a gorge side and leave them helpless. But if the man I was looking for didn't come where I expected him to after I had done my best to find him and kill him, that was not my fault. And there was not much chance that I had really guessed right. It was just the best that I could do.

There was still no light in the sky but moonlight. I turned away from the river where the land shelved back to some boulders and low trees, and felt around. Among the trees, which held the light from me, I could tell nothing except by touch. I put out a foot because I could reach farther that way. Something solid was there. I took a step toward it and was enveloped at once in branches and the stiff pine-hairs. I set the bow down and climbed into the lower limbs, which were very thick and close together, and went up until the tree swayed.

There was a little visibility through the needles, a little flickering light off the river, which the tree set twice as far off as it had been when I looked at it from the grasses at the edge of the cliff. I finally figured out that the part of the river I could see was where it came out of the turn from the last of the rapids below Lewis and Bobby, and calmed and smoothed out, losing its own thready silver for the broad-lying moonlight.

I went back down and got the bow and began to do what I could about setting up a blind in the tree. I had never shot anything—or at anything—from a tree before, not even a target, though I remembered someone's telling me to aim a little lower than seemed right. I thought about this while I worked.

Moving as though I was instructing myself—where does this hand go? Here? No, it would be better over here, or a little lower down—I cleared away the small-needled twigs between myself and the platform of sand. It was not hard to do; I just kept taking things away from between the river-light and my face until there were not any. When I was back against the bole of the tree, I was looking down a short, shaggy tunnel of needles; I would shoot right down that; it even seemed to help me aim. All the time I was clearing, I was aided by a totally different sense of touch than I had ever had, and it occurred to me that I must have developed it on the cliff. I seemed able to tell the exact shape and weight of anything at first touch, and had to put out no extra strength to break or strip off any part of the tree I wanted to. Being alive in the dark and doing what I was doing was like a powerful drunkenness, because I didn't believe it. There had never been anything in my life remotely like it. I felt the bark next to me with the most intimate part of my palm, then broke off a needle and put it in my mouth and bit down. It was the right taste.

I edged around the trunk one way and another to see if I could give myself any more advantages, or a slightly wider angle from which to shoot. I did not want to tear the tree up any more; it must look like a tree, with no danger in it; it must look like the others. I had my clear shot down onto the sand, down the dark tunnel, but I could not swing more than a foot or two either way. For me to kill him under these conditions, he would have to be thinking as I had thought for him, and not approximately but exactly. The minds would have to merge.

I took my good arrow off the bow quiver, nocked it by feel and drew it back, setting my feet firmly on two big branches and getting solid at full draw, leaning to the right a little from the trunk to clear my right elbow to go all the way back. I lined up the shot down onto the open place as accurately as I could, thought for a second about shooting the arrow down into the sand to make sure of my elevation, fought off the idea with a quick springing of sweat and relaxed the broadhead out from the bow, letting my breath come forward at the same time. It had been close; I had almost done it. Involuntary release would get me killed, and it was also likely to lose or damage the arrow so that I wouldn't have any chance at all, if the man came. If.

I got as comfortable as I could, and decided to stay in the tree until light. I began to practice stillness, for that was what I was there for.

It was very quiet, almost out of hearing of the river; I heard the rapids upstream from me as no more than a persistent rustle, mixing, I thought as I listened, with another sound that must certainly be coming from downstream: more rapids, I would have bet, maybe even a falls. If that were true, it increased the chances of my being in the right place. Everything about it was logical, though through all the logic I still had no real belief that the man would come; it was far more likely that I had figured the whole thing wrong. I was just going through motions, even though they were the motions of life and death. I was awfully tired and not very excited, except when I thought that I might have guessed right, and I would have to get into the last motions of all and go through them: to turn that broadhead down the tunnel of pine needles on a human body and let it go, forever.

But mainly I was amazed at my situation. Just rather dumbly amazed. It was harder to imagine myself in a tree, like this, than it was to reach out and touch the bark or the needles and know that I actually was in one, in the middle of the night—or somewhere in the night—miles back in the woods, waiting to try to kill a man I had seen only once in my life. Nobody in the world knows where I am, I thought. I put tension on the bowstring, and the arrow came back a little. Who would believe it, I said, with no breath; who on earth?

It was slow waiting. I looked at my watch, but the river had killed it. My head bent forward, and seemed to want to keep on going down. I snapped awake two or three times, but slower each time, with less snap; once I leapt up out of the oldest dream of all—the oldest and most dreamlike—the one about starting to fall. For a second I had no idea what to do or to grab for, and simply put out a hand. I straightened again, wedged back, and tried to take stock once more. There was no arrow in the bow. My God, I thought, I've done it now. I don't think I can get this crooked one even clear of the tree. Without a weapon I knew I would huddle helplessly in the tree, praying he wouldn't notice me, and stay there while he killed Bobby and Lewis. I knew that I wouldn't take him on with just a knife, no matter what advantage of surprise I had.

It was as dark as it had been, even darker. I hung the bow on a limb and went down the trunk. The arrow should have been on the ground, probably sticking up, but it was not. I crawled around in the needles, sobbing with fear and frustration, feeling everything and everywhere I could with hands, arms, legs, body, everything I had, hoping the broadhead would cut me, anything, but just be there.

It wasn't, though, and I could now feel a little light. I would have to go back up the tree. Maybe, when I could see better, I could do some kind of job of straightening on the arrow I had left, but I also knew that the confidence I could hit what I was shooting at was going to be hurt; there is no skill or sport, not even surgery or golf, in which confidence is as important as it is in archery.

But I found the arrow I had dropped, stuck in a limb below where the bow hung, and the plan I had set up locked together and rose up in me like marble. I had everything once more, and I went up to the bow and arranged myself into my shooting position again.

The needles were filling slowly with the beginnings of daylight, and the tree began to glow softly, shining the frail light held by the needles inward on me, and I felt as though I were giving it back outward. I kept looking down the tunnel, now not a massed darkness; there were greens. I opened my mouth so that my breathing would be more silent; so that a nostril would not whistle, or drag with phlegm.

I could see plainly now: the needled and rocky space just beneath the tree, and out from that to the sandy shelf, maybe ten feet wide, with its fringe of tall ragged grass, and beyond that down into space, the eye falling like a body, not dying, but coming to rest on the river. Bobby should be starting now. In a few minutes it would all be over; I would have been either wrong or right, and we would be dead or alive.

Or maybe he had already started, and slipped by me while I was looking for the arrow. There was no way to tell, and I cringed among the branches, waiting to hear a rifle shot from another place, a location I couldn't have guessed or known about.

None came, though. The light strengthened. My sense of utter concealment began to die out of me, and out of the tree. At the right angle, someone standing on the sandy shelf could look right up my tunnel of pine branches at me, and this could be either deliberate or by chance. A lot was hanging on chance.

I moved cautiously, as much as I could like a creature who lived in a tree, craning my neck and leaning out from the trunk to see a foot or two more of the cliff edge, to see if I could make out the canoe.

Something caught the tail of my left eye, and my stomach froze. I didn't turn my head at once, but slowly. I knew, though. I knew, and knew.

A rock clicked on another, and a man was walking forward onto the sand with a rifle. He had one hand in his right pocket.

This is it, I thought, but my first hope, one I could not keep off me, was that I could stay in the tree until he went away. My climb up the cliff had left me; all I wanted was my life. Everything in me was shaking; I could not even have nocked the arrow. Then I looked downward and saw my hands holding the bow, with the broadhead's two colors, sharpened and unsharpened, separating from each other. This steadied me, and I began to believe, once more, that I would do what I had come to do, in this kind of deadly charade. If he lay down with his back to me, I would shoot. I squeezed the first and middle fingers around the arrow nock, took a slow open-mouthed breath, and leaned back tense and still.

He was looking up the river and standing now with both hands on the gun, but with the attitude of holding it at his waist without necessarily thinking of raising it to his shoulder. There was something relaxed and enjoying in his body position, something primally graceful; I had never seen a more beautiful or convincing element of a design. I wanted to kill him just like that, and I prayed for Bobby to come into sight at that instant, but I could see nothing on the river, and he apparently couldn't either. He shifted around for some reason, with half of him framed by my tunnel of needles. Wait till he lies down, I said far back in my throat, and then hit him dead center of the back. Make it a problem. Try to break his back, so that even if you don't hit the spine you'll still hit something vital.

But he was still standing there, not indecisively or decisively; just standing, part of his body clear for a shot, but his head and the other part, not. I had better try now; he may move out of my line of fire. I tensed my arm to see if the muscles would work. The string took on a small angle. I looked right at him, and he gave a little more of himself to the hole in the needles. He was sideways to me, but if his face came into view, he had only to raise it a little to be looking directly at me. I knew that my next battle would be with hysteria, the wild hysteria of full draw, of wanting to let the arrow go and get the tension of holding the bow out of the body: to get the shot off and get it over with. I began to set up in my head the whole delicate routine of making a good archery shot, all the time aware that the most perfect form goes for nothing if the release doesn't happen right; the fingers of the right hand must be relaxed, and above all the bow arm must not move.

He seemed puzzled. He kept looking back from the river down at his feet, at the ground there, half sand and half rock, and every time his head inclined and his hidden face bent down he looked at a place farther from the river and nearer to where I was.

I closed my eyes, took a slow three-quarter breath, held it and leveled the bow inch by inch. When it was approximately in the position I wanted, I went to my muscles and drew. My back spread broader, drawing strength from the tree. The broadhead came back to the bow face along the arrow rest, the unborn calf. It chattered there with the unnatural tension of my body and a sound that was a sound only to the nerves in the palm of my left hand. I pulled the barb of the arrow firmly against the bow, and began checking things in the bow and the arrow and in my hands and arms and body, like a countdown.

He was just out of the frame of thread on the string; my peep sight. I had only to move the bow slightly for him to come into the peep sight and the right-left problem, except possibly for the release, was solved. Martha's orange and the target were now threaded and framed. That left only elevation, always the main problem when shooting downward, and the release. The tip of the arrow appeared, in my secondary vision as I looked at him, to be about six inches under his feet, and I brought it down another inch or so until, as I judged, it looked to me as though I were trying to shoot him through the stomach; looking through the string down the shaft and out the cave of needles, I could see the arrow as being in a plane extending through the middle of him.

We were closed together, and the feeling of a peculiar kind of intimacy increased, for he was shut within a frame within a frame, all of my making: the peep sight and the alleyway of needles, and I knew then that I had him, if my right hand just relaxed and let the arrow tear itself away, and if my left arm did not move, but just took up the shock of the vibrating bow.

Everything was right; it could not have been better. My anchor was good and firm, and the broadhead seemed almost rock-steady. I was full of the transfiguring power of full draw, the draw-hysteria that is the ruination of some archers and the making of others, who can conquer it and make it work for them.

I was down to my last two points, and he was still right there, stooping a little but now facing me just a shade more than he had been. Then he moved, slightly but quickly, and I fought to hold on to the arrow. He stirred the ground once with his foot, and I saw his face—saw that he had a face—for the first time. The whole careful structure of my shot began to come apart, and I struggled in my muscles and guts and heart to hold it together. His eyes were moving over the sand and rock, faster and faster. They were coming. When they began to rise from the ground they triggered my release. I never saw the arrow in the air, and I don't believe he did either, though he surely must have heard the bow twang. I had been at full draw so long that even in the instant of release I believed that I would no more have been able to move my left arm than a statue would. I was afraid that my concentration had blown apart under the recognition that he knew where I was, and some of it had; but not all. The shot had been lined up correctly; if the left arm had held, he was hit.

What happened next I was not sure about, and still am not. The tree thrummed like an ax had struck it, and the woods, so long quiet around me, were full of unbelievable sound. The next thing I knew there was no tree with me anymore, nor any bow. A limb caught my leg and tried to tear it off me, and I was going down the trunk backwards and upside down with many things touching and hitting upward at me with live weight, like arms. To this day I will contend that I spent part of the fall checking the fingers of my right hand to see if they were relaxed, had been relaxed when the shot went, and they were.

I tried also to turn in the air so as not to strike on the back of my head, and was beginning to turn, I think, when I hit. Something went through me from behind, and I heard a rip like tearing bedsheet. Another thing buckled and snapped under me, and I was out of breath on the ground, hurt badly somewhere as the gun went off again, and I could not get to my feet but clawed backward, dragging something. The gun boomed again, then again and again; a branch whipsawed in the tree, but higher than my head would've been if I'd been standing. There was something odd about the shooting; I could tell that even as I was, and I got to one knee and then to my feet from that, and crouched and crowhopped toward, to, and finally behind some rocks on the upriver side of the tree. I stayed low; the gun went off again. Then I slowly lifted my head over the rock.

He was staggering toward the tree, still ten or fifteen feet from it, trying to get the gun up as though it were something too long, or too limber to raise, like a hose. He fired again, but only a yard in front of his feet. The top of his chest was another color, and as he melted forward and down I saw the arrow hanging down his back just below the neck; it was painted entirely red, and was just hanging by the nock and flipping stiffly and softly. He got carefully down to his knees; blood poured when his mouth opened and seemed to splash up out of the ground, to have the force of something coming out of the earth, a spring revealed when the right stone was moved. Die, I thought, my God, die, die.

I slid down on my right side on the back of the rock and laid my cheek to the stone. What is wrong with me? I asked, as the rock seriously and gravely began to turn, as though it might rise. I looked down at my other side and an arrow, the crooked one from the bow quiver, was sticking through it, and the broken bow was still hanging to it by the lower part of the clip.

I put my head down, and was gone. Where? I went comfortably into the distance, and I had a dim image in my head of myself turning around, disappearing into mist, waving good-bye.

Mark Steadman

From *McAfee County*

Mr. McAllister's Cigarette Holder

1963: JUNE.

June.

McAfee County, Georgia, the month of June.

Five minutes before eight o'clock in the morning, and already the air is molasses warm and sticky. Summer comes fierce and early into the coastal counties of Georgia. For four months of the year everything seems to be melting down toward the ground like a landscape made of wax. Then, just before it all fuses together into a lump, the wind shifts around to the northeast and fall snaps in, bringing back the brittleness of October, so that things begin to separate and stand up straight again.

But the melting begins in June.

The McAfee County road-grubbing gang is impervious to it. Almost nothing like that bothers them. The slash pines are melting like candles into the flats on either side of the freshly graded road—the black water in the ditches turning to syrup—and they don't pay any attention at all.

One of the men says, "I seen me a fish coming to work this morning."

The other men look at him, waiting.

"About that high." He holds his hand up over his head to show them. "He's headed *up,*" he says, fluttering his hand.

The men are waiting for what it will be.

"Says he's going to find him a *dry* place if he's got to swum to the *moon.*"

The men laugh on the "*dry.*"

Dropline Richwine, foreman of the gang, stands a hundred yards down the road, squinting under his hand, looks at them milling around, forming up. "Here, Dewey," he says. He hands the small Negro boy a dime. "Dr. Pepper." The boy snatches the coin and runs away. A little over a mile down the road is a filling station owned by Phinesy Wooton. All day the boy will run back and forth fetching cold drinks for Dropline. Alternating Dr. Peppers and Seven-Ups. For every trip that he makes, he gets a penny tip. He won't earn enough during the day to buy a drink for himself, but will have to borrow the three or four cents from Dropline. By the end of the summer he will owe the foreman two and a half, maybe three, dollars.

Dropline holds his pocket watch out like a starter at a track meet, glancing at it, waiting for the big hand to touch twelve. When it does, he puts the watch into the pocket under his belt, cups his hands, and gives the signal.

"Goooo . . . to GRUBBING!" he says.

The gang spreads out, spans the black earth of the roadbed. Seven men. From the back they look like seven half-men—torsoless legs swinging along in an easy, apelike gait. From the front they look like the celebrants of some arcane and strenuous religious sect. Jack-knifed at the waist, their arms hanging loose and swinging. They make scooping motions with them as they move along.

Doing their job.

The grubbing gang follows the patrols—the road scrapers—grubbing out the roots and rocks and things from the topsoil that forms the roadbed, before the sheep's-foot rollers come along and pack it down. The work has to be done bending over. A break-your-back position. It is undignified and uncomfortable, but there isn't any choice. If a man keeps at it for more than a year, something snaps. His backbone takes on a permanent set, and he can't get it out. Young boys come along and work at it for a year or even two and don't seem very much bothered by it. They crouch around for a week or so after they quit the gang to go to work in the mill, or at the filling station, or wherever it might be, but soon they straighten up pretty well—or at least work the slump up into their shoulders, where it won't look so bad. But grown men who do it for more than a year take a permanent hitch. It won't ever come out.

"Shad Goety worked five years on the grubbing gang . . . ," it's their favorite story, the men on the grubbing gang—they tell it around, ". . . then he spent thirty-five years picking fruit—most of it off *high* branches. And when they buried him, they had to hinge the coffin and jackknife it to get him in." They laugh everytime.

Only Mr. McAllister is the exception to the rule.

He is a great, dignified, bear of a man who has worked nearly twenty years on the grubbing gang, but when quitting time comes he stands up straight as an arrow and walks to the truck like a man in a hurricane with the wind at his back. Dignity personified. And dignity triumphant. Even his clothes don't diminish him.

His bib overalls come from Shotford's Grocery Store and Filling Station, and his snapbrim straw hat from the same place. They are the same that everybody else in McAfee County wears, though Mr. McAllister has decorated his hat with a snakeskin band he made himself. Still, even with the band, it is the same kind of hat that stands on the top counter in Shotford's in nesting stacks three and four feet high. He wears no shirt at all for about half of the year. In the fall and early spring he has a long-sleeved flannel shirt that is red-and-black-checkered. For really cold days he puts on a cardigan sweater that his woman knitted for him out of purple wool. Though most of the men grub barehanded, Mr. McAllister wears white work gloves with blue knit ribbing at the cuffs.

Everyone calls him *Mister* McAllister. That's because of his own manner of speaking. "*Mister* Richwine . . . ," he will say. Or, "*Mister* Glanders . . ." Everyone is *Mister* to Mr. McAllister.

Mr. McAllister himself doesn't understand his own dignity. *He* thinks that the thing that sets him apart is his cigarette holder.

It is a cheap plastic one that he grubbed up in the roadbed one day a year or so after he joined the gang. When he first found it, he didn't know exactly what it was.

"What you reckon, Mister Richwine?" he said.

Dropline looked at the red plastic cylinder, holding it at arm's length, then drawing it up close. He pumped it in and out a couple of times, with the other men standing around watching him. "Cigarette holder," he said.

Mr. McAllister's eyebrows went up. "Shit you say," he said. "Red?"

Dropline pumped it in for another look. "Yes," he said.

Mr. McAllister took it back, holding it at arm's length. "Black," he said. "President Roosevelt. He had him a black one."

The only man Mr. McAllister had ever known to use a cigarette holder was President Franklin Delano Roosevelt, and he had had to go back a good many years to his green salad days to dig up that recollection.

Old Mr. McAllister, Mr. McAllister's father, had not been a church-going man, and religion had never been a strong part of his early training as a boy—just what his mother could work in on the sly when the father wasn't around. The old man's main interest had been politics. And, next to Huey Long, Franklin Delano Roosevelt had been his man. They didn't have the Praying Hands picture on the wall, or the Blond Jesus, or any of that kind of thing, but over the mantelpiece there had been a likeness of the President, painted on a cedar slab. Whenever he got drunk, old Mr. McAllister would take down the slab and talk to it—telling it his troubles. Mr. McAllister had the idea that his father was praying, and for a while he had gotten Roosevelt and God mixed up.

But God didn't have a cigarette holder.

After he had found the holder in the road, he took it home and polished it up with wax until it looked like new, and from that time on he was never without it. He kept it in his mouth while he was grubbing, for he was afraid that it would fall out of the pencil pocket of his overalls, and that it might get broken if he kept it in another pocket.

Now and then a young boy, new to the grubbing gang, would try to kid him about it, because most of them weren't used to seeing anybody really use a cigarette holder either. Mr. McAllister never lost his temper when it happened. He took them seriously and tried to answer their clatter rather than fend them off. Generally that worked. Just the same, every now and then a really deep-dyed cretin would come along—one who lived ninety percent of his life out of his spinal column—and he would keep it up and keep it up until even Mr. McAllister couldn't stand to hear it anymore.

"Hey, Mr. McAllister," said Dee Witt Toomey, the young boy on the gang in the summer of 1956, "how come you roll your own cigarettes when you got that fine holder?"

Mr. McAllister put the Bugler packet back into the front pocket of his overalls. He held the cigarette daintily in the fingers of his right hand and licked the seam.

"I seen a picture once," said Mr. McAllister, not looking at Dee Witt, but keeping his eyes on the cigarette, "in a magazine. It showed the inside of one of them cigarette plants. All you could see was cigarettes. Looked like they was a million of them. The words under the picture said they made a hundred thousand of them a day."

He put the cigarette carefully into the holder and lit it with a wooden kitchen match, snapped on his thumbnail.

"Anything that they make a hundred thousand of them a day," he said, "I don't want it."

Dee Witt thought this over for a while. Thinking was mostly a physical act for Dee Witt. He had to get his whole body in on it. You could almost trace the progress of his idea as he worked it up his ganglia, compressing and compacting it and squeezing it up toward his brain—getting it into a shape he could recognize. You finally expected to see something pop out of his mouth—like a Ping-Pong ball in a comic magic act.

"I bet they make a million of them Razorback overalls you're wearing every day," he said at last.

"May be," said Mr. McAllister, "but they's all Shotford's got. I got no choice. Don't count when you got no choice. When I got my choice, one of a thing is what I want."

The reply put Mr. McAllister out of Dee Witt's range, so he had to button up and go off without trying to make a reply. But he brooded about it for the rest of the day, and the next day he worked around until he got a chance, then he snatched the holder out of Mr. McAllister's mouth and ran off a little ways down the road.

"I got it now," he said. He held it up where Mr. McAllister could see it, in both hands, as if he was going to break it.

"Mr. Toomey . . . ," said Mr. McAllister.

"I got it now," said Dee Witt. "It's mine. Finders keepers." The way he was holding it, it looked like he was going to snap it in two.

Mr. McAllister had a rock in his hand that he had grubbed up. Before anyone could think what he was doing, he reared back and threw it. It caught Dee Witt just over his right eye with a hard, plonking sound. Dee Witt fell over backward, sprawling out, with the cigarette holder still in his right hand.

Mr. McAllister walked up to him, pulling out a marking stake that he kept in his pocket in case of snakes when he had to go into the woods for a piss call. He reached down and took the cigarette holder gently, lifting it out of Dee Witt's hand. Then he looked at the holder and at Dee Witt, back and forth, with his face swelling up and turning red like a balloon. Finally he raised the marking stake high up over his head and brought it down right in the middle of Dee Witt's forehead. The sound was duller—duller but harder—than the sound the rock had made. Dee Witt flinched his arms and legs when Mr. McAllister hit him, then he just lay there with his eyes rolled up into his head.

Mr. McAllister looked up at the other men, who were all watching him. "He oughtn't . . . ," he said. Then he put the holder in his mouth and walked off into the pine trees.

It took three days for them to find him out in the swamp, and another day to convince him that Dee Witt wasn't dead. If the law had come into it, he would have gone to jail. Dee Witt's eyes didn't roll back down to the right place for a month, and he never did see too well afterward, but other than that he wasn't really put out by it. The men on the grubbing gang decided that anything that happened to Dee Witt's head was bound to be an improvement, and when they saw he wasn't going to die, they handled the whole thing so the sheriff never got onto it, bringing Mr. McAllister out of the swamp and back to the grubbing gang. Good grubbing men were hard to find.

And Mr. McAllister was a good man.

He enjoyed his work. Finding the cigarette holder had opened up the possibilities of grubbing for him, and he began to notice the things that he found in the roadbed. Strange-shaped rocks and pieces of roots, buttons, arrowheads, and bones of animals. Best of all, mysterious objects he had to puzzle over and figure at without ever being able to settle *what* they were.

"What you reckon, Mr. Richwine?" he would say, holding up something that he had found, and turning it around for Dropline to see. "Petrified wood?" Petrified wood was his favorite. "See there. Like it's got a grain in it?" He would trace it out with his finger. "And a knot."

Dropline would take it and look at it. "Could be it was petrified wood, Mr. McAllister," he'd say. "I wouldn't want to say."

So Mr. McAllister would drop it into his pocket and take it home and add to his collection. He had a whole cupboard full of cigar boxes filled with things he had found just like that in the roadbed. One box was filled with arrowheads. Another was filled with buttons. Another was filled with teeth. The best one of all was the one that was filled with things that he never could figure out. That was his favorite. He would often take it down at night and go through the things, trying to decide what they were. Every now and then he would finally classify something—a piece of petrified wood that turned out to be just a rock—and it always saddened him to have to take it out of the mystery box and put it into one with a label on it.

Singularity—that was the quality that he prized above all others. It was the key to his character.

Some people said that the most singular thing he had in his whole house was Dora, his albino woman. She was one of a kind too.

The grubbing gang swore that he had grubbed her up out of the bottoms when the county road went through to Fancy Statin. The truth is that he found her in the Trailways bus depot at Rainbow, broke and crying, sitting on a cardboard box tied up with string. That had been in the early fall of 1956.

"I ain't never seen no eyes like that before," he said, crouching a little as he stood before her, his cigarette holder gripped in his front teeth, the corners of his mouth pulled up tight in the shape of a smile.

She gave him a long, dead look. "You kiss my ass," she said.

"Miss your bus?" he asked.

She shook her head, then looked away from him.

"Stranded?" he asked.

She nodded.

"Broke?"

She nodded again.

"Shit," he said. "Wouldn't you know?"

He stood looking at her.

"Albino," she said.

"What?" he said.

"I'm a albino," she said.

"Oh," he said.

"I'm a albino, so I got eyes like that."

He nodded.

"You satisfied?" she said.

He nodded again. "Yes'm," he said.

He looked at her for a while. "I got no money to help you with," he said. "I could put you up for the night."

She swung her pale eyes back to his. Her face was streaked from the crying. For a long time they looked at each other straight on.

"I ain't gonna fool around with you, lady," he said. "I just wanted to help you out."

She looked at him straight on for a long time again.

"Does it hurt?" he said.

"What?" she said.

"To be a albino," he said. "Does it hurt?"

She looked at him a minute with her eyes wide open. Then she laughed—a high-pitched, tearing sound. "No," she said. "It don't hurt a bit."

He laughed with her. "I thought so," he said.

After a while she wiped her eyes with her handkerchief and stood up. "Well," she said, "it's the best offer I've had. I ain't no Little Miss Fauntleroy. I guess it beats sitting here on my ass watching the cars go by."

"Yes," he said.

She picked up her cardboard box.

"Here," said Mr. McAllister, "I'll take that." He took the box from her arms. "Jesus," he said, "you sure are traveling light. Your clothes don't weigh nothing at all."

"Ain't clothes," she said.

"What is it?"

"Cotton," she said. "Finest long-staple cotton."

"Cotton?" he said. "What for?"

"Stuffing dolls," she said. "I make dolls, and the cotton is what I stuff them with. Good cotton is hard to find."

"I'll be real careful not to drop it," he said.

She looked at him and smiled. "You do that," she said.

"My name's McAllister," he said, shifting the cardboard box under his left arm, and putting out his right.

"Pleased to meet you, Mr. McAllister," she said, shaking his hand. "Mine's Dora."

"Yes," he said.

"How far is it to your house, Mr. McAllister?" she asked.

"Three mile," he said.

"Kiss my ASS," she said, trudging after him.

After they had lived together for about three years—it was the fall of 1959—Mr. McAllister asked Dora what she thought about getting married.

"I don't mind much one way or the other," she said. "I'll do it if it bothers you."

"We going to get married, we got to have us a ring to get married with," he said. He clamped the cigarette holder in his teeth the way Roosevelt used to do it. His head tilted back a little, the corners of his lips pulled up, showing the teeth at the sides of his mouth. His expression came close to being arch—as close as his dignity would let him. He was not an ironic man.

"How we going to get a ring?" asked Dora. "You going to grub one up out of the swamp for me?"

He had.

"Reckon this would do?" he asked. He held out a gold ring with a Masonic signet on it. "It ain't a wedding ring, but it *is* real gold. You could turn it so just the gold part showed."

Dora shrank from the ring. "I ain't going to put that thing on *my* finger," she said.

"What you mean?" he asked.

"That's a Mason ring," she said.

"I know that," he said. "You'd have to turn it around."

"My daddy was a Mason," she said. "He told me what they do to people who learn their secrets and they ain't Masons too."

"You wouldn't be learning no secrets, Dora," he said.

"Same thing," she said, "same thing."

He held the ring out to her, almost in her face. She shrank from it, fending him off with her hand.

"Put it up! Put it up, god damn it!" she said.

"You ain't no Mason!" he said.

"That's it! That's it!" she said.

Mr. McAllister gave the ring a long look, then he put it on the windowsill in the kitchen. He went to bed without saying any more about it.

For a week the ring stayed where he had laid it and for a week barely a word passed between them. Finally, seeing it hurt his feelings so much, Dora braided a cord out of white sewing thread, looped it through the ring, and put it around her neck. She wore it beneath her clothes where no Mason could see it, but it seemed to satisfy Mr. McAllister, and he began to speak to her again.

In the summer of 1963, Dora's birthday fell on a weekend, Saturday, June 22. Mr. McAllister planned a special treat for her.

"Look," he said when he came in from work on Friday evening. In his outstretched right hand were two bus tickets.

"What you got there?" asked Dora.

"Your birthday present," he said. "Two tickets to Tybee Beach. Round trip."

"We can't afford no trip to Tybee Beach," said Dora.

"And that ain't all," said Mr. McAllister. "This is for when we get there." He pulled two five-dollar bills out of his left pocket and waved them before her eyes.

"And this," he said, putting the tickets and the five-dollar bills on the kitchen table, and pulling a half-pint of Hickory Hill bourbon from his hip pocket, "is for when we get back." He put it on top of the tickets and the bills.

Flexing his knees and rocking back and forth slightly, he stood with his hands clasped behind his back.

"Happy Birthday, DORA," he said.

"Kiss my ass," she said.

They walked in the three miles to the Trailways bus depot at Rainbow, starting out at first light, since they weren't sure when the bus would arrive. It came at ten.

Mr. McAllister wore overalls and a red-and-green-checkered sport shirt with a wide collar, buttoned at the neck. Dora wore a purple voile dress. As they walked, Mr. McAllister dropped behind so he could watch her body moving inside the purple nimbus of the dress, silhouetted by the rising sun ahead of her. Every once in a while he would sing the "Happy Birthday Song" to her.

Now and again he would say, "You're a good woman, Dora." And he would add, ". . . for an albino." Then he would laugh.

When the bus came, Mr. McAllister boarded it ahead of her.

"Any special place you want us to sit?" he asked the driver.

"What?" said the driver.

Mr. McAllister took the cigarette holder out of his mouth. "You want us to sit any place special on the bus?" he repeated.

The bus driver looked at him a moment. "No," he said. "You can have any seat you want to."

"Much obliged," said Mr. McAllister.

He walked down the aisle until he found two vacant seats, then he slid into them, taking the one by the window. Dora sat down beside him.

Pretty soon everyone had gotten on the bus. Then the bus driver got on too, closed the door, started the engine, and pulled out onto the highway.

"Tybee Beach," said Mr. McAllister, looking out the window.

The front end of the bus nosed in toward the black shade of the awning outside the drugstore-bus-stop at Butler Avenue and Sixteenth Street. From the cool, green interior of the bus, the passengers stepped out into the yellow-white sunlight, paused for a moment blinking, then slid into the shade.

Mr. McAllister got off first, not looking at Dora behind him. He stepped into the shade and stood looking down the signs over the bars and souvenir shops on Sixteenth Street. At the end of the street, along the seawall-boardwalk, bathers counterflowed slowly in the bright summer sunlight.

"You take this," he said to Dora without looking at her, swinging his forearm back to the left, the palm up. The five-dollar bill was folded tightly and held lightly between the hard, swollen thumb and forefinger of his left hand. "I'll pay for the rides with mine." The sunsquint pulled the corners of his mouth up tight.

"You keep it," said Dora.

"You wouldn't spend it if I do," he said.

"I'll lose it," she said.

It seemed that the breeze might snatch the green bill away, so lightly was it held.

"Put it in your bosom," he said. He pronounced it "*boo*som."

"You keep it," she said.

"It's your birthday," he said.

She took it lightly, holding it away for a moment. Then she made a quick, deft loop with her arm, and the bill disappeared into the front of her dress.

They walked down Sixteenth Street toward the ocean.

"Look!" said Dora.

In the window of the store was a seashell and plastic palm-tree tableau, embedded in plaster of Paris, with a crucifix in the middle.

"Ain't that handsome?" she said.

Mr. McAllister looked down at the pale, watery-colored object, covered with dust in the window. Behind it a gaudy terrycloth towel stood improbably erect. Its colors garish and clashing—bright red and yellow and black. "Tybee Beach, Georgia—Come On In."

"What is it?" he asked.

"A Jesus," said Dora.

They stood contemplating it silently for a minute.

"Let's go look at it inside," he said.

The clerk met them at the door. They were the only customers in the store.

"How much is that there Jesus?" said Mr. McAllister.

"What?" The clerk's hair was dark and shiny, thoroughly combed and parted. In the back a few long strands levered up away from the rest, and when he walked they swayed in a gentle countermotion, like the tail of a fish.

"The Jesus," said Mr. McAllister. "The Jesus in the window."

"In the window over there," said Dora, pointing.

Together they pointed the clerk to the tableau.

"Ain't it handsome?" said Dora, looking at it in the clerk's hands. He did not offer to let them hold it.

"It's an excellent piece," said the clerk, "Look here"; he pointed to the plastic palm trees with his little finger, holding his hand palm up, the other fingers delicately curled. "And here"; he pointed out each of the features in turn, cradling the Jesus delicately in his left arm.

"And look," he said, leading them over to the counter. He plugged in the cord that extended from the back of the plaster-of-Paris base. Three red Christmas-tree lights lit up behind the shells in the front.

"Oh, that's handsome," said Dora. "That really is handsome."

"How much is it?" asked Mr. McAllister.

"Look what the red lights do to the flamingo," said the clerk, not answering him.

"It's nice, all right," said Mr. McAllister. "How much is it?"

"It's all handmade," said the clerk. "You really don't see many of them these days."

"It's all real pretty," said Dora, "but how much is it?"

"Five dollars," said the clerk. His voice was very quiet and he looked at them steadily, but moving his eyes from one to the other, cradling the tableau in his arm and swaying back and forth at his knees.

"Well," said Dora, bunching her eyebrows together a little, "that's a lot of money."

"It's your birthday," said Mr. McAllister almost under his breath, drawing his head back a little to look at the Jesus.

"It's a lot of money, though," said Dora, looking at the Jesus, not Mr. McAllister.

"They're hard to get these days," said the clerk, "because they're all handmade. Not many things handmade anymore." He jiggled the plug in and out so the lights flashed on and off.

"It's your birthday, Dora," said Mr. McAllister. "You want it, don't you?"

"But I think we better look around some more," she said. "We just now got off the bus."

"Why don't you just look around some more?" said the clerk, making an expansive gesture with his free hand. "Just go ahead and look around." He slid the Jesus gently onto the checkout counter where they would have to pass it on the way out.

"Oh, it'll be all right for us to just look around," said Dora.

"Don't sell it to nobody before we get back," said Mr. McAllister.

They began to walk slowly down the counters filled with combs and cheap dark glasses and souvenir key chains and ashtrays, spread out in glass-divided compartments in front of the bright beach towels with palm trees and pretty girls and "Tybee Beach, Georgia," printed on them. The clerk hovered along behind them, his shoulders hunched forward, rubbing his hands together.

"Dora!" said Mr. McAllister.

In one of the compartments of the counter in front of them was a pile of plastic cigarette holders, jammed out in different directions—a stiff, shiny nest of them. All with white stems and red, blue, and black barrels. As they looked, Mr. McAllister slowly took his cigarette holder from between his teeth, his mouth going slack. He poised his holder—comparing. They were the same. A pile that would fill two cupped hands.

The sign clipped to the glass divider said "29¢."

"Yes," said the clerk, stepping toward them. "Those are very nice. We sell a lot of those."

Under the awning the wind came in strong and cool from the ocean. Mr. McAllister sat looking at the napkin holder in the middle of the formica-topped table. His hand on the edge of the table. Beside his hand lay the cigarette holder.

"Eat your Corn Dog," said Dora.

"They was just like mine, wasn't they?"

"Ain't no two things *exactly* alike," she said.

"Mine ain't as shiny," he said, looking at the holder.

"Your red is prettier," she said.

"But it's just the same, Dora," he said.

"Well," she said, "eat your Corn Dog."

"I ain't hungry," he said, pushing the napkin with the Corn Dog on it over to her.

"I don't want it," she said, "but I hate to see it go to waste."

The napkin fluttered in the breeze, then wrapped around the Corn Dog.

"I ain't having much of a time," she said. "You want to go home?"

"It's your birthday," he said.

"I know," she said. "But I ain't having much of a time."

"Let's get the Jesus," he said.

"I don't want the Jesus," she said.

"I want you to get the Jesus for your birthday," he said.

"I don't want to go back in the store."

"I'll get it for you," he said.

"I don't want *you* to go back in the store either," she said. "Let's just go catch the bus back to town."

"It ain't much of a birthday," he said.

"I ain't never been to Tybee Beach," she said. "And we still got the Hickory Hill when we get back."

As they walked to the bus stop, Mr. McAllister kept talking to her about the Jesus. "We can't just come on down here to Tybee Beach and get you a Jesus anytime you feel like it," he said. "You don't get it now, and you ain't never going to see it again."

They stood under the awning next to the bus, Dora hugging her arms under her breasts, looking down at the sidewalk.

"Will you please go get the Jesus, Dora?" he said. A passenger brushed Mr. McAllister getting on the bus. "Will you please get it for me for your birthday?"

She hesitated, biting her lip.

"You better hurry, lady," said the bus driver. "Bus leaves at two on the dot."

"What time is it?" she said.

"Eight of," said the driver.

"Get us a seat," she said to Mr. McAllister. "I'll be back in a minute."

"Yes . . . ," said Mr. McAllister, nodding, ". . . and the Hickory Hill when we get home."

The bus was just ready to leave when she got back. In her hand she had a brown paper bag.

"That ain't the Jesus," said Mr. McAllister. "What you got in the bag?"

Dora didn't answer him. Instead she leaned out and slapped the man in the seat across the aisle from her. He jumped up in his seat and looked at her.

"You a Mason, mister?" she asked.

"What?" he said.

"I said, 'Are you a Mason?' " she said.

"No," said the man.

"Too bad," said Dora.

She hooked her finger into her dress and flipped out the cord with the ring on it.

"I'm thirty-five years old," she said, turning to Mr. McAllister. She sounded as though she didn't believe it.

Dora snapped the ring off the cord and put it on her finger.

"My daddy was a Mason," she said. She held up her hand, looking at the ring. "Never would tell us no secrets," she said. "The dirty son-of-a-bitch."

The man across the aisle looked out the window.

"What the hell come over you, Dora?" said Mr. McAllister, whispering.

She dumped the contents of the bag into her lap.

"What'd you do *that* for?" he asked.

She didn't answer. Instead she placed the open bag in his lap, then picked up one of the cigarette holders in both of her hands, snapped it, dropping the pieces into the bag. She kept on until she had snapped all of them.

"Seventeen," she said. "Seventeen of them all together. And I got this with the change." She handed him a piece of bubblegum.

He held it limply in his hand, looking at the bag full of broken cigarette holders in his lap.

Dora sat stiffly, her arms folded under her breasts, staring straight ahead at the back of the seat in front of her.

"Happy birthday . . . TO ME!" she said firmly.

She swung her left arm out and tapped the bag lightly with the back of her hand, not looking at it.

"Now," she said. "Throw that piss-ant out the window."

Mr. McAllister rolled a cigarette and put it into his holder. He leaned back in his seat, the corners of his mouth pulled up in a Roosevelt grin. Outside the windows the pines were sliding by under the summer sun, melting into the flats along the highway. Beneath him, the hard, black surface of the road unrolled eastward under the speeding tires of the bus.

Alice Walker

To Hell with Dying

"To hell with dying," my father would say. "These children want Mr. Sweet!"

Mr. Sweet was a diabetic and an alcoholic and a guitar player and lived down the road from us on a neglected cotton farm. My older brothers and sisters got the most benefit from Mr. Sweet for when they were growing up he had quite a few years ahead of him and so was capable of being called back from the brink of death any number of times—whenever the voice of my father reached him as he lay expiring. "To hell with dying, man," my father would say, pushing the wife away from the bedside (in tears although she knew the death was not necessarily the last one unless Mr. Sweet really wanted it to be). "These children want Mr. Sweet!" And they did want him, for at a signal from Father they would come crowding around the bed and throw themselves on the covers, and whoever was the smallest at the time would kiss him all over his wrinkled brown face and begin to tickle him so that he would laugh all down in his stomach, and his moustache, which was long and sort of straggly, would shake like Spanish moss and was also that color.

Mr. Sweet had been ambitious as a boy, wanted to be a doctor or lawyer or sailor, only to find that black men fare better if they are not. Since he could become none of these things he turned to fishing as his only earnest career and playing the guitar as his only claim to doing anything extraordinarily well. His son, the only one that he and his wife, Miss Mary, had, was shiftless as the day is long and spent money as if he were trying to see the bottom of the mint, which Mr. Sweet would tell him was the clean brown palm of his hand. Miss Mary loved her "baby," however, and worked hard to get him the "li'l necessaries" of life, which turned out mostly to be women.

Mr. Sweet was a tall, thinnish man with thick kinky hair going dead white. He was dark brown, his eyes were very squinty and sort of bluish, and he chewed Brown Mule tobacco. He was constantly on the verge of being blind drunk, for he brewed his own liquor and was not in the least a stingy sort of man, and was always very melancholy and sad, though frequently when he was "feelin' good" he'd dance around the yard with us, usually keeling over just as my mother came to see what the commotion was.

Toward all of us children he was very kind, and had the grace to be shy with us, which is unusual in grown-ups. He had great respect for my mother for she never held his drunkenness against him and would let us play with him even when he was about to fall in the fireplace from drink. Although Mr. Sweet would sometimes lose complete or nearly complete control of his head and neck so that he would loll in his chair, his mind remained strangely acute and his speech not too affected. His ability to be drunk and sober at the same time made him an ideal playmate, for he was as weak as we were and we could usually best him in wrestling, all the while keeping a fairly coherent conversation going.

We never felt anything of Mr. Sweet's age when we played with him. We loved his wrinkles and would draw some on our brows to be like him, and his white hair was my special treasure and he knew it and would never come to visit us just after he had had his hair cut off at the barbershop. Once he came to our house for something, probably to see my father about fertilizer for his crops because, although he never paid the slightest attention to his crops, he liked to know what things would be best to use on them if he ever did. Anyhow, he had not come with his hair since he had just had it shaved off at the barbershop. He wore a huge straw hat to keep off the sun and also to keep his head away from me. But as soon as I saw him I ran up and demanded that he take me up and kiss me with his funny beard which smelled so strongly of tobacco. Looking forward to burying my small fingers into his woolly hair I threw away his hat only to find he had done something to his hair, that it was no longer there! I let out a squall which made my mother think that Mr. Sweet had finally dropped me in the well or something and from that day I've been wary of men in hats. However, not long after, Mr. Sweet showed up with his hair grown out and just as white and kinky and impenetrable as it ever was.

Mr. Sweet used to call me his princess, and I believed it. He made me feel pretty at five and six, and simply outrageously devastating at the blazing age of eight and a half. When he came to our house with his guitar the whole family would stop whatever they were doing to sit around him and listen to him play. He liked to play "Sweet Georgia Brown," that was what he called me sometimes, and also he liked to play "Caldonia" and all sorts of sweet, sad, wonderful songs which he sometimes made up. It was from one of these songs that I learned that he had had to marry Miss Mary when he had in fact loved somebody else (now living in Chica-go, or De-stroy, Michigan). He was not sure that Joe Lee, her "baby," was also his baby. Sometimes he would cry and that was an indication that he was about to die again. And so we would all get prepared, for we were sure to be called upon.

I was seven the first time I remember actually participating in one of Mr. Sweet's "revivals"—my parents told me I had participated before, I had been the one chosen to kiss him and tickle him long before I knew the rite of Mr. Sweet's rehabilitation. He had come to our house, it was a few years after his wife's death, and was very sad, and also, typically, very drunk. He sat on the floor next to me and my older brother, the rest of the children were grown up and lived elsewhere, and began to play his guitar and cry. I held his woolly head in my arms and wished I could have been old enough to have been the woman he loved so much and that I had not been lost years and years ago.

When he was leaving, my mother said to us that we'd better sleep light that night for we'd probably have to go over to Mr. Sweet's before daylight. And we did. For soon after we had gone to bed one of the neighbors knocked on our door and called my father and said that Mr. Sweet was sinking fast and if he wanted to get in a word before the crossover he'd better shake a leg and get over to Mr. Sweet's house. All the neighbors knew to come to our house if something was wrong with Mr. Sweet, but they did not know how we always managed to make him well, or at least stop him from dying, when he was often so near death. As soon as we heard the cry we got up, my brother and I and my mother and father, and put on our clothes. We hurried out of the house and down the road for we were always afraid that we might someday be too late and Mr. Sweet would get tired of dallying.

When we got to the house, a very poor shack really, we found the front room full of neighbors and relatives and someone met us at the door and said that it was all very sad that old Mr. Sweet Little (for Little was his family name, although we mostly ignored it) was about to kick the bucket. My parents were advised not to take my brother and me into the "death room," seeing we were so young and all, but we were so much more accustomed to the death room than he that we ignored him and dashed in without giving his warning a second thought. I was almost in tears, for these deaths upset me fearfully, and the thought of how much depended on me and my brother (who was such a ham most of the time) made me very nervous.

The doctor was bending over the bed and turned back to tell us for at least the tenth time in the history of my family that, alas, old Mr. Sweet Little was dying and that the children had best not see the face of implacable death (I didn't know what "implacable" was, but whatever it was, Mr. Sweet was not!). My father pushed him rather abruptly out of the way saying, as he always did and very loudly for he was saying it to Mr. Sweet, "To hell with dying, man, these children want Mr. Sweet"—which was my cue to throw myself upon the bed and kiss Mr. Sweet all around the whiskers and under the eyes and around the collar of his nightshirt where he smelled so strongly of all sorts of things, mostly liniment.

I was very good at bringing him around, for as soon as I saw that he was struggling to open his eyes I knew he was going to be all right, and so could finish my revival sure of success. As soon as his eyes were open he would begin to smile and that way I knew that I had surely won. Once, though, I got a tremendous scare, for he could not open his eyes and later I learned that he had had a stroke and that one side of his face was stiff and hard to get into motion. When he began to smile I could tickle him in earnest because I was sure that nothing would get in the way of his laughter, although once he began to cough so hard that he almost threw me off his stomach, but that was when I was very small, little more than a baby, and my bushy hair had gotten in his nose.

When we were sure he would listen to us we would ask him why he was in bed and when he was coming to see us again and could we play with his guitar, which more than likely would be leaning against the bed. His eyes would get all misty and he would sometimes cry out loud, but we never let it embarrass us, for he knew that we loved him and that we sometimes cried too for no reason. My parents would leave the room to just the three of us; Mr. Sweet, by that time, would be propped up in bed with a number of pillows behind his head and with me sitting and lying on his shoulder and along his chest. Even when he had trouble breathing he would not ask me to get down. Looking into my eyes he would shake his white head and run a scratchy old finger all around my hairline, which was rather low down, nearly to my eyebrows, and made some people say I looked like a baby monkey.

My brother was very generous in all this, he let me do all the revivaling—he had done it for years before I was born and so was glad to be able to pass it on to someone new. What he would do while I talked to Mr. Sweet was pretend to play the guitar, in fact pretend that he was a young version of Mr. Sweet, and it always made Mr. Sweet glad to think that someone wanted to be like him—of course, we did not know this then, we played the thing by ear, and whatever he seemed to like, we did. We were desperately afraid that he was just going to take off one day and leave us.

It did not occur to us that we were doing anything special; we had not learned that death was final when it did come. We thought nothing of triumphing over it so many times, and in fact became a trifle contemptuous of people who let themselves be carried away. It did not occur to us that if our own father had been dying we could not have stopped it, that Mr. Sweet was the only person over whom we had power.

When Mr. Sweet was in his eighties I was studying in the university many miles from home. I saw him whenever I went home, but he was never on the verge of dying that I could tell and I began to feel that my anxiety for his health and psychological well-being was unnecessary. By this time he not only had a moustache but a long flowing snow-white beard, which I loved and combed and braided for hours. He was very peaceful, fragile, gentle, and the only jarring note about him was his old steel guitar, which he still played in the old sad, sweet, down-home blues way.

On Mr. Sweet's ninetieth birthday I was finishing my doctorate in Massachusetts and had been making arrangements to go home for several weeks' rest. That morning I got a telegram telling me that Mr. Sweet was dying again and could I please drop everything and come home. Of course I could. My dissertation could wait and my teachers would understand when I explained to them when I got back. I ran to the phone, called the airport, and within four hours I was speeding along the dusty road to Mr. Sweet's.

The house was more dilapidated than when I was last there, barely a shack, but it was overgrown with yellow roses which my family had planted many years ago. The air was heavy and sweet and very peaceful. I felt strange walking through the gate and up the old rickety steps. But the strangeness left me as I caught sight of the long white beard I loved so well flowing down the thin body over the familiar quilt coverlet. Mr. Sweet!

His eyes were closed tight and his hands, crossed over his stomach, were thin and delicate, no longer scratchy. I remembered how always before I had run and jumped up on him just anywhere; now I knew he would not be able to support my weight. I looked around at my parents, and was surprised to see that my father and mother also looked old and frail. My father, his own hair very gray, leaned over the quietly sleeping old man, who, incidentally, smelled still of wine and tobacco, and said, as he'd done so many times, "To hell with dying, man! My daughter is home to see Mr. Sweet!" My brother had not been able to come as he was in the war in Asia. I bent down and gently stroked the closed eyes and gradually they began to open. The closed, wine-stained lips twitched a little, then parted in a warm, slightly embarrassed smile. Mr. Sweet could see me and he recognized me and his eyes looked very spry and twinkly for a moment. I put my head down on the pillow next to his and we just looked at each other for a long time. Then he began to trace my peculiar hairline with a thin, smooth finger. I closed my eyes when his finger halted above my ear (he used to rejoice at the dirt in my ears when I was little), his hand stayed cupped around my cheek. When I opened my eyes, sure that I had reached him in time, his were closed.

Even at twenty-four how could I believe that I had failed? that Mr. Sweet was really gone? He had never gone before. But when I looked up at my parents I saw that they were holding back tears. They had loved him dearly. He was like a piece of rare and delicate china which was always being saved from breaking and which finally fell. I looked long at the old face, the wrinkled forehead, the red lips, the hands that still reached out to me. Soon I felt my father pushing something cool into my hands. It was Mr. Sweet's guitar. He had asked them months before to give it to me; he had known that even if I came next time he would not be able to respond in the old way. He did not want me to feel that my trip had been for nothing.

The old guitar! I plucked the strings, hummed "Sweet Georgia Brown." The magic of Mr. Sweet lingered still in the cool steel box. Through the window I could catch the fragrant delicate scent of tender yellow roses. The man on the high old-fashioned bed with the quilt coverlet and the flowing white beard had been my first love.

Harry Crews

From *A Feast of Snakes*

She felt the snake between her breasts, felt him there, and loved him there, coiled, the deep tumescent S held rigid, ready to strike. She loved the way the snake looked sewn onto her V-neck letter sweater, his hard diamondback pattern shining in the sun. It was unseasonably hot, almost sixty degrees, for early November in Mystic, Georgia, and she could smell the light musk of her own sweat. She liked the sweat, liked the way it felt, slick as oil, in all the joints of her body, her bones, in the firm sliding muscles, tensed and locked now, ready to spring—to *strike*—when the band behind her fired up the school song: "Fight On Deadly Rattlers of Old Mystic High."

She felt a single drop of sweat slip from the small of her back, hang for an instant, and then slide into the mellow groove between the flexed jaws of her ass. When she felt the sweat touch her there, she automatically cut her eyes to see if she could pick out Willard Miller, the Boss Snake of all the Mystic Rattlers, *her* boss Snake, pick him out from the other helmeted and white-suited boys scrimmaging on the other side of the track. When they made contact, their soft, almost gentle grunts came to her across the green practice field.

She tried to distinguish the sound of him from the sound of the others, and she thought she could, thought how amazingly the sound was like the ragged snorts he made into her ear when he had her bent brutally back over the hood of her Vette. There was hardly any difference at all in the noise he made when he scored on the field or scored on her. In whatever he did, he was always noisy and violent and wet, tending as he did to slobber a little.

She saw the band director raise his baton and she tensed, rolled her weight forward to the balls of her feet, and then the music was crashing around her, the tubas pumping, the drums rattling, and she was strutting like it was the end of the world. From the sides of the field came the dry, awesome rattle of the diamondback. Some of the fans had come out and they had brought their gourds with them. The gourds were as big as cantaloupes, shaped like crooked-neck squash, and full of dried seed so that when they were shaken they vibrated the air with the genuine sound of a snake. During a game, the home stands of the Mystic Rattlers put everybody's hair on end. You could hear those dried gourd seeds two miles away, buzzing like the biggest snake den God ever imagined. During football season, nobody in Mystic was very far from his gourd. Sometimes you could see people carrying them around with them in town, down at the grocery store, or inside Simpkin's, the only dry goods store in Mystic.

The band was strung out now in the shape of a snake. The band members used the yard markers to position themselves, double timing in place, drawing their knees high and waving their instruments, so that the entire snake vibrated in the sun. The snare drums were under one goal post, rattling for all they were worth and she was under the other goal post, standing in the snake's mouth, her arms rigid as fangs. She was at one with the music. She did not have to think to perform. Of all the majorettes—and there were five others—she marched in place with the highest knees, the biggest smile, the finest skin, the best teeth. She was a natural, and as a natural her one flaw—if she had one—was that her mind tended to wander. She didn't have to think, didn't have to concentrate like the other girls to get her moves right. Consequently she sometimes got bored with the drills and her mind wandered. Even now as she pranced in place, her back arched, her pelvis thrust forward, she was winking at Joe Lon Mackey where he stood under the end zone bleachers.

That was where he usually stood when he watched them practice and she was not surprised to see him there, glad rather, because it gave her something to think about. He wasn't twenty feet from her, standing in the shadows, a burlap sack in one hand and a brown paper sipping sack in the other. From time to time he raised the sipping sack to his mouth. He'd winked at her when she first stopped under the goal post. She'd winked back. Turned her smile on him. She'd always liked him. Hell, *everybody* had always liked Joe Lon. But she didn't really know him *that* well. Her sister, who was going to school at the University of Georgia in Athens, her sister, Berenice, knew him *that* well.

Her sister and Joe Lon had been a number in Mystic, Georgia, in all of Lebeau County for that matter, and Joe Lon could have been going to the University of Georgia in Athens or anywhere else in this country he wanted to except it turned out Joe Lon was not a good student. That's the way they all put it there in Mystic: Joe Lon Mackey is not a good student. But it was worse than that and they all knew it. It had never been established exactly if Joe Lon could read. Most of the teachers at Mystic High who had been privileged to have him in their classrooms thought he probably couldn't. But they liked him anyway, even loved him, loved tall, blond, high school All-American Joe Lon Mackey whose exceptional quietness off the playing field everybody chose to call courtesy. He had the name of being the most courteous boy in all of Lebeau County, although it was commonly known that he had done several pretty bad things, one of which was taking a traveling salesman out to July Creek and drowning him while nearly the entire first string watched from high up on the bank where they were sipping beer.

She missed the band director's whistle signaling that the snake was about to strike and consequently the five other girls making up the snake's head almost knocked her over. She'd been standing, her arms positioned as fangs, winking at Joe Lon where he raised his sack in the shadows and wondering if Berenice would come home for the roundup, when the girl right behind her, highstepping, hit her in the kidney with a knee and almost knocked her down. She caught herself just in time and hissed over her shoulder: "You want you ass kicked, do you?"

The girl said something back to her but it was lost in the pumping tubas. Under the stands Joe Lon Mackey took the last pull from a Jim Beam half pint and dropped the paper sack with the bottle in it into the weeds. He took out two pieces of Dentyne chewing gum and put them into his mouth. Then he lit a cigarette. He had been watching Candy—called Hard Candy by nearly everybody but her parents, Dr. and Mrs. Sweet—because she reminded him of Berenice and all the things that might have come true for him but had not. Two years ago Berenice had been a senior and head majorette and he, Joe Lon, had been Boss Rattler.

It was said that Joe Lon, on any given day of his senior year of high school, could have run through the best college defensive line in the country. But he had not. He had never set foot on a single college football field even though he had been invited to visit more than fifty colleges and universities. But that was all right. He'd had his. That's what he told himself about ten times a day: *That's all right. By God, I had mine.*

He reached into the back pocket of his Levis and pulled out a sheet of blue paper. It was almost worn through in the creases where it was folded. He shook it open and held it up to the light. It said: "I will see you at rattlesnake time. Love Berenice." There were some X's under the name. The letter had come to Joe Lon at the store three days ago. It had taken him most of the afternoon to be sure of the words and once he was sure of them, they had given him no pleasure. He had thought he was through with all that, had made his peace. He folded the letter and put it back in his pocket. But on the way to his pickup he took the letter out again and, using his teeth and his free hand, he carefully tore it into very small pieces and left them scattered behind him in the gloomy aisle underneath the stands.

He drove over to the little road that went by the practice field and watched Willard Miller run the ball. They were running him against the grunions, the smaller, second-string boys who came out for football for God knows what reason since they almost never got into a game and could only offer up their bodies as tackling dummies for the bigger, stronger boys. He watched Willard Miller fire three straight times up the middle. It was important to run him against grunions now and then. It gave him a chance to practice his moves without running the risk of getting injured. It also gave him great opportunities to run over people and step on them, mash their heads and their hands, kick their ribs good.

Joe Lon felt his own thigh muscles tick, as he watched Willard fake a grunion out of his shoes and then, after he had the boy entirely turned around and beaten, run directly over him for no reason at all. Well, what the hell, all things had to end, both good and bad. There were other things in this world besides getting to step on somebody. The main thing was to hold on and not let it bother you. Joe Lon turned on his lights and drove off into the early November dusk.

He had been drinking most of the day, but he didn't feel drunk. He drove out past the empty flag pole on the post office and past the jail, where he saw Buddy Matlow's supercharged Plymouth with the big sheriff's star painted on the door parked under a leafless Chinaberry tree, and on through town, where several people waved to him. He didn't wave back. Finally, two people shook their gourds at him though and he did raise his hand and smile but he only half saw them. He was preoccupied by the thought of going home to Elfie and the babies, that trailer where he lived in a constant state of suffocating anger.

He had the trailer just outside of town on the edge of a ten-acre field he'd bought and turned into a combination trailer park and campground. He drove slowly down the narrow dirt road leading to it and passed finally under a big banner that he himself had strung from two tall telephone poles he had bought secondhand from the REA. The banner was neatly printed in letters about two feet high: WELCOME TO MYSTIC GEORGIA'S ANNUAL RATTLESNAKE ROUNDUP.

The lights were on in his trailer, a double-wide with a concrete patio, and he could see the shadow of his wife Elfie moving behind the window in the kitchen. He parked the truck, took the burlap sack from the back, and walked out to a little fenced-in pen that had a locked gate on it. He took out a key and opened it. In the back of the pen were several metal barrels. The tops of the barrels were covered with fine-mesh chicken wire. He kicked two of the barrels and immediately the little enclosure was filled with the dry constant rattle of diamondbacks. He took a stick with a wire hook on the end of it from the corner of the pen, set the burlap sack down, and waited.

The mouth of the sack moved and the blunt head of a rattlesnake appeared. It seemed to grin and waved its forked tongue, testing, tasting the air. There was an undulation and another foot of snake, perhaps four inches thick, appeared behind the head. Joe Lon moved quickly and surely and the snake was twisting slowly on the end of the hooked stick.

"Surprise, motherfucker," said Joe Lon, and dropped it into one of the barrels.

For a long moment, he stared into the barrel after the snake but all that appeared there was a writhing of the darkness, an incessant boiling of something thick and slow-moving.

He put the chicken wire back in place, threw the hooked stick in the corner of the pen, and headed for the trailer.

Elfie was at the sink when he walked into the kitchen. From the back she still looked like the girl he'd married. Her hair was red and glowed like a light where it fell to the small of her back. Her hips were round and full without being heavy. Her calves were high, her ankles thin. But then she turned around and she was a disaster. Those beautiful ball-crushing breasts she'd had two years ago now hung like enormous flaps down the front of her body. And although she was not fat, she looked like she was carrying a basketball under her dress. Two inches below her navel her belly just leaped out in this absolutely unbelievable way. The kitchen smelled like she had been cooking baby shit.

"Smells like you been cooking baby shit in here, Elf," he said.

There was a fat eighteen-month-old boy strapped into a highchair. Right beside him in a blue bassinet was a fat two-month-old boy.

Elfie turned from the sink and smiled. Her teeth had gone bad. The doctor said it had something to do with having two babies so close together.

"Joe Lon, honey, I been trying to keep your supper warm for you."

"Goddammit, Elf," he said. "You ever gone git them teeth fixed or not? I given you the money."

She stopped smiling, pulling her lips down in a self-conscious way. "Joe Lon, honey, I just ain't had the time, the babies and all."

There was no dentist in Mystic. She would have to go over to Tifton, and the trip took the better part of a day.

"Leave them goddam younguns with somebody and git on over there and git you mouth looked after. I'm sick and tard of them teeth like that."

"Aw right, Joe Lon, honey." She started putting food on the table and he sat down across from the two babies. "Don't you want to wash you hands or nothing?"

"I'm fine the way I am."

She took some thin white biscuits out of the oven and put them in front of him. Along with everything else she was a terrible cook. He took one of the lardy biscuits off the plate, tore it open, and dipped some redeye gravy on it. She sat with her plate in front of her without eating, just staring at him, her lips held down tight in an unseemly way.

"Was it a bad day at the store, Joe Lon, honey?"

He had been all right when he came into the trailer, but he sat at the table now trembling with anger. He had no idea where the anger came from. He just felt like slapping somebody. He wasn't looking at her but he knew she was still watching him, knew her plate was still empty, knew her mouth was trembling and trying to smile. It made him sick with shame and at the same time want to kill her.

"I left the nigger at the store," he said. "I went snake hunting."

The biscuit and gravy was sticking in his throat and a great gaseous bubble of whiskey rose to meet it. He wasn't going to be able to finish it. He wasn't going to be able to eat anything.

"What all did you git?" she said in a small voice. When he didn't answer, she said: "Did you git anything?"

The baby strapped in the highchair had a tablespoon he was beating the tray in front of him with. Then he quit beating the tray and threw it into the bassinet and hit the other baby in the head, causing him to scream in great gasping sobs. It so startled the baby in the highchair that he started kicking and screaming and choking too. Joe Lon, who had felt himself on the edge of exploding anyway, shot straight out of his chair. He grabbed the greasy biscuit off his plate and leaned across the table. Elfie didn't move. She left her hands in her lap. Her eyes didn't even follow him up. She kept staring straight ahead while he stuffed the dripping biscuit down the front of her cotton dress, between her sore, hanging breasts. He put his face right in her face.

"I got sompin," he shouted. "You want me to tell you what I got? I got goddammit filled up to here with you and these shitty younguns."

She had never once looked at him and the only sign she made that she might have heard was the trembling in her mouth got faster. He kicked over a chair on the way out of the trailer, and before he even got through the door he heard her crying join the babies'. By the time he got to his truck the whole trailer was wailing. He leaned against the fender trembling, feeling he might puke. He almost never had an impulse to cry, but lately he often wanted to scream. Screaming was as near as he could get to crying usually, and now he had to gag to keep from howling like a moon-struck dog.

Jesus, he wished he wasn't such a sonofabitch. Elf was about as good a woman as a man ever laid dick to, that's the way he felt about it. Of course getting married with her three months gone and then putting another baby to her before the first one was hardly six months old didn't do her body any good. And it ruined his nerves completely. Hell, he guessed that was to be expected. But it didn't mean he ought to treat her like a dog. Christ, he treated her just like a goddam dog. He just couldn't seem to help it. He didn't know why she stayed with him.

He stood watching the ten-acre campground, knowing tomorrow it would fill up with snakehunters and blaring radios and noise of every possible kind and wondered if his nerves would hold together. He took a deep breath and held it a long time and then slowly let it out. There was no use thinking about it. It didn't matter one way or the other. The hunt was coming—the noise and the people—and whether he could stand it or not wouldn't change a thing. What he needed was a drink. He glanced once at the trailer, where the shadowy figure of his lumpy wife moved in the lighted window, and jumped into the truck and roared off down the road as though something might have been chasing him.

By the time he got to the store he had gone to howling. Through the open front door, he could see George sitting behind the counter on a high stool. There were no cars or trucks out front. Joe Lon sat next to the little store that was hardly more than a shed and howled. He knew George would hear him and it bothered him but George had heard him before. George would not say anything. That was the good thing about a nigger. He never let on that he saw anything or heard anything.

Finally Joe Lon got out of the truck and went inside. He didn't look directly at George because howling made him look just like he'd been crying, made his eyes red and his nose red and his face flushed. He was wishing now he had not torn up Berenice's letter. He wished he had it to look at while he drank a beer.

"Git me a beer, George," he said.

George got off the stool and went through a door behind the counter into a tiny room not much bigger than a clothes closet. Joe Lon sat on the high stool and hooked the heels of his cowboy boots over the bottom rung. He took out some Dentyne and lit a Camel. Directly, George came back with a Budweiser tallboy.

"What'd you sell today?" Joe Lon said.

"Ain't sell much," said George.

"How much?" he said. "Where's you marks?"

George took a piece of ruled tablet paper out of the bib of his overalls. The paper had a row of little marks at the top and two rows of little marks at the bottom. It meant George had sold twenty bottles of beer, five half pints, fourteen pints, and one fifth, all bonded. He had also sold ten Mason fruit jars of moonshine.

"Hell, that ain't bad for a Thursday," said Joe Lon.

"Nosuh, it ain't bad for a Thursday," George said.

"I got it now," said Joe Lon. "You go on home."

George stood where he was. His gaze shifted away from Joe Lon's face until he was almost looking at the ceiling. "Reckon I could take me a little taste of sompin? Howsomever, it be true I ain't got no cash money."

Joe Lon said: "Take yourself one of them half pints a shine. I'll put it on you ticket. Bring me one of them bonded whiskeys while you in there."

George brought the whiskey and set it on the counter in front of Joe Lon, dropping as he did the half pint of moonshine into the deep back pocket of his overalls.

Joe Lon had brought another ruled piece of tablet paper out of a drawer in front of him. "Damned if you ain't drinking it up bout fast as you making it, George."

"I know I is," George said.

"You already behind on the week and it ain't nothing but Thursday," said Joe Lon.

"It ain't nothing but Thursday an I already be behind on the week," said George, shaking his head.

George hadn't moved so Joe Lon said: "You don't want to borrow money too, do you? You already behind."

"Nosuh, I don't want no money. I already behind."

"What is it then?"

"Mistuh Buddy. He done locked up Lottie Mae again."

"Jesus."

"Yessuh."

"For what?"

"Say she a sportin lady."

"Jesus."

"Yessuh."

Buddy Matlow would take a liking to a woman and if she would not come across he would lock her up for a while, if he could. As soon as he had been elected Sheriff and Public Safety Director for Lebeau County he started locking up ladies who would not come across. They were usually black but not always. Sometimes they were white. Especially if they were transients just passing through, and a little down on their luck. If he got to honing for one like that and she wouldn't come across, he'd lock her up no matter what color she was, sometimes even if she had a man with her. He had been called to accounts twice already by an investigator from the governor's office, but as he kept telling Joe Lon, they'd never touch him with anything but a little lecture full of bullshit about how he ought to do better. Hadn't he been the best defensive end Georgia Tech ever had? Hadn't he been consensus All-American two years back-to-back and wouldn't he have been a hell of a pro if he hadn't blown his right knee? And hadn't he gone straight to Veet Nam, stepped on a pungy stick that had been dipped in Veet Nam Ease shit? Hadn't they had to cut his All-American leg off? Goddammit he'd paid his dues, and now it was his turn.

"I'll see about it," Joe Lon said.

"Would you do that, Mistuh Joe Lon? Would you see about it?"

"I'll talk to him tonight or first thing in the morning."

"I wisht you could axe him about Lottie Mae tonight."

"Tonight or first thing in the morning."

He cut the seal on the whiskey with his thumbnail and took a pull at it. George started for the door. Joe Lon waved the bottle in the air and gasped a little. He'd taken a bigger swallow than he meant to. He followed the whiskey with a little beer while George waited, watching him patiently from the door.

"Lummy git them Johnny-on-the-spots?"

Lummy was George's brother. They both worked for Joe Lon Mackey. They'd worked for Joe Lon's daddy before they worked for Joe Lon. They'd never been told what they made in wages. And they had never thought to ask. They only knew at any given moment in the week whether they were ahead or behind on what they'd drawn on account. Ahead was good; behind was bad. Everybody was usually behind on everything though and nobody worried about it much.

When George didn't answer, Joe Lon said: "The Johnny-on-the-spots, did Lummy git'm?"

Nothing showed in George's face. He said: "Them Johnny-on-the-spot." It wasn't a question. He'd just repeated it.

"Hunters'll start coming in tomorrow," said Joe Lon. "If the Johnny-on-the-spots ain't in the campground we in trouble."

"Be in trouble," said George.

"What?" said Joe Lon.

George said: "What it was?"

"The shitters, George!" said Joe Lon. "Did Lummy git the goddam shitters or not?"

George's face opened briefly, relaxed in a smile. He did a little shuffle with his feet, took the moonshine out of his back pocket, looked at it, felt of it, and put it back. "Sho now, Lummy come wif the shitters on the truck all the way from Cordele."

"I didn't see'm on the campground," Joe Lon said. "I should've seen'm."

"He ain't taken them shitters offen the truck, but he have'm everone. I seen'm mysef. Mistuh Joe Lon, them shitters be fine."

"Just so you got'm, and they out there when the hunters start rolling in."

"You drink you whiskey, Mistuh Joe Lon. Don't think twice. Lummy and me is put our minds on the whole thing."

The screen door banged shut behind him, and Joe Lon poured another dollop of whiskey down. It wasn't doing any good much, didn't seem to be taking hold. He knew nothing was going to help a whole lot until he saw Berenice and either made a fool of himself or did not. He had the overwhelming feeling that he was going to make a fool of himself. Tear something up. Maybe his life. Well, at least he got the Johnny-on-the-spots. Last year it had taken two weeks to clean the human shit up in Mystic. There'd been about three times as many people as there had ever been before.

The rattlesnake roundup had been going on now as long as anybody in town could remember, but until about twelve years ago it had been a local thing, a few townspeople, a few farmers. They'd have a picnic, maybe a sack race or a horse-pulling contest and then everybody would go out into the woods and see how many diamondbacks they could pull out of the ground. They would eat the snakes and drink a little corn whiskey and that would do it for another year.

But at some time back there, the snake hunt had started causing outsiders to come in. Word got out and people started to come, at first just a few from Tifton or Cordele and sometimes as far away as Macon. From there on it had just grown. Last year they had two people from Canada and five from Texas.

Mystic, Georgia, turned out to be the best rattlesnake hunting ground in the world. There were prizes now for the heaviest snake, the longest snake, the most snakes, the first one caught, the last one caught. Plus there would be a beauty contest. Miss Mystic Rattler. And shit. Human shit in quantities that nobody could believe. This year, though, they had the Johnny-on-the-spots. Chemical shitters.

The telephone rang. It was his daddy. He wanted Joe Lon to send over a bottle with George.

"Ain't here," he shouted into the phone. "He already gone."

"Send somebody else then. Damn it all anyhow, I want a drink."

"Ain't nobody here but me. What happened to that bottle I left by this morning?"

"I drapped it and broke it."

"Bullshit."

"Joe Lon, I'm gone have to shoot you with a gun someday, talking to you daddy like that."

"Who'd run the store if you done that? Maybe Beeder could run the goddam store. Tote you goddam whiskey. Maybe she'd quit with the TeeVee and act normal. Send her over here right now and I'll give her a bottle for you."

"You a hard man, son, making such talk about you only sister. Lord Christ Jehovah God might see fit to strike you."

Joe Lon wanted to scream into the telephone that it was not Lord Christ Jehovah God that struck his sister. But he did not. It would do no good. They'd been over that too many times already.

"All right," he said finally, "never mind. I'll bring the whiskey myself. Later."

"How later?"

"When I git a chance."

"Hurry, son, my old legs is a hurtin."

"All right."

Just as he put the telephone down, a car drove up. It stopped but nobody got out. Carload of niggers. He sighed. Joe Lon Mackey carrying shine for a carload of niggers. Who would have thought it? He looked down at his legs as he was going into the little room behind the counter. Who would have thought them wheels, wheels with four-five speed for forty yards, would have come to this in the world. Well, anything was apt to come to anything in this goddam world. That's the way the world was. He spat as he took down the half pints of shine from the shelf.

During the next hour he sold more than had been sold all day, most of it to blacks who drove up and stopped under the single little light hanging from a pole in front of the store. He wished to God they were allowed to come inside so he wouldn't have to cart it out front to them. Of course, they *were* allowed to come inside. Except they were not *allowed* to come inside. It had been that way for the twenty years his daddy had run the store and it had been that way ever since Joe Lon had taken it over. He hadn't really *kept* it that way. It had just *stayed* that way. Nobody ever complained about it because if you wanted to drink in Mystic, Georgia, you had to stay on the good side of Joe Lon Mackey. Lebeau County was dry except for beer, and since Joe Lon had an agreement with the bootlegger, his was the only place within forty miles you could buy you a drink.

He worked steadily at the whiskey in front of him, chasing it with beer, and by the time Hard Candy's white Corvette car pulled up out front, he was feeling a little better about the whole thing. The Corvette was Berenice's old car and it reminded Joe Lon of everything he had been trying not to think about. Willard came in ahead of Hard Candy. He was an inch taller than Joe Lon and looked heavier. He had a direct lidless stare and tiny ears. His hair was cut short and his round blunt head did not so much sit on his huge neck as it seemed buried in it. He was wearing Levis and a school T-shirt with a tiny snake printed over his heart. His worn-out tennis shoes didn't have any laces in them. He sat on a stool across the counter from Joe Lon and they both watched Hard Candy come through the door stepping in her particular, high-kneed walk that always seemed to make her prance. She took a stool next to Willard. Nobody had spoken. They all sat, unsmiling, looking at one another.

Finally Willard said: "Me'n Hard Candy's just bored as shit."

Joe Lon said: "I got a fair case of the cain't-help-its mysef."

"I don't guess a man could git a goddam beer here," said Willard.

"I guess," said Joe Lon.

"Two," said Hard Candy.

Joe Lon said: "Hard Candy, if you don't quit walking like that somebody's gone foller you out in the woods and do sompin nasty to you."

"I wish to God somebody would," she said.

"*Somebody* already has," said Willard.

Joe Lon got up to get the beer. When he came back he said: "You want to hold this whiskey bottle I got?"

"We et us some drugs to steady us," Willard said. "I don't guess I ought to drink nothing harder'n beer."

"Okay."

"But I will," Willard said.

"I thought you might," Joe Lon said.

"You shouldn't do that," Hard Candy said.

Willard bubbled it four times and set it on the counter. Hard Candy took it up.

"We'll probably die," she said, a little breathless when she put it down.

"Probably."

They sat watching the door for a while, listening to the screenwire tick as bugs flew against it.

"I think it's gone be a shitty roundup," said Joe Lon.

"Will if this hot weather holds," Willard said. "Must be fifty degrees out there right now. Shit, it's like summer. Won't be a snake nowhere in the hole stays this warm."

They sat and watched the door again. A car passed on the road beyond the light now and then. Hard Candy turned and looked at Joe Lon.

"You reckon we could feed one?" she said.

"Let's wait a little while," Joe Lon said. "Maybe somebody'll come in we can take some money off."

"You got one back there that'll eat you think?" asked Willard.

"I try to keep one," Joe Lon said.

They watched the door some more.

"Hell, it ain't nobody coming," said Willard. "Git that rascal out here and let'm do his trick."

"I'll bet with you," said Hard Candy. She opened the little clutch purse she was carrying and bills folded out of the top of it.

"I don't take money from my friends," said Joe Lon.

"If you gone bet with him on the snake," said Willard, "you might as well go ahead and give him the goddam money anyway. You sure as hell ain't gone beat him."

"I lose sometimes," said Joe Lon, smiling.

"Git the goddam snake," said Willard. "Shit, I'll bet with you."

"You ain't bettin with me," said Joe Lon.

"I'll make you bet with me," said Willard.

They were both off their stools now, kind of leaning toward each other across the counter. They were both smiling, but there was an obvious tension in the attitude of their bodies.

"You ever come to make me do something," said Joe Lon, "you bring you lunch. You'll be staying awhile."

"Maybe I can think of something you'll *want* to bet on," said Willard.

"Maybe," said Joe Lon.

He went into the small room at the back of the counter and they followed him. There was a dim light burning. It took a moment for their eyes to adjust. Bottles of various sizes lined the shelves of both sides of the room. One middle shelf toward the back had no bottles on it. It held, instead, five wire cages that were about two feet square and about that high. Four of the cages held a rattlesnake. The fifth cage had several white rats in it. Joe Lon slapped the side of one of the cages with his hand. The snake made no move or sound. Nor did any of the other snakes.

"I've had these so long I probably could handle'm," said Joe Lon.

"Why don't you," said Willard Miller, showing his even, perfect teeth.

"Would if I wanted to," said Joe Lon.

"Hell, let's make the bet then," said Willard. "The loser has to kiss the snake."

Joe Lon looked at him for a long moment. "You couldn't beat me at that either."

Willard Miller said: "I can beat you at anything." He was still smiling but something about the way he said it had no smile in it at all.

"You better back you ass out of here before you git it overloaded," said Joe Lon.

"If we don't never bet on nothing, how you know I cain't beat you?" said Willard.

"I know," said Joe Lon.

Hard Candy said: "I'll git the rat."

She went to the cage, opened the top, and reached in. When her hand came out she had a white rat by its long smooth pink tail. It hung head down without moving, its little legs splayed and rigid in the air. They followed Joe Lon out of the room to the counter, where he set the caged snake down.

"Ain't he a beautiful sumbitch?" said Joe Lon.

"Ain't nothing as pretty as a goddam snake," Willard said.

"I'm pretty as a snake," said Hard Candy.

They both looked at her. She was playing with the rat on the counter, holding its tail and letting it scratch for all it was worth. With her free hand she thumped the rat good-naturedly on top of its head.

"You almost are," said Willard, taking a pull at Joe Lon's whiskey bottle, "but you ain't quite."

Joe Lon took the bottle. "He's right, you ain't quite pretty as a snake."

"What would you two shitheads know about it anyway?" she said.

Joe Lon took a stopwatch from under the counter. It was the watch his coach had given him when he broke the state record for the two-twenty.

"Just for the fun what would you say?" asked Joe Lon.

"He'll hit the rat in a hundred and four seconds. He'll have it swallered in three and a half minutes."

"That's three and a half minutes *after* he hits it?"

"Right," said Willard.

Joe Lon bent down until his nose was only a half inch from the wire cage. The snake was in a corner, tightly knotted, with only its head and tail free. Its waving tongue constantly stroked in and out of its mouth. Its lidless eyes looked directly back at Joe Lon. The head was wide, wider than the body, and flat with a kind of sheen to it that suggested dampness. The tail was rigid now but still not rattling.

"This sucker'll hit right away, maybe twenty seconds. Yeah, I say twenty seconds. That rat'll be gone, tail and all, in two and a half minutes. That's total time. So I'm saying two minutes ten seconds after the hit." He had been staring into the cage while he talked. Now he straightened and backed off. "Drop that little fucker in."

"I'm playing," said Hard Candy.

"You already got the rat messed up and confused from thumpin him on the head," said Willard. "Stop thumpin him and do like Joe Lon says."

She held the rat up in the palm of her hand. She stroked its head with her thumb, gently. She pursed her lips and whispered to the rat: "Nobody's gone hurt you, little rat. We just gone let the snake kill you a little."

There was a spring-hinged door at the top of the cage that opened only one way. She set the rat on top of the door. It opened inward and the rat dropped through. The door immediately swung shut again. Joe Lon started the stopwatch. The rat landed on its feet, turned, and sniffed its pink tail. It looked at the snake in the corner, sat up on its hind legs, and started licking its front paws. The thick body of the snake moved and a high striking curve appeared below its wide blunt head.

None of them saw the strike; rather, they saw the body of the rat lurch as though struck by some invisible force. It sat for a split second without moving and then leaped straight into the air and landed on its back. The rattlesnake had retreated to the corner, its body again knotted and seemingly coiled about itself with only the dry flat head clear.

Almost immediately the snake came twisting out of the spot where it had withdrawn and very slowly approached the still rat. It touched the rat's back, ran its blunt head along the hairy stomach and legs, seemed to be taking the rat's measure. Finally, the snake opened its mouth, unhinged its lower jaw and, slow and gentle as a lover, seemed to suck the rat's head in over the trembling, darting tongue. Just as the head disappeared, the door of the store slammed open and a voice bellowed: "I caught you fuckers being cruel to little animals agin!"

They all turned together to see Buddy Matlow, wearing a cowboy hat and a wooden leg, standing in the doorway. When they looked back at the cage, there was nothing showing of the rat but the tail, long, pink, and hairless, sticking out of the snake's mouth like an impossible tongue.

"You degenerate sumbitches," Buddy Matlow said, watching the thin hairless tail disappear into the snake. "Never could understand how anybody could stand doing things like that to little animals."

Terry Kay

From *The Year the Lights Came On*

On those Sundays when we watched baseball at Harrison we did not attend Methodist Youth Fellowship at Emery Methodist Church. It meant not seeing Megan and Megan had become hauntingly important. The REA and Alvin had made summer alive and adventuresome, fuller than any summer, and I could feel energy spilling out of me, expiring in the heat of work and the heat of play. Yet, I missed Megan.

But there was the upcoming week of Bible school and revival, when Methodist members of the Highway 17 Gang and Our Side would meet for a week of play and treats, subtly conditioned by spirited tales of the Old Testament and nightly invitations to submit our worthless souls to the altar of the hymn, "Revive Us Again." I would see Megan then. I was even half-considering two or three occasions of conversion, just to impress her.

Wesley and I had been talking about Bible school and revival as we worked. Wesley was wondering about the qualifications of the guest preacher; I was concerned with a rumor that we would not have a final-day party. We often talked about different things in the same conversation. Wesley forgave me for being secular, and I forgave him for being ecclesiastical. We were very close.

We did not see Freeman, as he emerged from the pine stand below us.

"Hoooooo, boys!" he yelled.

He was shirtless and barefoot. In summer, Freeman became a bronze boy god. His skin turned deep brown the first day he peeled his shirt and he swam so much that the muscles of his chest knotted into tight bands of rope. He was only a year older than Wesley, but at least two inches taller, and in summer, with his bronze body, his faded-blue eyes and auburn-blond hair, Freeman could have passed for a sixteen-year-old.

"Slavin' away, I see," Freeman called cheerfully as he walked up to where we were mopping cotton for early boll weevils.

"Yea," answered Wesley. "You ever done any work, Freeman?"

"Nothin' as crazy as slopping molasses and junk on cotton. There's better ways, boys. Better ways."

"Yeah, doin' nothing," I said.

"Nothin'? Who said anything about nothin'? I'm about to take me a full-time job, ol' buddy."

"Doin' what?" I asked.

Freeman laughed and plopped down on the ground between two rows of cotton. "Well, you ain't gonna believe it, boys, but I'm goin' to work next week for Old Man Hixon."

"Hixon!" I exclaimed.

"Dupree's daddy?" asked Wesley. "You going to work for Dupree's daddy?"

"That's right, boys. That is absolutely, dead-on-it right."

"You know you ain't supposed to have anything to do with them," I protested. "Ain't that right, Wesley? What goes for me, goes for Freeman."

"Why, it ain't the same at all," Freeman argued. "I'm just gettin' me a job. Ol' Wesley's always after me for bein' lazy."

"It's the same," I snapped.

"Aw, c'mon, Colin, it ain't and you know it," Wesley replied. "How'd you get a job workin' for Mr. Hixon, Freeman?"

"Damndest thing you ever saw, Wes . . ."

"Watch your cussin', Freeman. I got sisters at the end of the row."

"Sorry, Wes. Anyway, Dover Heller's been workin' summers in the warehouse and cotton gin for Old Man Hixon for years, but he's caught on with the REA, bound and determined he's gonna be a line-man, or somethin'. So when Old Man Hixon asked him about work this summer, Dover turned him down, told him he ought to hire me. And, by God, that's just what he done."

"I bet Dupree's having a fit," I said.

"I don't care if he stands on his nutty head and rattles his brain," Freeman declared. "It don't make one whit to me. Ol' Dupree don't do nothin' but stand around that candy counter all day, playin' big shot. Anyhows, I'll be out in the warehouse. If I work it right, I won't even have to see him."

Wesley dabbed at the top of a cotton stalk with his mop. A black wad of calcium arsenic and blackstrap molasses rolled slowly to the edge of a leaf, pooled up, and thickened.

"Well, Freeman, I hope it works out," Wesley said. "I hope nothin' happens to get Dupree any madder'n he is at you."

"Hell, Wes, ol' Dupree stays mad at somebody all the time."

"Yeah, I reckon. Anyway, you better understand that his daddy expects you to be a hired hand, and he won't be puttin' up with any of your games, or cuttin' up. He'll fire you right on the spot, and you know it."

"Wesley, you worry too much, you know that? Anybody ever tell you that you're too plain serious about things? I know how to behave. You'd be shocked at how well I behave when I have a mind to."

"Freeman, I'd probably faint."

"Now, maybe you would, Wesley. Yessir, you just may."

Wesley picked up his bucket of molasses and dipped his mop into it. "Well, we gotta get to work, Freeman. Hope everythin' works out on the job."

"Tell you what, get me a bucket and I'll help you," Freeman volunteered.

"Naw. That's all right," Wesley answered. "Daddy'll think we takin' it easy if he sees you up here talkin' to us."

"Well, just thought I'd offer."

"We ain't got much more to do and we'll be finished," I said. "We quitting early so Mama can go have a meeting about revival."

"Revival," Freeman said suddenly. "Yeah. That's what I was gonna ask y'all about. You remember me tellin' you about ol' Preacher Bytheway? Well, he's havin' his Speaking-In-Tongues Traveling Tent Tabernacle revival next week over in Sosbee's pasture, down by the spring, and I thought maybe y'all would like to go over one night. It's a sight, boys! I'm guaranteeing you, it's somethin' not to be missed."

Wesley squinted at Freeman. Wesley did not like the way Freeman regarded a preacher's earnest attempt to spread the Lord's word. "Freeman," he said, "if you think it's a big circus, why do you go? Someday you're gonna need the help of the Almighty and you'll be sorry for everything you ever said about Preacher Bytheway."

Freeman grinned. He secretly enjoyed Wesley's sermonettes, because he knew Wesley cared.

"Yeah, Wes, you're right. Forgive me."

"It ain't me you need to be askin' forgiveness of, Freeman."

"You're right, Wes. Forgive me, Colin."

Wesley looked at Freeman and shook his head. "Someday, boy, you'll be regrettin' every little funny thing you ever tried to pull."

Freeman tried to suppress a giggle. He wiped his hand over his face and the smile disappeared. Then he looked up with a serious, pleading expression. "Yea, Wesley, I know. I know." The smile reappeared.

Freeman could not resist the temptation to tease and bewilder Wesley's simple confidence in spiritual matters. To Freeman, nothing was as joyful as being in Royston with Wesley and me on Saturday afternoons, and being confronted by a street preacher. The preacher would flail the air and gasp and quote something from the Bible, usually John 3:16, and he would pray and lay his hands on our heads and ask us if we had been saved. Freeman would tremble and quiver, and a whimper would rise out of his throat, and he would say, over and over, "Not till now, brother! Not till now! Oh! Oh! Oh! I feel it, brother! I feel it! The spirit's a-comin', brother! Lay on them hands, brother!" And the street preacher would get spastic and praise God from Horton's Drug Store to the Rialto Theater. Such behavior on Freeman's part would leave Wesley speechless and he would ignore Freeman for the rest of the day. I thought it was funny, because the same street preacher saved us an average of a dozen times each summer.

Freeman pestered Wesley until Wesley agreed to attend the

Speaking-In-Tongues Traveling Tent Tabernacle one night during the following week.

"You won't regret it, Wesley, ol' boy, and I mean it," Freeman promised. "That ol' Preacher Bytheway's a quality preacher, even if he does look like a skinny boar hog when he's took up with the spirit."

"Freeman!"

"Well, Wesley, he does. Ask your mama or daddy. I bet they know of him."

Wesley did ask Mother if she had ever heard of Bartholomew Bytheway.

"Who, son?"

"Bytheway," Wesley answered. "By-the-way. That's his name, Freeman said."

"I believe I have heard of him. A traveling preacher . . ."

"Yes'm. That's what Freeman said, too."

"Well, I don't remember what it was I heard, but I'll ask around. Maybe he's that old man that's kin to Hilda Marsh's first cousin. Hilda was a Sutherland before she married. I'll ask, Wesley."

Mother believed even then that Wesley would someday stand behind a pulpit himself and she radiated with gladness whenever he asked questions about religion.

"Well, I'd appreciate whatever you can find out," Wesley answered. "Freeman wants us to go over to hear him at revival next week, and since it's the only time Freeman ever gets to a church, I thought we'd go."

"That's nice, Wesley. Are Freeman's mama and daddy going?" asked Mother.

"Freeman didn't say. Maybe his mama. His daddy won't, I guess."

"Well, there's people like that, Wesley," explained Mother.

"Yes'm."

Mother did ask about Rev. Bartholomew R. Bytheway and learned only that he was a fixture in certain small towns in Georgia and the Carolinas. Freeman, in a remarkably incoherent session of laughter and half-sentences, told the better story of the good reverend and his famous tent.

The tent had been purchased at auction in Greenville, South Carolina, when a traveling carnival called it quits one Saturday afternoon because the show's only trick horse choked on some oats and died. The Rev. Bytheway had been street-preaching in Greenville, practicing his call to evangelism. He needed experience, and he knew it. Until his calling, Bartholomew Bytheway had been a fertilizer salesman grasshopping up and down the Savannah River Valley for the Green Grow Fertilizer and Plant Food Company. But he had had his troubles. He didn't know 6-8-6 fertilizer from 6-10-10 fertilizer, and each year he lost more and more customers in the small towns along the rich bottomland of the Savannah River. It had been his failure as a fertilizer salesman and the gnawing aggravation of believing he was meant for better things that had driven Bartholomew Bytheway to street preaching—that and one night at a Holiness church, where he had gone to please a potential customer. On that night, with the spirit overflowing, Bartholomew Bytheway put down his fertilizer catalogue and picked up a Bible.

And so it happened that Rev. Bytheway purchased his tent and promptly dedicated it as the Speaking-In-Tongues Traveling Tent Tabernacle. Two months later, he bought a retired school bus with a dying Ford motor and a Blue Bird body. He had a sign painter scrape off the county school inscriptions and cover them with a picture of a man speaking fire. The fire rose out of the man's mouth and ballooned over his head. In the balloon, the words BE SAVED! had been printed in letters that looked like spears. Bartholomew Bytheway had then hired two guitar players from Gaffney to travel with him, and he had begun his ministry in the same small towns of the Savannah River Valley where he had tried to peddle fertilizer. Things had worked surprisingly well for Rev. Bytheway. People loved him. They loved his name, his anger, his shouting, his pleading, his threats. They loved the way he danced around and the way he slapped his hands in a tambourine rhythm. In short, they loved his showmanship, and to prove it they were willing to fling themselves before him and declare personal salvation.

We went to the Speaking-In-Tongues Traveling Tent Tabernacle revival on Tuesday evening. Freeman came up from Black Pool Swamp wearing an old pair of crumpled Sunday pants and a white shirt frayed around the collar. Wesley and I were sitting on the front porch with our mother, who had fussed and dusted us off for over an hour. Her face was literally blazing with pride. In the middle of the week, her two sons were going to a revival meeting with Freeman, that poor, misunderstood child who had nothing but a tubercular mother and a drunken father. In her way, Mother loved Freeman as much as she loved us.

"Hello, Freeman," Mother said. "My, but you're sure lookin' smart tonight!"

Freeman tucked his head. "Yes'm. Y'all ready?"

"They're ready, Freeman. Oh yes, they're ready. Freeman, it's real nice of you to invite the boys to go to your church. Some Sunday, you'll have to go with them to the Methodist preachin'."

"Yes'm."

"Now, you sure you don't want me to drive you over?"

Wesley was quick. "No, Mama. It ain't far. We'll walk." Wesley knew that Freeman was too proud to accept a ride, even in a 1938 Ford.

"Yes'm. We'll walk. It ain't far through the swamp," Freeman assured her.

"But you might get all messy."

"No'm. I know the way."

Mother smiled and resigned herself to Freeman's determination. "Freeman, I do believe you know more about that old swamp than any man alive. I just can't believe you get around in it so easy in pitch dark."

"Yes'm."

Wesley stepped off the porch. "Well, Mama, we'll be in later."

"Be careful," Mother begged. She had never trusted the swamp.

But Mother was right about Freeman. He did know Black Pool

Swamp. He knew Black Pool Swamp the way other people know their homes. Freeman had charted every rabbit path, every squirrel nest, and every foxhole in the swamp. He could walk through the mud and mire and never make a footprint. In Black Pool Swamp, no man was Freeman's equal.

We crossed through the swamp, carefully following Freeman's exact steps. At the top of the hill overlooking Sosbee's Woods and Sosbee's Spring, we heard the faint singing of "The Old Rugged Cross."

". . . till my trophies at last I lay down . . ."

Their voices were muffled under the tent, and the wheezing of the tenors and altos pitched and bounced around the drooping canvas in a frenzy of discord wanting to escape.

". . . so I'll cherish the old rugged cro—osss . . ."

Freeman stopped and stood on a pine stump.

"You listen," he said happily. He smiled and spread his arms to hush us. "Hear ol' Preacher Bytheway singin' away?"

Preacher Bytheway's voice was clearly unusual. It came out of his nose and was compressed into a sound between the scratching of fingernails on a blackboard and the stripping of gears on Mother's old 1938 Ford.

". . . and exchange it some day for a crown . . ."

Freeman laughed aloud. "You ought to hear that fool doin' 'O For A Thousand Tongues to Sing.' Now that is class!"

We crossed into the pine-tree windbreak separating Sosbee's cotton field and Ben Looney's wheat field.

"C'mon, Methodists," Freeman said. "We are goin' to a circus!"

There were thirty-five or forty people sitting on wooden chairs that had been borrowed from the Emery Junior High School lunchroom. Fresh sawdust from Wray's Sawmill covered the ground and had been cooking all day under the heavy canvas. In the tent, it smelled like resin burning. People fanned themselves with fans that had a picture of Jesus knocking at a door without a handle on it. An advertisement for Higginbottom's Funeral Parlor was on the back of the fan, containing the message: GIVE YOUR LIFE TO JESUS, TRUST YOUR REMAINS TO US. Babies wiggled at their mother's feet, playing in the sawdust. Old men wearing bib overalls over starched, white shirts, sat rigidly still and mouthed the closing verse of "The Old Rugged Cross." Freeman and Wesley and I eased into three chairs in the last row, as the song ended.

"Glory! Oh, I say it again—glory! Glory! Glory! Glory! The Lord God Almighty and His holy house must be smilin' with pure pleasure sittin' out somewhere on a front porch of a cloud, rockin' and listenin' to such singing! Oh, I say it—help me, Jesus!—say it again! Glory! Glo-o-o-o-ry! Say it with me, good people! Say it so's the Lord God Almighty and His holy house can know we all feel the same wonderful way! Glo-o-o-o-o-o-o-ry!"

A half-dozen women answered.

Preacher Bytheway cupped his hand to his right ear and leaned forward, straining as though he had been struck deaf.

"What?! Now, the Lord God Almighty and His holy house couldn't hear that! Lordy, Lordy, Lordy! There's a reunion of angels and saints takin' place, havin' supper with the Almighty tonight, and they sure wanta hear that praise! Yessir! A big rush of wind come thunderin' by just as you let loose, and the Lord God Almighty knows you was drowned out by it, so He wants it again! Glo-o-o-o-o-o-o-ry!!!"

The two guitar players lunged forward together and strummed hard and Preacher Bytheway stepped out toward the congregation.

"Say it, brothers and sisters!" he ordered. "Say it!"

His voice was begging. He closed his eyes and raised his head. The congregation looked up with him, all the way to the top of the tent where a swarm of gnats and moths were circling an electric light that had been strapped to the tent pole by tape. The electric lines running to the tent had been strung and connected to the school, which fed from Georgia Power Company.

"Say it! Glory! Glory! Glo-o-o-o-o-o-o-o-o-rrrrr-rry!"

He lifted his arms and locked his wrists together as if they were handcuffed. He sucked in his lips until they wrinkled in the gaps where he had missing teeth, and he began to nod his head up and down. His eyes and nose and lips drew together until they were a scab on his skinny face. His hair looked as though some maniac with scissors had whacked gaps out of it.

"GLO-O-O-O-O-O-RY!"

The congregation was overwhelmed by Preacher Bytheway's frenzy.

"Glory! Oh, glory, glory, glory!" The women's voices were shrill screams. The men rumbled in bass counterpoint.

"Wesley," I whispered, "he does look like a skinny boar hog, like Freeman said."

"Shuttup! It ain't how you look, it's what you say," Wesley shot back.

"He's right, Wes," Freeman said.

Wesley whirled to stare at Freeman. Freeman grinned and jumped up. "Glory!" he shouted. Wesley grabbed him by the shirt and jerked him down.

"Freeman, you doin' that to make me mad, and I know it! Now you shut up, or I'm leavin'!"

Freeman giggled into his hands and slipped down to the edge of the chair. "Glory, glory, glory," he said in a snickering, low, mocking voice.

Preacher Bytheway had reached the takeoff in his trip to the outer space of evangelism. The two guitar players from Gaffney began a soft chording of "What A Friend We Have In Jesus," and Preacher Bytheway picked up the bass dips with his arms, still locked at the wrists.

"Oh, the Lord does love joyful noises! Help me, Jesus! Make a joyful noise unto the Lord! Yes! Yes! And you can do it! You can! You can do miracles makin' joyful noises unto the Lord! Help me, Jesus! Give it over! Let it roll out of your souls! Say it to the Lord! And He will hear! He will hear! He will hear!"

Preacher Bytheway's voice began to singsong. He began to siphon off great gulps of air, nodding up and down, pumping with his locked wrists, twitching in the knees.

"He will hear! Go—go out and preach! Go OUT! OUT! Oh, oh, yes! Preach the gospel! Gos-pel! TO ALL MY PEOPLE! TO ALL MY PEOPLE! Help me, Jesus! ALL OVER THE WORLD! And tell them—tell them—tell them—OF MY WORDS!"

In the back of the tent we could see the congregation beginning to sway and rock, leaning into the beat. Someone started clapping in time. And another. And another. A baby crawled out into the aisle and started eating sawdust.

"Tonight! Tonight! I tell you! We are goin' to talk about—oh yes, talk about—God's holy word in treatin' all the creatures of the world with love and kindness! And how—help me, Jesus—oh, how it is that hell's a-burnin' a thousand times hotter'n the sun to them that's mean and hateful and spiteful and—oh, help me, Jesus!—and stompin' on the weak and downtrodden! Oh, yes! Remember the Good Samaritan and how he stopped to help out the stranger! That's God's world a-workin' in God's word! Oh—oh, yes! It's there in the Bible! I say—help me, Jesus!—the Bible! It tells us about evil and good and how the two go 'round and 'round fightin', and how—oh, help me, Jesus!—how the Devil is sneakin' into every life he can find not tended by the good shepherd, Jesus . . ."

Wesley leaned forward in his chair. He could not believe Preacher Bytheway. He held his right hand over his heart.

"What's he sayin', Wesley?" I asked. "Is he all right?"

"He's being took. He's got the spirit," whispered Wesley.

I moved closer to Wesley. "I don't want it," I said.

"What?"

"Wesley, let's go home. That spirit may get down here."

"It ain't no spook, crazy! He's took with the Holy Spirit!"

"Oh," I said. Preacher Bytheway was retching on holy words stuck in his throat. "Wesley, anybody at the Methodist Church ever been took with the spirit?"

"Lots of 'em. Hush."

"I never seen any."

"There's different ways of being took."

Freeman leaned into Wesley. "That's preachin'! Now, Wes, ol' boy, you ever see such preachin'?"

Wesley shot Freeman a look that would have killed a snake. Freeman laughed and sat back in his chair and began clapping his hands out of rhythm.

Preacher Bytheway was again behind his pulpit, pounding on the Bible and declaring that an Atlantic Ocean of ice water wouldn't last a split second in hell, hell was so hot. He jerked in his shoulders, jabbed the index finger of his right hand in the air, and swatted at mosquitoes with his left. He broke in midsentence to talk about God's having a special love for animals and birds because He created them first and put them in the Garden of Eden and when it came time to flood the earth, he made ol' Noah gather up two of every kind and float them around until the rain stopped and the ark landed. The two guitar players broke out of a vamp and slipped into "Amazing Grace," and Preacher Bytheway started on a fox hunt of Scripture until he treed the passage about Jesus riding a donkey into Jerusalem, and that became his topic.

It was as though Preacher Bytheway had been jolted by a charge from an Atlas car battery. He broad-jumped from behind the pulpit in a convulsion. He landed flat with his back bent at an awkward angle, and he whipped forward bringing his right arm over his head, like Alvin letting fly a knuckleball. He then began to stutter step, dragging his left arm behind him. He snapped the fingers of his right hand and did his singsong about Jesus selecting a lowly animal—"Yes! Yes! A ass! It was a ass!"—and how that meant we all needed to humble ourselves.

"Amen! Amen! Amen, Preacher!"

A loud voice erupted from somewhere in the middle of the right side of the aisle. Rev. Bartholomew R. Bytheway stopped dead between twitches, startled by such quick response to his sermon.

"Yes, brother, that's what I say! Amen!" Preacher Bytheway echoed.

Suddenly, Laron Crook jumped straight out of his seat. "Oh, Preacher, I know what you mean! Oh, yes, I surely do!"

"Tell us, brother! Tell us all! Let it out! Praise God! Make a joyful noise unto the Lord! Is Jesus touchin' you?"

Laron was wringing his hands. His chin was revolving as if he had a chicken bone caught in his throat and he was trying to cough it up. "Jesus—oh, Preacher, Jesus is touchin' me! Helpin' me! Leadin' me!" Laron's chin was spinning. If Jesus had him, it was by the throat.

"PRAISE GOD! AND WHO IS THIS BROTHER?" shouted Preacher Bytheway.

Laron Crook was nearly forty years old. He was six feet, five inches tall, and he had a sunken chest. He was slightly retarded—retarded in that gray land of sad confusion. As long as he had lived in Emery, no one could remember Laron ever saying over a dozen words a day. Next to Alvin, before his conversion by baseball and Delores, Laron was the quietest man in north Georgia. He and his daddy had a farm near the Bio community and they traded mules, and sometimes field-trained them to know gee from haw. Occasionally, Laron's daddy would get drunk and wander around Emery yelling, "Gee" or "Haw" and he would conduct a mule-training lesson under the tin roof of the cotton gin. Laron would bring a two-horse wagon and drive his daddy away, as his daddy yelled out at the snickering crowd of onlookers, "Gee. Haw. Kick 'em in the ass." It would take weeks before Laron could speak to anyone without blushing.

"Tell us what the Lord's doin' for you, brother! Tell us all!" begged Preacher Bytheway, motioning for Laron.

Laron began to weave out to the middle of the aisle. There were a few restrained amens and everyone was stretching to see Laron.

"Jesus knew what He was doin', Preacher! Oh, I feel it! Feel it!"

"It's tinglin', ain't it, brother?!" encouraged Preacher Bytheway. "The spirit's tinglin', ain't it?!"

The two guitar players from Gaffney upped the tempo and cheated into a mild boogie sound. The applause picked up and matched the rhythm of the guitars.

"If you love this good brother, say amen!" Preacher Bytheway shouted. "Do you hear me, people?! A-a-a-a-men!"

"A-a-a-a-MEN! Hallelujah!"

"God bless you, Laron . . ."

"I'm prayin' for you, Laron . . ."

"Amen, Laron . . ."

"I'm filled with you, Laron . . ."

Laron moved slowly toward the front of the tent. The back of his neck began jerking involuntarily and he held his elbows close to his sides and began to pump his shoulder blades up and down. His head was bobbing to the bass beat of the two guitars and the hand-clapping swelled in stereophonic wildness around him. His feet were tapping out a buckdance step.

"Good God!" Freeman exclaimed. "Look at ol' Laron, Wesley. You see that? I'll be damned. Look at that fool."

"What's he gonna do, Freeman?" asked Wesley, slipping back into his seat. Wesley and I had never seen such behavior in the name of God.

"Depends on how took he is," replied Freeman. "Maybe talk in tongues."

Laron Crook, nearly forty, six feet, five inches tall, was took. He was seized. Obsessed. Possessed. Surrendered into and commanded by. Laron was converted.

"Preacher—Preacher—PREACHER! Uh—Inee! Ddaa—pogg—UH—EEE! Ahhh! GUNNNNN—UHHHHH! Gunnnnn—gunnnnn! AHHHHHHHHHH . . ."

Laron was talking in tongues. Preacher Bytheway was talking in tongues. The guitar players were playing in tongues, wild Latin-sounding dance music, and one of them was doing a click-click-click castanets sound with his lips.

Laron Crook's conversion made St. Paul's experience on the road to Damascus seem like a migraine headache in comparison.

Laron whipped up on his toes—I swear, his toes. He jabbed and hooked his arms like Joe Louis shadowboxing. He came crashing in on his heels on a downstroke by the two guitarists, held a quick freeze, and then broke into a couple of German goose steps.

"Show us the Lord, brother!" Preacher Bytheway urged, stepping out of Laron's way and waving him front and center.

"Amen, Laron . . ."

"We're with you, Laron . . ."

"God bless you and your daddy, Laron . . ."

Laron had circled to one side of the sawdust altar area. He began to jump and bicycle in midair. When he landed, he would skid into a split, claw at the air with his hands, and pull himself up. A couple of German goose steps and Laron would be leaping and bicycling in the air again. On his best jumps, he probably cleared four feet and he could pump three times with his legs before he hit ground.

Then Laron slowed the tempo. He began to stiffen and skip on his left foot. Suddenly, his body snapped and went rigid. He pulled his left arm close to him, cocked his elbow and folded his wrist under his chin. His right arm shot out, straight toward the ground, two inches below his knee. His right hand was hinged and opened, his fingers spread like web feet. His right foot was lifted ankle high and he hop-scotched in tiny, frantic steps across the sawdust.

Laron Crook looked like Red Grange stiff-arming a midget.

"God bless you, bro-THER!"

Rev. Bartholomew R. Bytheway annointed Laron Crook a preacher of the gospel of the Speaking-In-Tongues Traveling Tent Tabernacle, instructing him to continue the ministry of humanity that had moved him to the grandest, most spectacular display of being invested by God's mysterious spirit that anyone had ever demonstrated. It was a touching ceremony. Laron confessed to sins as fast as he could invent them. He told long, funny stories about how he had been taught to mistreat animals by being master over them, but how that had now stopped and how he believed the Lord God Almighty had called him to do something special with ". . . them poor creatures."

Everyone amened and hallelujahed and hugged Laron and wished him luck. Dover Heller promised he would quit kicking Bark in the head for chewing up rabbits. Laron said he'd work with Bark and try to train him with God's gentle help.

The Speaking-In-Tongues Traveling Tent Tabernacle left at the end of the week. It had been a triumph for Rev. Bartholomew R. Bytheway. He had attracted his largest crowds, had delivered the Thursday noon prayer following the Obituary Column of the Air on the Edenville radio station, and he had ordained his first minister. The fact that Laron was Preacher Bytheway's convert became the most exciting news event in Emery in years. Laron spoke up, proudly and often. If he wasn't talking, he was meditating. He put himself on a strict disciplinary program—prayer at morning, prayer at noon, prayer at night, and no more R. C. Colas between meals. If he was in God's service, Laron wanted to be in shape.

During his first days of spiritual growth and adjustment, Laron's constant companion was Freeman, when Freeman wasn't working for

A. G. Hixon in the warehouse and cotton gin. To Laron, Freeman was someone who had been misunderstood and poorly treated by life. It was a sympathy fired by the parallel of their childhoods, and oddly confirmed by their opposite personalities. If, in his new Born Again self, Laron could help out a fellow human being, it would be Freeman. Besides, no one in Emery knew animals as well as Freeman and Laron needed help in that commitment; Laron knew mules, but he had a way of repelling other creatures.

Freeman loved the attention. He amened at appropriate times. He allowed Laron to save his worthless soul at least twice a week. He had visions so fearful and vivid, Laron would hyperventilate with excitement as Freeman, wallowing on the ground, described scenes that made the Book of Revelations read like a Flash Gordon comic book.

On days when his personal evangelism fell on deaf ears, Laron would persuade Freeman to meet him in the late afternoon and they would go into the pastures and woods to communicate with God's animals. These were special missions for Laron, and his zeal was inspiring. He was kicked by a goat in Horace Wilder's pasture, chased across a cornfield by Otis Harper's breed bull, bitten by Bark, pecked in the face by a nesting hen, and Freeman left him one night in the middle of Black Pool Swamp hooting away with a distressed owl. Laron had no idea it was Freeman hooting back.

But Laron considered all these trials a test of his faith and, like Job, he would endure. "God forgive this dumb beast for kickin' me," Laron would say. "He knows not what he's doin'."

The injury and humiliation suffered by Laron was God's way of preparing him for a revelation. "When it happens, it's gonna be mighty," he claimed. "It's gonna come like a hold-up man at night, when I ain't expectin' nothin'."

He was right.

Laron was at Hixon's General Store one Saturday afternoon, sitting under a water oak, recuperating from a severe clawing he had received while trying to separate two cats intent on mating. We had been listening to his wonderful interpretation of Old Testament stories for an hour when Freeman asked his question.

"Laron, tell me something," Freeman said innocently. "How come there's a heaven for folks, but there ain't no heaven for animals?"

"Who said there ain't?" Laron replied. "Of course there is. Why, heaven ain't much different'n earth. Except that it's freed of sin, and maybe a little cloudier. What makes you think God don't believe in havin' pets? Why, think about how nice it must be up there with birds tweetin' and chirpin' all the time. Must be awful pleasin' to God and Jesus, and the saints and holy angels, to hear them birds."

"I thought they only had gold harps in heaven," Freeman said.

Laron peeled back the bandage and looked at a deep red wound on his hand. "Oh sure, they got harps. Gold harps. But they's only for special occasions. Like Sundays, or Christmas, or Easter, or the Fourth of July. Rest of the time, heaven's filled with birds singin' and dogs barkin' and things like that."

Freeman measured his words, folded them around in his mouth and dropped them like diamonds of pure wonderment. "But, gosh, I thought the only way you could get to heaven was by bein' baptized," he said.

Laron's head snapped like a whip. His eyes dilated. His sunken chest began to heave. You could see his heart pumping in his jugular veins. "That's it! That's it, Freeman! Praise God! That's what the Lord has called me to do! I know it, Freeman! You are an instrument of the Lord God Almighty Jehovah!"

Freeman crossed his arms over his chest, as if hiding from the fearful face of God. "What, Laron?!"

"The Lord God Almighty Jehovah, He who said I AM THAT I AM, has done delivered me a message, Freeman! Oh, yes! Not from no mountain, mind you, but from the mouth of a babe! I can hear it, Freeman! I can hear it!"

"Me, too, Laron! OH, YES! Go out yonder and baptize my creatures!"

"That's it, Freeman! Them's the Lord's words, right outa His mouth! Praise His holy tongue! Amen! A-a-a-MEN!"

For the next few days, Laron was lunatic in his determination to baptize every walking, flying, and crawling animal in Emery. He carried a Boy Scout canteen filled with water from Sosbee's Spring and if he couldn't lay his hands on a cow or a crow, he would flit water in their direction and declare the deed accomplished.

Laron was as crazy as Don Quixote, and, in his way, just as noble, but Wesley was greatly saddened by the spectacle of Laron chasing stray dogs and cats up and down the railroad track, and he blamed Freeman for encouraging such mad behavior.

"It ain't my fault," Freeman protested.

"Freeman, it is and you know it," Wesley preached. "Laron ain't got good sense, and all you're doin' is havin' a big laugh. What you don't understand is that Laron's all caught up in doin' what he thinks he ought to be doin'. It don't matter to him if everybody's laughing and making fun. He'd do anything anybody tells him, if it's said in the name of God. That's sad, boy, and you know it. Laron believes God's hidin' in that canteen of water and that He comes out like some magic monster everytime he flings some water around. Freeman, that ain't God. That's people sayin' God's a white-bearded old man floating around in the air somewhere, and that He's goin' around keepin' count on who is baptized and who ain't."

"Wesley, you know what it says in the Bible," argued Freeman.

"I don't need to read the Bible to know that water ain't gettin' you to heaven, Freeman. It ain't the water."

"Wesley, I'm tellin' you, Laron heard a voice."

"Freeman, what Laron heard was what you wanted him to hear. You think God's talkin' out loud, like Sam Spade on the radio? You really think such things?"

"Now, Wesley, that's what ol' Preacher Bytheway said."

Wesley was quiet. He wanted to say the right thing and say it in a way that even Freeman could comprehend him.

"Freeman," Wesley finally said, "if a man's got to learn about the Almighty by bein' scared to death because somebody's screaming about hell boilin' over with fire, or bein' fooled about heaven bein' paved with California gold, then he ain't learned nothing. That's just a way of trying to pin down something that can't be pinned down. If you got to say what God is, or ain't, you're just talkin'. That's all. Just talkin'. Knowing the Almighty don't need that."

Freeman did not understand a word Wesley said. Neither did I.

Raymond Andrews

From *Appalachee Red*

5

Yankee Town sits four miles up the Oconee, northeast of Appalachee, and is known chiefly as the site of the big state prison farm of the same name, the area's largest cotton mill, regional headquarters of the Ku Klux Klan . . . and no niggers. That is, no niggers except for those blacks who over the years have comprised the bulk of the population of the prison which sits surrounded by the town. But other than these convicts the only blacks allowed within the town's limits during the daylight hours are those who come on business to the prison or cotton mill located on the town's outskirts overlooking the Oconee, and they have to be in the company of at least one white male adult. Between sundown and sunup, no blacks are allowed in that part of Yankee Town not enclosed by the prison's walls under any circumstances. Scattered along the streets are signs warning of this fact.

The town got its name from the Union Army garrison, Camp Oconee, which was in existence from late 1864, when Yankee soldiers first entered the area, until all Federal troops were recalled from the South in 1877. But by this time the camp had left a permanent impression on this end of the Oconee, having drawn every two-legged scavenger ranging from prostitute to politician—providing any such gap between the two professions exists—in the region to pitch a camp of their own outside the gates of the garrison, seeking the favors and handouts of their conquerors and, for those blacks then present, saviors. For nearly thirteen years the countryside surrounding the camp reeked so of these human locusts that the area's decent folks feared to tread near this end of the Oconee, which was by now referred to derogatorily by these fearful citizens as "Yankee Town."

Then, shortly following the United States government's decision to hand the asylum back to its original inmates by recalling all occupation troops from the South, Oconee's former campgrounds, with barracks left intact, were utilized by the state as a prison farm, which came to have one of the largest inmate populations and worst reputations in the region. And for more than thirty-five years Yankee Town's economy depended solely upon the number of convicts the state allotted its prison, as during these years the town's residents consisted entirely of prison personnel and their families, plus a smattering of shopkeepers and surrounding farmers. Then came 1916, when a cotton mill was erected along the riverbank just outside town, eventually bringing droves of people to the area in search of work at the mill. Many blacks were included in this exodus along the Oconee in the beginning, but with so many of the area's poor whites in need of work as well, friction quickly developed between the two races over jobs at the mill. Such was the friction between these blacks and whites that an arbitrator had to be brought in from the outside to settle the dispute. Enter the Ku Klux Klan. And within a short period of time the matter of jobs had been settled with the mill, like its product, being purified into a lily-white production. So carried away did the Klan become over their duties that these refugees from the town's linen closets quickly extended their purification program to the whole of Yankee Town by sending all its few black residents running across the border, most left behind all their worldly possessions . . . some others their lives as well. Credit for this American-style pogrom and the revival of the Ku Klux Klan in the county belonged to one Ezra White, known to his many enemies throughout the region as the "Original Bastard of Yankee Town."

Ezra was dropped by his teenage mother, Kitty White, one of the original camp followers, outside the gates of Camp Oconee in the summer of 1865. Neither he nor his mother ever learned which of the many Yankee soldiers who made nightly visits to their tent (also scrounged from the U.S. Army) the child should've called Daddy. And even before the youngster had had a chance to get used to the word "Ma," Kitty had swum across the Oconee . . . splashing for dear life behind a deserting boy in blue who'd promised her Savannah just beyond the next levee. Young Ezra was reared by several of the nomads surrounding the camp and was destined to spend the next twelve years of his life in the midst of honky-tonks, prostitutes, pimps, gamblers, moonshiners, hustlers, scalawags, former slaves, and carpetbaggers, all competing for the Yankee soldiers' gold. And since he was one of the few youngsters living in the village during its formative years, Ezra grew up fast.

Once the soldiers had gone and the prison farm opened, Ezra, now an old fourteen, became the first Yankee Towner to find work at the new penal institution. In the succeeding years Ezra was destined to work his way up through the farm's system from general flunky to guard to captain of the guards to—finally, in the year 1910—prison warden, a position which made him the single most powerful person in Yankee Town. Ezra had gotten word years in advance of the possibility of a cotton mill opening in the vicinity and astutely began to buy up all the available real estate in and around Yankee Town. When the mill finally opened in '16, it went just as Yankee Town's Original Bastard had planned it. Practically overnight, shacks of all descriptions and materials were thrown up on Ezra's land to accommodate hordes of poor white millhands, who soon came to be commonly referred to as "lintheads." And since these lintheads had no choice but to live on Ezra's land, Ezra had little trouble convincing the mill's absentee owner to fill the key jobs in the mill with those members of the family White who didn't already hold similar jobs at the prison farm. And with nearly all of Yankee Town paying its monthly rent into his pocket, within a short period of years Ezra had jockeyed himself into position as the county and district political boss with his guaranteed offer of the linthead and prison-personnel bloc votes (a month's free rent for those who voted his way and ejection from house and mill, or prison job, for those who refused) to the area's political aspirants of his choice. And in assuring himself the confidence of all these mill and prison workers, Ezra reorganized the Ku Klux Klan in Muskhogean and personally led these hooded riders in cleansing Yankee Town and its environs of the nigger element. They were of no use to him at the polls, but the land they left behind when they were chased out of the area by the Klan Ezra himself confiscated personally to extend his linthead shantytown.

Of Ezra's eleven children, seven were boys and all but the youngest of these males were destined to spend their lives running Yankee Town's prison and cotton mill. The youngest, Clyde, born the year of his father's appointment as prison warden, from the beginning showed little interest in following in the careers of the older males of his family. During his late teen years he took to spending much of his time down the Oconee in the county seat. And when shortly following his twenty-first birthday he met and married an Appalachian girl, the brash young man drew the scorn of his father, who was well known in the county for his intense dislike of what he always referred to as the "nigger-loving passing-for-whites" of Appalachee. In fact the two towns had always shared a vehement hatred for each other which dated back to the origin of Yankee Town, when the Appalachian residents of that day first labeled the horde of camp followers living around the Yankee garrison as "a pile of poor white trash" and traitors to the South's cause. This label had stuck through the years, and when the Original Bastard of Yankee Town reincarnated the Ku Klux Klan in the county and chased all of the blacks out of his area onto Appalachee's doorstep, the two towns' hatred for each other became even more intensified.

But young Clyde had his father's temperament and determination; he got his way and settled with his bride in the county seat, and Ezra himself ended up clearing the way for his son by getting him a job on Appalachee's police force. And from the onset of his career as a lawman Clyde showed a fanatic's devotion toward his work. One of the very first things he did after getting the job was to buy himself a pair of high-laced black boots, a type worn at that time by the state patrolmen. The boots weren't a part of Clyde's regulation uniform, but Appalachee's Chief of Police at the time, Wade Mitchell, knew better than to remind the hot-headed youngster that he wasn't complying with regulations by sporting such footwear, because the Chief too had gotten his job as a lawman directly through the intervention of the county's political boss, Ezra.

In his early years on the force Clyde, a restless sort, never cared for the idea of sitting around the station house batting the breeze with his fellow workers or whoever happened to drop in to chat. Instead he preferred being out on the streets where things were happening, and he was gifted with the knack of helping them on. With his dark blue uniform especially tailored for a tight fit on his tall, slender frame and wearing those ever-glowing black leather boots with steel plated heels and toes, the youngest born of Ezra struck an imposing figure on the streets of Appalachee during the Depression Thirties. But it was along the narrow, gravel-strewn back street of the town, known among its black patrons as "the Alley," that Clyde most enjoyed strolling in his uniform. And it was back here that the awesome sight of the tall, arrogant, and swaggering policeman was met with fear and hatred by the blacks. Back here he was the Man.

Clyde's favorite time for visiting the Alley and its handful of small shops came, naturally enough, on Saturday, when most of the area's blacks came to town. His first patrol of the back street always took place in the early afternoon of that day. A hush would blanket the Alley once the blacks clustered back here on their big day in town would first hear the unmistakable sound of boots striking gravel, then look up to see the blue-clad figure of Clyde swaggering down the middle of the narrow little street with that loose-jointed gait of his. There would be a mad scramble to get out of the tall policeman's path as he strolled slowly along up and down each side of the street, peering out from under the bib of his cap, which rested almost on the tip of his pointed nose, wearing on his face a deep scowl while staring down each pair of black's eyes that dared to look his way. All the way down to the end of this short block and across the intersecting street, all that could be heard was the slow crunch . . . crunch . . . crunch . . . of those shiny black boots walking gravel.

Coming to a stop over across the street in front of Sam's Café, Clyde would stand for a moment or two before stepping up onto the porch, abruptly kicking open the door, and then stomping into the middle of the crowded, but now suddenly silent room. Standing here, he would glare around at the sea of black faces until one by one their white eyes would shift floorward. After staring everyone down to his satisfaction, Clyde would then spit in the middle of the floor, wheel around, and stomp out of the café with the sound from those steel-plated black boots reverberating off the walls. Leaving the door opened behind him, he would then walk south back toward the main part of town. The Man's big day of keeping the niggers in their place was thus officially under way.

During Clyde's first few weeks on the force, Chief Wade had condescendingly tried to discourage the youngster from making too many patrols in the back part of town, but this advice was quickly ignored by the son of Ezra, who had grown up well versed on Appalachians' "liberal" attitude toward their niggers. And after Clyde had discussed the chief's words with his father, the county's law enforcement agency, from the sheriff on down, was warned by Ezra not to interfere with his son while he was performing his duties as a lawman. Clyde now had his green light.

It was but a matter of days following this that Clyde had his first head-on clash with a member of the back-street crowd. And, as could've been expected, it came on a Saturday shortly after sunset when the policeman was strolling down the Alley in the company of a fellow patrolman. A tipsy black suddenly staggered from off the narrow sidewalk right into the path of the two lawmen . . . on Clyde's side. Stumbling against the policeman, the black man fell forward and, in doing so, automatically reached out to grab ahold of some means of support. And (pity the poor nigger man) that support turned out to be the front of Clyde's freshly pressed blue uniform shirt, which, quick as a flash, was yanked out from under the belt of those sharply creased trousers by the man's black, grasping fingers, sending little white buttons flying in all directions. And the man fell to the ground, with his head landing right next to those glossy toes of Clyde's boots. Pity the poor nigger man again. Stunned by the audacity of the black man, a now highly enraged Clyde started cursing and kicking the prone figure of the drunk about the head and body as the victim, not fully realizing what was happening, tried in vain to crawl out of the reach of those steel-plated black boots thundering down upon him and ripping his flesh. Clyde had first tried to go for his pistol, but his partner quickly grabbed his arm. Thus, he had to be content with kicking the black, who finally gave up trying to crawl away and just sank in an unconscious bloody pile at the edge of the sidewalk several yards down the street from where he had fallen. Getting some control over himself finally, but still cursing, Clyde ordered two of the blacks from the crowd that had gathered at a safe distance around the scene to pick the beaten man up off the street and follow the other patrolman with him to the police station, where the attacker was locked up. In the meantime Clyde, with the aid of his flashlight and several black youngsters, groped about over the gravel on the street until all but one of the buttons ripped off his shirt by his assailant had been found. Leaving the back street, the tall policeman walked over to the Morgan House where he had Willie Lee, the shoeshine boy working the stand in the barber shop of the town's lone hotel, wash the blood and dirt off his boots and put a fresh coat of polish and shine to them. This having been done to his satisfaction, Clyde then walked back to the police station, where he telephoned his wife to bring from home another one of his drycleaned uniform shirts. He sat around fuming until the shirt had been delivered and once donning it, and against the wishes of his station superiors, stomped out and back around to the Alley with more fire in his soul than ever—and this time alone.

But the back street's patrons, from years of experience, knew the Man would be back, and most of them had gone home when Clyde arrived this time. Sam's was the only place around here left open and the café's few remaining customers sat or stood quietly listening to the sound of the Man's boots kicking aside the gravel on the Alley, walking from one end of the small block to the other end . . . searching for that one missing button. No one in the café was to ever know whether or not Clyde came up with that one missing button, but one thing he did come up with on that night was the nickname of "Boots." The echo of those steel-plated heels and toes kicking aside gravel resounded down the Alley, into Sam's, and through the thoughts and conversations of Sam's late-night customers, who spoke in hushed tones as they pictured in their minds the light of the full moon glittering eerily up and down the sides and across the toes of those "nigger-stomping" boots.

Boots's stomping victim lived, but the back street crowd had gotten their first dose of bitter medicine from the tall bottle that held what was to prove a limitless supply, from Yankee Town. Following the missing-button incident, Boots stepped up his walking patrols on the Alley as his arrest record began to soar. Monday mornings now found the jailhouse with practically standing-room only as Boots locked up any black who he considered had given him so much as a look of "disrespect." Matters soon reached the point that when black husbands and sons didn't arrive home after Sam's Saturday night closing-time, their womenfolk would pack their food and bring it down to the town's jailhouse on Sunday morning where they, the missing, were more often found than not.

Boots soon began expanding his one-man harassment of the blacks by frequently riding through Dark Town (though always in the company of another patrolman, as the son of Ezra never ventured into the town's black community alone), raiding those houses known for harboring bootleg liquor, gambling, and whores. He even took to stopping blacks on the street, or in their motor vehicles or wagons, to search them for whiskey (including the smell of it), knives, razors, pistols, dice, playing cards, prophylactics, and pictures of white girls clipped from magazines and carried in wallets or loosely in pockets. And if any of these items were found on the suspect or in his car or wagon, an arrest would follow. Overnight and singlehandedly Boots had descended upon Appalachee and struck fear into the very heart of the black community and within a year of his joining the police force many blacks from outside the town had stopped coming in altogether. And most of those who dared venture into the county seat would take care of their business and get off the street before sundown. Saturday nights now found the Alley deserted except for the crowd over at Sam's. This crowd—predominantly male except for a handful of women whose reputations became soiled the moment they first set foot in the place—was a bullheaded bunch who accepted the fact that Boots was a nigger-hating white man and that the only difference between his kind and other whites was that he carried a pistol. And this bunch was determined not to let any cracker spoil their one night in town each week, even if it did mean getting their heads busted by the Man's blackjack or face kicked in from his steel-plated nigger stompers or, at best, spending the weekend in jail. Yes, they were a bunch of mean motherfuckers.

Following the death of his wife, Sam had started opening the café on Sunday in an effort to stay busy and keep to a minimum the time he spent sitting upstairs in his room alone. A fairly good crowd would frequent the café on Sunday and it was on a Sunday that the crowning blow was struck in the battle between the county blacks and Appalachee's one-man law. It was now the spring of 1936, and during Boots's nearly four years on the police force he had been able to cow down every single black he had come in contact with. But he hadn't yet come up against the town's biggest and toughest nigger, Big Man Thompson, who had just begun hanging out at Sam's late in the year before. Upon first seeing Big Man in the café, Boots couldn't help but notice the size of this new nigger and the policeman sensed right away the awe and respect the other blacks in the place had for the big man. And now whenever Boots went stomping into the café, everyone in the place would freeze in their places except one, Big Man Thompson, who would always be sitting playing pool as if he, his opponent, and the board and pieces were all that were in the room. Boots would always stop a few feet from where the game was in progress and stare down at the heads of the players. And whenever this happened, Big Man's opponent, no matter who, would look up nervously at the policeman before bowing his head and fidget about in his chair until Boots took his customary spit upon the floor, turn on his heels, and stomp out. But the big black one would never raise his eyes up from the board during this entire ceremony. And this simple fact soon began irking Boots, who believed firmly that anytime a white man walked among blacks, all their eyes should turn in respect toward him before they bowed heads. But the big black one never once looked up from his poo!board and in the back of his mind Boots knew that someday he and that big black scarry-faced nigger boy were going to have to lay the real raw red meat out on the table between one another. And in the spring of '36, the meat was laid out.

Shortly after coming on duty late on that fateful Easter Sunday afternoon, Boots had once again been mildly cautioned by Chief Wade about having the lockup too full of niggers from the night before. In a huff the son of Ezra strode out of the station and headed for what had become his second home, the Alley. In fact he spent so much of his on-duty hours on the back street that in kidding among themselves many of the town's whites at the time were saying that the policeman was slowly becoming "half-colored." And with Chief Wade's words still ringing in his ears, Boots stalked down the Alley and into Sam's in a redder rage than usual. Stomping his way to the center of the room, the red-faced, scowling policeman looked around the café until his eyes came to rest on the back of the broad black neck of Big Man as he sat playing pool with a fellow Dark Townsman.

"Ain' no checkah play'n 'lowed in heah on Sunday!" At long last words had been spoken by Appalachee's Man aimed directly at Dark Town's King, who greeted them with silence.

But as soon as Big Man's pool partner heard the Man's words he quickly jumped up from the table where the game was in progress and shuffled over to stand with bowed head alongside the wall on the Town Niggers' side of the room. Big Man continued to sit and stare down at the poolboard as if he was contemplating his next move and hadn't heard the words of the Man, or even noticed that he was now playing the game alone. (That was the way it seemed to the seven or eight people who were in the café that day, including Sam, though to anyone who listened to all the later versions of the story it must have seemed that at least half the blacks in the county had been present.) Big Man kept looking at the board, then proceeded to move one of his pieces.

"Gotdamnit, nigger! Ah said no checkah play'n in heah on Sunday!" Boots had quickly covered the few feet separating the two men while spewing these words of the law, and before anyone else in the place fully realized what was happening, one of the policeman's glossy black boots had flashed upward, sending the café's lone dining table crashing over with Big Man's homemade wooden poolboard and bottle caps going down with it. Now anyone who knew Big Man could've called Boots aside and told him in a nice sort of way that the black King of Dark Town didn't mind being cussed at a little, or even being called nigger from time to time, just so long as he felt no harm was meant. But nobody went around mistreating Big Man's poolboard . . . not even the white Man. The next thing everyone in the place knew was that Boots was lying flat out on his ass on the floor up near the front door, where Big Man had sent him flying with one blow from the back of his big fist. Then things began happening even faster. So fast in fact that it seemed no one present (or absent) on that day was ever able to tell the straight of things. There were those who said that after getting up from his chair, Big Man started walking towards the fallen Man, lying with face red with surprise, fear, and blood, to reach the front door at the policeman's back and get out of the café. And then there were those who swore that Big Man was walking up to the downed Man with the intentions of stomping the living shit out of him, for if this had not been the case, these believers contended, then Dark Town's King never would have gone and left his poolboard lying there on the floor where somebody was liable to step on it. However, no one was to ever learn the King's real intentions, because the moment the frightened Boots looked up and saw the giant approaching him, he was somehow able from where he lay to whip out his pistol and pump six bullets into Big Man's wide body. But even carrying all of this lead, the King, like a big bear, continued advancing towards Boots, who after firing his last shot somehow managed to scramble up and reach the front door just ahead of Big Man.

At the precise moment that the Man's ass first made contact with the floor Little Bit was walking slowly past the café on her way home from a short day's work. She often took the route past Sam's in the secret hope of getting a glimpse of her husband, sober and playing pool over on Blackshear's front porch. She suddenly stopped in her tracks at the sound of gunshots from inside Sam's. Then, for reasons unknown to her, the little woman turned quickly and ran toward the café. Halfway inside the front door she ran headlong into Boots who was trying to get out. Little Bit was running at such speed that when she hit the Man she sent him reeling back inside, where pandemonium had broken loose, everyone running about trying to find a way out of the café—other than through the front door, where Boots now stood clutching his still-smoking pistol. The first sight to catch Little Bit's eye was the huge figure of her husband standing in the middle of the café with a dazed look on his face. And although there was no sign of blood, Little Bit took one look at him and knew instantly that there was something all wrong with her Big Man. Screaming out his name, she ran up to her husband and tried to wrap her arms around him . . . her hands couldn't quite reach all the way around, but far enough to feel the blood gushing from those six bullet holes opening up his back.

"*Big Main . . . Big Main! Wha' dey dun dun to mah Big Main?*"

"De Main kicked ovah mah poolbode den shot me, Li'l Baby."

"*Wha' main?*"

"De law Main dar."

All the time she was crying and talking to her husband, Little Bit was slowly steering his big bulk over to the bench running along the wall on the Town Niggers' side of the room. Finally managing to get her heavy burden seated, the now frantic little woman opened her handbag and took out a freshly washed white handkerchief with which she began wiping from her husband's face the beads of perspiration covering his skin like great blisters. Not knowing what else to do for her Big Man, who she knew was dying right there in her arms, Little Bit began looking around the room in a desperate search for someone else's help. That was when for the first time she noticed Boots. The policeman appeared to be in a state of shock as he stood with blood running down the bottom of his face from what looked to be a broken nose and with long strands of blond hair hanging down from his bare head, partially covering a pair of glassy eyes aimed in the direction of the black man and woman. The front of his uniform was slightly ruffled, though no buttons were noticeably missing, and in his right hand he still clutched his now-empty pistol.

The moment Little Bit's eyes fell on the blue-clad figure of the Man, her hand automatically dropped down into her open handbag, to the handle of the razor she had gone back to carrying following her and Big Man's breakup some seven months earlier.

"*Gotdamn mu'fuck'n cracker!*" Screaming these words at the top of her voice, the little black woman tore away from the side of her dying husband and went straight for Boots. These incestuous words snapped the policeman out of his stupor enough for him to instinctively take a step backwards . . . yet not quite far enough. With one swipe of her razor the southpaw-swinging Little Bit carved a streak down the right side of the policeman's face, beginning just above the eyebrow and extending downward to the middle of his smooth pink cheek. Boots let out a piglike squeal, but before his attacker could strike again he had brought up the pistol he held in his right hand and slammed her alongside the head with the barrel. Quickly recovering from the surprise attack, Boots then took the butt of the weapon and with it began pounding Little Bit about the head while she was still off balance. The tough little black woman tried to fight back but the blows from the pistol had stunned her as she groped about with eyes fast becoming blinded by her own blood, trying to get out of reach of the crazed, swinging policeman and yet land another score of her own with her razor. And every time Boots landed with his pistol on her head she would call him a "motherfucking cracker" until finally the blows proved too much even for her to take and she crumpled slowly to the floor. Then Boots sent his boots into action and began kicking the woman from one end of the café floor to the other, but the more and harder he kicked the tough little Dark Town Queen, the louder she screamed "motherfucking cracker!"

When Little Bit dropped to the hardwood, Big Man, still sitting on the bench staring out across the room through fog covered eyes, began calling out his wife's name before trying to rise and toppling over face first onto the floor, bringing the Town Niggers' bench with him. Still calling Little Bit, he started crawling toward her while she dodged across the floor a few feet away from his outstretched hands, trying to get out from under those swinging black boots. And that was the last thing Big Man Thompson, the King of Dark Town, was to ever see in this world . . . those steel-plated and now red-smeared motherfucking nigger-stomping black boots of the Man crashing down upon the blood-covered head of his "Li'l Baby."

Olive Ann Burns

From *Cold Sassy Tree*

11

Mama didn't come down to dinner at all after Papa told her Grandpa and Miss Love had run off to Jefferson together.

I wasn't hungry, and Papa's appetite was down, too, judging by the way he picked at his food and picked at making conversation.

He had a habit at meals of telling things he'd heard at the store or read in the paper. But whereas I thought the big news today was Grandpa's eloping, the first thing Papa said was something about the average life span in America being forty-seven years.

Thinking any minute he would tell me what was really on his mind, I just said, "I declare." But what little he talked, it was about other things. Like for instance Papa said old man Plunket told him the train hit a mule and a cow at the same time yesterday just outside of Cold Sassy. "Killed'm both," Papa said, and reached for the pully-bone, my favorite piece of fried chicken except for the head. "And might-near wrecked the train."

By then I was just barely listening, because it had dawned on me that our time of mourning must be about over. If Grandpa could go get married, maybe I could go fishing.

Well, I'd just go. Today. I'd go to Cussin' Creek. Leave just soon as Papa went back to the store.

I never did like to fish by myself. So after whistling my dog out of the garden, where he was digging a hole to lay in and get cool, I went by the Predmore house to find Pink.

"He ain't to home," his little brother Harkness told me. "Him and Daddy rode the train down to Athens this mornin'."

Pink's mother was in the yard, hanging out clothes. "I was hopin' Pink could go fishin' with me," I told her.

"Well, he's gone to Athens."

"That's what Harkness said."

Mrs. Predmore didn't even mention Grandpa and Miss Love, so likely Mama was all wrong about folks being scandalized.

But when I got to Smiley Snodgrass's house I found out Mama was likely right. "What's this I heerd 'bout yore granddaddy, Will?" asked Mrs. Snodgrass, wiping her hands on her long white apron as she came to the door.

I couldn't tell how much she knew, so I just said, "I don't know'm."

"When they gittin' hitched? Not any time soon, I reckon."

"I don't know'm." They were already hitched, more than likely.

"I hear tell Loma's bad-mouthin' thet Simpson woman all over town. You cain't blame her." She waited for me to say something. When I didn't, she said, "Pore Loma. Pore Mary Willis. What a cross to bear, and Miss Mattie Lou not hardly cold in the grave. How's yore ma a-takin' it, Will?"

I couldn't make out whether Mrs. Snodgrass was embarrassed for pore Loma and pore Mary Willis or if she was thinking Mama and Aunt Loma would be pore in the future if Miss Love got aholt of their inheritance. One thing I did know, my mother sure would be upset when she found out Aunt Loma was talking outside the family—especially now that there wasn't any chance of changing Grandpa's mind. Mama thought private family matters ought to be just that. Private.

"Mama's takin' it all right, I s'pose," I said, as if widowers getting hitched right after the funeral was an everyday thing.

"I betcher Son Black's madder'n a wet hen, losin' Miss Love to a old man."

"I don't know'm. . . . Miz Snodgrass, where's Smiley at?"

"Down to the barn, cleanin' out the stalls. Bein' punished for back talk, so don't you go git him to slip off. You hear?"

"Oh, no, ma'am." I backed off the porch. Knowing that Mrs. Snodgrass would likely watch to make sure I left, I struck off down the street, pitching sticks for T.R. to go fetch. But after passing by the French Gordy house next door, I ducked around back to the Gordy stable and went through it to the pasture.

Mr. French had three cows. One of them, a tan Jersey named Blind Tillie, was Cold Sassy's champion milk producer. Born with milk-glass eyes, she was named for Blind Tillie Creek, where I sometimes fished. She always walked with her chin resting on the rump of another cow. That day, Tillie and the other two cows and I were all headed for a big oak tree near the barb wire fence, on the other side of which the Snodgrass's mule-headed Jersey cow had already laid down to chew her cud in the shade.

I crawled under the barb wire, stepped around a wet cow splat, and headed for the Snodgrass barn. There was old Smiley, leaning against a fence beside a big pile of manure, staring at the sky with his mouth open and his hands resting on the pitchfork handle—dreaming about girls, most likely. Seeing a pile of dried horse biscuits, I got me one and threw it just as Smiley's mouth stretched in a wide yawn. It went in nice and neat, like a baseball into a glove.

Boy, was he mad. He and I had us a great manure war then, throwing dried cow cushions and sheep pills and horse biscuits at each other and dying laughing. Just as I was fixing to talk about fishing, Mrs. Snodgrass yelled from over near the smokehouse for Smiley to come catch her a chicken. So that was the end of that.

Lee Roy Sleep was still out of town. He and his folks were up in the mountains at Tallulah Falls, visiting his grandmother. I thought about Dunson McCall, but remembered Dunse was picking peaches for Mr. Angus Tuttle, the depot man, who had an orchard out on the edge of town.

Mr. Tuttle hadn't offered me a picking job since that time us boys pulled up an acre of his onion crop to dam the stream between his pasture and ours. We were making a swimming hole. Our daddies paid for the onions and we all worked out the money, but Mr. Tuttle never forgave us.

Well, so I didn't have a soul to go fishing with but T.R.

T.R.'s real name was Theodore Roosevelt. He was just a puppy when Papa took me to Atlanta to hear the president speak; I named him Theodore Roosevelt when I got home that day—then shortened it to T.R. so folks wouldn't think my dog was a Republican.

Naturally I didn't carry a fishing pole. No use looking disrespectful of the dead. In one pocket of my overalls I had me a line, and my sinkers and my hooks stuck in a cork. Stuffed in another pocket were some biscuits, to wad up into dough balls to bait the hooks with, and five pieces of Queenie's fried chicken in case I got hungry. I would cut a pole at the creek.

Cussin' Creek was where us boys usually fished when an hour or two was all we had between chores. It wasn't far. Just a piece down the railroad tracks near Mr. Son Black's farm. Our train was a branch line of the Southern Railroad, which ran north from Athens through Cold Sassy, Commerce, and Maysville, connecting at Lula Junction with the Airline Railroad, which went on to Atlanta and Charlotte. I would get on the tracks at the depot just past the Cold Sassy tree.

That tree was close to a hundred feet tall and the only sassafras still left of the big grove our town was named for. On a bright fall day when the sun lit up its scarlet leaves, you never saw anything to equal it. People would ride the train to Cold Sassy just to look. Usually they'd read the plaque that was nailed to its trunk: "Sassafras: family *Lauraceae*, genus *Sassafras*, species *S. albidum*. Note how the leaves vary in shape on the same twig, some having no lobes, some two or three." Considering the number of train travelers we had, I thought the plaque ought to tell how unusual tall the tree was and something about how Cold Sassy got its name.

We used to have another big sassafras tree, which stood next to this one and had a knothole where bluebirds nested. Us boys used to rob the nest of its bluish-white eggs and blow out the insides. The railroad had taken that sassafras down some years earlier to make room for a bigger depot platform.

I saw Mr. Angus Tuttle out there on the platform now, but he didn't see me. He was too busy arguing with a fat old farmer in overalls. Like all depot agents, Mr. Tuttle was cow coroner for the railroad, so I guessed right off that this was the farmer whose cow and mule got killed yesterday. Death by train isn't unusual out in the country. Farmers don't keep their livestock tied or pastured up like we do in town. I gathered from the argument, which was getting pretty loud, that the farmer was mad about the amount Mr. Tuttle had offered to settle the claim against the railroad. I could still hear those two fussing after I passed the foundry, but then everything got drowned out as the 1:10 from Athens approached.

Stepping off the tracks to let it pass, I watched as the engine screeched and ground to a halt at the depot, belching smoke and steam. Back on the tracks and heading toward open country, I had a thought. "T.R., hot day like this, ain't no fish go'n bite at Cussin' Creek." I remembered then that Queenie's husband, big Loomis, said they were biting real good now under the trestle at Blind Tillie Creek.

There were hazards. The shortest way to get there was to follow the tracks in the opposite direction, which would not only take me back past the depot but also past our house and Grandpa's store, where I might be seen. Also, I'd have to go through Mill Town.

I had walked through Mill Town plenty of times, but never by myself.

I was about to call it a dern fool idea when it came to mind I might see Lightfoot McLendon. I hadn't laid eyes on her since school let out for the summer. Whistling to T.R., I turned and headed back—past the foundry, past Grandpa's house, past the Cold Sassy tree and the depot, past our house, which I detoured around, and on toward the hotel and the block of stores.

Walking along, I wondered about Grandpa and Miss Love. When would they get back? Would she come in and work on her hats, or would Grandpa drop her off at his house so she could sweep up some and cook his supper? Or since he was used to eating supper at Aunt Loma's, would they both go over there tonight?

I wondered if an old man who just buried his wife would take his bride on a wedding trip. I decided he wouldn't. Not just because of being stingy but also because, at fifty-nine, Grandpa had his mind on the store and not on what Queenie called "de sweet'nin' on de gingercake."

Well, right now my problem was not Grandpa and Miss Love but how I would get past the batch of stores without Papa and them seeing me, or old Crazy Tatum, who always sat in a rocking chair by the door to keep people out of his store. He put the chair just inside if it was cold, and out on the sidewalk if it was summer. If it looked like you might try to come in, he'd flap his arms like a bird and leap around, hollering and whooping. I knew if he went to whooping at me, Papa might chance to look out the store window and wonder why I wasn't weeding the garden like he said to.

I had figured on going behind the brick stores till I was clear of them, but when I saw the 1:10 leave the depot, headed towards us on its way to Lula, I whistled to T.R. and got off the tracks on the South Main side. Seeing me, the engineer put an arm big as a leg of mutton out the window and waved.

Since the store was across the tracks on North Main, we were hidden behind the moving boxcars, and I decided to keep on walking. The train was so long that before all of it passed us we were beyond the stores, the Confederate monument, the livery stable, the tanyard, the cotton gin, and Sleep's Ice and Coal, and nearly to Mill Town.

The factory soon came in view and, just beyond it, the river that powered the machines. On a railroad siding off the main tracks, men in linty overalls were loading big pasteboard boxes full of cotton thread onto a freight car. At a huge square opening in the factory wall, other men were taking bales of cotton off of a wagon. I recognized old Charlie Rowley up there on the driver's bench of the wagon. Old Charlie and his mule were both string-halted, each having a tight ligament in the leg that made him limp. But that didn't keep them from hauling for Grandpa's big warehouse—delivering to the mill or depot when farmers who stored their cotton with us finally sold it.

Charlie saw me and waved, and I waved back. Too late, I realized if he saw Papa later he might chance to mention seeing me on the train tracks going through Mill Town.

Hurrying by the factory, I came to where the mill hands lived in close-together little shotgun houses—three rooms in a row, like long boxes, with public wells and privies that served two or three houses each.

Cold Sassy was proud of its cotton mill, just as it was proud of the trains coming through. "Get you a railroad" and "Get you a cotton mill" was what big businessmen in Atlanta advised any town that wanted to grow. Having both, we were bound to grow, but Grandpa said he didn't see how the population could change any. "Ever time a baby's born, some boy joins the Navy." Still, Cold Sassy was considered up-and-coming. And like I said, already folks were talking about changing its name to something less countrified, the way Jugtown had been renamed Winder, and Garden Valley was now Pendergrass, and just four years ago Harmony Grove became Commerce—all of which, to my mind and Grandpa's, were awful improvements.

Our mill houses were a long sight better than in lots of places, but they looked more like repeating blobs of white than homes. There weren't any trees. No shrubbery. Families sat crowded on the hot little porches, cotton lint from twelve hours in the mill still clinging to their hair and overalls and dresses. I guessed they were night workers who hadn't gone to bed yet. Who could go to bed in those little houses on a hot day in July?

I kept glancing at the blank, stony, pinched faces of the men and women staring at me from steps and doorways, and at the children, all white-headed just like you see them in the Appalachians. They stared at me with sullen, mean eyes, like I was a strange animal. But whenever I looked right at them, their gaze dropped to the ground.

Mill Town was watching the Town Boy pass.

Nervous, I hurried my steps on the crossties. And T.R., who'd been running ahead like a brown and white flash, now walked stiff-legged close beside me, growling at any bony mangy dog that slunk too near. I went from hoping I'd see Lightfoot to hoping I wouldn't. It was one thing to like her at school and nobody know it. Here in Mill Town on my crosstie stage, folks would suspicion her if they saw me acting friendly. Also, I knew I'd be embarrassed if she was sweaty and lint-headed from the factory or if, Lord forbid, I saw her coming out of a privy.

I decided it was a lot harder to walk through Mill Town than to have our school cluttered up with snot-nosed children who had cooties and the itch, and who at dinnertime stayed at school to eat biscuits and syrup, making us town children feel guilty for going home to a big hot dinner. The mill boys were always picking fights with town boys—tripping us up or calling us names. Of course we did our share of tripping and worse. But it was our dern school, for gosh sake.

Before Lightfoot, I had a healthy disrespect for all mill children. Since Lightfoot, just being around them was like getting fussed at for wearing shoes in winter and having a cow and a family cook.

Lightfoot wasn't like the other mill children. Wasn't like any girl I ever knew, for that matter. Wasn't silly, wasn't always twiddling her plaits, didn't tattle or gossip, didn't hit boys over the head with books or scrape the back of your neck with a sweetgum burr when you weren't looking. She was quiet and sweet and smart. Ragged, of course, but real clean, and thin without having the bony-faced, sunk-eyed look of mill children who've been hungry all their lives. Lightfoot had what I thought of as the fresh free look of the hills on her.

The way I got to really know her, I had to stay after school one day for flipping spitballs, and she was staying late so Miss Neppie could help her catch up. This was back in January, soon after she came to Cold Sassy from the foothills of the Blue Ridge. At some point, when Miss Neppie went to Mr. McCall's office, I asked Lightfoot how come she left the mountains. "My mama always wanted us to move to Cold Sassy," she said. "My mama she had the TB, you know. Last summer, jest fore she passed, she wrote her brother in Mill Town and he said we was more'n welcome to stay with them. Mama kept sayin' Pa would have steady work in the mill and I could git me a good education and amount to something."

The girl didn't seem to have heard yet that nobody in Mill Town ever amounted to anything.

"So after the fall crop come in, my daddy he sold his plowin' steer and his piece a-land, and we caught the train to Cold Sassy."

"You got any brothers and sisters in the mountains?" I asked.

"Yeah, lots of'm. But they all married or dead, one."

As T.R. and I walked the railroad tracks past the sweaty, dirty, hostile faces of Mill Town, I couldn't help wondering if a summer of slaving at the spindles would take away Lightfoot's hopes—and my notion that she walked in a cloud of fresh mountain air. Fixing my eyes on the repeating crossties, I walked fast. And even faster as it dawned on me just how much I didn't want to see Lightfoot McLendon with lint in her hair.

I also didn't want to see Hosie Roach, a snot-nosed twenty-one-year-old mill boy in my class who stunk like a polecat and had tow-colored hair so thick and tangled it looked like a cootie stable. Hosie wasn't big as me, but whenever we had a fight—about once a week—he usually won. Gosh, what if he and a bunch of other mill boys ganged up on me.

Getting beat to a pulp might have been better than what happened later at the trestle. But of course I didn't know it at the time, so it was a grand relief when my dog and I got past all chance of seeing Hosie or Lightfoot, either one.

Once we were out in the country, we had a high old time. The dog romped through the daisies and weeds and tall grasses growing along the tracks. He scared up rabbits, barked at terrapins, caught gnats and flies in his mouth, and every few minutes looked back to be sure I was still coming along behind. Two bobwhites scooted across the tracks right in front of us, heads up and backs straight as tin soldiers', but they flushed before T.R. could point.

That dog must of wet every black-eyed Susan and every head of white Queen Anne's lace we passed. I never saw such a dog for doing Number One. Grandpa called it the sweet-pee trick. I know that's how dogs stake out territory and also how they find their way home, but looks like T.R. would know by now that all we had to do to go home was turn around and follow the train tracks.

Two or three times he stopped and stared back like he thought somebody was coming behind us. But then he would lower his head for a new scent and run ahead.

We saw a few mill people near the tracks, picking blackberries into lard buckets, and a whole family of colored people. The Negroes smiled and waved and held up their buckets for me to see. The mill people didn't.

It was hot, good gosh. My straw hat shaded my eyes, but that was all in the world good it did. "I guess I got about two hours," I muttered out loud. I knew the southbound train would cross the trestle over Blind Tillie Creek about when I ought to head home to milk.

You couldn't exactly tell time by that train, but it would be close enough. It always came back through Cold Sassy with a load of lumber from the sawmill at Lula, bound for the lumberyard in Athens, and usually there were some passenger cars carrying folks who'd been to Atlanta. In the fall there were always cotton buyers, and usually four or five drummers who would set up their merchandise in a hotel room, stay a few days, then move on to another little town. Grandpa called them "Knights of the Grip." When Mama and Aunt Loma were young, he never let them hang around the depot. Drummers liked to flirt, were fresh-shaved, and wore suits, patent leather shoes, and big smiles. Girls always liked them.

Less than a mile past Mill Town, I rounded a bend and saw the train trestle up ahead, marching through the air high above the wooded gorge where Blind Tillie Creek ran. Just before we got to the trestle I whistled for my dog and went slipping and sliding down a red-dirt path, past dusty briar bushes that reached out to scratch me as I ate my fill of blackberries.

It was a sight cooler by the creek than up there on the tracks. I cut me a pole and was soon perched on a stump, fishing and eating fried chicken. Later I cut a blackgum twig to chew on and settled myself comfortable on the ground with the stump for a back rest.

It was nice and peaceful there. Watching the shallow water splash and churn over rocks, I almost forgot how mad I was at Mama for making me stay in mourning, how mad I was at her and Aunt Loma for fussing about Grandpa marrying when he clearly needed a housekeeper, and how mad I was at him and Miss Love for not caring how the family felt. But then I got mad at Papa. Here I was at last—fishing—and I couldn't enjoy it for feeling guilty.

I had sense enough to know my daddy really needed me to be home working the garden. But I wished he knew what it felt like to have fun. All Papa had ever done was work. Before he was knee-high to a gnat, his own daddy had him picking bugs off of cotton plants, and he was hoeing as soon as he knew the difference between a weed and a cotton stalk, and milking soon as his hands were big enough to squeeze a cow's tit. I bet he never in his life had sat in the shade of a train trestle holding a fishing pole and watching dragonflies walk on water.

Grandpa Blakeslee bragged a lot about my daddy being such a dandy worker. I was proud he wasn't lazy like his own daddy, who spent the summer days on his porch swatting flies and even had him a pet hen to peck up the dead ones. Grandpa Tweedy always claimed he couldn't work. "My veins is too small," he'd say. "My blood jest cain't git th'ew fast enough to let me do much." Naturally he had a beard. He was too lazy to shave. He was even too lazy and self-satisfied to go anywhere, except to preaching over at Hebron or to Cold Sassy to sell his cotton. Wasn't ever on a train but once, when he went to Dr. Mozely's funeral in Athens. All of us went, but first Grandpa Tweedy and my daddy had to decide if it was all right to ride that train. Being Sunday, it might be a sin.

Like Grandpa Tweedy, Papa worried all the time about sin on Sunday. He never let us read anything but the Bible and the *Christian Observer* on the Sabbath, and once talked Mr. Tuttle into locking up everybody's Sunday Atlanta papers at the depot till Monday morning. The fact that Cold Sassy put up with that for a month or more shows how much they respected my father. I respected him, too, as I said before. But I wished he knew what it felt like to need to go fishing.

My bait was gone again. I wasn't going to catch anything here. It was too hot and the creek too low. Might as well go home and get to work. But glancing around, I saw a mess of logs and brush on the other side and remembered the deep hole there. If any fish were in Blind Tillie Creek, that's where I'd catch them. I was just fixing to get up and wade across when I chanced to look up at the train trestle.

I had walked trestles plenty of times. I used to play on one out in Banks County with Cudn Doodle and them. But I'd never been on Blind Tillie Trestle. From where I sat, leaning against my tree stump and looking up, it seemed higher than a Ferris wheel. Higher even than the new Century Building in Atlanta, and it spanned a wide, deep gorge.

Miss Bertha at school had told us about the si-renes—the mermaids who used to sing to Greek sailors and they'd go off course to follow. Looking at that trestle, I felt like I was being sung to. Or maybe it was more like when the fire bells clang on Cold Sassy's horse-drawn fire engine and you just got to go chasing after it to where the smoke is billowing up.

That's how Blind Tillie Trestle called to me that day.

The longer I stared up at it and the blue sky and fleecy clouds beyond, the more it seemed like a bridge across the world. I wanted to see how things looked from up there. I don't even remember winding the fishing line around my pole, but all of a sudden I was clambering up the bank. Old T.R. raced me to the top and then barked at me till I got up there.

At the edge of the trestle, a brisk breeze had whipped up, and the tracks seemed to soar across the sky.

It never once occurred to me to be scared. But it occurred to the dog.

12

Following behind me, T.R. crouched low and took a few careful steps onto the trestle. Then, whining, he turned and crawled back to solid ground, tail behind his legs, and commenced begging me to come back, too.

When the dog saw I was laughing at him, he wet on the rail,

scratched with his back paws in the dirt, and dashed off, trying to get me to play chase. After that didn't work, he bounded down the brambly path to the creek below, where we had just come from, and splashed over to the other side, trying to show me a better way to get there. Standing in the shallow water, T.R. barked and bragged his white-tipped tail like he'd done something to get praised for.

"Old yeller belly!" I called down to him, laughing. My voice echoed spooky between trestle and water and gorge. I sure wished Pink Predmore and them were up here with me.

I put one bare foot on the rail. It was hot but not enough to burn, so I walked on it a piece, arms spread-eagle, balancing with my fishing pole like a tightrope-walker at the circus. I remember wondering if any birds ever walked through the sky up there instead of flying over the gorge. I soon passed the sand barrel that was bolted onto the trestle beside the tracks. People have been known to jump into a trestle barrel if a train comes at the wrong time and they get trapped.

Two thirds of the way across, I stepped off the rail onto a crosstie and sat down, elbows on knees, to look around. I thought about putting a penny on the tracks for the train to flatten, then decided not to. The penny would fall in the creek. So I just sat there, looking way off, and tried to think who lived in that little white farmhouse with green shutters down in the valley. From up here the house looked like a fresh-painted toy. I wondered why nobody ever painted their houses out in Banks County, where Grandpa Tweedy lived. He didn't know what a can of paint looked like.

Enjoying the breeze, I stretched out, face down, to look through the crossties at the water below. Leaves floated on the creek like tiny boats. And here came a long stick, a wake trailing behind it. When the stick turned against the current to swim toward the bank, I saw it was a water moccasin and threw a cinder at it. I missed the snake, but my next cinder hit the white spot on old T.R.'s rump. He barked at me till he got distracted by a big terrapin crawling on the creek bank.

It sure beat being in mourning.

All of a sudden I saw T.R. raise his head to listen. Then he dashed up the path on the far side of the creek, barking all the way, and went to jumping around at the edge of the trestle. He like to had a fit for me to come on. Shoot, you'd think he heard the train or something. Wasn't near time for the train. I didn't hear anything myself except that dern dog barking.

But just to make sure, I moved my head over to the rail and put an ear against it, lazy-like, and—I could hear the clickety-clack! The train was coming! Well, I could make it easy. But as I scrambled to my feet, the fishing pole got wedged somehow between the rail and crosstie. Couldn't leave it that way. Might derail the train. By the time I got it loose, the clickety-clacks were plain as day and getting louder, *louder,* LOUDER!

I stumbled and fell. Jerking myself up, I saw I couldn't possibly get off the trestle before the train moved onto it. Like a fox who runs into a hound, I turned and sprinted the other way. From somewhere, as in a dream, I heard a scream and looked back just as the big smoking engine roared around a bend.

I knew the engineer saw me. His whistle was going *whoo-whoo-whoo* in quick fast blasts. The trestle shook like a leaf as the train hit it.

I thought to aim for the sand barrel.

God A'mighty help me, I wasn't go'n make it! *Jump!* No, too far, creek too low. . . . Whistle screeching in my ears. . . . Train heat almost at my heels. . . . *Whoo-whoo-whoo!*

At that moment I thought FALL!

Like a doll pushed from behind, I fell face down between the rails and lay flat and thin as I could, head low between crossties, arms stretched overhead. As I was swallowed up in fire and thunder, I hugged my arms tight against my ears.

The engine's roar pierced my eardrums anyway, making awful pain. I was so scared I could hardly breathe, and there was a strong smell of heated creosote. Hot cinders spit on me from the firebox. Yet even as the boxcars clacked, knocked, strained, ground, and groaned overhead, it came to me that I wasn't dead. If there wasn't a dragging brake beam to rip me down the back, I was go'n make it!

Boy howdy, I did some fancy praying. All it amounted to was "God save me! Please God save me!" And then it was "Thank you, Lord, thank you, God, thank you, sir. . . ." I guess what made it seem fancy was the strange peaceful feeling I got, as if the Lord had said, "Well done, thou good and faithful servant," or something like that. I wasn't dead! Boy howdy, boy howdy, boy howdy! I was buried alive in noise, and the heat and cinders stung my neck and legs and the bottoms of my feet. Still and all, that was what kept reminding me I wasn't dead.

I found myself counting boxcars, by the sound of them, which was a long sight different in this position, with my eyes shut tight against the dust and cinders, from being in Cold Sassy waiting for the train to get by so I could cross from South Main to North Main. The train had to end. Trains always do. It seemed like this one never would, but brakes were screeching and the clickety-clacks on the rails were slowing, so I knew the engineer was trying to stop.

I felt blistered from the heat. My straw hat was gone. My arms were so tight against my head that my ears felt numb, yet it wouldn't have hurt more if knives were being jabbed into my eardrums.

But boy howdy, I was alive! Thank you, Jesus.

All of a sudden I felt sunshine overhead. Opening my eyes and raising my head, I saw the red caboose getting smaller and smaller as it neared the end of the trestle. The shaking of the trestle stopped. All sounds were muted, as if I had a wad of thick cotton in both ears or was shut up in a padded closet. I felt limp and dizzy. And as knowledge of what could of happened hit me, I started shaking and crying.

I heard T.R. barking from what seemed like far off, but all of a sudden his tongue was on my face! By gosh, he had run out over that trestle he was so scared of! I grabbed and hugged him, crying, "Good ole dog, good ole T.R.!"

When the train finally stopped, its caboose was maybe a hundred feet beyond the trestle. Just then, despite being deafened, I heard a girl's voice scream out, "Will! Will Tweedy! You awright, Will?"

And then she was on the trestle running toward me, her arms outstretched. "I'm a-comin', Will!" she called. "I'm go'n holp you!"

13

The girl running toward me was Lightfoot McLendon, which didn't surprise me at all. If you've been run over by a train and you're alive to know it, what can surprise you after that?

She ran over the crossties barefooted, surefooted, lightfooted like her name. I wanted to quit crying and shivering, but what did it matter, anyhow? I was alive!

I no longer felt so boy-howdy about it, though. I was numb, I was half-deaf, I was sick, shaking, stinging, and smudged with dirt and oil. I fixed my eyes on Lightfoot as if she was one of Granny's angels come to fetch me, and put my arms tight around T.R. He crowded me—licking, wagging, whimpering. When Lightfoot reached us, I grabbed her, too, and the dog licked both faces. Hers and mine, hers, mine, hers, mine. She was crying, too.

She said something that must of been "Lemme holp you up, Will," and tried to pull me to my feet. WHOOP! Both of us nearly toppled off into the creek below. I tried not to look down.

"I don't . . . I cain't . . . I don't know if I can stand up," I mumbled. My voice came out of a well inside my head. She said something I couldn't understand.

Lightfoot bent so close that her long flaxen hair brushed against my face. It was tied with a string instead of plaited and I can still remember how sparkly white it looked in the sun. She yelled into my ear, "Kin you crawl, Will? If you cain't, them men comin' out'n the train can holp you."

I looked up to see men, women, and children rushing towards the trestle, and others swinging themselves out of passenger cars. Reminded me of bugs pouring out of a rotted cantaloupe if you kick it on the ground. The sight was enough to get me moving. Nobody was go'n tote me off that trestle.

"You go on first, Lightfoot!" I yelled. I reckon I was thinking if I couldn't hear her very good, she couldn't hear me, either. "I'll come behind you!" Grabbing a rail, I pulled myself up to a squat—but didn't have the nerve to turn loose and stand up. I was still shaky. The girl stood up, but swayed and then dropped down to her hands and feet, like me, and we moved on all fours, holding to crossties. Later somebody said we looked like spiders coming off that trestle.

As we neared the end of it, there were shouts and whistles and cheers from the folks crowded there, and finally a burst of clapping. The last few steps of the way, hands reached out to pull us to our feet. Then I was caught up in the arms of a huge man wearing overalls and a train cap—the engineer who'd waved at me in Cold Sassy. Giving me a bear hug, he shouted, "God a'mighty, boy! God a'mighty!" It was like I was his own son. He'd never even seen me before that day, I don't think, but it was like I was his own son.

In bed that night, going over and over what all happened, it dawned on me that by saving myself, I had saved the train engineer from running down a life, never mind it wouldn't of been his fault. That's why he was so glad to see me.

He was still holding me tight when I looked back and saw that T.R. was right out there where we'd left him on the trestle. Yelping and whining, he crouched forlorn between the rails, yearning towards us but not moving.

"T.R.!" I yelled, pointing at him, and the crowd took it up.

"Come 'ere, boy!" a man called, giving a loud piercing whistle.

"Here, boy! Here, boy!" from someone else.

"Come on, pup, you kin make it!"

More whistles. Arms outstretched toward him. And me shaking worse than ever, too weak to yell again. The dog wouldn't budge. Howling, barking, whimpering, he finally tried to crawl, but quit when one hind leg slipped through the crossties. He just let it hang there. He was frozen.

"Won't somebody g-go get him?" I was weeping now. "That's my dog!"

But the engineer, one bulging arm still around my shoulders, suddenly yanked me towards the train. "We gotta git outer here, boy! Come on, folks, git back on the train!" he hollered. "They's another'n comin'!" Then, handing me over to the conductor, he and the fireman sprinted toward the engine, way up the tracks.

The conductor, a tiny man in a beaver hat and Prince Albert coat, was jumping up and down like a tin clown. "Make haste, folks!" he yelled, waving his hat and pushing me toward the caboose. "We had to put on two trains! Other'n will be along any minute! Got to clear the tracks!"

"I ain't go'n leave my dog!" I said, turning back.

Lightfoot sprang forward. "I'll go git him, Will!"

The conductor grabbed her. "We ain't got time! I ain't go'n let you be on that-air trestle for the next train to hit. Besides, you cain't tote that big dog, honey. You too little bitty."

A new voice swept by like a wind, deep and booming. "I's gwine git him, Mr. Will!" It was big black Loomis, Queenie's husband, six feet six and three hundred pounds, hat on and coattails flapping. Racing by me, without even slowing down he hit the trestle like it was no different from the tracks in Cold Sassy. T.R. recognized Loomis right off and started crawling in, belly scraping the crossties.

Some of the passengers rushing to get back on the train stopped to watch as Loomis loped over the trestle. It was like they were hypnotized. But the conductor and the regular train travelers sure weren't hypnotized. They kept yelling for us to come on.

As the crowd pulled and pushed me toward the cars, my head corkscrewed back just in time to see the black man swing T.R. up and drape him around his neck, like in the Bible picture of the lost lamb and the shepherd. Then I got handed up to the conductor, who stood on the steps of the caboose—Lightfoot right behind me. The conductor was screaming for folks to run on up to the other passenger cars. "Ain't room for nobody else on this here caboose!"

But they let big Loomis on. He handed up the dog. Then, ducking, he swung himself through the door just as the train lurched forward. T.R. licked my face, wagging his tail into a blur, while I and the others cheered the black giant.

Some of the passengers didn't make it back onto the train. We saw men, and women, and children pull back into the bushes and brambles as the train got rolling. They looked anxious but most smiled and waved. Those of us who were by a window waved back.

Big Loomis had moved onto the little platform at the back. I figured he didn't feel right, being in the same car with white folks, though Lord knows nobody cared right then. All of a sudden Loomis yelled, "Jesus save us, dare's dat dar udder train! He ne'ly at de trestle!"

Fear spread over faces. A lady screamed. I felt like screaming. Clapped a hand over my mouth so I couldn't. Lightfoot caught my other hand and held it tight, her eyes wide, her face gone white. Somebody yelled, "Conductor, cain't you run faster?"

The oncoming engine hit the trestle, whistle screaming WHOO-WHOO-WHOO. The question was could it be braked fast enough and could we speed up fast enough. . . . The chasing engine got bigger and bigger as the gap between us closed, then shrunk as our engineer picked up speed. The last I saw before we rounded a bend, the other train had stopped and was picking up everybody we'd left beside the tracks.

Lightfoot sat by me on the short run to Cold Sassy. T.R. lay across my feet. Loomis had come back in, and he stood with one hand on my shoulder, his black face shining with pride and sweat. Hot as he was from running, he kept on the long black jim-swing coat till he saw me shivering, and then he put it around me. Queenie had sewed that coat. Weren't any white men in town big enough to where Loomis could wear their old clothes, so she had to make nearly everything he had. The cloth smelled sweaty, but I didn't care. I didn't know there was lubricating oil on my overalls and in my hair, where it had dropped off the engine parts, and I'm afraid it got on the coat that Loomis was so proud of. Shouting above the train noise, I told him much obliged for saving T.R.

"You be's welcome, Mr. Will. You know dat."

I loved Loomis. His whole name was Annie Mae Hubert Knock-about Loomis Toy. After his mama had ten boys, she said the nex' baby gwine be name Annie Mae no matter whut. She always called him Annie Mae, but nobody else did. His daddy was owned by the Toys is how he got his last name. Loomis worked for us off and on all my life—milking till I got big enough, plowing the garden till I got big enough, fixing fences and chopping wood till I got big enough. He beamed down at me now, showing his two gold front teeth, and rolled his eyes toward Heaven. "You sho got you a frien' Up Yonder, Mr. Will. Sho nuff! I speck it cause yo daddy and mama be sech good peoples. Lawdy, Lawdy, it gwine be a happy time at yo house t'night!"

I hadn't thought that far. Good gosh, Papa would be mad as heck about my sneaking off!

The train rocked on toward Papa.

Lightfoot was scrooched up in the corner of the bench, swaying with the motion of the train. I looked over at her, red-faced from the heat and sweaty and dirty as me. Her long whitey hair hung in damp strands and there were briar scratches on her hands. Tears brimming in her blue eyes suddenly spilled over. I figured she was picturing me flattened like a penny on the trestle rails. But what she said, in a wail hard to understand over the train racket and me still part deaf, was "I left my bucket in the blackberry bushes, Will! Hit were might near full!"

I couldn't think what to say. If she hadn't rushed to help me, she wouldn't of lost the bucket, and I knew those blackberries weren't picked to make a pie with or to put up as jam or jelly or wine. They were for supper. Like as not, all else her folks would have was fried fatback, cream gravy, and corn pone.

The girl blushed, like it just dawned on her that she had let out how poor and hungry she was, and turned her face away from me.

Trying to sound like I thought berry-picking was just something she did for fun, I said, "Why'n't we go pick some more early in the mornin'? Mama's been astin' me every day when am I go'n get her some blackberries."

As a matter of fact, Mama never asked me to pick anything anymore, except in our garden. Between her and Papa and Grandpa I was too busy with home chores and store work to go hunting wild fruit. Mama bought our blackberries and yellow plums and muscadines from little colored boys who came by, or from doddery old colored men, or from fat black women with shy stair-step children, each toting two lard buckets full.

"If we go back to Blind Tillie Trestle we can find your bucket," I said. "How bout tomorrow?"

Soon as that was out of my mouth I didn't know why I said it.

For one thing, I didn't particularly want to walk through Mill Town again. For another, I felt sick. Sick at my stomach. For another, I'd never hear the last of it if Pink and them somehow found out a girl was waiting for me under Blind Tillie Trestle. Guffaw and haw!

And if Mama and them found out it was a mill girl, I'd be hard put to explain it. No town boy or girl from a nice home would be caught dead with a linthead.

I was about to make up some excuse when I felt the clickety-clacks slow down and saw Cold Sassy going by the train windows. Remembering Papa, I forgot all about Lightfoot's blackberry bucket. Him laying on the strap wouldn't be the half of it. He'd keep me in the store, garden, and stable the rest of the summer.

Sick at heart, I knew I didn't even want to meet Lightfoot tomorrow.

I tried to think up some excuse, but no matter what I said, it was such in Cold Sassy that she would read *mill girl/town boy* written all over me and she'd hate me the rest of her life, despite she had helped me up from under the wheels of death, so to speak.

Passing the Cold Sassy tree, I felt a new wave of nausea. Amidst the jolts and grinds and the whoosh of steam as the engineer braked into the depot, big Loomis pulled me to my feet and said again, "Lawdy, Mr. Will, yo ma and pa dey gwine be sho nuff proud dis eeb'nin'."

I never found out why Mr. Tuttle was way back there at the caboose when the train pulled in. I just knew that when I looked out the window I found myself staring right into his hard little eyes.

Loomis half pushed, half carried me to the door. I was shaking like the palsy and scared to death I'd puke or start crying. If the earth had opened up and dropped me clear to China, that would have been just dandy with me.

14

When I try to put together the rest of July 5, 1906, it seems hazy. And not just because eight years have gone by now. It was hazy at the time.

I remember worrying after I got to bed that night about not telling Lightfoot good-bye or thanking her. I guess she followed me and Loomis and the dog off the train, but I never saw her after I got surrounded by the other passengers. They were touching me, patting my arm, congratulating me. A tall old man with bulging eyes and a big goiter on his neck pressed a five-dollar gold piece in my hand and got back on the train without saying a word. One little boy begged for a piece of my shirt. I felt foolish, but I pulled off a loose button and gave it to him.

Loomis pushed me through the crowd, bowing and scraping to the white folks, but pushing all the same. "Pleas'sir, let dis here boy pass. . . . Please'm, we's gotta git dis here boy home."

There were Cold Sassy folks at the depot and of course they were puzzled why I was such a hero. I saw Shoeshine Peavy, a young colored boy. He was staring at me, and so was the dwarf, little old Thurman Osgood, who always watched the trains come in. Mr. Beach drove up in his buggy, bringing his wife and little girls to catch the train to Athens. They and others pressed around me, asking questions. "What happened, Will?" "You git hurt?" "Somebody tell us what happened!"

"Please, white folks, let dis boy pass. He don't feel lak talkin'. . . ."

Then the big engineer ran up. "Lookit this 'ere boy!" he shouted, like he was a barker at the county fair and me the prize pig. Waving in my direction, he boomed out his news: "This 'ere boy just now got run over by this 'ere train! Look at him good, folks! Ran over by a train on the trestle and livin' to tell it! Not a hair on his head hurt, folks, not one Goddamn hair, praise be the good Lord!"

Normally I didn't mind being on stage. But what with shaking and shivering and about to cry and vomit and all, I just wanted to get home. It was awful, everybody crowding around like I was a side show, asking how'd it happen and what was I doin' on the trestle anyhow, and what you mean, ran over?

"Mr. Will he ain't feelin' too good," Loomis kept insisting. "He need to git on home." He was still talking polite, but not smiling.

About then Mr. Tuttle got to me. "Engineer said you was on Blind Tillie Trestle. You know you shouldn' a-been up there, boy!"

I didn't answer. I figured Mr. Tuttle was picturing me cut to pieces and himself down at my house trying to settle, cheap, my folks' claim against the railroad. Gosh, would I be worth any more than a dead cow and mule? Or would Mr. Tuttle have sat in our parlor and argued about it.

When Mr. Beach offered to carry me home in his buggy, I said, "Thank you, sir, I'd sure be much obliged." We just live across the street and two houses down from the depot, but I wasn't certain I could walk it, and I sure as heck didn't want Loomis totin' me like a sick calf.

You can imagine how it was when we got to my house and Mr. Beach told Mama what happened. Trying not to cry, she led me in and made me lay down on the black leather davenport in the front hall. I was shivering like a wet dog; she put a heavy quilt over me. She was wiping the dirt and grime from my face with a wet washrag when Papa tore through the front door.

"Loomis said—" he began, then must have been too mad to say any more, because he just stood over me. Fastening my eyes on his knees, I saw they were shaking. I waited for him to take off his belt. When he didn't, I got the nerve to look up at him.

Tears were streaming down Papa's cheeks. He had his straw hat across his chest like folks do when a Confederate veteran's funeral procession passes on its way to the graveyard. I stared up at him, tears wetting my own cheeks. Suddenly he knelt down beside Mama, put his hat on the floor, grabbed my right hand in both of his, and held on like he'd never let go. I couldn't help it; I sat up and threw my arms around my daddy's neck. He held me tight for a long time, till I quit shaking. He didn't say a word.

Papa hadn't hugged me I don't reckon since the day I was twelve years old.

Well, then he put his arms around Mama. "Oh, Hoyt," she whispered. "The little grave we've got in the cemetery . . . I don't think I could stand it if—oh, Hoyt, our boy is alive!" Then she grabbed aholt of me and cried like I was dead.

At some point my daddy walked toward the back hall and was gone a while. When he came back in he said, "You don't have to worry about the milkin', son. I did it."

It's not to my credit that I had forgot all about the cow. Well, I reckon he needed to go get aholt of himself.

I didn't want any supper, and they didn't, either. Mama just brought some buttermilk and cold corn lightbread and they sat there by me in the hall to eat it.

About first dark, Cold Sassy arrived.

Good ole Loomis, he must of galloped all over town telling about my escape on the train trestle, because everybody seemed to know all about it. Just the same, they kept asking questions that I didn't feel like answering.

Lots of ladies brought cake or pie—like if somebody had died.

I wanted to see Grandpa Blakeslee. I almost asked if him and Miss Love were back yet from getting married, but there wasn't any use giving Mama another headache.

I remember Aunt Loma and Uncle Camp coming in. The baby, fat and sweaty and dumb-looking, was fast asleep on her shoulder. I don't know if I mentioned it before, but Campbell Junior was the fattest baby ever seen in Cold Sassy. Aunt Loma looked furious. She didn't so much as ask how I was feeling. Why would my getting run over make her so mad? Maybe she was mad because I'd lived to tell it.

But for once it wasn't me she was mad at. "How could Pa have run off with That Woman!" she whispered to Mama.

"Hush, Loma," said Mama, placing her hand on my arm. "That's not important right now. Not compared to Will."

I felt like the Prodigal Son. When my mother headed for the dining room, her eyes shining with joy, I knew she was fixing to get out her gold and white china dessert plates.

Pink and Smiley and Dunse McCall came in, tiptoeing over to me like I was a haint or a corpse, or like they planned to yessir and no-sir me from now on. Finally Pink mumbled, "You didn't have to go do a fool thing like that, Will." He was proud of me and jealous both, I could tell.

"Aw, go get you a piece of pie," said I. Propped on my elbow, holding up my head with my hand, I grinned at the three of them. They grinned back, and Smiley kind of joshed my shoulder as they moved toward the dining room, where Aunt Carrie and Miss Sarah, French

Gordy's wife, were slicing cakes and pies. I could hear the dessert plates rattling as Mama took them out of the china cabinet.

I could also hear several ladies talking low over near the front door. I knew by the crackledy voice that Miss Alice Ann Boozer was one of them. She said somebody seen Rucker Blakeslee and the Simpson woman havin' supper at the ho-tel. "A weddin' supper, I s'pose you'd call it. Rucker didn't never spend one dime takin' Mattie Lou to no ho-tel. Bet you she haints them two t'night."

"Well, I heard little Loma threw a pure fit down at the store today," said somebody else. "You want my opinion, Rucker's been hopin' to git shet a-Mattie Lou ever since he laid eyes on the milliner. But be ye not disencouraged. The Lord says vengeance is His'n."

Miss Sarah heard this last as she came through the hall with the big plate of sliced cake. Going over to the talking ladies, she whispered, "I saw her and Rucker right after they come in from Jefferson. He called me over to say they'd just got married. 'She wants a weddin' pitcher,' he said, and they went in Mr. Hale's photo shop. I couldn't believe the nerve."

"I heard Mr. Hale refused to take the pitcher," said Miss Alice Ann.

"Well, good for him," said somebody. "Imagine, a weddin' pitcher this soon after Mr. Hale took a funeral pitcher of Mattie Lou laid out in her coffin and all them baskets of flowers around her."

I knew Mr. French would be upset about the wedding. His mother having married Granny's daddy, they grew up together like brother and sister. The day Granny died, Mr. French said to Mama, "Mr. Blakeslee is a good decent man. But Mattie Lou done all the givin'."

The talkers moved on then, because a covey of Presbyterian ladies were coming in. I shut my eyes like sleeping as they marched over to stare at the corpse.

"Dear boy, hit just wadn' his time to die," Miss Looly said softly.

"S'pose it wadn' his time to die but it was that trestle's time to fall?" her sister breathed, touching my cheek. "Or what if it was that train engineer's time to die? What would of happened to Will?"

"Shet up, Cretia," whispered Miss Looly. "Hit ain't for us to ast sech questions. Hit were the Lord's will for the boy to live. All we got to do is be thankful."

For a moment I swelled with importance, getting talked about like that. Then for no good reason I saw myself as Raw Head and Bloody Bones, spinning into nothing under giant wheels and thunder. I felt sick again, and scared. I didn't want to be a nothing.

I wished Grandpa would come, but I knew he wouldn't. Not on his wedding night.

Pat Conroy

From *The Prince of Tides*

In September school began and Savannah and I entered first grade together, our mother and grandmother walking us to the bus stop on Briarcliff Road. Luke was going into second grade and was put in charge of seeing that we got to school safely and on time. The three of us had notes pinned to our white cotton shirts. My note read, "Hi, I'm Tom Wingo, a first grader. If you find me and I'm lost, please call my mother, Lila, at the following number: BR3-7929. She'll be very worried about me. Thank you, neighbor."

We carried new lunch boxes and wore brand-new saddle shoes. The first-grade teacher was a small, shy nun built like a child herself, who made our entry into the frightening realm of human knowledge as gentle and enriching as any act of love could be. My mother rode the bus with us that first day and told us we were about to learn to read and write, that we were embarking on our first adventure of the mind.

I did not cry until she left me on the playground, slipping away quietly, unnoticed and tenative, when I looked up and saw her on the sidewalk by Courtland Avenue, watching the nun lining up the first graders. I looked around and tried to find Luke, but he was disappearing with the other second graders through a side door.

When I cried, Savannah cried, and we both bolted from the line of suddenly motherless children and ran to our mother, our lunch boxes beating against our knees and thighs. She ran to us and knelt down to receive our charge into her arms. The three of us wept and I held her in the most passionate fury of abandonment and wanted never to be torn away from those arms.

Sister Immaculata approached us from behind and, winking at my mother, led the three of us into her classroom, where fully half the students were crying out for their mothers. Mothers, looking like giants as they moved along the aisles of diminutive desks, consoled each other as they pried their children's arms from around their nylon stockings. There was terribly affecting pain and sorrow loose in that room. Loss and the passage of days showed in the eyes of those gentle women. The nun ushered them from the room one by one.

The nun showed Savannah and me the reading book we would use that year, introduced us to Dick and Jane as though they would be neighbors of ours, and placed us in a special corner to count out apples and oranges the class would have for lunch. My mother looked back at us from the door, then slipped away unseen. Sister Immaculata, with her soft white hands flowing through our hair and over our faces, began the process of creating a home away from home in her classroom. By the end of the day, Savannah had learned the alphabet by heart. I knew it up to the letter D. Savannah sang the ABC's to the class and Sister Immaculata, touched with the wizardry of the fine, unpraised teacher, had given a poet the keys to the English language. In her first book, the poem "Immaculata" would speak of that frail, nervous woman trussed in the black drapery of her order, who made the classroom seem like a part of paradise spared. Years later, when Sister Immaculata was dying at Mercy Hospital in Atlanta, Savannah flew down from New York and read the poem to her and held her hand on the last day of Immaculata's life.

I did not cry again that day until I found a note in my lunch box from my mother. Sister Immaculata read it to me. It said, "I'm so proud of you, Tom. I love you and miss you so much. Mommy." That's all. That's all it had to say and I wept in that good nun's arms. And I prayed the Korean War would last forever.

In the house on Rosedale Road, Papa John Stanopolous lay in the back bedroom, taking his own good time about dying. My mother required absolute silence from us when we were in the house and we learned to speak in whispers, to laugh noiselessly, and to play as quietly as insects when we drifted through the rooms that led to Papa John's door.

Each day when we returned home from school, we would eat cookies and milk in the kitchen and tell what we had learned that day. Savannah always seemed to learn twice as much as either Luke or me. Luke usually recited the latest atrocity committed in the name of Catholic education by the dread Sister Irene, and my mother would frown, disturbed and worried, by Luke's tales of distress. Then she would lead us quietly to the back bedroom and let us visit with Papa John for a half-hour.

Papa John rested with his head propped up on three soft pillows, and it was always dark in his room. His face would materialize out of the half-light and the venetian blinds, half drawn, would divide the room in symmetrical chevrons of light. The room smelled of medicine and cigar smoke.

His flesh was pale and sickly, his chest as hairless and white as a pig's back. There were books and magazines scattered on the night table beside him. He would lean over and turn on the lamp when we entered. We would scramble onto his bed and cover his neck and face with kisses with my mother and grandmother warning us to be careful. They stood watching in soft attendance. But Papa John, his eyes luminous and bright as a retriever's, would wave them off. He would laugh as we crawled over him and tickle us under our arms with his heroic, shadow-casting awning of a nose.

"Be gentle with Papa John, kids," my mother would call out from the doorway. "He's had a heart attack."

"Let the children be, Lila," he would say, caressing us.

"Show us the nickel in your nose, Papa John," Savannah would demand.

With an ostentatious sleight of hand and a few magic words of Greek, he would extract a nickel from his nose and hand it to Savannah.

"Are there any more nickels up there, Papa John?" Luke would shout, peering into his dark spacious nostrils.

"I don't know, Luke," Papa John said sadly. "I blew my nose earlier today and there were nickels shooting out all over this room. But look here. I feel something funny in my ears."

We would search his great hairy ears and find nothing. He would repeat the Greek phrases, wave his hands theatrically, cry "Presto," and pull two nickels from behind his fleshy lobes and place the coins into our eager hands.

At night, before we went to bed, our mother permitted us to return to Papa John's bedroom. Freshly bathed, clean as snow, we arranged ourselves around his pillows like three bright satellites around a new moon. We took turns each night lighting the cigars the doctor had forbidden him to smoke. Then Papa John would lean back, his face framed in a nimbus of fragrant smoke, and tell us a bedtime story.

"Should I tell them about the time I was captured by two hundred Turks, Tolitha?" he asked my grandmother as she stood by the door.

"No, don't scare them before their bedtime," my grandmother answered.

"Please tell us about the turkeys," Luke begged.

"Turks," Papa John corrected. "Not turkeys, Luke."

"They won't sleep a wink if you tell that story, Papa John," my mother said.

"Please, Mama," Savannah said. "We won't sleep a wink if we don't hear about the Turks."

Each night this thin, withered man took us on miraculous, improbable voyages around the globe where he encountered perfidious Turks attacking him in countless, inimical battalions, and each night he would devise ingenious ways to repulse them and return safely between the white sheets of his bed, where he was dying slowly, painfully, and without the companionship or intercession of Agamemnon's soldiers, dying without honor, surrounded not by Turks but by three children as he weakened daily until the stories became as important and essential to him as they were to us. His imagination lit fires in that room in a final shimmering ignition. Papa John had never had children and these stories poured out of him in bright torrents.

Behind us, watching and listening, were our mother and grandmother. I did not know who Papa John was or where he came from or how he was related to me and no one would explain it to any of us children. We had left my grandfather in Colleton and all of us wept as we left him. My mother and father carefully instructed us to call our grandmother by her given name and never under any circumstances reveal that she was my father's mother. Papa John might have been a gifted storyteller, but he had nothing over my grandmother.

At bedtime, there would be one more story. Then my mother would lead us out of his room, into the dimly lit hallway, past the door that led to the dread basement, and up the winding stairs to the large bedroom on the second floor where we, the children, made our home. If a wind was blowing, the branches of the hovering oak trees would scratch the windowpanes. There were three beds set side by side. Savannah had the middle bed, flanked by her two brothers. A small bedside lamp was the only light in the room. We cast enormous, superhuman shadows on those slanted enclosing walls.

Once a week my father would write and my mother would read those letters to us right before we went to sleep. He wrote in a clipped, military prose that read like an order of the day. He described each mission to us as though he were speaking of an errand to buy bread or fill the car up with gas. "I was flying recon with Bill Lundin. We were watching a squad of our grunts winding up some mountain when I spotted something funny going on just above them. I radioed Bill and said, 'Hey, Bill, you see what I see?' I look over and see Bill straining his eyes. Sure enough, ol' Bill sees it too. About halfway up the mountain, there were about three hundred North Korean regulars waiting to ambush these poor grunts. So I get on the radio and I radio down to the grunts and I say, 'Hey, boys, call a halt to your little daytrip.' 'Why?' the guy asks me. 'Because you're walking into the arms of half of North Korea,' I say. He gets my drift. Then Bill and I decide to go down and ruin those nectarines' entire afternoon. I go first and lay a few napalm on their heads. It certainly got their attention. I saw thirty of them trying to wipe flames off their bodies like they were cleaning lint from their coat. But it don't work that way. Then Bill lays a few more eggs and we got us a party going on. I radioed back and a whole squadron lifted off to help us. We chased that battalion for three days. Refueling, then hunting, then refueling and hunting again. Finally we caught what was left of them crossing the Naktong River. Caught them in the open. Turned the river red. It was fun but it didn't do an ounce of good. Folks breed like mink over here and there's plenty more where they come from. Tell the kids I love them very much. Tell them to pray for the old Dad and to watch out for their Mama."

"Who is Papa John, Mama?" Savannah asked my mother one evening.

"He's Tolitha's husband. You know that," she answered.

"But who is he to us? Is he our grandfather?"

"No. Your grandfather Amos lives in Colleton. You know that."

"But Tolitha's our grandmother, isn't she?"

"She's your cousin when we're up here. She doesn't want Papa John to know you're her grandchildren."

"But she's Dad's mother, isn't she?"

"When we're here in this house, she's your father's cousin. Don't ask me to explain. It's too complicated. I don't understand it myself."

"Why isn't she still married to Grandpa Wingo?"

"They haven't been married for years. You'll understand it later. Don't ask so many questions. It's none of your business. Besides, Papa John treats you as though you're his grandchildren, doesn't he?"

"Yes, Mama," Luke said, "but is he your father, Mama? Where's your mother and father?"

"They died a long time before you were born."

"What were their names?" I asked.

"Thomas and Helen Trent," she answered.

"What were they like?" Savannah asked.

"Very handsome people. They looked like a prince and princess. Everyone said so."

"Were they rich?"

"They were very rich before the Depression. The Depression wiped them out."

"Do you have any pictures of them?"

"No. They were all burned down in the fire that destroyed their house."

"Is that what killed them?"

"Yes. It was a terrible fire," my mother said without emotion, her face drawn and apprehensive. My mother, the beauty. My mother, the liar.

As children, we had but one duty. In the basement, in rows of dusty Mason jars, Papa John kept his collection of black widow spiders, which, as a hobby, he sold to biology teachers, entomologists, zoos, and private collectors around the country. We were given the job of caring for those small malignant spiders, which floated like black cameos in their jars. Twice a week, Luke, Savannah, and I would descend into the moist glooms, switch on the naked exposed bulb, and feed those mute arachnids, any one of which, we were assured by a garrulous Papa John, "could kill us deader than a stone." We had helped feed poultry since we could walk, but these descents required a courage and agitated sense of commitment no chicken ever inspired. When the feeding hour approached, we would gather in Papa John's bedroom, listen to his careful instructions, then descend the wooden staircase to face the minuscule, satanic livestock who watched us in stillness like the approach of flies.

On Saturdays we brought the jars of spiders up to Papa John for his inspection. He would wipe the jars clean of dust with a linen cloth. He eyed the spiders with discrimination. He would question us closely about their feeding habits. He would count the pear-shaped egg sacs and make notations in a small notebook whenever there was a crop of new spiders. Cautiously, he would remove a spider and let it walk back and forth across a dinner plate, turning it with a pair of tweezers when it neared the edge. He would point to the red hourglass delicately tatooed on the female spider's abdomen and say, "There. That's what you look for. That hourglass means 'I kill.' "

"Why do you collect black widows, Papa John?" Savannah asked one day. "Why not goldfish or stamps or something pretty?"

"Because I was a shoe salesman, sweetie," he answered, "a shoe salesman and a damn good one. But being a shoe salesman is the most common thing in the world. I wanted to do something no one else I knew did. Something special. So I became the shoe salesman who raised black widows in his basement. It's an attention getter."

"Do they really eat their husbands?" Luke asked.

"These are very stern women," Papa John answered. "They eat their husbands right after they mate."

"Can they really kill you?" I asked.

"I think they can kill a child fairly easily," he said. "I'm not sure they can kill a full-grown man, though. The guy that got me started in this business had been bitten a couple of times. He said it made him sick enough to think he would die. But he was still walking around."

"How did he get bit?" I asked.

"Black widows are kind of shy except when they're defending their eggs. Then they're a mite aggressive. He liked to let them walk around on his arm," Papa John said, smiling.

Savannah said, "That makes me sick to think about it."

"He sure raised pretty spiders, though," Papa John said, studying his pets.

The care of black widows inspired a patience and concentration rare in young children. We took our responsibilities seriously and studied the life cycle of the spiders with the supercharged zealotry born of caring for creatures who could kill us. My lifelong love of spiders and insects began with my nose pressed close against Mason jars, observing the tedious and horrifying existence of black widows. They hung motionless in webs spun out of their viscera. They lived dangling and still, black in the high wires of their jar-shaped lives. When they moved quickly, it was to kill. Over the months, we watched the females kill and devour the males. We became attuned to the seasons of spiders and time poured out of the red hourglasses in shimmering, ill-formed webs. We watched egg cases exploding into spiders newly minted, scattering like brown and orange seeds across a jar. Our fear of them turned to fascination and advocacy. There was such beauty in the economical structure of spiders; they moved across webs with the secret of lace making and silk screening implied in their loins, aerialists in a quart of Georgia air. They were good at doing what they were born to do.

Behind the house, a large deciduous forest, circumvallated by a low stone fence, stretched all the way to Briarcliff Road. There were "No

Trespassing" signs posted along the fence at thousand-foot intervals. Our grandmother informed us in a breathless, conspiratorial voice that "very, very rich people" lived on the property and that under no circumstances were we ever to cross the fence to play in those verboten woods. This was the Candler family, the heirs of Coca-Cola, and whenever my grandmother spoke of them it was as though she were describing a collegial association of some scrupulous peerage. According to my grandmother, the Candlers were the nearest thing Atlanta had to a royal family, and she would not allow us to desecrate their walled baronage.

But we would approach that fence after school each day, that deep-green, perfumed realm forbidden to us, and smell the money coming through the trees. We longed to glimpse a single member of that noble and enchanted family. But we were children and soon we were climbing the fence and taking a few forbidden steps into the forest, then racing back to the safety of the stone wall. The next time we would step off ten paces into the woods before we lost our nerve and returned to our own yard. Slowly, we began to demythologize the outlawed woods. Soon we knew the acreage of that forest better than any Candler ever had. We learned its secrets and boundaries, hid in its groves and arbors, and felt the old thrill of disobedience buoyant in young hearts gallant enough to ignore the strange laws of adults. Surrounded by trees, we hunted squirrels with slingshots, watched from the high branches of trees the lucky Candler children, looking serious and bored, cantering thoroughbreds down forest paths, and spied on the gardener fertilizing banks of azaleas.

And one warm November night, we slipped out of an upstairs bedroom, climbed down the immense oak that ruled our quadrant of the house, and walked through the forest all the way to the Candler mansion itself. Lying on our stomachs, we crawled toward that opulent Tudor mansion through the thick grass and watched, through the silver light of French doors, the great family itself at dinner. Servants were wheeling in food on elaborate dollies. The Candlers, erect and pallid, ate their meal as if they were attending a church service, such was their seriousness, their unruffled ecclesiastical mien.

In awe we watched the meal consumed, the blaze of candelabra lifting off the table like buckheads on fire, the tender light of chandeliers, the lethargy and restrained grandeur of wealth. Lying in a field of freshly mown grass, we attended to every detail of that casual, slowly evolving meal. There was no laughter or conversation from the royal family, and the rich, we assumed, were silent as fish. The servants moved stiffly in penguinesque charades through the room. They measured the pace of the meal, poured wine into half-filled glasses, floated like undertakers from window to window, unaware of our presence. At that very moment, disguised as night creatures, we inhaled the delicious aromas of that meal, watching as secret Candlers, initiates into the extraordinary rites and customs of the Coca-Cola princes. They did not know we owned their forest.

The house was known as Callanwolde.

In the woods of Callanwolde, we found a fitting substitute for the island denied to us by the Korean War. We built a treehouse in one of Callanwolde's extravagant oaks. We resumed our interrupted life as country children in the middle of the South's largest city. Quails called to us at dusk. A family of gray foxes lived beneath an uprooted cottonwood. We would come to the forest to remember who we were, what we had come from, and where we would be returning. Once we had crossed the fence and made our claim on that prohibited acreage, Atlanta became a perfect city.

It was only later that I realized I loved Atlanta because it was the only place on earth I had ever lived without a father. By then, Atlanta had darkened in the imagination. By then, the woods of Callanwolde had become a fearful place. By then, the giant had come into our lives and the children, unafraid of spiders, would learn the harsh lesson that they had much to learn and fear from the world of men.

It was early March and the dogwoods were just beginning to bloom. The whole earth shivered with the green tumult of ripening, sunsoft days, and we were walking through the woods, looking for box turtles. Savannah saw him first. She froze and pointed at something ahead of us.

He was standing beside a tree covered with poison sumac, relieving himself. He was the largest, most powerful man I had ever seen and I had grown up with men of legendary strength who worked around the shrimp docks in Colleton. He grew out of the earth like some fantastic, grotesque tree. His body was thick, marvelous, and colossal. His eyes were blue and vacant. A red beard covered his face, but there was something wrong about him. It was the way he looked at us, far different from the way adults normally studied children, that alerted us to danger. The three of us felt the menace in his disengaged stare. His eyes did not seem connected to anything human. He zipped up his pants and turned toward us. He was almost seven feet tall. We ran.

We made it to the stone fence, clambered over it, and ran screaming into our back yard. When we reached the back porch, we saw him standing at the edge of the woods, observing us. The fence we had to climb over barely came to his waist. My mother came out of the back door when she heard our screams. We pointed toward the man in the woods.

"What do you want, mister?" my mother shouted, taking a few steps toward the man.

She saw the change in his face too; she sensed the demonic, unjoined quality in his eyes.

"You," he said to my mother, and his voice was strangely high-pitched for such a large man. He did not seem cruel or imbalanced; he simply seemed inhuman.

"What?" my mother asked, frightened by his lack of affect.

"I want you," the giant said, taking his first step toward her.

We ran for the house and as my mother locked the back door I saw him watching her through the kitchen window. I had never seen a man stare at a woman with such primitive lust until I saw that stranger looking at my mother. I had never studied eyes that were born to hate women.

My mother saw him through the window and she walked over and pulled the shade.

"I'll be back," the man said, and we could hear his laughter as my mother dialed the number for the police.

When the poice came, he was gone. The police combed the woods and the only thing they found was our treehouse and a single footprint from a size nineteen shoe. My mother spanked us for trespassing on Callanwolde property.

In our minds, I think we children truly believed that we had summoned the visitation of the giant, that he was the manifestation of our willful disobedience, that he had been called out of the netherworld as an instrument of divine, unappeasable justice to punish us for crossing the fence into the taboo frontiers of Callanwolde. We had profaned the lands of the rich, we thought, and God had sent this giant to punish us.

We never entered the Callanwolde property again, but the giant had already exposed the gravity of our sin. He would require expiation. He would bring Callanwolde into our home. He would come as the lordly inquisitor and punish the sins of the Wingo children in a perverse and imaginative way. He would not punish the sinners for their crimes, for he understood well how to punish children most grievously. When he came, he would come for our mother.

Another secret was added to that house of endless intrigue. We could not tell Papa John about the intruder from the forest. "Because he's got such a weak heart, honey," my grandmother explained to me. I thought he should be told immediately, feeling with enormous justification that we needed someone on our side who could slay two hundred Turks if the giant returned. But my grandmother assured us that she and my mother were big girls and could take care of themselves.

During the next week we were vigilant and cautious, but the days passed without incident and the streets of Atlanta erupted in a white flaming of dogwood. Bees moaned in the ecstasy of clovers and azaleas. My mother wrote a letter to Grandpa Wingo that week, telling him the exact date we would be returning to the island after my father returned stateside. She asked him to hire a black woman to clean up the house for their arrival. She was careful to mention that my grandmother sent him her kindest regards. Then she let each of the children write "I love you, Grandpa" at the bottom of the letter. She addressed the letter to our house on Melrose Island, knowing that he checked our mailbox more frequently than he did his own. Placing the letter in the mailbox on Rosedale Road, she raised the red metal flag to alert the postman as we left for school on Friday morning. It was only when we returned to the island that summer that we learned my grandfather never received that letter. The letter would not be delivered for more than a decade.

On Sunday evening we were watching television in the living room. My mother and grandmother were sitting in brown overstuffed armchairs, watching the *Ed Sullivan Show*. I was sitting on the floor between my mother's legs. Luke was lying on his stomach, watching the screen and trying to finish his math homework. Savannah was sitting in my grandmother's lap. My mother passed me a bowl of hot popcorn. I took a generous handful and spilled two kernels on the rug. I picked them up and ate them. Then I felt the room go dead with fear and heard Savannah say the single, electrifying word: "Callanwolde."

He was standing on the porch in darkness, staring in at us through the glass-paneled door. I do not know how long he had been watching us but there was a quality of vegetable stillness about him, as though he had sprouted like some dissident, renegade vine as we sat there. His eyes were fixed on my mother. He had returned for her and her alone. His flesh was morbidly pale, the color of a tincture of alabaster, and he filled the doorway like a column upholding a ruin.

Placing one enormous hand on the doorknob, he twisted it violently and we heard the strain of the metal. As my mother rose she said to my grandmother, "Walk very slowly into the hallway and call the police, Tolitha."

My mother walked toward the door and faced the stranger.

"What do you want?" she asked.

"Lila," he replied, and my mother took a step back in shock when she heard him use her name. His voice was ill-fitting and still high-pitched. He smiled a hideous smile at her and turned the knob again.

My mother then saw his penis, exposed and enormous, rising out of him, the color of pig flesh. Savannah screamed when she saw it and I saw Luke moving up from the floor.

"The police are coming," my mother said.

Suddenly, the man broke a pane of glass on the door with a brick and his long arm thrust into the hole. He reached for the lock on the door. Glass cut him and his wrist began to bleed. My mother reached for his arm, trying to keep him from unlocking the door. She grappled with him briefly but he backhanded her across the chest, knocking her to the floor. Somewhere I could hear Savannah and Luke screaming but they seemed displaced and faraway, like voices heard underwater. My whole body lost feeling, like a Novocained gum. He undid one lock, then struggled to turn the key that held him away from us. He was twisting the key, a low animal whine issuing out of him, when Luke approached him, swinging a fireplace tool. Luke crashed the poker across the man's wrist. The man shouted in pain and withdrew his arm. He tried to put his arm through the window again but Luke was there waiting for him, swinging that poker as hard as any seven-year-old kid on earth.

I heard something behind me, the sound of my grandmother's slippers sliding down the polished floors of the hallway. I turned and I saw her round the corner with a small revolver in her hand.

"Duck, Luke," she ordered, and Luke dove to the ground.

Tolitha opened fire on that glass door.

The giant ran when the first shot pierced a windowpane close to his head. He ran with his penis flopping against his leg. He sprinted off the porch and toward the safety of the Callanwolde woods. We heard the sound of police sirens far off on Ponce de Leon.

My grandmother yelled into the darkness from the porch: "That'll teach you to fuck with a country girl."

"Your language, Tolitha," my mother said, still in shock. "The children."

"The children just watched a guy with his dick in his hand trying to get to their mother. A little language won't hurt 'em much."

When it was over, my mother found me eating popcorn, watching the *Ed Sullivan Show* as though nothing had happened. But for two days I could not speak. Papa John had slept through the entire attack and had not even awakened to the gunfire or the coming of the police. When he wondered at the reason for my silence, my mother said "laryngitis" and my grandmother seconded her lie. They were southern women who felt a responsibility to protect their men from danger and bad news. My silence, my pathetic wordlessness, affirmed their belief in the basic fragility and weakness of men.

For a week the police parked a patrol car on Rosedale Road and a plainclothes detective circled our home several times during the night. My mother could not sleep at night and we would find her hovering over us after midnight, obsessively checking and rechecking the locks on our bedroom windows. Once I awoke and saw her framed in moonlight, staring out toward the forests of Callanwolde. As she stood there, I noticed her body for the first time, observed in guilt and terror its soft, voluptuous features, admired the shape of her full breasts and the curve of her waist as she scanned the moonlit yard for the approach of her enemy.

The word *Callanwolde* changed meaning for us, and, following Savannah's example, we began to refer to the man as Callanwolde. "Did Callanwolde come last night?" we would ask at breakfast. "Have the police caught Callanwolde yet, Mama?" we would ask as she read to us at bedtime. It became a catchall, portmanteau word for everything evil or iniquitous in the world. When Sister Immaculata described the terrors of hell in her sweet voice, she was explaining the boundaries and perimeters of Callanwolde to me and Savannah. When my father wrote in a letter that his plane had been hit with machine-gun fire and he had fought his plane all the way back to the air base, losing oil pressure and altitude, trailing black smoke, afraid that the plane would explode in midair, we called that dreadful flight a Callanwolde. It was a specific person, a specific place, and a general condition of a world suddenly fearful and a fate uncontrollable.

After two weeks of diligent patrolling, the police assured my mother that the man would never return to the house.

He returned that night.

The phone rang in the house that evening. Again we were watching television and eating popcorn. My mother answered the phone in the hallway and we heard her say hello to Mrs. Fordham, the old woman who lived in the house next door. I saw my mother turn white and watched as she put the receiver down on the side table and say in a drained, uninflected voice, "He's on the roof."

We lifted our eyes slowly to the ceiling and heard the faint sounds of his footsteps walking down the slanted shingles on the roof.

"Don't go upstairs," my mother said. "He might be in the house."

She phoned the police.

For ten minutes we listened to him moving unhurriedly about the roof. He made no attempt to enter an upstairs window. This visit had no meaning, except to establish his credentials in our lives again and to inspire a renewed panic in our hearts. Then the sound of sirens burst far off in the city, hovered over Atlanta like the cry of redemptive angels. We heard his footsteps run across the roof and felt him enter the limbs of the huge oak that grew beside the driveway. My mother walked to the bank of windows in the music room and saw him as he reached the ground. He paused, looking back, and saw her through the window. He waved at her and smiled. Then he ran in an easy, untroubled gait toward the dark harboring forest behind us.

The next day the police took bloodhounds through the Callanwolde forest but they lost his scent somewhere along Briarcliff Road.

He did not come again for two months.

But he was there even when he was not there. He inhabited each alcove and recessed corner of that house. We could not open any door without expecting him to be waiting behind it. We came to fear the approach of night. The nights he did not appear were as spiritually exhausting as the ones when he did. The trees outside the house lost their healthy, luxuriant beauty and became grotesque in our eyes. The woods of Callanwolde became his domain, his safe hermitage, and a region of inexhaustible dread in our imaginations. His face was portrayed subliminally in every window. If we closed our eyes, we saw his image imprinted on our consciousnesses like a face on a veil. He sundered our dreams with his murderous eyes. Terror marked my mother's face; she slept during the day and roamed the house checking locks at night.

With my mother's permission, we moved the forty jars of black widows out of the basement and transported them with great and serious concentration to our upstairs bedroom. None of the children could bear to descend into the terrifying depths of the basement when

Callanwolde was threatening the house. The basement also had a door that led to the outdoors and the police had told my grandmother that this provided the easiest entrance into the house. She was as relieved as we were when we arranged the jars of spiders in long rows on an unused bookshelf in the far corner of our bedroom. When Sacred Heart School had a Pet Day, each of us brought a single black widow to school and collectively won the prize for most unusual pet.

At night, with the lamps gleaming brightly, the interior of the house felt like an aquarium and we floated from room to room, feeling Callanwolde's eyes study us from beneath the glooms of oaks. We assumed he was watching and appraising us; we assumed he was omnipresent and was biding his time, awaiting the perfect moment to launch his next sortie against us. Swimming through the electric light of that besieged house, we waited in the charged, breathless atmosphere of our own obsessions. The police checked our house twice a night. They searched the bushes and trees with flashlights. They entered the woods. They would leave and the night would belong to him again.

It was the year that Luke flunked second grade, a fact that humiliated Luke but caused Savannah and me great joy, since the three of us would now be joined happily in the same classroom when we returned to Colleton. It was the year I lost my first tooth, the year Savannah and I got the measles, the year a tornado destroyed three houses in Druid Hills, but in our memories, in the trackless shadows of our subconsciouses, it became the year of Callanwolde.

It was a week before my father's return from Korea. We had all gone into Papa John's room to kiss him good night. He was drawn and wasted and he was forbidden by his doctor to tell us bedtime stories, so we had taken to speaking to him in whispers. We had witnessed his daily diminishment, the leaking out of his fervent vitality, and he taught us a little bit about death each day as he fell further and further away from us. His eyes had already surrendered the light. My grandmother had begun drinking heavily in the evenings.

My mother was feeling safer now that my father's approach was imminent. All of us looked upon my father as the heroic figure, the redeemer, the knight errant who would deliver us from harm's way and the fear of Callanwolde. I no longer prayed for my father to die. I prayed for him to be near me. I prayed for him to save my mother.

That night when she read a chapter of *The Yearling* to us a strong wind moved the trees against the house. We said our prayers together, and she kissed each of us good night. She turned out the light and although we heard her footsteps descend the winding stairs, her perfume lingered in the darkness. I fell asleep listening to the wind in the trees.

Two hours later I awoke and saw his face in the window, staring at me. He put his finger to his lips and bade me to be silent. I heard the knife cutting through the screen like the tearing of cheap silk. I did not move or speak. A paralysis of exquisite, impenetrable terror entered each cell of my body. His eyes transfixed me and I lay as rigid as a bird before the copperhead's approach.

Then Savannah awoke and screamed.

His foot broke through the window in a brutal showering of glass.

Luke rolled off the bed, shouting for my mother.

I did not move.

Savannah grabbed a pair of scissors from her nightstand and when that great arm entered the window and moved along the sill toward the lock, Savannah struck with those scissors and the blade stuck in his forearm. He howled with pain and withdrew his arm. Then he began kicking out the window frame with his foot and pieces of wood and glass splintered and fell into the room.

His head, lionesque and cruel, peered into the room, and he smiled when he saw my mother standing in the hallway looking at him.

My mother, trembling, begged, "Please, go away. Please, go away."

Savannah threw a hairbrush at his face. He laughed. He laughed again when he saw my mother try to control her trembling.

Then the first jar broke against the wall above his head.

Luke threw the next jar straight at Callanwolde's face; it missed and exploded against the windowsill.

Then the man's head disappeared and we saw his huge leg swing into the window, slowly entering as he tried to make himself smaller and squeeze through the opening. Luke opened four jars and emptied them on his trouser leg. Savannah ran to the bookcase and returned with a jar. She hurled the contents at the advancing leg and the jar exploded against the floor. My mother was screaming for my grandmother. The man's other leg slid through the window and he arched his spine, preparing to slide into the room, when the first black widow sent her venom shooting through his bloodstream. It was that enormous howl of pain we would remember most clearly later. In the light of the hallway we saw those huge legs withdraw as a small civilization of spiders found themselves on the loose and alarmed in the folds and creases of his trousers. He felt them moving on him and he rolled down the roof, panicked now, hurting and out of control. We heard his body hit the ground outside the window. He was screaming now, confused, rolling on the ground, beating at his legs and groin with his immense hands. Then, rising, he looked up toward my mother watching him from that destroyed window, screamed again, and ran toward the woods of Callanwolde as if on fire.

We never learned how many spiders bit him. The dogs came the next day and lost his trail by the gas station on Stillwood Avenue. The police alerted every hospital. But no seven-foot giant with a red beard who had been bitten by black widows presented himself for treatment at a Georgia hospital. His disappearance was as mysterious and open-ended as his sudden appearance had been.

My father returned the following weekend and we left the same day for the island. Our mother forbade us to tell our father a single thing about the man who had so shaken our lives. When we asked her why, she explained that our father had just returned from a war and had a right to come back to a happy family. More darkly, she suggested that our father might think that she had done something to invite the attentions of Callanwolde. My father often said to her that no woman was raped who had not asked for it. She told us this matter-of-factly and said there were many things that men could not understand.

Luke, Savannah, and I spent the next three days trying to recapture the missing spiders. We found half a dozen in our bedroom. We found two in the attic and one in one of my old tennis shoes. We never slept in that room again. After we left my grandmother continued to find black widows in different places around the house. When Papa John died, she released all of them deep in the Callanwolde woods. She, nor any of us, ever killed a spider again. The spider became the first of a number of sacred species in our family chronicle.

Many years later while going through some clippings in the Atlanta Public Library, I came upon a photograph and the following news item: "Otis Miller, 31, was arrested in Austell, Georgia, last night for suspicion of having raped and murdered Mrs. Bessie Furman, a local schoolteacher separated from her husband."

I made a photocopy of that story and inked a single word across it: Callanwolde.

Mary Hood

Nobody's Fool

Floyd headed up the hill to feed the dogs. They had been hoping for him, pacing the length of the near fence, for an hour. He was that much later than usual; it was his day to shave. A man with the shakes would be a fool to shave fast. When Floyd opened the door to the shed to get the food, Goldie padded down to the gate and poked her muzzle through the gap by the latch, sniffing, her blind eyes blue as the sky. Cinder, the puppy, tromped over the empty pans, dumping the water basin in his clumsy hunger. The bald patch on his hip was hairing over and he no longer limped. He looked as if he had been rolling in ashes. He always could find trouble.

"Now, listen," Floyd said, pleased as he always was by their boiling-over welcome. He staggered a little under the weight of the chow sack. It was hard to open. He tugged at the string, then took out his knife and cut it. He should have done what Ida said, put some food in a bucket and not carried the whole bag, but how could he, after she said it? The bag only weighed twenty-five pounds. That wasn't too much for a man. She was at work. She'd never know it if he didn't do what she said, and why should he? Just because she said?

"It'll weigh even less going back downhill," he told the dogs. They were busy eating. He stood in the open gate, watching them. They weren't doing anything but eat. They ate loud.

"All you think about's your belly," he said.

It was nice weather. Floyd liked spring. He thought he'd get the rake and sweep up those last oak leaves. Ida said for him not to get up on the ladder and do the gutters, but he could still rake. He'd rake.

Then—before he could say more than "Whoa"—the dogs got out, got past him, escaped, tore away across the yard as if they'd been planning it for weeks. Cinder was leading, Goldie at his heels. For a blind dog, Goldie was keeping up.

"Y'all don't," Floyd said.

But they did. Straight down across Ida's rye grass, under the cedar fence, and free, barking out of sight as if they were closing on a coon. Floyd listened for the squeal of brakes—nothing—so that was all right, they made it across the highway, heading for the woods behind the shopping plaza. He could imagine them pelting on like that for hours, till their dinner gave out and they circled back for supper.

"They'll be back before you get home," Floyd said aloud. He hoped so. He didn't want to hear from Ida about it. She'd say he couldn't even manage that, to leave it to her to do from now on.

"I was just trying to save you from walking up here in the mud and ruining your shoes," Floyd said.

He'd remember to mention that, if the subject came up. Let her think about *that* for a while. "The world ain't all me-me-me," he said.

He stooped to scrabble up the dog chow that had spilled from the sack while the dogs had his attention. He toed the rest over onto their pans and left the gate open.

"They'll be back," he said.

He started down to the house, the sack of chow in his arms like a baby. Ida had been a difficult child, sure of her ways and disapproving of everybody else's, from day one. Things had to be nice and they had to be all her way. Or she'd kick sand. Or do without. Or starve. She was proud. Nice about things, always wanting better. "Like her mama," he said.

Once Ida had gone without her lunch. Refused to eat it. Opened her brown sack at school and announced, "This isn't mine. Someone stole my lunch," in that flash and fury against all things wrong and second best that carried her through high school, chin high, and on past college too, to tell the world, for her living, how it was doing things wrong too. That day, she said, "My mama don't make black banana sandwiches." The teacher sent home a note. Floyd remembered it like yesterday. He laughed.

He set the chow sack against the shed door and sighed. It had been easier on the downhill. "A sight easier," he said. The pain in his shoulder eased in a minute, but he thought he would rest some more before he started raking. He sat on the patio and chewed. It was pouch tobacco, not his usual plug. Ida had bought it for him. She didn't approve, and didn't see any difference. Besides, Piggly Wiggly didn't carry Bull of the Woods, and Piggly Wiggly was where she got double coupons.

"No use in telling you," Floyd told her.

All day long he'd talk to her like that, till she came home from work. They'd eat in silence, or else she'd talk, talk, talk at him. It wasn't always quarreling, but it wore him out, so he'd go to his room and listen to the radio till bedtime. Ida liked her TV in the evenings. She laughed along. Sometimes she talked on the phone at the same time.

It was ringing now.

Floyd spit into his soup can and had a sip of Coca-Cola before he answered.

"Hay-lo," he said. "This here's Floyd."

"I'm Bob, the computer," the voice said. Floyd listened. He didn't know Bob.

"Did you say computer?" Floyd asked.

The voice talked on without pause. It didn't matter if you were listening or not, Floyd thought. He hung up. "Bad as you," he told Ida. He had better to do.

Ida said, "All you had to do was shut that gate."

"I was just trying to save you from some trouble," he said.

"Then why didn't you shut the gate?"

They were driving slowly along. All the yards they passed were empty. Everyone was at work, or indoors, watching TV. There was only one dog in sight—a Doberman.

Floyd said, "Those'll kill you soon as look at you."

Ida stopped the car and got out. The Doberman danced as he barked, his clipped ears, healing in their splints, white as horns.

"Somebody's bad news," Floyd said.

Ida got in and drove them on. They turned left. Her window was rolled down so she could whistle. She beat on the side of the car with her hand. Cinder and Goldie were nowhere to be seen.

"They'll come home when they get hungry," Floyd told her.

"You're the one who's hungry," Ida said. "That's why you want to give up looking." Whatever Floyd knew, she knew better.

Floyd took some tobacco and packed his cheek.

"And don't you spit from that window," Ida said. "I ran this car through the Bubble Wash this afternoon."

"I'd swaller it first," Floyd said.

They went past the shopping center. At the mud lane into the pines where the dirt bikers roared on weekends, Ida slowed.

"You reckon my babies got this far?" she said.

"I hope I'd have more sense," Floyd said. "Why do they dock them dogs like that? Ears and tail too. Didn't leave him more than a nub."

Ida said, turning onto the mud, "It's dry enough. We won't get stuck." She rocked them slowly along the ruts, trying not to splatter her clean car. Floyd sat up straight, his fist on the door handle. They ran over a piece of chrome from a junked car. There was a mattress sagging against a dinette chair. Ida edged past. Then they came to the scrap roofing and old tires, blocking the way.

"Trash is all they are who'd do a thing like that," Ida said. She had to saw the car, back and forth, back and forth, to get them turned around and headed back to the road. When she got to the highway, she blew out her breath and just sat there.

"Ain't nothing coming," Floyd said. "Either way."

"You-can-give-me-a-minute," Ida said, like she was counting out change, each coin clicking down to pay a righteous debt.

"Just trying to help," Floyd said, folding his hands.

"Help like yours I need like a hole in the ground," Ida said. "All you had to do was *shut that gate*!"

Floyd opened the door and got out. He had to spit. He worked on that.

She leaned across the seat and yelled, "You going to run off too?"

He swiveled around. "Better for both of us if I did."

"Wipe your chin," she said. She handed him a Kleenex. She was always right there with her Kleenex, her coasters, her spray wax, her dictionary, her Lysol, her vitamin tablets, her salt substitute.

He turned his back on her. "Ain't good for nothing no more," he said, just loud enough if she cared to deny it. He could set off, walking, if he knew which way was north. He could find friends. He checked the sun, held his hand forth, counting the hours between it and the horizon. He still wore his watch on his grandpa's chain, but it was broken.

"Get in this car, Daddy," she said, gunning it. Next thing she'd be blowing the horn.

"Maybe I'll walk," he said. "I've walked further'n that."

"Right now, Mister," Ida said.

"Many a day," Floyd said. But he was already trembling, like he'd gone miles. That lint cough, the one the mill had retired him for, bent him over, blind. He didn't even notice it any more. He stood up, wiped his eyes, and eased back into the car.

"Pore as a snake," he said, catching his breath.

She just stared at him. "Why do you do this? Behave like a child? I've had students no worse than you. They don't waste *my* time, not a minute. I send them out."

She drove toward home, fast. The tire made a flap-flapping sound on the asphalt. Floyd heard it, but didn't mention it. Maybe they'd wreck.

She heard it too.

She slowed, eased over onto the shoulder, past the sign that said: BOILD P'NUT AHEAD FRESH HOT GOOD. Closed till summer.

"Well, check and *see,*" she said. "Can't you even do that?"

Floyd got out and looked. There was a piece of board stuck to the right rear tire. The tire went on down to flat as soon as he had kicked the board loose. The long nails left holes like snakebite.

Ida got out and looked, too.

"I don't suppose anyone'll stop," she said. "Why should they?"

Floyd said, "I can fix it."

She didn't count on that, he could see. "I'll trouble you for them keys," he said.

When he got the trunk open and was fiddling with the jack—it had to fit in those holes in the bumper and he couldn't get it right—a truck pulled up behind them and a man in a camouflage jumpsuit offered to help.

It didn't take him long.

Floyd unbuttoned his front pocket and unwadded three bills from his snap purse. He handed them to the man. "Many thanks," he said. "If there's ever anything I can do for you some day . . ."

The man pushed the money back. He laughed. "Keep it, old-timer. Buy yourself some Red Man." He swung up into his truck and drove away.

Floyd stood there for a minute. Ida was already back in the car, washing her hands on a little towelette. Floyd flung the dollars into the sedge. He kicked at one of the bills that fluttered by.

Ida started the engine. "Daddy?"

When he shut his door, it hung up.

"*Slam* it!" Ida said. "Can you?"

Floyd said, "Don't worry about *me.*"

They rode along not talking.

Just before they turned onto the street where Ida's house was, Floyd said, "If you was to need a transplant, I'd be who to ask. You can have anything I've got that'd do you any good."

Ida aimed the car up the drive, braked sharp, rammed the lever into park, then jerked out the keys. "I don't need anything presently," she said. She laughed.

Floyd just sat there, thinking. Ida went on into the house. She didn't look back out, or wonder.

The dogs came home on their own. Ida was out at the fence welcoming them, pouring red-eye gravy on their chow, talking to them like children past nine o'clock that night. Floyd watched from the kitchen door. He couldn't have gravy. Ida read where it was bad for his heart.

Floyd went to his room and packed.

He didn't know whether to tell her or just leave a note, but if he told her, she'd have something to say.

"Nothing I ain't heard," he decided.

He stayed in his room till she had left for work the next morning. As she left, she tapped on his door.

"Daddy? Daddy?"

When he didn't answer, she went on to school. He could hear her muttering, "Like a rock . . . whole place could burn down around him . . . thank Jesus he doesn't smoke . . ." She had to be at school by 7:30.

Floyd waited till her taillights were good and gone. Then he tied up the pillowcase with his extra overalls and Sunday shirt. Ida hated his overalls, hated the very sight and color of denim, but Floyd didn't mind it. He'd spent his life making it, so why should he mind? He was drawing seventy-five cents a day—"A *day,*" Floyd said—at the sawmill when he got hired on at the cotton mill for three dollars a day. It made a difference in their life right from the first paycheck. Ida didn't know how to be grateful, that was what it was. Floyd had his Bible in the sack, too, and the photograph of all of them, that summer day at the river when he got himself baptized and stopped drinking for all time. A man could change for the better, Floyd knew. He liked to keep the evidence at hand. He put his knife in his pocket and counted what was left of his pension. He had enough.

He reached down his hat from the closet shelf, and put it on, by touch, from long experience. Floyd knew who he was. He could shave in the dark. His hat had that trademark billiard-rack block to the crown. Ida hated that hat. Said a sock cap, like babies wear, was warmer. She bought him one, and a muffler to match. Floyd left it in the box, saying, "Where's my mittens, Mama?" and wouldn't even wear it to feed the dogs.

Floyd dug out his pencil and licked it twice.

Now Ida, he wrote, *dont bother. I done it before and I no how to live. A man has to pull his own weight at least. I done fed the dogs. When I am settled I will let you no.*

Yore dad, Floyd.

He added at the bottom: *no usen caling me,*
it'll be long distance.
No usen hunting me.
I don't like it hear.
All you do is fuss.

In fairness, he marked that out so she'd read: *All we do is fuss.*

He set out, walking strong. If a man offered him a ride, he'd consider it. But he felt strong enough for miles, if no one did. When he saw just the right sapling he carved it down some and kept it in hand.

"To scare off varmints," Floyd said, nobody's fool. He read the papers.

He was meeting all the traffic on its way to town jobs. He wasn't going that way. Nobody even slowed. Some of them had on their headlights. The wisps of fog off the river blew into pieces as they drove through it. Even without the traffic, there was a wind. He stopped to put on his extra shirt. As he bent to retie the pillowsack—caught between his legs as if he were shoeing a horse—his hat blew off, skipping along, teasing him into chasing it with his stick.

Then the wind played a trick. Lifted the hat over the railing of the bridge and tossed it up, sailing it out on a curve, into the water below. Floyd watched it settle into its reflection, sinking slow. It was considerably oiled after years, randomly waterproofed by Wildroot. A little fishing skiff putted up to the rocks below the bridge and their mere trolling wake sent it under.

"Adios, hat," Floyd said.

He walked on across the bridge, then, bare-headed, clear-headed, undizzy. There was more to think about than a lost hat.

"I played here as a boy," he told the fisherman at the other end of the bridge. "Used to jump right off the mill into the deep over yonder."

The man looked where Floyd pointed.

The lake covered it now. And the fields he'd run. "Prettiest cotton," Floyd said. He saw the fisherman didn't remember.

"It's this new road," Floyd said, irritated. "It don't go where it used to, just to town and back. Look over *yonder,*" he said. "That hill?"

The man looked again.

"Me and this old boy hauled Book Gravely up it with ropes and mules to be buried close by. Drownded himself in the mill. Nowhere else to swim, but you had to be strong against the tow. Dry summer."

The man said, "Drought, huh?" He was busy with his fishing. He took out a little red and white lure from his box and hooked it on his line. Floyd watched it swing out and down, and the ripples spread wide, from such a little thing.

"Grass growed in the riverbeds so cows could graze," Floyd said. "Only green left in the county." He got thirsty remembering. He wiped his face.

"Things was different then," Floyd said. "Book didn't have no kin and it being hot, we couldn't ship him. We did it as decent as we could."

"Back then, folks was different," the fisherman said. "Cared for each other, you know."

"It's so," Floyd said. He studied the man for likeness. "You from around here?"

"My mama was from over at Rose Creek."

"Maybe she knowed her," Floyd said.

"Who?"

"The lady who come on toward nightfall and laid weeds on Book's grave. We rolled a rock on it to mark it but nobody knowed who she was, never did."

"Weeds?" He was pulling in his fish, a little one, not worth keeping.

"Weeds was all he got, and a fieldstone, but that was more than he might've, considering."

"Mama never said nothing about that," the man said.

"We always wondered," Floyd said.

The man went back to his fishing. Floyd looked out at the lake.

"Nah, mama never said nothing about that," the fisherman said again.

Floyd checked his dead watch. It was a habit, marking time. He always had to be doing something useful, or he felt he was slacking. He said, "I could talk all day," and the man said, "Yeah, I know what you mean. I could fish for a living."

"Same thing," Floyd said. "Back to work, then, son." He took up his sack and headed on up the hill. He told the man, as he went on, "Take it easy on them crappie, son, save some for the rest of us."

Floyd struck off up the hill strong, past the Marina, not looking back. He had to rest his breath, though, at the top. He stood poking at the crumbly shale on the bank by Spain's old place, honeysuckled over now, boarded up.

"Dead now," Floyd said. "I knowed him good as a brother. His little sick wife. All them flowers he growed for her to look at."

Floyd blew his nose.

When the chicken truck stopped, Floyd told the man, "I won't say no," and got up in the cab. He had to leave his hickory stick behind. He glanced back, to memorize *where*, in case he got back by there. "I hope not," he said. They were rolling. The radio was on, and the heater. Floyd sank asleep almost at once.

The lady at welfare said Floyd *had* to tell her his name. He didn't see his way clear to do that. He said he'd manage, then, without her help. Could she recommend a rooming house? She wrote the directions on a scrap of paper and he took that—and his pillowcase—and stepped off toward town, steady as he could in case she was watching from the window. "I'm no hobo," Floyd said.

At the rooming house it turned out he had enough money for one week, if he ate lean. Floyd knew how to manage that, too.

He couldn't change his Social Security till the next week. The agent only came to the courthouse on Tuesdays. Even so, it meant the next check would go on to Ida's, too late to stop it now.

"If I was to die, mid-month, she'd have to pay it all back," Floyd said. He thought that through, how she'd look when she got the letter saying IMPORTANT and she read how she'd have to miss work to get it straightened out.

"Ida, she hates paperwork," Floyd said.

Every day he walked the streets, looking for work. He got a few little jobs—mainly handyman chores—mainly for widows who couldn't even change the light bulb in their ovens. Floyd had a little problem with that, too, till the man at Otasco told him to buy the heat-resistant bulb. That woman told him, when he came back with the right bulb and explained he wouldn't charge her for his mistake, "You're not too handy but you're sure a man."

He did better on raking. Hammermill had a lot of oaks.

"They bad to hold their leaves till spring," Floyd said, door to door. He had all the work like that he needed. He piled the leaves up and burned them if they didn't want them turned into their gardens. He didn't know anything about that ordinance against burning.

"I ain't from around here," he told the police. They didn't hold him. He wasn't a vagrant. He didn't have any money to pay a fine. They could see that. They didn't shame him into crying or telling Ida's name. He didn't even feel bad about it till he got to his room to rest. He lay on his cot, weak. He couldn't even go out the next day, to straighten out about Social Security. He kept a fever, and his cough was worse.

He thought Ida had found him. He thought Ida was spying on him. He told Mrs. Sloane, when she came around to get the rent, "Look." He showed her the markings, their code, the way they numbered his room when they came checking up. She laughed.

She said, "Ridiculous!" just like Ida.

"It's where the cash register tape got in some water," she told him. "The ink's left a stain on your table, that's all."

He knew by the way she laughed it off that she was one of them. He couldn't stay any longer. But he paid her what he could, so she'd think he was going to.

That night he took his Bible and extra clothes and left by the back door, while Mrs. Sloane and the others were in the front room, watching TV. He could hear them laughing.

It was twelve steps down to the back yard. Floyd took them in one. He landed hard on his arm. He crawled back up to the house and into bed before he called for help.

"I heared it snap," he told the doctor.

They didn't know to look for his things. They lay out in the rain all night. His Bible was ruined.

Floyd had paid Mrs. Sloane all the extra he had, and the hospital wanted more. If he gave them his real name for Medicare, he was as good as back with Ida again. They'd call her before the plaster dried.

He wasn't going to be handed back. He had legs.

Floyd walked out of the hospital. It was easy.

"They weren't expecting *that*," he said, getting clean away. He headed back to Mrs. Sloane's, and when she was talking to the milkman, he slipped around and got his things. He took the alleys and lanes, walking like he had business. He had his sleeve pulled down over the cast. He fit in. No one noticed. He staggered, bummed up from the fall, but he kept on going. He loosened up as he pressed on. He could feel the heartbeat in his broken bone. He didn't dwell on it.

It wasn't raining now. That was a good thing. He sat on one of the benches in the park by the post office. He needed to think. He needed his tobacco. His head was clearer than it had been. Day was just getting going. The sparrows and starlings were awake, drifting down from the eaves and clock tower. From the courthouse roof the pigeons rose with a sound like worn-out cards being shuffled. Floyd watched them wheel. He always did like first light best. He felt young. Like he was on his way to school. Or to the mill. And none of the things that went wrong had yet come to him.

Then he thought, But they're behind me, at least, if they had to happen. The *pastness* was something. If he was young, it'd all be ahead, even if he didn't know to dread it. What was ahead now? He didn't know that, either. So it was like being young.

"If ignorance is peace," Floyd said, "I oughta be getting more out of it."

He felt for his Bible. It was swollen and damp, its pages sealed to each other around the photograph of his baptizing.

"Never mind," he said. He knew by heart what was in there. He knew what he had to do before sundown that very night. He stood. After he got moving, he was warmer. His feet woke. He picked up speed heading down the sidewalk toward the railroad. He didn't even feel hungry any more. At the depot he turned south.

It was Saturday. Plenty of traffic going both ways. He got a ride in the first mile that carried him as far as the river. After that, he rode, wind-whipped, with the sun in his eyes, in a plumber's truck that got him down to the four-way stop. There were three in the cab already. He didn't mind riding in back. "Take it easy," they told him.

"Or any way I can get it," Floyd said. He felt good. As if it were home he was nearing, not just Ida's. He walked up the drive fast.

Ida was still in her housecoat and slippers. She answered the door with a half a biscuit in her hand. She just stood and stared, without swallowing. She looked hollowed out, like she could use that biscuit and some sleep too, Floyd thought. He saw, in that light, she looked way past grown, on the downhill side, like him.

"Daddy?" She reached for his hurt arm.

"I just have this one thing to say," Floyd said. "Let me say it."

She turned him loose.

"I think I made a mistake about that dog gate," he said. "That's what I think."

She kept staring.

"Next time I won't," he told her.

She still didn't say anything.

"What do *you* think?" he wondered. She had about gripped a hole all the way through the biscuit. She took another bite and leaned against the door.

"You still mad?" Why didn't she say something?

"Talk at me," he said.

If he could just get her started, it'd be all right again. He didn't have to listen.

"Ida," he said, priming the pump, "I throwed away my hat."

Ferrol Sams

Fubar

It never crossed my mind that any of them was crazy, and now I look back on it most likely they all was. There's some things a few years'll give you if you keep your eyes open and your guard up. One of them's a little sense. Maybe not a whole lot, but then a little sense is better'n none atall. I finally got myself some and that's the only reason I'm living today. Course along with the sense come a whole new set of friends, and that helped, too.

I didn't aim to get in no trouble, but at that age I guess I sure wasn't aiming to run away from any either. At the time I had done convinced myself that all I wanted was a job, and I was hell-bent and determined I was going to get one at Freddy's. I had run with the Sunday School crowd ever since my daddy died when I was eight years old. I'd joined the Boy Scouts because Elbert lived next door and his mama gave us a ride to meetings, but I never got past Tenderfoot. I was one of them boys that grow off fast, and besides I was large of my age and I didn't like being bigger than all the scouts in my troop. On top of that, all of them still had their daddies, and back then that was still an ache in my gut worse than being hungry, tired, or sick or all three at once. Mama never would cry, so that sure didn't leave no room for a big boy like me to cut loose, but there were times I'd watch my friends with their daddies, or just listen to them drop a remark about something one of them had said, and I sure wanted to sit down and cry till I hiccupped.

My granddaddy taught me to work and he learned me to be tough and not ever cry about anything. Just like he learned my mama and all her brothers and sisters. School teachers all tell you that you ought to say *taught* instead of *learned,* but my granddaddy taught me how to work and he learned me not to cry, and if anyone can't tell the difference, all I can say is one of them lets you talk to folks and guide them and the other one just needs a set jaw with an eye that can shrivel your feelings like salt in a snail's shell. By the time I was ten he had me on a tractor; by the time I was twelve I could fix anything that broke on it and I could work in the fields way past dark. I'd do it, too. I'd do it and be real proud of it, just to watch my granddaddy spit tobacco juice and hear him tell somebody at the store, "That boy works hard as any nigger you ever saw and better'n most white men you'n find nowadays. Ain't like when I was a boy," he'd go on. "All of us was raised to work and didn't know nothing else. He's got a lot of git-up and go about him." I wanted him to love me so bad I'd have done anything he wanted. That's where I learned how to work and got it so in my bones that to this day I feel guilty if I ain't working. I wanted him to love me and I wanted him to step in and be a daddy in my life. Looking back I realize he didn't do neither of them.

When I was thirteen years old I looked like a grown man and was strong as a bull. The coaches started talking football to me, but back then we didn't have a junior varsity team and wasn't no way I could play till I got to the ninth grade. I got my growth and my build from my daddy's side, but I still felt like a little kid inside. A six-foot two-inch kid. I asked my granddaddy about my daddy one day; told him I still missed him so bad I couldn't hardly stand it. My granddaddy hadn't ever mentioned my daddy to me, and yet I knew they'd worked together a long time. I could remember my daddy on the tractor and my granddaddy with a hoe, both in the same field. And I could remember my granddaddy stepping over to the store for a Co-Cola or setting for a half hour under a shade tree to fan with his straw hat while my daddy kept that tractor chugging and clanging, never letting up till dinnertime.

When I said I missed my daddy, he rared back and spit a long stream and told me that my daddy never would have amounted to nothing if it hadn't a been for him. My daddy, he said, was wild as a buck and didn't study nothing but laughing and having a good time, and he never would have settled down and held a regular job. My granddaddy set him up in the produce business and taught him all he ever learned about farming. Why, the only reason he was able to afford that nice brick house for me and my mama, which we didn't really need nohow, was because of what my granddaddy had done for him; he never would have amounted to a hill of beans otherwise. Then he told me in a real flat voice my daddy was dead and gone and I had to put the past behind me and the cantaloupes was overdue for turning.

Well, sir, I felt like the hungry man they talked about in church who wanted fish and got a serpent and then asked for bread and got nothing but a cold, hard rock. I asked about my daddy and got my granddaddy. Big I, little you. That was when I commenced thinking my granddaddy didn't really care about anybody but himself. He never even laughed about anything unless it was a put-down on somebody he didn't like, and there sure were a heap more folks that he didn't like than he did. All the things he told wound up making him look smart and important and the other fellow dumb and trifling.

I asked my mama if I had to work for Granddaddy, and she gave me a look and then set her jaw and turned off. In a minute she said one word. "No." We never mentioned it again. My mama is not somebody you do a lot of talking to, and I sure didn't dare tell her about Daddy. She never talked about him, but she's never dated another man and that in spite of her being the best looking woman in the whole county.

Anyhow, that's how I come to be looking for a job. And the reason I wanted to work at the Freddy's Fubar Filling Station was because everybody who hung out there laughed all the time. They laughed at things other folks were scared of. Seemed like all the funny folks in town swarmed to Freddy's. It was on one of the corners across from the courthouse where the two highways crossed and was easy to get to, but I always felt like the same folks would have hung out there if it had been down behind the burying ground. I know they would if Freddy had run it because he was the one that drawed them in and kept them coming. You never knew what Freddy was going to say next.

First time I personally run into anything out of the ordinary there was the first time I ever went in there. It wasn't a place that school kids felt welcome in. We all went another block on down to the drug store or else some of the tough guys would head over town a couple of blocks to Burson's Cafe where you could play pool and cuss a little and get a thumb dog from Buck. You couldn't cuss much because Buck wouldn't stand for anybody saying the Lord's name and the F word or he'd threaten you with a cue stick, but you could use all the others and he'd just grin. That and his weenies was part of growing up in our town. Buck's weenies were just regular old weenies; it was watching him fix'em that made them special. He'd grab a bun and then lick his thumb like some folks do to turn a page in the phone book. Then he'd spread the bun open with that same thumb and reach in the water and pull a weenie out with his hand and lay it in there. It was fun to watch a guy the first time he ordered a hot dog at Buck's. It wasn't no place for a candy ass, I'll tell you that.

The afternoon I went into Freddy's for a Coke was right after I started watching my granddaddy and deciding he didn't really ever think about nobody but himself. There was about a half dozen in the station, a couple of them playing checkers and Boss cleaning out his fingernails with his Barlow, and nobody paid me any attention. I got my Coke out of the box and put my nickel on the register, and about that time Lamar Hester rolled up in his sawmilling truck. He came in hollering for Freddy and said he needed a drink and needed one bad. Freddy said yeah, he had a drink and he'd let him have one, but just one. And he reached up under the register and pulled out a bottle of liquor and handed it to Lamar. I'll never forget it. Lamar stood spraddle-legged right in the middle of the filling station between the stand for maps and the butane heater. There was two fly swatters hanging on the wall next to the bathroom door underneath a calendar with a picture of Miss Turpentine Queen on it. Just the ends of the fly swatters were showing, for they hadn't been used in four months. Lamar took the cap off the bottle, throwed his head back, and swung that bottle straight up. When he did, Freddy stuck the muzzle of his pistol right behind Lamar's ear and said, "If your Adam's apple moves more'n once, I'll blow your goddam brains out the other side your head."

Well, sir, I tried to squeeze in between the fan belts and the glass case with the Moon Pies and goobers in it, but nothing happened. Lamar took one swallow and laughed and handed the bottle back, and Boss kept working on a split nail with that old pocket knife and it seemed like business as usual at Freddy's Fubar Filling Station. One of the checker players jumped a king and said, "Freddy, you got to watch that damn fellow. It's just three o'clock in the afternoon and he might be one of them alkyhawlics. Hand that bottle around, why don't you? I didn't know you had an extry one hid out or I'da done been in it."

Nobody said a word when I come in, and far as I know nobody said a word when I went out, but from that day on I was fascinated with Freddy's.

His name wasn't even Freddy. It was Carter Lee Cantrell III, but most folks in town had plumb forgot what his name really was and couldn't of told you any more'n they could sing out the real names for Boss Cleveland or Mouse Stinchcomb or Polly Parrott or Custard Mize, let alone Miss Bunch Brown. Come to find out he'd got his nickname from the Li'l Abner comic strip where everybody went around for weeks asking, "Are you ready for Freddy?" and Freddy finally turned out to be the undertaker. Carter Lee had picked up the name because he could outdrink all his buddies, and when they'd get to talking about how liquor was going to kill him, he'd brag that when all of them was dead, he'd embalm 'em in half his Old Crow and drink the rest. And then he'd laugh and yell out, "Are you ready for Freddy?" And the name caught on.

When he took over the filling station, he personally put the sign up, and when I found out what Fubar had meant to Freddy and everybody else who went off to World War II, I nearly died and thought for sure the missionary ladies would run him out of town for it. But nobody ever objected that I heard of, and I finally decided that either the missionaries didn't know what it meant or that it wouldn't have been genteel to notice it. Sort of like you're not supposed to notice or snicker if somebody poots when there's company around, although your mama will frail hell out of you if you slip up and do it when there's just homefolks there. Mama don't talk much but she's hell on pooting.

I got up my nerve to go back to the Fubar a coupla days later. The same two guys was playing checkers and far as I knew they played there every day but Sunday. They didn't neither one ever go to church but they'd been raised not to play checkers on the Lord's day. There was a different crowd warming the butane heater and they was laughing at old Harley Prince. There was a bottle going around in a sneaky way with folks turning it up but looking sideways out the window while they swallowed. It was against the law to drink in public back in them days and we had a marshall in town who'd make a case against you in a minute if he caught you at it. Harley Prince wasn't in the Fubar but he had just left and they was all laughing at what he'd said. Harley was a newcomer to our town, hadn't been there more'n ten or twelve years, and he'd been to college and smoked Parliament cigarettes and all that, but still he hung out at the Fubar now and then. He talked fine proper English all the time and he'd get off these real good zingers without ever cracking a smile. He didn't rightly have no business hanging out in the Fubar, what with his college education and all, but he hadn't been raised here and didn't know any better.

Seems he was at the heater and had just took a drink when Hardup Betsill come in. Hardup always deserved a heap of credit, I thought, for growing up in the middle of ten sisters who babied him to death and still getting in the produce business and winding up rich. The only thing was he never could keep from bragging. Lots of times he was lying, too.

Once they said he was with a crowd of fellows in Atlanta and they all told the waitress that Hardup was going to pay the bill, and he was good-natured and said he would but that she'd have to get him a blank check. And when she asked him what bank he wanted it on, Hardup said, "It don't make no difference, I got money in all of them." Folks in town just took things like that as his ways and didn't pay it no attention. Except to laugh at him.

That afternoon he'd wandered into Fubar's and bought himself a pack of crackers and a Pepsi because his third wife wouldn't let him drink no liquor and she was about thirty pounds heavier'n him and twice as mean, so he minded real good. He turned around to Harley Prince and said, "Harley, I've told everybody else but I ain't seen you. Did you know I'd bought my wife a house in Florida?"

And Harley dead-panned it and said in that kind of lofty way he had, "No, I didn't, Hardup, but I'll tell you right now if she's going to run it herself you'll lose money."

And it went plumb over Hardup's head. He said, "Oh, it ain't for rent, it's just for pleasure." Hardup is pretty slow about everything but produce, and since Harley Prince never cracked a smile but just said, "Indeed?" everybody else in the Fubar felt like they weren't real men if they give it away by laughing, so they all held it till Hardup and Harley Prince had done walked out together.

That was the day I asked Freddy for a job and that was the day he give me one. I felt like I was going to belong somewheres and on account of that I was going to amount to something.

It didn't take me long to figure out that except for Hardup everybody that hung out at Freddy's Fubar had one thing in common and that was liquor. Freddy had liquor hid out everywhere and the only place that made me nervous was the tire casings. If you snatched a tire off the pile without feeling around in it first, you were liable to sling a bottle out and break it, and that created more commotion than a weasel in the hen house for sure and certain.

Most of the regulars brought their own, but Freddy was always good for a drink if any of them had run out. Freddy hisself killed two quarts every day. He drank vodka before dinner time and bourbon in the afternoon, and I never saw him when he was thick-tongued or staggering. He usually had a smart answer for everything and laughed at things you'd never thought was funny till Freddy got hold of them.

Him and Lamar Hester used to crank up and laugh at each other every day about six o'clock. Lamar'd come in from the sawmill and set there till he got to feeling good, and then him and Freddy would start jowering with each other about who was going to live the longest. Freddy and his folks went to the old doctor in town, who had moved in as a young man but hadn't ever really been looked on as anything but a newcomer cause he wasn't born here and even had a wife who come from Michigan. Lamar's family had all took up with the young doctor. He'd been raised in our county and come home to practice medicine, and he might still have a lot to learn, which he did, but at least he was one of us. Old Doc talked proper all the time and wouldn't get out of bed at night unless you was born a Calhoun or a Carmichael. Young Doc was the one everybody took their field hands to and Lamar liked him because he'd see his sawmill hands when they was sick or cut. Old Doc said "whiskey" and Young Doc said "likker." Each one of 'em said that was what was going to kill Freddy and Lamar. Freddy and Lamar would get to laughing about it and turn their bottles up. They even had a bet about who was going to live the longest. Only thing kept 'em from putting the money up was they couldn't agree on somebody they could trust to hold the stakes. They talked tough but you got the feeling they was friends.

"Here you come as wall-eyed as a hung-up dog and it barely six o'clock in the evening," Freddy said one day. "That means you ain't got your own bottle again and that you're ready for Freddy."

"Here's my bottle, you spindle-legged tumble turd," Lamar fired back. "I even brought you a drink, and don't say I never gave you nothing. Punch Stinchcomb made this batch his own self. Run it through a radiator down on Ginger Cake Creek and caught it in his mama's slop jar. I think he might have even rinched it out first. It's been aging ever since yesterday and it's guaranteed to clear your head and shrink your liver. You look like you're nine months pregnant and you're the one what's ready for Freddy. Drink up."

"Shut up, boy. That whiskey's going to kill you. Your eyes are redder'n a fox's ass in pokeberry season."

"You're flat out wrong, Freddy. Whiskey's going to get you. Likker's what's going to kill me, and I got a medical opinion to back me up. But I still bet you five hundred dollars I outlive you by at least ten days. Have a swallow!"

"Lamar, I wouldn't drink that shit if you had a gun drawed on me with the hammer cocked. I've always heard that the worst liquor ever came through this county was back in thirty-two when Judge Ballard paid off an election bet with a gallon that'd been made out of ice cream cones. Even Ferrol McFarland and Lawrence Hightower couldn't drink it. Mr. Lawrence told me he couldn't get it past his nose even when he held it out at arm's length and come in fast as a wood duck. That stuff you've got is stinking up the whole station. You'll have to drink it in the bathroom or under the grease rack."

"Trouble with you, Freddy, is you done drunk whiskey instead of likker until you ain't nothing but a sissy. You don't know bad likker. In New Guinea oncet I had buddied up with a coupla yankees. Wasn't nothing else in the outfit to buddy with or I never would of sunk that low. They was always making fun of me being from Georgia and the way I talked and all. Nobody but the officers had any alcohol on the whole island. Them two yankees and me got hold of a whole mess of dehydrated potatoes and some sugar from one of the mess sergeants and set us up a still out in the jungle. They'd never heard of such, but there sure wasn't anything else to do on that goddam island. I mixed up the mash and rigged a condenser out of parts from the motor pool and we let it sit for about a week before we decided it was time to run it. It was a little green but the weather was awful hot and we had to run it. Now that was bad likker.

"One of them boys was from the Bronx and other from Brooklyn and they had trouble drinking it, but I shamed 'em into it. I drunk the most of it trying to set them an example, and when I come to you know where I was? I was tied up like a hog, slung from a pole with my head hanging down backwards and a bunch of barefooted savages was trotting through that jungle with me. The soles of their feet was tougher'n Biscuit Tarpley's. Come to find out them fuzzies come by the still when I passed out. Bronx and Brooklyn sold me to them. The CO seen Bronx and Brooklyn come walking across camp rubberlegged and laughing and stopped them. He had got used to seeing three of us wherever one of us went.

" 'Where's Georgia?' he asked. And they giggled and he says, 'You're drunk! Where's Georgia?' And they commenced dying alaughing and told him I'd passed out and they'd sold me to some black folks and when I woke up I'd be a slave and that'd teach me a lesson about being from Georgia. The which is a bunch of bull shit, for none of the Hesters far as I know ever had no slaves back in the old days, and I sure as hell wouldn't be bothered with owning one of the sorry bastards now; it's all I can do to pay 'em sawmill wages and kick they asses home ever night. You couldn't give me a slave. But yankees think we all used to be up to our elbows and butt-holes in them and they ain't nothing going to change a yankee's mind about the South. Ever.

"Thank God the Captain stepped in. He hollered, 'Hell, these people don't own slaves. They're going to eat him.' And Brooklyn laughed louder and told old Bronx I'd be upset but that I'd probably think it was better'n none atall, and the Captain plumb exploded and said they'd have to find me before I was carried into a village or it'd be too late, that they was gonna cook me and eat me. And he got up a detail and found the path I was on and rescued me. He had to buy me back; those spooks didn't want to turn me loose. They was bandy-legged and fuzzy-headed and all of 'em had big thick scars they'd cut into they faces and sharp pointy teeth. One of 'em had a chicken bone through his nose, and none of 'em spoke no English to amount to nothing. The Captain wound up trading three machetes and two sacks of sugar for me and throwed in two boxes of matches for boot. I had the worst headache I ever had in my life."

Freddy laughed, "It's a damn good thing for you that captain was in charge, Lamar. If it had been me they'd never have got but one machete and no sugar at all. Hell, no wonder the government's nearly bankrupt; squandering money and overpaying for sorry trash like that."

"You kiss Old Rusty, Freddy. What hacked me was that Brooklyn and Bronx had sold me in the first place for only two coconuts and a string of beads. And come to find out those natives do eat folks. They call it 'long pig,' and that's what everybody in the outfit called me after that night, 'cept they finally just made it plain 'Pig Hester' and it followed me plumb through the service. Here, take a drink outa my bottle."

By then Freddy'd done got to where he could drink anything. "Don't care if I do. How'd you get even with Brooklyn and Bronx?"

"I never did. When we left New Guinea, Brooklyn got hit in the leg going in on a beach head. Bronx and me dragged him through the water and commenced trying to run with him and a sniper got Bronx square between the eyes and then sprayed Brooklyn's guts all over my face and he died in my arms hollering Jesus and cussing Japs. Ain't nobody called me 'Pig' since and better not, by God, nobody ever do it again. Hand me your bottle. Mine's empty. You're right about my liquor stinking, but it don't smell as bad as Brooklyn's guts did."

With that he threw his bottle up against the wall and broke it into a thousand pieces, and Freddy laughed fit to kill and hollered, "That ain't no fireplace, but kill this'n and throw it, too. You got a home in the Fubar."

Now, you think after that I'd ever be satisfied working anywhere else? I could have played football for three years and plowed cantaloupes for twenty and missed all that story.

One of my favorite folks was ole man John Jenkins. He come in ever morning at eight o'clock just before I left for the school house, got a Co-Cola and a sack of roasted goobers without speaking to nobody, and locked hisself in the toilet. He was always still in there when I left for school and I asked Freddy once what time did he come out, and the Fubars started watching and he always stayed in the toilet exactly an hour. Freddy took to banging on the door ever now and then when he'd think about it and hollering, "Whatcha doing in there, Mr. John? Everthing coming out all right?" But old man John always stayed his full hour and when he did come out, he still didn't speak to nobody and just walked on out the Fubar. I never saw him in the house or out lest he had his hat on. He died in his sleep one night. Lamar Hester asked Freddy did he reckon the Co-Colas killed him and said he'd of been safer drinking liquor. Freddy laughed, but every morning after that between eight and nine he locked the restroom door. If a stranger came in and wanted to use it, Freddy would bang on the door and holler, "Mr. John, everthing coming out all right?" Then he'd tell the man he'd have to wait till nine o'clock cause Mr. John was in the john. Harley Prince said he was glad Mr. John's last name hadn't been Trapper.

Freddy always opened up the Fubar hisself and heap of times I knew he'd slept there all night. It wasn't that he got too drunk to go home. I never did figure out why he'd sleep in that old station now and then. I guess he stayed drunk all the time but he never seemed drunk to me, just didn't give a damn and made jokes about most everything. Real early one morning this car load of folks from out of town pulled up and Freddy came prancing out the station all dressed out in one them wide hats and a shawl with a hole in it that somebody had brought him back from Mexico. He was running forwards two steps and backwards one and bowing from the waist. He had a ukulele in his hand and when the driver rolled down his window, he bowed real deep and hollered, "Good morning! Are you ready for Freddy?" and the driver acted real dignified and said, "Fill it up, please."

And Freddy said, "Fill it up? Fill it up? I can play you a tune, but I can't fill'er up for another half hour." And the man smiled real nice and wanted to know how come, and Freddy hollered out, "Cause, by God, it's too early in the morning! I ain't even puked yet!" Then he laughed like crazy and that's the first time I ever saw a fifty-year-old man scratch off. Most of our trade was local.

That was also the morning Harley Prince insulted the Masons. Masons was the only thing in our town stronger'n the Baptists, and everybody that amounted to anything seemed like was in the Lodge, and they was also the only people, the way I could see it, who took themselves as serious as the Baptists. Bobby Lee Bowers had worked up to Shrine and come by the Fubar selling tickets to the barbecue they had every year up at the Lodge Hall. Everybody in the Fubar had bought at least one. Harley Prince walked in all straight-back and dignified, and Bobby Lee walked up and said, "Mr. Prince, I'd like to sell you a ticket," and Harley said, "A ticket to what, my good man?" And Bobby Lee said, "To the Masonic barbecue." And Harley barks out, "Sorry. I do not support Communist Front organizations." And everybody sucked in their breath except Freddy. He let out a laugh and whooped, "You're really ready for Freddy." Then he grabbed his pistol and shot straight up and everybody cleared out for a while.

Hawk Forts was the mayor and he wasn't a regular except on Monday and Friday mornings. He had the concession on the condrum machine in the men's toilet, and he took out the quarters on Monday and put in the rubbers on Friday. The Forts family had a heap of money and at one time had owned nearly the whole town, but everything was tied up in the estate and Hawk sold them rubbers to get his spending money. He got elected mayor every year and that paid twenty dollars a month. Harley Prince said when he observed the qualifications for public office in our town that he did believe he would offer for City Council his own self, even if he hadn't been born and raised there. Freddy kept at him and promised he'd support him, and Harley actually announced. He might have overcome Freddy's endorsement and insulting the Masons and got elected, too, because his opponent didn't amount to nothing and was sorry as gully dirt, if he'd only kept his mouth shut.

About a week before election, Mel Johnson tracked him down in the Fubar and gave him a check and that did it. Mel had the insurance agency, and the Baptist preacher's wife had run into Harley's car when his wife was taking their little girl to school and tore up a fender. Mrs. Prince was pregnant again and Mel Johnson had the preacher's car insured. When the check came in, he hunted Harley up and give it to him because Mel was always real prompt and dotted his i's and crossed his t's. And Harley looked at the check and then swung around to everybody in the Fubar and announced real formal, "I accept this check for damages to my automobile, but I proclaim before God and these witnesses here assembled that if my unborn child grows up to be a Baptist, I still have a claim against Johnson Insurance Agency." Freddy got so tickled he shot twice that morning, but sure enough Harley got beat. He come by the Fubar on election night and took so drunk they had to take him home. He still talked real formal, drunk or not.

I'd been working for Freddy about six, seven months I reckon; at any rate I'd done turned fifteen and I was muscled out more'n ever and was six-three and shaved every day. Whenever one the Fubars happened to notice me, they'd say I looked like my Daddy and that always made me feel good and I wouldn't have left Freddy by now for nothing. On a Friday evening just before supper time, there was a crowd of Fubars there. It was summer time and they was setting on benches out front and it wasn't good dusk-dark yet. Bob Marston had just come up and somebody said to him, ain't it been a pretty day. Bob was bad to look on the dark side of things ever since he'd been sheriff all them years and had to put up with criminals and also their kinfolks on visiting days, and he hardly ever smiled anymore. That evening he had just dropped by for a minute. You could tell because he didn't have his bridge across his upper front and his tushes was all that kept his upper lip from sucking in all the way, and he was in his undershirt with his galluses hanging down. And he growled back, "Yeah, it has been so far, but it ain't too late yet for some sonbitch to come along and mess it up."

About that time here come Harley Prince and somebody asked how he was and he said he was very upset and Freddy says, "How come?" And Harley looked real mournful and says, "I discovered that my wife doesn't trust me." Freddy comes back with, "Whatcha mean?" And Harley says, "She's gone to visit her sister in Birmingham and I just found out that she took the diaphragm with her." Well, sir, Freddy got out the pistol and shot and everbody laughed, including me, although it was going on two years before I caught on to what was funny. Bob Marston laughed for once till he nearly choked and said, "I just be goddam." After that everybody passed their bottles around and broke up and started home.

When Lamar Hester drove up that evening wasn't nobody left but Freddy and me and Hardup and Burdell the black boy that Freddy'd hired to wash cars since I'd built up his mechanic business so much I didn't have time to wash and shine. Burdell was about forty, forty-five years old and would probably have worked for nothing because he couldn't hold no regular job, and I'd caught him a hundred times sneaking drinks from Freddy's bottles. I hadn't never told on him and he was my friend as much as he could be anybody's friend. He'd had so many fits his brains was addled like a setting of eggs in a thunderstorm. He had to take pills every day to keep from having spells, and he still stayed with his mama.

I'd found out a long time ago that black folks don't "live" anywhere.

They "stay." You ask one of 'em where he lives, and he may have been in the same house for twenty, twenty-five years, and he'll say, "I stay on Redwine Road." Burdell's mama worked in the grammar school lunch room, and every now and then she'd drop by the Fubar to bring her boy his pills when she found out he'd forgot them.

That particular evening Lamar Hester got on my case. "What kind likker you drink, boy? Or has Freddy got you fubarred on whiskey?" I sort of sidled off and grinned and never said nothing. But he wouldn't leave it alone. "Freddy, big as that boy is it's time he had a drink." Now I hadn't ever had the slightest desire in the world to even taste whiskey, but somehow he had me on the spot and feeling like I wasn't tough.

"Come on, boy, you don't even have to drink my white likker; old Freddy'll give you some of his bottled in bond, I bet."

"Lamar," I said, "I don't want no drink. If I did, I'd take one."

"What's matter? You fraid you'll be one them alkyhawlicks from the Fubar? You scared you'll turn out to be like Freddy?"

That struck me wrong. "Freddy ain't no alcoholic. He can quit any time he wants to. And what's wrong with being like Freddy? I wouldn't mind that atall."

Lamar laughed so hard he sprayed spit five feet. "He'n quit any time he wants to! I told that to Young Doc oncet and he said, 'You dumb bastard. That's what every alkyhawlic in the country says. Go ahead and drink yourself to death; nobody else can stop you.' And that's been eight years ago and I been doing my dead-level best to follow his advice, but them dumb damn doctors don't know everything; I ain't dead yet. Freddy don't want to quit! But you're wrong! Ain't no way you'd want to turn out like that bird-legged, pussel-gutted turd head. You probably couldn't hold your likker nohow."

I'd done got hot. "I'n drink good as any of you if I take a notion. And I'n put it down fast as any of you, too."

"Boy, you done lied now. When I's your age I killed a quart in ten minutes on a bet. You ain't in the class with no real drinking man."

"That ain't nothing. Anybody could do that."

"Awright, you muscle-bound young smart aleck. I got a hundred dollars says you can't swallow no quart of likker in ten minutes."

Freddy had a quart of rum in the old tire casing by the water cooler. I don't know what come over me but I grabbed it out and broke the seal and turned it up and never let it down till it was gone. It didn't take two minutes. Lamar Hester let out a yell.

"Foul! I call foul! That had to be colored water. You couldn't do that."

Freddy says, "You're wrong. That was a brand-new bottle. And you gotta pay me for that in addition to his hundred." Lamar hollered. "I been took. Can't no kid ain't never had his first drink do that in a thousand years."

I reached in the hole in the plaster down behind the candy machine and pulled out a new quart of Freddy's vodka. Mr. Boston it was.

"I still got five minutes. I'll show you," I told him.

To this day I don't remember getting more'n half way through that second bottle, but Freddy told me later that I drained it and then made it to the grease pit before I fell. He said in about ten minutes it come back. Said it shot straight outa me like a busted hydrant. Went ten feet out and he thought it'd never stop. Young Doc said later that was the only reason I didn't die, but it was three, four years before I told him about it.

I slept till Sunday. Freddy and Lamar had dragged me to Freddy's cot in the store room and Freddy called my mama and told her Mr. Laverne Williams and his boy had come through and invited me to Steenhatchie, Florida, to fish for the weekend. Told her we'd tried to call her and Freddy had give me ten dollars and permission to go. Freddy said he'd rather have faced two mad dogs and a turpentined bobcat than my mama if he took me home drunk. He was more'n likely right.

When I woke up on Sunday I felt worse'n hell. The bad part was not remembering. Freddy was feeding me Red Rock ginger ale and tomato soup, and I noticed his hand shaking and asked him what was the matter.

"You got to me, kid. I ain't ever before in my whole life had anybody say they wanted to be like me. And I decided maybe I am an alcoholic and that I'm by God going to quit. I haven't had a drink since Friday night when you fell out and scared the living shit out of me. I can quit cause now I want to quit."

It was Tuesday morning before they had to take him off. I'd always heard that you saw snakes when you got the DT's, but Freddy didn't. He had grasshoppers. He'd be talking good sense to you and then all of a sudden he'd jump and yell and start brushing on his shoulder or snatching the air in front of his eyes or even picking 'em off your sleeve. At first everybody thought Freddy was just going on with his foolishness, but then the sweat commenced to pouring off him in gallons. Lamar Hester and Hawk Forts was alaughing and pretending to stomp the grasshoppers on the floor and Lamar was really having a good time.

"Freddy, you're a real sissy. Comes from drinking whiskey instead of likker. I got the shakes and horrors that time they locked me up for a week where I couldn't git at no likker, and I had snakes in my cell crawling all over me. In and out the bars. And even out the nose of another prisoner. What kinda man sees hoppergrasses? You want I should get the fly swatter for you."

I could see Freddy's eyes. The blue was all gone and all you could see was the black. He was scared to death and the sweat had soaked every thread on him and he was beginning to blow when he breathed. I sneaked around to the phone and called Bob Marston. Freddy didn't have no kin left in town except for an old maid cousin, and she worked in Atlanta at the tag department and was so big in the Baptist Church I sure didn't want to call her. Bob growled and grumbled but he took care of it.

They had to cuff Freddy to take him off, but I told him I'd run the Fubar till he came back and he hollered to me that he still wanted to quit and wasn't no grasshoppers gonna make him break his promise to me.

They took him to the VA Hospital. Bob came back by the Fubar and told me they put him on the floor where they had the alcoholics and mental cases, and when he left they had Freddy in a strait jacket and you could hear him hollering two floors down even on the elevator.

"They got him in a semi-private room with a goddam nigger. That's the U.S. gov'mint for you. Us veterans go off and fight for this country and then they don't respect none of our rights atall. I don't know what this country's coming to. Looks like it's going to be the schools next, in spite of hell."

Well, the black man did bother Freddy but not the way Bob thought it would. Which that word *nigger* is one I have done got completely out of my vocabulary. Ain't nothing in the world would make me madder'n being one except for somebody to call me one. You got to consider other people's feelings in this world. Now I'm trying to remember to say "mobile home" instead of "trailer"; folks have done got touchous about that. Freddy's room was right next to the elevator, and every time it would stop at that floor the elevator bell would go "ding." Hardup said it sure did sound for all the world like a car pulling into the Fubar. And every time the bell would go "ding," Freddy would pull and jerk at the strait jacket and try to sit up in bed. He'd look over at his roommate in the other bed and yell, "Get up off your goddam black ass and check the oil and tires and wipe that windshield!" And the poor fella didn't know what to think and would lay there and pull the sheet over his head and get as far over on his bed as he could.

This went on for three days no matter how much medicine they give Freddy. The nurses were about to go crazy and I guess the poor black man did, from hearing it so much. When Freddy finally come to himself and quieted down and they took him out of restraints, all of a sudden the black man went wild. They had to put him in the strait jacket and every time the elevator would go "ding" he'd rare up and yell over at Freddy, "Get up off your goddam white ass and check the oil and tires and wipe that motherfucking windshield!" And Freddy would pull the sheet over his head and edge away as far as he could.

Freddy sent me word that he hadn't forgot his deal with me and for me to clean out the station as only I would know how to do. I knew what he meant, and I got shed of every bottle he had hid out, including the one behind the trap door in the ladies' rest room and the one buried in a box under the drum of used motor oil.

Like I didn't have trouble enough, Burdell the black boy got hold of one of the bottles and also forgot to take his medicine at the same time. Him and I was there by ourselves, and I had put him to work on a lube job while I patched a tire so Mrs. Turnipseed could pick it up on her way back from Ruby's Grocery. I heard this godawful noise like a wild animal crying on a werewolf show, and Burdell was sort of in a half crouch with both arms swinging back and forth like Mr. Muggs. He kept on with that high-pitched wail and his eyes was looking plumb through me and it scared me so bad I couldn't help but start to run. And about that time I heard this crash and looked back. He had fell over and cut half his face in two on a tire rim and was jerking and flopping like a chicken when you wring its neck. I was afraid he'd trip the hydraulic catch and the car'd squash his brains out, so I run back and snatched him out through the blood and grease, and he was still jerking and flopping and chewing his tongue. You could tell he'd wet his overalls and it smelled like he'd done the other, too. I knew better'n to call Old Doc, even if Freddy did use him and it was Freddy's station and all. I got ahold of Young Doc and he come and give Burdell a shot in the vein and stopped his fitting and then called the colored hearse and sent him off to Grady Hospital. That was my first and only epileptic fit.

I'd of quit then, but I couldn't let Freddy down. The Fubars turned out not to be so damn funny when you had to do all the work at the station and were having to step over them to get it done. Freddy left out the hospital before they wanted him to. The black man had got to him with that "goddam white ass" business, not to mention the "motherfucking windshield" and he flat out left. He walked out that hospital in nothing but a split-tail hospital gown and showed up in the Fubar right after sun-up one morning barefooted as a yard dog with no drawers on and nothing but little strings holding that gown together in the back. He never would tell how he managed to get out of that hospital and plumb across Atlanta and back home in that outfit. He swore he couldn't remember, but it's something I have always wondered about. Freddy could talk anybody into anything when he set his mind to it.

He didn't drink no whiskey. First news you know he had a new Co-Cola sign. It left off the Fubar and just said Freddy's Filling Station. It had been up over a week before anybody noticed it. Harley Prince said, "We have this day sacrificed honesty and diluted euphoria, I see," and that was the end of it. That Harley Prince was educated. Not that he ever done anything with it but he sure as hell had it. He always walked straight and toted his head too. He has been a credit to our town.

Lamar Hester didn't let nothing change him. "What's the matter with you, Freddy? Them doctors get to you? They die, too, you know. It's just that when we do it, it's the likker what kills us. They don't actually live any longer, it just seems that way. You don't really want to quit, you're just trying to prove you can."

Within two weeks Lamar Hester was dead. He'd set up a sawmill way the hell out in Shakerag, and he commenced throwing up blood 'bout middle of a Monday morning. They had to bring him out in a logging truck and he died in Young Doc's office before he could get the ambulance. Young Doc told Lamar's brother that he had varicose veins coming out his liver and wrapped around his isogaphus and he never stood a chance. Freddy closed the filling station and put a wreath on the door for Lamar's funeral.

Next day Lamar's oldest sister, the one who never married and lived over in Jonesboro, come by the station. She was pale but she wasn't but a little red-eyed from crying, and when I told her that Freddy had gone to the post office, she give me an envelope for him.

"Please give this to Mr. Cantrell. Lamar gave it to me five years ago and made me promise on the family Bible I'd deliver it when he died."

The envelope had printed on it in pencil, "You win. Have one for me." When Freddy opened it, there was five one-hundred-dollar bills so crisp and new-looking you couldn't hardly get them apart. I heard Freddy say, "Well, I'll be a son of a bitch. Why hadn't I thought of doing that?" Then a minute later he said, "He really was ready for Freddy."

For two, three days Freddy was right quiet and didn't laugh much. I figured he was grieving the best he could for Lamar and I felt like he really needed me, so I worked hard as I could and never said nothing. The Fubars were pretty quiet, too.

Then one afternoon Freddy took drunk. Where he got it I don't know, for I am sure and certain he never left the station. I reckon I had missed some when I was cleaning up. I have said that Freddy could take a drink and never show it, but this time he got falling down, limber-legged, tongue-tied drunk. I guess it was from being dried out so long. Anyhow, he finally passed out and I put him to bed on the cot in the stock room.

When I got to work the next morning, he was up and sober and had swept out the tire bay, and I thought everything was all right again. Then 'bout seven o'clock I come through to get a screw driver and caught him turning his bottle up. It wasn't more'n a third empty, so I knew he'd just started on it that morning. I never said nothing about it and he acted like I hadn't seen him nor him me.

Harley Prince come by for a minute and one of the checker players said, "Welcome back from your fishing trip, Harley. Did you catch anything?" And Harley said, "I'm not sure. I'm on my way to the doctor to find out." And Freddy laughed like always.

I got busy pumping gas and lining out work for Burdell and it was about eight-thirty before I realized Freddy wasn't around. I looked in the station and the rest room door was locked. I even knocked on the door, to keep up tradition and all, and said, "Mr. John, Mr. John, everything coming out all right?" Then I saw Freddy's keys laying on top the cash register, and I knew he was somewhere around, for he had locked the toilet door as usual. I wondered how come he had laid his keys down, for he usually kept 'em on his belt with a chain, but 'bout that time the bell went "ding" and I went running out to check the oil and tires and wipe the windshield.

Later on the checker players had settled in and one of them yelled at me, "Where's Freddy? It's nine-thirty and the door's still locked and I need to step out."

I grabbed up the keys and unlocked the door and there was Freddy. I took one look and commenced dying laughing. He had his head twisted way over to one side and was bugging his eyes almost outa his head and was running his tongue out at me like some kid playing Ugly Face. He was the tallest and skinniest and stretched outest I'd ever seen anybody, and all of a sudden he sorta swung around real gentle and passive like and I saw that he was hanging from the pipes by an electric cord. I realized that he'd stepped off the toilet seat and that he'd meant to do it and I hollered so loud they never did find all the checker buttons.

They sent for Bob Marston and Young Doc, and a bunch of 'em cut Freddy down and took him away. I was sitting on the cement propped against a gas tank crying my guts out. I couldn't help it and couldn't stop it and I didn't even think about who might see me. Young Doc come over to me and squatted down a while and didn't try to say anything. Just patted me. I finally managed to tell him how horrible it was that I had laughed. Then he told me that he'd been called to a heap of hangings and always had the same impulse, said the face of a hanging victim was ridiculous and one we usually associated with comedy, that nobody thought of sticking your tongue out in a tragedy. Then he left, and directly I picked myself up and went home.

Well, I'm playing football now. Coach is proud, says he'll get two good years out of me. I'm staying full-time with my granddaddy. We've got the best crop of turnip salad he's ever seen and we start cutting it for market on Monday. After that the collards will come off.

My granddaddy is still mean and tight and he still don't ever think about anybody but hisself. It don't bother me anymore that he won't cry. I'm cried out my own self. For the rest of my life, I suspect. We don't laugh much, neither.

He hasn't changed. I'm staying with him because nobody else will and because whether he'll admit it or not, he needs me.

He may not have changed, but I have. I have come to see that in his own way he loves me. He loves me because he does need me. And I need him, too. You know why? I need him because I love him. There's a difference there. I know that, even if I don't understand it yet. Someday I will.

Charlie Smith

From *Shine Hawk*

V

We heard the singing before we saw the lights. We heard it, low and sibilant, smooth as the flow of water, floating up the dark river toward us. Nobody remarked on it—though Frank and I stopped paddling—as we eased down between distant banks upon which the trees of night heaped themselves in the copious darkness. The music was beautiful. People, a crowd of people, were singing a spiritual, one of the old songs we had listened to all our lives, "Let the Light Carry Me Home." We had fallen silent already, snugged into the relief of labor, each of us wandering along in our own thoughts, letting the high-riding night sweep on above us, pulling on in the steady reach and gather of river travel. Then we came around a bend and down at the end of a long stretch upon which shown their reflection we saw the lights, lanterns blazing on the bank.

We weren't shy about coming down. And we didn't explain anything to ourselves. Paddling with the coffin in the stern was awkward, but the current did enough work. As we got closer I saw that someone had built a tower right at the edge of the water. It was about thirty feet high and appeared to be constructed of fresh lumber haphazardly nailed together. Beyond it, on ground that sloped gently upward, was an open park space, grassy under isolated oaks and sweet gums. There were people everywhere, a hundred or more, sitting on the ground and standing, holding lanterns and candles. At the top of the slope among the trees and just before a rank of large oaks were parked campers, small trailers, and cars. Two long rows of tables covered with white cloths and piled with food were set out near the vehicles.

A woman sat in an armchair on the tower. She leaned over her knees speaking loudly to people who stood on the ground underneath, the way a person would lean off a front porch to talk to somebody in the yard. She was monstrously fat and wore a dress of bright purples and reds that glittered and shimmered on her body. Over her shoulders and across her back was a cloth and leather harness that was attached to two ropes which were twined together and looped over the heavy branch of a large sycamore above her head. It was the kind of harness trapeze artists wear in practice to catch them if they fall.

We saw all this as we glided down the lighted path of the river, paddling and pausing to look, not speaking. Hazel hummed along momentarily with the spiritual and fell silent. Along the riverbank fires burned in buckets set on top of tall poles and there were strings of colored lights laced up into the trees and swinging in long sagging arcs over the open ground. The people who sang were not arranged in a group; they stood around, almost separate, almost like strangers waiting at a station, like people in a musical comedy who in the midst of regular life break into harmonic song. They swung the lanterns or they stood in couples or separately, but they were all singing and all of them were looking up at the fat woman on the tower.

We pulled in a little ways upstream and got out. The bank was grassy and unarticulated; it gave out like a flooded pasture into the water. A couple of tall guys with candles standing nearby came down and helped us drag the boat up. Then they stepped off closer to the tower and resumed singing. They didn't say anything to us. "They're good people but they've got business to tend to," Frank said chuckling.

"Indians?" I said.

"What else?"

The guys who had helped us looked Indian but I saw others in the crowd who did not. There were blonde-headed kids—as the counterman said there would be—and a couple of red-headed girls stood next to a tall woman with white skin under a big dogwood; the woman on the tower was black.

Off to the side of the tower, parked among a low heap of gallberry bushes, was a new scarlet Cadillac. It was close enough for me to read the stamped plastic sign on the driver's door: Hercules Red Dawn, Chief, Eastern Creek Nation. The Creeks in Georgia were a remnant of the old tribe that had fled to the woods or intermarried with whites when Andrew Jackson's soldiers rounded everybody up in the 1830s for the Trail of Tears march to Oklahoma. They didn't stand out in the little southern towns they lived in; like the Catholics and the Jews they were a minor minority, just some black-headed kid over in the corner of the classroom, a dark, humble boy with a middle name like Five Rivers that he never mentioned himself, his father an assembler out at the mobile home plant, mother home in a housedress preparing a supper of mustard greens laced with hog grease—maybe only a little kink in the blood, some dream of the woods familiar as a house, blown along like a scarf before the wind, some already unpronounceable word, and a glance from dark eyes, something too fleeting to catch all that was left of the old times, of the times when they were free and all the people were acrobats in the great shining feat that the world was.

As we stood there getting our bearings—Frank scanning the crowd for any sign of the cops—the driver's door of the Cadillac opened and a man got out. He too was immensely fat and Indian dark with straight black thinning hair that hung to his shoulders. He wore a gray summer suit and black patent leather slip-ons split along the toes to give his corns air, and he carried a small stick with a couple of colored feathers attached to one end. He hailed us with the stick and then leaned back against the car grinning.

I gave him a small wave and said, "I think that's the fellow we need to talk to."

The song ended as we walked over to the chief—that was who he was—and people got up and began to move around. I noticed the fat woman looking down at us; when she caught my eye and smiled a big gold-toothed smile I looked away. I didn't know what I wanted to get into here—maybe nothing. As we reached the chief he took a step forward and shook our hands. "I welcome you," he said.

As he spoke the passenger door flew open and a thin man in a straw cowboy hat got out and came around the side of the car. He wore a pink cowboy shirt with silver snap buttons and jeans tucked into boots that looked as if they were made from reptile skin: pebbly and glossy and green in the light of lanterns. He stepped in front of the fat man and shook our hands again and said, "I'm Dennis Chowan." His teeth were very white and gapped and his ears stuck straight out.

The fat man was the chief and Dennis was his son. This was the eastern Creek tribe, a far-flung collection of mostly half-caste Indians who met several times a year for socializing and, to my surprise, pentecostal preaching. This gathering, Dennis explained, was a preachment and a special one. "That's my mother," he said, when I asked him who the fat woman on the tower was, and she was about to give her farewell sermon before retiring as head of Mother Pentecost Holiness Church, which was the Indian denomination the tribe had devised for itself. "I hope we're not interrupting anything," Hazel said and Dennis assured her we weren't. I wanted to ask if the cops had showed up, but I didn't—Frank didn't say anything either—because I was afraid that if I did we would have to explain why we wanted to know. A few of the people drifted by to look us over, guys in jeans or stiff suits, women dressed in the cheap finery of department store basements. There were campfires burning here and there; people sat around them on the yellowed grass in small groups. From time to time in one of the groups another song would start and slowly the other folks would take it up until everybody was singing. All the while the woman on the tower continued to chatter away to one or another standing on the ground below her. Candles in tin cups burned on the arms of the chair she sat in, which was a gold wing chair like the ones Esmé and I had on the boat. A small wind stirred the sycamore leaves above her head and the smell of woodsmoke drifted over us and the lantern-lit air was hazy. The night was cool but still comfortable and the river gurgled on its way. The white look was back in Frank's eyes, the look that had been there this afternoon when he sat on the bed reading the letter, that had been there as he sat in the truck in front of the restaurant; I figured he was about to pull something else, some other breakaway that would have us all scrambling for footing and I began to draw into myself, wondering what it might be. I was about to suggest that we head on down the river when Dennis Chowan took him by the arm and began to lead him toward the tower. His father the chief walked behind with Hazel and me. "We are all so glad you have come," he said and I thanked him for having us. He walked with his small soft hands clasped on his belly.

He asked us if we had had supper and Hazel said no. He told us that when the preachment was over food would be served at the tables under the trees. I asked him why his wife was stepping down. He said it was because she was old and tired and she wanted time for meditation. "She looks familiar to me," Hazel said. "What is she called?"

"The Morning Queen Jeserea," he said and began to tell us the history of the tribe and the history of the religion they were a part of. It was one of those stories about oppressed people overcoming.

There was a wide bed of ferns and pine boughs spread on the ground about thirty feet back from the tower and he settled us there. The rest of the tribe wandered up and took seats. They chattered and affectionately jostled one another, just like folks would at a Baptist picnic. The chief and his son sat side by side, with Frank on the other side of Dennis Chowan and Hazel and me beside the chief.

The Morning Queen beamed down at all of us. Her bright red tongue licked around her dark lips and she made smacking noises. Half a dozen women in white wearing headscarves of blue and red—the Provisioners, the chief called them—herded small children down in front of us. They arranged the children in a semicircle and sat down among them. I kept looking around to see if the police were creeping up on us. The chief noticed, leaned over his big lap, and said, "They've already come and gone. You won't get in any trouble here."

I wasn't too sure of that, but I thanked him without asking what he knew. We hadn't done anything that bad anyway. Hazel leaned her shoulder against mine and for a moment I tried to think what our married life might be like, busy on the boat in St. Lukes, careening around the streets of the Village, but I couldn't really picture it. I touched her hair, which was loose and still damp from the river. "Are you two getting along all right?" I said.

"No," she said, "we aren't."

Something in me shied, as it had when I was a child lying in my narrow bedroom listening to my parents as they argued their way through the night downstairs. "Someday," I said, "I want you to tell me about it. I want you to tell it graphically and in detail; I want you to make it come alive for me, but I'm not sure that day will be on this side of heaven."

She said, "You've got to find a way to live after your dreams shatter. You have to be prepared to go on."

"I don't think any of us is able to do that."

"You mean the three of us."

"Yes. We're a little group of resurrectionists, grave-diggers. Maniac Dr. Frankensteins, trying to pump life into a corpse. I sat in the grass last night listening to the two of you shouting. It was like you were shouting at me, accusing me."

"We love you. You're our anchor and our hope."

"Yes," I said. Again the thought came that somewhere else, in some equivalent and distant place, there were others sitting out on the grass on a balmy fall night, talking about their troubles. In another state—on another planet maybe—the woman turned to one of the men and, as she looped a strand of rich dark hair over her ear, looked at him with eyes that filled with tenderness and hopelessness, and asked for nothing. As long as I lived she wouldn't ask me to save her, she wouldn't even ask me to preach over her as she went down.

I looked at Frank, who was reared back, his head held so high his bull neck looked stalky, glaring sullenly at the crowd as if he would spring on anybody who spoke to him. He had spent years trying to get Jake to straighten out, but one day he just gave up on it. "Ten thousand prayers wouldn't save my brother," he said and walked away. He wouldn't have anything to do with him anymore. When Jake got jailed for raging through the streets drunk and called Frank, he wouldn't talk to him. He hung up on the sound of his brother's voice. He was the only one in the family who would turn Jake away. His mother and his aunts pleaded and nagged but they let him in the house. They covered for him too. If the neighbors asked, Jake was in hotel management, he was sensitive, he was recovering from a long illness. They told just the sort of lies that Jake had raged against all his life, but which, at least in the last years, he depended on for survival. His aunt Canty tried to get him to go to church—the only answer as far as she was concerned—but he wouldn't. He didn't get angry though, when, stiff in her gray clothes, she raised her jewel-less hands to implore him—he didn't scoff or insult her, but something in his eyes would go blank, and if you were looking into them, the eyes that were hazel, almost the gold of orange-flower honey, you might think, suddenly and with a pain that shot to your heart, that what lived behind them was big enough and ravenous enough to eat God—if there was such a being in this world—to obliterate him.

Frank had shunned him, he had cast him off—but no, that wasn't true. I wondered if he'd saved the letter from the burning trailer. Maybe that was why he had run back in.

I shuddered. If there was a fence around the world, we were climbing it. We were on the way out. Perhaps this was how de Kooning felt that winter and spring in New York when the great eidolonic body of a woman split into its grinning pieces and he found himself staring into the screeching mystery. I looked up at the woman in the chair. She leaned out over us grinning. Her harness creaked and the candles on her chair flickered. Her face was shiny with grease or sweat. She was so fat her body billowed. The chief looked at the tower, nudged his son with an elbow, and said, "I still don't think that thing is safe. I don't think it's going to hold her."

"Stop worrying," his son said, "Jose and Jerry did a good job. It'll serve its purpose."

A small boy at my feet—black-headed, stringy under his clothes—edged back until he was between my legs. I pulled him into my lap. He nestled his head against my chest and looked up at me with large, assessing eyes. "Howdy, pardner," I said. He giggled and squirmed closer. Hazel stroked his hair.

And there was Jake beached in his box on the shore of the Congress. His life had come to an end. Though in the cells of his flesh the molecules whirled and jumped, there was no life. Lungs, liver, lights—all dark. What was the deal here?

Behind us the rest of the tribe sat in small groups under the trees and on the open ground. Torches lit the road that angled down from the highway. I could hear the low murmur of conversation and somewhere off toward the campers a radio was playing the soft whining despair of a country western love song. I looked straight up, checking for stars, but the night must have clouded because the sky was empty. It looked chill and high, as if in the eaves of heaven winter was building.

"Children!" It was the voice of the Morning Queen. She had risen to her feet and stood now at the edge of her platform, her body swaying as if to music. She was shorter than I had supposed and below her dress her legs looked like creosoted fence posts. Her eyes were closed and she held her face up. Slowly her arms lifted, palms up, until they were above her head. There were sweat patches the size of faces under her arms. Gold bracelets fell down her wrists.

"Children!" she cried again, her voice heavy and distinct. A thin echo, faint as a whisper flew back across the river. The murmuring died out around us. I looked down the line and saw Dennis Chowan make the sign of the cross, backwards, as they do in the Greek Orthodox church. What are we into now? I thought, pressing my shoulder against Hazel who pressed back. Baby, baby, baby.

"My sweet, dying children," the Morning Queen said.

"Yes, yes," I heard in a murmur behind me.

Her arms fell to her sides, her chin jutted, and she surveyed the crowd, her mouth opening and closing over gold teeth. Her voice rang out. "I'm going to tell you about Jabbo Jesus; yes, I'm going to tell you about that gentleman. You think he's dead? You think he's rode away to heaven in a silver sports car? You think he aint walking around here among us?"

"No, Sister, no," the answer came back. Breeze made the lantern lights tremble, the candles flicker.

"Thas right, children, because I tell you if you think that you're crazy. He's right here. He's sitting here tonight. He's right next to you. He's leaning over your shoulder and he's whispering in your ear. That boy, that old Mr. Jabbo Jesus, he lived just like you and me live. He got up in the morning scratching at the flea bites and went out into the kitchen and asked his mama what was for breakfast. . . ."

"Yes he did, Sister," somebody shouted. This was a strange group of Indians.

"Yes, yes. He say, 'Mama, why can't I have fried eggs?' and she say, 'Boy, it's cause we're poor, it's cause we aint got no money,' and Jesus he say, 'Whoo Lord, that's a rough situation. I don't like that.' You think Jesus grew up on the Riviera? You think he was raised in a penthouse in New York City?"

"No, Sister."

"Thas right. He didn't see no penthouse. He had to go to the back door too."

"Tell us, Sister."

"I'll tell you. Now his daddy was a carpenter, he was good, he built houses and barns and he had hands that moved so sweet he could turn a piece of wood into a thing of beauty. He was real good, but it was the time of the Romans and the Romans didn't pay much money. They liked to keep the Jews down; they didn't like no trouble with the Jews. His daddy say, 'One day, boy, you gonna take over this business; I'm gonna teach you everything I know—you gon be a better carpenter than I ever dreamed of being.' And old Jabbo Jesus he believed his daddy. He liked to sit back there in the shed and watch him plane those boards. He was a little boy. He liked to cup his hands and catch those shavings of cedar and pine and bring them up to his nose and smell that rich scent. It made him dizzy, it made him full of life. . . ."

There was agitation in me. Her voice had that swooping rise and fall of the preachers from my childhood. I looked at Hazel; she looked back. I mouthed silently, "Everybody's drunk," and she laughed, caught the laugh in her hand and shushed me. Frank bent over his lap, swinging his head. The Morning Queen was saying,

"Then he began to feel something stir in him. He felt his manhood rise up like the sap in a tree. It was strong, it was powerful; it roared in his body. It tickled him and it teased him and it filled up his head with a strong voice. He'd get lost to hisself til his daddy would rise up from his workbench and say, 'Boy, what's the matter with you—you sick or something?' and then old young Mr. Jabbo he'd look up at his daddy and he'd say, 'Daddy, I don't know what it is; I feel something jumping inside of me. It's scary, but I like it.' And his daddy was afraid because even though he had other children none of them acted like this, none of them spoke this way, and he went to his wife Miss Virgin Mary and he said, 'Darling, I don't know about that boy. He's a queer duck and I don't know what's going to become of him.' And Miss Virgin Mary, she'd just smile, because she knew, she remembered what old Gabriel told her about how her boy was going to become a great king, and she'd give old Joseph a pat and say, 'Now honey, don't you worry; that boy's gonna turn out fine. . . .'"

The Morning Queen paused long enough to drink from a glass balanced on the arm of her chair. She raised the glass and drained it all at once. The water spilled over her face as she gulped it down, her throat muscles working like a hammer, her big stomach heaving. She set the glass down hard on the chair arm and looked at us with her eyes full of mischief and a cunning smile just edging along at the corners of her full mouth. "You believe me, children?" she cried, and the answer came back: "Yes, Sister, yes, Sister; yes, we believe."

The Morning Queen threw her head back and the smile filled her face. "That's right, children, that's right. All through his growing up Jesus felt funny cause this thing moving around on the inside of him started to come on him real regular—it wahnt just when he looked at a pile of clean shavings, it was anytime; it was when he was looking up at a flock of birds settling into the sweet gum tree at night; it was when he looked out across the cornfields and saw how the light laid down like a golden coat on the tops of the corn; it was there when he watched his mama take the new baby to her breast. He thought, Lord, I'm going crazy, I don't know what this business is; I sure wish it would go away. Shoot, he was a young man, he was learning the carpentry business from his daddy and he was good at it too; he could make a house that stood up plumb, he could set a window so the sash would slide up and down smooth as butter. He was worried about these feelings; he wanted to shake em; he wanted to go on about living; he wanted to be a success in the world. But they wouldn't quit; this scary sweetness kept filling him and moving around inside him until finally it got so bad he went to visit his cousin old John, the circuit preacher over in the next county.

"Now John he was a strange old fella; he dressed real shabby and he camped out in the woods, and he'd eat anything: berries, honey, even old hoppergrass—any of you seen any of those old hoppergrass around here that come out around June time'll know how strange it is to eat some mess like that—ooo—but old John he was a man of God. He had limitations and he knew it. What he specialized in was baptizing; he liked to go around the country and whoever he came on that accepted the Word of the Lord he'd take him down to the river and dunk him. This was something new, before that folks only gone in for waving smoke over each other's heads—incense—and maybe a little sprinkling, but old John he liked to put em under—he said the water stood for God's spirit that washed their hearts clean. Old John probably wahnt the kind of boy you'd go to unless you were pretty bad off, which is probably why he had to live out in the woods away from town in the first place—he couldn't work up enough of a congregation to pay the rent on a house. But he was Jesus' cousin, so Jesus went to see him. Now you know what old John did—you know?"

The voices came back, "What did he do, Sister? Yes, Sister, what did he do?" I leaned over to Hazel: "I think these folks have gone through this before." She stroked my arm—touch of fire—and looked up at the Morning Queen.

"Jesus said to John, 'Cousin, I don't know what this is going on inside of me; I mean it feels like a wind and it sounds like a voice and it keeps springing up on me when I don't want it to. Why last night I was eating a plate of biscuits and cane syrup and I swear if I didn't look down at that plateful of syrup, at that gold color, the way it spread out over those buttered biscuits, and I just got mesmerized, I mean I was charmed until I forgot where I was; I forgot *who* I was, and then I heard this voice speak to me; it said, '*I am the long lost*

Lover' and I said, 'What did you say?' and it said again; '*I am the long lost Lover*' and I swear if Daddy hadn't popped me on the back of the head with his spoon I might've lost my mind right then and there—what do you think that is?' Well, John studied him a minute and then he said, 'Come on down here to the river; I think it's time you got baptized.' But Jesus, he didn't want none of that. 'Not me, boy,' he said, 'I've heard about all that and I believe I'll pass on it. Besides, I got on new clothes.' John said, 'Nah, it'll be all right; you're going to like this, I promise,' and so, because John was his cousin and because he knew his reputation for craziness and he was a nice boy who didn't want to cause a fuss, Jesus went down to the river with him and John took him out into about four feet of water and dunked him under. And you know what happened then—you know what happened?"

"What, Sister; Sister, what?"

"When Jesus came up he was different. Old John stepped back and he gasped because around that boy's head was a pure white light, a light white as snow, white as the full moon, and as he looked John saw that light change itself into a white dove that flew off into heaven and John—who had trouble with always hearing things anyway—heard a voice say, 'This is my beloved son with whom I am well pleased.' Well now, let me tell you, if you saw a hair full of light change itself into a bird and fly off, and then you heard this big old voice say 'This is my beloved son,' I mean you might not just shrug it off and go back so easy to your whittling and spitting. Well, old John he fell back and he cried out, 'I'll be damned—you're the Son of God. You're the one I heard about.' And he knelt down right there in that water and he worshipped. He worshipped. This young fella from down at Nazareth who was working as a carpenter for his daddy, this fella who was good to his mama and who, except for right now, had probably never been out of the county in his life—at least since he was a baby—this fella was the Son of God, born to change the world."

She hawked and spit over the side of the platform and a gentle, beatific look came into her face. She pulled a big blue bandanna from her belt and wiped sweat off, dabbed at her lips. Then she looked around smiling at the crowd, which looked back at her from under the trees and the open ground around the tower. People had set their candles at their feet; they threw a yellow, trembling light over their bodies, flickering at the shadows.

The Morning Queen drew herself up. "Now don't let anybody tell you that Jesus wahnt no man. He had all the troubles and joys that any of you sitting out here's got. You think his pecker didn't get hard when he saw a beautiful woman? Don't you believe it. This aint no sugar Jesus. You think he didn't like to stay up late and get to carrying on with the boys? You think he didn't shit and piss like the rest of you? He did, he rightly did."—I looked across the chief and his son at Frank, who was fidgeting, squeezing his hands into bleached fists. His face was dark with blood. "—But let me tell you something. When old Mr. Jesus came up out of that water and Mr. John the Baptist fell back in awe because he understood that his little cousin standing there in front of him with river water dripping off his new clothes was the authentic and prophesied Son of God and he fell down on his scabby knees right there in the river Jordan, you know what Jesus did—you know what old Jabbo Jesus did?"

"What did he do, sister? What did he do?" Something was muscling up in Frank, something too large for him. His mouth opened; he swung his head.

The Morning Queen cried, "He raised that man up; he raised that shabby crazy man, that man who was so stung by the Word of God that he had to live out in the woods and eat the black hoppergrass, raised him to his feet, and looked in his eyes, and he said, 'You *too* are the Son of God!' Children! I say this to you now; I say this to you, all my sisters and my brothers, on the final evening of my life as a preacherwoman; I say this to all you little ones sitting out there on the grass on this fine fall evening; I say you the truth: You are all the children of God; you are all his sons and daughters. That spirit, that sweet ghost fluttering down out of the heavenly blue is upon you all. . . ."

As her arm swept down, her pointed finger passing over the crowd, I saw Frank leap to his feet, and I heard his voice, low at first and far back in his throat—the voice of a man tearing himself out of silence—cry out: "Raise my brother up!" Dennis Chowan reached for him, grabbed his arm, but Frank brushed him away. "Raise my brother up," he shouted stamping his feet.

The Morning Queen cried, "The spirit of God is in you," but I couldn't tell whether she meant in Frank or in the rest of us in general. But then she looked down at him with such a look of baffled sweetness that I wanted to throw myself down on the ground in front of her. There were other voices, other short songs sung out in the flickering camplight, but only Frank was on his feet, only Frank cried out, demented and relentless, "Raise my brother up!"

The chief began to push himself up from the ground. He looked at Frank with scared eyes. But Hazel didn't move. She gazed at her husband as if he was performing magic tricks. As he cried out—anger in his voice, a petulance, as if the Morning Queen held a sweet she would not give him—she looked up at Frank with something rapturous in her eyes, something that gave full permission and acceptance. I started to get up as he cried again. "Raise my brother up," as he shook his fist at the Morning Queen who leaned now looking down at him, as the people behind us stirred and a murmuring ran through the crowd, but before I could get to him he was running at the tower crying his talisman phrase, and as I started after him he leapt upon the rickety structure and began to climb, scrambling like a desperate commando at a battlement. The tower swayed, the Morning Queen cried out, "Whoa, boy, back off," and the chief, his son, and I rushed to retrieve him, but we were not quick enough to grab him as he crabbed up the pale yellow struts crying out as he went. The tower trembled, creaked, the Morning Queen stumbled and swung against her harness; she whooped, "Oh, Lord," as she grabbed the ropes rising from her waist; the structure groaned and shuddered and then a board broke under Frank's foot and he almost lost his balance, but he caught himself and pulled up higher even as the beams and struts began to give out around him and the whole tower began to lean away from us like a stately gentleman passing out, and then it began to topple slowly backwards as both of them, Frank and the Queen, let loose shrill cries. The front legs rose off the ground and, as Frank, coming momentarily to his senses, glanced around—a look on his face of such comic surprise

I almost laughed out—it fell with a great groaning and splintering into the river.

The Morning Queen hung in her harness thirty feet above us; Frank, who clutched the tower all the way down like a bull rider, shoved up out of the black water as the tower bobbed beside him, its shape crazily askew. Hazel, who had leapt to her feet, crying out as he fell, ran into the shallows and waded out to him. "I'm all right," I heard Frank say. "Baby," Hazel cried.

I stood on the bank looking at the scene. The Morning Queen bobbed in the air so that the sycamore branch that held her swayed, shaking leaves. A few spiky seed balls dropped onto the grass. "Undo these ropes," she cried. The two ropes that had been twisted around themselves slowly unraveled, revolving her on a slow wheel.

"She's beautiful," I said to an old man standing beside me. "She should have made her sermon hanging up there like that."

The old man, whose face was knotted with age, looked at me out of slitted eyes that were as black as black jewels. "She's purposeful," he said, "just like your friend."

The Morning Queen's red and purple dress flowed softly around her legs; her broad back, humped at the shoulders with fat, appeared, then her side that showed dark sweat patches under her upraised arms, then her swollen front.

"Get me down," she cried, "This thing hurts my bosoms." She looked down at Frank. "It'll be all right, son," she said.

Frank stood in water up to his waist looking around as if he didn't know where he was. Hazel, her green skirt billowing out around her, waded out to him and took him in her arms. The chief and his son helped a couple of men in bright cowboy shirts undo the rope and let the Morning Queen down. She spun slowly as she descended, kicking her legs a little as if she were swimming. "Lord, what an experience," she said. When her feet touched ground she collapsed. A woman near me cried out, but the Queen was not hurt, only weary. The chief and Dennis Chowan helped her to her feet. She unbuckled the leather harness and shoved it away from her. "I told you, son," the chief said, "that tower wouldn't hold."

The Morning Queen shook herself; "We all doing fine," she said to the crowd which had drawn closer. A few of the women came up and brushed her clothes, their hands fluttering over her large body like the wings of birds. "That's fine, that's fine," the Morning Queen said to them, gently pushing their hands away. She turned and looked at Frank who stood in the water with Hazel. "You a crazy boy, aint you—you suffering," she said.

Frank waded to the bank and stood there as if he didn't want to come out. I heard the silvery cry of a woodthrush. The river sucked lightly at his legs. "My brother's over there in that boat, dead," he said.

Someone in the crowd gasped and a look of dismay passed over the chief's face. "Now we will be in big trouble," he said, but his wife raised her hand to shush him. "What you mean?" she said to Frank.

Frank, quickly, his voice staccato, gripped in a vise, told her about Jake's death in Calaree, about our mission of retrieval. "So he's right there in that coffin," he said. "We're his traveling pallbearers you might say."

She didn't even scold him for knocking her tower down. She talked to him as if he had come into her office for counseling. "You'll just have to face up to it," she said, "it wahnt your fault."

Frank grimaced. "That's not the kind of help I want right now," he said. "You're a preacher woman—I want you to raise him from the dead."

"Honey, I can't raise nobody from the dead. God and Jesus bout the only ones that can handle that matter."

"No, that's not true," Frank said. "I know it says in the Bible that he gave the disciples the power. Well, you're some kind of disciple; you ought to be able to do it."

"Frank," Hazel said. She had taken his hand and she tugged it slightly to make him look at her, but he disengaged himself and stepped ashore. He said, "I can't convince you to do it, but you'd be doing me a great favor if you'd try."

He sounded like a farmer trying to convince his machinist to make a difficult tractor part.

"We rise in the spirit," the Morning Queen said. "We only die in the flesh. Your brother's spirit lives on now. He's with the angels."

"Yeah, I know, but I can't talk to him in that condition. I've got more things I'd like to say to him. Besides," he said, cocking his head, "I heard you got the power. You're known all over as a woman with the power."

"That power belongs to the Lord," the Morning Queen said. "Aint nobody here on earth can manufacture it theyself."

"That's what I mean," Frank said. "You got access. I just need a little access right now."

"Come on, Son," I said. This sounded stupid to me and I wanted to go on.

"It's okay, Billy," he said and then he grinned at me so that I wondered if the whole thing, the assault on the tower, the demand, was nothing more than Frank's version of a country drama, just another episode of the vigorous antics he had been pulling all his life. I turned away to Dennis Chowan, who stood fidgeting beside me and said, "Did you mention something about having supper?"

"You're surely right there," his father said reaching across Dennis and shaking my hand. "Come along; we're getting prepared."

"Wait a minute," Frank said. "I want to know if this woman is going to raise my brother." He looked at her. "You're supposed to be able to do that sort of thing."

"Boy, you playing me for a fool," the Morning Queen said. "Besides, this is the night of my retirement."

She shook her arms, making her bracelets clatter; she shook them as if that were one of her devices—the gleam and clatter drawing attention to what she wanted heard. And suddenly I thought of my own father shaking the ice in his highball glass as he explained to me when I was twelve that my mother was in heaven now, that she was living with God, and how that frightened me, the picture of my mother living with this huge gray man who was not her husband and not her father and too strong for me to take her away from, protect her from. I said, "This is a bunch of bullshit and we got miles to go and we better get going."

"Come on, darling," Hazel said and I felt anger well up in me against her; I wanted to pull her arms away that were raised to touch Frank's washed face, wanted to scream at her that she had betrayed me, fooled me, that she should have let me stay. Perhaps the Morning Queen saw the look that slid into my face, because she turned to me and drew up close. I could smell the sweat on her and underneath it the trickling sharp odor of a candy perfume that was the exact equivalent of the perfume the girls wore to the dances years ago at the youth center when Frank and I took turns slow-dancing with Hazel under the party lights. The Morning Queen touched my face. Her hand paused for a moment on my forehead and I felt the fingers tense on my skin, press inward. My eyes, for the briefest second started to close, the light seemed to blink away as if a gap had suddenly opened in the moment; I seemed to see the blackness pulling like a curtain across a bright window, but it was a blackness that itself opened into space, into another version, a blackness like the surface of the river, blackness which contained life and movement and something big and muscular that I could not bear to see—I gasped and pulled back. The imprint of her fingers burned on my forehead—"No," I cried, "not me." I looked at her, a distance closing fast between us, and she smiled at me, a smile full of benevolence and wry understanding. "You just about ready," she said. "You on the verge."

I felt my face flush and I looked away, humiliated and frightened. "It's all right, boy," she said, "You'll be all right."

Then she put her hand out to Frank who came dripping out of the river and took it, his red face still working with the acid of his needs, followed by Hazel, who held the tail of his shirt like a child tagging along.

"I want you to consider doing the favor I'm asking of you," Frank said. "It's very important to me."

"I know it rightly is," the Morning Queen said, "and I don't defend you from making the request. I only defend myself from honoring it."

Then she led us toward the line of tables that had been set on trestles under the trees, where women in long dresses with their hair pinned up in bright headrags placed food out for the assembled.

Warren Leamon

Papaya

Sometimes late at night when I can't sleep I think of roads. I remember vividly the exact route my family took from our home in Atlanta to Florida thirty-five years ago: U.S. 41 to Barnesville, U.S. 341 to Perry, U.S. 41 to Lake City, U.S. 100 to Bunnell, U.S. 1 to Daytona Beach. Then I'm in the backseat of the Chrysler coupe or the Hudson Hornet; my head leans against the window and the countryside rolls by, mile after mile, until the steady rhythm of trees and signboards and roadside stores and filling stations and cows and leaning shacks rocks me into dreams.

I seldom remember the dreams, but then, I don't remember many of the places we stayed or what we did. I remember the sea, of course, but it's as though the roads I traveled, like my distant memory of them, lulled me into sleep and forgetfulness. And then, on a rainy winter day when I'm driving through the town I live in now and my son asks me what Spanish moss is, suddenly I see the clump that hung on the lower limb of the dogwood tree in front of my house. It was as out-of-place in that Atlanta suburb as a palm tree or a black family would have been yet no one seemed to notice or remark on it; and a few days after I hung it there, even I had forgotten about it. Which seems strange when I consider how it got there.

Every summer we went to Florida for our vacation because my father, who traveled the South for Sears, supervising the remodeling of mail-order stores, managed to wrangle a job in a beach town. I suppose I get my obsession with routes and maps from my father, who could—and on the slightest provocation would—tell you how to get from Pascagoula to Birmingham or from Hahira to Pulaski, complete with all detours and shortcuts. Moreover, he could tell you how long it took to get from town to town; and once he had you hooked, he would start in on his records: "The fastest I ever made it from Gainesville to Opelika was . . ." or "I once drove from Memphis to St. Augustine without stopping for anything but gas." It was this last record, and the endurance it involved, that tormented my family through all my childhood.

While I was still a child, and for a long time afterwards, I thought that my father's obsession with roads, with getting from one place to another, was a conditioned response, that the job itself, a job he took during the Depression when one took *any* job, had formed his attitude. It never occurred to me that he might not even have cared about getting from one place to another, that there might have been another explanation, another reason why, when he took the family on vacation in the summer, he was incapable of changing his attitude.

My mother knew what to expect and tried to prepare for it, much as Arabs must prepare for trips across the desert; but there were six of us in the family—myself, my mother and father, my brother and sister, and my grandmother, my father's mother—so there wasn't much room for provisions. There wasn't much room in the car for anything but feet and legs and shoulders. My father filled up the tank the night before the trip, we ate breakfast in the dark and left at dawn, "to beat the traffic." Mother never ceased to be hopeful. "Maybe we can do some sightseeing along the way," she suggested. "We're leaving so early, we don't have to hurry." And always my father was very agreeable and at the beginning of every trip he vowed to stop at the Stephen Collins Foster Museum or Cypress Gardens or Silver Springs. I think he even intended to; he was basically a good-hearted man. But a highway was to him what whiskey is to an alcoholic.

So this journey, like all the others, started pleasantly enough. More pleasantly, in fact, since, being about my son's age (twelve or thirteen), I had begun to think of the beach not as a place of fierce waves and sand-castles but in terms of girls: girls on the sand and girls on the boardwalk; girls in the dark game rooms, their slim arms propelling the ski-balls, their hips moving with the silver balls in the pinball machines. They danced in my head as we passed through Barnesville and Fort Valley and Perry and the great expanses of peach orchards. They sustained me when the land began to flatten, the sun rose higher in the sky, and the damp morning air gave way to the blistering heat of south Georgia. All the windows were rolled down and the hot wind that swirled through the car couldn't even dry the sweat that rolled down our foreheads and bodies. But the thought of those girls, of their golden hair and their smooth tanned skin and their long legs, kept me from the reality of the car for a while longer. Finally we began to shift about, trying to get our legs in new positions, bumped into one another and squabbled. My grandmother told us to stop fighting.

"Let's stop and stretch our legs and get a Coke," my mother said.

My father stared ahead, one sunburned arm hanging out the window as he clutched the steering wheel with a hand that held a cigarette wedged between two fingers, the ashes blowing into the backseat from time to time, and said nothing.

"Look," she said, pointing to a roadside sign. "There's a Stuckey's in ten miles. Let's stop there."

Our spirits rose as the signs rolled by: Stuckey's 8 Miles; Stuckey's 6 Miles; Stuckey's 3 Miles; Stuckey's 1 Mile.

"There it is," Mother said.

"I can't stop now. I'd have to pass all those trucks again."

And Stuckey's, filled with happy people drinking Coca Colas and orange juice, flew by. I turned and, much as Lot's wife must have looked wistfully back before she turned into a pillar of salt, watched it fade in the rearview mirror. We could deceive ourselves no longer. Our only hope now was the gas tank. From the backseat I peered over my father's shoulder and watched the needle on the gas gauge fall. It was like watching the hour hand on a clock.

"I have to go to the bathroom," said my sister.

"So do I," said my brother.

"I'm thirsty," I chipped in.

"Calvin," my grandmother said sternly. "We must stop at the next filling station. Elizabeth has to go to the bathroom."

"All right."

The next filling station "probably didn't have a bathroom." The next one was "too dirty." We crossed the Georgia-Florida line. My mother stared out the window, her face filled with despair as my grandmother told us that "Calvin's always been this way. Even when he was a little boy he was stubborn as a mule."

"It looks like we'll make Lake City in six hours," my father announced, his voice filled with excitement. "And we're getting good gas mileage."

I peered over his shoulder once again. The needle had fallen to the quarter tank mark. My stomach rumbled with hunger and my kidneys ached. Over the car there fell a deadly silence that lasted mile after flat hot Florida mile. We gave up pointing to filling stations; signs announcing the small towns we passed through meant no more than the "Come Again" signs that flashed by soon after. The turnoff to the Stephen Collins Foster Museum came and went like a half-remembered dream. Our only hope was the car, which, unlike my father, had its limits. Or so I thought.

"Calvin, the gas gauge is on empty."

"We can make it to Lake City," he shot back as we passed a sign that read, "Lake City 17 Miles."

I fixed my eyes on the odometer and watched the numbers tick off: 16, 15, 14, 13. Then I gave up; it was hopeless. We would never get to Lake City. We would never get anywhere. We were doomed to die in a car that never stopped moving because, miraculously, it never ran out of gas. My brother groaned, my sister was rolled up in a tight ball, Grandmother's eyes were glazed, my mother put her arms on the dashboard and rested her head on them. And the last thing I remember seeing before I closed my own eyes was my father, cool and determined, staring straight ahead. Without doubt he would drive straight through the state of Florida and on to the South Pole.

"Calvin, please," my mother moaned. "We're on vacation."

I collapsed into a hot blackness.

"Lake City."

A sound, far in the distance. No. My father's triumphant voice. I looked up and before me, swimming in my sticky, sweat-filled eyes, stretched a wide street lined on either side with filling stations. I didn't believe it at first but when my father said, "We made it," I knew I wasn't dreaming. Then he said, "Let's find a good one," and my heart sank; as far as I could tell, there was no such thing as a good filling station.

But then the car began to sputter and jerk.

"What the hell."

My mother lifted her head from her arms. "Gas," she mumbled. "We're out of gas."

And my father, muttering angrily, steered the car into a filling station.

I sometimes wonder what the attendants at the station thought when they saw a medium-priced late model car die before a gas pump and then explode. All doors flew open and we tumbled out and made a dash for the rest rooms. My brother and I ran side by side. I threw a glance back at my sister, who was hunched over and limping toward the women's room, my mother next to her, helping her along. Only my grandmother retained her dignity. She stepped slowly from the car, rose to her full height, straightened her hat, swept the wrinkles from her black skirt, and glared at her son for a moment.

But he already had the map spread on the hood of the car and was studying the route for the remainder of the journey. Of course he knew the route; he knew how to get from Lake City to anywhere in the South. But there he was, off the road but still on it, traveling it with his finger, lost in relentless movement and the hum of the engine, oblivious to the desperate orgy of his family as it emerged from the rest rooms, descended upon the office, and gulped down soft drinks and pumped money into the candy machines. "Buy anything you want," my mother said grimly as she dispensed nickels. "This is our only chance." We came out of the office loaded down with peanut butter crackers, Moonpies, candy bars, and soft drinks. The stunned attendant came to his senses long enough to say, "Hey, lady, you got to pay for those bottles if you take them with you."

"It's all right!" my father shouted. He was refolding the map, anxious to get started. "We'll stop for drinks down the road."

My mother glared at him for a moment, then said to the attendant, "How much?" He could have said, "A dollar a bottle," and it wouldn't have mattered.

"Okay, let's get going," my father said. He was back behind the wheel and, clutching our provisions, we wedged back into the car. The doors were still closing as we roared away from the pump. In horror, we realized that he was trying to get to the highway ahead of a truck that was nearing the station. "No, Calvin, we can't make it!" my mother shouted and at the last moment he slammed on the brakes. The truck roared by and he muttered, "Damn. Now I'll have to pass him again."

As the car pulled onto the highway, I looked out the back window and saw the attendants standing in front of their ransacked station and staring at us in utter bewilderment. Slowly they faded, became specks in the distance and disappeared. "A hundred and twenty-seven miles to go," my father said. "If we don't hit too much traffic we'll make it by four o'clock." He swung the car out into the oncoming lane and repassed the truck. "I think that was the only one," he said.

We all settled back, looked out the windows at the Spanish moss trailing from the limbs of the trees, fingered our crackers and candy and drinks, and tried not to think of the miles that lay between us and the beach. The worst was over. One way or another we would survive.

I think it was then, as I was slumped in the seat, my head resting against the window, my eyes fixed on the monotonous flat wasteland that stretched as far as the eye could see in all directions—a desolation between the squat stolid suburbs of Atlanta and that other stretch of endless reality, the sea—I think it was then that the words leaped out of the bewildering maze of billboards that lined either side of the road. Billboards advertising oranges and grapefruits and lemons and orange juice and beach towels and suntan lotion and . . . papaya juice. *Papaya*. I had seen the word on previous trips; I even knew how to pronounce it. But I had seen Spanish moss before, too, only now the two merged, the mysterious sound echoing in my head through dark mysterious forests draped with the gray hanging plant.

Explain it any way you like: adolescent fantasy, ignorance, exhaustion, the desire to escape the car and the family I was trapped in. Whatever, the word came to represent all the exotica of the tropics—rain forests and strange animals and thatch huts beneath the burning sun. Every time the word appeared beside the road I saw myself as a traveler moving through the lush sun-drenched colors of countries whose names I could hardly pronounce. They were all somewhere *south*, farther south than Florida, farther south even than Cuba and Haiti. That's where papaya (whatever it was) came from. At times I was sure I could smell it, a rich pungent odor, like that of overripe oranges with a hint of banana mingled in. But different.

That night as I lay on the screened porch of our cottage and listened to the surf, I pronounced the word over and over again until I strolled along another beach, a semicircle of soft white sand embracing water so clear I could see the small brightly colored fish swimming in it. And behind me as I walked a deep green jungle stretched to the mountains that loomed dark in the distance. At first I walked by myself, a lonely brooding man, but gradually there emerged beside me another figure—vague, shadowy—that made me tremble with emotion.

By day the beach came to lose all its charm. I had no desire to tumble with the younger children in the breakers and I was disgusted by the motels and hot dog and raft rental stands that stood between the sea and the road. Ski-ball was boring; the chicken that danced when I put a nickel in the slot wasn't funny; even the pinball machines—an old obsession—didn't interest me. There were the girls, of course, their tanned skin bulging against their tight bathing suits, but they roamed the beach in giggling packs, moving fortresses that could be assaulted only by packs of boys as loud and aggressive as they. A loner like myself had no chance. I could only watch them from a distance or stroll casually by them as they lay stretched on the sand and cast furtive sidelong glances at their bodies. They were what I had come to the beach for; they were exactly as I had imagined them in Atlanta, in the car. And now, surrounded by them, I found myself drifting away although my heart still pounded when I imagined my hands touching their flesh.

"What's wrong with you?" my mother asked. "You don't seem to be having any fun."

But I couldn't explain to her how the word *papaya* had altered my life. I couldn't even explain it to myself, anymore than I could explain why I refused to drink papaya juice. It was sold everywhere but for two weeks I held back, pronounced the word over and over again but refused to drink it.

Maybe she said something to my father, told him something was wrong with me. How else account for his turning up at the beach in the middle of the afternoon? Since arriving I had seen him only in the early morning when he left for work and late in the afternoon, sometimes after dark, when he came back to the cottage, ate and went to bed. Now he stood on the beach, and had he been a pine tree he couldn't have looked more out of place in his tie and dark pants and heavy leather shoes.

"How are you doing?" he asked.

"Fine."

He stared out at the sea.

"Are you all right?"

"Yeah. Sure. How come you're not at work?"

He hesitated. "We're almost finished. I could take a little time off."

"Oh."

He looked at me, started to say something, then turned his eyes back out to the sea. "Just think," he said, "if you keep going out that way," he pointed to the horizon, "you'll hit . . . what? Africa? Europe?"

"Africa, I think."

He looked down, kicked the sand. "Boy, it's hot. How do you stand it?"

I didn't answer.

"Well, I just wanted to make sure you're having a good time." He hesitated again, looked at me for a moment, then turned his eyes down the beach. "I've got to get back."

"Okay."

He walked toward the road but when he got to the dunes he turned and shouted, "You look out for the girls!" and laughed.

"I will!" I shouted back.

That evening my mother asked me, "Did your father talk to you today?"

"Yes."

"What did he say?"

"Oh, nothing much. The usual, you know. He asked me if I was having a good time."

"And that's all?"

"More or less."

She was standing at the sink, her back to me as she washed dishes. "He wishes he could spend more time with you. But he has to work so hard. It hasn't been easy for him. He had to quit school in the seventh grade. When you consider that, it's amazing what he's done." She stared into the dishwater much as he had stared at the sea. "He's a good man. He'd do anything for you."

"I know."

But what did I know? My mother always brought up my father's lack of education, as though that explained everything, but I didn't know what there was about my father to be explained. Moreover, she seemed to find great significance in what was simply the routine of our lives, a routine I never questioned because nothing else seemed possible. And when my father came in after dark with a slight smell of bourbon on his breath and complained about how badly the job was going, the routine seemed as unbreakable as ever.

As the two weeks passed and the girls faded farther and farther beyond my reach, my shadowy companion took shape—or rather *she*, for it was most certainly a *she*, formed and dissolved beside me over and over again. Sometimes she was tall, dark and willowy; sometimes she was petite, fair and delicate. But always her breasts were the same: impossibly erect, large and at once firm and soft (though I never touched them; they merely brushed against my arm from time to time as we strolled along the beach).

On the night before we left I couldn't sleep, haunted as I was by the fear that I had gotten halfway to a place I would never see. To the north lay Atlanta, my brick house on East Wesley Road, the steam radiators that would hiss through the winter, North Fulton High School, its dingy halls and classrooms. To the south lay my dream of paradise, a dream growing from the smells of sea and sand, smells the gaudy trappings of Daytona—the neon lights and cars and the stench of hamburgers—couldn't obliterate. I got up, tiptoed out of the cottage, eased the screen door shut behind me, and made my way over the dunes to the beach. A half-moon hung low in the sky and sent streaks of pale light along the shifting surface of the sea, light that rose and shattered on the sand with the waves. The stars in the heavens, the sound of the surf, the rippling moonlight. Yet there was nothing I could touch, could feel. No, not even the woman who stood beside me—as solid and distant as the stars, as solid and ephemeral as the sound of the waves. To come so close . . .

And then it rushed away, flew backward as the car hurtled forward through dreary flat stretches of land toward Lake City. Farther and farther away. The car encapsulated the world that lay ahead: my brother fretted about missing the first day of football practice, my sister clung to her stuffed donkey and struggled against car sickness, my grandmother pontificated on the evils of the modern world, the immorality of the beach, and the almost naked women.

I panicked. Everything was fading, vanishing forever. Papaya was my only hope, a miserable hope offered by a small sign stabbed into the sand by the side of the road. "All the Orange juice U Can drink 25¢." And below that, among "Cantaloupes, Grapefruit, Lemons, Limes"—buried among them, the last letters squeezed against the edge of the sign, "Papaya juice." I pronounced the word aloud. "Papaya."

"What?" my mother asked.

"Papaya juice. The next place has papaya juice. I want to stop."

"We just started," my father said. Actually we had been on the road for over an hour.

"I don't care," I whined, a little ashamed because my voice was like that of a six-year-old. "I want to stop."

"We'll stop at the next place."

"That's what you always say. And you never stop. I want to stop at *this* place!" By now I was shouting, and even my brother, who never noticed anything, was looking at me. And so was my mother. *What is it?* her eyes asked. How could I answer? What could I say?

"Please stop, Calvin," she said. "It won't take but a minute. We'll just let him jump out and jump back in."

"Stop for papaya juice. He's had two weeks to drink papaya juice. Damn it, I wanted to make . . ."

"Please." She lowered her voice. "Can't you see there's something wrong? Please."

He looked at me in the rearview mirror. "All right. I'll stop for two minutes. That's all. Understand?"

He pulled the car off onto the sandy parking area in front of a small sagging fruit stand, behind the center of which stood an enormous fat woman who was swatting flies off herself and the fruit stacked in front of her.

"Okay, now the rest of you stay in . . ."

But already all the doors were open. Nobody was going to miss what might be our only chance for hours.

On one side of me stood my brother, gulping down glass after glass of orange juice; on the other side of me my sister was telling my mother that she was sick and needed a bathroom; behind me my grandmother complained about how filthy the fruit stand was; my father sat behind the steering wheel and stared grimly ahead. And on the counter in front of me stood my small cup of papaya juice. I had no way of understanding what I felt at that moment. Only years later when I read Keats, especially the line, "O for a beaker full of the warm South," would I experience some understanding of that feeling. I reached out, raised the cup to my mouth, and drank.

The sticky sweet taste was revolting. It oozed about my mouth, caught halfway down my throat and almost made me gag. I stared at the cup and, unable to withstand another swallow, I pronounced the word *papaya* aloud.

"What is it?" my mother asked. "Don't you like it?"

The word that had held such promise, had transformed the dreary world around me, now became a part of that world, as disgusting as my gluttonous brother, my whining sister, my overbearing grandmother. But before I could answer, my father, who had bolted from the car, was upon us, flapping his arms and shouting. "Come on! We've got to get back on the road! Hurry up!"

I wandered away from the group, off to the edge of a little clearing. Behind me I could hear my father haggling with the fat woman.

"He gave some of it to the others," she said. "Nobody could drink that much orange juice."

"The hell he did. Your sign says all you can drink for a quarter and that's all I'm paying."

There stretched before me, as far as I could see, trees draped with Spanish moss. The taste of papaya juice that still lingered in my mouth clashed with my vision of the trees, gloomy and mysterious. I recalled what I had felt two weeks before when the Spanish moss first loomed before me. I wandered in among the trees and—without really knowing what I was doing—I began pulling handfuls of it from the lower branches and stuffing it in my pockets. The feel of it against my hand seemed to take the taste from my mouth and, obsessed, I filled my pockets and piled it in my arms. I would carry it back with me, carry the paradise it foretold back to Atlanta.

My family had gathered in a semicircle around the fat woman. She was threatening to call the state police, my father was threatening to sue her, my mother was trying to pull my father away and my brother was shouting, "I didn't give any away! I drank it all myself!"

I stuffed the moss under the front seat and between the cushion and the back of the rear seat. And I kept a small clump clutched tightly in my fist. A talisman, a charm against the world.

We were well into south Georgia before my sister began to complain of itching. My own arms had been itching for quite a while but I had hardly noticed it, so caught up was I in my own visions. Then my grandmother began to scratch her legs. Soon everyone was scratching and cursing. "What is it?" my mother asked. The car swerved as my father tried to scratch and drive.

"What's this?" My brother, who had reached down to scratch his foot, pulled a swatch of the plant from under the front seat.

"O Jesus!" moaned my father. "It's Spanish moss. The goddamn stuff is full of chiggers."

"Calvin! Don't talk like that."

"How the hell did it get in the car?"

"There's more," said my brother, and he pulled up another handful. And another.

"It's behind the seat, too," my sister said.

"It's everywhere! The car is full of it!"

My father pulled off the road, and soon we were standing around the car, scratching and pulling the Spanish moss out as fast as we could.

"Who did it?!" my father roared.

But of course he and everyone else knew who had done it.

"Why?" he asked me, his voice expressing genuine bewilderment. "What the hell were you thinking about?"

The question, like life itself, had no answer. All I could do was say that I didn't know it had red bugs in it.

"Have we gotten it all?"

"Yeah. That's it."

But it wasn't. There was still the clump in my pocket. It would remain there, chiggers or not, all the way to Atlanta.

"What are we going to do?" my sister asked. Her legs were covered with red splotches.

"We need clear fingernail polish," my mother said. "If you cover the bites with it, it kills the chiggers. It's the only cure."

"Goddamn it, we'll need about a gallon."

We stopped in the next town—Unadilla, I think—and bought the fingernail polish. By the time we reached Atlanta, long hours later, we were covered with sores that glistened with their coating of lacquer. And we were still scratching, as we would be for days.

After everyone was asleep, I got out of bed, pulled on my blue jeans, and slipped out of the house. Once again, a half-moon hung low in the sky, but now it illuminated the silent solid houses that stretched all around me, their low-slung serenity broken only by the steeple of the Baptist church a block away. The only sounds were the occasional whine of an automobile and, far away, the wail of a train whistle. But when I reached in my pocket and touched the Spanish moss, I could hear the sound of the sea pounding on the beach. For a moment I stood alone between the ocean and the stars. Then I took my talisman from my pocket and draped it from the lower branch of the dogwood tree that stood in the front yard.

"What are you doing?"

I turned. My father was a dark shape standing on the porch.

"Nothing."

"You better come in the house. You shouldn't be out there."

"I don't want to. I want to stay out here."

He leaned forward and the moonlight caught his face. He started to say something, just as he had started to say something that afternoon at the beach. His lips even began to move. And then he stopped. For a long time he stared at me.

"All right," he said. "Do as you please." And his face fell back into the darkness.

The Spanish moss hung from the tree year after year. And then it was gone. Maybe the limb it hung from was pruned; maybe it fell off; maybe someone pulled it off. I don't know. As I said, I forgot it was there and no one else ever noticed it, ever asked how a clump of Spanish moss came to be hanging from a dogwood tree in Atlanta, Georgia. I don't know how long it had been gone before I noticed its absence. Nor do I know how long the tree itself had been gone when, coming home for a visit years later, after I was married and had children of my own, I noticed—no, felt—that something was missing in the front yard. It must have been gone for a long time because there was no trace of it, no clue as to where it had once stood, only a flat expanse of grass, indistinguishable from the rest of the lawn. And what came back to me, as I leaned against my car on a hot summer day, was not the Spanish moss or the taste of papaya juice or the sea or that shadowy companion—no, what I remembered was my father's face, the way it glowed in the moonlight, and the expression on it as he abandoned whatever stern command his lips were forming. A wistful expression, at once joyous and sad. At the time inscrutable as the sea. Only now do I begin to understand his words, how they embodied a thought as solid and ephemeral as the sound of waves breaking on the sand.

Biographical Sketches

CONRAD AIKEN (1889–1973). Although Aiken was born in Savannah, Georgia, and lived there until the age of eleven, his parents were New Englanders and he considered himself one as well. He moved to Massachusetts in 1901 to live with an aunt after his parents' murder-suicide. At Harvard his classmates included Heywood Broun, Walter Lippmann, Van Wyck Brooks, and T. S. Eliot, to whom he gave his poems for criticism. Aiken wrote more than fifty books of fiction, poetry, criticism, drama, and autobiography. The volume and the difficulty of his work may account for his relative neglect by critics and readers. Nonetheless, he was a significant figure on the modern American literary scene. In 1930 he won the Pulitzer Prize for his *Selected Poems* (1929), and his 1953 *Collected Poems* earned the National Book Award in 1954. He was consultant in poetry for the Library of Congress in 1950–51, recipient of the Bollingen Prize in Poetry in 1956, of the Academy of American Poetry Fellowship in 1957, the Gold Medal of the National Institute of Arts and Letters in 1958, and the National Medal of Literature in 1969. He spent the last years of his life passing his summers in Cape Cod and his winters in Savannah. Governor Jimmy Carter named him Georgia Poet Laureate in 1973. Important works include (novels) *Blue Voyage* (1927), *Great Circle* (1933), *King Coffin* (1935), *A Heart for the Gods of Mexico* (1939), *Conversation; or, Pilgrim's Progress* (1940); (poetry) *The Coming Forth of Osiris Jones* (1931), *Preludes for Memnon* (1931), *Time in the Rock: Preludes to Definition* (1936); (others) *Ushant* (1952), *The Short Stories of Conrad Aiken* (1950).

RAYMOND ANDREWS (1934–91) was born the son of a Madison, Georgia, sharecropper. He held numerous jobs during his youth, served in the U.S. Air Force from 1952 to 1956, studied at Michigan State University in 1956–57, and worked for KLM Royal Dutch Air Lines from 1958 to 1966. He left the airlines to write in 1966. His central achievement is a trilogy of novels set in the fictional north Georgia county of Muskhogean: *Appalachee Red* (1978), *Rosiebelle Lee Wildcat Tennessee* (1979), and *Baby Sweets* (1983). All three novels were illustrated by Andrews's brother Benny. Originally published by the Dial Press, they were reprinted in 1987–88 by the University of Georgia Press. Using the oral and tall-tale traditions of Southern and African-American humor, they explore racial interrelationships among the inhabitants of Muskhogean County. They are humorous, sometimes violent and wild, and vividly evocative of the lives of their characters. *Appalachee Red* won the James Baldwin Prize for Fiction. Andrews's memoir *The Last Radio Baby* appeared in 1990, and his two novellas, *Jessie and Jesus; and Cousin Claire*, in 1991.

VEREEN BELL (1911–44) graduated from Davidson College in 1932 (B.S., political science). Unable to find work as a journalist, he turned to free-lance writing. He began publishing stories about wildlife and the outdoors in the late 1930s, mostly in *Colliers* and the *Saturday Evening Post*. He explored the Okefenokee Swamp in both Florida and Georgia and talked extensively with the people who lived there to prepare for his first novel, *Swamp Water*, published in 1941. It was later made into a successful movie starring Dana Andrews and Walter Brennan. When the Second World War began, he enlisted in the Naval Air Force and volunteered for intelligence duty. He rose to the rank of lieutenant before being killed in action in 1944 near Samar in the Philippines.

OLIVE ANN BURNS (1924–90). Born in Banks County, Burns attended Mercer University in Macon for two years and graduated in 1946 with a B.A. from the University of North Carolina at Chapel Hill. She wrote for the *Atlanta Journal and Constitution* Sunday magazine from 1947 to 1957 and also did an advice column from 1960 to 1967 under the name of "Ask Amy." Her husband, Andrew Sparks, also wrote for the Atlanta newspapers. Burns worked on her novel *Cold Sassy Tree* for more than eight years, part of which time she was undergoing treatment for cancer. It was published in 1984 to laudatory reviews and became a best seller. Burns freely admitted that the novel was based on the life of her own great-grandfather of Commerce, Georgia. To write the novel she interviewed family members in an attempt to recover her grandfather's story: "What I was after was not just names and dates; I wanted stories and details that would bring the dead to life" (*Contemporary Authors*, 120, p. 68). The book is a gently comic, faintly nostalgic, often hilarious account of small-town life in north Georgia before urban sprawl and the modern world's arrival. A recurrence of cancer interrupted her work on a sequel, ten chapters of which she had finished at the time of her death.

ERSKINE CALDWELL (1902–88) was born a preacher's son in Newnan and grew up in Wrens. He attended Erskine College in South Carolina, the University of Virginia, and the University of Pennsylvania, though he never graduated. He was four times married, including once to the photographer Margaret Bourke White, with whom he collaborated on several projects. During the first half of his career, he worked often as a journalist. He spent 1925–26 at the Atlanta *Journal*, served three screen-writing stints in Hollywood, and worked as a foreign correspondent from 1939 to 1944. His first important publication was in *Scribner's Magazine*, edited by Max Perkins. The Scribner's publishing house printed several of his early books, including *American Earth* (1930) and *Tobacco Road* (1932). Caldwell was best and most notoriously known for his portrayal of Southern whites in such novels as *Tobacco Road* and *God's Little Acre* (1933), though whether his portrayals are accurate has been the subject of considerable discussion, including a lawsuit. In style Caldwell worked in the traditions of both American realism and old Southern humor. His best-known writings are about Georgia, though for much of his life he lived elsewhere.

PAT CONROY (1945–). Conroy lived much of his childhood on military bases or at his maternal grandparents' home in Atlanta. His father was a Marine Corps pilot from Chicago, his mother a native of Rome, Georgia. Much of Conroy's fiction seems autobiographical, based on his relationship with his family (*The Great Santini*, 1976; *The Prince of Tides*, 1986), his college experiences at the Citadel, from where he was graduated in 1967 (*The Lords of Discipline*, 1980), or his work as a teacher of poor black children on Daufuskie Island (*The Water Is Wide*, 1972). Conroy writes of the South with a more critical eye than many of his contemporaries. Family conflict, racial discrimination, the occasional insanity and violence of modern life frequently mark his novels. Four of his books have been made into successful films: *Conrack* (1974, based on *The Water Is Wide*), *The Great Santini* (1979), *Lords of Discipline* (1983), and *The Prince of Tides* (1991).

HARRY CREWS (1935–) was born a farmer's son in Alma, Georgia. After four years in the Marines, where he rose to the rank of sergeant, he left the military and studied writing at the University of Florida under the direction of Andrew Lytle. He earned his B.A. in 1960 and his M.S. Ed. in 1962. He joined the faculty as a creative writing teacher in 1968. Crews's first novel, *The Gospel Singer*, appeared in 1968, followed by *Naked in Garden Hills* (1969), *This Thing Don't Lead to Heaven* (1970), *Karate Is a Thing of the Spirit* (1971), *Car* (1972), *The Hawk Is Dying* (1973), *The Gypsy's Curse* (1974), *A Feast of Snakes* (1976), *A Childhood: The Biography of a Place* (autobiography, 1978), *Blood and Grits* (1979), *The Enthusiast* (1981), *Florida Frenzy* (essays and stories, 1982), *A Grit's Triumph* (1983), *Two* (1984), *All We Need of Hell* (1987), *The Knockout Artist* (1988), *Body* (1990), and *Scar Lover* (1992). Crews projects a dark, comic, often gruesome vision of life in the modern South. His fiction is marked by frequent violence, a romantic pessimism bordering on the existential, and a remarkable array of dispossessed characters.

JAMES DICKEY (1923–) was born in Atlanta and graduated from North Fulton High School. After a year at Clemson University, he became a fighter-bomber pilot, flew eighty-seven missions in the Pacific during World War II, and was awarded a Silver Star and two Distinguished Flying Crosses for valor. He graduated Vanderbilt University magna cum laude in 1948 and earned his M.A. there in 1950. He held teaching positions at Rice University and the University of Florida, served in the Air Force during the Korean War, and worked as an advertising writer in New York and Atlanta. During the 1950s Dickey began writing poetry intensively. His first book of poems, *Into the Stone*, appeared in 1960; his second, *Drowning with Others*, in 1962. He received a Guggenheim Fellowship in 1961, traveled in Europe, and taught at a number of American colleges. His volume *Buckdancer's Choice* in 1966 won the National Book Award and his collection *Poems: 1957–1967* secured his reputation as a major poet. Other volumes of poetry include *Helmets* (1964), *The Eye-Beaters, Blood, Victory, Madness, Buckhead and Mercy* (1970), *The Zodiac* (1976), *The Strength of Fields* (1979), *Puella* (1982), and *The Eagle's Mile* (1990). His 1970 novel *Deliverance* was a best seller and was made into a movie, for which he wrote the screenplay, featuring Jon Voight, Burt Reynolds, Ned Beatty, and Dickey himself in a small role as a sheriff. A second novel, *Alnilam*, appeared in 1988. Dickey has also published four collections of highly original criticism. He lives in Columbia, South Carolina, where he is poet-in-residence at the University of South Carolina.

AUGUSTA J. EVANS (1835–1909) lived only the first few years of her life in Georgia. She was among the most popular of nineteenth-century American novelists and was well known to many Georgia readers well into the present century. She was born in Columbus, Georgia, but after her father's business failure her family moved to Texas and later to Mobile, Alabama. She wrote her first novel (*Inez: A Tale of the Alamo*) at the age of fifteen, though it was not published until 1855. The three novels that followed were extremely popular: *Beulah* (1859), *Macaria* (1864), and *St. Elmo* (1866). Evans was an ardent secessionist and a conservative in most other causes as well. Despite occasional portraits of strong, independent women, her work is sentimental and marred by flowery language and wooden, stereotyped characters. Other novels include *Vashti* (1869), *Infelice* (1875), *At the Mercy of Tiberius* (1887), *A Speckled Bird* (1902), and *Devota* (1907).

BERRY FLEMING (1899–1989). Born in Augusta, Fleming studied art at Harvard but abandoned that calling after being advised that he was not suited for it (though he continued to paint throughout his life). He graduated from Harvard in 1922. In the same year his first novel, *The Conqueror's Stone*, was accepted by Berenice Baumgarten, a literary agent and wife of novelist James Gould Cozzens. It was published in 1927. Other novels followed. In 1943, *Colonel Effingham's Raid* was chosen as a Book-of-the-Month Club selection, became a best seller, and was adapted in 1945 into a film featuring Charles Coburn and Joan Bennett. Shortly after this success, Fleming decided to act as his own agent and severed his relationship with Baumgarten, a decision he later regretted. His popularity and his sales soon declined. After the failure of *The Fortune Tellers* in 1951, he wrote very little for twenty years. *The Make Believers* in 1973 marked his return to writing, but it did not sell well, and he could not place later novels with New York publishers. Late in the 1980s Fleming contacted the Second Chance Press, a small publishing house devoted to reissuing the works of neglected writers. The press subsequently reissued seven of Fleming's novels and published a new one as well, *Who Dwelt by a Churchyard*, in 1989. Fleming died in his ninetieth year, just as readers were beginning to rediscover his work. Other novels include *Siesta* (1935), *To the Market Place* (1938), and *Lucinderella* (1967).

WILL N. HARBEN (1858–1919). A prolific writer associated both with the New South movement and with late nineteenth century American realism, Harben was born in Dalton, Georgia, where he lived until, at the age of thirty, he moved to New York City and began to write. His best work was about his native South. *Northern Georgia Sketches* (1900), which contained "The Heresy of Abner Calihan," won the admiration of William Dean Howells. The realism of much of his work about struggling poor Southern whites is often tainted by a New South optimism which prevented him from recognizing the full reality of the region and the people he described. Still, he produced an impressive body of writing. Among his works are *White Marie* (1889), *The Land of the Changing Sun* (1894), *Westerfelt* (1901), *Abner Daniel* (1902), *The Georgians* (1904), *Pole Baker* (1905), *Ann Boyd* (1906), *Gilbert Neal* (1908), *Dixie Hart* (1910), *Jane Dawson* (1911), *The Inner Law* (1915), *The Hills of Refuge* (1918), and *The Divine Event* (1920).

JOEL CHANDLER HARRIS (1848–1908). Born illegitimately in Eatonton, Harris was befriended at the age of thirteen by farmer and newspaper editor Joseph Addison Turner, who introduced him to the worlds of journalism and literature. Harris's life on Turner's plantation gave him much of the knowledge about Georgia plantation life that he later used in his writing. He moved his family to Atlanta in 1873 and began working for the *Constitution*, under the editorship of Henry Grady, with whom he became friends and whose biography he later wrote. He developed the character of Uncle Remus in columns during the middle 1870s, and his first collection of Uncle Remus stories appeared in 1880, followed by three more volumes, in 1883, 1892, and 1905. Harris's Uncle Remus stories, along with his other writings about Southern blacks and plantations, earned him a national following and the respect of no less a writer than Mark Twain. The stories are noteworthy for their relative accuracy in the presentation of African-American folklore, their psychological understanding of the racial situation in the post–Civil War South, their humor, their variety, and their nostalgia. Harris published a number of often distinguished works on other subjects as well. Although he at first was a strong supporter of Grady's New South movement, he became increasingly disenchanted in his later years with the direction it had taken and worried that the South would lose its distinctiveness to northern commerce and industry.

MARY HOOD (1946–) is the author of two story collections, *How Far She Went* (1984) and *And Venus Is Blue* (1986). Born in Brunswick, Georgia, she earned her B.A. from Georgia State University in 1967. She first came to the attention of Stan Lindberg, editor of the *Geor-*

gia Review, the first magazine to accept one of her stories, "Doing This, Saying That, To Applause," published in 1978. The *Georgia Review* has published five other stories by her as well. *How Far She Went* won the 1984 Flannery O'Connor Award for Short Fiction and the Southern Review/Louisiana State University Short Fiction award. The story "Inexorable Progress" was included in *Best American Short Stories 1984*; "Something Good for Ginnie" won the National Magazine Award in fiction for 1986; *And Venus Is Blue* earned the Townsend Prize for Fiction in 1988. Contemporary in many of her concerns, her fiction is usually set in the small towns of the North Georgia hills just outside the suburbs of Atlanta. It is noteworthy for economy of form, precision of language, and perceptive treatment of human character. Hood lives in Woodstock, Georgia.

TERRY KAY (1938–) was born into a farming family in Hart County, Georgia. He earned his B.A. from LaGrange College in 1959. He worked first for the Atlanta *Journal* as a sports writer and then as a theater and drama critic from 1962 to 1973. After a term in the Peace Corps in 1973–74, he worked in public relations during much of the rest of the decade. His first novel, *The Year the Lights Came On*, appeared in 1976, *After Eli* in 1981, *Dark Thirty* in 1984, and *To Dance with the White Dog* in 1990. Kay is married and the father of four children. He lives in Lilburn, Georgia.

JOHN OLIVER KILLENS (1916–88) was born in Macon, Georgia. He attended Brown and Howard universities, and studied law at Columbia, New York University, and Terrell Law School. He served on the National Labor Relations Board from 1936 to 1942 and in the United States Amphibian Forces in the South Pacific from 1942 to 1945. After the war he helped found the Harlem Writers Guild and at various times was writer-in-residence at Fisk University, Howard University, and Medgar Evers College. His first novel, *Youngblood*, appeared in 1954, followed by *And Then We Heard the Thunder* (1963), *'Sippi* (1967), *The Cotillion, or One Good Bull Is Half the Herd* (1971), and *Great Black Russian: A Novel on the Life and Times of Alexander Pushkin*

(1989). He wrote several plays, screenplays, and children's novels as well. Working deliberately in the activist tradition of such African-American writers as Langston Hughes and Richard Wright, Killens explored in his fiction the black experience in America: racism and racial conflict, identity, the discovery of a heritage. Although he is not widely known, many critics regard him as one of the most important black novelists of the century.

SIDNEY LANIER (1842–81). Born into a cultured family in Macon, Lanier showed an early interest in music. He attended Oglethorpe University, graduated in 1860, and enlisted in the Confederate army in 1861. Made prisoner of war in 1864, by the time of his release he had contracted tuberculosis, which eventually caused his death. His novel *Tiger-Lilies*, written in three weeks, was published in 1867 and is based in part on his Civil War experiences. He married Mary Day of Macon in the same year; they became the parents of four sons, all raised in the poverty to which a poet-musician's income destined them. Lanier moved to Baltimore in 1873 and, when his health permitted, played the flute in an orchestra there. He composed most of his important poems during the last three years of his life. In 1879 he became a lecturer in English at Johns Hopkins University. Lanier is noted not only for his poetry but also for his theories on the relationship of music and poetry. He was one of the major American poets of the nineteenth century.

WARREN LEAMON (1938–) was born and reared in the Buckhead district of Atlanta. He attended Davidson College and then the University of Georgia for his B.A., Vanderbilt for his M.A., and University College in Dublin for his Ph.D. in Anglo-Irish literature. Leamon has published stories, poems, and criticism in a number of popular and scholarly journals, including *Southern Review*, *Sewanee Review*, *Georgia Review*, and *South Carolina Review*. His novel *Unheard Melodies* was published by the Longstreet Press in 1990. Leamon currently teaches modern Irish, English, and American literature at the University of Georgia, where his excellence as a teacher has been repeatedly recognized. He is finishing another novel and a study of the contemporary novelist Harry Mathews. He lives in Athens with his wife Patsy and three children.

AUGUSTUS BALDWIN LONGSTREET (1790–1870). Born in Augusta, Longstreet studied at Yale, attended law school in Litchfield, Connecticut, and returned to Georgia to practice. He served as a judge and a state legislator before turning to newspaper editing. During the 1830s he began writing humorous sketches which he collected in an 1835 volume entitled *Georgia Scenes, Characters, Incidents, etc. in the First Half Century of the Republic. By a Native Georgian*. Edgar Allan Poe praised the sketches in the *Southern Literary Messenger:* they were "heartily welcome," their author was "imbued with a spirit of the truest humor," they were "a sure omen of better days in the literature of the South." A second series of sketches published in 1843 was less successful. After becoming a Methodist minister in 1838, Longstreet served as president of a number of Southern schools, including Emory University and the University of South Carolina. Embarrassed over what seemed to him the vulgarity of *Georgia Scenes*, he published a temperance novel, *Master William Mitten*, in 1864, perhaps to make amends. It lacked the vigor of *Georgia Scenes*, which he was fortunately never able to live down.

CARSON MCCULLERS (1917–67). Born in Columbus, Lula Carson Smith early in life studied music. She moved to New York in 1934 to attend Juilliard and Columbia University but lost her tuition money on the subway and had to support herself through various odd jobs. Her study of writing under Sylvia Chatfield Bates at New York University was a crucial experience. At the age of twenty she married Reeves McCullers. Her first novel *The Heart Is a Lonely Hunter* appeared in 1940, followed by *Reflections in a Golden Eye* in 1941, *The Member of the Wedding* in 1946, and *The Ballad of the Sad Cafe* in 1951. Her marriage was stormy and unstable. She divorced her husband in 1941 after discovering that he was forging checks in her name. They remarried in 1945, but not happily, and Reeves committed suicide in

1953. McCullers often suffered from ill health, beginning with a bout of pleurisy, pneumonia, and a stroke in 1941, followed by another stroke in 1952. She was ill throughout much of the fifties and sixties until her death of a massive stroke in 1967. McCullers's fiction explores themes of alienation, isolation, and human identity. Frequently interested in Southern "grotesques" and in adolescence, her best work portrays her characters with sympathetic insight, but with pessimism as well.

CAROLINE MILLER (1903–). Caroline Pafford was born in Waycross and in 1921 married her high school English teacher William Miller. She raised three sons and also managed to write her first novel, *Lamb in His Bosom*, published in 1933. Its main character is a strong woman, Cean Carver, who faces, often alone, the rigors of life and motherhood in the Georgia backwoods. Anne Goodwyn Jones observes that through Cean, the novel "challenges the Victorian stereotypes of fragility and dependence." The book won both the 1934 Pulitzer Prize for fiction and the *Prix Femina Americain* in 1935. After a divorce in 1936, Miller married again and published a second novel, *Lebanon*, in 1944.

MARGARET MITCHELL (1900–1949). No Georgia writer has achieved more worldwide fame than Margaret Mitchell. Her one novel *Gone with the Wind* has sold well over thirty million copies and has been translated into twenty-seven languages. Mitchell claimed not to have shown any early inclinations toward writing. When her first marriage in 1922 ended in a matter of months, she began writing for the *Atlanta Journal Sunday Magazine* and, eventually, for the daily paper as well. In the middle 1920s she began writing her novel. Harold S. Latham of the Macmillan Company saw the manuscript in 1935, and his company soon after offered to publish it. Meticulously concerned with historical accuracy, determined to tell the South's story honestly, Mitchell spent several months checking, revising, and rewriting the manuscript. The novel was published in 1936 to general acclaim. Though Mitchell had no involvement in its production, the movie based on the book brought her more attention, and she spent much of the rest of her life answering letters from admirers. Though pressured to do so, she never wrote a sequel to her novel. In August of 1949, while crossing Peachtree Street, she was struck by a car and died several days later.

MARION MONTGOMERY (1925–). Born in Thomaston, Montgomery studied in the University of Iowa writing program and earned B.A. and M.A. degrees in English from the University of Georgia. He became an instructor at the university in 1954, where he taught creative writing, lyric poetry, and modern literature until his retirement as a full professor in 1989. Montgomery's life has been primarily that of a writer and scholar. He has published three novels, two volumes of poetry, and numerous essays and volumes of criticism, including a massive three-volume study of his friend Flannery O'Connor and of western culture in general entitled *The Prophetic Poet and the Popular Spirit*. In retirement Montgomery continues to write and lecture. He would not hesitate to acknowledge that he is a latter-day spokesman for Southern agrarianism. Making full use of Southern tradition, folklore, and idiom, his writing offers a fierce indictment of what he regards as a corrupt and secularized modern world.

FRANCES NEWMAN (1883–1928). Born in Atlanta, Frances Newman is the most unfairly unread modern Georgia writer. She was a largely self-educated woman whose learning and wit won the admiration of James Branch Cabell and H. L. Mencken. After one year at Agnes Scott College, Newman attended the Atlanta Carnegie Library School in 1912. For much of the rest of her life she worked as a librarian, first at the Florida State College for Women (1913), then the Carnegie Library in Atlanta (1913–23), and finally at the Georgia Institute of Technology (1924–26). She also studied at the Sorbonne in 1923. During this time she began writing book reviews and in the 1920s turned to fiction. Her first and only published story, "Rachel and Her Children," appeared in Mencken's *American Mercury* in 1924 and won the O. Henry Memorial Award for that year. Her first novel, *The Hard-Boiled Virgin*, was published in 1926 and her second, *Dead Lovers Are*

Faithful Lovers, in 1928. Both novels are rendered in a highly original, crafted, and stylized prose in the tradition of Virginia Woolf and James Joyce. They center on young women struggling toward individuality against domestic, social, and romantic pressures which push them toward conformity. Newman's novels won her an audience that promised to grow, but in 1928 a mysterious eye ailment sent her to specialists in New York for treatment, where she died either by suicide or natural causes.

FLANNERY O'CONNOR (1925–64). One of the leading writers of short fiction in American literature, Flannery O'Connor attended the Georgia State College for Women in Milledgeville, graduating in 1945. She earned her M.A. at the University of Iowa and presented as her master's thesis a collection of stories entitled *The Geranium*. She lived for a time with the translator Robert Fitzgerald and his wife Sally in Ridgefield, Connecticut. When she began suffering from lupus in 1950, she returned to her mother's Milledgeville home. In general, except for her illness and her writing, the remainder of her life was uneventful, though her active correspondence with other writers (preserved in *The Habit of Being*, edited by Sally Fitzgerald) reveals a fertile intellectual existence. O'Connor wrote two novels: *Wise Blood* (1952) and *The Violent Bear It Away* (1960). Her first story collection, *A Good Man Is Hard to Find*, appeared in 1955 and the second, *Everything That Rises Must Converge*, in 1965 shortly after her death. O'Connor's fiction blends a fiercely moral, devoutly Catholic vision of a fallen modern world with a comic talent for characterization, description, and dialogue.

BYRON HERBERT REECE (1917–58). Reece grew up in the North Georgia mountains outside Dahlonega. He began writing at an early age and his high school teachers recognized his talent. He enrolled at Young Harris in 1935, dropped out, and reenrolled in 1938, writing poetry all the while. His poems caught the eye of Atlanta *Constitution* editor Ralph McGill, who met him while on a visit to Young Harris. Reece left college without graduating in 1940 and returned to his parents' farm to work. His poetry attracted the attention of Kentucky writer Jesse Stuart, who helped convince E. P. Dutton to publish Reece's first volume of poems, *Ballad of the Bones*, in 1945. Other volumes of poetry followed: *Remembrance of Moab* (1949), *Bow Down in Jericho* (1950), *A Song of Joy* (1952), and *The Season of Flesh* (1955). Reece received two Guggenheim fellowships in creative writing, served as poet-in-residence at UCLA in 1950, and spent a brief summer in an artist's colony in California. He never married, worried constantly over his parents' health and his own, and spent too much time preparing lectures and grading papers at Young Harris College, where he taught on and off from 1953 to his death. He committed suicide in 1958, apparently in despair over progressing tuberculosis. His novels *Better a Dinner of Herbs* (1950) and *The Hawk and the Sun* (1955) are unrecognized literary gems.

FERROL SAMS (1922–). A medical doctor and a long-time resident of Fayette County, Sams was born in Fayetteville. He graduated from Mercer College in 1942 and attended Emory Medical College. He began writing in 1978. His first novel, *Run with the Horsemen*, appeared in 1982, followed by a sequel, *The Whisper of the River*, in 1984. Both are loosely autobiographical. A collection of stories, *The Widow's Mite and Other Stories*, appeared in 1987. Married to the former Helen Fletcher, also a doctor, Sams is the father of four children. He practices medicine at a family clinic in Fayetteville with his wife and two sons. Other books include *The Passing: Perspectives of Rural America*, with Jim Harrison (1988), *Christmas Gift!* (1989), and *When All the World Was Young* (1991).

CHARLIE SMITH (1947–). The son of Georgia legislator Charles Smith, Sr., and a native of Moultrie, Smith graduated from Duke University. He served two years in the Peace Corps, studied at the University of Iowa Writer's Workshop, and edited the Clayton *Sun* newspaper before his first story, "Crystal River," was accepted by the *Paris Review* in 1977. It won the Aga Khan Prize for Fiction. Smith's first novel, *Canaan*, appeared in 1984. *Shine Hawk* followed in 1988, and *The Lives of the Dead* in 1990. *Crystal River*, a collection of three short novels, appeared in 1991. Smith is also a distinguished poet. His work is marked by an intense lyricism, violence and eroticism, and psychological explorations into the contemporary human psyche. He lives in New York City.

LILLIAN SMITH (1897–1966) lived with her wealthy family in Jasper, Florida, until the age of seventeen, when business failures forced her father to relocate to Clayton, Georgia. She attended Piedmont College in Demorest, Georgia, for one year, studied music at Peabody Conservatory in Baltimore on and off for four years, and later attended Teachers College of Columbia University until her father's death in 1930 cut short her schooling. Her three-year experience as a music teacher in China during the early 1920s apparently was a major influence on the development of her liberal attitudes toward race and Southern society. In 1936 she began publishing a literary magazine called *Pseudopodia*, which under various names continued on until 1945. It was the only Southern literary journal of the time to publish black writers. Her first novel, *Strange Fruit*, about a love affair between a black man and white woman, was published in 1944 and immediately became a controversial best seller. In 1949 she wrote a nonfiction study of Southern culture entitled *Killers of the Dream*. Smith spent much of the rest of her life lecturing, crusading for civil rights, and writing. Later books include *The Journey* (1954), *One Hour* (1959), *Memory of a Large Christmas* (1962), and *Our Faces, Our World* (1964).

MARK STEADMAN (1930–) holds both an M.A. and Ph.D. in English, earned at Florida State University. A native of Statesboro, he completed his undergraduate work at Emory University. Among those writers who influenced him, he cites Caldwell, Sherwood Anderson, Ring Lardner, S. J. Perelman, Faulkner, and Hemingway (*Contemporary Authors*, 37–40, p. 520). Steadman writes firmly in the intertwined Southern traditions of gothicism and frontier humor. Both are evident in his books: *McAfee County: A Chronicle* (1971), *A Lion's Share* (1976), *Angel Child* (1987), and *Bang-Up Season* (1990). He teaches at Clemson University in South Carolina.

WILLIAM TAPPAN THOMPSON (1812–82) was born in Ravenna, Ohio. Educated as a lawyer, he lived most of his adult life in Georgia. For a time he worked for the Augusta *States Rights Sentinel* with A. B. Longstreet, whom he admired and imitated in his own writings. While editing journals in Macon and Madison, he began the sketches which in 1843 he collected as *Major Jones' Courtship*. The book amounts to a novel told in the form of letters to a newspaper editor. They recount in genteel, homespun fashion life in the Georgia countryside, most especially Major Jones's courtship and marriage and the early years of family life. Among Thompson's other books are *Chronicles of Pineville* (1845) and *Major Jones' Sketches of Travel* (1848). Like Longstreet's *Georgia Scenes*, Thompson's Major Jones sketches were extremely popular. *Major Jones' Courtship* alone was reprinted thirty times before 1900.

JEAN TOOMER (1894–1967). Nathan Eugene Toomer was born in Washington, D.C. His maternal grandfather, the controversial P. B. S. Pinchback, was a Macon native who served as acting governor of Louisiana during Reconstruction. In his youth Toomer frequently changed schools, political persuasions, career plans, and religions. He spent only three months in Georgia, serving as temporary principal of an industrial and agricultural school for blacks in Sparta, but from that brief stay came the novel for which he is remembered. *Cane* was published in 1923 to general acclaim and is one of the most important works of the Harlem Renaissance. Later in his life Toomer became evasive about his race, stopped writing about the black experience, and became an adherent of the spiritualist self-realization movement of Georges Gurdjieff. With the exception of one privately printed book, he published only occasional pieces after *Cane* and left at his death a large body of unpublished work.

ALICE WALKER (1944–). If the poems of James Dickey seized the southern imagination in the sixties and seventies, Alice Walker's fiction, especially *The Color Purple*, seized it in the eighties. Born into a large sharecropping family in Eatonton, Walker graduated first in her high school class and attended Spelman College in Atlanta for two years before transferring to Sarah Lawrence College in New York. In Atlanta she was active in the civil rights movement, and at Sarah Lawrence she studied writing under Muriel Rukeyser. Her first book, a collection of poems, *Once*, appeared in 1968; her first novel, *The Third Life of Grange Copeland*, followed in 1970. Walker is especially skillful as a writer of short fiction, as her collection *In Love & Trouble: Stories of Black Women* (1973) demonstrates. Two stories from the volume ("Everyday Use" and "The Revenge of Hannah Kemhuff") appeared in *Best American Short Stories* for 1974. Her 1976 novel *Meridian* in part concerns the transformative effect of the civil rights movement on one of its participants. In the 1970s Walker served as an editor of *Ms.* magazine and in 1977 won a Guggenheim Fellowship. *The Color Purple*, her widely acclaimed novel about an oppressed young black woman's gradual struggle toward self-discovery, appeared in 1982. It was a best seller and won both the Pulitzer Prize and the American Book Award in 1982. A film based on the novel appeared in 1985. *Living by the Word: Selected Writings, 1973–1987* appeared in 1988, and another novel, *The Temple of My Familiar*, in 1989.

DONALD WINDHAM (1920–) was born in Atlanta and graduated from Boy's High School in 1937. He worked briefly for Coca-Cola, and at the age of nineteen left for New York City. Though he rarely returned to Atlanta, a number of his works, including *The Dog Star* (1950), *The Warm Country* (1960), and *Emblems of Conduct* (1964), are set there. In New York, he became friends with Tennessee Williams. Together they wrote a play, *You Touched Me*, in 1942–43; it was produced on Broadway in 1945. Their friendship is chronicled in Williams's *Memoirs* and Windham's edition of *Tennessee Williams's Letters to Donald Windham, 1940–1965* (1977). Although Windham insists he is a Southern writer, European influences, especially Joyce and Proust, are evident throughout his work. His other novels include *The Hero Continues* (1960), *Two People* (1965), *Tanaquil* (1972, revised 1977), and *Stone in the Hour Glass* (1981).

FRANK YERBY (1916–91). Most of Yerby's "serious" writing was done early in his career, in the 1940s, when he wrote several promising stories. "Health Card" was cited as an O. Henry Memorial Prize Award story for 1944. But he soon turned to the popular fiction for which he is best known. He was born in Augusta and studied at Paine College, where he earned his B.A. in 1937. He earned an M.A. from Fisk University a year later and then studied for a year at the University of Chicago. After brief service as an English teacher at Florida A&M and Southern University, he worked during World War II for Ford Motor Company and Fairchild Aircraft. Yerby mainly wrote popular historical novels. Many concern white characters, while others depict the black experience in the antebellum South and in more recent times as well. Among them are *The Foxes of Harrow* (1946), *The Vixens* (1947), *Pride's Castle* (1949), *The Garfield Honor* (1961), *An Odor of Sanctity* (1965), *Judas, My Brother* (1968), *Speak Now* (1969), and *A Rose for Ana Marie* (1976).